CONTENTS

Unit 5 EMPLOYMENT IN THE MARKET ECONOMY

Unit 6 FINANCIAL TRANSACTIONS AND MONITORING

Unit 7 FINANCIAL RESOURCES

Unit 8 BUSINESS PLANNING

INTRODUCTION FOR THE STUDENT

The second edition of *Business: A Student's Guide* is dedicated to all students and staff who are pursuing GNVQ Business at Advanced Level.

A whole army of educational administrators, curriculum designers, publishers, textbook writers, teachers and their support staff have worked hard to develop a stimulating and exciting – GNVQ – way of preparing students who wish to make a career in the world of business or public administration.

I very much share their enthusiasm for the GNVQ Business Awards and, with the much appreciated help and support of my wife, my publishers, contributors and many organisations who have made illustrative material available, have 'campaigned' hard to produce a textbook which follows directly and comprehensively the GNVQ specification for the mandatory Advanced Level Units. The text also provides both helpful build-up tasks and a series of evidence-building activities at the end of each Unit which cover all the Elements and Performance Criteria of the Advanced Level in Business.

The following notes are intended to assist you in making the most of this second edition, which has been extensively revised to meet the finalised and current programme specifications. I wish you every success, both in your course of study and in your future career!

HOW TO MAKE THE BEST USE OF THIS TEXTBOOK

Structure and contents

Business: A Student's Guide 2nd edition comprises eight Units, which correspond to the mandatory units of Advanced Business, and share their titles. Each of the text's Units contains information and material which relate to the GNVQ Unit Elements in these ways:

- **to provide the detailed knowledge and understanding which relate to the Units' specifications** and which provide a source of reference in preparation for the externally assessed Unit Tests

- **to supply insights and explanations of current business procedures, practices and approaches** through the inclusion of models, diagrams, examples and specimen documents etc.

- **to encourage lively discussion and debate** about current business issues and developments

- **to include opportunities for both individual and group assignments and activities** from which you will practise and acquire skills you will need throughout your business career.

Element and Performance Criteria references

To assist you in studying each mandatory unit of your Advanced Level programme as you progress through it, each of the text's Units is supplied with **references to the Performance**

Criteria to which each portion of text refers on a page-by-page basis, including diagrams and charts. Sometimes the reference extends over a single paragraph and sometimes over several pages if the subject matter stays the same.

Study tips

- use the GNVQ references and overviews at the beginning of each Unit as a quick way of locating sections of the text relevant to your study topic of the moment. Also, remember to use the index at the back of the text to locate specific items such as: *grievance procedures or colour photocopiers* etc.

- Make a regular practice of reading and re-reading those referenced sections of each Unit of the text which correspond to the topics of your weekly studies. This will help you to assimilate and remember important points and information.

- Use the text to help you in writing up your notes of classwork and your own research studies; these will help you to recall essential facts and techniques.

- Make a habit of checking back over examples and models, such as the job description or the marketing break-even chart as they occur in your studies, so that you acquire a thorough grasp of the content and format of business documents and techniques.

- Take notes of the main points which occur in class discussions or group presentations on topics from the text, since some very useful ideas and responses are bound to emerge.

Unit tasks and activities

In addition to providing you with a helpful source of knowledge and understanding of current business practice, *Business: A Student's Guide* 2nd edition, also supplies a range of tasks and activities which relate directly to specific sets of Performance Criteria (and are thus handily referenced) and which will enable you to practise and perfect newly acquired skills and competences. Your teacher/lecturer may decide to employ these activities as 'rehearsals' or 'practice goes' prior to your undertaking centre-devised activities, or may use them as the means of your building up evidence for your portfolio.

Tips on undertaking tasks and activities

- Always take the trouble to read the content of each activity scenario and instructions carefully – if you misunderstand what you have been asked to do, you will waste a lot of precious time!

- Whether singly or as a group member, make notes on how you plan to tackle the task or activity and how it progressed in the event. You will find these to be an invaluable part of your evidence for your portfolio – but remember to follow your teacher's directions in this regard as well.

- When you are undertaking an activity which requires you to carry out research locally, remember that you have a network of willing and easily contactable assistants – your parents, relatives, neighbours and friends who are already working, and may have accumulated many years of know-how and experience. So tap into it by arranging to talk to them about the activity you are pursuing and to ask them 'how it is done' where they work, as well as what tips and advice they can provide on good practice.

- This certainly does not mean that you get such 'assistants' to do your assignment for you, but it does mean that you should make sensible use of such handy sources of expertise.

- A number of activities may require you to make arrangements to meet local business or public sector managers or officers. Always take the trouble to prepare your questions or interview material well beforehand, to be punctual and polite. This includes the sending of 'thank-you' letters which may well keep a useful door open for another similar visit. And always remember, if you pick up information about an organisation during a visit or attachment, to obtain the permission of your contact manager before you share it with your class. Business people are rightly anxious to avoid confidential or sensitive information 'leaking' without their knowledge or approval, and carelessness could wreck an invaluable local contact not only for you but your GNVQ successors.

■ Before you submit activity evidence for assessment, take the time to check it through carefully for your use of English and completeness. Cross-check each item of evidence against the Performance Criterion it meets and ensure that you have given it a clear and unique PC reference. Also, make sure you have filled out accurately the forms which accompany your evidence.

Careful storage of your portfolio and notes

Make a habit, right from the outset of your studies, of keeping your portfolio as it builds up, in a safe place along with the notes you accumulate for each Unit. Use a ring-binder or folder to transport study materials daily to school or college and **transfer its contents daily** to your main files. Where especially precious pieces of evidence are concerned, take a photocopy of them before parting with them for whatever reason.

This text and other sources of evidence

Lastly, keep in mind always that a textbook, such as this one, which embraces a very wide range of business-related topics can, at best, provide only a limited amount of information, some of which is conveyed in overview, survey or summary form.

If you wish to do well in your Advanced Level Business studies, you will undoubtedly need to make full use of the reference and learning resources of your school/college library, public library and other information databanks. For this reason, each Unit includes at its close a select listing of *Further Sources of Information* to help you in finding more detailed and specialised sources of information.

Acquiring the study habit

Textbooks are very much like milestones; they can point the way along main routes and highways along which to travel, but they can't do the journeying for you!

So the pains you take to acquire the study habit will prove well worthwhile in both the short and long term. The pace of technological change and product/service innovation in the world of business is now so hectic and permanent that every business executive – whether he or she realises it or not – is engaged in a career-long process of study to acquire and develop continually changing and evolving skills and expertise!

All being well, *Business: A Student's Guide* 2nd edition and the above notes will act as good milestones. But your own journey now awaits you. I very much hope it will prove enjoyable and rewarding, even if it is sometimes strenuous and uphill. Good luck and good studying!

Desmond W Evans
March 1994

ACKNOWLEDGEMENTS

I should like to thank Barry and Susan Curtis for writing Unit 5: Employment in the Market Economy. Their contribution was much appreciated. Thanks are also due to Barbara Darby who wrote Units 6 and 7 for the first edition, parts of which have been reproduced in the second edition, as well as to the team at Bradford and Ilkley Community College – namely Stan Goleb, Peter Horton, Mike Leake, Peter Rooney and Graham Wood – for new input to this second edition. No author can succeed without an encouraging editorial back-up, and I thank Catriona King and Ian Little for the skill with which they enabled me to meet their production deadlines, and to extract from me inner resources of stamina I did not know I possessed!

In particular, I should like to convey my warm thanks to Howard Bailey, Chief Editor at Pitman Publishing, who, with their design team, put together this text from my manuscript. Howard and I go back a long way, and without his unstinting enthusiasm, patience and expertise, my texts would not have displayed the visual appeal which users have been kind enough to compliment.

I also gratefully acknowledge the generous help and support of executives and staff of the following organisations for the textual illustrations and case study material etc. they made available.

ACAS: Advisory Conciliation and Arbitration Service
Aldus Pagemaker Limited
RG Anderson, *Data processing*, Macdonald & Evans Limited
Barclays Bank
The Body Shop International and Body Shop Supply Company
British Standards Institute
British Telecom
M Buckley and Longman Group Ltd
R J Bull, *Accounting in Business*, Heinemann Butterworth
Business Equipment Digest Magazine
Canon (UK) Ltd
Cave Tab Limited
CBI *Quarterly Industrial Trends Survey*
Centaur Limited
Chichester & District Angling Society
The Corporation, Chichester College of Technology
The Department of Trade and Industry, *A Summary of the UK Economy*, Mentor Publications, Dublin
John Dunn and Longman Group Ltd
J R Dyson and Pitman Publishing
Employment Gazette
EOC
Fellowes Manufacturing UK Limited
Fretwell-Downing Data Systems Limited
GEC Plessey Telecommunications Limited
H T Graham & R Bennett, *Human Resources Management*, M & E handbooks, Longman UK Limited
The Guardian
Hargreaves, *Starting a Small Business*, Butterworth Heinemann
John Harrison, *Finance, First Levels of Competence*, Pitman Publishing
John Harrison & Ron Dawber, *Clerical Accounting*, Pitman Publishing
Headway Computer Products
Heinemann Professional Publishing
Her Majesty's Stationery Office
J Hopkins, *Finance for BTEC*, Pitman Publishing
Peter Hingston of Hingston Associates
ICI
The Independent: Images change as joblessness affects all social classes (John Arlidge) article
Institute of Chartered Accountants
Institute for Employment Research Alan Jones & Associates

D Keenan & S Riches, *Business Law*, Pitman Publishing
Kodak Management Information Systems Limited
Lake Publishing Company
J Lambden & D Targett, *Small Business Finance*, Longman Group Limited
Marshall Editions Limited
Midland Bank plc
Minolta UK Limited
Muirfax Systems Limited
National Westminster Bank – and especially Ms Marion O'Connor
New Earnings Survey 1992
Sheila Robinson, *Frank Wood's Business Accounting AAT Student's Workbook*, Pitman Publishing
G L Thirkettle, *Wheldon's Business Statistics*, 8th ed., Macdonald & Evans
Times Newspapers Limited: Road to the Busy Aisles Article, Leading Tabloids Chart, Mars Marketing Article
Torus Systems Limited
Waterlow Business Supplies
A West, '*A Business Plan*', Natwest and Longman Group Ltd
West Sussex County Council
Western Riverside Waste Authority
G Whitehead, Heinemann Professional Publishing Limited and Longman Group Ltd
Frank Wood, *Frank Wood's Book-keeping and Accountancy* and *Frank Wood's Business Accounting*, Pitman Publishing

The unit specifications of the Advanced General National Vocational Qualification in Business shown at the beginning of each Unit in this book are reproduced by kind permission of the National Council for Vocational Qualifications.

Throughout this text I have endeavoured to demonstrate that a chief executive, manager, supervisor, assistant or operative may be either male or female. Sometimes, simply for the sake of syntax and simplicity, I have employed the generic 'he'. Similarly, I have sometimes used chairman, in preference for 'chair' or 'chairperson'. This use does not in any way imply an under-estimation of the valuable contribution which women make – at every level of activity – in both the private and public sectors of our economy.

Desmond Evans

The Purpose of Industry

'The purpose of industry is to create goods and services to meet human needs.

It is not to make money for its own sake.
It is not to make profits for shareholders, nor to create salaries and wages for the industrial community.

These are necessary conditions for success but not its purpose.'

Dr George Carey, Archbishop of Canterbury
Derby Cathedral May 1992. Service of Dedication to mark the advent of the Single European Market

BUSINESS IN THE ECONOMY

Element 1.1
Explain the purposes and products of business

Element 1.2
Explain government influences on business

Element 1.3
Investigate the supply of goods and services by business

Pages

Element 1.1: Explain the purposes and products of business

5–34

Performance criteria:

1 demand for goods and services is identified and described 34–47
2 demand in relation to particular product is identified 34–47
3 industrial sectors are identified and described 5–7, 48–53
4 the product of businesses in different industrial sectors is identified and described 5–7, 48–53
5 purposes of selected business organisations are explained 5–34

Range: **Demand:** needs, wants and effective demand; consumption and income; demand and price; elastic and inelastic 34–47

Industrial sectors: primary, secondary, tertiary 5–7, 48–53

Product: goods; services 5–7, 48–55

Purposes: profit-making; public service; charitable 5–34

Evidence indicators: An analysis of selected businesses with an explanation of why businesses exist, an explanation of their product and an explanation of demand in general and demand in relation to particular product. Evidence should demonstrate understanding of the implications of the range dimensions in relation to the element. The unit test will confirm the candidate's coverage of range.

Element 1.2: Explain government influences on business

57–80

Performance criteria:

1 government approaches to economic management are explained 57–80
2 governmental interventions in national and international markets are described 61–71
3 reasons for governmental intervention are explained 57–80
4 effects of government and EC policy on business decisions and actions are explained using relevant examples taken from business 71–5

Range: **Economic management:** free market; mixed/social market; command economy 5–34

Intervention in national markets: government policy; EC policy 71–82

Intervention in international markets: protectionism, trade agreements (e.g. General Agreement on Tariffs and Trade) 75–82

Reasons for governmental intervention: to support competition; to eliminate barriers to competition; to eliminate inequality of opportunity; to subsidise essential needs; to support politically favoured business; to sustain employment 57–80

Government and EC policy: interest rates; competition; employment; regional; transport; environmental protection; common standards; taxation (company & VAT) 71–82

Evidence indicators: A brief explanation of different approaches to managing economies. A detailed explanation of UK government and EC policies which affect business organisations. Relevant examples taken from selected businesses should illustrate the explanation. Evidence should demonstrate understanding of the implications of the range dimensions in relation to the element. The unit test will confirm the candidate's coverage of range.

Element 1.3: Investigate the supply of goods and services by business

Performance criteria:

1 the supply of goods or services by business sectors is investigated using economic relationships

2 different ways of evaluating the supply of goods and services are illustrated by the use of relevant information drawn from various sources

3 information and relationships as tools for investigation are evaluated

Range: Business sectors: public, private

Relationships: costs, supply and prices; wealth and welfare (e.g. when a company sponsors sport this could contribute to the nation's wealth or welfare)

Evaluation: in relation to trends in the UK and Europe; quantitatively in financial terms; qualitatively

Information sources: UK government, EC, business press, reference texts, media, sources within businesses

Evidence indicators: An explanation of the product of one private and one public sector business using economic relationships to evaluate the supply of goods and services and different perceptions of product. The explanation should incorporate a discussion of the usefulness of information and relationships to understand the supply of goods and services by businesses. Evidence should demonstrate understanding of the implications of the range dimensions in relation to the element. The unit test will confirm the candidate's coverage of range.

Unit 1 provides a detailed examination of the economic environment in which both business and public sector enterprises operate. It provides a thorough treatment of the principal economic concepts such as: needs, wants, scarcity, supply, demand, price, elasticity and so on and relates them to the macro-economic activities of the developed economies of the UK, European Community, USA and Japan as well as Third World States.

In addition, Unit 1 examines how different types of economy – market, mixed and command – work, and how governments seek to influence business activities in their economies through the implementation of fiscal and monetary policies, and various other types of support and intervention such as regional aid and industrial subsidy.

Unit 1 also examines the impact upon the UK economy of its membership of the European Community since 1973 and its role within the EC in terms of its world trade and international economic policies.

Lastly, Unit 1 explains how the supply of goods and services is underpinned by extensive networks of economic relationships, and how perceptions of economic activity depend on particular positions and interests within the network, such as overriding requirements for profit, ecological considerations or political advantage and so on.

In particular, Unit 1 explains:

- activities within primary, secondary and tertiary sectors of an economy
- the concepts of added value, profit and wealth creation
- the business activity cycle of an economy – expansion, recession, expansion
- the major activities which comprise the infrastructure of a developed economy
- the main types of business, public sector and charitable organisation: sole trader, partnership, private and public limited companies, franchises, multinationals, public corporations and charitable trusts
- the principal government agencies which interact with business
- the key features of market, mixed and command economies
- key economic concepts including: needs, wants, scarcity, supply, demand, price, price equilibrium, production and quantity
- the impact of economic structural change upon regions and communities, and how changes in lifestyles affect business activities
- the influence of government upon business: growth of social expectations, 'earth-mother' role of government and the implementation of specific policies such as privatisation
- government's needs to sustain: full employment, economic growth, low inflation, a healthy balance of payments, social equalisation etc. and the levers available to it, such as the control of public expenditure, money supply, exchange rates, direct and indirect taxation and public sector borrowing etc.
- the impact of European Community membership upon the UK economy and its international economic and trading activities
- the interplay of economic relations upon the supply of goods and services including: government economic policies, industrial and commercial climates, environmental issues, consumerism, legal requirements, international trading circumstances etc.
- principal sources of economic and business information available: government and EC statistics, business sector abstracts and digests, regularly published journals and bulletins, private sector data, including computerised databases etc.

'**It is the business of the wealthy man to give employment to the artisan.'**

Hilaire Belloc

Within the doggerel verse of the above quotation lie a number of ideas which inform an introduction into the world of business. Hilaire Belloc well understood, for example, the need for money to flow around in a kind of circle within an economy as a means of creating further wealth. He also understood the importance of enabling those without personal wealth to prosper from gainful employment of hand and brain.

Thus, with Hilaire Belloc's help, we can identify three important components of business enterprise:

1 The importance of putting money to work by investing in buildings, plant and the equipment needed to make a product or provide a service.

2 The need to employ the skills and energies of a workforce – sometimes referred to as human resources, manpower or labour – and in so doing both to promote business enterprise and to enable people to live and prosper.

3 The need to create a cycle of business activity in which invested money facilitates the purchase of materials and people's work in order to create added value in a product or service.

To complete this basic economic cycle of business activity, the following activities also need to be identified:

4 The selling of the created product or service at a profit to either home or overseas customers.

5 The reinvestment of accumulated profits in purchasing more materials and labour to sustain the making and selling cycle and to enable the business to grow.

6 The spending of the wages and salaries of the employees on numerous needs and wants which in turn sustain the business cycles of many other enterprises in the economy.

The diagram in Fig 1.1 illustrates the circular nature of business enterprise.

■ Primary, secondary and tertiary business sectors

As Fig 1.1 illustrates (see also Unit 3 on Marketing) in many national economies the cycle of business extends across three major sectors.

Primary sector

The primary sector comprises the getting of raw materials, the growing of food and the catching of fish. Industries in this sector include: mining for oil, coal, iron and other minerals; forestry, agriculture, fish farming and land reclamation, etc.

In the primary sector are also included the energy-making utilities like coal, oil and nuclear-fuelled power stations, gas-making plants and hydroelectric schemes.

Secondary sector

This sector refines, processes and manufactures and includes industries like petrochemical

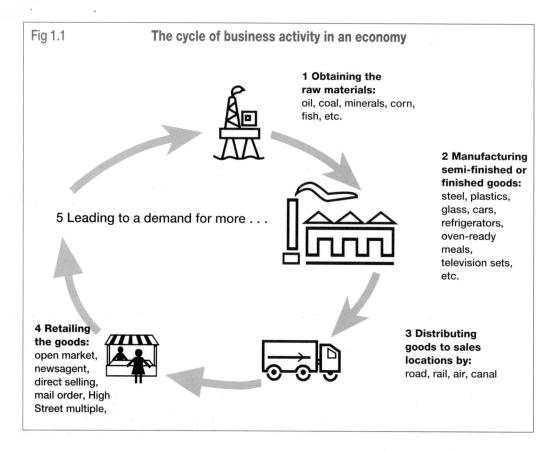

Fig 1.1   The cycle of business activity in an economy

1 Obtaining the raw materials: oil, coal, minerals, corn, fish, etc.

2 Manufacturing semi-finished or finished goods: steel, plastics, glass, cars, refrigerators, oven-ready meals, television sets, etc.

3 Distributing goods to sales locations by: road, rail, air, canal

4 Retailing the goods: open market, newsagent, direct selling, mail order, High Street multiple,

5 Leading to a demand for more . . .

refineries, steel-making mills, factories for making equipment and machinery for industry and goods for consumer purchase.

Tertiary sector

In this sector are the businesses which distribute and retail the manufactured goods; they include transport companies which deliver goods by air, sea or land, wholesalers breaking bulk from warehouse to retail store, retailing chain stores and multiples, franchised shops, newsagents and supermarkets, etc.

Also included in this sector are the service industries which sell commodities like information, training, legal advice and finance cover provided by insurance companies, banking services, on-line database providers, office cleaning companies and telephone companies, etc.

■ Operating across the sectors

Many businesses inhabit only one of the above sectors and sell on to the next. Extractors of iron ore, for example, may sell it on to a steel mill, or manufacturers of lawn-mowers may sell them on to wholesalers. Some firms, however, choose to operate in two or even all three sectors by, say, owning farms which grow wheat, mills which process it into flour, bakeries which produce bread and cakes and shops which retail the end-products. Such companies are said to be vertically integrated and they benefit from the profits generated at each stage of the process.

KEY CONCEPTS OF THE BUSINESS ACTIVITY CYCLE

Before proceeding to examine different types of business and the ways in which they are organised, it is important to understand a number of key concepts which tie individual businesses into a national economy and which impact upon them, however big or small they are.

■ Supply and demand

The way in which the business cycle moves round – from the extraction of raw materials in the primary sector to the sale of finished goods and services in the tertiary sector – depends almost entirely upon the basic free-market rule of supply and demand. For example, when a country's economy is in a buoyant phase, consumers will demand the latest model of motor car, caravan, refrigerator or garden furniture suite. This demand tracks back to wholesalers as increases in orders from retailers, and correspondingly to manufacturers from the wholesalers. As a result of such an upswing in demand, more iron ore will be needed to make steel, more oil to convert into plastic and more energy to fuel the whole business cycle.

In the same way, exporters of raw materials or finished goods will respond to demands from overseas customers.

When, however, the national or international cycle of business activity turns down (as it did in the 1970s because of a fourfold increase in the price of oil on world markets), then the process goes into reverse. A lack of demand in consumer markets because of unemployment or the fear of redundancy knocks on through wholesale and distribution industries to cause a drop in demand for manufactured goods and thus for raw materials. Additionally, producing companies cut back on investments in capital – plant, equipment and buildings – which in turn hurts firms supplying industry.

In this way all businesses in an economy are affected by the levels of supply and demand. Sometimes the effects are restricted to regions within a country and sometimes to particular industries.

Another important aspect of supply and demand is the effect it has upon prices. By and large, when demand for goods or services exceeds supplies of them, then their prices go up to 'what the market will bear' – what people or companies are prepared to pay. For example, when a district power failure occurs after a flood or storm, some retailers quickly increase the price of their candles, gas bottles, lanterns and cookers knowing that consumers will pay inflated prices for light and energy during a lapse in their supply. Correspondingly, when supply exceeds demand, prices for goods and services tend to fall. During the recession of the early 1990s, for instance, the sale prices of houses in the south of the UK dropped by as much as 30 per cent because their owners had to accept what people were prepared to pay if they wanted to achieve a prompt sale.

■ Adding value and creating wealth

A key concept in a free market is that of adding value to a good or service. For example, a seam of coal lying some two miles offshore and several hundred metres below the North Sea is virtually without value until British Coal extracts it, brings it to the surface, washes it, and transports it, say, to a coal-fired power-station. This process adds value to it, since it becomes a saleable commodity. Moreover, the same coal has more value in the power-station's yards than it does at the pit-head because of the costs of transportation. Thus a key concept in the business cycle is:

Investing capital in plant, equipment and human resources	**To add value to a product (or a service)**

The same process is evident in the manufacture of, say, a house or office block from assembled parts and fixtures. And it is important to note that additions in value to products or parts arise not only from a manufacturing process – prestressed concrete pillars from sand, cement and steel rods – but from their location. Saloon cars protectively waxed and standing in fields around motor car factories have one value but another when polished and gleaming in dealers' showrooms.

Thus the making, distribution and selling of appliances, furniture, food, clothing and the myriad of other items which support both consumer and industrial needs and wants is a process which creates wealth by adding value.

The same concept is applicable to the wide range of services which support business in all three sectors of the economy. For example, a computer software applications company will invest in computers, disks, printers and allied products and hire expert systems analysts and programmers to write software programs which will, for example, coordinate and record a firm's entire accounting procedures. The fruits of their labours will be installed on disks which are easily transported and stored in dealers' shops. While the intrinsic value of the disk and manual of the accounts package may be a pound or two, such programs sell for hundreds of pounds because of the added value they embody in supplying a system which enables accountants to work faster and more accurately. In this way, value is added in a servicing context, whether it be legal advice from a solicitor, business start-up help from a clearing bank or the sale of a property by an estate agent.

■ The concept of profit

Perhaps the most central concept in the business activity cycle is that of making a profit. For hundreds of years, the concept of profit has had a bad press. In the Middle Ages it was associated with usury – the setting of crippling interest rates on loans given; in the nineteenth century it was linked to the greed of some textile-mill and coal-mine owners who paid bare subsistence wages, part of which were tokens which could only be spent in company shops selling poor quality, high-priced goods. Nearer to our times the profit concept has been adversely affected by unscrupulous landlords securing high rents for derelict slum properties, and in the excessive mark-ups which characterise some companies in the defence, perfume and food industries.

However, the concept of making a profit from the added value given to products or services should not be 'rubbished' by the activities of the greedy and unscrupulous. Without a mechanism allowing goods and services to be sold at a profit, raw materials and semi-finished goods could not be bought in, machines and plant could not be acquired or renewed and employees could not be paid. Moreover, the shareholders in a business enterprise – individuals or companies putting up risk capital to float a business or aid its expansion – could not be paid any dividends or returns on their investments.

WHY BUSINESSES NEED TO MAKE PROFITS

Businesses in every sector of the economy need to make profits:

- To buy in more finished goods or raw materials in order to sustain their cycle of business activity.
- To meet the bills they incur in operating the business – energy, labour, business rates and professional services (e.g. legal) etc.
- To pay employees and directors and to fund employers' contributions to pension and health schemes.
- To create surplus cash to plough back into the business in the form of new or replacement premises, plant and equipment.
- To build up emergency reserves to guard against any future hard times.
- To finance growth and expansion – by buying existing companies or creating new ones.
- To service loans taken out from banks or credit houses.
- To pay government taxes.
- To contribute if so desired to charitable and community projects.

Relating the concept of making a profit to the above checklist provides it with a legitimacy which far outweighs the bad press given to it as a result of the actions of a few discreditable companies and entrepreneurs.

■ The business activity cycle and its infrastructure

The process of transforming extracted or grown raw materials into goods for consumption in either industrial or consumer markets could not proceed successfully without an infrastructure to support it. This infrastructure is illustrated in the second business cycle diagram (Fig 1.10) which overlays the first.

Fig 1.10

The cycle of business activity in an economy including infrastructures

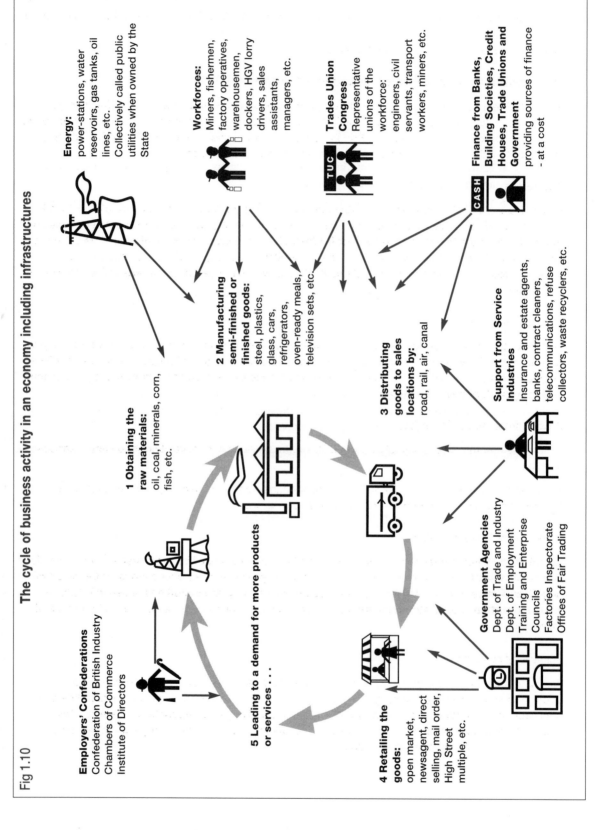

Energy:
power-stations, water reservoirs, gas tanks, oil lines, etc.
Collectively called public utilities when owned by the State

Workforces:
Miners, fishermen, factory operatives, warehousemen, dockers, HGV lorry drivers, sales assistants, managers, etc.

Trades Union Congress
Representative unions of the workforce: engineers, civil servants, transport workers, miners, etc.

Finance from Banks, Building Societies, Credit Houses, Trade Unions and Government
providing sources of finance - at a cost

1 Obtaining the raw materials:
oil, coal, minerals, corn, fish, etc.

2 Manufacturing semi-finished or finished goods:
steel, plastics, glass, cars, refrigerators, oven-ready meals, television sets, etc.

3 Distributing goods to sales locations by:
road, rail, air, canal

Support from Service Industries
Insurance and estate agents, banks, contract cleaners, telecommunications, refuse collectors, waste recyclers, etc.

Employers' Confederations
Confederation of British Industry
Chambers of Commerce
Institute of Directors

5 Leading to a demand for more products or services . . . .

4 Retailing the goods:
open market, newsagent, direct selling, mail order, High Street multiple, etc.

Government Agencies
Dept. of Trade and Industry
Dept. of Employment
Training and Enterprise Councils
Factories Inspectorate
Offices of Fair Trading

THE MAJOR COMPONENTS OF THE BUSINESS CYCLE INFRASTRUCTURE

The major components supporting the business cycle are:

The organisations supplying energy to industry and commerce

In order to keep the wheels of industry turning, vast amounts of energy are needed. This energy is supplied by coal, oil, gas and nuclear-fuelled power-stations which generate electricity sold on to the regional electricity boards. Similarly, British Gas and oil companies like British Petroleum and Shell UK plc sell on their products in both industrial and commercial markets.

Workforces

Ever since the industrial revolution began some 200 years ago, people have moved to where work is to be found, for example, to the South Wales collieries, to the shipyards of the Tyne, the factories of the Midlands or the textile mills of the North-West. The assembly of workers who become skilled in specific industries is a key factor in developing a modern economy, as the development of the Japanese Nissan car factory in Sunderland illustrates, where a new workforce was trained to work in a new industry.

Access to finance

Central to the business infrastructure are the banks and credit houses which lend out venture capital to businesses. This service industry provides a specialist brokerage by bringing together – at a fee – people or institutions with spare cash to invest and businesses seeking to borrow money to finance general growth or a special project.

Support from service industries

Industry and commerce today rely enormously on the services of specialist firms to supply services such as:

• insurance cover • legal advice • software applications • contract cleaning • refuse collection • laundry services • telecommunication channels, and so on.

Trade unions and associations

Established by industry-specific groups of employees over the past 150 years, trade unions provide a source of collective support for a wide variety of employees in diverse occupations. Full-time officers negotiate with companies and employer associations over pay and conditions of service. Their influence and position is strong in times of full employment but correspondingly weak in periods of recession.

Employers' confederations

Just as trade unions emerged to safeguard the interests of workforces, so confederations of employers in engineering, shipping and retailing, etc. evolved to secure a consensus of policy and approach across entire industries or commercial sectors. They also negotiate with relevant trade union officials. Both employers and trade union leaders act as consultants to governments over industrial and commercial policy-making.

Government agencies

The government of the day plays an important part in the infrastructure which supports business activities. Through its various departments, it provides statistical and factual data to inform marketing and corporate strategies. It supports the activities of exporters (who help governments to balance the payments for imported goods and services). It also funds agencies like Training and Enterprise Councils (TECs) which coordinate with Further Education and private sector trainers the vocational training and education of employees.

Furthermore, governments (and the EC Commission) inject finance into regions whose economies are ailing as the result of, say, the decline of industry which has become uncompetitive.

Also, through its central bank, the Bank of England, and through the Treasury, government exerts a significant influence on business activity – say, by raising the bank rate (the interest which the Bank of England charges the clearing banks for loans) – which dampens demand for goods and services, or by decreasing the amount of corporation tax paid by companies, thus leaving them with more money to purchase equipment and raw materials and so to build demand.

All governments seek to promote an economy in which business flourishes but inflation is held down; where the currency is kept strong but its goods offered for sale abroad at keen prices. No mean achievement for any government today!

PC
1.1.5

DISCUSSION TOPICS

1 What do **you** see as the essential purposes of industry and commerce?

2 What advantages do you think a business enterprise might secure which elected to operate in all three sectors (primary, secondary, tertiary) of the economy?

3 What reasons can you supply to explain why developed economies tend to move in cycles or waves from expansion to recession and then back to expansion? Can the recession phase – with all its accompanying human suffering and deprivation – ever be eliminated? How would **you** go about eliminating it?

4 Do you believe that some companies in developed economies make excessive profits? Or is there no such thing as excessive profit in a free, competitive economy?

PC
1.1.3
1.1.5

TYPES OF BUSINESS AND PUBLIC SECTOR ORGANISATION

As we have already established, business organisations are created to service the wants and needs of perceived markets, such as:

- Government agencies, e.g. Ministry of Defence
- Industrialist enterprises, e.g. Imperial Chemical Industries plc
- Consumers nationwide, e.g. Marks & Spencer plc

■ Consumers locally, e.g. F. Williams & Son Family Butchers

Figure 1.11 illustrates a kind of pathway up through which enterprising business people tend to travel as their businesses grow and prosper – from small-town sole trader to transcontinental conglomerate!

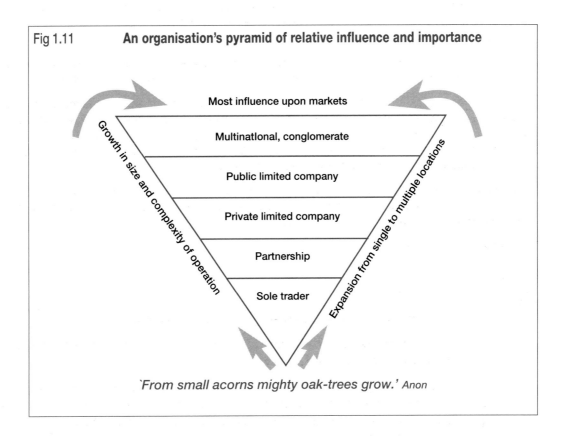

Fig 1.11   **An organisation's pyramid of relative influence and importance**

Most influence upon markets

Multinatlonal, conglomerate

Public limited company

Private limited company

Partnership

Sole trader

Growth in size and complexity of operation

Expansion from single to multiple locations

'From small acorns mighty oak-trees grow.' Anon

■ The sole trader

PC
3.1.5

Modestly situated at the foot of the inverted organisations pyramid is the sole trader. Sometimes referred to as a 'one-man-band' kind of business organisation, it is often just that. Usually, however, it is a family concern with either husband or wife taking a leading part. The small trader may rent modest premises such as a corner grocery shop or newsagents, may work from home, or journey as a roundsman selling fresh fish or greengrocery products.

As a rule, sole trader businesses tend to be launched on very modest capital and operate on tight margins between the selling price of goods and services and the cost of operations. This is in no small part due to the inability of the small trader to benefit from bulk purchasing discounts. Though nowadays associations of small retailers group together to buy collectively and thus secure better terms.

In legal terms, it is very simple to become a sole trader, provided that the trading name and trade mark employed are not in existing use and comply with the Business Names Act 1985.

Sole traders currently need to register for VAT if annual sales are likely to exceed £37,600.

Also, they are obliged in law to maintain proper records both for the payment of taxes and as an employer once staff are taken on. Prudent sole traders also take out public and employee liability, fire and theft insurance policies.

The trading edge in a local community enjoyed by the sole trader is summarised in Professor Schumacher's aphorism: 'Small is beautiful!' Communication is so easy if limited between a sole trader and his or her customers; decision-making is prompt if only a 'committee of one' has to be consulted. Similarly, business opportunities – to buy in stock at a bargain price, to spot a newly emerging fad or trend and to capitalise upon it – tend to be quickly spotted and taken. And it is much easier to keep a close eye and tight rein on sales and gross profits. All these benefits stem from running a small business enterprise with just a few people.

However, unless the business has been set up as a private limited company, the sole trader or business proprietor is entirely and personally liable for all debts that the business may incur once trading has commenced. Moreover, all the sole trader's personal assets and possessions could be sold from under him or her in order to pay off creditors in a bankruptcy action.

Given the modest cost of purchasing an existing but mothballed private limited company (about £100), it is astonishing that many sole traders still suffer in this way.

■ The partnership

PC
1.1.5

Often a business enterprise is created because of the shared expertise of two or more people and the fact that they can work well together. Customarily, partnerships are formed by between two and twenty partners (though there are exceptions). The relationship and respective job roles of partners is set out in articles of partnership, which will also make clear the respective share in profits due to each partner (according to the amount of capital brought into the partnership or the agreement made with other partners).

Like the sole trader, a partnership is required to maintain proper records and to comply with the relevant clauses of the Partnership and Companies Acts. Also in common with the sole trader, the business partner's liability for the debts incurred by the trading activities of the partnership is unlimited – though such liability is shared out pro rata to the partnership articles.

A typical business partnership evolves an effective division of labour – say, where one partner makes and the other sells, or where one partner oversees production while another coordinates administration. Alternatively, a partnership may comprise some active partners who run the business and one or more 'sleeping partners' who have invested in it and who secure an annual share of any profits made. Examples of business partnerships include management consultants, chartered accountants, retailers, architects and solicitors.

■ The private limited company

PC
1.1.5

In the mid-nineteenth century, the concept of limited liability was introduced into Great Britain. Initially it was aimed at limiting the liability of shareholders in failed companies but soon came to be used by the owners (as directors and shareholders) of small businesses as a means of separating their business and personal assets and liabilities. This was possible since, if a business went bankrupt, then its creditors could only seek repayment of monies owed from the sale of any assets which remained intact. The company as a legal entity had unlimited liability, but that of its directors was limited to the amounts they had invested in it.

Today private limited companies may be set up with a share valuation of a few hundred pounds divided among directors. If such businesses are launched on the basis of extensive loans from a bank, and if both premises and equipment are rented, then in the event of business failure very few if any realisable assets are likely to survive.

For this reason, detailed credit-worthiness references are required when a private limited company seeks to purchase goods or services on account. By the same token, a bank as a prospective investor in the business and as the lender of pump-priming, start-up finance will require security for any such loans. The securities the bank will want take the form of agreements to surrender to the bank the assets specified should the loan be defaulted upon. A bank will also set prudent limits on any overdraft facilities which are unsecured.

In this way, lenders to private limited companies seek to minimise the risks they take, which they claim justify the comparatively high rates of interest they charge on such loans.

PC
1.1.5

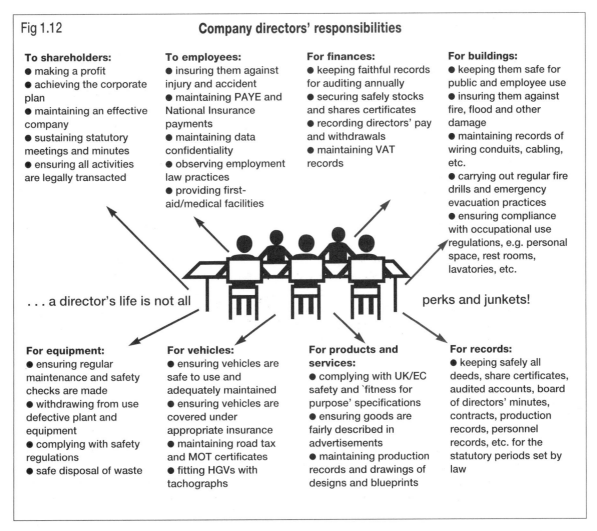

Fig 1.12   **Company directors' responsibilities**

To shareholders:
- making a profit
- achieving the corporate plan
- maintaining an effective company
- sustaining statutory meetings and minutes
- ensuring all activities are legally transacted

To employees:
- insuring them against injury and accident
- maintaining PAYE and National Insurance payments
- maintaining data confidentiality
- observing employment law practices
- providing first-aid/medical facilities

For finances:
- keeping faithful records for auditing annually
- securing safely stocks and shares certificates
- recording directors' pay and withdrawals
- maintaining VAT records

For buildings:
- keeping them safe for public and employee use
- insuring them against fire, flood and other damage
- maintaining records of wiring conduits, cabling, etc.
- carrying out regular fire drills and emergency evacuation practices
- ensuring compliance with occupational use regulations, e.g. personal space, rest rooms, lavatories, etc.

. . . a director's life is not all

perks and junkets!

For equipment:
- ensuring regular maintenance and safety checks are made
- withdrawing from use defective plant and equipment
- complying with safety regulations
- safe disposal of waste

For vehicles:
- ensuring vehicles are safe to use and adequately maintained
- ensuring vehicles are covered under appropriate insurance
- maintaining road tax and MOT certificates
- fitting HGVs with tachographs

For products and services:
- complying with UK/EC safety and 'fitness for purpose' specifications
- ensuring goods are fairly described in advertisements
- maintaining production records and drawings of designs and blueprints

For records:
- keeping safely all deeds, share certificates, audited accounts, board of directors' minutes, contracts, production records, personnel records, etc. for the statutory periods set by law

Private limited companies are required by law to draw up articles and memoranda of association. Such documents detail the precise nature of the business to be undertaken, the names and addresses of directors, the trading name and registered office of the company (usually located at the offices of its chartered accountant) and the value and allocation of shares issued. The directors will be responsible for supplying annual accounts for auditing by the company's appointed accountants prior to their despatch with an annual tax return to the allocated Inland Revenue Office. In addition, an annual return (Companies Form No 363) to the Registrar of Companies is required. This return updates any changes in directors and provides details of mortgage debts and issued share capital. It provides little or no information as to the trading performance of the company.

The various Companies Acts, and in particular the Act of 1985, define the legal liabilities of company directors of private (and public) limited companies. These include the calling of regular (usually annual) shareholders meetings, responsibility for tax and VAT returns and responsibilities under various Acts such as:

- The Factories Act 1961
- The Health and Safety at Work Act 1974
- Offices, Shops and Railway Premises Act 1963
- Employers' Liability (Compulsory Insurance) Act 1969
- Data Protection Act 1984

The trading edge of private limited companies lies in their protection from hostile takeovers (their shares are not available for sale on public stock exchanges), the privacy they enjoy from competitor scrutiny (they do not have to publish detailed annual accounts), and their ability to react swiftly to changes in market trends. On the downside, however, it takes them time to establish credit-worthiness, and they tend (as smaller businesses) to have limited collateral with which to secure loans to expand. They are unable to benefit on the whole from volume discounts, and they often suffer – quite inexcusably – from the unwillingness of larger companies to pay up on time for purchased goods, which can so harm their cash flow that they fail.

■ Public limited companies

PC
1.1.5

Just as a private limited company is denoted as, say, Anvil Engineering Limited, so a public limited company uses the abbreviation plc to show the nature of its incorporation: Project Office Furniture plc.

The major difference between a private and public limited company is that the public version has its shares available for anyone to purchase on a stock exchange – it is in this sense 'public'. In order to become a public limited company, a company needs to have £50,000 worth of its shares purchased and a quarter of them must be fully paid up. That is to say, their owners must have paid to the company the full asking price. Sometimes, as in the various government privatisation share issues, shares can be bought in tranches at intervals until their full cost is paid off. Such shares are deemed partly paid.

When a company becomes public, it may elect to issue different types of share. Some, called preference and debenture shares, have a higher status than ordinary shares and their owners are paid first – either pre-set annual dividends or according to company performance. Also, if the company is involuntarily wound up (goes broke), such preferential shareholders are high up the ladder of creditors likely to receive some payment.

A public limited company may at times elect to offer an issue of shares for sale (called a rights issue) in order to acquire fresh capital for expansion or to fund new projects or takeover bids etc. Existing shareholders usually get first call on such issues pro rata to their holdings.

Public limited companies tend to be in 'the big league' or first division of business companies. 'Money makes money' and many plcs take the form of multiples – companies with many branches, stores or outlets – that have steadily grown over the years by acquiring other companies or by building new factories or shops.

As a result of such activities, a plc may construct itself as follows (say it is Industrial Chemicals plc):

INDUSTRIAL CHEMICALS PLC

CENTRAL HOLDING COMPANY

WHOLLY OWNED SUBSIDIARY COMPANIES

IC Paints Limited   IC Fuels Limited   IC Plastics Limited

In such a plc, the issued shares of the subsidiary companies would all (thus wholly) be owned by the parent 'holding' company, and could not be purchased unless the parent company wished it or was taken over entirely. Each subsidiary would be responsible for its activities (as instructed) and would keep separate accounts. Again, a large plc may retain a single company structure but organise itself into divisions.

The trading edge of the larger public limited companies derives from the capital and human resource skills they command. A company like Glaxo or Wellcome Laboratories can pump millions of pounds into research and development and sometimes come up with a world-beating drug. National chain store plcs are able to set up for business in almost every centre of population and cream the business from prime site locations. They are also able to benefit from economies of scale in production and the power of bulk buying ability in distribution and retailing. Where their products or services command high profit margins, they are also able to establish strength in depth by maintaining a high staff presence in areas like customer relations and technical services.

The downside of large plcs lies in their bureaucratic inertia. They tend to create too many layers of management; their systems and procedures become too complicated – orders take ages to process and complaints too long to remedy and so on. Top decision-makers become too remote from customers and market trends. Innovation suffers from office politics. Moreover, since the company's shares are transferable through stock exchange dealings, if it is not careful, an unwary plc may wake up one morning and find itself 'under new management'! Thus prudent plc directors are careful to control the ownership of at least 51 per cent of the shares – if they can!

DISCUSSION TOPICS

1 Is 'small' really 'beautiful', or is Professor Schumacher's axiom merely a myth when it comes to operating a successful business?

2 Should there be a ceiling on the amount of net profit a company makes on a given turnover ? Or is the sky the limit in a free economy ?

3 What in your opinion is the ideal balance of power between business managers and employees? Should all companies, for example, be obliged to include representatives of the workforce on their boards of directors? Has the right to strike been made too difficult to action by trade unions, or were they irresponsible in the 1970s thus deserving of a harder-line treatment today?

4 Are there too few large companies today in the UK controlling too much of the national market in their sphere of activities ? Are small shopkeepers and sole traders doomed ?

■ Conglomerates and multinationals

A further development among plcs is for them to become multinational or conglomerates – or both. Marks & Spencer plc, for example, has set up stores in France and also trades in Canada. The Hanson Corporation has been very active acquiring and building up companies in the USA, while organisations like International Business Machines Incorporated – IBM – is well established in all four corners of the world. Sometimes there are straightforward reasons for a plc becoming a multinational. In the oil business, for example, it makes good sense for a company like Royal Dutch Shell or British Petroleum to control the operation from extraction to petrol-tank filling, which may well start on an oil rig in the China Seas and end up in a filling station in Ealing Broadway, London!

Another reason for the growth of multinationals lies in the benefits which accrue from having a business operation in, say, a Third World economy where abundant raw materials or foods are to be found, and to be able to buy in very cheap labour and allied services on the spot. While controlling the costs of distribution to richer countries such multinationals are able, for example, to sell pineapples, bananas, hard woods or guano at premium prices but with low production and distribution costs.

The term conglomerate is used to describe organisations which operate quite different types of business. The Lex company in the 1960s, for example, was a network of garages and motor car dealerships. Its directors then decided to use accrued profits to move into the hotel business. The reason for successful plcs expanding into quite different business sectors has much to do with spreading the risk of their business activities. Just as a stockbroker will vary the portfolio of an investor between government gilts, equities and unit trust certificates, so some plcs deliberately choose to distribute their capital around totally different sectors on the basis that they are unlikely to go through a bad patch all at the same time.

The trading edge of multinationals lies particularly in their ability to use the differences in the value of various national currencies and the economic growth and recession phases of different countries to their own advantage. Also, their huge size gives some of them the buying power and influence of many a nation state! The downside lies in the distance between multinational centres and complexes (though this is now very much offset by electronic mail, fax and teleconferencing), and the problems in creating any sense of international corporate identity. Also, critics consider that multinationals wield too much power through their financial muscle but exercise too little responsibility, not being accountable to any unified group of voters or government.

While a deliberate policy of expanding into a number of different business areas as a conglomerate protects a firm from the risks associated with operating in a single market, it takes an extraordinarily able holding company board of directors to coordinate the whole enterprise. As a result, what starts off as a business diversification programme often ends in asset stripping an acquired company (selling it off in component parts) to get rid of a problem purchase.

■ Public corporations and utilities

PC
1.1.5

So far, this survey of different types of business organisation has examined private sector organisations. In a mixed economy, however (one in which the operation of a free market is offset by a degree of government control and operation of certain industries), the role of what are called public corporations or sometimes utilities is very important.

In the UK, the following industries have either been or still are run as government-controlled public corporations:

- coal mining; gas and electricity manufacture, distribution and retailing; nuclear-fuelled power-stations;
- steel-making;
- rail transport, road haulage;
- docks, harbours and airport authorities; telecommunication services;
- water services.

As the above checklist shows, in the UK this century various governments have been most interested in controlling energy supplies, transport and communication services, together with key areas of heavy industry. Part of the reason for such government involvement lies in the enormous costs involved in designing and building, say, a nuclear-fuelled power-station or in maintaining a national railway network. Also, governments have been concerned to ensure that no single conglomerate or multinational should gain control of such an important economic resource as, say, energy production.

Nationalisation and privatisation

PC
1.2.1
1.2.2

Since 1946 consecutive Labour and Conservative governments have followed a zig-zag policy of delivering certain companies into public ownership (called nationalising them) and subsequently selling them back into private ownership. British Steel is one such industry whose development has been affected by such 'yanks on its tiller'. In various post-war administrations, as part of their belief in the benefits of public ownership, Labour governments nationalised some nineteen industry areas including:

- The Bank of England
- The Coal Industry
- British Road Services
- The Iron and Steel Industry
- Civil Aviation
- British Rail
- The Gas and Electricity Industries

With the election of Mrs Thatcher in 1979, the Conservatives developed a central policy of privatisation of nationalised industries. As a result, companies like British Telecom and British Gas were established by selling shares in them to the public at large, backed up by City financial institutions. Other utilities like electricity and water were also privatised in the 1980s in the same way, and private companies now supply these essential services to the UK's regions.

While public corporations have some degree of independence from government intervention, ultimately they lie under government control and may aid a government's policies in these ways:

■ they are employers of large workforces and thus give government influence over the number of people in work

■ through their pricing policies they enable governments to influence supply and demand on a significant scale

■ if a government so chooses, industries and consumers can benefit from subsidised prices for, say, energy and travel

■ they provide a means of developing social policies – like maintaining a coal mine or steel mill in an area of high unemployment

The critics of public corporations – those wishing to return them to the private sector – identify these shortcomings in them:

■ they suffer from overmanning – too many employees producing too little – and are therefore inefficient

■ they breed bureaucracy – their managers adopt work cultures associated with the less attractive characteristics of central government civil servants

■ because they often work as state monopolies they lose touch with the competitiveness of free market companies

■ they absorb – like blotting-paper – ever-increasing sums from the public purse sometimes with little or no increase in profitability or output

■ Privatisation in the 1990s

The re-election of the (Major) Conservative government in April 1992 for a fourth term resulted in the continuance of the privatisation programme. Next on the list for returning to the private sector are British Rail and British Coal, with the Post Office as another possible target.

■ Charitable and non-profit-making organisations

As well as the organisations of the private and public sectors, there is a third area occupied by organisations called the voluntary sector.

This sector is characterised by organisations such as:

■ Registered charities: like Oxfam and Save the Children

■ Charitable trusts: which often run schools, homes for the elderly or small hospitals on the income from willed monies and endowments

■ Companies limited by guarantee: which are not established to make a profit, such as national examination boards and certain schools and colleges

Such organisations are normally exempt from paying taxes, since they generally are performing socially valuable work while administering their activities at low costs. The Registrar of Charities exercises a careful control on what kind of activity may be so registered so as to prevent unscrupulous organisations from siphoning income due for tax into such an organisation, or evading tax payment altogether.

DISCUSSION TOPICS

PC
1.1.5
1.2.1
1.2.3

1 If Professor Schumacher is right and 'small' really is 'beautiful', why is it that so many national chain store and multiple businesses emerge in the consumer market and so many multinationals in the industrial field ?

2 What do you see as the major problems and challenges facing a company as it grows in size?

3 Is limited liability in the consumer's interest?

4 To what extent do multinationals and large conglomerates become immune to government control? Should their activities be more closely monitored? If so, how?

5 Should all public corporations be privatised ? Or only some? What do you see as the pros and cons in the nationalisation–privatisation argument?

6 To what extent should a government become involved in business enterprise? What do you see as the advantages and disadvantages of government intervention in an economy?

INDIVIDUAL ACTIVITIES

l Find out how a typical partnership agreement is drawn up. Report back to your group on what you discover.

2 Research into the structure and content of private limited company articles and memoranda of agreement (a solicitor will help you find out about formats and customary clauses). Brief your group on what you discover.

3 Find out where the responsibilities of company directors are set down and draw up a short fact-sheet on them to share with your group.

4 Research into one of the following organisation's activities and range of wholly owned subsidiaries and/or divisions and give a suitably illustrated oral presentation to your group:

    The Hanson Trust Limited
    Imperial Chemical Industries plc
    Barclays Bank
    Unilever plc
    British Rail

5   Find out how the work of the Charity Commissioners protects the general public.

CHECKLIST OF CENTRAL AND LOCAL GOVERNMENT DEPARTMENTS AND AGENCIES WHICH INTERACT WITH BUSINESS ORGANISATIONS

The Inland Revenue; collector of the government's taxes (see Treasury).

HM Customs & Excise; collector of Value Added Tax and other duties.

European Community; through its Commission, the EC issues and monitors a number of Community laws and directives with significant impacts upon industry and commerce, covering a host of areas from cheese-making to VDU screen use.

Government departments of:

Agriculture, Fisheries & Food; works with, inspects and develops the agricultural industry.

Trade & Industry; supportive of industry and commerce; directs government policy and resources and assists exporters, etc.

Energy; coordinates energy policies and assists energy industry development.

Employment; helps industry to train and develop its human resources – see also Training & Enterprise Councils.

Treasury; publishes detailed economic analyses and surveys; produces annual budgets and tax policies, etc.

Transport; coordinates transport policy and EC directives on transport administration and law.

Bank of England; issues currency and acts as the government's banker; monitors activities of national and private banks.

Central Office of Information; publishes regular reports, forecasts, surveys and statistics often useful to industry and commerce.

Health & Safety Commission; health, safety and care of employees and customers on premises, etc.

Factories, Public Health Inspectorates; corps of inspectors set up to carry out in-situ inspections of factories, restaurants, shops, etc. to ensure that relevant health and safety requirements are in place.

Registrar of Companies; maintains a national registry of private limited companies and details of shareholdings, etc. Monitors use of trade names and marks.

Office of Fair Trading; public watchdog on trading practices and legality of activities.

Monopolies and Mergers Commission; set up to monitor any potential establishment of monopolistic business activities, with powers to stop acquisitions and mergers if deemed 'not in the public interest'.

Industrial Tribunals; listen to industrial/employment law disputes and adjudicate – for example, on unfair dismissal or sexual/racial discrimination.

Advertising Standards Authority, and Independent Television Commission; monitor advertising standards and regulations and investigate complaints.

County and District Councils; implement various Acts of Parliament bearing upon business, including public health, trading standards, planning consents, collection of business rates and taxes on premises, etc.

The above checklist – by no means exhaustive – indicates both the range and depth of government involvement in trade and industry. This interest varies from the rigorous collection of VAT payments to support for exporters at foreign trade fairs. Much of what the government agencies do lies in monitoring and checking to make sure that the relevant Acts of Parliament are in fact being adhered to. To some this smacks of Big Brother interference, but many employees and consumers have good reason to be grateful to vigilant equipment or kitchen inspectors, or watchful trading standards officers whose actions may prevent the loss of a limb, or an eye, or a nasty attack of salmonellosis.

INDIVIDUAL ACTIVITY

PC
1.2.1
1.2.2

By arrangement with your teacher, investigate one of the above government departments, agencies or arms and produce a summary of its main activities and involvements with business on about two sides of A4 typescript, keeping your points short and sharp.

Collate your group's individual briefing sheets into bound booklets and issue one to each member of the group as a source of reference.

GROUP ACTIVITIES

PC
1.1.4
1.1.5

1 In pairs, arrange to interview two or three sole traders in order to find out what they see as their major preoccupations and essential activities and report back with an oral briefing of 5–10 minutes to your class.

2 Arrange in pairs to meet with members of a business partnership – solicitors, accountants, small traders etc. – and find out how some of the partners view the partnership type of business structure and why they prefer it to, say, a private limited company.

3 In groups of three, research into the duties and obligations which directors of private limited companies have to discharge and then report back to your class with an illustrated short presentation.

4 In pairs, select one of the Acts listed on page 26. Research into it and then design a factsheet on one side of A4 which summarises its main features. Circulate this factsheet to your class members as a study aid.

5 In pairs, find out why large public limited companies such as the IBM Corporation and ICI plc decided to decentralise their activities and to give more autonomy to their wholly owned subsidiary companies. Report back to your class in a short oral presentation.

6 In groups of two or three carry out your research into the activities of one of the following:

The Bank of England, The Monopolies and Mergers Commission, Oftel, The Training Education and Enterprise Directorate (TEED), The Charities Commission, The Department of Trade & Industry (DTI),

and produce a factsheet outlining clearly why it was established and how it interacts with UK business/economic/charitable activities.

REVIEW TEST

1 Explain briefly the stages of the business activity cycle in an economy.

2 What is meant in economic terms by 'added value'? Give an example.

3 Why is it so important in an economy to generate profit?

4 Outline the activities of the primary, secondary and tertiary sectors of an economy.

5 Explain how the economic concepts of supply and demand work in (a) a mixed economy and (b) a command economy.

6 List five activities which form part of an economy's infrastructure.

7 List the main types of business activity in the UK economy, including those which lie outside the private sector.

8 Explain briefly the difference between:

   a sole trader, a partnership, a private limited company, a public limited company and a charitable trust.

9 What are the following: a conglomerate, a multinational, a chainstore group, a public utility?

10 List four UK industries privatised since 1945.

11 For what is the Office of Fair Trading responsible?

PC
1.1.3
1.1.4

HOW TO RUN AN ECONOMY: THREE MAJOR SYSTEMS – MARKET, MIXED AND COMMAND

Macro-economics – economic systems viewed from both a national and international perspective – are inextricably linked to the political systems through which nation states run their affairs.

Over the past two thousand or so years, three major and contrasting ways of structuring a state's economy evolved as follows:

■ The market economy

This economy (and its over-arching political system) is based upon the twin concepts of capitalism and free enterprise. Essentially, such an economic ideology supports these views:

■ the market operates most efficiently and vigorously when it is free to operate according to the forces of supply and demand

■ free competition (unrestricted by interventionist government policies) tends to result in the creation and continuance of markets which are healthy – since fierce competition benefits both consumers and industrial organisations. Weak and inefficient companies do not survive, and so scarce resources – materials, land and people – are employed most efficiently

■ by minimising as far as possible its impact upon the free market economy, the government does not waste its resources on projects which may prove abortive, nor does it 'skew' the market by supporting lame-duck firms or obsolescent regional economies

■ the free market is allowed to fix its prices for labour, materials, premises and equipment on the basis of 'what the market will bear', as opposed to 'how much the government is willing to pay in subsidies'

The essence of capitalism in an economic sense is to encourage the free range of entrepreneurial vigour and enterprise, with a minimum of government intervention and control. However, in such a market economy approach, the needs of the socially inadequate, poor and sick, disabled and disadvantaged may take very much of a back seat, since it tends to breed societies in which 'you get what you can pay for'! But, such an economic system also tends to avoid the waste, 'feather-bedding' and over-manning created by powerful but unaccountable bureaucracies.

■ The mixed economy

A state operating within a mixed economy seeks to achieve an ongoing balance between a free-market entrepreneurial system interwoven with a government involvement in economic affairs. The government of such an economy will retain money created within the economy from the winning of raw materials, their manufacture into finished products and ultimate sale (allied to the sale of services such as insurance) to spend on providing those goods and services to which it committed in its last election manifesto and economic plan.

Such spending in modern, developed economies tends to concentrate upon: defence, health, social services, education, state pensions and public housing. In many Western states today, governments themselves spend about a half of the total income which their national economies generate. They tend to obtain the finance involved from direct and indirect taxation of both individuals and companies, and also by borrowing money from national and international banks and financiers.

■ The command economy

Unlike either the market or mixed economies, the command economy seeks to control entirely all the resources available to it: land, transport and telecommunication infrastructures, labour and managerial resources, all buildings and premises – mines, refineries, factories, offices and shops etc.

All the resources of production, distribution and sales are organised from a central planning secretariat. In the former communist United Soviet Socialist Republics (USSR), and its eastern European allies (COMECON), as well as in the People's Republic of China, such central economies were directed and governed by a series of successive five-year plans. Also, such centralised economies accorded with the communist ideology in which the State owns all the resources within its boundaries.

In theory the command economy planners were able to ensure that the laudable principle of 'To each according to his needs, from each according to his ability'. In practice, without the disciplines of a free market regulating supply and demand, goods and services which people did not want were over-supplied, while chronic shortages occurred in essential, staple products. Moreover, as the economies of the USSR and its European allies became progressively more subordinate to communist political beliefs, they slipped into a completely introspective and archaic pricing structure for goods and services, so that their currencies became non-convertible – no state wanted payment in USSR roubles or Democratic Republic of Germany (DDR) Ostmarks. However, such states were able to offer their citizens a life-long expectation of full employment, in contrast to the all too frequent dumping of employees on to the scrap-heap of long-term unemployment which characterises Western capitalism in its phases of recession and slump.

PC
1.1.3

DISCUSSION TOPICS

1 Which of the three above economic systems would you consider most suitable to a state which possesses:

(a) a developed, industrialised economy?

(b) an emerging, Third World economy?

(c) an under-developed, highly populated economy?

2 Do you think that there will always be a variety of economies operating in different nation states across the world, or is there likely to be eventual harmonisation into a true world economy? What evidence can you provide to support your views?

3 What do you see as the problems which the emergent democratic states of the former USSR have to overcome in transforming their economy from a command to a mixed one?

PC
1.1.1
1.1.2
1.3.1

SUPPLY AND DEMAND

The concepts of supply and demand lie at the very heart of business. They govern the dealings of the market-place. As Mrs Thatcher once remarked, 'You can't buck the market!' They also form – in free, market economies – the foundations of all private sector business activities. So deeply have these twin activities become rooted in our way of life, every public-house economist and the proverbial man on the top of a London bus will observe sagely from time to time: 'It's all a matter of supply and demand!'

But how do supply and demand occur? For what do these concepts stand, exactly? To supply answers to these two questions, it is necessary to go right back to the origins of human beings living in social groups, and to understand first three more economic concepts, namely:

NEEDS   WANTS   and   SCARCITY

■ Needs

In order to survive, human beings must satisfy basic and essential needs – for warmth (either in the form of heating or clothing), for food and drink and for safety (in the form of a secure haven). Until these fundamental needs are met, mankind usually has little interest in goods or services which lie at the margin, such as jewellery, entertainment or prettily decorated drinking vessels etc.

■ Wants

However, once they have been satisfied, man promptly moves up a gear into another level of activity, where wants emerge into his consciousness. At this stage, an assertion has to be accepted which has more to do with human nature than abstract economic theory:

Human beings are governed by a desire to satisfy a seemingly endless series of wants.

As the stone-age cave paintings all over Europe illustrate, early on in his social and economic evolution man began to adorn his habitations with colourful paintings, to fashion jewellery and to weave cloths of pleasing design. Markets emerged in which wines were exchanged for skins (or slaves!) between Celts and Phoenicians and a whole series of wants were progressively identified in the classical world, including beautiful sculptures, gardens, perfumes, garments and hairdressing fashions.

Over the past two thousand years, hundreds of industries have been created to satisfy markets which only consider wants – rock music on CDs, package holidays to the Mediterranean or adventure holidays to the Amazon, fast cars with computerised diagnostics and four-wheel drive, Broadway musicals, telephone banking, computer games, cosmetic surgery and so on – the list is only limited by man's imagination and temporary satisfactions!

■ Economic scarcity

While man's needs and wants were relatively modest, his numbers reckoned in the low millions instead of billions, and his technology limited to his muscle-power, both needs and wants were relatively well met – though winter starvation was common in Europe only a few hundred years ago.

In today's over-populated and materialistic world, however, very many needs and wants are governed by economic scarcity. In other words, while man's needs and wants combine into an infinite shopping list, there is a finite limit to their supply. Some nation states are currently blessed with:

■ extensive and varied natural resources – oil, gas, coal

■ fertile, well watered agricultural land in a kind climate

■ a technologically advanced society

■ low numbers in the population to feed, clothe, house and educate and keep well

Such nation states find it comparatively easy to satisfy both needs and wants, since their resources – in the form of either goods or services – are in plentiful supply. Moreover, if such states are able to export surplus production or services to others, then their affluence improves markedly, and, like Japan today, they are able to sustain a trading surplus (with the rest of the world) of some $100 billion each year.

However, the harsh reality of the current world economy is that there is a wide gap – if not a chasm – between the distribution of scarce resources among the rich and poor countries of the world. The leaders of most states have continually to make choices about what they spend their available income on, and how they allocate what resources they can keep in their internal markets. For example, in the USSR of the 1920s and 1930s, Joseph Stalin elected to build a steel industry, almost from scratch, so as to keep pace with other developed nations such as Germany and the USA. But, given the poverty of the USSR, Stalin could not provide both steel and consumer goods at the same time. And so the people went without. German militarists during the same period offered their citizens 'guns or butter', and guns were selected as a means of reversing their sense of ignominy after their defeat in the First World War.

For Third World countries the uncaring laws of economic scarcity seem to have been designed to keep them in both a trough of despair and a poverty trap. They have to sell their produce (usually food or raw materials) on world markets, since they themselves lack the expensive technology to transform them into goods to which considerable value has been added. Gourmet mushrooms grown in Afghanistan high valleys sell there for 40p a pound. In high-class London restaurants they make £15.00 for a half-dozen on a plate! Similarly, there are large differences in price between the bauxite ore at a Latin American pithead and the alloy wheels on a Ferrari Testarossa! And, sad but true, developed Western nations have a vested interest in keeping world prices for raw materials (latex, copper and cotton) as well as foodstuffs (cocoa-beans, bananas and rice) as low as possible, since this improves significantly their buying-in and selling-out margins.

Just as scarcity in the distribution of raw materials, technological know-how and the power of strong financial reserves create the differences in the economies of nation states as they trade around the world, so they also shape the economic activity of the individuals in their populations.

■ Scarcity and market segmentation

Markets for many goods and services become highly segmented (broken up into distinct, separate parts) simply because of the differences in spending power of various socio-economic groupings of consumers. The motor-car industry provides a good example. A vast array of models, from Rolls-Royce to Citroen 2CV, has been produced to suit the pockets of motorists, ranging from the chairman of a multinational to a research student finishing off a PhD. Indeed, most people are continuously engaged in juggling their incomes to pay for a mix of wants and needs – mortgage, food, heating, retirement, holidays and hobbies as one month or week succeeds another.

DISCUSSION TOPICS

1 What evidence can you think of which either justifies or refutes the assertion that 'Human beings are governed by a desire to satisfy a seemingly endless series of wants.'?

2 Given that raw materials, a fertile land and a kind climate are not equally or fairly distributed among the nations of planet Earth, what economic steps can a country not blessed with them do in order to develop its economy?

3 Can you see any economic advantage to the developed countries of the world in providing more extensive financial aid to Third World countries? For example, should the massive debts they have incurred with the developed world states be written off, or is their poverty trap unavoidable?

4 Can you envisage a situation in which there is an equalisation of the economies of the world's nation states? If so, how? If not, why not?

5 To what extent are individuals able to resist the impact of economic scarcity in their own countries? How do supply, demand and scarcity affect the market for labour?

■ Demand, supply, price and price elasticity of demand

Demand

The demand for a product is the amount or quantity of that product that consumers are willing to buy.

The market demand for a product is the total amount that will be bought in a specific market over a specified time period, e.g. the number of cars bought in the UK in January.

INDIVIDUAL ACTIVITY

List five other examples of market demand. Make them as varied as possible.

Factors influencing demand

Demand for a product is dependent upon several factors. Changes in any or all of the following factors can increase or decrease demand:

■ price of the product
■ price of other products
■ size of household income
■ tastes and fashion
■ expectations
■ potential market size
■ distribution of wealth

These factors will now be considered in more detail.

Demand and price

Changes in demand caused by changes in price are represented by movement along the demand curve. An example is shown in Fig 1.2.

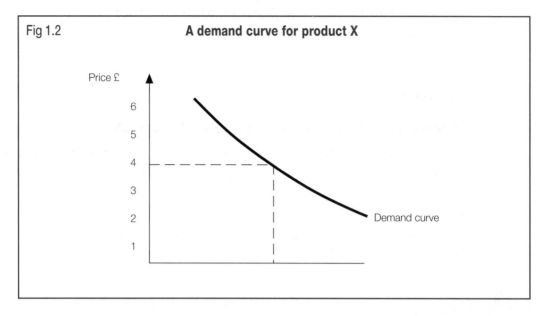

Fig 1.2   **A demand curve for product X**

INDIVIDUAL ACTIVITY

1 If we want the quantity demanded to increase to 10 what price should we set?

2 Think of a product for which demand increases as the price increases and explain why this happens.

An increase in demand due to factors other than price would move the curve upwards (D_2) and a decrease would move it downwards (D_3) (see Fig 1.3)

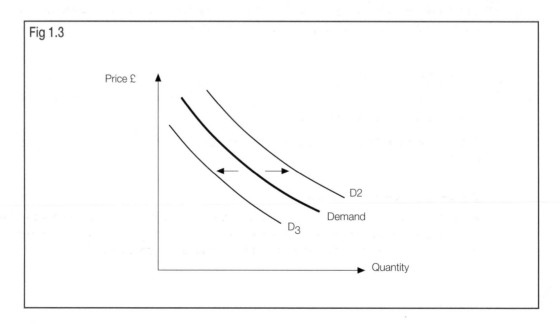

Fig 1.3

Demand and income

As household income increases, the demand for products will change.

1 The demand for normal goods, such as clothing, will rise.

2 The demand for basic goods, such as milk, will reach a maximum.

3 The demand for inferior goods will decrease.

INDIVIDUAL ACTIVITY

1 Think of two examples of normal goods, basic goods and inferior goods.

2 Briefly explain why demand for these products increases or decreases with a change in household income.

Demand and fashion

Tastes and fashion can change for psychological, social or economic reasons. It is therefore very difficult to predict their effect on demand.

INDIVIDUAL ACTIVITY

1 Think of two examples where demand has increased owing to changes in tastes or fashion and two where demand has decreased.

2 Could these changes have been predicted?

Demand and expectations

The things that people expect to achieve or acquire throughout their lives affect their demand for particular products. Expectations change as a result of changes in economic and social conditions, for example, in the United Kingdom home ownership has become an expectation for many people in the last 20 years.

INDIVIDUAL ACTIVITY

1 List some of your life expectations.

2 How do these affect the products that you demand?

Demand and the distribution of wealth

A society in which the majority of people have a middle income will demand different quantities of certain products than a society where the majority of the population are on lower incomes. In this way the distribution of wealth affects demand.

INDIVIDUAL ACTIVITY

Study the income distributions of country A and country B shown in Fig 1.4. How will demand differ between the two countries?

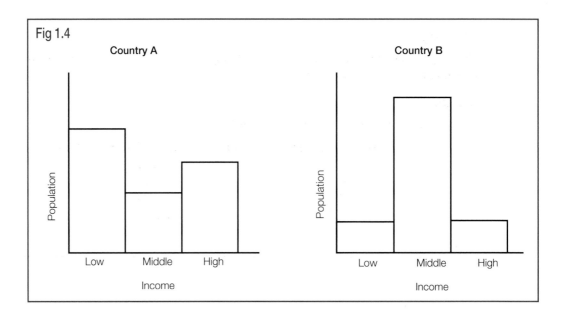

Fig 1.4

GROUP ACTIVITY

Choose any product and explain fully how each of the factors discussed have influenced or could influence demand for it.

Supply

The supply of a product is that quantity which existing or potential suppliers are willing to produce for the market.

The quantity supplied may vary as suppliers can increase or decrease the amount they allow on to the market, and firms can enter or leave the market.

Factors influencing supply

The factors which influence the quantity supplied are all related to prices and costs. These are:

- the price obtainable for the product
- the price of other products
- the cost of producing the product
- changes in technology
- changes in weather

The supply curve

The supply curve illustrates the relationship between the price of a product and the quantity supplied at that price.

Example

The supply schedule for product Y is as follows:

Price per unit (£)	Quantity supplied at this price (Units)
100	10,000
150	20,000
300	30,000
500	40,000

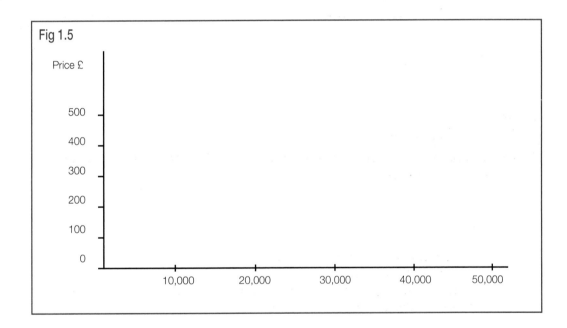

Fig 1.5

Price

Price is the common factor influencing both the demand for and the supply of a product in a market economy.

Price determination

As firms decide which products to supply and consumers decide which products to buy, both suppliers and consumers influence the price of products.

The quantity demanded and the quantity supplied will be equal at a certain price. This price, P_1, is known as the equilibrium price (see Fig 1.6)

INDIVIDUAL ACTIVITY

Referring to Fig. 1.6 answer the following questions:

1 What will happen if the price is set above the equilibrium price at P_2?

2 What will happen if the price is set below the equilibrium price at P_3?

3 In a market economy how are the situations in (1) and (2) rectified?

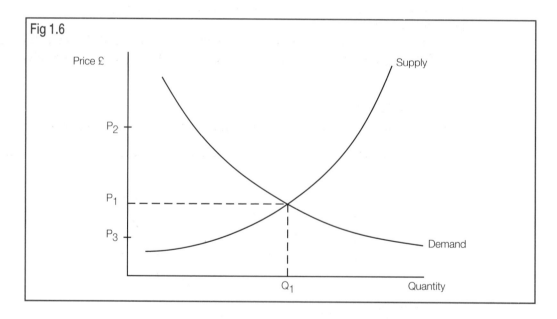

Fig 1.6

Price regulation

When prices are regulated or set by government policy, the market forces of supply and demand are no longer the main determinants of price.

Maximum price legislation

The graph in Fig 1.7 illustrates the effect of setting a maximum price.

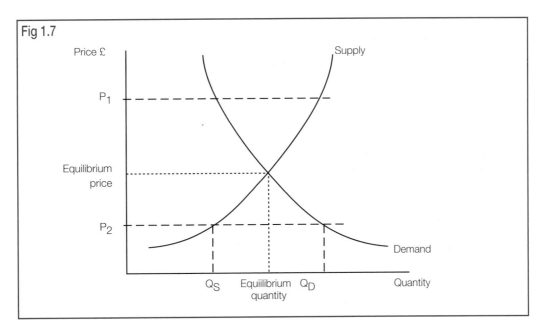

Fig 1.7

If the maximum price is set at P_1 there is no effect as suppliers can still choose the equilibrium price.

If the maximum price is set below the equilibrium price at P_2, then the quantity demanded, Q_D, is higher than the quantity supplied, Q_S, and a shortfall results.

Minimum price legislation

The graph shown in Fig 1.8 illustrates the effect of setting a minimum price.

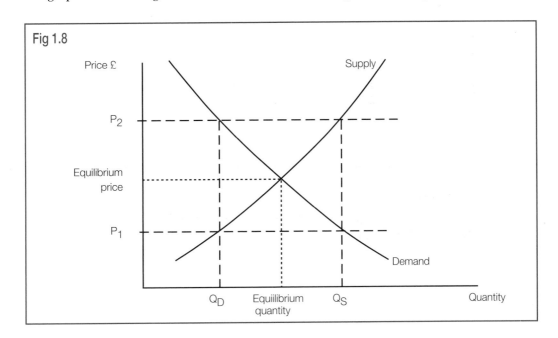

Fig 1.8

INDIVIDUAL ACTIVITY

Think of examples of products which have been in short supply. How were these shortages dealt with?

A minimum price, P_1, below the equilibrium price has no effect, but a minimum price above at P_2 leads to a higher quantity being supplied, Q_S, than quantity demanded, Q_D, giving a surplus.

INDIVIDUAL ACTIVITY

What has been the effect of minimum price selling for European agricultural products?

GROUP ACTIVITY

The Potato Market

Price	Amount demanded	Amount supplied
(Price per kilo)	(Kilos per week)	(Kilos per week)
7	30	62
6	35	60
5	41	57
4	45	53
3	49	49
2	53	45
1	57	41

Using the data shown in the table above:

1 Draw the supply and demand curves for the potato market.

2 State what the equilibrium price would be and why.

3 Say what would happen if the government set a minimum price of 4 pence per kilo.

4 State what the new equilibrium price would be if demand per week increased by 8kg at all prices and supply remained the same.

Price elasticity of demand

The price elasticity of demand (PED) for a product is a measure of how much the quantity demanded is affected by changes in price. Demand is said to be elastic if it increases and decreases greatly due to only small changes in price.

Calculating the price elasticity of demand

The PED for a product can be quantified using a simple calculation.

$$PED = \frac{\text{The percentage change in quantity demanded}}{\text{The percentage change in price}}$$

shortened to $PED = \dfrac{\%\Delta Q_D}{\%\Delta P}$

The percentage change is worked out as follows

$$\%\Delta Q_D = \frac{(\text{New } Q_D - \text{Old } Q_D)}{\text{Old } Q_D} \times 100$$

$$\%\Delta P = \frac{(\text{New P} - \text{Old P})}{\text{Old P}} \times 100$$

Example

If the price of product A increases from £1.50 to £1.75, the demand decreases from 1,000 units to 600 units.

The PED for product A can be calculated.

$$\%\Delta Q_D = \frac{(600 - 1,000)}{(1,000)} \times 100$$

$= 40\%$ decrease in quantity demanded

$$\%\Delta P = \frac{(1.75 - 1.50)}{1.50} \times 100$$

$= 16.7\%$ increase in price

$$PED = \frac{40\%}{16.7\%} = 2.4$$

The price elasticity of demand for product A is 2.4.

INDIVIDUAL ACTIVITY

Calculate the PED for product B whose quantity demanded decreases from 1,000 to 800 when the price changes from £2 to £4. Which is the more elastic, product A or product B?

Interpreting price elasticity of demand

A product is said to be elastic if its PED is greater than 1 and inelastic if its PED is less than 1.

INDIVIDUAL ACTIVITY

Referring to Fig 1.9, which demand curve shows an elastic product and which an inelastic product? Can you also calculate the changes in total revenue for both (a) and (b)?

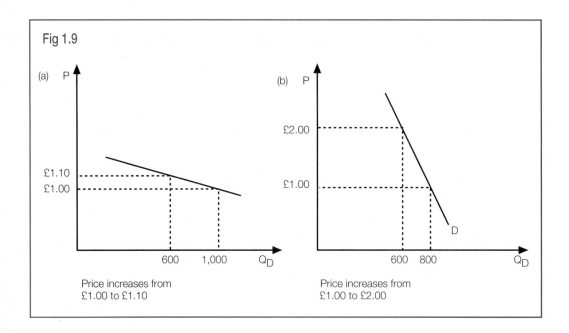

Fig 1.9

(a) Price increases from £1.00 to £1.10

(b) Price increases from £1.00 to £2.00

The price elasticity of demand for a product allows interested parties to predict the effect of a price change on the quantity demanded. They can then determine the optimum price to maximise revenue.

Factors influencing price elasticity of demand

1 *Strength of consumer demand*

Stronger for essential items or those purchases influenced by habit or fashion.

2 *Household income*

Changes in income will affect the proportion spent on each product, e.g. the gas bill for a person on a State pension may be 30 per cent of income over a given period; for a company chairman it may be 3 per cent.

3 *Availability and prices of substitute products.*

INDIVIDUAL ACTIVITY

1 Explain how the above factors would affect the price elasticity of demand.

2 List five products which are inelastic and explain why.

3 List five products which are elastic and explain why.

DISCUSSION TOPIC

Discuss how the Government has used, or could use, PED in setting their policy on VAT.

SUPPLY AND DEMAND IN THE MARKET-PLACE

There are a number of factors in the market-place which bear upon the *demand for* and therefore the *supply of* a good or service. These major factors are:

■ the amount of the good/service which can be readily brought to the point of sale at any given time

■ the size of the demand which exists (or which can be created) for the good/service

■ the asking (sales) price for the good/service

■ the ability of the would-be purchaser to pay the sales price

■ the willingness of the would-be purchaser to pay the sales price

■ Supply shortages, buoyant demand and price increases

All of the above major factors are flexible and bear upon each other. For example, during a wet summer, soft fruits like strawberries may rot where they grow and a shortage in supply may ensue. But the number of strawberry-lovers remains constant. The strawberry (in its punnet on the market) thus becomes a product with a scarcity value because the growers cannot grow more within the strawberry season. Demand therefore now exceeds supply. In such a market, the economic law which obtains is that the price for strawberries will rise. The seller will seek to maximise profits by testing out how much more consumers are willing to pay in order to enjoy their summer treat of fresh strawberries. Prices per punnet will thus rise until their sales begin to flatten out into a plateau. Would-be buyers begin to balk at the higher prices being demanded. In other words, a new equilibrium or balance has been negotiated between the seller and the buyer because the strawberry is in short supply.

■ Over-supply, satisfied demand and price decreases

The reverse scenario can exist, however, in the same soft-fruit market when ideal growing weather, allied to too many growers in the industry, combine to produce a glut, say, of apples, which do not keep well. In order to shift their perishable produce promptly, retailers will begin to offer such apples at a discount on the normal price for the season, and shoppers will begin to shop around for the best price they can get. In this way, a steep fall in the price of apples occurs since there is a significant over-supply. The market (which has a finite size) becomes swamped with such produce and 'the bottom falls out of the market'.

In order to avoid such a calamity, growers will sometimes destroy a proportion of such crops in the fields so as to maintain the price (and profit margin) of the remainder when it does get to market.

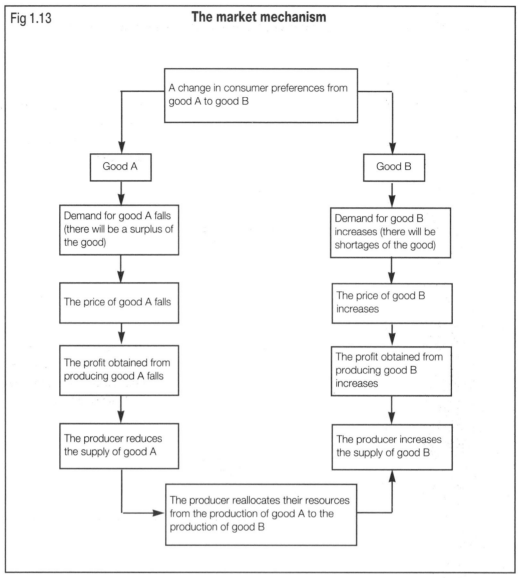

Fig 1.13 — **The market mechanism**

A change in consumer preferences from good A to good B

Good A → Demand for good A falls (there will be a surplus of the good) → The price of good A falls → The profit obtained from producing good A falls → The producer reduces the supply of good A

Good B → Demand for good B increases (there will be shortages of the good) → The price of good B increases → The profit obtained from producing good B increases → The producer increases the supply of good B

The producer reallocates their resources from the production of good A to the production of good B

(Source: *Economics*, S Ison, M&E Handbooks)

PC
1.1.1
1.1.2

■ Price equilibrium in the market-place

The above examples serve to illustrate the existence of market forces in the form of these variables:

■ how much product is available in how large a market

■ how open competition is – fierce, or monopolistic

■ how sensitive is the demand for the product when its price is rising or falling

When the market is open and not rigged (by, say, one supplier controlling all access to the product), and when buyers are able to access information easily about price movements in the market-place, then the pendulum of price equilibrium for the product will swing either to an upper or lower level, depending on whether supply exceeds demand or vice versa.

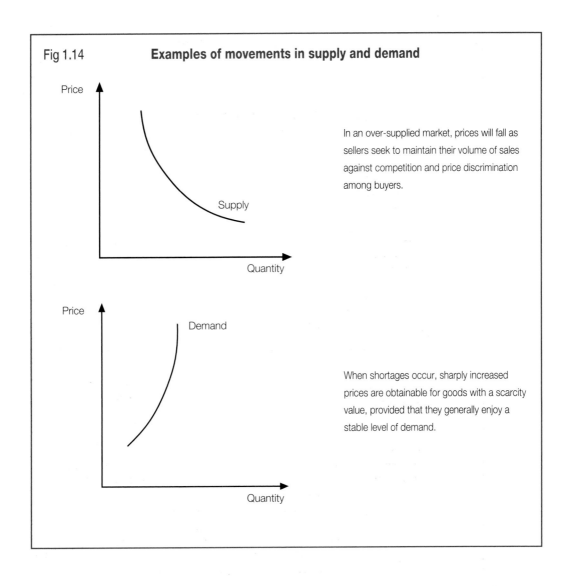

Fig 1.14   **Examples of movements in supply and demand**

In an over-supplied market, prices will fall as sellers seek to maintain their volume of sales against competition and price discrimination among buyers.

When shortages occur, sharply increased prices are obtainable for goods with a scarcity value, provided that they generally enjoy a stable level of demand.

■ Supply and price equilibrium

The factors leading to a movement along and a shift in the supply curve

---

A movement along the supply curve for chocolate bars

The quantity of chocolate bars supplied will

fall if:
- the price falls

rise if:
- the price rises

A shift of the supply curve for chocolate bars

The quantity of chocolate bars supplied will

fall (shift to the left) if:
- there is an increase in price of another product
- there is an increase in the price of a factor of production
- there is a deterioration in the technology used in the production of chocolate
- there is the introduction of a tax on the product

rise (shift to the right) if:
- there is a reduction in the price of another product
- there is a reduction in the price of a factor of production
- there is an improvement in the technology used to produce chocolate
- there is the introduction of a subsidy on the product

INDIVIDUAL ACTIVITY

Draw up a table similar to the one above relating to a shift in **demand** for chocolate bars.

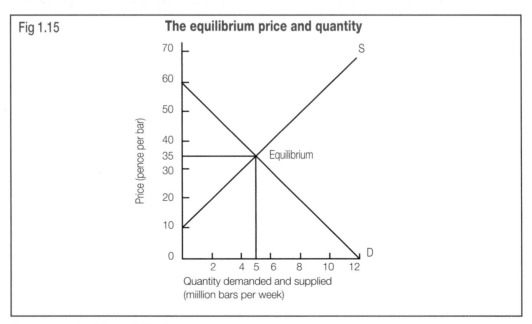

Fig 1.15   **The equilibrium price and quantity**

(Source: Economics, S. Ison, M&E Handbooks)

■ Supply, demand and production

PC
1.1.1
1.1.2

Producers of goods and services are always very conscious of what it costs to bring their products to the market-place. In normal circumstances, they will seek to obtain the highest return possible on the capital they have invested in making the product.

Factors bearing upon the return achievable (the profit margin) often depend on:

■ the perceived value of the product, such as its high-technology design and structure (like a Tornado fighter-plane)

■ the complexity and cost of producing it, which results in few competitors participating in the industry (as in sea-based oil platform construction) so that little competition exists

■ whether the perceived market is large or small (long production runs bring about economies of scale and facilitate cheaper manufacturing costs per unit)

■ whether the existence of fierce competition impacts upon the sales price because products of similar design and build costs are easily brought to the market

And all of the above are closely affected by the state of the economy in the boom–recession cycle, which will have a strong bearing on demand in both consumer and industrial markets.

■ Low volume high cost; high volume low cost

Given that such factors are important determinants in the supply/demand equation, manufacturers tend to need (and get) higher prices for goods which are expensive to produce and for which the available market is small, for example, the manufacture of operating tables as opposed to kitchen ones. In the case of the manufacture of kitchen tables, as they are relatively easy to make, and since the potential market is huge, a higher number of companies will enter the market attracted by the lure of high profits. But as the Kiwi Fruit case history below illustrates, such markets may prove hard to survive in.

CASE HISTORY

The Kiwi Fruit: from gourmet's delight to grandma's fancy!

Some ten or so years ago, pleasantly green slices of fruit with interesting little black pips in them (each slice the size of a small cucumber in circumference) began to appear on plates of gourmet food – especially cuisine minceur – in London restaurants. The kiwi fruit had arrived from New Zealand! Because of its environmentally friendly appearance, delicate flavour and low-calorie make-up, the kiwi fruit quickly came to dominate the up-market trade in exotic fruits, finding its way not only into Belgravia mixed salads, but also into King's Road Chelsea fish garnishes. Demand for this delicacy combined with its scarcity value enabled fruiterers and supermarkets to ask for, and obtain, 50+ pence per little plum-shaped kiwi.

However, no sooner did the kiwi fruit take off in European supermarkets than other profit-hungry Antipodean and Channel Islands fruit-farmers moved in smartly on 'a nice little earner'!

Thus, increased supply began to shift the kiwi fruit off its gourmet delicacy podium downwards on to the 'Get us a couple of kiwi fruit, love, for a bit of colour' platform, and from its place on the top shelf of the supermarket gondola next to its passion and star fruit companions down to a spot next to the satsumas and Granny Smiths. The price of a kiwi fruit fell in a relatively short time – from 50+ pence to 11+ pence each.

The brighter kiwi fruit growers quickly came to realise that it was time to get out of kiwis and back into a better paying alternative crop. Thus the kiwi fruit market settled into a more mature and equilibrial state. Prices moved back up a little, and became more stable.

The case history of the kiwi fruit illustrates the important role played by suppliers in the market-place, since prices are not only demand-created. Manufacturers will invade or quit a market, depending upon whether a satisfactory return on investment is achievable in the long as well as the short run. In this way mature markets, which may have been volatile at their outset, become established but stabilise when a price structure is established which both buyer and seller come to accept as 'fair and acceptable' given the extent of the work done in adding value – whether in growing, making or distributing.

CHECKLIST OF FACTORS INFLUENCING THE QUANTITY OF A GOOD PRODUCED

From the supply viewpoint

Cost to research and develop

Cost to make

Relative complexity of manufacture

Size of the estimated market and whether it is likely to grow, and by how much annually

Nature and extent of the competition – currently and in the future

Likely demand for the product

Price the market will bear for each unit of production

Long-term prospects for the product

Profits achievable – in both short and long terms

From the demand viewpoint

Utility of the product – how suitable will it be for its intended use

Features and specifications – 'what's it got that competing products haven't'?

Its cost relative to directly competing products

Its safety features

Its environmental friendliness

The nature and extent of attached warranties and guarantees

Its product life and reliability – how long before another one is needed?

How easily obtainable are parts and spares?

The cost of repairs and maintenance

The extent of the quantity of a good made (the length of its production runs and product life cycle) depends on how well the product meets both the needs of its manufacturer and its purchaser as illustrated in the twin listings above.

DEMAND, QUANTITY, PRICE AND ELASTICITY

Economists use the term *elasticity* to describe the ways in which the demand for a good or service and the quantity produced, are or are not, affected by upward or downward movements in their prices.

For example, goods which form part of the essentials of life – flour, water, heating or petrol – are much more likely to remain at a given level of demand, even though their prices may increase, since consumers will make economies in other purchasing areas in order to continue to be able to afford these items, since they are essential to them.

On the other hand, the demand for other goods which are 'wants', as opposed to 'needs', such as snack sweets, mouth fresheners or hobby magazines is much more likely to fall if their prices are increased, since consumers can do without them, and these goods may only be able to command a given level of demand as long as their prices continue to lie within pricing bands which are regarded as either trouser pocket change money, personal indulgence money, whim or impulse purchasing money and so on.

Such goods are said to be *elastic* in demand terms, since demand for them is affected by changes in their prices. Such a sensitivity is termed:

Price elasticity of demand

Price elasticity of demand can also occur when there is a reduction in price which leads to a corresponding increase in the purchase of the goods or services concerned.

Where the demand for goods or services is relatively insensitive to movements in prices, then they are said to be *inelastic*.

Factors affecting elasticity/inelasticity are:

- the degree of availability of alternative, substitute products to which a purchaser may switch – say from one brand of toothpaste to another – which has become cheaper because of a price increase in the favourite brand

- the relative purchase cost of the goods compared with money available – price movements measured in pennies for a newspaper affect demand much less noticeably than an increase of hundreds in the cost of a foreign holiday as far as most consumers are concerned

- consumer purchasing habits and patterns – fans of a particular rock group may continue to purchase its tapes or CDs at the same levels of demand even though the marketing pundits of the music publishing company hike their prices 'through the roof'; brand loyalty impinges upon the price–quantity relationship

- conspicuous consumption – people able to afford a Ferrari so as to demonstrate their financial power position are likely to continue to buy such status symbols even though the price demanded is increased by several thousand pounds.

PC
1.1.1
1.1.2

CHECKLIST OF DETERMINANTS OF PRICE

A number of economic factors combine to determine the price of a good or service in the market-place:

- its relative scarcity, when it is in demand – the quantity available compared with the number of willing purchasers

- its relative abundance when there is a scarcity of interested potential buyers

- the nature and extent of competitors in the market

- whether the size of the market allows for economies of scale in production

- its sales price, compared with the price being asked for similar, competing products

- the cost of the raw materials and/or component parts used in its manufacture

- the cost of its manufacture, distribution and sale

- the loading upon it of Customs and Excise or VAT tax

- the likely duration of the demand for the good/service (where research and development costs having been recouped a lowering of the sales price is feasible)

- whether the good/service is a continuous widespread need or a temporary, faddish want

- the position of the good/service in its product life-cycle – does the price reflect the need to recover R&D and production tooling-up costs, or have these been recovered?

- how affordable it is in terms of the finance available (from either consumers or industries) to pay for it; in times of recession prices tend to fall because 'money is tight'

- the relative availability of credit-purchase schemes or bank loans (the 'buy now, pay later' effect) which makes expensive goods or services more readily 'affordable'

- the pressures exerted by governments such as, for instance, the increase of interest rates which makes money more expensive to borrow and thus increases production costs

GROUP ACTIVITIES

In groups of two or three research into one of the following activities and then report back to your class in a suitable form:

1 Research into the 'poverty trap' of a selected Third World country and find out why and how this trap tends to be reinforced by supply and demand conditions in world trade.

2 Research into the sale of the following products in three or four outlets and then produce a report which explains how and why they differ in terms of their response to supply, demand and price elasticity:

- petrol for private vehicles

- pineapples

- beach holidays in southern Europe

- (retail) refined sugar

3 Find out what laws and activities the government has in place in order to discourage the setting-up of illegal business cartels and monopolistic dominations of the market-place.

4 Find out how 'the economic laws' of supply and demand affect what is offered for sale in your school/college shop and refectory.

5 Undertake a survey of your class-mates to find out what they consider as 'needs' and 'wants' in their own personal buying habits. See if any common items are identified.

■ Costs and cartels

As you will have realised, manufacturers, distributors and retailers of products in markets which are price sensitive often have to work within tight margins and overcome problems which are caused, say, by increases in imported raw materials.

Where a product embodies a *price elasticity of demand* sensitivity, then it may not be possible to pass on price increases to customers – they would simply switch to an alternative. Such costs often, therefore, have to be absorbed through improvements in the production process, use of advanced technology, more cost-effective use of labour and so on.

For this reason, many companies operating in the same market would prefer to 'come to gentlemen's agreements' on what prices to charge to purchasers. Given the chance, they would like to establish cartels based upon price-fixing agreements.

However, such business practices are illegal under the Restrictive Trade Practices Act of 1976 and would be promptly investigated by the Office of Fair Trading.

By the same token, consumers and industrial purchasers are protected under European Community law against unfair business practices within the 1992 Single Market, including individual governments supplying an unfair advantage to 'home-grown' products by protectively subsidising them so as to skew the market in their favour.

ECONOMIC FORCES – OPERATING LOCALLY, NATIONALLY AND INTERNATIONALLY

Few economists can agree on the extent to which a government is able to influence an economy. Some maintain that market forces are the over-arching agents of all business change.

Certainly all businesses have to be responsive to trends and changes in the markets they serve if they are to survive. However, the processes by which markets are formed, mature and eventually wither away – to be replaced by others – are complex and sometimes contrary. At times entire industries fail as a result of developments in countries half a world away with which it may prove impossible to compete. The following case history reinforces this point:

Scottish, Tyneside and Belfast shipbuilding

Ever since the advent of the steamship, and until the 1960s, the yards along the Clyde, Tyne and in Belfast enjoyed a world-class reputation for both naval and merchant ship-building.

However, a combination of factors in Far Eastern countries like Japan and Taiwan radically changed the market for merchant ships in the 1970s and 1980s:

- Rapid post-war economic recovery provided finance to invest in constructing vast yards for building the new bulk oil tankers.

- The steel-making industries of Pacific-Rim countries benefited from state-of-the-art technology which helped to keep construction costs down in the shipyards.

- Skilled labour was generally cheaper and not liable to strike or cause expensive stoppages over industrial disputes.

Such developments allied to the meeting of delivery dates and aggressive marketing to oil and bulk carriers proved at the time an irresistible attraction to shipping magnates who, naturally enough, gave their orders to those yards which could best meet their demanding specifications.

As a result, order books in UK shipyards became thinner and some yards were forced to close. Moreover, the world oil crisis of 1973–74 which increased the world price for oil threefold, also caused a massive downturn in demand for oil-based products. As a result, many Western economies went into recession. This state of affairs had a further adverse effect on the UK shipbuilding industry – large users of various kinds of steel – and thus upon the steel mills of centres like Sheffield, Middlesbrough and Consett.

As a result of the Far Eastern investment in shipbuilding, the oil crisis and subsequent recessions in Western economies, there is still today an over-supply of merchant ships, which causes demand for new ships to proceed at reduced levels. Further, the collapse of communism in the USSR and Warsaw Pact states has created a 'peace-dividend' in which fewer ships are needed for NATO and allied defence needs.

As the above case history briefly outlines, international market trends can have a devastating impact upon entire regions within a particular country – in this case the UK. Thanks to their determination and hard work, UK shipbuilders are staging a comeback by targeting particular 'niche' markets for specialist ships like ice-breakers and minesweepers, but the past thirty years have marked a significant decline in the UK shipbuilding industry, which today constructs only 3 per cent of the world's new ships.

The impact of structural change on people

When heavy industry goods can no longer be sold cost-effectively in national or international markets, the consequences for entire towns and their inhabitants can be dire. Industries like steel-making, coal-mining, shipbuilding and motor car manufacturing tend to require workforces in the thousands – all employed on single or adjacent sites, such as Ravenscraig, Consett, Sheffield, the Rhondda Valley, Coventry and Dagenham.

Such industries also require extensive business infrastructures – to supply components, effect specialist maintenance, run canteens and launder overalls. Large service industries are also necessary to feed, clothe, educate, entertain and otherwise cater for the needs of the thousands of employees located in housing estates or villages adjacent to factories and plants. If a large works is closed down – as has happened all too frequently in UK industrial centres over the past twenty years – then some of the main effects upon the local town and its inhabitants are as in the panel shown below.

MAJOR EFFECTS OF STRUCTURAL CHANGE ON AFFECTED COMMUNITIES

- Redundancy on a large scale occurs which swamps the number and availability of alternative jobs in the district; long-term unemployment results for both middle-aged former employees and school-leavers; the resulting mental stress affects marriages, personal health and even local law and order.

- Families living in owner-occupied accommodation with mortgages to pay find themselves in a Catch-22 trap – they cannot sell their houses since no one wishes to move into a depressed area, and so find it hard to move out to regions where work may be available.

- Middle-aged men and women have to retrain to find work – often undertaking radical career changes – from, for example, steel-worker to male nurse.

- Small businesses tied to the economic well-being of the local large works close down and contribute further to the local unemployment problem.

- Young, single people drift away from the area in search of work and a better environment and the normal age distribution curve of the population is skewed towards the middle-aged and retired.

As the above checklist illustrates, structural changes in a region's economy have a profound impact upon the lives of the local people. However, many local authorities, chambers of commerce and central government agencies have already worked wonders in cities and districts adversely affected by the decline of long-established industries by putting into action strategies like these for recovery and renewal:

STRATEGIES FOR RECOVERY AND RENEWAL

- Introducing new industries and businesses such as tourism, computing, car-making (Nissan; Sunderland) or light-engineering into the area, etc.

- Building programmes to attract businesses and consumer trade – new business parks, shopping malls, theme parks, relocated government office complexes, entertainment centres, etc.

- Tax incentives to encourage businesses to move into the area (from both UK Government and EC Commission sources).

- Government sponsored retraining and re-skilling programmes undertaken by local Training and Enterprise Councils, FE colleges and private sector trainers,

- Inner-city redevelopment to demolish run-down areas and encourage the repopulation of deserted centres,

- Construction and renewal of transport infrastructures – road, rail and city airport – to improve access and encourage trade.

- Restoration of the surrounding countryside – by landscaping slag-heaps and mining-waste mounds and by creating urban parks and gardens.

- Tackling pollution 'turn-offs' by cleaning soot-blackened buildings, rivers and streams, by removing graffiti and by improving local waste-disposal systems.

Changes in local markets

As has already been demonstrated in cities like Sheffield, Liverpool, Glasgow and Bradford, a combined effort by central and local government, district business people and interested action groups can transform an ailing city and breathe new life into much needed small businesses. Newsagents, boutiques, cafés and record stores and so on are often revitalised in purpose-built covered shopping centres or arcades.

Also, the changes brought about by introducing new regional industries and by effecting urban reconstruction sometimes result in entirely new businesses being set up. For example, the building of a large new leisure centre may aid the opening of a specialist shop selling only sports shoes and trainers; a newly opened large shopping mall may enable the start-up of a contract cleaning company or security business.

Local businesses are not only responsive to changes on a regional scale, but also to the endless shifts and moods which consumers demonstrate as they respond to trends in fashion and lifestyles.

The following checklist provides some interesting examples:

PC
1.1.1

HOW LIFE-STYLE CHANGES IMPACT ON LOCAL BUSINESSES

- Public houses now provide attractive hot food menus to cater for the increase in demand for plated meals; twenty-five years ago, a pork pie, a cheese sandwich or a packet of crisps represented the available menu. Pubs also enjoy much more flexible opening hours today because of public demand for changes in licensing hours.

- Supermarkets have installed bakeries to provide freshly baked bread, and pizzas with custom-filled toppings for immediate takeaway and subsequent baking.

- Garages provide car-wash facilities routinely since many drivers would rather pay £5 a wash and wax than devote an hour of personal weekend 'quality-time' to the chore.

- Dress has become far more casual over the past ten years; denim jeans, cotton T-shirts, white trainers, anoraks, bermuda shorts, highly patterned men's shirts and flower ties (if ties at all) have ousted blazers and sports jackets, black, polished Oxford shoes, long dresses, fitting overcoats and long-sleeved white shirts or blouses. More men and fewer women now carry handbags. The trend towards more casual clothing not only reflects changing life-styles, but also the much higher costs of more formal clothes like suits and woollen jackets and trousers. Family business drapers and outfitters in High Streets have largely been replaced by chain-stores which discount Third World imports aggressively through high-volume sales.

- Oven-ready meals in a pack and video films are replacing fresh foods and books on the shelves of companies like Marks & Spencer and W H Smith, reflecting the fact that both partners work full-time in many households and would rather heat up than cook, and view, rather than read in their spare time.

- City-centre small businesses are fighting to retain customers who are defecting in large numbers to outer ring-road hypermarkets and malls, where easy parking exists for the ever-increasing number of cars which choke and clog urban streets.

- Charity-run clothes and jewellery shops mushroom as recurrent recessions oblige people to shop (discreetly) for second-hand, low-cost goods. Similarly, car-boot sales and flea-markets flourish.

- Small-business proprietors become willing to haggle to effect a sale, and the question 'How much off for cash?' is no longer too embarrassing for consumers to utter.

- Retail businesses and service sector branches are obliged to improve the quality of their customer services and warranties to match competition and meet the requirements of more discerning consumers – witness the six-year warranty on car bodies and paintwork against rust, and 'no quibble' guarantees on consumer durables and white goods which are less easy to sell when consumers are reluctant to buy on credit.

INDIVIDUAL ACTIVITIES

PC
1.1.1
1.1.2

Select one of the activities set out below. Carry out your research and then report back to your group in the manner shown:

1 Find out why the British-built motorbike virtually disappeared from motorcycle showrooms at the end of the 1960s. Brief your class orally on what you discover.

2 Find out how the city of Bradford responded to the demise of some of its major industries in the period between 1974 and 1983. Present your findings as a two A4 page typescript survey. Include a summary which identifies the reasons for Bradford's successful recovery.

3 Select **one** of the following industrial centres and research into the ways in which it is responding to the decline of the industry listed:

   a The steel mills in Sheffield–Rotherham

   b The textile mills north of Manchester

   c The coal mines of South Wales

   Present your findings in an illustrated talk to your class.

4 Find out what actions are taken by the management of a large works in liaison with local and central government agencies to minimise the consequences of job-loss on a large scale in the event of its closure. Present your findings in the form of a case history relating to a particular works.

5 Select a business activity in your locality which you think has been extensively affected by change over the past five or so years. Arrange to interview selected key employees and find out how the change affected them and the work they did and now do. Present your findings in the form of an article suitable for a business magazine such as *Marketing Today*.

6 Arrange to interview approximately five males and five females in **one** of the following age-groups:

   16–20, 21–25, 26–30, 55–60, 65–70

   Before doing so, devise a checklist of about 15 questions aimed at obtaining specific information and concrete examples of the ways in which their working and/or personal lives have been affected by change the past five to ten years. Find out what kinds of change are considered to have been most significant to them and what changes they found most difficult to adjust to.

   Present your findings in the form of a written report of about 500 words.

■ The small versus big battle

In the local business markets of Britain's towns and cities, a battle to win and keep customers is constantly being fought between the small, family-owned kind of business and the national chain store or multiple outlet.

Before the Second World War, the general grocer, fruiterer and hardware corner shops were features of most terraced-house street blocks. Post-war housing redevelopments, however, favoured shopping parades of six to ten shops with parking lay-bys: post office, butcher, newsagent, wool shop and hairdresser, etc. to service suburban and local residential needs. Housewives tended to use such local shops and venture only into city shopping centres on the bus for occasional large items.

The advent of price-cutting supermarkets, carpet and furniture discount stores and DIY centres in the 1950s heralded a significant shift in the purchasing habits of UK consumers which was supported by the introduction of hire-purchase schemes.

As a result, many suburban retail shops went out of business. However, others survived by joining buying cooperatives like SPAR and yet others like fast-food outlets and hardware stores were aided by negotiating franchising deals with well-known organisations like Colonel Sanders' Kentucky Fried Chicken.

Other small businesses located in the suburbs of large cities struck back by offering enhanced services to locals such as being 'open all hours'. Few hypermarkets open in the mornings at 6.00 am to sell newspapers, cigarettes and breakfast foods and are still open at 10.00 pm at night to provide video rental, snacks, six-pack beers and bottles of wine! Similarly, a 24-hour laundrette or filling-station shop service is a boon to shift-workers and those working unsocial hours. In such ways, small businesses were able to combat the changes in post-war consumer shopping habits and lifestyles by identifying niches – areas where a distinct demand was identifiable, which the small business could supply better than its chain store or multiple competitor.

By providing personalised and user-friendly services, other small firms such as:

■ car insurance broker

■ mobile fish-monger/ butcher

■ home-delivered, ready meal caterers

■ 'eight til late' dry-cleaners

■ TV aerial and satellite-dish fitters and even

■ drain clearers and call-out locksmiths

are able to combat big business successfully. They identify and develop a business niche which is profitable, which responds to changes in consumer or commercial market needs, but which is not so simple to operate as to encourage a host of local imitators.

DISCUSSION TOPICS

1 Consider your own locality. Can you identify any local small businesses which have either been established over the past three to five years and then prospered, or which have successfully competed against larger local firms **because they were responsive to changes in local consumer trends and life styles?**

2 Given that small businesses are unlikely to beat big ones on buying-in prices, can you think of any other, innovative ways in which they can win the local battle for business?

3 The term 'niche marketing' has become popular in businesses like publishing and supermarket retailing as a label for the process of identifying a small, yet worthwhile market and then producing the good or service to meet its needs – at a satisfactory profit.

What market niches can you identify in your locality which would be worth exploiting with the sale of innovative services or products?

GROUP ACTIVITY

In groups of two or three, consider the following mini case studies:

1 A small engineering works employing 25 employees makes trailers for towing behind saloon cars or vans and is located in a small-town industrial estate. Demand for the trailers is falling locally as residents now prefer to go on foreign package holidays rather than UK-based camping holidays.

2 A large tea-room family business occupies a central corner site of a market town in which a second, fast-food multiple outlet has just opened; while tourism is growing in the town, visitors seem to prefer hamburgers and soft ice-cream to cream teas and rounds of buttered toast.

3 A family jobbing builder business employs six men and two women and works out of a set of elderly but sound post-war prefabs in an affluent, semi-rural area. The business possesses an ample yard and covered storage space. Due to the recession in the construction industry, business is bad, but bills have to be paid and income earned to support two families.

Assuming that the directors/proprietors of each of the above enterprises believes that the business is likely to fail unless some changes are soon made, what sort of options are open to them which might help to rescue the situation to the benefit of all participants in each enterprise?

BUSINESS PLAN ACTIVITY

Select one of the above business scenarios, and when your group has decided upon a most likely restructuring strategy for it, make a checklist of the key features of your strategy which would need to be taken into account in devising a successful business plan.

■ Glossary of macro-economic specialist terms

The term macro-economic simply describes a national or international economy within which individual businesses function. The following glossary explains some of the major terms you will encounter when researching business activities on a nationwide scale:

Balance of trade: the position which results from a nation's imports and exports being measured against each other; an adverse balance of trade is where the cost of imports exceeds the earnings secured from exports.

Bank of England: the UK's central bank which acts as the government's banker and controls the levels at which clearing banks lend out money.

Bank rate: the level of interest charged by a country's central bank for providing loans to commercial banks who use it as a means of setting their own lending rate – at a number of percentage points above it.

Capital: another collective term for the various components – buildings, equipment, raw materials, finished and semi-finished goods and money and transport fleets of lorries and cars available to an enterprise which are used as the 'building blocks' of business.

Commodities: this term serves as a combined label for both items or products which are manufactured and more intangible services such as legal advice.

Competition: the existence of entrepreneurs or businesses which vie with each other to supply the needs of a perceived market: note the term 'perfect competition' – a concept in which many businesses produce similar commodities at an equal advantage and in which newcomers can become established readily.

Corporation tax: a tax which is imposed upon businesses by the Inland Revenue in order to secure money for redistribution; also used by the government as a kind of regulator to discourage inflation, since high rates of corporation tax slow down growth and thus affect demand.

Demographic trends: this term describes movements and changes in a nation's population caused by factors such as the distribution of age-groups, immigration and emigration, employed and unemployed ratios, racial mix, levels of education, gender split and so on.

Elasticity: demand for some products is closely affected by the price at which they are sold in relation to the prices of competing commodities; where a change in price produces significant changes in demand, a commodity is termed 'elastic', when demand is almost unaffected, it is called 'inelastic'.

Free market economy: an economy in which prices are allowed to fluctuate according to variations in supply and demand and the availability of resources; compare this with a centralised or command economy such as existed in the Soviet Union, which set prices centrally for commodities and controlled the distribution of resources.

Gross domestic product (GDP): the total in pounds sterling of all the internal or domestic goods and services produced by a nation.

Gross national product (GNP): the total in pounds sterling of a what a nation produces, including income from overseas earnings such as insurance and other 'invisible' exports.

Inflation: a condition in which the spending power of money declines because too much money is chasing too few commodities.

Labour: a term used to describe the workforce in an enterprise or available for work in an economy; sometimes referred to as human resources.

Mixed economy: an economy which is partially 'free' and partially controlled by the state through the public ownership of certain industries such as energy and transport.

Monopoly: legally a situation in which a single business controls 25 per cent or more of a specific market; note the existence of the Commission for Monopolies and Mergers, the government agency which rules on whether a monopoly has been created and imposes strict penalties on guilty parties.

Opportunity cost: whenever a new proposal is considered to produce a product or service, an estimated cost will be drawn up; thus an opportunity cost is the cost of not being able to do something else with the sum devoted to the new project.

Output: a measurement of work achieved by an individual operative, a factory or a national economy; output may be measured in pounds sterling gained by the sale of goods made within a timescale, or the number of units produced, or the number of man-hours taken to achieve a set task, etc.

Production: the process of making a good or product; economists have traditionally viewed the production process as requiring capital, land, labour and business ingenuity or enterprise.

Profit: profit is generally defined as the difference between the amount received from the sale of a commodity and its cost of production – after overheads and other running costs are taken into account; other factors impinge on such a profit, such as directors' remunerations, dividends awarded and taxes due.

Resources: in economic terms, resources may be: money, materials, labour, land and know-how; the comparative availability of such resources, say, between competing trading nations,will significantly affect their ability to bring goods to the market which will sell and secure profits. For example, scarce resources such as uranium or a world-class pharmaceutical chemist will command high prices where an established demand exists.

Supply and demand: a central concept in macro-economics which serves as a kind of shorthand for market-place transactions in which the makers of commodities and their prospective purchasers between them evolve a market price for an item, being that at which they are respectively willing to sell and buy.

INDIVIDUAL ACTIVITY

Keep a notebook handy for jotting down specialist terms like those above and make a point of looking them up in a dictionary of economic or business terms – or ask your teacher to explain them.

Also, make a point of browsing through the business and financial pages of a good quality newspaper in your library during your studies, since seeing terms like those described above used in a current business context will help bring them to life and help you to absorb their meaning.

GROUP ACTIVITIES

In groups of two or three, carry out one or more of the following activities and report back to your class on what you discover:

1 Find out what the major impacts of the 1988–93 UK recession were and how the UK government sought to re-create an expansion phase in the economy.

2 Find out more about the ways in which UK governments work to exercise influence and control on the macro-economy.

3 Research into the supply and demand concept as it operates in today's UK and world economies. Decide whether there are any permanent rules which may be said to govern the pendulum swings of supply and demand.

4 Find out how manufacturing cost accountants monitor the adding of value to products as they go through the manufacturing process.

5 Research into the role of trade unions and associations in industry and commerce and seek to ascertain why their power and influence has waned in the period from 1980 to the present time.

REVIEW TEST

1 Explain the main differences between a market, a mixed and a command economy.

2 How does an economic need differ from an economic want? And how are they both linked to the economic concept of scarcity?

3 What main economic factors are involved in the determination of the price of a good or service in a competitive market?

4 What do you understand by the term 'price equilibrium'? What economic forces are involved in the creation of a price equilibrium state for a good or service?

5 What economic factors influence how much of a product is manufactured in a market economy at a given time?

6 What do you understand by the term 'elasticity' in the context of supply, demand and price?

7 How does structural unemployment come about in a developed industrial economy? What can governments do to minimise its effect on people's lives?

8 Supply three examples of how changes in people's lifestyles have led to economic change in the UK economy over the past 10–15 years.

9 What is meant by the terms: (a) balance of payments (b) balance of trade?

10 Why is high inflation considered by economists to be so dangerous to the economic welfare of a modern economy?

11 What is meant by the term demography? How do economists use demographic trend data?

12 Explain the following abbreviations: GDP, GNP. What is the major single factor which distinguishes them?

13 What do you understand by the term opportunity cost? Supply an example of an opportunity cost in an economic context.

GOVERNMENT INFLUENCE ON BUSINESS

■ The impact of one hundred years of social evolution

During the past one hundred years, the involvement and influence of successive UK governments upon business and the national economy has grown steadily – to the point where, today, the government itself spends almost half of every pound earned by private sector enterprises and consumers.

How did such a large-scale involvement come about? For much of the nineteenth century, economic theorists held strongly to the view that government intervention into the world of business should be minimal. Prevailing economic theory held that the economy of Britain was more likely to grow and prosper in a free-market environment in which open competition was actively encouraged and business entrepreneurs were given a free hand to 'speculate and accumulate'.

However, the government did intervene from time to time, as for example in 1856, when the Limited Liability Act for companies was introduced so as to encourage wider investment without the risk of investors and directors being imprisoned for the debts incurred by a failed limited company, having surrendered all their possessions to help pay creditors.

Despite such liberalising moves, however, there was a wide gulf in Victorian England separating the rich from the poor and the educated from the barely literate. As a result, strong pressure was exerted between 1860 and 1910 for both Liberal and Conservative governments to:

■ make education available to all (Education Act 1870)

■ introduce secondary education (Education Act 1902)

■ extend the authority and roles of local government in areas such as public health and medical officers to inspect and improve amenities (Public Health Act 1848)

■ construct a rudimentary 'safety net' for the very poor (Poor Law Act 1834)

■ The growth of social expectations (1850–1990)

Thus during the last 50 years of the nineteenth century, largely as a result of pressure groups like the Trades Union Congress and Salvation Army and the development of a more educated public opinion, successive governments were encouraged to lay the foundation stones for:

■ universal, free education – to 16 plus, paid for out of national taxation

■ a comprehensive national health service paid for out of a national insurance levy from all in employment together with employers' contributions

■ a social services 'umbrella' to assist all those in need of support as a result of poverty arising from ill-health, prolonged unemployment, disability, family break up etc. paid for out of national taxation and insurance contributions.

■ The mounting costs of enlarged social expectations

Indeed, the extent to which governments over the past 150 years have progressively taken up the responsibilities of education, health and social welfare are evidenced in the amounts spent upon them today. For example, the National Health Service costs *over £100 million per day* to run. In mid-1993, *over £16 billion per annum* was being spent by the government to provide income support to one person in six of the UK population (including claimants' dependants) as a result of hardship arising from the deep recession of 1990–93. Spending on education more than doubled between 1981 and 1991 from £13.4 billion to £29.5 billion (before taking inflation into account).

Defence spending has similarly spiralled over the past 150 years. Twice in the twentieth century Britain (with her allies) fought in two world wars, and, during the Cold War era between 1945 and 1991 when the threat of nuclear war hung over the capitalist west and communist eastern blocs, UK governments felt obliged to channel billions into defence, devoting in 1991 over £27 billion (some 15 per cent of all government expenditure) to the national security provided by the armed services.

■ An 'earth-mother' role for government evolves

What in effect took place in Britain over the past 150 years was a radical change in how its citizens viewed the role of government. 'They' – the government of the day – in the eyes of the populace became progressively responsible for ensuring:

- that parents secured a good education for their offspring
- that 'free' (paid out of taxes) health treatment was promptly and universally available
- that a reliable and affordable transport infrastructure was first constructed and then efficiently maintained
- that citizens could move about safely and sleep securely, thanks to a vigilant and efficient police force
- that a welfare-state safety-net would catch and care for all falling upon hard times, such as becoming homeless.

In this way, the role of government has expanded since 1850, when its workforce of civil servants numbered only a few hundred to its present day 'earth-mother', cradle-to-grave, over-arching social role which requires a mammoth central, local and public corporation bureaucracy employing 5 million people or almost one person in four of the UK working population!

CHECKLIST OF ACTIVITIES ADMINISTERED BY CENTRAL/LOCAL GOVERNMENT AND FINANCED OUT OF GOVERNMENT INCOME

- Defence
- Health
- Education
- Social Security
- Provision of an Independent Legal System
- Housing and Community Amenity
- Fuel and Energy
- Transport and Communications
- Mining and Mineral Resources
- Agriculture, Forestry and Fishing
- Services and Support for Commerce and Industry
- Recreational and Cultural Affairs
- Tax Collection
- Police Services
- Fire Brigades
- Planning
- Environmental Protection
- Consumer Protection
- General Public Services

As the above checklist (by no means exhaustive) readily illustrates, there are today few areas of national or local activity which remain outside of an arm of government interest and involvement.

■ The political dimension of government involvement in the economy

Political activists tend to join political parties in order to bring about changes – political, social or economic – which they believe will satisfy the wants and needs of that segment of the national population they represent. Members of Parliament, for example, though they become elected representatives for *all* the electorate within their constituencies nevertheless take up their party's Whip, which in practice results in their faithfully voting along party lines in almost all parliamentary divisions. Thus the ideologies and principles of policy which political parties evolve and publish in manifestos inevitably colour the statutes and directives which are enacted and issued by the government of the day. Moreover, such dearly held party principles can have a sometimes bewildering impact upon the world of business and the UK economy. A number of economic sectors, for example were set upon wasteful zig-zag courses between 1945 and 1979 when opposing Labour and Conservative governments nationalised and then re-privatised industries such as Transport, Steel, British Road Services (freight transporters) and various commercial docks, such as the London Port Authority. Since Mrs Thatcher's first Conservative administration in 1979, the following previously state-owned industries have been privatised, with private UK citizens as well as companies and financial institutions being actively encouraged to buy shares in many of the new public limited companies:

MAJOR INDUSTRIES PRIVATISED SINCE 1979

- The energy utilities of: gas, electricity and water, broken down into regional providers
- The Civil Airport Authorities – now British Airports Authority
- British Telecom (formerly part of the Post Office)
- British Leyland – now The Rover Group
- The aerospace industry – now British Aerospace
- The local bus transportation services – now segmented into many small-business companies

Expected to be privatised in the near future:
- The National Coal Board – the mining industry
- British Rail
- The Post Office
- The Prison Service

Another political reason for all governments wishing to influence business and the overall performance of the national economy is the sword of Damocles which is always hanging over their heads – the desire for re-election with a comfortable majority! As one senior politician succinctly put it: 'No party can introduce and implement change while in opposition.' For this overriding reason, most governments seek to construct economic cycles in which the peaks of boom periods coincide with national elections, and defer any unpleasant economic medicine such as the need to increase taxation until they are securely returned to office. Hence the label of 'give-away' added to budgets which immediately precede elections and in which the electorate (according to its political colours) is wooed variously by a reduction in the highest band of taxation and extended tax relief on mortgages or a freeze on council-house rents and increases in child and income support benefits etc.

Broadly speaking in the UK, each major party draws its support particularly from:

Conservative Party:	upper, middle/professional class together with an unpredictable tranche of blue-collar workers
Labour Party:	working class, with support from some white-collar and managerial workers
Liberal Democrats:	in essence, voters who fall broadly in their politics between the Labour right and the Conservative left wings.

Each party relies extensively upon funds made available to it from the associations which represent large groupings of its supporters. For example, the Labour Party is largely funded by trade unions, and the Conservative party by private sector organisations. It is therefore not surprising that their respective economic policies will inevitably favour either company owners, directors and managers, or employees and their trade associations or unions.

■ The common ground of economic influence sought by all governments

Whatever the political complexion of a given government, it will seek to improve the economic well-being of its electorate by:

■ seeking to obtain full employment

people suffering the hardship of joblessness are most unlikely to vote for the party they perceive as responsible for their predicament; moreover, such people are net receivers of government money in the form of unemployment benefit, income support and mortgage relief etc. While unemployed, they are not making any contribution towards the increase in the nation's wealth, and thus the enlargement of the government's revenues, which it wishes to employ to achieve its political aims. Furthermore, people inhabiting the outer fringes of society, in terms of deprivation and demoralisation, may turn to crime or acts of anti-social behaviour which may destabilise the localities they inhabit

■ seeking to win and maintain economic growth

only by creating wealth on a continuous, rolling basis is a country able to sustain the levels of affluence which its populace has either come to expect, or to which it aspires. A steady growth in a country's economy enables government to:

○ achieve the social, political and economic objectives it was elected to deliver

○ build new road, rail and air arteries in the transport infrastructure, so as to further strengthen the economy

○ facilitate financial investment by companies in order to replace worn-out plant and premises

○ improve and sustain educational, health and security provisions by means of increased revenues from corporate and individual taxation

When a nation's economy slides into reverse – in say, a recession or slump – a decrease in government revenue inevitably results because of a steep decline in trading income. Further, unemployed people do not provide the government with income from taxes but they do require increased financial support from social services funds. Thus the government of the day may be obliged to borrow money – either at home or abroad – and, as a result, create a downward spiral of an ever-increasing national debt, which burdens the economy and diminishes hopes of recovery.

Such deficit economies have a limited life, since the international value of the currency involved also spirals downwards relative to others, which makes the purchase of imports ever more expensive. This in turn tends to fuel inflation – hence the term 'stagflation', to identify economies with a declining trading performance allied to inflation caused by governments 'bailing themselves out by printing money', instead of achieving the much harder goal of improving economic performance and re-establishing an economic equilibrium, where imports are largely paid for by exports.

However, within the overall world economy, there are inevitably winners and losers in terms of creating and sustaining economic growth. Some economies are blessed with raw materials like copper, bauxite and oil which are in constant, world-wide demand. Others can grow and export efficiently crops of wheat, coffee or rice, or supply timber, wool or cotton to buoyant world markets. Yet others capitalise on superior technological know-how and production processes to sustain a marketing edge on their competitors, while others may rely on cheap labour costs and high volume outputs. Nevertheless, in world markets, it generally 'takes money to make money', and in the world's economic performance league, it is Third World countries that are currently suffering from having their margins relentlessly squeezed by the economic muscle of states with developed economies. As a result, they are unable to generate sufficient operating surpluses to plough back into their own economies and thus strengthen them on a long-term basis.

Controlling inflation – the enemy of all economies

In addition to seeking virtually full employment and sustained economic growth, all governments strive to maintain and control inflation. As you already know, inflation occurs when too much money is available to spend – a high demand for goods or services enables suppliers to increase prices while maintaining the level of sales, for a time. However, the downside of inflationary spirals includes:

- a general loss of international competitiveness, as goods cost more to produce for export
- a progressive downward movement in the value of people's investments and savings, since their worth (buying power) may be decreasing at 10–20 per cent each year
- consumer-led purchasing of foreign goods which leads to adverse balance-of-payments problems
- an increasing downturn in saving and investment as more money is needed to maintain families and firms in a 'hand-to-mouth' situation
- an eventual slide into recession as companies start to fail to sell from an over-stocked position, and begin to lay workers off and cut production, as confidence in the economy plummets.

Such a situation occurred in the UK in the late 1980s, following upon a sudden inflow of money into the economy as a result of significant tax reductions. The economy – especially in its consumer segment – overheated and sucked in large volumes of foreign goods. Building societies were offering young men loans so they could take their girlfriends out for curry suppers! Interest rates zoomed upwards in order to keep overseas investment in the UK at a time when the innate value of the pound sterling was being undermined, but this had the effect of making bank loans much dearer for UK businesses, and thus depressed the economy further. Moreover, in order to redress this worsening situation, Sir Norman Lamont, the then Chancellor of the Exchequer was obliged to use the interest rate lever in order to continue to restrict the supply of money to the private sector and so reduce inflation. Only gradually – at a half point at a time – were interest rates allowed to fall, as inflation was brought slowly under control between 1991 and 1993. Base rate fell from a peak of 14 per cent to some 6 per cent during this period, while inflation also dropped from 10.2 per cent in 1990 to 1.3 per cent in 1993. But, unemployment rose from 1.6 million in 1990 to 3 million in 1993, and the government's Public Sector Borrowing Requirement (the amount it needs to borrow in order to balance its income and expenditure) changed from a surplus of 1.5 per cent of the UK Gross Domestic Product in 1989/90, to a deficit of some 8 per cent of GDP in 1993/4 – amounting to a need to borrow about £1 billion each week!

Indeed, the social costs of such strong economic medicine are that it tends to throw millions out of work, force the closure of thousands of businesses each year and oblige building societies to repossess homes from people unable to maintain mortgage payments. At the same time, the welfare costs of unemployment benefit, income support and social services place huge financial burdens on the government.

Achieving economic growth without fuelling inflation has, for successive UK Chancellors, proved as difficult as squaring the circle! Hence the sequence of 'stop–go' government economic policies since 1945, where violent yanks on the UK's 'brake lever' have been deemed necessary every few years in order to restrain a demand-led economy from accelerating into inflation.

Sustaining a healthy balance of payments

All trading nations import goods and services as well as exporting them; some states with large reservoirs of natural resources may enjoy a natural healthy balance, where they are able to sell abroad far more than they need to import. Others, such as Japan and the UK, rely largely on human resources and skills to refashion imported raw materials into exportable goods. Such states also tend to develop 'invisible exports' such as banking insurance and telecommunications services which they can profitably sell overseas.

Whatever a country's economy produces, it will, sooner or later, need to balance the books of its international trading. By selling its own goods or services to a country from which it is importing, a state facilitates 'payment by exchange' – the cost of the goods (of an equal value) reciprocally bought and sold can be effected without the currency having to leave either country.

Where states do not possess a currency which is internationally accepted – like the rouble of the former communist USSR – then payments for goods purchased abroad would have to be made in a respected currency such as the US dollar, German Deutschmark or Japanese yen. Otherwise such a state would need to resort to barter – rare furs for engineering plant.

Severe economic penalties face states which fail to balance their payments books over a prolonged period:

■ a balance-of-payments deficit is run up which has an adverse effect upon the rate of exchange at which other states will buy the currency of the weak economy – a crisis of confidence builds up regarding the overall economic well-being of the country concerned

■ the government of such an unfortunate country is obliged to borrow money – at high interest rates – in order to pay for imported goods. Or, if it has any, it will need to draw upon its reserves. In the case of the UK, these would be held in gold (or a stable currency) by the Bank of England

■ Once such a country's credit-worthiness and reserves have been depleted, it will have to 'put the bar down' on all imports, including medicines and essential equipment spare parts, and set up strict import and exchange controls. A final strategy open to it – as happens sadly all too frequently in Third World countries – is for the government to meet with its overseas creditors in order to seek a rescheduling of the debts incurred, to reduce annual repayments over a more extended period

The balance of payments in the UK is recorded statistically as follows:

	1992 £
Visible trade	– 14 billion
Invisible trade	+ 2 billion
Balance of payments, current account	– 12 billion

While the UK's invisible balance of trade has been in surplus through the 1980s, its visible balance has worsened since 1983, peaking at £ –24 billion in 1989, and still £ –14 billion in 1992.

Policy steers towards social equalisation

Ever since the French Revolution of 1789, Western governments have taken mind of the revolutionary consequences of too wide a gulf separating the rich from the poor. 'Ability to pay' has characterised the imposition of *progressive direct taxes* in the UK (which in the early 1970s rose to a dizzy height of 98 per cent on personal income above £150,000 per annum! Currently the first PAYE tax band (after single and married persons' allowances) levies 20 per cent on the first £3,000 of income, 25 per cent on additional income up to £23,700 and 40 per cent on all income over £23,700.

Other efforts by successive governments to equalise the relative affluence of its citizens are evidenced by zero-rated VAT on children's clothes and food, and by the creation of a floor of some £5,165 below which no PAYE tax is levied upon a married person. Current Conservative Party views hold that a ceiling of 40 per cent on all income over £23,700 encourages able entrepreneurs to create wealth from which all members of society benefit.

The imposition of indirect taxes, such as VAT are considered by some economists as being more equitable, since they are only levied from those who choose to purchase such a taxed good or service. However, the purchase of petrol (for a car) by a rural resident whose bus service has long been discontinued, may be deemed a need rather than a want! Similarly, the proposal to levy VAT on fuel purchases aroused widespread hostility in 1993.

Other means of encouraging the equalising of UK citizens' wealth take the form of stamp duties on house purchases, inheritance taxes and capital gains taxes on the profit made from the purchase and sale of shares etc.

PC
1.2.2
1.2.3
1.2.4

■ The levers available to government to influence the UK economy

Given that governments of all persuasions see advantage in the creation of full employment, low inflation, a healthy balance of payments and sense of equal opportunity in a generally affluent society, they will naturally use the levers and controls which are available to them as the government of the day. The levers or 'influencers' they employ tend to be:

- control of public expenditure
- control of the money supply
- raising or lowering the base rate of the Bank of England, which effectively controls the interest rates offered by the clearing banks
- seeking to control the rate of exchange at which the pound sterling is bought and sold on international stock exchanges
- raising or lowering consumer and company direct and indirect taxes and national insurance contributions
- providing grants and subsidies to particular industrial sectors (such as information technology and telecommunications) and subsidising businesses in regions suffering economic hardship
- borrowing money from individuals, corporations or institutions (in the form of government gilts and bonds offered for sale) in order to balance its public spending books in the short term
- seeking to influence public and business opinion through mass media advertising campaigns to 'buy British', or 'think green', to 'save electricity' or to 'buy British Telecom shares'.

PC
1.2.1
1.2.2

DISCUSSION TOPIC

Some political and economic commentators believe that governments are far less able to influence the workings of the UK economy than they would have us believe. The proverbial man in the street blames all his economic ills on the incompetence of the government of the day. To what extent do you consider governments *are* able to influence the direction of an economy such as the UK's mixed economy ?

■ The control of public expenditure

PC
1.2.1
1.2.2
1.2.3

Of all the levers and 'influencers' available to a government, that exercised over its own expenditure would seem the easiest to control. Each year the Treasury requires what are called spending ministers of state – those running departments like education, defence and social services to supply estimates of the costs of their spending plans for the coming financial year. Similarly, Treasury civil servants estimate – for the Chancellor of the Exchequer – the amount of government revenue or income which can be expected to be raised in the same year from direct and indirect taxation, the sale of government products and services, and interest on any government investments etc.

Budgets and autumn statements

Chancellors of the Exchequer make their pronouncements upon the control of public expenditure in their annual budgets and autumn statements. Traditionally the budget took place in March each year and the autumn statement in November. The March budget tended to concentrate on the govemment's fiscal and taxation strategies, and the autumn statement on its spending plans. However, from 1993 onwards the government announces both its spending and taxation plans every autumn.

The budget deficit problem

In some years, as in 1987, the amount of money flowing into the government's coffers exceeded that which it spent out. As a result, it was able to pay off some of the long-term debts which it holds, referred to as the national debt. Sadly, however, there have been very few such repayments made over the past twenty or so years, since most UK governments have worked within an economic or budget deficit framework, ending up each year spending more than has been received as revenue.

Indeed, in 1993, this deficit was running at the rate of £1 billion pounds each week, or £50 billion per annum! As a result, when Sir Norman Lamont resigned his Chancellorship, and Kenneth Clarke took over, his main concern was to reduce this enormous drain upon the public purse by supervising necessary but unpleasant cuts in public spending, since no government can continue to spend at such a rate without passing on an unmanageable debt to its future adult citizens. Moreover, such a debt requires a significant amount of wasted money being spent on servicing the loans which the government is obliged to secure, and makes overseas investors very nervous about the pound's future, thus tending to devalue it, unless a corrective economic policy is seen to be forthcoming.

Governments as paymasters

It is also worth remembering that the government is the paymaster of some 5 million UK public sector workers – civil servants, teachers, servicemen, postmen, railwaymen, nurses and doctors etc. – and can exercise significant fiscal power by limiting their pay rises. In 1992, for example, the government limited all public sector employees' pay rises to 1.5 per cent – a figure which was at the time below the level of inflation.

In addition to making cuts in, say, the amount of income support, child or unemployment benefit in order to reduce government expenditure, a government may choose to postpone or cancel capital building projects, such as schools, hospitals or roads, or naval vessels or aircraft due to be built or refitted.

Keynes and public spending in a recession

Governments do not always cut back on public expenditure, even in times of recession. President Roosevelt in the world slump of the 1930s elected to follow the advice of economists like J M Keynes (to use public spending as a way out of the slump) by building roads, dams and public buildings.

■ Public spending control and politics

While, at least in theory, all governments have the power to exercise tight control over public spending, in practice they find it very hard to control. The reasons stem from the politics involved. Whereas backbencher MPs tend to find it easy to support public spending cuts in general and in the abstract, they find it much harder when such cuts become specifically targeted, affecting, say, large numbers of their own constituents. By the same token, spending ministers tend to protect their budgets fiercely from any Treasury onslaught, as if any reduction would undermine their power and influence in cabinet and appear as a slight upon their public image. Perhaps this is why public spending rose so sharply between 1989 and 1993 during the recession.

DISCUSSION TOPIC

Why do you think public expenditure rose sharply during the 1989–93 recession? Would you expect it normally to rise or to fall during a recession? What evidence can you provide to support your views?

PC
1.2.1
1.2.2
1.2.3

■ Control of the money supply

Most economic theorists agree that when too much money is available in an economy to purchase goods or services – by both consumers and businesses – the effect over a period of time is inflationary. Freely available finance, especially when on offer at low lending rates from banks or building societies, helps to create a surge in demand. As we have already seen, when demand exceeds supply, prices tend to increase until a price equilibrium is established at a higher level. In short the goods and services cost more to acquire, and thus the currency of the economy buys less.

■ The interest rate lever

In order to combat such inflationary trends, governments have at their disposal the major lever of interest rate adjustment. A government wishing to depress demand and so to encourage a deflationary spiral can instruct the Bank of England to increase the base rate. This is the rate at which it will lend money to the clearing banks. If the rate the Bank of England charges is higher than the prevailing market rate, the clearing banks will promptly adjust their own rates upwards. By raising or lowering the base rate, the government is able to increase or restrict the amount of money which consumers or businesses borrow to spend on goods or services, and thus help to encourage growth or cut-backs in the economy.

Ever since the Second World War, successive Chancellors of the Exchequer have sought – without much success – to promote a smoothly growing UK economy. In reality, they have tended to use 'hikes' in interest rates or 'give-away' tax cuts as crude levers to promote growth or cut back, depending whether the economy was in an expansionist or recessionary wave of the economic cycle. Hence the terms 'boom or bust', 'stop and go' were used to describe governments' economic policies over the past fifty years.

While the use of the interest rate lever or weapon may be justly regarded as crude, it is nevertheless effective. In 1990 inflation in the UK was running at some 10.2 per cent per annum. During that year, the interest rate peaked at 15 per cent dropping to 14 per cent when the UK entered the Exchange Rate Mechanism of the European Community. By employing a prudent policy regarding the use of the interest rate mechanism, the Chancellor at that time, Norman Lamont, was able to bring down interest rates from 14 per cent in January of 1991 to 6 per cent in 1993, with a corresponding drop in the rate of inflation from 10 per cent to 1.3 per cent. The downside of this policy, however, was the sharp rise in unemployment, bankrupted businesses and private house repossessions by building societies.

DISCUSSION TOPIC

Do you think that a government is entitled to use the interest rate lever as a means of control in the UK economy? Or do you think that such mechanisms should be employed – as in Germany – by a central bank which is independent of government?

■ The taxation lever

Perhaps the most effective lever at the government's disposal at any time lies in its ability to increase or decrease the taxes paid by individuals or businesses.

Direct taxation

Few employed people are unaware of the proportion of their gross wages taken from their pay-packets in the form of Pay As You Earn (PAYE) direct tax. At present PAYE taxation is paid in three tranches after personal and married persons' allowances have been deducted:

Income Band

20% rate:	first	£3,000
25% rate:		£3,000 – £23,700
40% rate:		£23,700 and over

Corporation Tax – the tax which companies pay on their profits – currently runs at 33 per cent for the full rate of tax, with small companies paying 25 per cent on profits up to £250,000.

In addition to PAYE and Corporation Tax, both employees and companies are obliged to pay National Insurance Contributions to the government. Some economists regard such payments as a form of taxation, in that the money goes into a 'global pot', from which the National Health Service and Social Services are funded. Currently employees' contributions* range from 2 per cent on weekly earnings of £56 per week to 8 per cent on earnings over £420 per week, with the employer also contributing between 1.6 and 10.4 per cent pro rata. (*In the government's 'contracted in' scheme.)

In general terms, the more direct tax a government takes from individuals and companies, the more deflationary the impact upon the economy, since less money remains for consumers to spend on cars, hi-fi stacks, washing machines and holidays, and for company directors to spend on raw materials, capital equipment, premises and employees' pay.

However, if the government decides to spend *itself* the extra revenue it obtains from increased taxation, this of itself is likely to fuel inflation! Further, when direct taxes become too high, they engender serious disincentives – for employees to work overtime or to seek financial advancement, and for companies to invest in new equipment or to expand. Thus a policy of high taxation may only work in the short term in order to damp down demand. When the highest rate of direct taxation on individuals reached an incredible 98 per cent in the early 1970s, many highly successful entrepreneurs moved abroad and took their financial interests with them. Punitive levels of direct taxation may therefore cause harm to an economy by creating poor morale and disincentives in national workforces and flight to greener pastures by national wealth creators. High taxation also tends to lead to significant growth in a country's black economy, where people work and pay for work without declaring it, thus diminishing the income from taxes due to the government.

PC
1.2.1
1.2.3
1.2.4

DISCUSSION TOPIC

States which levy high taxes also tend to have a high profile of intervention – through the funding of social services, health services, education, leisure activities, state pensions, state housing and the like. States which levy low taxes, tend to have a lower profile through the encouragement of private enterprises to supply such services at a cost to the individual, paid for as health insurance, school fees and personal pensions schemes etc.

Which system do you think preferable when thinking of a country's population as a whole? What do you see as the pros and cons of either approach to direct taxation?

Indirect taxation

Indirect taxation in the UK takes two main forms: value added tax (VAT) on specified goods and services and customs and excise duties payable on specific goods, such as alcoholic beverages, transport fuels, betting and tobacco products.

Value added tax

VAT, introduced in 1973 to replace purchase tax (called in the USA a sales tax), is levied upon a wide range of goods and services. VAT in the UK is currently levied at 17.5 per cent of the sales price. Certain products, such as food, children's clothing, books and newspapers are currently exempt from VAT (zero rated) on social grounds, but future governments may well take a less liberal view as the need to reduce the Public Sector Borrowing Requirement (PSBR) becomes more urgent.

There is both an input side and an output side to VAT, since all sole traders or companies engaged in business (except for those making and selling zero-rated goods) are, in effect, unpaid tax collectors for the government. An enterprise, say, in the primary sector selling on raw materials to a manufacturer will add VAT to the sales price. The manufacturer of the finished goods will likewise add VAT to the price of the goods to the distributor and the retailer to the eventual consumer. VAT levied during manufacture is regarded as an input tax, and on the eventual sale as an output tax. Where a business incurs VAT charges on goods or services bought in as a necessary part of running costs – say petrol, cleaning materials, stationery and office equipment etc. – such costs may be set against the VAT collected on all 'vatable' sales, which must be remitted to HM Customs and Excise quarterly.

Excise duties

In addition to VAT, the government, through its Customs and Excise arm levies taxes on a number of products or pursuits, such as alcoholic drinks, petrol, tobacco products and betting and gambling, notably horse-racing.

Council taxes and business rates

Other sources of revenue for the government are the locally collected Council Tax and Uniform Business Rates. For decades until 1990, local taxes for individuals had been based upon the levy of a local rate from householders who either owned or were purchasing their homes. (Council house tenants were exempt.) The amount of rates paid was worked out by means of a formula which computed a notional income arising if the owner-occupier were to rent out his or her house. Over many years this form of indirect taxation operated on the basis of a not too unreasonable 'ability to pay', but was also seen to be unfair, since some residents using local facilities paid nothing and others, such as widows and old-age pensioners, were penalised if they remained in larger houses. The Thatcher Government therefore decided to introduce a Community Charge in 1990 (promptly called a poll tax by its opponents) on all 18-plus adults, with special reductions for students, pensioners and people on income support etc.

This tax proved wildly unpopular – especially in Scotland and in poor districts – where reassessments gave rise to steep increases in charges payable. Also, widespread resentment resulted from the very wealthy and the very poor in many cases paying identical Community Charge taxes. So unpopular was this tax, although in many ways inherently fairer than its antecedent, local rates, that the Conservative government was obliged to restructure it as a 'Council Tax' in 1992–93 by going back to a system based on the estimated value of owner-occupied accommodation.

Uniform business rates

During the same period, companies and partnerships also saw the new, nationally fixed uniform business rate increase the valuation of their business premises sharply in many instances, sometimes by as much as 300 per cent on the former local business rates valuations. Many small businesses cited this increase as a major factor contributing to their collapse during the 1990–93 recession.

Miscellaneous indirect taxes

Over the past two hundred years, successive Chancellors and their ingenious senior civil servants have devised a number of other forms of indirect taxation. Eminent among these are:

- Stamp duty – a tax levied on the sale of property
- Inheritance or wealth tax – a tax levied (above a nil rate band currently up to £150,000) of some 40 per cent
- Capital gains tax – a tax charged upon individuals at their PAYE rates – on profits made from the sale of assets over and above a base level of £5,800 per annum
- Motor vehicle tax – a tax levied on cars and trucks which are then licensed to use public roads for a period of six months or one year, depending on the licence purchased
- Television and radio licences – a tax levied on the users of TV and radios who also are obliged to purchase annual licences

When the revenue from direct and indirect taxation is totalled and then divided by the number of adult UK citizens, it is not difficult to see how the government comes to spend some 40 per cent of the entire gross domestic product of the UK!

PC
1.2.1
1.2.2
1.2.3

■ The pound sterling's exchange rate

Like every other currency which is generally accepted among international trading nations as a convertible currency (in effect, acceptable by foreign states for goods purchased) the pound sterling has a rate of exchange *vis-á-vis* other currencies, notably the US dollar, the Deutschmark, the Japanese yen and the French franc.

The gold standard

Until 1931, the pound sterling (along with major currencies like the US dollar) enjoyed a value which was fixed to that of gold. Such an arrangement proved a great stabilising influence, since there was very little change in value between currencies – as long as they could maintain the link to the value of gold. However, the world slump of 1929 resulted in the UK no longer being able to maintain the value of its currency in this way.

The US dollar standard

With the emergence of the USA in 1945 as the world's dominant economy, the link with gold was substituted by a link with the US dollar – a marker as to the pound's international value which still exists today. After the pound came off the gold standard, it was allowed (largely) to float in the international markets regarding its value relative to other major currencies. Sadly, the cost to the UK economy of the Second World War and the repayment of debts incurred to the USA greatly affected post-war economic reconstruction, and the pound drifted inexorably downwards in the 1950s and 1960s relative to the value of the US dollar and Deutschmark.

The European Community and its exchange rate mechanism

With the creation of the Common Market between 1951 and 1957, a movement began to harmonise the economies of the participating European states. By 1986 the twelve member states of the evolved European Community had progressed far along a path of not merely creating a free-trade area, but of moving towards a form of unified federal government.

Crucial to such an evolution was the creation of a single market and a single currency. The EC Single Market – in which internal tariff barriers were scheduled to be progressively removed by 31 December 1991 – was duly established.

The creation of a community operating within a European Monetary Union, however, proved far more complex. In 1979 the Exchange Rate Mechanism (ERM) was set up and progressively joined by nine of the twelve member states during the 1980s (the UK, Greece and Portugal remaining outside it).

Essentially, the ERM was designed to provide a stable relationship between participating currencies. Economically strong participators such as Germany and France opted to link their currencies within a narrow band of pegged, related values, while less strong member states were permitted to let their currencies float between a wider band of related values. All participating currencies would be given a corresponding ECU value (European Currency Unit). The hope was that, in this way, EC states could, with little economic pain, proceed to a single currency and monetary union. Also, by obliging member states to link their currencies to the robust Deutschmark, it was hoped that EC inflation would remain low and that a climate of financial prudence and responsibility would prevail. It is worth noting that the 'mechanism' aspect of the ERM included the support by strong states of weaker ones in this way: when a currency of a member state was in danger of hitting the bottom of its band, the strong states were committed to intervening and buying the currency on international markets as a means of maintaining its exchange rate value.

John Major took the UK into the ERM in October 1990, and – as events proved – made the fatal mistake of over-valuing the pound sterling against the Deutschmark, pegging it within a band of some 2.78–3.13 DM.

'White Wednesday'

By October 1992, it had become clear that the pound sterling could not be maintained within its ERM band parity, and on 'White Wednesday', 16 September 1992, international speculators struck, and within a matter of hours, forced the government to come out of the ERM after a devaluation of the pound by some 15 per cent.

During the hectic trading period on the London and international stock exchanges, the Chancellor, Sir Norman Lamont, through the customary intervention of the Bank of England spent some £7 billion on buying pounds in order to seek to maintain their value. But this incredible amount of buying proved in vain, and devaluation was accepted as inevitable. The Conservative government was very bitter at the time about the alleged failure of the German Bundesbank to buy pounds according to the ERM agreement.

Return to a floating pound

With the return of the pound to a floating role (at a position some 15 per cent cheaper than it was within the ERM) UK exporters were given a heaven-sent opportunity to increase their sales both with the EC and internationally, and this opportunity was heralded by many politicians as a god-send in aiding the UK recovery from recession – hence the label 'White Wednesday'. Indeed, UK government agencies advertised widely in Germany the opportunities to German business of moving their factories to Britain so as to take advantage of low costs and prices.

The limitations of exchange rate interventions

As the above case history of the pound's October 1992 exit from the ERM amply illustrates, government intervention in international exchanges either to maintain the value of the pound or to encourage its reduction (by either buying or selling sterling), while it may work within small movement margins, cannot of itself combat the concerted efforts of an alliance of international currency speculators. Such efforts are especially doomed when such speculators are convinced that the pound is over-valued by as much as 15 per cent, and are prepared to gamble billions (by selling pounds and then buying them back at a lower value) to back their judgement!

REVIEW TEST

1 Why has the role of the UK government in the economy grown so dramatically during the past 150 years?

2 List three main arguments both for and against the privatisation of state-run industries.

3 What are the major economic policies which virtually all democratically elected governments seek to achieve? Explain briefly the rationale for each one.

4 What is meant by the term social equalisation? Why should a government be concerned to sustain a policy of social equalisation?

5 In what ways can a government influence the activities of a mixed economy?

6 What is likely to happen in a developed economy if its budget deficit is allowed to increase uncontrollably?

7 What do you understand by the term Keynesian economics?

8 Explain what part is played in the UK by the Public Sector Borrowing Requirement.

9 What case can you make for preferring a system of indirect as opposed to direct taxation?

PC
1.2.1
1.2.2
1.2.3

GROUP ACTIVITIES

In groups of two or three carry out one of the following activities and then report back to your class by means of an illustrated oral presentation of 10 – 15 minutes duration:

1 How and why successive UK governments became more involved in the operation of the UK economy between 1840 and today. Your presentation should highlight major milestones and developments.

2 What activities the present-day UK government undertakes in its efforts to secure full employment and the return to work of unemployed people.

3 What actions post-war (1945) UK governments have taken to contain the Public Sector Borrowing Requirement within manageable limits, and to prevent budget deficits from growing out of control.

4 Select **one** of the central/local government activities on page 59. Research into its main operations and how it supports or impacts upon UK industry and commerce.

5 Research into **one** of the privatised industries listed on page 60 and find out how the process of privatisation affected its operations and activities.

6 Find out what types of direct, indirect and excise taxes are currently levied upon business organisations and consumers and what contribution is made to the national exchequer by each tax you identify.

7 Research into the ways in which a UK government borrows the money it needs in order to balance its books when running a budget deficit.

8 Research into the problems which have to be overcome in order to introduce a single European currency for use among all EC member states. Suggest what you believe to be the best way to achieve this goal of currency union.

THE IMPACT OF UK GOVERNMENT AND EUROPEAN COMMUNITY POLICIES UPON BUSINESS

PC
1.2.2
1.2.4

Since the Treaty of Rome was signed in 1957, the influence of the European Community has grown strongly, embracing all economic sectors and activities. The crops grown by UK farmers are now monitored by EC satellite cameras, the production of foodstuffs and manufactured goods have to conform to an encyclopaedia of regulations and EC articles, and business-related services such as finance and insurance also now have to comply with EC regulations.

The economic policies of the EC include:

■ the establishment of a tariff-free internal market among member states – the Single Market of 1992 was established by the Single European Act of 1988; the creation of an open financial services market further underpins this development (*Directive 92/12/EEC and the Investment Services Directive 1990*)

■ the free movement of individuals and enterprises among member states in order to work or set up businesses, together with a progressive harmonisation of trade and professional vocational qualifications (see *Certificates of Experience*)

■ working towards monetary union based around the ECU – the European Currency Unit. The Exchange Rate Mechanism (ERM) was established to harmonise the relative exchange rates of member states within a set of wide and narrow bands allocated respectively to less and more economically powerful states (see the *European Monetary System 1979*)

■ the progressive creation of a unified system of company law and underpinning regulations to integrate and harmonise areas like contracts, product advertising and descriptions, quality, health and safety standards etc. (*Directives 89/666/EEC, 88/627/EEC, and especially the European Company Statute COM/91/174*)

- the removal of unfair barriers to trade (*Article 30*) and the implementation of fair competition laws (*Single European Act 1988, Articles 85/1 and 86*)
- the harmonisation of working conditions for employees – the Social Chapter of the Maastricht Treaty (Articles 117–122 of Maastricht Treaty)
- the progressive harmonisation of Value Added Tax percentages for goods and services of a common type (*Directive 91/680/EEC*)
- the further development of a Common Agricultural Policy (CAP) and the establishment of common food and animal transportation and slaughtering laws (*Directives 77/94, 79/112, 89/109/EEC, 89/397/EEC 91/628/EEC and 92/5/EEC*)
- the standardisation of procedures and practices for governments procuring goods and services so as to eliminate bias towards a member state's own businesses and utilities (the *Supplies, Works, Services, Utilities and Remedies Directives*)
- a unified policy for consumer protection (*Directives 84/450/EEC, 85/374/EEC, 88/314/EEC and 87/102/EEC etc.*)
- a common environmental policy for protecting the natural resources of all member states (*The Single European Act 1988*, and some 338 directives covering areas like water pollution, dangerous chemicals and the protection of rural areas etc.)
- an open systems policy for unifying information technology and computer systems (*the Open Network Provision Directive, and 92/38/EEC on television signal broadcasting by satellite*)

(*Source: The Single Market: The Facts*, published by the Department of Trade and Industry, August 1992)

Other policy areas covered by EC Directives, Articles, regulations include:

- transport
- standards
- intellectual property
- pharmaceuticals
- health and safety
- collaborative research and development

As may be seen by the above (by no means exhaustive) checklist, European Community business and economic policy has – over a period of some thirty years – been supplied with an impressive set of 'teeth' in the form of directives, articles and statutes. These enable the European Commission and the judiciary of member states to enforce laws which aim to create a unified set of standards of business activity and to construct a legal and bureaucratic infrastructure which will lead, inexorably, to 'an ever-closer union' of the Community's member states.

UK GOVERNMENT INTERVENTION IN INTERNATIONAL MARKETS

■ As a member of the European Community

Currently about a half of all of the UK's overseas trade is with other members of the European Community. Indeed, the transition away from trading predominantly with British Commonwealth countries like Canada, Australia and New Zealand, to Germany, France, Italy and the Netherlands has been remarkable since the United Kingdom joined the European Economic Community in 1973. Understandably, UK economic policy is now to promote strenuously the expansion of UK businesses into the EC Single Market through fiscal incentives (such as the fortuitous devaluation of the pound sterling in September 1992) and government-sponsored export drives and initiatives from the Department of Trade and Industry in particular.

■ As a member of the General Agreement on Tariff and Trade (GATT)

Since joining, the UK has naturally been obliged to harmonise its own international trade and economic policies with the unified positions adopted by all member states as European Community policy. A recent example of this was in the 1993 series of negotiations of the Uruguay Round of talks on the General Agreement on Tariffs and Trade (GATT). GATT was established in 1948 as a forum for some 25 states which wished to encourage mutual trade by reducing as much as possible the tariff barriers erected by members to protect their own national industries from external competition. Such protectionism was found to be counter-productive to sustaining general economic prosperity in the long run.

Following upon the setting up of GATT, series or rounds of trade negotiations were held every few years. The Uruguay Round started in 1986 and a new set of tariffs and agreements was finally agreed in principle in January 1994.

In the spring of 1993 the USA imposed additional tariffs on steel imports to protect its own industry (in deep recession) and rowed with the French who were being intransigent over allowing USA cereals into France at the levels the USA wanted. At the time, general agreement on the Uruguay Round was very close, and other member states, including the UK, put pressure on both the USA and France to make concessions so as to avoid a total GATT break-down. This would have had the effect of a melt-down on the recession-hit economies of the GATT member states, since ensuing protectionism and tariff barrier hikes might well have led to a world slump.

In the summer of 1993, at a Tokyo summit of the G7 Group (the seven most economically powerful states in the world) President Clinton led the Group into a set of agreed compromises which saved the GATT negotiations and rescued the prospect of bringing an end to the international recession and to creating an economic climate in which some 40 million unemployed people could be got back into work.

■ Promoting UK exports

Against this GATT background it is not difficult to see why successive UK governments are constantly negotiating with trading partners of all complexions to:

- ■ reduce tariffs and quotas
- ■ encourage reciprocal amounts of trading (so as not to upset balance of trade and payments equilibriums)
- ■ open up new markets and seize upon new trading opportunities

■ The Organisation for Economic Cooperation and Development

To support such international trading policies, the Organisation for Economic Cooperation and Development (OECD) which includes EC states, USA, and Japan focuses upon helping poor, Third World economies to develop trading links with GATT and G7 member states.

■ Intervention to prevent unfair subsidising of imported goods and dumping

The counterpart for UK governments to encouraging trade with foreign countries lies in preventing unfair trading practices such as dumping and excessive overseas governments' subsidies of imported goods. Such practices lead to significant influxes of foreign imports into the UK which are offered for sale at prices well below those which UK manufacturers can match. For example, in order to gain a foothold in an affluent nation's economy some foreign governments may well provide significant financial support for the production of personal computers, the growing of foodstuffs or the extraction of raw materials.

By the same token, goods like cotton garments, motor-vehicle tyres, and timber may be produced in countries where labour, production and partial distribution costs are significantly lower than in countries like the USA, Japan or EC states. Such products – given the chance – may well be dumped into overseas markets. To prevent such practices, governments usually restrict their importation by imposing swingeing import duties and quotas (ceiling totals of goods which may be imported in any year). It is often difficult to see in some national economies where justified intervention ends and unwarranted protectionism begins.

■ International trade and regional policy

The government of the United Kingdom as a member state of the EC receives finance from the European Regional Development and Social Funds which are specifically targeted on regional areas whose economies have suffered, for example, from structural economic decline resulting from the demise of a traditional industry such as mining, shipbuilding or fishing. Such funds are often used to pump-prime the creation of new industries – information technology, telecommunications, tourism etc. – which will attract foreign currency either through exports or an increase in overseas tourists. They are also employed to provide reskilling and retraining programmes for local inhabitants made redundant from obsolete occupations.

GROUP ACTIVITIES

1 In pairs, select one of the policy areas listed on pages 73, 74, carry out your research into the relevant Directive(s), Article(s) and EC regulations, organise your findings suitably and then deliver a 5–10 minute oral presentation to your group on what you discovered.

2 In groups of two or three, research into the founding and subsequent effects of GATT upon the development of trade among member states and the rest of the world. Produce your findings as a factsheet, agree on which group produced the best one, and distribute it to all class members as a reference source.

3 In pairs, research into one of the following:

the OECD, G7, the European Development Fund, the European Social Fund

Present your findings in the form of a 5-minute illustrated briefing to your class.

ECONOMIC RELATIONSHIPS AND BUSINESS INFORMATION

The supply of goods or services by the private and public sectors of the UK economy may be viewed and evaluated in a number of different ways, depending upon who is doing the evaluating and what their economic interests happen to be.

At the centre of the concept of economic relationships is the process of exchange. In primitive societies this often took the form of barter (in the absence of a generally accepted currency).

Today, the exchange concept may take a variety of forms including:

■ work (of hand or brain or both) for pay

■ the acquisition of goods or services for money in payment (whether cash, cheque, credit card transaction or IOU)

■ the influx into a public company of finance in return for a prescribed number of shares which offer the promise of a return on the capital invested on demand plus an annual dividend as a percentage of the accumulated value of the shares purchased

■ an expectation on the part of national government of a return on its investment in, say, regional economic redevelopment in the form of an increase in regional employment and thus a decrease in the cost of social services allied to an increase in tax revenues from re-employed people.

Other economic exchanges may take the form of contributions to football clubs' incomes from sponsorship by businesses who in return receive televised publicity for their product or service or brand loyalty-building exchanges in which, say, petrol purchasers receive a given number of tokens per litre of petrol purchased which may eventually enable them to obtain a 'free' gift.

Economic relationships example chart

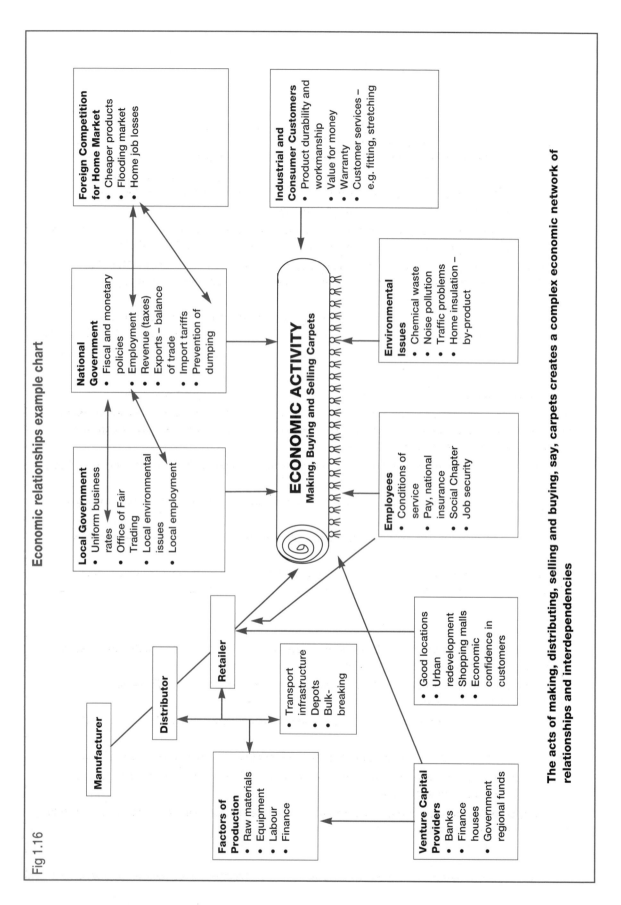

Fig 1.16

Foreign Competition for Home Market
- Cheaper products
- Flooding market
- Home job losses

Industrial and Consumer Customers
- Product durability and workmanship
- Value for money
- Warranty
- Customer services – e.g. fitting, stretching

National Government
- Fiscal and monetary policies
- Employment
- Revenue (taxes)
- Exports – balance of trade
- Import tariffs
- Prevention of dumping

Environmental Issues
- Chemical waste
- Noise pollution
- Traffic problems
- Home insulation – by-product

Local Government
- Uniform business rates
- Office of Fair Trading
- Local environmental issues
- Local employment

ECONOMIC ACTIVITY
Making, Buying and Selling Carpets

Employees
- Conditions of service
- Pay, national insurance
- Social Chapter
- Job security

Manufacturer

Distributor

Retailer

- Transport infrastructure
- Depots
- Bulk-breaking

- Good locations
- Urban redevelopment
- Shopping malls
- Economic confidence in customers

Factors of Production
- Raw materials
- Equipment
- Labour
- Finance

Venture Capital Providers
- Banks
- Finance houses
- Government regional funds

The acts of making, distributing, selling and buying, say, carpets creates a complex economic network of relationships and interdependencies

EXAMPLES OF ROLES, POSITIONS AND VIEWPOINTS IN THE CONTEXT OF ECONOMIC RELATIONSHIPS

The UK Government

- **as customer** for defence contracts, NHS work by doctors, nurses and paramedics, road-building and a host of other items for which it foots the bill (out of levied taxes)
- **as investor** – in run-down regional economies, 'sun-rise' industries such as CADCAM and robotics, training and career re-orientation through agencies such as Training & Enterprise Councils and higher education courses which it finances
- **as banker** – as part of its role in the various world banking organisations such as the World Bank, International Monetary Fund and a wide range of aid projects across the Third World
- **as supplier** – of extensive services, such as information provision through its HMSO publishing house, its policing, medical, defence, education and social services, its provision of postal services, its legal aid and so on
- **as employer** – of literally millions of UK citizens, spanning thousands of different kinds of jobs in: the civil service, local government, the NHS, the armed services, the police, transport services etc.

The worker

- **as employee** and source of manual, technical, professional or managerial expertise
- **as consumer** – with considerable power over the economy, depending upon whether he elects to spend or to save, and whether he is employed and is confident in his job-security or part of a cohort of long-term unemployed UK citizens
- **as business part-owner** – through the acquisition of shares in public limited companies (perhaps as a result of the privatisation issues of the 1970s and 1980s)
- **as donor of money or gifts** to charitable organisations such as OXFAM, MIND, Help the Aged, NSPCC etc.
- **as a seller** – of goods or belongings at car-boot sales, auctions or sales of work, whether for personal gain or charity
- **as a payer of taxes** – both to central and local government in the form of: income tax, council tax, VAT, stamp duty, inheritance tax, customs and excise levies and so on

The company director/ business proprietor

- **as seeker after financial loans** – to assist the start-up or further expansion of the business in return for interest payments on a given loan
- **as supplier of goods and/or services** – purchased by either private or public sector organisations or consumers
- **as 'unpaid tax collector'** – collecting and holding VAT income until payment falls due each quarter
- **as a source of funds through sponsorship** of either business or charitable organisations
- **as a payer of taxes in return for services** – in the form of corporate tax, uniform business rates and various types of indirect taxation
- **as a responsible person for the legal entity** which is the limited company or business which he or she owns in whole or part

As the above three tables illustrate, governments, individuals and the legal representatives of companies and businesses are all intertwined in a complex series of economic relationships in which they each may adopt at some point the contrasting roles of both supplier and purchaser, employer and employee, tax payer and tax beneficiary (through supplied services).

PC
1.3.1
1.3.2

DISCUSSION TOPICS

1 What do you see as areas of tension or problem which may arise from conflicts of interest between the UK Government's roles as: employer, balancer of the Public Sector Borrowing Requirement (PSBR) books and investor in economic pump-priming activities, say, to assist recovery after a recession? Can you supply any examples? Hint – growth and expansion without inflation?

2 How might an individual's views of 'big business' change after he or she became a shareholder in, say, a multinational like British Telecom, The Hanson Group or ICI plc?

3 The 'poll tax' introduced in the late 1980s became so unpopular that the government was obliged to withdraw it (at great cost) and to replace it with a 'council tax' which returned to home owner-occupiers and property valuation as the basis for its scale of payments.

   In many ways the 'poll tax' imposed a potentially much fairer system of taxation upon all 18-plus adults. So what aspects of the economic relationships it brought about caused its vehement rejection in some quarters of UK society ?

4 What **is** a motor-car? Is it simply a means of transporting its occupants from A to B? Is it the outward symbol of its owner's personal success and status? Is it a much loved 'toy' and companion called Betsy? Is it a collector's item and thus an investment? Is it a symbol of a young man's virility or woman's career independence? Is it a means of generating profits and dividends for shareholders and company directors whose firm builds and sells it? Is it merely a milch-cow source of income to a government with an insatiable need for increased tax revenue? Or is it basically a major threat to human beings as an atmosphere pollutant, killer and maimer?

   Can you think of any examples – say from advertising, government information commercials, people's remarks you remember etc. which confirm any of the above questions?

   Can you suggest how an individual's, government department's or car-making firm's responses to the above questions might affect various aspects of the buying, selling and taxing of motor vehicles?

PC
1.3.3

■ Social and political trends in economic relationships

The various economic roles, perceptions and activities of UK governments, businesses and consumer-employees have all been significantly affected over the past 70 years by the tremendous advances made in telecommunications. As a result, an endless, daily flood of information and opinion washes over the population of developed countries through television, radio and newspaper news, advertisements and debate.

As a result, the citizens of such countries are today far more critical and aware of economic events, trends and developments. For example:

The geographical and population characteristics of California, together with its population's love-affair with the motor-car has led to the introduction of harsh laws prohibiting harmful car-exhaust emissions. By the end of the decade all cars driven in California will have to comply with such laws. As a result, radical changes in motor-vehicle engine and exhaust

designs have been forced upon car manufacturers – largely as a result of mobilising public opinion through public telecommunications.

A similar response has been made throughout the EC in terms of lead-free petrol and catalytic converters.

DISCUSSION TOPIC

Can you think of any other examples in which changes in people's views and perceptions have altered the basis of an economic relationship in, say, the area of supply and demand for a given product or service?

Another area in which significant changes in economic relationships lies is the public's perception of quality relating to a good or service. Such changes have resulted in EC countries largely as a result of the influx of consumer goods from countries like Japan, Taiwan, South Korea and Malaysia which combine high levels of design with build quality delivered at extremely competitive prices.

As a result, EC consumers have become far more demanding as to what they expect from, say, a television-set, hi-fi stack or personal computer. This in turn exerted tremendous pressure on EC manufacturers either to improve their own quality standards or to lose significant market share. By the same token, the workforce of such firms were exposed to much more rigorous work practices and procedures, simply just to survive and keep their jobs in the face of high quality, inexpensive imports.

In this way, the economic relationship between a more demanding consumer of manufactured goods and Asiatic suppliers well placed to meet such demands has led to fundamental changes in the patterns of manufacture and work in EC states.

SOURCES OF ECONOMIC AND BUSINESS INFORMATION

PC 1.3.3

A welter of government, public and private sector, European Community and international agency information is published at regular intervals of economic trends, outcomes, forecasts and results to assist both business and government economic analysts and financial services managers. The following list of such information sources is by no means exhaustive, but includes some of the most respectable and frequently quoted:

Her Majesty's Government (UK)

United Kingdom National Accounts (annual publication), CSO* referred to as 'The Blue Book'

Public Expenditure Analyses (annual publication), HM Treasury referred to as 'The Brown Book'

Financial Statement and Budget Report (annual publication), HM Treasury referred to as 'The Red Book'

The Employment Gazette, Department of Employment, HMSO (published monthly)

Social Trends, Economic Trends, Financial Statistics, CSO

Annual and Monthly Abstract of Statistics, CSO

Labour Market Statistics and Quarterly Reports, Department of Employment

Bank of England Monthly Factsheets and Quarterly Bulletins

Monopoly and Mergers Commission Reports

Overseas Trade Statistics of the UK

*Central Statistical Office

European Community sources

European Commission Publications, e.g. Eurostat, Annual Economic Reports etc.

European Central Bank (ECB)

European Parliament, UK Information Office

DTI: Single Market Bulletins and Booklets, e.g. 'Europe Open for Business'

Office For Official Publications Of The European Communities, Luxembourg

EC and international government-funded agencies

The Organisation For Economic Cooperation and Development (OECD)

The General Agreement on Tariffs and Trade (GATT)

The International Monetary Fund (IMF)

The World Bank

The World Resources Institute

International Labour Organisation (ILO)

UK private sector and professional institute information services

The Market Research Society

Phillips & Drew Monthly Economic Forecasts

Mintel Information Sources

Datastream, Dataline, Extat and ICC Eurocompany Information Services

Clearing Banks' Economic Reviews, e.g. Natwest, Royal Bank of Scotland

Building Society Quarterly and Annual Reports

UK Financial and Economic Publications

Financial Times

The Times, Daily Telegraph, Independent, European newspapers (and their Sunday publications)

The Economist (weekly magazine)

REVIEW TEST

1 What do these abbreviations stand for: ERM, ECU, OECD, GATT, G7?

2 List five ways in which Britain's membership of the EC since 1973 has affected the government's relationship with the UK economy.

3 List five different economic policies which currently impact upon the UK economy.

4 What is meant by the term 'dumping'? What can a government do to prevent it?

5 How does GATT seek to develop international trade?

6 Draw up a list of the interested parties which are drawn together into an economic relationship in the activities of the UK motor-car industry. Explain briefly the main interests of each party you identify.

CASE STUDY

The Safeway way

Read the following case study carefully, and then carry out the assignments which follow.

Road to the busy aisles

Why the group is big in Britain

America's Safeway Stores first signalled an interest in the United Kingdom in 1954 when it registered Safeway Food Stores, a UK subsidiary, with a nominal capital of £100, Derek Harris writes.

Not until seven years later, however, did the Americans strike out from their toehold. The subsidiary's capital was hoisted to £2 million as Safeway decided that Britain was ready to follow the American grocery retailing path to big, self-service, one-stop stores, at which a customer would do a bumper weekly shop.

After months of speculation as a Safeway team sized up the expanding UK retail scene, it was announced in the middle of 1962 that an association was being negotiated with the supermarket offshoots of John Gardner of London. There were eight supermarkets, plus warehousing, trading under two different fascias, Gardner and Prideaux, reflecting an earlier merger.

The arrangement was finalised on September 20 1962. The Gardner parent company was given £1 million in cash and a third interest in the new company. Safeway Food Stores was in business, with a mainly British directorship and management.

While the negotiations were going on, the British Safeway had started developing its first store, at Bedford, with selling space of 20,000 sq ft. It is hard to grasp the impact then of such trading methods on Britons. When the Bedford store opened in 1963, police had to be brought in to control the crowds.

As the Gardner stake in Safeway dwindled until its interests were bought out by Safeway, expansion was pursued. The first Safeway store in Scotland opened in 1965 in Glasgow. By 1969, Safeway sales were breaking the £20 million barrier. The following year, it opened a state-of-the-art central distribution centre at Aylesford in Kent.

In 1975 Terry Spratt, formerly the Prideaux manager, became chairman and managing director of the UK Safeway operation. By 1982, expansion had increased the work-force to more than 10,000.

The next year was marked by the opening of the 100th Safeway store. Profits exceeded £20 million.

The watershed years for Safeway were 1986 and 1987. Its American parent, which had run into problems, sold the UK operation.

In February 1987, the Argyll Group, which traded mainly as Presto, bought the UK Safeway with its 132 stores for £681 million. Argyll wanted to pick up the Safeway magic: its trading techniques, management expertise and methods. That year, seven big Presto stores were converted to Safeway outlets. As they were converted, staff were retrained to Safeway standards.

When Safeway opened its first store in Wales, at Colwyn Bay, in 1987, sales exceeded £1 billion for the first time.

Eventually, 140 transformed Prestos swelled the Safeway chain. The combination of conversions from Presto stores, plus greenfield store openings, meant that by the middle of 1989 Safeway owned 250 stores, and 275 by November. In that year, too, Safeway appointed a director with responsibility for environmental issues on store and product fronts, and set up an environment policy committee.

Safeway had already begun to collect awards for its fresh food and "green" policies. By 1990, Safeway was accounting for 72 per cent of Argyll's £4.1 billion turnover.

Twenty-three new Safeway stores opened during the year. By the end of 1990, Safeway had 310 stores operating and its new Coventry outlet became the 200th store with laser scanning checkouts. Coventry, with its 24-hour petrol station, rated "flagship" status as it came into operation just before Christmas, with nearly 40,000 sq feet of selling space.

The following year, Argyll, mainly through the Safeway expansion, became the third force in food retailing after J Sainsbury and Tesco. Operating profits rose by 27 per cent to £285.3 million. By now, 50,000 people were on the Safeway payroll – 30,000 more than when Argyll acquired Safeway. That year, at Bellshill in Scotland, Safeway opened Europe's biggest food distribution centre, which from May 1991 supplied nearly 300 stores with three temperature-graded goods – ambient, chilled and frozen.

The retailer has been working to close the UK's food and drink trade gap in a project co-sponsored with farmers and manufacturers aimed at creating more sales opportunities for British food suppliers.

Now 322 Safeway stores include more than 50 in-store pharmacies, nearly 270 bakeries, more than 40 coffee shops, ten post offices, seven dry-cleaners and more than 30 petrol filling stations

ASSIGNMENTS

Group activities

In groups of two or three, read the above history of Safeway's start-up and development in Britain and then carry out the following assignments:

1 Identify what you think were the key factors in Safeway's growth in Britain, from a company with a nominal capital of £100 in 1954, to 1992, when its turnover was in excess of £2.95 billion. Present your conclusions in a written discussion which compares Safeway's approach with that of other food stores you are familiar with in your own locality.

2 From your reading of the article, consider the extent to which Safeway's retailing approach differs from that of other food retailers. First list the differences your group identifies and then, in a class discussion, identify what you believe to be the essential ingredients for successful food retailing in today's consumer food market.

3 If your group were part of the top management team at Argyll, what would be the main planks of your development strategy for Safeway until the end of the present decade? Produce your answer as an illustrated oral presentation including a clear rationale and give it to your class. As a class, decide which group devised the strategy most likely to succeed.

Individual activities

4 Research into Safeway's recent financial performance and compare it with that of other major food retailing multiples. Present your findings as a short, written briefing, highlighting the aspects you think most significant.

5 Find out how companies like Safeway organise their nationwide operations and how they seek to maximise efficiency and effectiveness through their organisational structures. Present your findings in an oral presentation to your group.

Discussion topics

1 Given the economies of scale which an operation like that of Safeway can achieve, which can be translated into very competitive sales pricing policies, is there a future for the 'corner shop' grocer and general store? If so, what sort of business and marketing plans would be likely to prove successful for such stores in an age of vast shopping malls and supermarkets?

2 If you were in charge of Safeway, would you decide to go for vertical integration from food growing to food retailing? If so, to what extent, and with what products initially?

What do you see as the comparative advantages and disadvantages of vertical integration for companies like Safeway, as opposed to a policy of sticking firmly to tertiary sector food retailing only?

British Rail – the privatisation plans

British Rail was founded in 1948 with the amalgamation and nationalisation of loss-making private railway companies. The present government plans to reverse nationalisation and privatise BR during its present term of office. A White Paper was published in 1992, giving details of the privatisation plans for BR.

In recent years BR has been making huge losses. This presents a problem for privatisation. Who would want to buy an organisation making such large losses? Other major utilities which were privatised (such as gas, water and electricity) had some prospect of being turned into profit-making businesses. The prospects for BR are not as good because it is obliged to run loss-making services for a mixture of social, economic and political reasons.

For example, in the year ending March 1991, a decline in fare revenues and a fall in profits from the property holdings, resulted in losses of £93m, twice the previous year's losses. This was even after the government increased its subsidy to BR by 20 per cent from £500m to over £600m.

However not all BR's divisions make losses. InterCity, in spite of the economic recession, made profits of £50m before interest payments. The Railfreight division usually makes profits but made losses of £55m in 1990/91.

The two divisions which make the greatest losses are (i) Regional Railways (ii) Network SouthEast. Regional Railways made losses of £503m in 1990/91. This is the provincial train service burdened with the obligation to run a network of loss-making services considered to be socially desirable but not commercially viable.

Network SouthEast is the London commuter service. It made losses of £155m in 1990/91. This division has a virtual monopoly in commuter transport and could become commercially viable if fares are increased by over 50 per cent. Naturally such an option is not politically attractive.

With this pessimistic analysis, the government will not consider selling off BR as a single entity. To do so would simply change a public monopoly into a private monopoly.

The move to privatise BR can be divided into two phases (a) the deregulation of Britain's railways (b) privatising the railways. BR's statutory monopoly of train operations will end. At present other trains run on BR's tracks only with its permission. After privatisation other trains will have automatic access to the tracks and a statutory regulatory body (similar to Oftel in telecommunications i.e. a type of 'Ofrail') will ensure that BR charges fair prices for use of tracks.

The second stage is privatisation through a graduated sell-off or franchising-out of certain BR divisions.

1 **InterCity** – all of this profit-making division will be offered for sale complete with tracks and trains. InterCity will have to give other operators access to its tracks which will be a source of revenue but not necessarily competition as the main competitors for InterCity are planes and cars.

2 **Railfreight** – even though it made losses in 1990/91 it is regarded as having great potential for profits. As it owns very few tracks, it would depend on the official regulatory body to get fair treatment on track charges.

3 **Network SouthEast** – as it is currently making heavy losses, it cannot be sold in the near future. The government will retain the tracks and franchise out train services to private owners. This could attract private buyers as 45 per cent of the costs of running train operations relate to infrastructure (i.e. tracks and stations etc.). New private owners will have to pay for use of the tracks but these costs will be reduced by any subsidies available to keep fares at a reasonable level for commuters. Franchises will come up for renewal every few years.

4 **Regional Railways** – this division is so dependent on subsidies, it cannot be sold in a privatisation sale. Its tracks will be owned by the state. Private sector companies will be invited to submit tenders for five-year contracts to operate services.

The government's plans for privatising BR will be met with both criticism and praise. Long-suffering users of the present system will hope that changes will be for the better. Critics of the proposed changes will point to the many questions left unanswered – who will be responsible for safety? Will fares increase? Will uneconomic lines be closed? Will continued subsidies be available for loss-making services? Will the breakdown of private trains entitle other users of the same track to compensation for delays?

Reproduced from *A Summary of the UK Economy '92/93'* (editor D.C. McCarthy) Mentor Publications Dublin.

PC
1.2.1
1.2.2
1.2.4

CASE STUDY ASSIGNMENTS

Discussion topics

1 What arguments can you produce either in favour of or against the privatisation of British rail?

2 Given that most European governments subsidise their railway networks, what sort of services do you think a private operator would need to concentrate upon in order to make a profit out of railway transportation? Give reasons for selecting the services you identify.

3 What sort of freight services would a private operator need to develop in order to compete successfully with road haulage companies?

4 What safeguards would the government need to introduce into its privatisation bill in order to support those citizens with low incomes or on income support (and who do not possess motor-cars) who rely on rail transport within their local districts? What is likely to happen if a private operator decides to stop an uneconomic service or close an uneconomic line?

Or are such considerations no longer a government problem after privatisation?

5 To what extent is privatisation likely to lead to the profitable parts of BR being taken up by entrepreneurs (along with the profits generated), leaving the British taxpayer to continue paying for the unprofitable parts which cannot be sold? Can you suggest ways to resolve this dilemma?

6 How important in the privatisation of BR debate is the very high cost – and who will bear it – of replacing items of capital equipment such as track, buildings and bridges, trains and rolling stock?

PC
1.2.1
1.2.2
1.2.4

Group activities

In groups of two or three:

1 Find out how privatisation plans are likely to affect BR's services in your locality and report back with an oral presentation to your class.

2 Find out how one of the following countries runs its railway network and how its management differs from that employed to run BR:

Germany
France
USA

Brief your group orally on what you discover.

3 Discuss the sort of checks and balances you would want to have written into the powers given to a public watchdog organisation – Ofrail – with the brief to ensure that key public needs and interests are protected after privatisation. Brief your class on your decisions in a general debate.

1 Find out how the recessions of 1981–83 and 1988–93 affected industry and commerce in your district, and what actions local business associations (like the Chamber of Commerce) and local/national government agencies (like the Training and Enterprise Council – TEC) took to help businesses to survive and recover.
PC
1.1.1

2 Carry out an audit of the principal industrial and commercial business activities which characterised your district over the past 50 years. Research particularly into how they have changed and why, and how such changes have combined to shape your local community into its present form.
PC
1.1.3

3 Arrange to interview:
PC
1.1.1
1.1.2

   a   three sales/marketing managers in a manufacturing firm

   b   three managers/owners of retail shops

   c   three managers of a service industry – e.g. a bank or insurance company

   and find out how they view the current workings of supply and demand upon their businesses and their effect upon sales and profitability

4 Find out what services and monitoring activities your local county and district councils undertake which impact upon your local economy and businesses and why they are undertaken
PC
1.2.2
1.2.4

5 Find out how the government policies of privatisation have affected your local community. Interview a cross-section of local inhabitants to ascertain their views in a structured way.
PC
1.2.4

6 Arrange to interview a series of managers – sales, marketing, company secretary, production etc, – in order to find out how Britain's membership of the European Community, and in particular the creation of the 1992 Single Market, have affected the work they do and the activities of their organisations.
PC
1.2.4

7 Select a charitable organisation – Oxfam, Help the Aged, MIND, NSPCC etc. – which is active in your locality and find out how it is run, and how the regulations governing its activities differ from those required of a private sector organisation.
PC
1.2.2

8 Research into Britain's membership of the EC Exchange Rate Mechanism between 1990 and 1992 and brief your class on what you discover and how the UK economy was affected.
PC
1.2.2
1.2.4

9 Find out the reasons why **one** of the following industries has declined in the UK since 1945:
PC
1.2.2

   shipbuilding, coal-mining, textiles, steel, heavy industry, manufacturing

10 Research into the government's fiscal and monetary policies since 1988 and the reasons which were given for pursuing them.
PC
1.2.1
1.2.2

11 Find out how the European Commission works and how its activities impact upon the UK economy.
PC
1.2.4

12 Find out how the advent of the 1992 Single Market and Eurotunnel will affect the UK economy over the next ten years.
PC
1.2.4

13 Research into the provision of regional aid in the UK from both the UK government and the EC and how such aid is assisting economic recovery and replacing obsolete industries with new ones
PC
1.2.2
1.3.1

<table>
<tr><td>PC
1.2.2</td><td>14 Having first gathered your data, make a case for an independent Bank of England.</td></tr>
</table>

PC
1.2.2

14 Having first gathered your data, make a case for an independent Bank of England.

PC
1.1.1
1.1.2

15 Research into the rebirth of the UK car industry since 1985 and the reasons for its newfound success in home and international markets.

PC
1.2.4

16 Find out how the privatisation of either:

British Telecom, British Gas or a Water Board

has changed the ways in which they operate and the services they provide. Make a reasoned analysis of both the up and downsides resulting from the privatisation.

PC
1.3.1

17 Find out why out-of-town shopping malls have become so popular over the past 10 years and what economic impact they have had upon small, traditional local businesses.

PC
1.1.1
1.1.4

18 Research into the economic changes in the former Soviet Union which have taken place since the end of communist rule and the transition from command to mixed economy. Concentrate upon the efforts being made to create a competitive, entrepreneurial culture and to transform the rouble into a convertible currency.

PC
1.2.4
1.3.1

19 Research into the economic relationships between the world's developed industrial states and Third World nations and analyse the efforts being made (or not made) to lift the burden poor countries have from being indebted to the developed states over a long period of time. Decide whether the Third World can escape from their so-called economic poverty-trap, and if so, how.

PC
1.2.4
1.3.1

20 Research into the Rio Accord which resulted from a meeting in early 1993 of world statesmen seeking to protect the earth's natural environment from economically inspired pollution and destruction. Decide whether sufficient action is currently being taken by the world's political leaders in this area.

EVIDENCE-BUILDING ACTIVITY FOR YOUR PORTFOLIO

Element 1.1 Explain the purposes and products of business

In your locality, select **three** businesses, **one** of each from the following economic sectors:

a   primary, e.g. agriculture, mining, fishing

b   secondary, e.g. manufacturing

c   tertiary, e.g. distribution, retailing, financial services

Research objectives

For each of the businesses you select, you should obtain evidence which provides information explaining:

1   the economic wants or needs which the business seeks to satisfy

2   the nature and purpose of the specific products or services which the businesses market

3   how the businesses work within the supply and demand relationship in your locality and in general

4   the outcomes which the business operations aim to achieve (such as: expansion, profit-making, providing a public service, charitable work etc).

Presentation of evidence

Present your researched evidence as three profiles of about 600 words each which are factually based and which compare and contrast the operations of your three selected businesses against a back-drop of your local economy and its place in the UK economy. Your profiles should explain simply and clearly why it is your think the businesses exist at all, the purposes they serve in the context of the supply and demand relationship and how **what they do** affects their structures and activities.

Method of producing evidence

You should either hand-write or word-process your evidence and provide illustrations (photographs, charts, graphs etc) as you think appropriate.

Performance criteria covered

1.1.1, 1.1.2, 1.1.3, 1.1.4, 1.1.5

Core skills Level 3

Communication
3.1.1–3.1.4, 3.2.1–3.2.4, 3.3.1–3.3.3, 3.4.1–3.4.3
Information technology (if wp software used)
3.1.1–3.1.7, 3.2.1–3.2.7, 3.3.1–3.3.5
3.5.1–3.5.5 (by means of logged notes on how any errors or faults were handled and how compliance with HASAW requirements was effected)

Element 1.2 Explain government influences on business

In this Activity, there are two tasks which you must complete, which are set out below:

Task 1

Research objectives
Select **three** countries, where one of each operates an economy (as closely as you are able to determine) in one of the following ways:

a)   as a free, market economy

b)   as a mixed economy

c)   as a command economy

Next, carry out your researches into each of your three selected countries so as to find out the major features of its economic policies and activities which characterise it as either a market, mixed or command economy. You should ensure that you secure some concrete examples to illustrate your task which is to produce an article of about 800 words which compares and contrasts the three economic systems you have researched.

Presentation of evidence

Your article should be intended for a readership of business studies students as part of a monthly publication entitled: *Business Today*. The aim of the publication is to impart up-to-date business information and views in a lively and readable way, without sacrificing accuracy and correctness.

Method of presenting evidence

Either word process or hand-write your article. You should include graphical information where appropriate to illustrate your text.

Task 2 (This task should be carried out in groups of three to five students)

Research objectives
In your locality, select:

a) a large, private sector organisation

b) a local or central government agency or organisation

c) a small business

Having made your choice (bearing in mind your network of contacts such as relatives who work in such organisations) arrange a series of interviews and research activities which will enable you to find out:

1   the nature of various government economic policies and underpinning directives and regulations which have impacted upon each of the organisations you have selected over the past three years.

2   the EC initiatives directives and regulations which have similarly had an effect upon them

3   the likely effect upon the three organisations of economic interventions and agreements of international bodies such as:

GATT   Group 7   APEC   OPEC   and   NAFTA

Your researches should concentrate upon:

a) legal requirements

b) importing and exporting aspects

c) quotas, tariffs, dumping practices

d) effects upon unemployment and conditions of work

e) the impact of government fiscal and monetary policies (e.g. taxation levels)

f) effects upon local, national and international competitiveness

Presentation of evidence

Provide your evidence in the form of an illustrated oral presentation to your class of about 20 minutes, in which each group member plays a roughly equal, active part. Your presentation should include audio-visual aid (AVA) support and a factsheet hand-out for your co-students.

Method of presentation

Provide your teacher with a set of notes which detail the sources of your data, and how you set about collecting it. Produce three to five illustrative OHPs and a factsheet of two sides of A4 which summarises your findings and conclusions. Your teacher will assess your oral presentation (along with your co-students).

Performance criteria covered
1.2.1, 1.2.2, 1.2.3, 1.2.4

Communication
3.1.1–3.1.4, 3.2.1–3.2.4, 3.3.1–3.3.3, 3.4.1–3.4.3
Information technology
3.1.1–3.1.7, 3.3.1–3.3.5
3.5.1–3.5.5 (by means of logged notes on how errors and faults were handled and how compliance with HASAW was effected)

Element 1.3 Investigate the supply of goods and services by business

Group activity for two or three students

Private sector	*Public sector*
a clearing bank	a county council department*
an insurance business	a district council department*
a hotel	a citizens' advice bureau
a fast-food café	a tourist information centre
a shoe shop	a job centre
a chemist	a job club
a card shop	a charity shop
a car dealership	a BR railway station

In this Activity your tasks are as follows:
Firstly, select **one** type of private sector business and **one** type of public sector organisation. You may decide to choose your pair from local organisations where you have contacts, you may select your pair from this checklist:

* Choose a department which markets a public sector product or service such as a leisure centre or 'compulsory competitive tendering, department such as a county council's commercial group which tenders for providing school meals, cleansing services or road mending etc.

   Alternatively, you may decide to make your own selection of a private and public sector business pair.

Your second task is to research into a single product (or service) which is provided by your pair of organisations (one for each), and to explain how it is perceived and evaluated by the different people brought together by the economic relationship its marketing brings about.

Research objectives
Firstly, decide precisely upon the two products or services you will research. Next, make arrangements to talk to various people involved in their supply and use. This may involve you in meeting factory operatives, managers, long-distance lorry-drivers, inland revenue officers, factory inspectors, trading standards officers, customers, service technicians, refuse-collectors and so on, depending upon the type of product or service you select. Try to find as varied a list of people economically related to your selection as possible.

   Next, before meeting your selected interviewees, draw up appropriate sets of questions for each which aim to obtain information on how they see the product or service they make, sell, buy, use or service etc.

Presentation of evidence

Having carried out your interviews, produce a written report of your findings (which may be illustrated with any helpful factual information you acquire).

Your report should provide the following information:

1   A detailed explanation of the various perceptions of the products/services which the people held whom you interviewed.

2   Your explanation of why you think they held the views they relayed to you.

3   The impact of the various perceptions you found upon the economic profile of the product or service – in supply and demand terms, perceptions of worth and added value, price determination, nature of the market it is in and so on.

4   Your report should also include a discussion on how information about a product or service and an understanding of the economic relationships which surround it help someone in business (or the public service) to appreciate better the supply of goods or services to customers who may also be the general public.

Method of producing evidence

You should produce your evidence as follows:

1   A set of notes which explains how your group undertook this Activity.

2   The sets of questions which you asked your interviewees.

3   The findings which you acquired in the form of a report (using one of the currently accepted report formats).

4   A 10–15 minute oral presentation to your class on your findings (in which each group member plays an equal, active part)

You may either present your evidence in hand-writing or as word-processed A4 printed copy.

Performance criteria covered

1.3.1, 1.3.2, 1.3.3

Core skills Level 3

Communication
3.1.1–3.1.4, 3.2.1–3.2.4, 3.3.1–3.3.3, 3.4.1–3.4.3
Information technology
3.1.1–3.1.7, 3.2.1–3.2.7, 3.3.1–3.3.5
3.5.1–3.5.5 (by means of logged notes on how any errors or faults were handled, and how compliance with HASAW requirements was effected.)

FURTHER SOURCES OF INFORMATION

The Organisation in its Environment, 4th Edition, J Beardshaw and D Palfreyman, Pitman Publishing, 1990.
ISBN: 0 273 03268 2

Economics, N Palmer, Folens Publishers, 1986

Introductory Economics, 5th Edition, G F Stanlake, Longman, 1989. ISBN: 0 582 03695X

An Introduction to Positive Economics, 6th Edition, R G Lipsey, Weidenfeld & Nicolson, 1983. ISBN: 0 297 78265 7

The Economy in Focus 1992/93, A Anderton, Causeway Press Limited, 1992. ISBN: 1 873929 013

Applied Economics: An Introductory Course, A Griffiths and S Wall, Longman, 1986 ISBN: 0 582 29730 3

Economics Made Simple, 14th Edition, G Whitehead, Made Simple Books, 1992.   ISBN: 0 7506 0526 X

Business and Enterprise Studies Made Simple, G Whitehead, Made Simple Books, 1990 ISBN: 0 7506 0730 0

European Studies, A A Scott, Pitman Publishing, 1992. ISBN: 0 273 03813 3

The Single Market: The Facts (Europe Open for Business Series) 10th Edition, Department of Trade & Industry,
HMSO, 1993

Business in Europe Series, Department of Trade & Industry, HMSO, 1993

Europe on the Move Series, Office for Official Publications of the European Communities, 1990 on

Public Administration in the UK, D Farnham and M McVicar, Cassell, 1982. ISBN: 0 304 30338 0

A Summary of the UK Economy Series, D C McCarthy (Ed.), Mentor Publications, 1992–93 on

Economics and the Banks' Role in the Economy, G Lipscombe, Pitman Publishing, 1988 ISBN: 0 273 02882 0

2

BUSINESS SYSTEMS

Element 2.1

Investigate administration systems

Element 2.2

Investigate communication systems

Element 2.3

Investigate information processing systems

Pages

Element 2.1: Investigate administration systems

98-114

Performance criteria:

1 purposes of administration systems in business organisations are explained

98-114

2 administration systems to support legal and statutory requirements are described

98-112

3 a business organisation's administration systems are investigated and described

98-127, 186-7

4 effectiveness of systems in supporting the functions of the business organisation is evaluated

186-7

5 users' opinions of investigated administration systems are described

191

Range: **Purposes:** routine functions; non-routine functions; supporting human, financial, physical resources; recording and monitoring business performance

98-114

Legal and statutory requirements: health and safety; Companies Act (e.g. annual accounts); employment law, fiscal – VAT; PAYE; pensions

180-2

Administration systems: accounting; sales; distribution; personnel; services (e.g. maintenance, catering)

98-127

Evaluation criteria: efficiency of operation, effectiveness of control of business functions

183-5

Evidence indicators: An account of an administration system in a business organisation showing how the system meets the needs of the organisation and reporting on users' opinions. Evidence should demonstrate understanding of the implications of the range dimensions in relation to the element. The unit test will confirm the candidate's coverage of range.

Element 2.2: Investigate communication systems

115-80

Performance criteria:

1 purposes of communication systems used by business organisations are explained

115-80

2 a business organisation's communication systems are investigated and described

191

3 effectiveness of systems in supporting the functions of the business organisation is evaluated

191

4 users' opinions of investigated communication systems are described

191

5 electronic technology changing communication systems is identified

127-80

Range: **Purposes:** internal, external; handling information, taking decisions, informing actions

98-180

Communication systems: internal, external; face to face; correspondence; telecommunications; computer-aided

115-35

Electronic technology: network computer systems, electronic mail, enhanced telephone systems

115-80

Evaluation criteria: accuracy, efficiency, cost-effectiveness, security

183-92

Evidence indicators: Examples of communication systems within a business organisation indicating how new technology is changing communication systems and an evaluation of accuracy, efficiency, cost-effectiveness and security of systems. Evidence should demonstrate understanding of the implications of the range of dimensions in relation to the element. The unit test will confirm the candidate's coverage of range.

Element 2.3: Investigate information processing systems

Performance criteria:

1 purposes of information processing systems used by business organisations are explained

2 a business organisation's information processing systems are investigated and described

3 effectiveness of systems in supporting the function of the business organisation is evaluated

4 effects of the Data Protection Act on users and operators of information processing systems are identified and explained

5 effects of computer technology on users and operators is identified

Range: Purposes: storing information, distributing information, using information, communicating information

Information processing systems: manual, electronic

Evaluation criteria: security, efficiency, cost-effectiveness

Data Protection Act: individual rights, access to information, security, ownership

Effects of technology: speed, accuracy, costs, health, skills, access to information

Evidence indicators: Examples of information processing systems used by a business organisation illustrating the purposes of the systems and the effects of legislation and changing technology on users and operators. Evidence should demonstrate understanding of the implications of the range dimensions in relation to the element. The unit test will confirm the candidate's coverage of range.

INTRODUCTION

This Unit explains how business and public service organisations employ systems and procedures to perform their operations and activities. It examines the ways in which information technology in the forms of electronic office equipment and telecommunications networks have revolutionised organisations and how they administer their activities.

The transition from paper-based business administrative procedures is carefully explained. In particular the IT-based systems which interlink computers, facsimile transceivers, printers, PABX telephone networks, video-conferencing data packet-switching and so on are examined in detail. The issues of systems management are also covered in the context of cost-effectiveness, security and efficiency.

In particular Unit 2 examines:

- the impact of twentieth-century technologies and complex interrelations in society upon the development of business information systems
- an examination of the various types of information which businesses need and employ
- the varying kinds of information used in the major types of company department – from R & D 'state-of-the-art' scientific abstract, to market research field survey, to after-sales service records
- major sources of primary and secondary information
- informational needs and applications at strategic, tactical and job-specific levels in businesses
- the applications of historic, current and futuring information
- using the systems approach to managing information in business
- the transition from manual, paper-based systems to computerised, networked counterparts
- a survey of IT-based, electronic office equipment and its applications – LAN/WAN systems, open systems integration (OSI), convergence and connectivity, integrated services digital network (ISDN), facsimile transmission, viewdata and videotex, Prestel, computerised automatic branch exchanges (CABX) telephone systems, printers, photocopiers and desktop publishing systems
- filing systems – paper-based, electronic and microform: classification techniques, inputting, storing and accessing
- how to set up an effective business information management system

BUSINESS INFORMATION SYSTEMS AND 20TH CENTURY TECHNOLOGY

■ Information is power!

Accurate, up-to-date and reliable information is the most precious resource an organisation possesses. This sweeping assertion may be justified in this way. Over the past two hundred years, the effect of the first industrial revolution has been to create highly complex, technology-led societies in developed countries across the world. As a result many multi-layered networks of interdependence have been created, linking, say, the research chemist to the ulcer sufferer in an extended chain of relationships. Such sophisticated chains of interdependence can be identified across a myriad of occupations and activities in all developed economies.

■ Networks of information need

The nexus or thread linking these relationships is that of information need. The research chemist on the treatment of ulcers relies on the scientific papers published by his eminent colleagues. The pharmaceutical production manager needs to know about the latest pill-making equipment, and the GP needs to have easily assimilable information on the effectiveness of the pill and any side-effects it may have. His patient needs to know how the pill will work and what the outcome will be. And so on.

■ Informational interdependence

Rapid technological development has therefore brought about a remarkable degree of dependence upon specialists and a reliance upon the effective exchange of information. For example, today's householders depend upon technicians to install and maintain telephones, heating and lighting systems, televisions, and microwave ovens. As consumers they rely upon complex banking processes to wire money abroad, process cheques or authorise credit payments. As holiday-makers they take for granted the ability of local travel agents to make instantaneous bookings with remotely located tour operators, airline companies and car-hire firms. As employees, they remain unmoved at the telephone company's ability to identify a single, selected telephone among millions of handsets in London or Tokyo and to make it ring within seconds.

■ The creation of the information society

The creation of what some social scientists call 'the information society' began in the post-war reconstruction era of the 1950s. The development of first valve- and then microchip-driven computers between 1940 and 1970 transformed the ways in which scientists, engineers, civil servants, manufacturers, retailers and teachers processed information. Calculations, which previously would have taken mathematicians thousands of man-hours to work out, could be computed in seconds! Lengthy drafts of reports, which formerly took days to retype, could be edited through word-processing techniques in minutes. Complex manufacturing cost changes could similarly be recomputed promptly with the help of a spreadsheet's cell-linked formulae.

The silicon chip (first marketed by Intel (USA) in 1971) which made such computer-based advances possible also transformed telecommunications. In moments, business people a world apart could be connected, by fax, telephone, video-conferencing or electronic mail messaging, routed through satellite telecommunications, fibre optic cable or radio signal.

■ The impact of information technology

PC
2.2.1
2.3.1

The rapid expansion of information and communications technology in the second half of the twentieth century caused radical changes in the ways in which people acted as householders and consumers, and in the ways in which business organisations functioned to meet consumer and industrial market needs.

At the heart of all this change one need has remained a constant in all organisations – to have in place reliable systems and procedures for managing the inward and outward flow of information upon which their success and survival depends.

It is for this reason that an understanding of how business information systems are designed, installed and maintained is an important part of a preparation for a career in business. This Unit provides a thorough examination of a business's information needs, the types of information it employs, the equipment used to process information and the techniques for creating and maintaining effective information systems.

DISCUSSION TOPIC

PC
2.2.1
2.3.1

The impact of IT

1 Some economists now refer to the 'information industry' in the same way as they talk and write about manufacturing and business service industries. Are they right, or is the term an unjustified overstatement?

2 One major manufacturer of hi-fi equipment recently commissioned a survey on how well its customers were able to operate the range of stacks they sold. To their surprise, it turned out that most customers only carried out the most basic of operations, and barely scratched the surface of the sophisticated features built into each model. Similarly, in America, industrial psychologists have identified an increasing trend among office workers of feeling more and more inadequate in the face of ever more complex software programs and computer systems, which they call 'computer stress' or technophobia.

   Should such reactions to chip-driven equipment be simply regarded as teething troubles at the dawn of a new era, or are they further evidence of the ongoing mistrust of man for machine?

3 Has IT **really** changed the ways we work and live, or is its impact still largely superficial when the broad range of people and jobs in society is considered?

THE EVOLUTION OF INFORMATION TECHNOLOGY IN BUSINESS

1714 Henry Mill typewriter patent.

1837 Samuel Morse (USA), telegraph line.

1839 Wheatstone & Cook, London, telegraph.

1843 Facsimile transmission invention – patented by A Bain.

1868– Scholes invents mechanical typewriter (USA) which
1874 Remington market.

1876 Alexander Bell – first voice transmission by telephone.

1882 Vertical filing system introduced into businesses.

1897 First cathode ray tube invented by K. F. Braun.

1901 Guglielmo Marconi sends first radio signal from Cornwall to Newfoundland.

1913 First vacuum tube amplifier (valve) developed by H. D. Arnold and first long-distance telephone cable laid.

1920 Electric typewriters introduced.

1925 John Logie Baird produces first real television transmission.

1936 BBC transmits first world TV programmes.

1946 ENIAC – Electronic Numerical Indicator and Calculator developed – the dawn of the computer age in Pennsylvania!

1947 Brattain and Barden invent the solid state transistor to replace the valve.

1949 EDSAC computer with memory storage developed in Cambridge, England.

1950s Long-distance direct dialling available in UK.

1956 IBM Corporation develop the computer disk-drive.

1958 First international message routed by satellite.

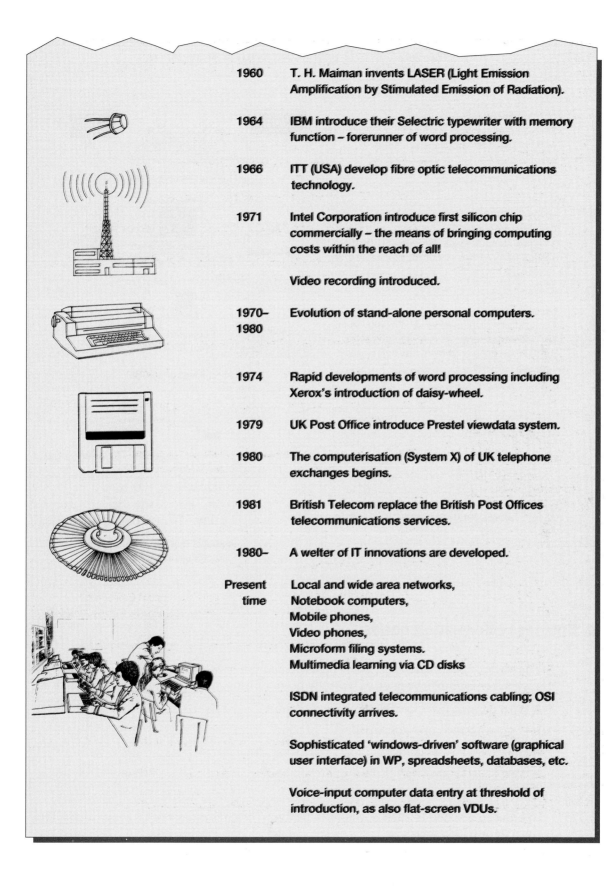

1960	T. H. Maiman invents LASER (Light Emission Amplification by Stimulated Emission of Radiation).
1964	IBM introduce their Selectric typewriter with memory function – forerunner of word processing.
1966	ITT (USA) develop fibre optic telecommunications technology.
1971	Intel Corporation introduce first silicon chip commercially – the means of bringing computing costs within the reach of all!
	Video recording introduced.
1970–1980	Evolution of stand-alone personal computers.
1974	Rapid developments of word processing including Xerox's introduction of daisy-wheel.
1979	UK Post Office introduce Prestel viewdata system.
1980	The computerisation (System X) of UK telephone exchanges begins.
1981	British Telecom replace the British Post Offices telecommunications services.
1980–	A welter of IT innovations are developed.
Present time	Local and wide area networks, Notebook computers, Mobile phones, Video phones, Microform filing systems. Multimedia learning via CD disks
	ISDN integrated telecommunications cabling; OSI connectivity arrives.
	Sophisticated 'windows-driven' software (graphical user interface) in WP, spreadsheets, databases, etc.
	Voice-input computer data entry at threshold of introduction, as also flat-screen VDUs.

Fig 2.1   **The evolution of IT information systems in the office**

1870s – 1970s

The stand-alone typewriter was the office workhorse – from mechanical manual to electric, to electronic and electronic with memory

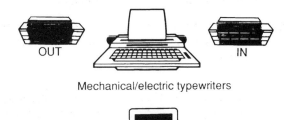

Mechanical/electric typewriters

1970s – 1980s

The dedicated, stand-alone wordprocessing personal computer was introduced (Could only perform WP tasks with 'built-in' software)

Dedicated word processors

1980s – 1990s

'Connectivity' or 'convergence' evolved: local and wide area networks (LANs and WANs) interlink computers, printers, fax, telex, view-data, copiers, etc.

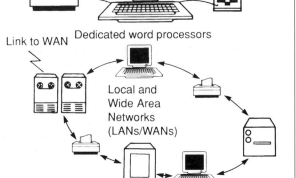

Link to WAN

Local and Wide Area Networks (LANs/WANs)

1990s – on

Open Systems Connection introduced internationally – protocols are developed to enable computers of different manufacture, using different operating systems, to communicate with each other

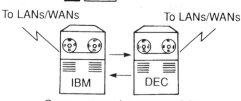

To LANs/WANs   To LANs/WANs

IBM   DEC

Open systems interconnectivity of computer networks

■ Business information needs

The kinds of information needed by business and public sector organisations are many and varied. For example, businesses typically need information answering questions such as:

- What do our customers want?
- What are our competitors up to?
- How are our sales going?
- Are we making enough profit?
- Where should we be in three years' time?

In order to respond to such questions effectively, organisations need to have available to them information which is:

DIFFERENT TYPES OF INFORMATION USED BY ORGANISATIONS

Type of information	Examples	Typical applications
1 Number-based in chart form (sometimes called quantitative information):	Tables, graphs, pie-charts, ratios, formulae	Sales performance analysis, share of market, level of profits, wastage rates, proportion of bad debts, etc.
2 Oral or written word based: rational, logical, analytical treatments of researched information (sometimes called qualitative information)	Investigatory reports, factsheets, briefings, abstracts, summaries, specifications	Problem-solving reports, product specifications, technical updatings, operating manuals, etc.
3 Audio-visual information (sometimes called graphic information):	Videos, over-head viewfoils, audio-cassettes, slides, films, colour graphic charts, photographs	Presentations, opinion-leading advertising, training, briefings, etc.
4 Persuasive information: Influencing, promoting, convincing (sometimes called subjective information)	Advertisements, sales literature, posters, newsletters, oral presentations, meetings, press-conferences	Sales and marketing, public relations, team-building, internal communications, etc.

Accurate, up-to-date, easy-to-digest information is the life-blood of all organisations, without which purpose, direction and effective management are all soon lost!

- up-to-date
- accurate
- relevant
- reliable
- significant (from a statistical viewpoint)

For example, if a manufacturer of sweet snacks surveys customers' current preferences across a representative area of the country and a cross-section of consumers, the following responses may be obtained:

- Three-quarters of the respondents preferred snacks with a low-sugar, low-calorie content.
- Two-thirds disliked 'gooey centres', preferring 'chewy' ones.
- Ninety per cent preferred to buy snacks which, if consumed between meals, did not make them feel guilty.

If such a survey had been conducted only two weeks ago, among a sufficiently large sample (so as to make it 'statistically significant'), and if it had been compared with similar surveys carried out over the past two to three years, then the information it contained would meet the conditions outlined above. It would provide up-to-date, statistically significant data. When the costs of introducing a new product on to a production line and bringing it to the market are considered (and they may run into the hundreds of thousands of pounds), then the importance of high quality information is readily appreciated.

It is in this way, as an aid to effective decision-making, that information is power in organisations.

■ Sources of information

As the chart in Fig 2.2 illustrates, a medium to large manufacturing company needs to obtain, analyse and respond to an enormous amount of information across some eight departments and embracing both internal and external sources.

Primary sources of information

Primary sources of information are those that provide data which is usually original in its content and specific to a particular organisation's needs. For example, a firm wishing to develop a new product, say, a blend of coffee, may well identify a sample of targeted customers, who might be young professionals in the 22–30 age range. This group might be invited to test the new blend over a period of time, during which they return questionnaires and attend marketing feedback sessions. The information gleaned by such an activity is technically said to come from a **primary source**. Primary sources of information are valued because they are tailored to meet specific needs, are confidential to the organisation and represent the very latest in available data.

Other primary sources of information could include a selection of customers (who have recently purchased an upgraded product), regional groups of dealers or retailers belonging to specified turnover sizes and so on.

Secondary sources of information

All departments make extensive use of sources of secondary information. Basically this is information obtained and compiled by others which, nevertheless, has a value to the organisation. For example:

- Reviews of new software and updates in monthly computer user magazines.
- Surveys of economic indicators and trends published by the Department of Trade & Industry.
- Regular updatings on legislation and EC directives published by the specialist press, such as *Croner's A–Z of Business Information Sources*.
- Revisions and introductions of specifications by the British Standards Institute.
- Changes to personal taxation and/or VAT rates following upon the annual government budget and accountants' interpretations and advice on such changes.

  and so on.

Fig 2.2

Sources of information that organisations seek out

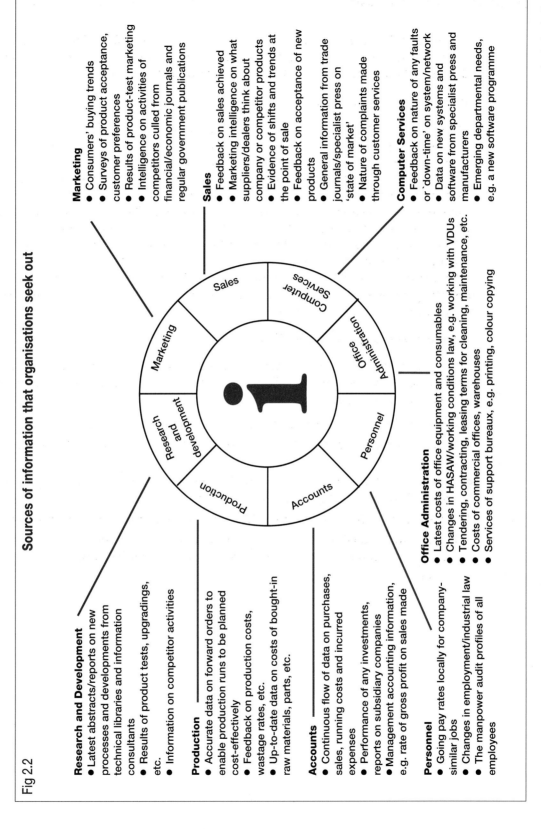

Research and Development
- Latest abstracts/reports on new processes and developments from technical libraries and information consultants
- Results of product tests, upgradings, etc.
- Information on competitor activities

Production
- Accurate data on forward orders to enable production runs to be planned cost-effectively
- Feedback on production costs, wastage rates, etc.
- Up-to-date data on costs of bought-in raw materials, parts, etc.

Accounts
- Continuous flow of data on purchases, sales, running costs and incurred expenses
- Performance of any investments, reports on subsidiary companies
- Management accounting information, e.g. rate of gross profit on sales made

Personnel
- Going pay rates locally for company-similar jobs
- Changes in employment/industrial law
- The manpower audit profiles of all employees

Office Administration
- Latest costs of office equipment and consumables
- Changes in HASAW/working conditions law, e.g. working with VDUs
- Tendering, contracting, leasing terms for cleaning, maintenance, etc.
- Costs of commercial offices, warehouses
- Services of support bureaux, e.g. printing, colour copying

Marketing
- Consumers' buying trends
- Surveys of product acceptance, customer preferences
- Results of product-test marketing
- Intelligence on activities of competitors culled from financial/economic journals and regular government publications

Sales
- Feedback on sales achieved
- Marketing intelligence on what suppliers/dealers think about company or competitor products
- Evidence of shifts and trends at the point of sale
- Feedback on acceptance of new products
- General information from trade journals/specialist press on 'state of market'
- Nature of complaints made through customer services

Computer Services
- Feedback on nature of any faults or 'down-time' on system/network
- Data on new systems and software from specialist press and manufacturers
- Emerging departmental needs, e.g. a new software programme

MAJOR SOURCES OF SECONDARY BUSINESS INFORMATION

● Government department official publications	published by HMSO
● Professional institute magazines e.g.	*Banking World*
	Management Today
● Specialist trade journals	*PC User*
	Marketing Weekly
	Business Equipment Digest
	The Grocer
● Specialist 'state of the art' reports published by information consultants like Frost & Sullivan Inc., e.g. Note: Multinational companies and other large organisations may commission such reports for their own, exclusive use.	'The Implications for the Food Industry of the EC Legislation on Labelling, Presentation and Advertising of Foodstuffs For Sale': (Document 89/395) published 20 June 1992
● National/ international newspaper cuttings and clippings, e.g.	*Financial Times*
	New York Herald Tribune
	The Times
● Annually published yearbooks and handbooks, e.g.	*Annual Abstract of Statistics*
	Post Office Guide
	Kompass (listings of UK and European companies and products) etc.

Secondary information and technical libraries

Large organisations maintain their own technical libraries which stock standard references, subscribe to relevant trade, institution and professional association journals and provide connections to national and international computer databases. Their librarians may also produce abstracts on demand of specialist articles and papers for company research scientists, marketing executives and so on.

Desk research: sources of in-house information

External sources of primary or secondary information may be supplemented as a general rule by accessing information from within the organisation. All organisations are obliged to store certain types of information, such as annual balance sheets for up to 30 years. In addition to information which has to be retained by law, organisations also store details for their own convenience and assistance:

- Plans, designs and specifications of products developed and produced.
- Account customer records and purchasing patterns.
- Listings of suppliers and buying terms.
- Registration records of equipment sold to customers – for warranty and customer service reasons.
- Inventory of plant and equipment and details of date of purchase.
- Personnel records – salary progression, promotion, relocations, etc.

And so, whenever an executive is given an investigation to undertake, he or she will probably start at the office desk by sifting through the data which is readily available from within the organisation – hence the term 'desk research'.

PC
2.2.1
2.2.2
2.2.3
2.2.4

INDIVIDUAL ACTIVITIES

First carry out your researches and then report back to your group in an illustrated oral presentation:

1 The major primary and secondary sources of information currently in use in your department either at work, in your college or in your school.

2 The regular publications produced by one of the following government departments/agencies to aid commerce and industry:

 a The Department of Trade & Industry

 b The Department of Employment

 c The Bank of England

 d The Treasury

 e The Central Office of Information

3 The different types of data and information available in your local reference library which would be useful to your local business community.

4 Make arrangements to interview the manager of one of the following local businesses:

 a A major car dealership;

 b A building society branch;

 c A supermarket;

in order to find out what sort of top priority information they need to be able to run the business successfully, and what information they are most interested in at present.

■ How businesses use information

PC
2.1.3
2.2.3
2.3.3

How businesses and public sector organisations use information depends very much upon the level of operation of executives or officers. Consider, for example, the diagram shown in Fig 2.3.

In its rough and ready way, the chart illustrates the different timespans of decisions and the extent of their impact in an organisation. It is also useful to highlight the different types of information which tend to be employed at various levels in the organisational pyramid.

At corporate director level

Information needs to be presented in summarised, analytical form – say, as the comparative breakdown of last month's sales in the seven regions of a national company. This data will be expressed as 'Actual to Target'. Other information may be expressed as a forecast of market share over the next three years, or as a quarterly set of trading accounts.

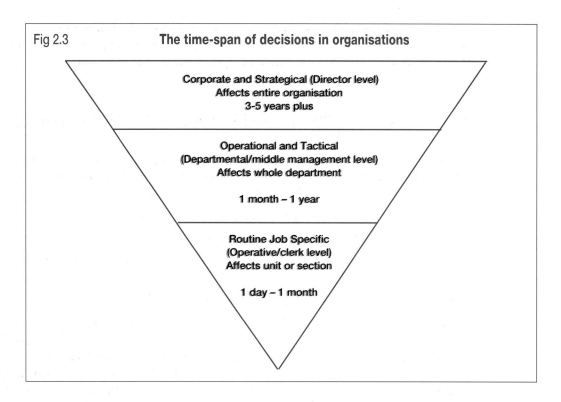

Fig 2.3 — The time-span of decisions in organisations

Corporate and Strategical (Director level)
Affects entire organisation
3-5 years plus

Operational and Tactical
(Departmental/middle management level)
Affects whole department

1 month – 1 year

Routine Job Specific
(Operative/clerk level)
Affects unit or section

1 day – 1 month

Much of senior management's information needs tends to be of the quantifiable type, which covers the entire scope of company activities. Such data is usually provided in reports, surveys, abstracts, reviews, analyses and so on. It is as though the managers are continually monitoring the firm's pulse-points, and measuring present against past performances, while seeking to meet anticipated future needs. And indeed, it is just such constant monitoring that informs and influences the rolling corporate plans produced by senior management annually, which deal with the coming (financial) year in detail, and the subsequent two years in overview.

At the operational and tactical level

Middle and departmental managers also need number-based information to enable them to monitor how they are matching up to targets allocated in annual business plans; they also tend to require direct, word-of-mouth feedback from operatives or office support staff on daily events and activities, so as to be kept 'in the picture'.

While directors and public service executives concentrate on long-term cycles of activity – the strategic dimension – middle managers are primarily concerned with: this month's sales compared with last month's; next month's projected production; output for the third quarter of this year compared to the same quarter last year and so on. Their management activities are said to be tactical, and rarely span more than a year.

At the job-specific, routine level

Inevitably, the job-role of the clerical assistant or factory operative is limited – say, to the maintenance of a section of a company's accounts, or to the assembly of a small part of a washing machine. Consequently, much of the informational needs at this level take the form of orally delivered instructions, short-life data schedules or amendments to operating routines.

At the operative level of activity information tends to be limited to current daily or weekly cycles of activity and to remain within a tightly controlled framework of routines and procedures, where there is limited scope for the use of discretion.

■ Business information systems and the decision-making pyramid

PC
2.2.1
2.2.2
2.2.3

If a business information system is to be effective, it must meet the needs of, the organisation at each level of activity. By the same token, its designers must take fully into account the needs of its users for information which may be:

- Historical – reviewing past achievement and keeping records

- Current – monitoring processes as they occur

- Futuring – anticipating and forecasting what is likely to happen next month or next year.

The need for 'after the event' or 'historical feedback'

In order to assess the success (or otherwise) of a project or operation, organisations need to have set up procedures for monitoring the activities they undertake. For example, both the shareholders of a company and the Inland Revenue receive at 12 monthly intervals a set of company accounts which provide an in-depth profile of the company's financial position on a particular day of the year – usually at the end of its annual trading period. The information provided by the set of accounts summarises the overall sales achieved by the firm, the costs it incurred in making the sales, the amounts of money it owes to others and the amounts others owe to it, as well as the computed value (at the time the accounts were produced) of the stock it has in hand, the value of its plant and equipment as well as of any property and other assets it owns.

Other examples of the evaluation of information which is 'historical' – by the time it is available – are:

- reviews of sales achieved compared with targets set

- running expenses incurred in maintaining a sales force on a regional basis

- the number of sales the company has achieved in a specific trading period and their value in pounds sterling etc.

Unless procedures are established for monitoring the success or cost-effectiveness of activities as soon as possible after their occurrence, a company has no way of knowing whether it is on or off track in meeting preset budgets, targets or planned costs – hence the common question among sales representatives, factory foremen and accountants: 'How did we do?'

EXAMPLE OF QUANTITATIVE INFORMATION USED IN AN HISTORICAL POST-EVENT WAY

A Company's Balance Sheet

Remember that a balance sheet is like a snapshot and is only accurate for a single point in time, here 31/10/199–

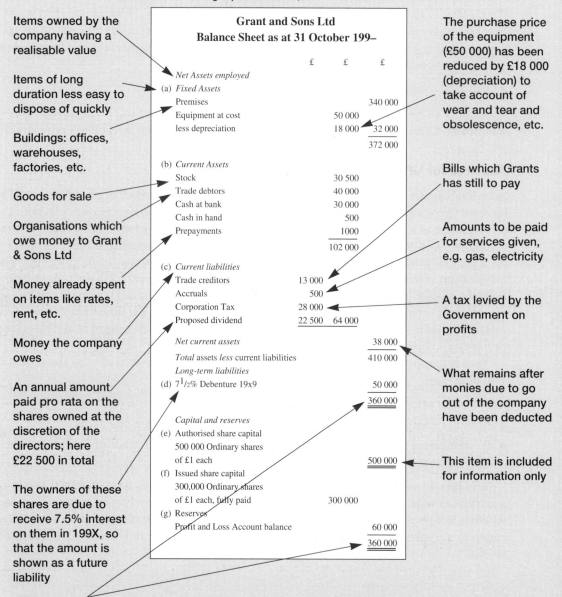

Items owned by the company having a realisable value

Items of long duration less easy to dispose of quickly

Buildings: offices, warehouses, factories, etc.

Goods for sale

Organisations which owe money to Grant & Sons Ltd

Money already spent on items like rates, rent, etc.

Money the company owes

An annual amount paid pro rata on the shares owned at the discretion of the directors; here £22 500 in total

The owners of these shares are due to receive 7.5% interest on them in 199X, so that the amount is shown as a future liability

The purchase price of the equipment (£50 000) has been reduced by £18 000 (depreciation) to take account of wear and tear and obsolescence, etc.

Bills which Grants has still to pay

Amounts to be paid for services given, e.g. gas, electricity

A tax levied by the Government on profits

What remains after monies due to go out of the company have been deducted

This item is included for information only

Grant and Sons Ltd
Balance Sheet as at 31 October 199–

	£	£	£
Net Assets employed			
(a) *Fixed Assets*			
Premises			340 000
Equipment at cost		50 000	
less depreciation		18 000	32 000
			372 000
(b) *Current Assets*			
Stock		30 500	
Trade debtors		40 000	
Cash at bank		30 000	
Cash in hand		500	
Prepayments		1000	
		102 000	
(c) *Current liabilities*			
Trade creditors	13 000		
Accruals	500		
Corporation Tax	28 000		
Proposed dividend	22 500	64 000	
Net current assets			38 000
Total assets *less* current liabilities			410 000
Long-term liabilities			
(d) 7$\frac{1}{2}$% Debenture 19x9			50 000
			360 000
Capital and reserves			
(e) Authorised share capital			
500 000 Ordinary shares			
of £1 each			500 000
(f) Issued share capital			
300,000 Ordinary shares			
of £1 each, fully paid		300 000	
(g) Reserves			
Profit and Loss Account balance			60 000
			360 000

Here is the 'balance' of the Grant & Sons total Balance Sheet. The sum of £360 000 is represented by £300 000 invested by shareholders in the business, plus £60 000 retained profit from the Profit and Loss Account.

To an expert eye, a Balance Sheet is like a 'frozen frame' picture showing how healthy and wealthy (or otherwise!) a company is.

Balance sheet reproduced from *Finance for BTEC National* by John Hopkins, Pitman Publishing.

The need for operational information

PC
2.1.3
2.1.4
2.2.3
2.3.2
2.3.3

While some kinds of information serve to summarise events which have already happened, other kinds are needed to monitor activities **as they occur**.

Take, for example, the involved process of developing and manufacturing a new model of saloon motor car. In order to be in a position to sell the model at a preplanned level of output per month and to maintain a precalculated profit, the following operational costs have to be analysed very closely as they arise in the overall development and production process:

- Research and developmental costs.
- The buying-in costs of raw materials or finished/semi-finished parts.
- Labour costs in the production phase.
- Overhead charges to be apportioned from the expense of providing: energy, light, heat, rental and rates charges, etc.
- Value-added taxes to be borne at each phase of the production to sales process.
- The costs of distributing the product to bulk-breaking wholesalers or to retail outlets.
- The expenses incurred in printing and mailing catalogues price-lists, sales brochures, merchandising displays, trade journal and newspaper advertising, etc.
- Providing customer service facilities (such as the availability of customising add-ons like CD-players or mobile phones).

As the above checklist illustrates, bringing a motor car to the market is a highly complex operation. It requires systems – nowadays extensively computerised – which make continuously available various measures and ratios of quantitative (number-based) information for teams of accountants and allied staff to analyse.

For instance: If 500 sheets of lightweight alloy have been calculated to produce 20,000 wheel-trims, how many were actually produced to company quality standards and what was the percentage wastage rate?

Similarly, if a pre-launch mailshot to established dealers expects a positive response from 8 per cent, what was the actual percentage of dealers who placed orders compared with the planned response level?

Only by introducing detailed methods for obtaining information relating to such operational activities can a car maker keep within the levels of costs allowed, and produce the percentages of overall profit which have been planned.

And this is why the question 'How are we doing?' is asked at regular intervals by all involved in making and selling operations.

Assuring the organisation's future

While detailed information is needed to assess past performance and compare it with similar preceding data like:

   this month – last month
   this year – last year (first quarter)
   etc.

and while it is important to monitor information relating to ongoing operations, perhaps the most important information an organisation needs to obtain and sift is that which will inform the crucial question: 'Where are we going?'

If this question fails to be answered, or prompts the wrong answers, then as night follows day, the commercial undertaking concerned is headed for the slippery slope descending to Carey Street, 'Queer Street', or in other words, bankruptcy!

For this reason, large investments of time and money are devoted to gaining just this kind of futuring information:

PC
2.2.3
2.3.3

INFORMATION NEEDED TO ASSURE THE FUTURE

Research and Development:
- What technologies and scientific processes currently or newly developed are most likely to affect the products or services we sell?
- What should be our developmental priorities?
- In what general directions is research going?
- Are we keeping pace in our field?

Marketing:
- What introductions or changes do we need to plan for now in order to ensure that our goods or services remain in high demand in three to five years' time?
- How do we maintain a competitive edge over our competitors in terms of these future offerings?

Production:
- How can we refine and improve our manufacturing processes so as to increase output, reduce waste and remain cost-effective?
- What new plant do we need? What training and development does the factory workforce require?

Personnel:
- What kind of workforce does the organisation need in the coming five years in terms of age, qualifications, skills and experience?
- What manpower planning steps need to be taken – recruitment, early retirement, retraining, fast-track development, etc. – to generate the right employee profile in good time?

Finance:
- Are the levels of profit currently being produced sufficient to ensure that the corporate development plan for the next three years can be financed?
- Should the company:
  - obtain further capital by a rights issue of shares (i.e. offer new shares in the company to existing or new shareholders)?
  - or restructure its activities so as to improve both cash-flow and profits in key sectors?

As the above examples illustrate, senior executives in organisations devote expensive time and energy to acquiring the information needed to answer such crucial, corporate questions.

PC
2.1.4
2.2.5
2.3.2

■ Modelling and forecasting

The advent of high-capacity, networked computers in the 1980s gave corporate futuring – anticipating future possibilities which could affect the organisation's success – a powerful thrust.

Researchers were able to create computer models of:

- specific national and international markets;
- trends in consumer lifestyles and purchasing patterns;
- comparative costs in complex products related to the use of alternative parts and/or processes;
- design options to meet high/low build schedules, costs and quality specifications.

Such models provide answers to questions like:

- What happens to product sales if consumers continue to be influenced by environmental issues at the present rate?
- By how much should the price of our vacuum-cleaner increase if our energy costs rise by 8 per cent next year, and the costs of our bought-in electric motors by 6 per cent?

In a similar way, computers enable likely future trends to be forecast as a result of analysing historic and current results. For example, market-makers and stockbrokers use highly sophisticated software to record the hourly, daily, weekly and monthly fluctuations of the stock market so as to gain insights into the likely future movements of particular shares. Such information influences the prices at which they are prepared to buy or sell.

Government departments and public sector organisations also make extensive use of computer modelling techniques. Civil servants in, say, the National Health Service need to explore the impact upon the provision of geriatric wards and day-care centres of the current trend of people living ten to fifteen years longer than they did fifty years ago. Similarly, staff in the Department of Social Security need to secure realistic estimates of the likely costs in income support for single parents across the country should the current divorce rate remain at some 40 per cent of all marriages.

GROUP ACTIVITIES

PC
2.1.3
2.2.3
2.3.3

In a group of two or three, first undertake your researches and then report back to your group in a ten to fifteen minute illustrated oral presentation:

1 The kind of 'historical snapshot' information about a company's business activities and financial state provided in its annual balance sheet.

2 The historical information published by a company in its annual report to its shareholders.

3 The sort of data which project planners assemble when using PERT – Programme Evaluation and Review Technique – in order to manage a project.

4 The information used to design a business plan prior to opening a small business.

5 The sort of information a company like *Laura Ashley*, *Halfords* or *Body Shop* would include when drawing up their corporate plan for the coming three years.

INDIVIDUAL ACTIVITIES

First carry out your researches, then report back to your class as indicated:

1 Find out how a microchip is designed and manufactured. Provide your class with an illustrated briefing on the process lasting about ten minutes.

2 Find out what is meant by a 'statistically significant sample' and report back orally to your class with some examples.

3 Assume that a students' hall of residence is to be built on your school or college campus to cater for both UK and overseas students. What primary and secondary sources of information can you think of which might be needed during the design and building of the hall? Make a checklist to share with your co-students.

4 Select one of the following commercial/industrial company departments:

Research and Development   Production   Marketing   Personnel   Sales

Then make arrangements to interview a senior manager working for a local firm in the department you select. Your task during your visit is to find out what kind of information is needed most frequently and used most often by the department.

Report back to your group orally and produce a set of notes for each member which summarises your findings.

DISCUSSION TOPICS

1 The Information Revolution is placing ever more reliance upon impersonal computers and their support equipment to minister to our everyday needs – like personal finance, shopping, travelling and recreation – as well as in our daily working lives. Are we in danger of creating an impersonal and uncaring world in which only electronic logic rules?

2 How many different types of information can you identify? Or is information incapable of being broken down into different types?

3 'Would that the infernal Information Revolution had never reared its ugly head! Contemporary society and its business concerns are becoming buried beneath an avalanche of information – most of it unasked for, time-consuming to absorb and, in the event, trivial and unnecessary!'

Do you agree with this jaundiced view of the I990s?

THE SYSTEMS APPROACH TO INFORMATION

So far, this Unit has examined the need for information in organisations, the wide variety of the forms it takes, where it comes from and – in outline – what it is typically used for.

In order for the welter of information generated by an organisation or available to it to be of any value, it has to be systematically managed. One particular management approach which was developed, notably by Kenneth Boulding in the 1950s, has come to be called systems management. The concept of systems management is illustrated in Fig 2.4.

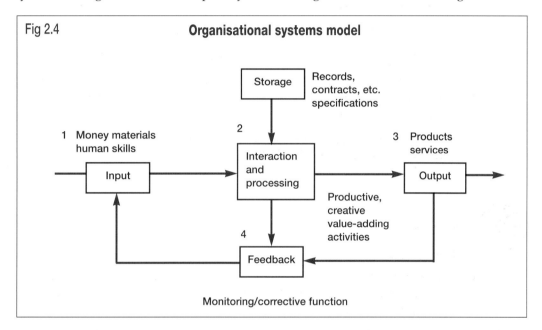

Fig 2.4 **Organisational systems model**

1 In order to function and maintain itself, an organisation needs continual inputs of money, materials and human skills. In the above systems management model, this process is called **the input phase**.

2 The ingredients of finance, materials and human skill are then mixed together in a number of ways, depending upon the work of the organisation – in, say, the process of manufacturing a product, writing software programs, or supplying legal advice and services, etc. This activity is called **the process phase**. The storage of records, files, prototypes and so on is included in this phase.

3 The process of making, designing or advising may result in making a 36-piece china tea-set, writing a desktop publishing program or drawing up a new will. Whatever their form, in systems management these end results are termed **outputs**.

In the process of transforming inputs into outputs, value is added, which forms the source of profit and of further money inputs so that the system can continue.

4 In order for the system to work effectively, the process phase needs to be continuously monitored. Thus feedback is supplied – either that all is going according to plan, or that faults, break-downs, incorrect data, bottle-necks, etc. have occurred which threaten the system.

The systems management approach to running organisations arose primarily from the interest of scientists, such as botanists and biologists, in how living organisms maintained themselves and from engineers who understood thoroughly the interactions of, say, an internal combustion engine, where inputs of fuel underwent an explosive burning process which was turned into output energy to drive wheels, and so on.

■ Responsiveness to change

As the theory of systems management for organisations developed, further ideas were introduced. For the organisation to survive, for example, it was considered essential that it be capable of adapting to changes in its environment. If, say, a government suddenly imposed a 30 per cent purchase-tax surcharge on luxury goods, then a sports car manufacturer might need to switch promptly into making low-cost family saloons. However, such a sudden lurch from one production model to another might well make the car firm unstable; it might need to borrow too much cash, or lack a suitable distributor network in the short term. Therefore, as far as possible, systems management seeks to maintain a stability or equilibrium in the process phase.

■ Self-administered health checks

Just as the human body constantly monitors its own health and produces antibodies to fight infection, so the organisational system maintains similar internal health checks. In this way, its accountants may keep a watchful eye on cash flow, so as to ensure that sufficient money is always available for the payroll and to pay for purchases and so on. Other 'health checks' include regular machine maintenance, quality assurance systems, customer complaints analysis etc.

■ Open and closed systems

Within the systems management model, two different types of system were identified, the open, and the closed. Open systems – like human bodies or business companies – are able to interact with their environments and adapt themselves to changes which they experience. Closed systems – like a musical box, or a looped, repeating advertising tape – cannot change from their preset routines and do not interact with anything outside their 'environment'.

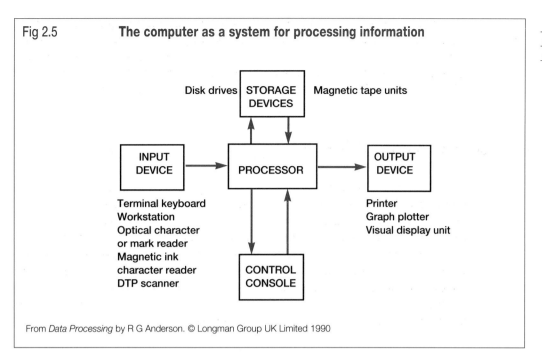

Fig 2.5   **The computer as a system for processing information**

Disk drives **STORAGE DEVICES** Magnetic tape units

INPUT DEVICE

PROCESSOR

OUTPUT DEVICE

Terminal keyboard
Workstation
Optical character
or mark reader
Magnetic ink
character reader
DTP scanner

Printer
Graph plotter
Visual display unit

CONTROL CONSOLE

From *Data Processing* by R G Anderson. © Longman Group UK Limited 1990

■ The systems approach to information

The approach of systems management, embodied in the INPUT – PROCESS – OUTPUT – FEEDBACK model above is particularly suited to the design and management of business information systems. Indeed, from its earliest development, computerised data processing has been explained by using virtually the same model to illustrate the way in which computers work (see Fig 2.5).

The diagram in Fig 2.6 fleshes out the INPUT–PROCESS–OUTPUT computer model with a number of examples of input, process, storage and output media and processes.

■ From paper to computerised systems

Since the introduction into western Europe of movable-type technology in the fifteenth century, the communication of ideas has been largely paper-based. Even Victorian etchings and early photographs were distributed in a paper medium.

It is not unnatural, then, that businesses should have developed over the past five hundred years information systems which relied on complex cycles of document exchange. Consider, for example, the eight main stages (each one capable of being transacted by means of a paper document) of making an account sale (see Fig 2.7 on page 119)

As the diagram at Fig 2.7 illustrates, instructions and authorisations are effected by the physical movement of paper documents – from mailroom (in) to sales department to warehouse to despatch, to accounts department and back to mailroom (out).

As a consequence of the limitations of the paper-based system, a number of complications inevitably arise:

THE DOWNSIDE OF PAPER-BASED INFORMATION SYSTEMS

● The same information has to be repeated a number of times on different forms at various stages in the process.

● Copies of issued forms have to be sent around the organisation to maintain essential communications among those involved.

● The process of issuing dockets, notes and forms is expensive in both time and money and keeps the customer waiting.

● Records of the transaction need to be kept, and over a period of time, storing paper is costly in terms of floor space occupied, and document recovery time. Currently 1 in 10 of all paper documents filed becomes lost for ever!

● Maintaining paper-based information systems is labour-intensive, and therefore costly.

Fig 2.6   **A systems model of the information processing function in the office**

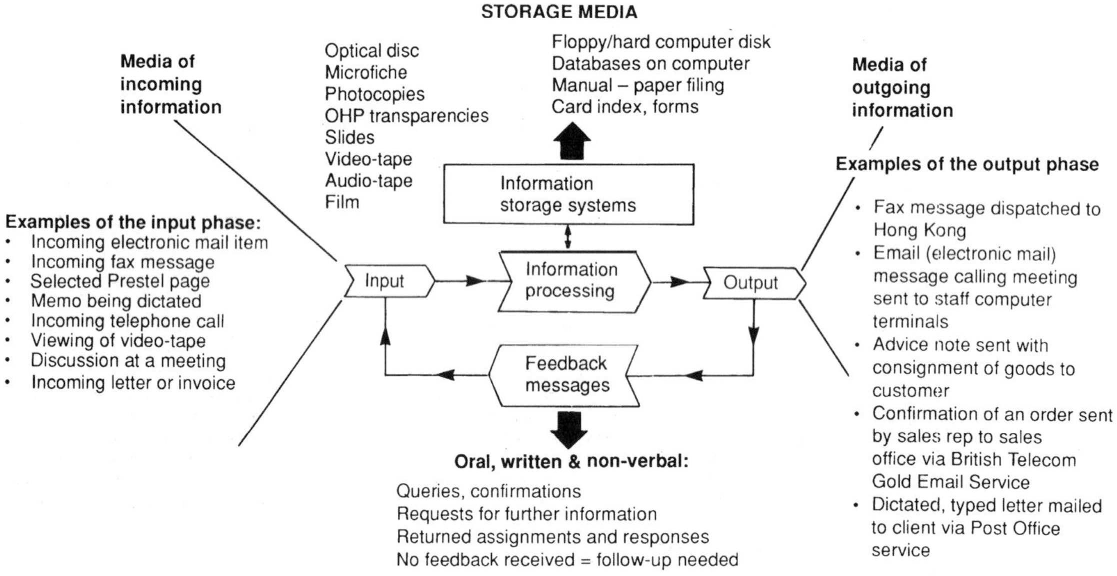

STORAGE MEDIA

Media of incoming information

Optical disc
Microfiche
Photocopies
OHP transparencies
Slides
Video-tape
Audio-tape
Film

Floppy/hard computer disk
Databases on computer
Manual – paper filing
Card index, forms

Media of outgoing information

Information storage systems

Input → Information processing → Output

Feedback messages

Examples of the input phase:
· Incoming electronic mail item
· Incoming fax message
· Selected Prestel page
· Memo being dictated
· Incoming telephone call
· Viewing of video-tape
· Discussion at a meeting
· Incoming letter or invoice

Examples of the output phase

· Fax message dispatched to Hong Kong
· Email (electronic mail) message calling meeting sent to staff computer terminals
· Advice note sent with consignment of goods to customer
· Confirmation of an order sent by sales rep to sales office via British Telecom Gold Email Service
· Dictated, typed letter mailed to client via Post Office service

Oral, written & non-verbal:

Queries, confirmations
Requests for further information
Returned assignments and responses
No feedback received = follow-up needed

Examples of the process phase:
· Keying an appointment into an electronic diary
· Entering fresh figures on to a spreadsheet
· Producing a staff holiday rota for visual display
· Revising a report via word processing
· Arranging the time, date and location of a meeting for dissemination via electronic mail

All kinds of information is received via various media, dealt with and processed into appropriate forms of message for onward distribution. Copies, records and back-up files are stored in a wide range of paper and media, as archived data or for future reference.

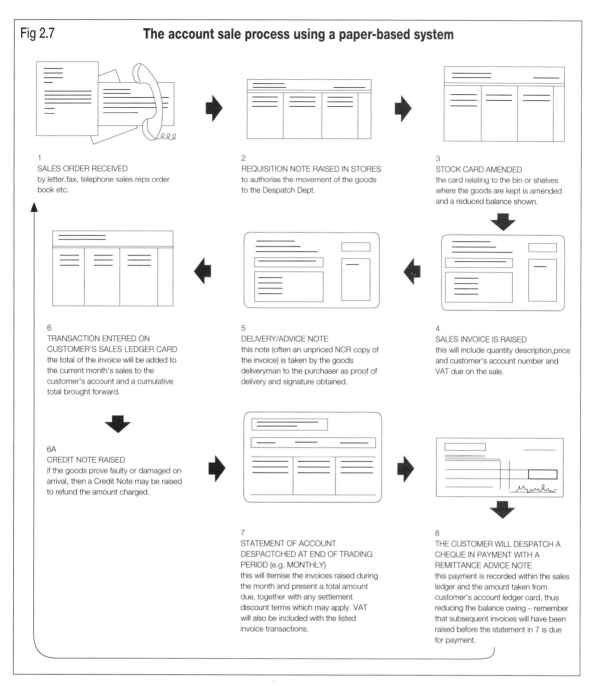

Fig 2.7   **The account sale process using a paper-based system**

1
SALES ORDER RECEIVED
by letter,fax, telephone sales reps order book etc.

2
REQUISITION NOTE RAISED IN STORES
to authorise the movement of the goods to the Despatch Dept.

3
STOCK CARD AMENDED
the card relating to the bin or shelves where the goods are kept is amended and a reduced balance shown.

6
TRANSACTION ENTERED ON CUSTOMER'S SALES LEDGER CARD
the total of the invoice will be added to the current month's sales to the customer's account and a cumulative total brought forward.

5
DELIVERY/ADVICE NOTE
this note (often an unpriced NCR copy of the invoice) is taken by the goods deliveryman to the purchaser as proof of delivery and signature obtained.

4
SALES INVOICE IS RAISED
this will include quantity description,price and customer's account number and VAT due on the sale.

6A
CREDIT NOTE RAISED
if the goods prove faulty or damaged on arrival, then a Credit Note may be raised to refund the amount charged.

7
STATEMENT OF ACCOUNT DESPACTCHED AT END OF TRADING PERIOD (e.g. MONTHLY)
this will itemise the invoices raised during the month and present a total amount due, together with any settlement discount terms which may apply. VAT will also be included with the listed invoice transactions.

8
THE CUSTOMER WILL DESPATCH A CHEQUE IN PAYMENT WITH A REMITTANCE ADVICE NOTE
this payment is recorded within the sales ledger and the amount taken from customer's account ledger card, thus reducing the balance owing – remember that subsequent invoices will have been raised before the statement in 7 is due for payment.

The illustration in Fig 2.8 further emphasises the complex processes involved in maintaining a paper-based, double-entry bookkeeping system. In the chart, five stages are explained:

1. The original document data entry phase
2. The input to the Books of Original Entry phase
3. The posting to the Ledger phase
4. The extraction of the Trial Balance phase
5. The preparation of Final Accounts phase

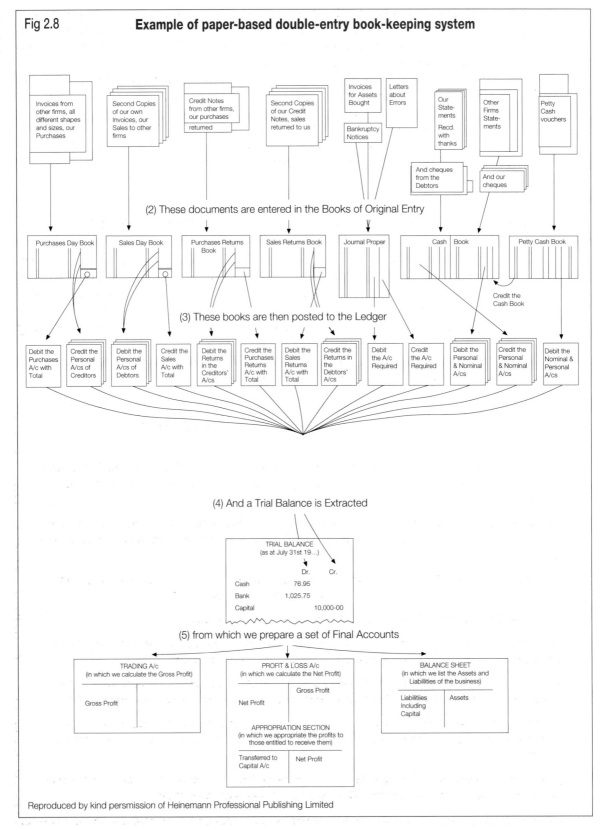

The illustration depicts twelve different document sources and types in phase one and seven different books of original entry in phase two. It is not difficult to picture the paper-chase which used to characterise many large commercial and industrial accounts departments dealing with thousands of transactions daily!

It is therefore little wonder that accountants were among the early converts to computerised business information systems. Software houses like Fretwell-Downing recognised the huge potential market that was awaiting the programmers who could devise a software application package which would remove extensive accounting drudgery by carrying out double-entry bookkeeping postings, extracting trial balances and issuing management accounting reports automatically.

■ Fretwell-Downing data systems business management system

As the diagrammatic presentation of the software package on pages 122 and 123 reveals, the package is both flexible and cost-effective. Items like updated pricelists, trial balances, outstanding purchase order details, and so on, may be printed on demand, and until needed, occupy a minuscule storage space within the computer's hard disk.

Managers and support staff can call up any data for checking in a trice on their desktop VDUs (on-line review) and have more time to audit and monitor the sales and purchase order process since so many tasks – like posting to the sales or purchase ledgers – are automatically effected through the software's commands.

PC
2.3.1
2.3.2
2.3.3
2.3.5

THE UPSIDE OF COMPUTERISED INFORMATION SYSTEMS

- Software applications may be designed to promote 'one-touch football', in other words once-only entry of data which is automatically relayed to any part of the information process where it is needed.

- Accuracy is built in; provided the software has been rigorously tested, and provided that data is entered correctly, the subsequent manipulations of the data within the computer are not prone to human error.

- Security of sensitive information is good; while no program is hacker-proof, password systems and levels of access are much more secure than metal filing cabinet locks.

- Access to files and records is far faster than in paper-based systems.

- The equivalent of wall-lengths of vertical or lateral paper filing systems is available in the 40cm square processor housing the hard disk memory of a personal computer.

- The advent of computerised networks (see page 126) made it possible for files and data to be transmitted not only between office block floors, but also continents in seconds and in safety!

- Provided sufficient investment is made in data entry resourcing, the system may be developed into an overarching database, housing all an organisation's records and in-house informational needs.

- The worldwide development of specialist computerised databases is extending fast and the day when 'all you need to know' can be called up on your VDU is not far distant.

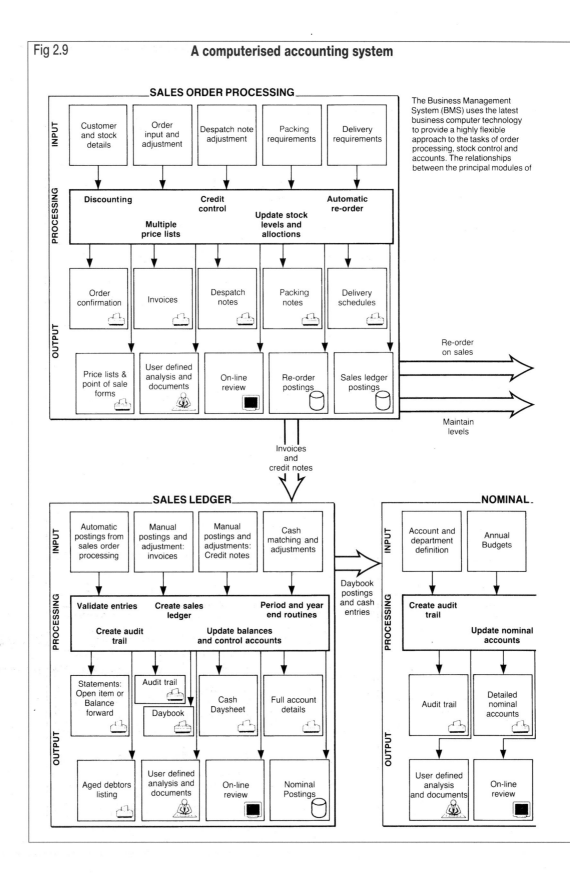

Fig 2.9 **A computerised accounting system**

The Business Management System (BMS) uses the latest business computer technology to provide a highly flexible approach to the tasks of order processing, stock control and accounts. The relationships between the principal modules of

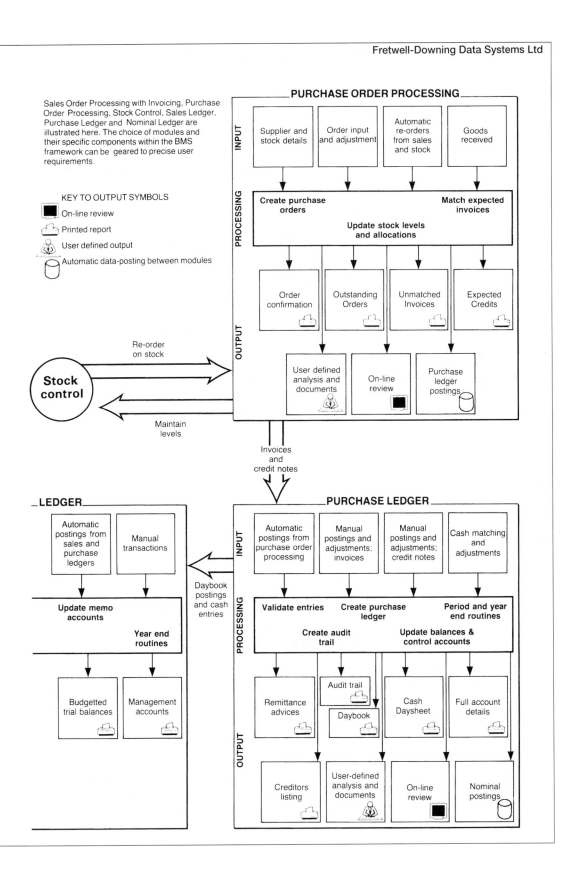

Sales Order Processing with Invoicing, Purchase Order Processing, Stock Control, Sales Ledger, Purchase Ledger and Nominal Ledger are illustrated here. The choice of modules and their specific components within the BMS framework can be geared to precise user requirements.

KEY TO OUTPUT SYMBOLS

- On-line review
- Printed report
- User defined output
- Automatic data-posting between modules

PURCHASE ORDER PROCESSING

INPUT

| Supplier and stock details | Order input and adjustment | Automatic re-orders from sales and stock | Goods received |

PROCESSING

Create purchase orders   Match expected invoices

Update stock levels and allocations

OUTPUT

| Order confirmation | Outstanding Orders | Unmatched Invoices | Expected Credits |

Stock control

Re-order on stock

Maintain levels

| User defined analysis and documents | On-line review | Purchase ledger postings |

Invoices and credit notes

LEDGER

| Automatic postings from sales and purchase ledgers | Manual transactions |

Update memo accounts

Year end routines

| Budgetted trial balances | Management accounts |

Daybook postings and cash entries

PURCHASE LEDGER

INPUT

| Automatic postings from purchase order processing | Manual postings and adjustments; invoices | Manual postings and adjustments; credit notes | Cash matching and adjustments |

PROCESSING

Validate entries   Create purchase ledger   Period and year end routines

Create audit trail   Update balances & control accounts

OUTPUT

| Remittance advices | Audit trail / Daybook | Cash Daysheet | Full account details |

| Creditors listing | User-defined analysis and documents | On-line review | Nominal postings |

TYPICAL FILES CREATED AND STORED ELECTRONICALLY

Department	Application software package	Type of file
Sales	Database	List of account customer particulars and purchasing limits
	Spreadsheet	Records of salesforce, actual to target sales
	Sales tracking (the progress of prospective sales is closely monitored)	Sales representatives' expenses
	Word processing	Sets of mailmerged sales circular letters – easily updated
R & D/Production Marketing	Project management	Introduction of a new product – from prototype to launch
Marketing	Graphics and modelling software	Analysis of market penetration/client types/market share, etc.
	Desktop publishing	Advertising copy – display ads, leaflets, brochures, etc.
Personnel	Database	All employee records
	Database	Training/staff development notes Promotion/pay increase records
Accounts	Spreadsheet	Management accounting reports and ratios
	Integrated accounts package	All ledgers – sales, purchasing, nominal, etc. plus payroll
Transport	Database	Fleet servicing records
	Tailor-made	Optimum journeys and routes to distribute goods
All departments All staff	Unified database	Specifically designed data files relevant to the organisation's work
Manager/PA – Secretary	Local area network operating software Integrated modular management package (allows data to be merged from one application to another)	Email messages, notes to self, diary, appointments and meetings schedulers, etc. Letters, reports, tables, calculations, graphs and charts, database records, etc.
Created by technicians and secretaries for managers	Desktop publishing	News sheets, bulletins, invitations, reports, etc.
PA/secretary	Word processing	Letters, memos, reports, minutes, abstracts, press releases, pricelists, etc.

Note: The above chart indicates the extent to which business/public service application software packages have mushroomed since the original dedicated wp software of the mid 1970s. As the section on convergence which follows indicates, the arrival of computer networks meant that such files could also be shared amongst the different users on the network.

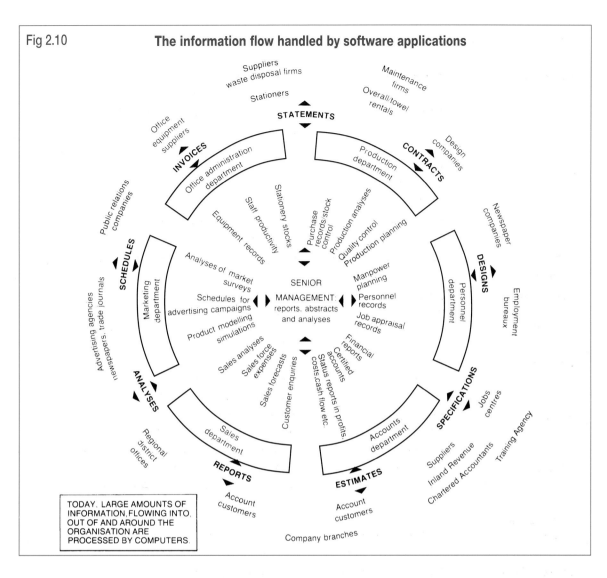

Fig 2.10 **The information flow handled by software applications**

TODAY, LARGE AMOUNTS OF INFORMATION, FLOWING INTO, OUT OF AND AROUND THE ORGANISATION ARE PROCESSED BY COMPUTERS.

DISCUSSION TOPICS

1 How valid do you think the systems model is as a means of explaining how organisations function? Does it oversimplify the way that organisations work, or is it a fair reflection?

2 In the 1970s, over-eager supporters of IT were proclaiming the imminent arrival of 'the paperless office'; in the 1980s they modified the slogan to 'the less paper office'; today, most managers complain that they are being deluged by more paper to wade through than ever.

   Does this trend suggest that IT has failed to deliver a promised freedom from 'bumf', or that, deep down, we much prefer to rummage around the A4 paper sheets on our desks than to gaze for hours at a colour VDU screen ?

3 The preceding pages of this Unit have emphasised the 'downside' of paper-based information systems and the 'upside' of their computerised counterparts. Can you think of any 'upside' points in favour of paper systems, and 'downside' ones against computerised alternatives?

Fig 2.11   **LAN installed in a multi-storey head office linked to a remotely located branch office**

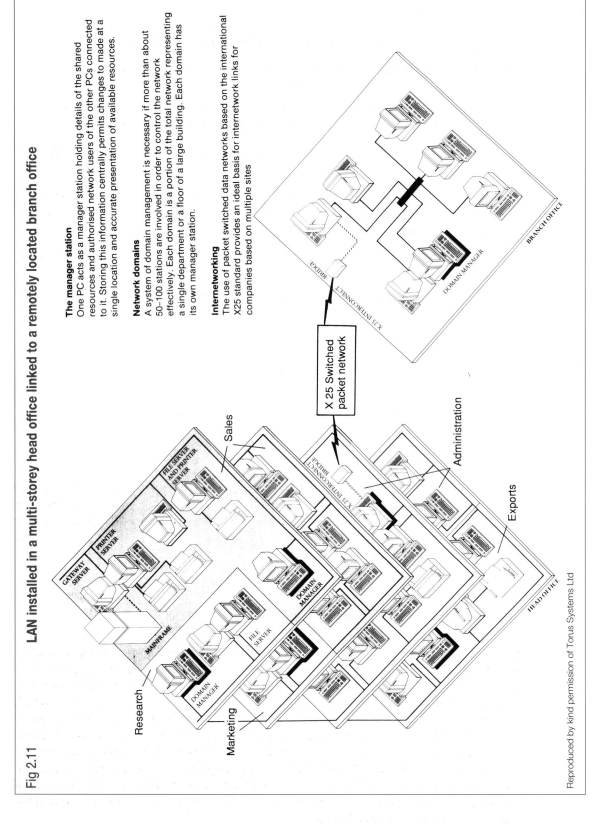

The manager station
One PC acts as a manager station holding details of the shared resources and authorised network users of the other PCs connected to it. Storing this information centrally permits changes to made at a single location and accurate presentation of available resources.

Network domains
A system of domain management is necessary if more than about 50–100 stations are involved in order to control the network effectively. Each domain is a portion of the total network representing a single department or a floor of a large building. Each domain has its own manager station.

Internetworking
The use of packet switched data networks based on the international X25 standard provides an ideal basis for internetwork links for companies based on multiple sites

INDIVIDUAL ACTIVITY

First undertake your researches, and then report back to your group in an illustrated oral presentation:

1 Examine carefully the type of information which your organisation uses (firm, school or college) in terms of the inputs–processes–outputs–feedback systems model.

   Then design a diagram to illustrate the system and include the mechanisms of boards, committees, task groups or working parties, etc. which are employed to link the system's parts.

2 Find out what the acronym EDI stands for and how it is currently revolutionising the purchasing–supply interface of large manufacturers.

3 Reread the account sale process using a paper-based system on page 119 and then with the help of family and friends, obtain examples of the documents referred to used by local businesses. Post them on your base-room noticeboard as a group briefing.

4 Find out what an 'audit-trail' is in an accounts software package and why the Inland Revenue insists on its presence and effective working.

5 Find out what management accounting reports are routinely used in a manufacturing company and why.

'WE HAVE THE TECHNOLOGY!' LOCAL AND WIDE AREA NETWORKS

The advantages of improved speed, security and lower costs of computerised information systems became rapidly apparent in the early 1980s. Yet there remained the stubborn problem of how to move information around the managers and support workers who needed to interact with it without having to revert to paper in the form of hard-copy printouts, or as distributed source documents.

■ LAN – messaging at the speed of light!

This problem was solved ingeniously by computer scientists who developed cabling systems interconnecting desktop terminals which were capable of transmitting messages in electronic form, either up and down a 'bus' (a kind of electronic high-speed motorway with spurs leading to connected terminals), or around a kind of ring-main to which terminals were linked. Such systems came to be called Local Area Networks partly because, initially, the furthest a terminal could be from its host file-server (a kind of central processing unit) was some 200 metres. The two transmission systems moving the messages around the network which became most popular are Ethernet (line bus system) and Token Ring ('ring-main' system). The unique attraction of the LAN system in terms of information interchange is that its electronics circuitry enables messages to zip around the network at virtually the speed of light!

As the diagrams in Figs 2.12 and 2.13 illustrate, LANs may be networked in a number of ways – along a line, as a ring or as a star. Whatever their structure, the principle of their operation remains the same. 'Messages' intended for one or several LAN terminals are directed around the network – virtually at the speed of light – by the central processor or file-server. The speed at which the message pulses travel around the LAN is in the order of 10 million (10 megabits) per second. Each terminal in turn interrogates the message to see if it is the intended recipient. If it isn't it passes it on. Only the one bearing the correct 'address' retains the message and displays the fact of its arrival on its VDU as, for example, 'New Mail For You'.

In the initial stages of the development of LANs, computer terminals were inter-connected by a kind of coaxial cable. Nowadays technology has made possible LANs and WANs which are linked by radio signal, thus removing the geographical restrictions of having to provide a kind of cable ring-main connecting the system.

Fig 2.12　　　　　**Examples of LAN connection layouts**

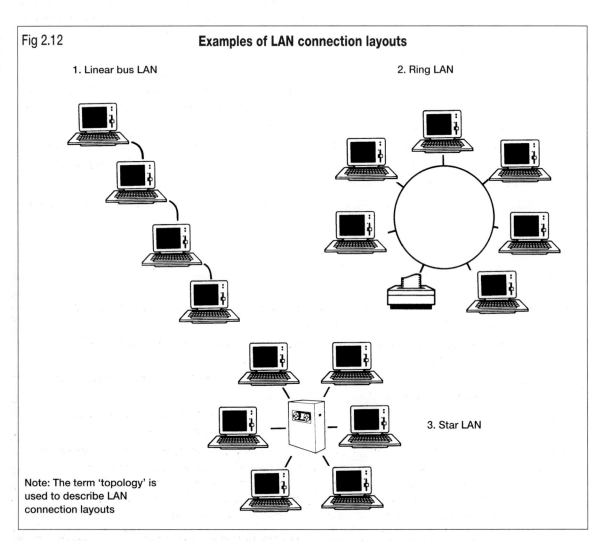

1. Linear bus LAN

2. Ring LAN

3. Star LAN

Note: The term 'topology' is used to describe LAN connection layouts

■ The file-server: multi-tasking and multi-serving workhorse

At the heart of the LAN/WAN system is the file-server, the nerve-centre of the system. A file-server may take the form of a mainframe or mini-computer, or in smaller networks it may be a terminal similar to all the rest, but possessing a large hard-disk memory of 100 plus megabytes.

The attractiveness of the LAN network lies in the flexibility and versatility of its operation. Because of the speed at which it can send information around the system to all or some users it can:

■ multi-serve

In other words, simultaneously attend to the **individual** needs of 250 or more users, whether they are in the process of booting-up their terminal, using a software package, importing artwork via a scanner or printing out completed work. The file-server manages to do this by sending high-speed, interrupted message parts to each terminal. But so fast are the interrupted pulses, that each user 'sees' them as a continuous stream.

■ multi-task

As a result of its powerful memory and drive, the file-server is able to download multiple versions of any of the software application passages stored on its hard disk. As a result, each of four adjacent users could be word processing, desktop publishing, working with a spreadsheet or designing a colour graphic.

Just as the file-server attends to the needs of multiple network users using software packages, so a network print-server ensures multiple access to a network printer with a minimum of delay.

The LAN's ability to multi-serve and multi-task provides its users with the following facilities:

USER FEATURES PROVIDED BY A LOCAL AREA NETWORK

- Sending or receiving electronic mail (email) messages; messages may either be emailed to individuals or simultaneously to designated groups.

- Any file produced by a user whether by word processing, spreadsheet, graphics or DTP package, etc. may be 'clipped' to the email note and transmitted with it.

- Files produced by a remote user which are stored centrally on the file-server may be called up (with authorisation) by any other user.

- Created files may be imported or exported to any software application package being used on a given terminal, e.g. from a spreadsheet on to a report being word processed.

- By employing a package like an electronic diary, a user may call a meeting of, say, five members of a project team on the first possible day and time when all are available; the computer interrogates each user's electronic diary to check for a common available slot. Similarly, if kept in open mode, any diary may be called up by any user wishing to arrange to see a colleague. Sophisticated LANs also enable users to book meeting rooms and audio visual aids equipment!

■ From LANs to WANs

All the above features of the network system are available in wide area networking, which works on entirely the same principle, save that the terminals may be thousands of miles apart and electronic messages may need several power boosts to keep them going along the route. One company which makes extensive use of the WAN system is IBM Incorporated. As a multinational computer manufacturer, IBM has offices and factories all over the world. Wherever IBM has a terminal installed, its user, whether production manager, marketing executive or research scientist is able to communicate with a co-worker – perhaps on the other side of the world – in a matter of seconds. Not only does IBM's WAN system permit its staff to communicate swiftly, it also enables messages to be sent to a WAN electronic address overnight, to be 'opened' by its recipient in the same way as incoming letter post. Moreover, recent developments in telecommunications have made it possible for interconnected WAN users to work simultaneously via their visual display screens on, say, the design of an architectural plan, the wording of a joint diplomatic communiqué or set of spreadsheet figures.

PC
2.2.2
2.3.2

Fig 2.13

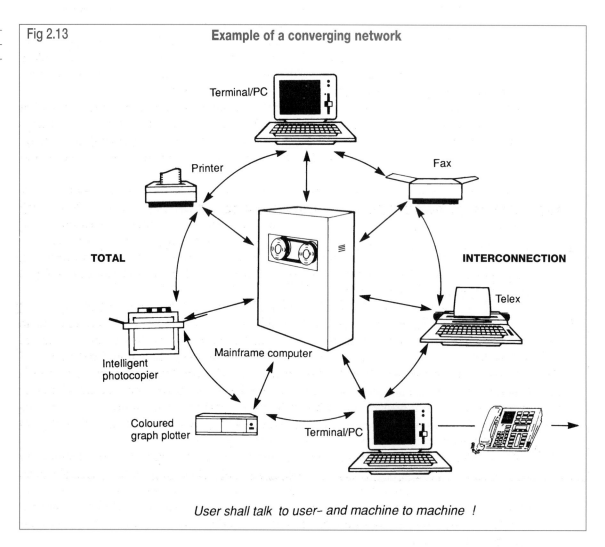

Example of a converging network

User shall talk to user– and machine to machine !

LANs and connectivity

The commercial introduction of the local area network in the 1980s formed only a part of what computer scientists came to call the 'process of convergence'. As you will be aware, the verb to converge means to come together, and that is exactly what systems analysts and computer engineers brought about – a coming together or interconnection of all the electronic office equipment available to an organisation's personnel. The label for this process which caught on was 'connectivity', but whatever the label, this electronic wizardry transformed yet again the capacity to communicate – on a local or worldwide basis – from each and every desktop workstation, as the diagram in Fig 2.13 above illustrates.

Open systems, connectivity and the office worker

PC
2.3.5

Anyone who has ever purchased a ball-point pen knows (usually through bitter experience) that you have to buy a refill made by the same company that made the pen. Others simply don't fit. Indeed, wily manufacturers take steps to ensure that they don't fit, since they are in the refills as well as the new ball-point market!

For the past ten to fifteen years, a similar kind of situation has obtained among computer and peripheral equipment manufacturers. The problem area that emerged as the kink in the pipe of increasing computer sales and improving business information systems was the computer's operating system, or rather systems.

Equipment designed for use with one operating system would not 'fit' or talk to similar equipment using a different operating system. Various manufacturers since earliest days had constructed IT equipment to work either on DOS (short for Disk Operating System), UNIX, CP/M (control program/monitor) or other operating systems none of which could talk to each other.

The result was that organisations became wedded to a particular system where computers using, say, DOS, could not communicate with others using UNIX. Such isolationist developments were preventing the open communications essential for establishing a worldwide infrastructure vital to the further development of IT. And so international interested bodies – makers, dealers and users, etc. – set about introducing network designs which would conform to an International Standards Organisation/Open System Interconnection (ISO/OSI).

At present the process of OSI still has some way to go, but the future of truly open and intercommunicating networks looks bright, since competing manufacturers have come to see the market potential of a much more interactive and more widely spread climate of 'connectivity' which will encourage more users to use more systems more frequently.

Easy connectivity (see Fig 2.14) between computer, printer, photocopier, facsimile transceiver (fax), PABX telephone switchboard, telex, viewdata (Prestel), optical character readers (OCR scanners), etc. – whether in-house or worldwide – will bring an enormous range of communications media and opportunities literally to the keying-in fingertips of each office workstation user!

And a further development in the incredible surge of telecommunications technology which is central to the development of open systems and connectivity is ISDN, short for Integrated Services Digital Network. This telecommunications technology enables a variety of digitised (data converted into streams of numbers or digits) messages to be transmitted simultaneously either along a fibre optic cable or as radio signals. A single cable network is therefore able to handle:

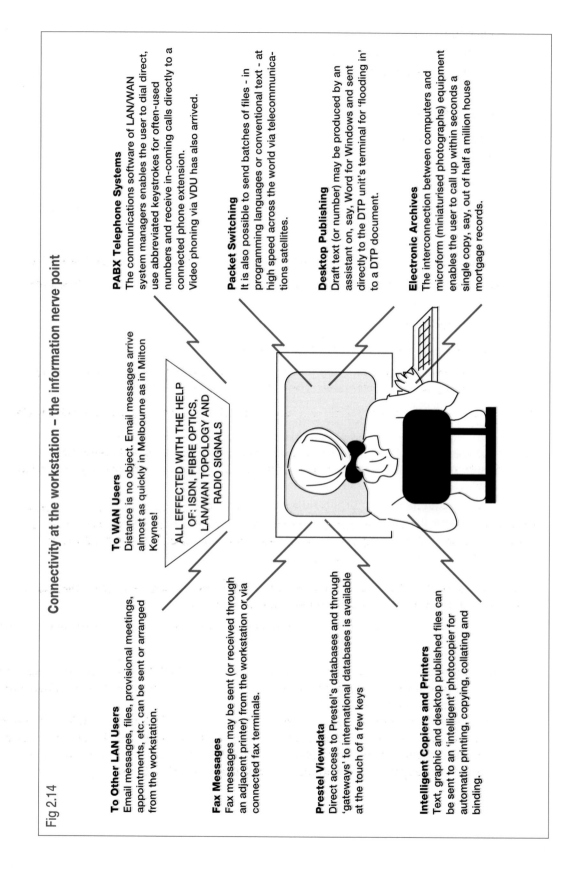

Fig 2.14

Connectivity at the workstation – the information nerve point

To Other LAN Users
Email messages, files, provisional meetings, appointments, etc. can be sent or arranged from the workstation.

Fax Messages
Fax messages may be sent (or received through an adjacent printer) from the workstation or via connected fax terminals.

Prestel Viewdata
Direct access to Prestel's databases and through 'gateways' to international databases is available at the touch of a few keys

Intelligent Copiers and Printers
Text, graphic and desktop published files can be sent to an 'intelligent' photocopier for automatic printing, copying, collating and binding.

To WAN Users
Distance is no object. Email messages arrive almost as quickly in Melbourne as in Milton Keynes!

ALL EFFECTED WITH THE HELP OF: ISDN, FIBRE OPTICS, LAN/WAN TOPOLOGY AND RADIO SIGNALS

PABX Telephone Systems
The communications software of LAN/WAN system managers enables the user to dial direct, use abbreviated keystrokes for often-used numbers and receive in-coming calls directly to a connected phone extension.
Video phoning via VDU has also arrived.

Packet Switching
It is also possible to send batches of files - in programming languages or conventional text - at high speed across the world via telecommunications satellites.

Desktop Publishing
Draft text (or number) may be produced by an assistant on, say, Word for Windows and sent directly to the DTP unit's terminal for 'flooding in' to a DTP document.

Electronic Archives
The interconnection between computers and microform (miniaturised photographs) equipment enables the user to call up within seconds a single copy, say, out of half a million house mortgage records.

- telephone calls
- digitised DP data transmissions
- email on LAN/WAN systems
- teleconferencing
- video telephone calls
- fax/telex transmission

    etc.

PC
2.2.2
2.2.3
2.3.5

THE INFORMATION AND COMMUNICATION SUPPORT AVAILABLE FROM ISDN – INTEGRATED SERVICES DIGITAL NETWORK

- Files expressed in a computer language like COBOL for high-speed, batched packet-switching.

- Two-way telephone conversations, including the newly introduced videophones which operate through PC workstations.

- Fax and telex transmissions.

- Electronic mail messages and files on LAN/WAN systems.

- Closed-circuit television transmissions or video-cassette playbacks (which can be distributed simultaneously to, say, 200 retail branches as part of a training programme).

- Audio and teleconferencing – live hook-ups linking remotely located colleagues and/or clients via phone or TV monitor.

- Shared screening and co-working on computer software applications files between remote locations – two electronic engineers 15,000 kilometres distant are able to modify, say, the design of a microchip.

- The interrogation of specialised databases – like the legal LEXIS database which provides case precedents and judgements, etc. and interaction with CD ROM libraries of information (a mixture of film, slides, computer package, textual and graphic data – all displayable on the VDU and capable of being browsed through at will).

Throughout the 1990s, ISDN will revolutionise the information available – either through a home TV/computer console or a workplace, desktop workstation.

The diagram (Fig 2.15) of Plessey's GPT ISDX System Architecture provides a 'see-at-a-glance' explanation of the Integrated Services Digital Network which will dominate office communications in the 1990s.

ISDN can distribute not only telephone conversations but also fax, telex, viewdata, electronic mail and digitised inter-computer packet switching. As the Plessey diagram shows, all an organisation's messaging in-house, local, national and international, can now be distributed at high speed and high volume thanks to ISDN technology.

Fig 2.15   Example of the range of IT and telecommunication services supported by an 'all-in' ISDN system

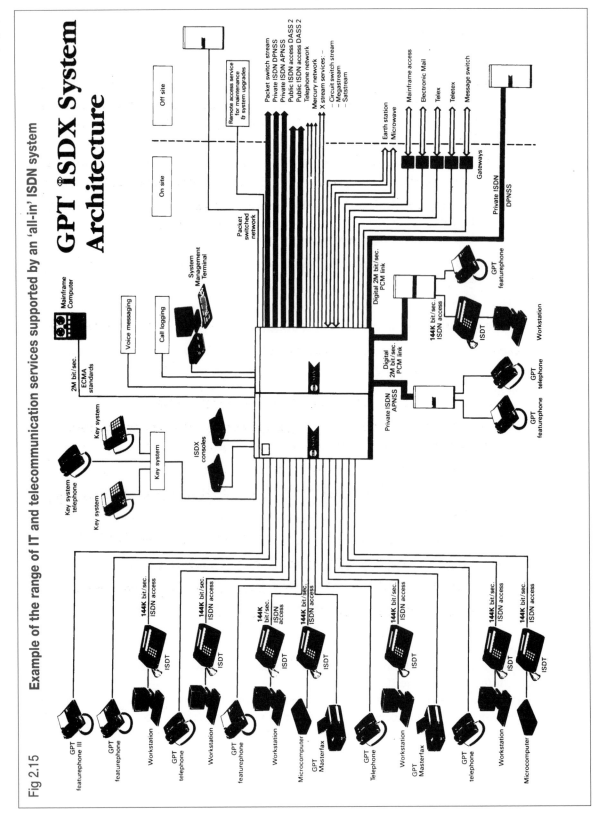

GPT ®ISDX System Architecture

Information issues

1 With the rapid expansion of national and global telecommunication systems, which can now bring the world to any manager's desk, what steps should organisations take to protect their executives from the information overload which prevents them concentrating on the organisation's key objectives?

2 Is the abundance of data nowadays readily available to large and small organisations a help or a hindrance to effective decision-making? Can a manager know too much as well as too little?

3 Is the trend of routing all kinds of communication to staff's desktop terminals likely to result in the loss of valuable face-to-face direct communication? If it did, would it matter?

REVIEW TEST

1   Why was the development of the silicon chip in the late 1960s so important to the IT revolution?

2   Why is there still so much paper around in offices?

3   How is it hoped OSI will assist international communications?

4   In what ways would you categorise the information used in organisations?

5   Make a checklist of the kind of information typically used in two of the following departments: Accounts, Personnel, Marketing, Production.

6   Explain the difference between primary and secondary sources of information.

7   Contrast the type of information needed at the corporate and middle-management levels of an organisation.

8   What is meant by modelling and forecasting in terms of information needs and the future?

9   Describe briefly and simply the systems approach to managing information.

10 List five advantages a computerised information system has over its paper-based counterpart.

11 Explain how LAN/WAN systems can improve information exchange.

THE IT EQUIPMENT USED IN INFORMATION SYSTEMS

As we have already seen, business information systems today rely increasingly on the connectivity of computerised, electronic equipment. In order to understand how current information systems work, it is necessary to be thoroughly familiar with the operating principles of the equipment involved.

This section, therefore, examines in detail the following equipment:

■ Facsimile transceivers

■ Telephone systems

■ Viewdata – Prestel

■ Photocopiers

■ Printers

■ Filing and microform record systems

■ DP packet-switching

■ Facsimile transmission

Known universally today as fax, this telecommunications system has become extremely popular with the managers and secretaries in all kinds of organisational departments, largely as a result of the speed and versatility which IT technology has given to it over the past decade. Fax can transmit to local, national and international locations all kinds of messages – handwritten notes, word processed printout, maps, diagrams, or even photographs and can accept messages in the same range of media. Transmission is effected in the space of a few seconds or minutes, depending upon the length of the document and can be undertaken (through BT and international telephone networks or through private telecommunications circuits) directly or at cheap, off-peak times in order to minimise costs.

Fax transceivers are given a rating depending on the speed at which they can transmit. A Group 3 fax transceiver can take as little as 20 seconds to transmit or receive a typical A4 page business letter. A Group 4 series carries out the same task in about six seconds.

Feedback confirmation of the safe arrival of a fax message and the facility to transmit messages confidentially are further important features of fax. The latest transceivers can also handle high-quality, plain-paper faxes.

How fax works

The way in which facsimile transmission works may be compared to the way in which a photocopier takes a copy of a document and the way a telephone line carries an oral message, which becomes an electronic signal along the telephone line and is converted back into speech at the receiver's end. In a similar way, the fax transceiver converts the text or image of the original for transmission into a series of electronic pulses or signals so that they may be transmitted over a telecommunications network of either telephone lines or satellite communication radio signals.

At the reception end (another fax transceiver), these signals are converted back into their original form, as either text, photograph or diagram etc.

The diagram (Fig 2.16) illustrates the principal routes of fax transmissions.

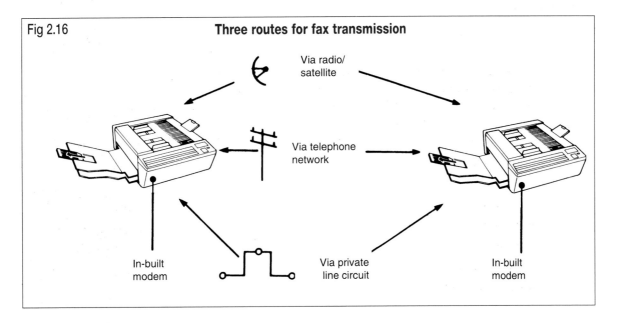

Fig 2.16

Three routes for fax transmission

Via radio/satellite

Via telephone network

In-built modem

Via private line circuit

In-built modem

Sending a fax message

1 Initial checks are made to ensure the transceiver is powered up and has paper loaded.

2 The document is fed into a document feeder for encoding. Note: if multiple documents are being transmitted care must be taken with their alignment.

3 A test copy is taken whenever the light/shade tones of a document need to be checked prior to transmission. The fax transceiver can regulate this aspect just like a photocopier. Also, fax transceivers generally provide a dual means of document transmission (fine or standard) according to the variety of shades in the original.

4 The document's recipient (another fax transceiver) is contacted by dialling the appropriate fax number. Note: fax transceivers for extensive use incorporate a feature which provides for 50–100+ fax numbers to be accessed through abbreviated codes.

5 Transmission may be effected either automatically or after telephone verbal contact with the recipient, to talk through any relevant matters or to arrange for confidential message reception etc.

6 The fax transceiver returns to a state of readiness for document acceptance once the transmission is completed.

7 A print-out of a message confirmation report detailing the date, time, transmission time, receiver machine identification code, number of pages and confirmation of the message's safe arrival may also be obtained from the transceiver.

Delayed transmission

In order to save costs or avoid busy peak transmission times, most fax systems allow the user to 'stack' a number of messages for onward transmission until a predetermined transmission time – say overnight UK time. At the appropriate moment a timer is activated to set the transmission sequences into operation. This function is usually set up at the end of the office day when no further messages are to be sent by normal means.

Status reports

A very useful feature of fax transmission is the intermittent (say after 50 transmissions) issuing of a status report which lists the number of calls made, their date, time and transmission duration, their destination and the number of pages transmitted. This provides a means of monitoring the fax bills when they arrive.

Receiving a fax message

1 A check must be made to ensure that the fax transceiver is switched on to an automatic reception mode (i.e. AUTO RECEIVE).

2 Care must be taken to ensure that sufficient paper is loaded into the transceiver to print out the anticipated number of incoming messages while fax is on auto receive. Note: fax transceivers can also be set up for the manual reception of an individual message (see 5 above).

3 At the end of each document's reception, the transceiver guillotines it and stores it in its document stacker. The date, time, and sender machine code number are printed out on each incoming message.

4 Reception polling: this device enables the receiving transceiver to accept an incoming message once a password command has been transmitted to the sending fax, and so enables a message to be despatched and received confidentially. Polling transmission techniques also allow messages to be sent to a preselected number of fax transceivers simultaneously, once passwords have been exchanged.

Facts on fax

Specifications

All fax transceivers are built to meet international (CCITT) specifications and are given a group rating. Group 1 is now almost obsolete. Group 2 operates at about 5-6 minutes to process a typical A4 sized letter. Group 3 does this in about 20 seconds. Group 4 machines do the same job in about 6 seconds. Group 4s can 'talk' to Group 3s, but at Group 3 speeds only. Many fax transceivers possess a variety of resolution facilities – 'fine' for delicate work, 'standard' for normal documents and some have a 'half-tone' facility for photographic work. The size of fax rolls of paper for printing upon is a compromise between UK, European and USA paper size standards in order for respective users to be able to accept each other's documents.

Paper and printing

For a long time fax transceivers used thermal copying paper which did not give a particularly good copy. Recently office equipment manufacturers have developed the means of printing out fax messages to letter quality standards on laser/ink-jet printers.

Fax and the future

The future of fax looks assured. It is extremely versatile, being able to transmit handwritten notes, typed/printed text, images and diagrams and photographs in seconds. One major telephone company reckons to be able to guarantee a fax transmission to anywhere in the world within two minutes, given that there are no faults in the telecommunications network! Fax equipment is becoming cheaper to buy (machines now under £400) and run. Worldwide users now surpass telex in number. It is user-friendly and simple to operate. Its

(Status Report Print Out)

Below you will find an example status report and an explanation of its components.

Example Status Report

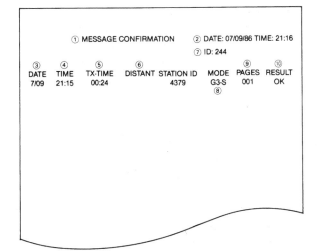

```
                    ① STATUS REPORT

                                        ② DATE: 20/09/86 TIME: 17:24
    ⑧ TOTAL TIME  TX = 00:09'     RX = 00:01'

                                        ④ ID: 0081 3 432 3211

     ⑤      ⑥       ⑦             ⑧            ⑨      ⑩      ⑪
    DATE   TIME   TX,RX-TIME   DISTANT STATION ID   MODE   PAGES   RESULT

                                                                           ⑫
    09/09  13:12   00'36"              6294        G3-S    001     OK     0000
    09/09  13:27   01'09"              6294        G3-S    003     OK     0000
    09/09  15:54   04'32"              6294        G3-S    006     OK     0000
    09/12  15:01   00'24"          03 432 1519     G3-S    001     OK     0000
    09/17  11:28   00'44"                          G3-R    000     NO     9081
    09/18  10:26   00'08"                          G3-S    000     STP    9080
    09/18  18:28   00'35"                          G3-S    000     NO     9081
    09/19  09:02   00'00"        0PPP432-1519      G3-S    000     NO     9999
    09/19  09:04   00'00"        0PPP432-1519      G3-S    000     NO     9999
    09/19  09:05   00'34"          03 432 1519     G3-S    001     OK     0000
    09/19  09:08   00'00"        0PPP432-1519      G3-S    000     NO     9999
    09/19  09:10   00'34"          03 432 1519     G3-S    001     OK     0000
    09/19  09:12   00'00"        0PPP432-1519      G3-S    000     NO     9999
    09/19  09:13   00'00"        0PPP432-1519      G3-S    000     NO     9999
    09/19  09:15   00'00"        0PPP432-1519      G3-S    000     NO     9999
    09/19  09:16   00'00"        0PPP432-1519      G3-S    000     NO     9999
    09/19  09:25   00'38"              6294        G3-S    001     OK     0000
    09/19  09:33   00'47"          03 432 1519     G3-R    001     OK     0000
    09/19  15:48   00'09"                          G3-R    000     STP    9080
```

Explanation of Status Report Components

① Title of Report
② Date and time report is made
③ Total transmission and reception time
④ TSI/CSI data (Your 9550's telephone number)
⑤ Date of each facsimile transaction
⑥ Time at which each transaction started
⑦ Time taken for each transmission (TX) or reception (RX) transaction
⑧ Identification of the remote machine
⑨ Communication mode for sending (S) and receiving (R) operations
⑩ Number of pages transmitted or received for each transaction
⑪ Result status of transaction
⑫ Four-digit code used by servicing engineer

Example codes for possible result problems:
STP (stop button pressed)
BUSY (partner fax did not answer)
NO (problem with partner machine or telephone line)

(Message Confirmation Report Print Out)

Below you will find an example Message Confirmation Report and an explanation of its components.

Example Message Confirmation Report

```
            ① MESSAGE CONFIRMATION      ② DATE: 07/09/86 TIME: 21:16
                                        ⑦ ID: 244

     ③      ④       ⑤            ⑥               ⑨      ⑩
    DATE   TIME   TX-TIME   DISTANT STATION ID   MODE   PAGES   RESULT
    7/09   21:15   00:24             4379        G3-S    001     OK
                                                  ⑧
```

Explanation of Message Confirmation Report Components

① Title of Report
② Date and time of report
③ Date of the communication mode
④ Time at which communication began
⑤ The length of time the communication took to complete
⑥ Remote machine identification data
⑦ TSI/CSI data (Your 9550's telephone number)
⑧ Communication mode
("S" = Transmission, "R" = Reception)
⑨ Total number of pages transmitted
⑩ Result status of communication

confidential transmission service and message integrity features are making fax increasingly popular with senior managers, and its incorporation into LAN/WAN systems is offering a versatile and express service to a fast increasing number of organisations.

A TYPICAL FAX FEATURES CHECKLIST

- Storage of telephone numbers via a predetermined code.
- Automatic call initiation
- High speed automatic dialling facility.
- Automatic storage of last number called.
- Call Progress Monitor.
- Tone detection: Ring, Busy, Equipment Engaged, Unobtainable.

- Repeat attempt facility.
- Auto clear from originating end.
- One touch auto dialling and auto polling.
- Automatic copying of transmitted documents.
- Delayed transmission facilities.
- Reception and transmission polling.
- Provision to supply status and management reports on fax transmissions and receptions.

■ Viewdata and videotex

You will be forgiven for experiencing some confusion about the labels which the experts have given to various telecommunications systems. We have already learned to distinguish between telex, teletex and teletext and now have viewdata and videotex to unravel!

Actually, there is no problem here for they are both terms which are used to describe the same system. British Telecom employ viewdata to describe its Prestel service, while videotex is the internationally agreed term to label the interactive services based on a central computer, telephone transmission lines, modem, and a monitor and keyboard capable of accepting colour graphics and text.

How does videotex work?

The UK viewdata system widely in use is BT's Prestel service. At its heart are ten regionally located computers which contain a large database of information on all sorts of topics. Some of this information is provided by government and public bodies – such as data on university courses – and some is provided by private companies such as hotel brochures or car-hire offers.

Each Prestel user needs a VDU screen adapted to accept Prestel transmissions, a computer and keyboard to relay instructions and a modem with call-up facilities to link the computer terminal to the appropriate Prestel computer. Indeed, any desktop PC may be adapted to accept Prestel.

Prestel is accessed by keying in a customer identity number and password. Once connected, costs are incurred by the minute for the duration on on-line connection.

Prestel information is viewed and interrogated as a series of screen colour pages of information made more interesting by the inclusion of graphic diagrams and designs. Private and public organisations (Information Providers) pay Prestel a fee for having a page of data included in the Prestel database. Each page is given a unique number which is used to locate and display it on the user's screen. The Information Provider may update, modify or withdraw a given page by arrangement with Prestel.

At the present time there are some 360,000 pages of information available for scrutiny and the database is divided into the following sectors:

Agriculture, Banking, Education, Finance-Citiservice, Insurance, Microcomputing (including a hobbyists' network), Teleshopping and Travel.

Prestel advertisers of interest to the secretary include:

■ air travel ■ advertising rates (Press) ■ bank services ■ British Telecom services ■ business equipment ■ car hire ■ cleaning services ■ computer services ■ employment agencies ■ ferry services ■ financial advice ■ hotel booking ■ insurance ■ entertainment ■ office services ■ shopping services ■ teleshopping ■ tourist information ■ *What's On*, etc.

Technically, the Prestel database is termed a branching or hierarchic database. The user starts at an initial menu or index listing the major sectors and then proceeds along the chosen one, branching off at will. For example, Business Information can take the user on to advertising or money markets or statistics and so on. Alternatively, a simple command will transport the user into an entirely different sector. Prestel pages are generally accessed by keying in a desired number once this is known, and the Prestel Directory lists keywords and numbers in blue and page numbers in black.

Perhaps the most important feature of Prestel is its interactivity. The user may locate, for example, a page which lists hotels in Birmingham and there and then effect a booking for a manager. Or, a secretary may be able to check what shows are on in London and book tickets for a musical for some visiting foreign clients. Prestel also offers such time-saving interactive facilities in banking, travel arrangements, hotel reservations, office services bureaux and so on.

A further useful feature of Prestel lies in its ability to connect the user – at a fee – to private computerised databases of information via 'gateways' – a simple term used to describe the sophisticated electronic network which links two remote computers to the user. Thus a manager in Edinburgh can browse through the menus of a United States university's database on, say, American taxation laws or registered patents on inventions!

BT also offer private versions of Prestel to larger organisations entirely for their own use. The travel industry, for example, uses a videotex system connecting tour operators with travel agents so as to reserve flight seats and hotels at the time of enquiry (subject to confirmation and deposit). City financiers also use viewdata systems to relay up-to-the-minute share prices to dealers.

Additional Prestel features include: an electronic mail system called Mailbox, which has been extended to link in with BT's Telecom Gold service; Closed User Groups services which link specific users privately; a means of accessing BT's telex service, and the facility of communicating with other databases through BT's gateway services.

What does Prestel cost to use?

Given the speed, range of data, interactivity features and user-friendliness of Prestel, its costs are very reasonable to the public user. The connection charges to a Prestel computer are priced at *local call rates* and using Prestel at cheap rate times improves value for money, as does the taking of a page of data as a printout instead of reading it while on line to Prestel. All Prestel users also pay a quarterly standing charge and a time charge which acts as a further tariff on top of the telephone charge.This charge is not levied after 6.00 pm on Mondays to Fridays, nor from 1.00 pm on Saturdays until 8.00 am Mondays. Some frames or pages of information display a number which indicates an extra charge payable levied by the information provider.

Viewdata videotex and the future

Prestel originally got off to a slow start and some telecommunications experts consider that the service should have been concentrated on the business user rather than the man in the

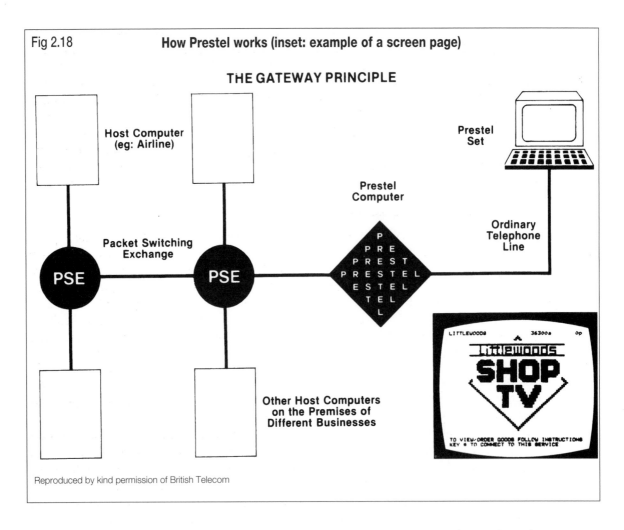

Fig 2.18 **How Prestel works (inset: example of a screen page)**

THE GATEWAY PRINCIPLE

Host Computer
(eg: Airline)

Prestel
Set

Prestel
Computer

Packet Switching
Exchange

PSE

PSE

Ordinary
Telephone
Line

Other Host Computers
on the Premises of
Different Businesses

street. That the technology offers a marvellous opportunity to bring the information in reference books, research documents, encyclopaedias, timetables, catalogues, etc, swiftly and easily to the office executive and secretary is beyond doubt. That its two-way communications system offers tremendous savings in time and effort for making bookings and confirming travel arrangements and so on is also not in dispute. It remains to be seen how BT will develop Prestel so as to make its database less dependent upon the commercial interests of some information providers and more comprehensive as a public information service.

■ Telephone services in organisations

Nowhere in today's office has IT brought about more changes than in the telephone systems linking in-house, local, national and international calls. Indeed, the current global network of telephone lines not only carries several hundred billion telephone calls around the world each year, but it also routes similarly huge amounts of data between computers and their users via modems and multiplexing (a means of enabling telephone lines to transmit varying data voice and computer language based – much faster).

It is therefore becoming increasingly difficult to view the telephone system – as it once was – as a totally distinct medium of communication. Indeed, British Telecom is currently installing an **Integrated Services Digital Network (ISDN)** in the UK which joins together voice-based telecommunications via Private Automatic Branch Exchanges (PABXs)* and the **Public Switched Telephone Network (PSTN)** with computer digital data switching networks, like BT's **Packet Switched Services (PSS)** – Datel, Satstream and Kilostream. In this way, communications in the media of voice, telex, fax, videotex, Confravision and digitally processed data will become fully exchangeable through a unified telecommunications network, instead of in today's piecemeal fashion in which some equipment cannot 'talk to' similar equipment of a different make and design, because they are not compatible.

Telephone services and the office

Essentially, there are two kinds of telephone service available in any office. Firstly there is the private line which connects its user directly to the PSTN exchange which is known as a Direct Exchange Line. Some senior managers have such telephone lines connected to a personal desktop handset so as to be able to make confidential business calls in complete privacy.

Secondly there is the extension line which connects the user to a central switchboard. In large organisations several switchboard operators are kept busy routing incoming calls to desired extensions and obtaining telephone numbers for staff wishing to make outgoing calls. At the turn of the century such connections were made by plugging large sets of cables into a board by means of jack plugs – 'trying to connect you . . .' Today such arm-aching activity has been replaced by pressing touch-sensitive buttons on a desktop computerised switchboard no bigger than a ring-binder which may control as many as 50–100 extensions!

For many years small firms like accountants', solicitors' and doctors' practices used systems which linked some 8–12 handsets. Any one user could accept an incoming call and route it if need be to a companion extension. By the same token, any one user could access an outside line. Such systems, however, offered no protection from unauthorised use.

As a result, large organisations preferred to employ systems which allowed centralised control. For example, current computerised systems provide a number of monitoring features:

- **Outside line access limited to local call-making only:** usually by dialling 9 on any extension given this facility
- **Call barring:** outside calls may only be made through the switchboard operator or not at all.
- **Call interrupting:** audio or visual prompts are activated in handsets when calls go on for longer than a pre-arranged time (say 5 minutes)
- **Call override:** a switchboard operator or senior manager may break into a call if the caller is urgently required.
- **Call logging and reporting:** sophisticated equipment exists to monitor all incoming and outgoing calls by extension number and to calculate ongoing costs and the time a handset is active; such measures help to keep down telephone costs and to enable accounts departments to allocate to each department an accurate proportion of the single, all-in telephone bill it receives quarterly.

Following upon the privatisation of British Telecom a number of UK telecommunications manufacturers like Plessey and Ferranti introduced a range of C/PABX (sometimes simply referred to as PBX) computerised telephone systems capable of supplying the needs of

*Note increasingly Computerised Automatic Branch Exchanges (CABX) are replacing their PABX counterparts.

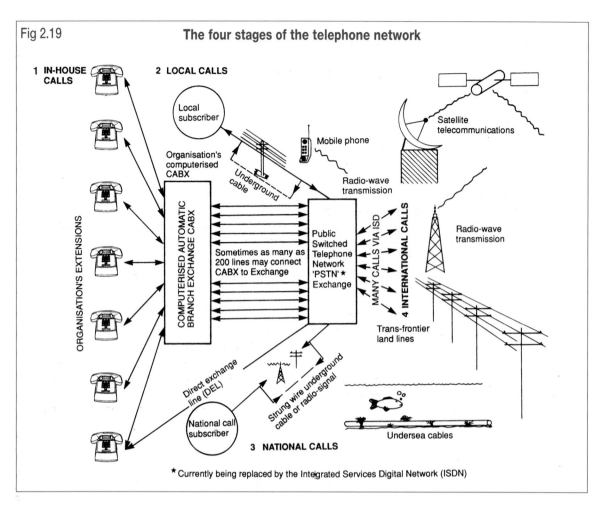

Fig 2.19 The four stages of the telephone network

1 IN-HOUSE CALLS

2 LOCAL CALLS

Local subscriber

Organisation's computerised CABX

Underground cable

Mobile phone

Radio-wave transmission

Satellite telecommunications

ORGANISATION'S EXTENSIONS

COMPUTERISED AUTOMATIC BRANCH EXCHANGE CABX

Sometimes as many as 200 lines may connect CABX to Exchange

Public Switched Telephone Network 'PSTN' ★ Exchange

MANY CALLS VIA ISD

4 INTERNATIONAL CALLS

Radio-wave transmission

Trans-frontier land lines

Direct exchange line (DEL)

Strung wire underground cable or radio-signal

Undersea cables

National call subscriber

3 NATIONAL CALLS

★ Currently being replaced by the Integrated Services Digital Network (ISDN)

8–250+ extension users. Such manufacturers vied with each other to include yet more sophisticated features in order to win orders and to provide a better service. Some of the more commonly occurring ones are described on page 145.

Key system and CABX

In concentrating upon the CABX as the telephone system which the office worker is more likely to use in a larger organisation, it is important not to overlook the sales boost which IT has given to key system telephone networks. Essentially the key system telephone network has been around for many years in the form of the small user Post Office Telephones plans which enable any telephone extension (usually up to 8–12) to accept any incoming call and to route it to an alternative if that was where the call needed to be connected.

MAJOR TYPICAL FEATURES OF A LARGE CABX SYSTEM

This table is based upon the Ferranti GTE OMNI System and is kindly made available by Ferranti GTE Ltd)

Some of OMNI's system features

Administration message recording – to provide usage reports
Dictation access – providing a link to dictation services
Group hunting – seeking out any one of a working team's extensions available to take an in-coming call by trying each in turn
Intercom groups – linking users via intercom speakers
Music on hold – playing a soothing tune over the phone while a caller is waiting to be connected
Paging and code calling access – ability to activate pagers used by roving staff
Standby power – facility to keep system going in event of power failure
Call barring – ability to restrict the range of connections availability on any extension

Some attendant features

Automatic recall re-dial – system keeps trying to connect to a busy number
Break in – facility to break into an active conversation in case of urgency
Call waiting – provision to alert extension user of another call awaiting attention
Camp on busy – ability to wait, having dialled a number until it becomes available and then to ring dialler's extension having effected the connection
Conference – linking of several extension users so all can converse with each other over the phone system can also include outside callers

Some extension features

Abbreviated dialling – often used numbers are given a short 1/2 digit code to save time
Boss–secretary – direct interconnection
Call forwarding follow me – instruction for incoming calls to be routed from a customary extension to others near to a roving staff member
Call hold – facility to keep line open to caller while specific staff member located
Direct inward dialling – facility to enable incoming calls to be routed directly to selected extension by adding its number to normal organisation's number
Direct outward dialling – facility to access PSTN directly
Do not disturb – cuts phone off while meeting etc. taking place; avoids irritating interruptions
Extension to extension calling – for direct in-house phone calls

Other major features included in CABX systems are:

Amplifying speech – to enable an incoming call to be heard across a room
Night service – enables incoming calls to be answered by late staying staff after switchboard staff have left
Call parking – the ability to divert an incoming call to another extension
'No answer' transfer – facility to re-route a call to another, specified extension

Note: Many of the above features of computerised switchboards are available to the general public with the introduction of BT's System X digital exchanges.

The key system telephone network comprises extension units linked in a circuit where each extension is able to display the status of incoming call/extension connections which are active and this does away with the need for a switchboard operator. Any free extension user is able to answer an incoming call and usually one member of staff has this duty as a priority. Key systems are being designed with increasingly useful features for small businesses and professional partnerships, and today's secretary in training may well end up with a major responsibility for coordinating a key system telephone circuit.

Executel

A new telephone switchboard with a display unit and loudspeaker facility, storage capacity for a 20-year electronic diary, telephone number directory and reminders for external and internal calls, together with an inbuilt calculator. It may also be used as an Email and viewdata terminal for Prestel or telex via the Prestel Line.

■ Using a CABX system

In order to make optimum use of a CABX computerised telephone system by means of an extension handset, it pays to have an informed understanding of how the system is structured and what the switchboard operator does and how he or she may be able to provide support. In many ways the CABX may be regarded as an upgraded version of preceding key and lamp PABXs but one which offers a much wider range of services both to callers ringing in and users of its internal network.

Operations at the console

The CABX at the console end embodies a noticeably slimmer and sleeker switchboard and handset for internal enquiries. The console generally possesses these features:

1 A series of panels which may be lit and made to flash in order to convey the status of each exchange line – in use or free – and a system which causes each lit panel to pulse or flash in various ways to indicate, for example, whether an incoming call is ringing on the desired extension or whether the operator has parked it while finding an alternative free extension by using the group hunting feature.

2 The CABX console will possess a numeric keypad for keying in call numbers and, usually, a number of keys – like command or function keys on a PC keyboard – which activate specific operations, like retrieving a call which has been put on 'hold' or 'park', or breaking into an active call in case of urgency, etc. Indeed, it is the wide range of such features which makes computerised versions of these systems so attractive.

3 In addition, many CABX consoles include an LCD panel on which messages are displayed to aid the operator during a series of busy transactions. For example the panel may advise that an incoming call and a specific extension number are connected, or it may display the digits of an external number as it is being keyed in on the keypad, to provide a visual check.

4 The console also features a series of ringing codes or patterns which alert the operator to an incoming call or extension user dialling the switchboard and the CABX will include a number of distinct ringing patterns and tones to convey different messages such as:

- line is busy
- there is a call waiting to be connected to your extension

- you are connected to an outside line
- the number you dialled is not obtainable

5 The operator has a number of support features available at the console, including abbreviated dialling codes for numbers often used by the organisation, 'repeat last number' if connection not immediately made, and overdialling for storing the IDD prefix parts of long overseas telephone numbers in regular organisational use.

Fig 2.20   **Plessey's ISDX switchboard**

Operations at the handset

Firstly it is important to remember that all computerised systems are programmable. This means that any individual handset may be allocated a variety of permitted functions. Any extension may be programmed as a master phone with full facilities or may have a number of activities barred so that, for example, it may only make 999 calls out, or only dial local numbers direct, or only national ones.

The range of features available to the extension handset user naturally varies according to the size and hence sophistication of the system used. It is very important for newly appointed staff to acquire as quickly as possible after appointment a thorough understanding of the organisation's system, even if this means requesting a short training course, since inadequate telephone techniques such as losing or cutting off an incoming caller cause much loss of face and dent the office's image. The following features are available to the extension user on most systems:

Dialling out

Extension users normally access the console operator by dialling 0 and acquire an outside line by dialling 9. On many systems it is possible also to dial an extension number on the organisation's private line circuit by dialling 7 followed by the number.

Handling calls coming in to the extension

Remember that an important part of the role of support staff is to act as a preliminary filter of calls and to handle them accordingly. Here the computerised systems offer many useful features which may be activated (if the system operates MF4 handsets) by pressing the R button and then dialling various codes:

- Putting an incoming call on HOLD. This enables the extension user to talk without the caller hearing – for instance, to check with the manager whether he is 'in'.
- *Transferring* incoming calls to another extension – for example when it becomes apparent that another department or staff member is needed.
- *Parking* an incoming call; sometimes it is necessary to keep a call in suspension while checking a matter with another extension user etc.
- *Shuttling* between an incoming call and an extension; this feature enables an extension user to move back and forth between two lines without either hearing the other and the user talking.
- *Conferencing* is a feature which permits a number of internal extensions and external lines to be linked by the extension users dialling up a code. Secretarial staff may be expected to 'line up' such conferences for their manager.

Note: codes are available to retrieve calls put on 'park', 'hold' or 'transfer'.

In the context of taking calls, it is important to remember that most managers have the system programmed so that their secretaries' extensions intercept all incoming calls to the manager for prior screening.

Making calls

Outside calls may be made either by dialling 9 followed by the prefix and number needed or via the console operator after dialling 0. The following internal features are also available to the extension user:

- *Automatic ring back* allows the system to ring the user's number when contact has been made with a number which was not immediately obtainable. The user does not have to hang on to the extension receiver while waiting. This feature also comes into play if an internal extension number is busy when dialled.
- *Ring back when in* is a feature where the system notes an extension number is not being answered and then retries the user's call after it picks up the fact that the desired extension has just been used.
- *Ring back for an exchange line* contacts the extension user (the bell rings) when an exchange line becomes available if all were busy when the user wished to dial out.
- *Piggybacking* is a jargon term used to describe a feature which enables the extension user to contact other extension users on a different but connected CABX system – say of a sister company or subsidiary.

Other useful features

Most systems enable assistants and managers to have incoming or extension calls forwarded from their home extensions to other assigned extensions. For example, if you plan to spend some time in the reprographics unit, you may arrange for incoming calls to be rerouted there.

- *Call forward* diverts calls to another extension and prevents the home extension being used.

- *Follow me* allows calls to be routed to further extensions as the user moves around the organisation's buildings.

- *Alarm call* allows any user to arrange for a call to be made to a given handset in order to act as a reminder for, say, an important meeting. Staff who know they become engrossed in their work use this feature to help them remember priority appointments or overseas calls to be made, etc.

- *Night service* allows an extension user to make and take calls after the operator has gone home.

- *Call waiting and intrusion* are features where the handset user is made aware of other callers queuing to talk to him/her (call waiting) and of a need for a priority user to access the line being used or to access the caller directly in an emergency (intrusion).

- *Do not disturb* allows the user of any given extension to put a bar on receiving any calls until further notice – vital if sensitive and important interviews and meetings are not to be interrupted, or if a priority task is under way.

EXAMPLES OF BRITISH TELECOM TELEPHONE SERVICES TO BUSINESS

PC
2.2.2
2.2.5

Audio conferencing – Providing regional/national/international telephone hook-ups for meetings etc.

Call cost indication – Informing user of the cost of a telephone call just completed.

Citicall – Information service on stocks and shares.

Yellow Pages – 1.4 million listed business services in district directories, and as an electronic database.

Credit authorisation – Acceptance of credit payment for phone calls, etc.

Pay card sales – Sale of units of phone call time via a plastic card: many public phone boxes accept this form of payment and erase time used from the inserted card (cards sold in units of 20, 40 and 100).

Freefone service – Businesses accept sales enquiries by phone and pay for the incoming calls – up to a preset time limit.

Mobile radiophone and car/train phone service – Mobile, cordless telephones connected by radio to BT telephone network; equipment is sold by Cellnet and Vodaphone for national use via BT's Cellnet system to route messages over more than short local distances.

Ship's telephone service – Long-established passenger phone service routed via radio signals and/or satellite.

Star services – Eight services provided by System X exchanges: call waiting warning signal; abbreviated call coding, up to 27 numbers' repeat last call; charge advice; call diversion; 3-way calling; call barring.

Telephone credit cards (national and international) – Internationally placed calls are accepted and placed by the operator upon the citing of your credit number; especially useful for sales representatives.

Radio paging – Individuals are 'bleeped' anywhere in UK by radio signal and asked to get into telephone contact. Note: some pagers only emit certain tones, others will communicate short messages on an LCD strip.

Data sources: British Telecom and *The Telecom User's Handbook*; and Telecommunications Press

---

■ Summary

Information Technology has made a tremendous impact upon telephone systems. The number of potential contacts – customers, government officials, organisation managers, etc. – who may call up a given executive has increased greatly as a result of national and international direct dialling and the extension of private line circuits. Similarly, the ways in which such callers may be handled by a CABX system have become much more sophisticated.

No two CABX or key system circuits are the same and so it becomes most important for all new personnel to acquire an informed understanding of typical routines and features and once in a post to acquire an absolutely thorough mastery of the system employed by the organisation.

PC
2.3.2
2.3.5

■ Mobile phones for mobile people

The early 1980s saw a rapid uptake among managers, executives, professionals and self-employed businessmen of the mobile phone and its 'sidekick' the radiopager.

The system developed by both Telecom–Securicor and Racal–Vodaphone under licence is called a cellular telephone network. As the diagram (Fig 2.21) illustrates, it enables different types of mobile telephone (powered by either car or inserted batteries) to transmit a radio signal which is, in effect, like the dialled telephone call. This radio signal is picked up at the perimeter of the cell (the area picked up by one British Telecom exchange) in which the user finds himself and relayed to a telephone exchange where it connects with

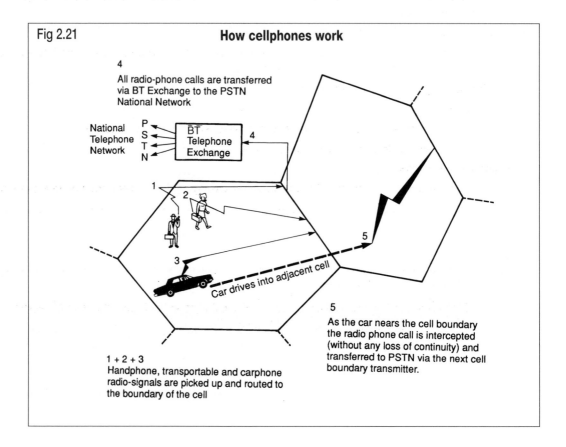

Fig 2.21   **How cellphones work**

4
All radio-phone calls are transferred via BT Exchange to the PSTN National Network

National Telephone Network   P S T N   BT Telephone Exchange   4

1
2
3
Car drives into adjacent cell

5

1 + 2 + 3
Handphone, transportable and carphone radio-signals are picked up and routed to the boundary of the cell

5
As the car nears the cell boundary the radio phone call is intercepted (without any loss of continuity) and transferred to PSTN via the next cell boundary transmitter.

the national PSTN system. As the mobile telephone user moves from one cell to another in his car, the radio signal of the continuing telephone call is relayed on to the next cell in the network.

A further development of mobile telephoning in the 1990s is that of telephone points. Within densely populated urban areas, mobile phones can link into networks of a form of relay station – called a phone point – which may be situated in a restaurant or shop. These relay stations route the mobile phone call into the nearest PSTN exchange, and hence into national and international systems.

Radiopaging

A less expensive form of contacting mobile staff is through radiopagers. These are small devices which are sometimes called bleepers, which pick up a radio signal which causes them to emit a bleeping sound. Such a signal alerts the person carrying the radiopager to telephone his office, say, from an internal extension in a large hospital, or from a payphone in the world at large if he does not possess a cellphone. The latest type of radiopager includes a LCD panel which can accept transmitted brief messages via radio signal, such as: CONGRATS! GLOBAL CONTRACT IN THE BAG! or, MOST URGENT YOU RING 071-345-9876 DIRECTLY. British Telecom offers a range of services to enable customers to transmit such messages over the UK as a whole to remotely located radiopager holders – even veterinary surgeons knee-deep in Farmer Giles' water meadows!

CHECKLIST OF USEFUL TELECOMMUNICATIONS DIRECTORIES

Effective fax and telephone systems users ensure that they have easy access to the following internal and external directories:

- Up-to-date Directory of Internal Telephone Extensions
- Personal Directories of Frequently Used Phone and Fax Numbers (note the ability of PCs and fax transceivers to store these through macro abbreviations)
- BT/Mercury Local Telephone Directories
- Thomson Local Directories
- Thomson Yellow Pages (Local Commercial Businesses) and electronic database
  Note: also now available as a national computerised database
- National BT Fax Directory
- Directory of Private Line Numbers (If organisation is leasing a private telephone network system)

INDIVIDUAL ACTIVITY

Choose one of the above external directories, find out what range of information it provides and provide a suitable briefing about it to your group.

PC
2.2.2

First undertake your researches and then report back to your group on:

1 How an organisation controls the costs of acquiring and maintaining its office equipment systems.

2 The current range of services provided by British Telecom, Mercury or Cable and Wireless plc for one of the following:

   a personal call networks (PCNs)

   b teleconferencing

   c private line packet switching

3 How Integrated Services Digital Network (ISDN) systems work and how they are likely to develop in the near future.

PRINTERS, PHOTOCOPIERS AND DESKTOP PUBLISHING IN IT SYSTEMS

■ B–IT: before information technology!

As you already appreciate, new technologies seldom advance on a broad, even front. Usually there are advance parties of early new technology users and pockets of diehard resisters. The area of reprographics – reproducing text, number and graphic image – is no exception. At the forefront of IT-based systems are laser colour printers and colour copiers and at the rear of the field – and fast becoming obsolete – are the spirit and ink duplicators and heat-transfer copiers. 'Before IT' reprographics tended to rely on three methods of reprography: either a combination of heat, light and chemically treated paper, or a means of transferring ink through a cut stencil (ink duplicating) or by transferring ink (by typewriter) on to a master sheet in a kind of embossed way so that the text thus produced could be activated by a spirit – spirit duplicated. These last two types of duplication imprint lines of text (or drawings) on to sheets of paper passing under a roller on to which the master is attached.

The technology widely known as 'plain paper copying' also preceded the IT office age but has been enhanced by IT rather than overtaken by it (see below).

■ Printers

Electronic printers

The advent of the widely distributed desktop PC in the late 1970s meant that users either needed access to an adjacent personal printer or the opportunity to share a faster, more sophisticated and more powerful one. And to complicate matters, while office DP managers were seeking to provide a prompt and easily accessible service to executives, secretaries, clerks and WP operators, printer manufacturers were busy developing four quite different major types of electronic printer, known as thermal, dot matrix, ink-jet and laser. Each has its advantages for use in many different types of office application and thoughtful office staff will ensure they know which type of printer offers the best cost-effective approach for various tasks.

The dot matrix printers

This printer's name stems from the way in which it imprints characters on to paper. Early dot matrix printers possessed a print head made up of nine wires which stuck an inked ribbon in various patterns so as to imprint, say, the letter A, the number 2, or the percentage sign %. A close examination of 9-wire dot matrix printing reveals the rather ragged outline made in this way:

An example of dot matrix printer

The use of nine wires meant that each character was in effect nine dots high and text was printed by the printer running bidirectionally – left to right then right to left for consecutive lines of text. The 9-wire dot matrix printer could print at roughly 100–200 characters per second (cps) in what is called now draft quality typescript – that is to say with a print quality only suited for internal consumption and not up to letter quality. Dot matrix printers at the upper end of the market operated at both draft quality (DQ) and near letter quality (NLQ). The NLQ speed is appreciably slower because the print-head passes twice over each character in a slight skew to fill out its ragged edges. Dot matrix printers have proved extremely reliable workhorses for many managers and office staff. Typical ribbons last for some 3 million characters and print-heads for 100 million characters. Most low-cost dot matrix printers are used with tractor feed continuous paper which is also cheap. An additional feature of the dot matrix printer is its ability to print graphs, charts and other computer-originated diagrams. The computer directs the printing operation (as it does in the case of all electronic 'on line' printers, i.e. printers which accept their instructions from the computerised software program). As a result, modern software can produce very useful and flexible print-out very cheaply using dot matrix printing technology.

In 1985 some 85 per cent of the electronic desktop printer market in Europe was dot matrix; however, the arrival of ink-jet and laser printers at more affordable prices caused dot matrix printer manufacturers to look to their laurels as users demanded a higher quality of print appearance – up to letter quality standards. As a result, a 24-pin (or wire) dot matrix printer was developed by leading manufacturers. This offered a much enhanced print appearance of letter quality and offered speeds of some 400 cps in draft mode and 50–60 cps in letter quality mode. The introduction of 24 wires improved character resolution over two and a half times. Current upper end of the market dot matrix printers embody several different types of fount (or font; a design of typeface) and can also accept single, cut-sheet paper inserts without tractor-fed continuous stationery having to be removed. Also, some modern dot matrix printers can accept a colour ribbon add-on and so print documents in different colours – i.e. vary the colour in which consecutive lines of text are printed. Thus a use of different typefaces and colour at low cost makes it possible to produce appealing sales leaflets and house magazines, etc.

While the low purchase and running costs of dot matrix printers makes them attractive, the noise of their impact printing is much less so. A market for acoustic covers to limit noise soon arose, and users need to balance low cost with impact printer noise levels.

Ink-jet printers

These printers operate within a quite different technology. Ink is drawn up from a cartridge into a series of tubes which focus on to a central printing point. An electrical pulse ejects the ink on to the awaiting paper page which has been electrostatically treated so that the ink sticks to those parts which carry the text. The ink dries almost immediately.

While less ragged than draft quality dot matrix printed text, ink-jet text does not always convey the same high quality of appearance of either daisywheel or laser printed text. However, the quality of an ink-jet printer depends on its price and the one with 32 jet nozzles at the more expensive end of the market acts like the 24-pin dot matrix counterparts and upgrades the text to NLQ at a typical speed of 100 cps.

Like the dot matrix printer, the ink-jet can take continuous fan-fold paper and cut-sheet paper and generally possesses both tractor and sheet feed options. It will also accept roll paper.

Both types of printer are able to print text in the following ways: emboldened, underscored, proportionally spaced, expanded, double height, double width and italics, all effected through keyed-in computer commands. Ink-jet printers are cheap to acquire at their lower market range and can accept normal office paper. They operate at a much quieter level than impact printers. Typical speeds are: draft quality using 10 pitch – 200 cps and near letter quality – 75 cps

Ink-jet printers are currently finding a growing market as portable printers linked to notebook computers, battery powered and about 50 cps at NLQ.

Laser printers

The laser printer is generally regarded as the very best of the electronic printers. Its technology uses a concentrated laser beam of light to transmit the computer's printing instructions (the text or image for printing) on to a cylindrical drum as a line of text or a line of a photograph or image in the making. The drum or roller moves over the sheet of paper on to which the text/image is to be printed. Those parts of the drum which have not been exposed to the laser beam's light accept the toner (black carbon dust) from a loaded cartridge and become the black printed letters or shades of black and grey in a photograph or drawing. The print resolution of laser printers is very high – 300 dots per inch, or 90,000 dots per square inch! As a result, text and images look crisp and sharp and of very good letter quality.

Also, the laser printer's print speeds are high compared to those of their counterparts. Some specialist (professional printing) laser printers can print at a rate of 200 A4 pages per minute. Typical office desktop laser printers operate at about 8–10 pages per minute, or about one A4 page every 6–8 seconds! However, this speed drops appreciably if the page for printing is complicated and includes several images.

In addition to high quality appearance, laser printers are extremely versatile – some have as many as 40 different print founts inbuilt with the facility to access others from slot-in electronic cards. Such printers provide a virtual printing house in the office!

Like its counterparts, the laser printer not only offers a very wide choice of founts, it also prints in the variations indicated above – italics, emboldened, proportional spacing, subscript and superscript, etc., and, because of its high resolution facility, can print type from very tiny sizes (printers would refer to 'four point' type) to very large sizes – say, 'seventy-two points' in printers' jargon. The term point is a measurement of print height and width.

The laser printer tends to use A4 cut sheets stacked in a feeder and some models accept multisize stacking trays and can switch from A4 to envelopes or to labels directly. It also tends to be used by larger firms to produce their own forms and stationery cheaply, and its memory can retain the design of an extensive number of forms and schedules.

Line printers

It is worth noting that a high volume printer called a line printer is used in large organisations to produce computer DP printout in collated and bound report form.

Printers and paper

All the above printers will accept A4 cut sheet paper if appropriate feeders are fitted to them. Depending on their width, they will also accept continuous stationery up to some 400 mm or 16 inches in width. Dot matrix and ink-jet printers accept most types of office paper, but laser printers require high quality bond paper for best results.

Printers and costs

As you might expect, there is with electronic printers a direct relationship between quality output and cost. The following factors affect such printing costs:

- Capital cost or leasing cost of the printer.
- Cost of maintenance contract (can be significant).
- Renewal costs of: toner cassettes, cartridges and laser drums or black/colour ribbons or print wheels.
- Cost of electricity to drive the printer.
- Cost of paper used and amount used per month.

Note: some printer and photocopier suppliers levy monthly charges based on the number of pages/copies printed.

When costed out at an all-in price per sheet, such costs vary considerably depending on the above factors and type of printer employed, with laser printers proving most expensive to run.

■ Photocopiers

Choosing the right copier for the right job

PC
2.3.2
2.3.3
2.3.5

At present there are some 175 different types of photocopier on the market and larger organisations will employ a family of photocopiers for different purposes and applications. These range from the small, personal desktop machines for very low volume 'one-off use' through middle or departmental copiers which may produce some 6000–20,000 copies monthly, up to systems machines which are used in a central reprographics unit or printroom and may copy as many as 200,000 pages per month. In this situation it is important to be fully aware of the comparative costs of copying on a small copier as opposed to a systems machine – large print runs are made much more economically on large, purpose-built photocopiers and runs of 20–50 copies are very expensive by comparison on a single-sheet feed copier. Office staff tend to pay little heed to copying costs, and expect their work to be copied instantly – by any machine available. However, efficient secretaries control and route such reckless copying demands!

Fig 2.22 **A typical departmental photocopier**

Photo courtesy of Canon

Low volume desktop copiers

The low volume desktop copier works slowly, but is reliable and cheap to buy. It is designed to handle occasional copying needs such as making a copy of an incoming letter three to four times to circulate to section heads, or to copy internal memos, notices or bulletins a few at a time.

Such copiers operate at approximately 8–15 copies per minute (cpm) and will only copy on one side of the paper at a time – to copy the reverse of a sheet requires reinsertion. The low volume desktop copier generally incorporates these features:

- Hand-feeding of single sheets (a laborious process).
- Light–dark adjustment to compensate for good/poor originals.
- Toner level indicator – to warn when toner is becoming used up.
- Paper jam indicator.
- Simple trays to hold paper passing through the copier before and after the process.

The mid-range or departmental copier

Such copiers have become increasingly popular since they occupy little space – not much more than a desktop – yet provide a very much larger range of features, while the cost of the modest single sheet copier is a few hundred pounds, the middle range copier (sometimes referred to as a departmental copier) will cost anything from £1500–£10,000. As with all office equipment, the buyer tends to get what he pays for. The following checklist illustrates some typical features of the mid-range copier:

- Able to copy from A6 postcard and A5 to A3 paper sizes.
- Automatic enlargement and reduction.
- Automatic document feed – for copying sets of different originals.
- Bypass feed to do a quick single-sheet copy in the middle of a long job.
- Automatic exposure control – to adapt to originals of varying quality.
- At least a 20-copy stacking bin which automatically collates copies into sets of reports, minutes, etc.
- User control system – either a security lock or insertable type of credit card which meters copies made.
- At least two automatic paper feed trays (A4 and A3). Note: some models automatically activate the appropriate paper 'cassette' tray according to the size of original.
- Capacity to hold at least 1 ream (500 sheets) of copy paper – many will hold 2000 sheets or more.
- Automatic enlargement and reduction features both by predetermined ratios (according to paper sizes A5, A4, A3, etc., or by percentage from, say 50 per cent to 150 per cent of original by single percentage steps – sometimes referred to as 'zoom magnification'.
- Emergency override switch to halt the photocopying process in the event of a mistake or machine fault.

Such is the pressure of competition to sell photocopiers – a market leader sold over half a million worldwide in one year alone – that even the above range of features in the middle tier of copiers is being increased by such sophisticated facilities like:

- Editing board and stylus – rather like a computer's VDU and light-pen, this additional equipment enables the user to edit existing originals on a screen electronically and to blank out unwanted portions (image overlay), to join together parts of different originals without tell-tale lines showing and to adjust margins for right or left hand sheets in a bound document.
- Automatic double-sided copying (sometimes called duplexing) – a feature which prints simultaneously on both sides of the paper from two originals placed side-by-side (tandem copying).
- Colour printing – the incorporation of red, blue, sepia, etc., colours one to a single sheet (not to be confused with full-colour copiers which can reproduce colour photographs) at the touch of a button.
- Copying of three-dimensional objects, such as jewellery for insurance purposes and bound books without showing dark areas where light has been let in.
- Automatic electrical power saving mode operated when the machine is not in active use (to save electricity and costs).

Given the present pace of copier design development, such features and facilities are being extended and improved virtually every month as a new or upgraded model is introduced.

Therefore the effective user will take steps to become fully proficient on the equipment his organisation employs and keep an eye on incoming sales leaflets and office equipment magazines to stay up-to-date. Local exhibitions of office equipment mounted in hotels, etc., are very useful in this respect.

The systems photocopier

The systems photocopier or print-room model will copy at speeds of 40–200 cpm and handle an output of millions of sheets per year. Such copiers will carry out all the above applications and will also:

- accept the continuous fan-fold paper for computer data copying;
- adjust to various specialist modes for, say, converting colour photo originals to black and white with good clarity;
- collate, staple/bind extensively paged documents and insert coloured chapter pages and front/back covers;
- conduct complex enlargement, reduction and automatic document reversal operations;
- handle a wide range of paper sizes – A5 to poster size from automatic feeder trays and effect runs up to 9999 copies long without stopping.

Colour copiers

Over the past five years or so a wide range of full-colour photocopiers has been marketed which brings exciting design and presentation within the reach of the office manager in medium-size to large organisations.

Such machines can reproduce colour photographs and paper copies of original photographs with remarkable faithfulness, and one market leader's model can provide up to 64 tones of each major colour! Such machines operate on the laser principle and are revolutionising the quality of in-house document and quick-response sales brochure standards. Such copiers work at about 5 cpm.

Photocopying costs

The factors which go to make up photocopying costs are very similar to those for electronic printers (see page 155). Most office administration managers circulate offices with regularly updated costs per sheet according to machine used, paper size, type of copying and volume etc.

Photocopying paper varies widely in cost and the office staff with a stationery buying role should take care to select copying paper which can accept print on both sides, will not cause jams, for example, because it is too light in weight, and which is problem-free from insert to collation stage for ream after ream.

In terms of recurring photocopying costs, it is worth remembering that, while the photocopier with more automatic facilities may cost more to buy or lease, it will undoubtedly save money each month in saved personnel time – compare the time taken to hand-feed single sheets with a fully automated feeding and collating operation which may be left unattended.

Photocopiers and the future

The next phase in photocopier development is already under way with one leading Japanese manufacturer marketing a copier which is also a fax and telex transceiver and scanner! Such multifunctioning equipment is only made possible by the extensive use of reliable microprocessors and clever design.

In addition, copier manufacturers will undoubtedly want to develop further the editor board and stylus operation which resembles the kind of page creating and modifying ability fast becoming popular with users of desktop publishing equipment (see below).

We can certainly expect to see a rapid introduction of 'intelligent photocopiers' in offices with LAN networks so that text may be originated at an individual's desk and networked to the office copier for automatic duplication according to copy commands which the user keys in at the end of the text and which instruct the copier accordingly, much like existing computer print commands. Equinox, for instance, is a new electronic system for combining the function of photocopier, word processor, laser printer, fax, modem and document scanner, with a desktop publishing system, and is also IBM compatible.

■ Desktop publishing (DTP)

PC
2.2.2
2.2.3
2.3.2
2.3.5

Desktop publishing (sometimes referred to as electronic publishing) has been one of the fastest growing IT developments of the past decade. Its rapid uptake was the result of a number of factors and influences, principal among which was that the equipment was already in existence – PC desktop computer with hard disk, laser printer, scanner and mouse. What was the vital additional ingredient was of course the software to do the creative job.

In a nutshell, a desktop publishing system provides its user with the means of producing

Fig 2.23   **The screen on this desktop publishing unit shows graphics and text combined on the Aldus PageMaker system, with the mouse cursor control in the foreground**

page-by-page and document-by-document highly attractive and well printed copy – that is a mix of:

- text in a wide variety of typefaces and sizes,
- photographs, drawings, graphs and charts all capable of being enlarged or reduced to fit a predetermined space,
- lines, rules, shading, cross-hatching and frames which either make reading easier or create visual appeal as part of the overall page design,
- imported artwork (known as clip-art) from the DTP software which can be quickly positioned on to a given page.

Previously, such printed matter had to be given to a printing house to set and print. The development of DTP, however, has had a profound effect upon the production of organisational documents and the presentation of information, as it has brought the printing house – with many of its visual and graphics devices and effects – right into the heart of office information processing.

Indeed, at the end of the 1980s some 50 per cent of everything we read was produced by a DTP system!

How desktop publishing works

Perhaps the best way to view DTP is as a kind of enhanced word processing and visual image combining system. Desktop publishing creates an electronic page of text on the PC's visual display screen using aspects of the mix outlined above. The text for this mix is usually originated by means of a current commercial word processing package and, in a similar way, previously devised charts and graphs, etc., may be installed into the DTP system from a graphics software package. Photographic or drawn images are installed by means of a scanner. Once all the desired ingredients have been 'loaded' into the DTP system, the process of designing each page of the document may commence.

Desktop publishing: step-by-step

1 The mock-up phase

A mock-up of the desired page or document is created (called a style sheet) which provides the DTP editor with a clear idea of such aspects as the nature and required size of illustrations – quarter page, 3 cm × single column etc., and the way in which text is to be displayed – in simple paragraphs, in columns divided by rules, with emboldened paragraph titles, or with a reversed white text in a black box, etc. The mock-up will also show the size of any required headline for eyecatching effect.

In organisations where DTP is established, the mock-up phase will also include a choice of typefaces (technically known as founts) and the respective sizes of typefaces for use in different areas of the page. The sizes of different founts varies considerably – just think of the size of some newspaper headlines and the small print of some books and documents – and is measured in points (a printer's term). The illustration (Fig 2.24) provides a clear idea of the range of fount sizes between 6 and 30 points and newspaper banner headline founts are even larger.

2 The text/graphics installing phase

The text (often called 'copy' for desktop publishing) is usually produced in organisations by departmental secretaries – as the wording for an advertisement, a handbook to set out a product's specifications, items for the organisation's house journal or as a sales brochure, etc. This copy may be produced via hard or floppy disk.

Where the text producer is familiar with the organisation's DTP system and its software is compatible with the WP package in departmental use, the WP copy may be given format/editing instructions to assist the subsequent DTP editing process, but it may fall to the DTP operator to work on the wordprocessed text in order to make it suitable for DTP editing (this may involve taking out underscoring or emboldening instructions if the DTP page is to be reformatted from scratch). This process is termed 'flooding in' the text.

3 The editing phase

The text and graphics having been installed into the DTP system, the editing process may begin. In order to design each page – using the mix of typefaces and graphics outlined above – a mouse is used as the DTP's control mechanism to move the cursor rapidly around the screen. It can pull down (bring into play or activate) various DTP menus of instructions – such as the shading of a space, the reversing of black on white, the 'cropping' or cutting to a required size of a picture or the enlargement of the page on the VDU either to see it as a whole or to see a magnified portion of it. In addition to the mouse, the PC keyboard is used with its command keys in the editing process.

At the outset of the editing process, the DTP operator will check the mock-ups and, to save time, will select a style sheet (sometimes called a template) from the DTP's memory which most closely resembles the desired page design. Such a sheet is a kind of skeletal blank page with, for example, the rules and columns already set, and margins already specified etc.

The operator may then 'pull down' the various menus which contain the instructions which he wishes to use to design the required page. These menus include the following:

- **File** for loading data on to the page and subsequently storing it – simply the setting up of a file in the normal way.
- **View** to provide enlarged or reduced displays and to check illustrative material
- **Page** to add page sequencing and numbering features, to set up right-hand and left-hand page alignments and to set the ongoing page structure, etc.
- **Frame** to insert lines, rules, boxes to a desired size.
- **Graphic** to add illustrations on to page designs.
- **Type** to enable the operator to select the chosen fount or typeface and its size.

Note: Various DTP software applications have similar functions grouped in similar menus, and to provide an extended range of instructions which the operator can select or 'tag' in order to build up the page with the desired typeface, graphics and layout. Also, for ease of use, icon 'tool kits' are available for selection by mouse to draw lines, circles and move items around the page, etc.

4 The printing phase

When the editing phase is completed, the printing process via laser printer is begun. The laser printer with its high quality end product and ability to print in an extensive range of typefaces (founts) and type sizes (points) is what makes DTP so incredibly versatile and useful in larger organisations. Even so, it should be kept in mind that a laser printer with a resolution of at least 300 dots per inch cannot compare for print quality with professional printing by the phototypesetting process in which a resolution of some 1100 dpsi is used. However, if need be, the DTP print command sequence can be relayed on to a phototypesetter.

Fig 2.24   **Examples of founts available on desktop publishing**

LePrint & JLaser

from

Headway Computer Products

LePrint will enhance any text and is suitable for use with Wordstar and any WP that can produce an ASCII file.

Characters can be varied in size from 4 point to 700 point (nearly 10 inches high).

A large range of Type Styles is available.

This is 12 point Old English... and this is Prestige.

Here is the Courier type style.

LCD gives a futuristic look to your documents.

All this is achieved by the use of dot commands within the text, which are recognised by LePrint. The capability of the system is further enhanced by Headway Computer Products JLASER board.

LePrint is the low cost alternative to a shelf full of font cartridges. It runs under MS DOS on IBM's and compatibles and utilises the power and versatility of the Laser Printer. LePrint will also function with a wide variety of Dot Matrix printers.

Contact HEADWAY today for more details or a demonstration of

LePrint and JLaser

This document was produced using LePrint and JLaser and printed on a Canon Laser Printer.

HEADWAY COMPUTER PRODUCTS
Headway House, Christy Estate,
Ivy Road, Aldershot, Hants. GU12 4TX.

Tel: 0252 333575 Telex: 859518 Fax: 0252 314445

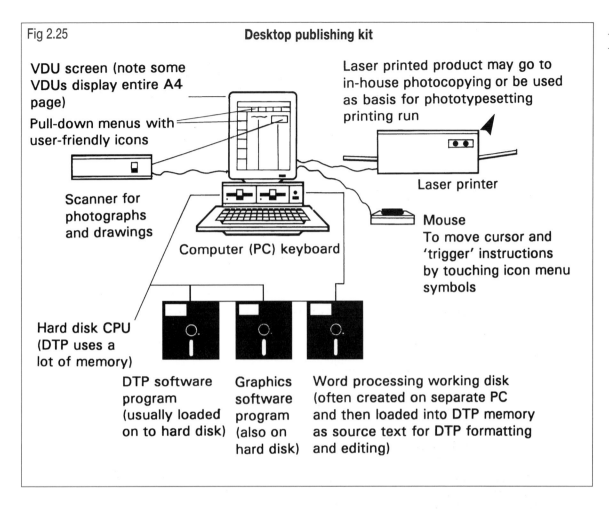

Fig 2.25 **Desktop publishing kit**

VDU screen (note some VDUs display entire A4 page)

Pull-down menus with user-friendly icons

Laser printed product may go to in-house photocopying or be used as basis for phototypesetting printing run

Laser printer

Scanner for photographs and drawings

Computer (PC) keyboard

Mouse
To move cursor and 'trigger' instructions by touching icon menu symbols

Hard disk CPU (DTP uses a lot of memory)

DTP software program (usually loaded on to hard disk)

Graphics software program (also on hard disk)

Word processing working disk (often created on separate PC and then loaded into DTP memory as source text for DTP formatting and editing)

GROUP ACTIVITIES

In groups of two or three first undertake your researches then report back to your group as indicated.

1 Investigate the current costs (and how they break down) of leasing for a two-year period a departmental group photocopier.

Compare the comparative costs of outright purchase as opposed to leasing, if the department you work in typically produced: (a) 20,000 or (b) 12,000 A4 copies each month.

2 Find out about the range of printing features available in a mid-range laser printer relevant to in-house desktop publishing.

3 Ascertain what services are available from a local reprographics bureau – e.g. colour copying, photocopying, photo-enlarging, report binding, 3-colour printing, etc. and what they cost. Devise a short fact sheet to communicate your findings.

4 Produce a 'what you get for what you pay' chart to compare and contrast the features of mid-range 24-pin dot matrix, ink-jet and laser printers which would be of use to a departmental manager seeking to update his printing facilities.

FILING AND RECORDS MANAGEMENT

■ Office records: classifying, filing, storing and retrieving data

Initially in this Unit the organisation was examined as an information processing centre, able to take in, process, store and disseminate large volumes of information and data. Indeed, some large offices process more than 20,000 items of information each day thanks to automated office records systems and equipment.

In some offices the filing and storage of data, whether in the form of paper letters, invoices or memos or as computerised electronic files, is regarded sometimes as a chore or necessary evil. And, not surprisingly, it is in just these same offices that tempers become frayed and staff frustrated and irritable when vital documents cannot be found before, say, a meeting which the MD is attending! Indeed, a recent survey found that one in every ten documents or files stored become immediately lost for ever, thanks to inadequate and careless filing techniques and practices.

Accomplished records management skills and techniques form a most important part of an office staff's repertoire today, particularly since developments in electronic office automation are transforming the speed at which data may be stored and accessed and extending massively the amount of data which organisations wish to retain and refer to at intervals.

Systems for classifying data

Dewey decimal system

For many years now, librarians, lexicographers, data processing managers and scientists have devised various logical methods for organising and classifying information. For example, compilers of dictionaries in the 17th century used, not unnaturally, the alphabetical sequence from A to Z to list words and their definitions. Dr Peter Roget in the mid 19th century devised six major categories in which to organise his *Thesaurus of English Words and Phrases*, ranging from abstract relations to emotion, religion and morality. Melvil Dewey, father of modern library classification techniques developed his 'Dewey Decimal System' in Albany, USA, in 1876, by dividing all areas of human knowledge into eleven expandable sectors. For instance, the area between 600 and 699 was given over to technology; within it 651 was allocated to the area of business English and, by introducing sub-divisions behind a decimal point, Dewey was able to add any new entry or item to his system indefinitely:

651.74: English for business students
651.77: committees
651.78: report writing

Hierarchical system

More recently, data processing specialists have devised systems for organising information which include the decision-tree system which provides the user with a single starting point and then arranges data according to a series of dividing branches taking him into ever-increasing detail, as shown in Fig 2.26.

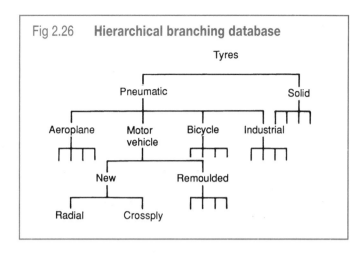

Fig 2.26   Hierarchical branching database

Decimal point reference system

Another system for organising information frequently used in the composition of long reports is to number each consecutive major section as follows:

1.0 2.0 3.0 4.0 5.0

Sub-divisions within each major section are then divided thus:

1.1, 1.2, 1.3 etc.   3.1, 3.2, 3.3 etc.

Within each subdivision further subsections may be created by the addition of another decimal point and number:

1.1.1, 1.1.2, 1.1.3,   4.1.1, 4.1.2, 4.1.3 etc.

Such a system provides a very quick method for referring to a detailed topic within the body of such reports:

. . . in the case of lost of misfiled documents (para 3.6.4 refers) . . .

As you can see, a varied range of systems exists for ordering and classifying the knowledge which we need to access, and it is held in all sorts of storage media — books, filing cabinets, card-indexes, microfiche film, computer files on floppy or hard disk, film slides, audio tapes, video cassettes, multimedia CD-ROM disks and so on.

The following section concentrates on examining those record storage systems and techniques which are most frequently found in today's offices. However, you should take the trouble to extend and deepen your own appreciation of current systems for storing information since the ability to obtain and present data quickly and skilfully from a wide variety of sources is extremely valuable and much esteemed by perceptive managers.

Factors influencing the design of record management systems

The following factors affect the ways in which records are kept and the methods and media employed:

■ The length of time for which a record must be kept. For some items this may be as long as 30 years!

- The extent or volume of records for storage and the rate at which this volume is expected to grow.

- The speed at which access to a given record is demanded or expected, together with the estimated number of people needing to be given access and the frequency of requests for the item.

- The duration of the short-term, active life of a document or record and the long-term period of its passive existence as an archive.

- The nature or form of the original record – paper letter, computer file, photograph, etc.

- The cost of storage: paper files occupy much more floorspace than their microform counterparts.

- The extent of legal requirements: certain documents may be vital originals like deeds, contracts or share certificates which must be kept in fire-proof safes.

As the above checklist illustrates, record management is by no means a dull or boring chore. On the contrary, secure and efficient records administration requires constant imaginative planning and anticipation as well as a logical and consistent approach.

PC
2.1.2

GUIDE TO CURRENT ARCHIVE RETENTION PRACTICE

Agreements	12 years	Medical certificates	1 year
Balance sheets	30 years	Expired patents	12 years
Bank statements	6 years	Power of Attorney	30 years
Cheque counterfoils	1 year	Prospectuses	30 years
Correspondence files	6 years	Paying-in books	1 year
Credit Notes	6 years	Purchase orders	6 years
Customs & Excise VAT records	6 years	Quotations, out	6 years
Delivery notes	1 year	Royalty ledger	30 years
Directors' reports	30 years	Sales invoices	6 years
Expenses claims	1 year	Product specifications	6 years
Insurance claims forms	6 years	Tax records	6 years
Expired leases	12 years	Share applications	12 years
Licences for patents	30 years		

This guide is reproduced by kind permission of Fellowes Manufacturing UK Ltd and Business Equipment Digest magazine

PC
2.1.5
2.3.5

INDIVIDUAL ACTIVITY

By arrangement, visit the offices of, for example, a local district or county council department, an estate agent, an insurance office, an architect or your school/college and obtain a briefing on the kinds of filing systems used and their various advantages and disadvantages. In particular, find out how computerised record systems are improving records management. Make notes of your findings and report back to your group to exchange information by means of an oral/AVA presentation.

To help you draw up a useful checklist of questions beforehand, refer to the checklist above and on page 165, 'Factors influencing the design of record management systems.

■ Major features of popular office filing systems

At the heart of all commonly occurring office filing systems lies the need for them to be simple enough so that a range of staff can use them competently, to be totally logical in the way in which files are classified and sequenced and to be capable of locating and presenting required information quickly and accurately.

The type of filing system an office will employ naturally varies according to the nature and characteristics of source documents or materials – large maps need to be handled very differently from extensive batches of customer invoices or from sets of colour slides. The following checklist includes the principal systems currently in use in office filing systems:

Files may be arranged in:

1 Numerical order

Files may be numbered from 1 to 1000 and major sections may occur at regular intervals (100, 200, 300 etc.) as in the Dewey decimal system. Sub-sections within a file may be introduced by the addition of a decimal point: 100.1, 234.35 etc.

Advantages: Such a system is capable of infinite expansion and can cope with a very large number of sub-sections, sub-divisions and diverging branches of data.

Disadvantages: In order for the numbers to convey readily what they mean, it is necessary for an index to be created, e.g.;

600 Technology
650 Business Practices
658 Management etc.

This system is therefore more time-consuming to use than one in which each file is given an instantly identifiable name.

2 Alphabetical order

Here files are arranged in a sequence which follows that of the A–Z order of letters. A number of protocols or rules for filing alphabetically must be committed to memory:

■ 2.1 The alphabetical sequence must be strictly adhered to: abbess comes before abbot and Richards before Richardson.

■ 2.2 Files or entries are sequenced letter by letter:

Dun
Dunn
Dunstable

■ 2.3 Indefinite and definite articles (a, the) are ignored in entry titles.

■ 2.4 Abbreviations are filed as written: Messrs Smith and Williams.

■ 2.5 Abbreviated names like BBC, ITV, TUC, etc, are filed according to their abbreviated letter sequence.

■ 2.6 St is filed as Saint and foreign versions like San or Sainte are filed as spelled. Some filing systems treat Mc, Mac or M' as quite different versions of 'mac' and file them according to their individual letter sequence; others treat them all as 'Mac'.

■ 2.7 As a rule entries which are shorter come first:

Elizabeth
Elizabeth I
Elizabeth I, Queen of England

■ 2.8 Personal names are normally filed surname first:

Richards, Jack
Richards, Dr John
Richards, Sir Gordon

Titles like Mr, Mrs, Dr, Prof, Sir etc, are ignored, save for forming part of the entry after the initial surname shown.

■ 2.9 Where the same word occurs as a name, then the convention is to enter forename followed by surname, followed by corporate name, followed by name as subject:

Heather
Heather, Arnold
Heather Products Limited
Heather, British species

Advantages: Alphabetical filing enables files to be read and accessed quickly; the system is also readily expandable.

Disadvantages: Items within a named file require some additional system of classification – letters to an account client may need to be numbered or filed chronologically, making cross-referencing laborious.

Note: items 2.1–2.9 have been adapted from the British Standard on filing and indexing: BS 1749 specimen filing sequence.

3 Chronological order

Sometimes it is necessary to file items according to the day/date received – such as applications for permits or licences or the dates when vehicles in a company fleet were serviced:

May 19XX
   1   Ll95 BXP   30,000 service
   2   K256 DFX   48,000 service etc.

Advantages: particularly useful when actions need to be taken on a cyclical basis – like relicensing sales reps' cars annually; good for cross-referencing – file on vehicle and relicensing date records quickly matched. Ideally suited to computerised database all vehicles due for re-taxing on say 31 August 19XX may be located and displayed on the VDU in a trice!

Disadvantages: Need for index and explanatory back-up system. Time-consuming to access data held in manual filing system.

4 Geographical order

Many organisations file data according to geographic region, area or locality, such as sales turnover by region or international sales division; public service departments hold many records in regional, county, district and parish council sections and sub-sections.

Advantages: Such a system enables statistics to be held in manageable and comparable units and also permits a large or 'macro' figure or total to be evaluated in terms of its 'micro' or component parts.

5 Decision–tree branching

As records are being stored increasingly on computer files, new methods of accessing data are being more widely introduced. Popular among these is the decision-tree system for moving from root or basic entry points into a system of offshoots or branches of information which has been classified according to a logical form of progression or division of data. Some such systems operate on the basis of providing alternative routes according to whether a question is answered by a 'yes' or a 'no':

Must the paint used be waterproof?

YES: (VDU displays menu on marine/outdoor paints)

GOOD PRACTICE TIP

It is good practice in maintaining a filing system to make a habit of:

● Cross indexing: making a reference in one file of related or helpful/additional data held in another file.

● Noting files in use: a file borrowed without a record of who has it, when it was removed from the filing system, etc., is a file lost! Make sure you have a 'file in use' set of slips to be filled out showing: user, date out, date due back, etc.

● Maintaining security: some files will certainly contain highly confidential data; make sure you control who may access what and keep a secure system for sensitive files.

■ Manual and paper/card-based filing systems

PC
2.1.3
2.2.2

Alongside the rapidly growing computerised records management systems are still their traditional, paper-based counterparts in which the office assistant also needs to be fully expert.

Such systems use the various numerical, alphabetical, geographic and chronological classification methods outlined above, and the approach is inherently the same. Nevertheless, a number of important features remain to be examined, and these are set out below.

Vertical and lateral filing systems

In considering paper-based records systems, a practical starting point is to remember that, essentially, the vast majority of items to be stored will take the form of either individual paper documents of A4 or A5 size or sets of A4 sheets collated into minutes, reports, brochures etc. As a result, the techniques of filing associated with them all derive from the design of folders, wallets, receptacles and enclosing boxes or cabinets which permit such documents to be stored safely, accessibly and with a minimum of office space occupation.

The vertical filing system

As its name suggests, the vertical filing system describes a means of document or file storage which uses V-shaped wallets suspended from a set of parallel rails constructed within a drawer or compartment of a cabinet which may comprise two to four drawers.

Each V-shaped wallet acts as a receptacle for the papers to be filed under the title or name given to it and is identified by means of a flag or tab.

Fig 2.27   **Lateral filing with colour coding, showing 'out' markers**

Reproduced by kind permission of Cave Tab Ltd

Within the file, letters, memoranda and other documents are likely to be stored chrono-logically. For example, a file may be set up to hold all the documentation which a sales department creates or receives in its business with, say, Alpha Products Limited. All received and transmitted correspondence held in the file is likely to be stored by date with the most recent letters lying at the top of the storage folder. Also, a system may be employed in which all letters sent out to Alpha Products limited are numbered consecutively, where Our ref: JJ/PD APL 128 refers to the one hundred and twenty-eighth letter composed since the file's creation.

Where a correspondence, say about an insurance claim, is protracted, the outgoing series of letters and replies received may be clipped together as a temporary working file.

The alphabetical system is frequently used in vertical filing and where a numerical system is employed, a key index is commonly kept at the front of the filing drawer for ease of reference.

Note: Some manufacturers of vertical filing cabinets market a means of joining wallets together in a kind of concertina shape at the top to avoid papers falling to the bottom of the drawer and thus becoming lost: always be on the guard against this type of mishap.

The lateral file

Again, the term lateral is descriptive, since in this system, files are stored side by side and their flags or tabs stick out for the user to consult from one side. A series of wallets hang from tracks which are suspended at heights within the filing cabinet which correspond to the depths needed to accommodate files lying on their sides (see Fig. 2.27.)

As a rule, filing cabinets are some 2 metres high and 1.5 metres wide, with a capacity of five to six tiers of files. They are thus useful for offices which operate a significant number of active files. and security is achieved by means of lockable cabinet doors. However, lateral filing cabinets take up a good deal of office floorspace and are a luxury in expensive city locations. Similarly accessing top and bottom-most tiers is cumbersome, and tags in such tiers may be hard to read.

Automated/mobile lateral systems

Centralised filing units – such as a company's technical library – often install automated filing systems in which racks of lateral files are constructed so as to move around upper and lower cogs, rather like an endless loop of trays. Thus the operator can summon up a required tier at will. A further source of assistance in such systems lies in the use of colour coding on files and tags or spines for prompt recognition and identification of a correct file location – a single blue strip in a block of red quickly identifies a misfiled wallet!

Visual filing systems

In addition to vertical and lateral filing designs, a range of visual systems exist, aimed at optimising ease of use and prompt location of data. Indeed the terms 'visual' or 'visible' are used to describe such systems, which include the following:

Rotary filing systems

Here files are inserted into free-standing, circular shelves constructed in columns which users can walk around. Visibility is good but they absorb a great deal of space.

Year planners and project charts

A variety of card or wipe-over charts are available either to pin or hinge to the office wall which display information like staff holiday rotas, key dates, branch visits, plant maintenance records, etc.

T-card slot indexes

This system takes the form of a large metal framework of slots – like rows of breast pockets – into which coloured cards shaped like the letter T are slotted: main titles or labels are written across the lateral bar of the T and more detailed data down its vertical bar which rests inside the pocket. Such T-cards may be moved around the frame and this system is popular in offices controlling projects or the work of personnel who move from job to job.

Strip indexes

Strip indexes often take the form of metal-edged frames with removable transparent inserts, beneath which a series of strips of card have been aligned in a particular sequence, each of which displays a piece of relevant information. For example, the displayed data may take the form of the names, addresses and telephone numbers of frequently used suppliers in a garage workshop to which mechanics may refer without greasing up a telephone directory .

Note: Sometimes such strip indexes are fixed around a central plinth as a rotary index.

Wipe-over whiteboards

Many office managers like to jot down memory-joggers and important information on wall-mounted whiteboards using coloured marker pens: while not particularly sophisticated this system is most effective in highlighting key information.

Desktop card indexes

Managers and secretaries alike often insert frequently used information on card-indexes stored in small boxes or pop-up A-Z files encased in spring-loaded metal containers.

PC
___
2.3.2
___
2.3.3

■ Micrographics, microform and microfilm

An important method of records management takes the form of the miniaturisation of original documents on to frames of film/photographic media. In the USA, this process is called micrographics. For years in the UK it has been known as microfilming, but perhaps it ought to be called 'microform' since this term reflects the various photographic forms that the miniaturisation can take.

Essentially, microform records are produced by the reverse of the process which enables us to have enlargements made of photographs which start out as contact prints. In microforming, special cameras take photographs of, say, A4 documents and reduce them by up to 105 times. In many popular processes, the reduction ranges between 24 and 48 times. As a result, an entire textbook could be transferred on to a set of microfiche cards or 100 foot roll of microfilm!

Furthermore, at higher ratios of reduction it is possible to store the Bible on a strip of microform known as Ultrastrip no more than 20 cm long!

Fig 2.28 **Information management system using optical disk, desktop scanner and laser printer; the system integrates document capture, indexing and computer-assisted storage and retrieval**

Reproduced by kind permission of Kodak

It is little wonder, then, that microform has been a popular source of record storage and archiving since its invention over 100 years ago. During the past decade, microform technology has taken a new lease life by combining with computer-based data creation and retrieval techniques to produce Computer Output Microform (COM), Computer Input Microform (CIM) and Computer Aided Retrieval (CAR) see below.

Types of microform

Roll film

As its name suggests, this type of microform comprises a continuous strip or roll of film made up of juxtaposed frames. Roll films occur primarily in 100- or 200-foot spooled lengths of 16 mm, 35 mm or 105 mm widths. A roll film may contain 2000–4000 individual frames, each one capable of holding the text and/or images of an A4 document on 16-mm film) or set of plans or designs on 105-mm film. While such a medium is ideal for archiving high-volume documents like sales invoices or purchase orders, it is a cumbersome way of storing data which needs to be referred to often, since the operator has to spool through the roll of juxtaposed frames in a linear sequence to arrive at the desired one. However, motorised scanning equipment has improved this situation – but at a price.

Microjackets and fiches

Two popular media of microform are microjackets and microfiches, which resemble one another. Both usually are constructed as a kind of card some 15 cm x 10 cm. The microjacket takes the form of a transparent sleeve into which strips of microfilm (say 12 frames long) or individual frames may be arranged in any desired sequence. A typical jacket might hold 30–40 frames. The microfiche embodies a similar structure but is made up of a

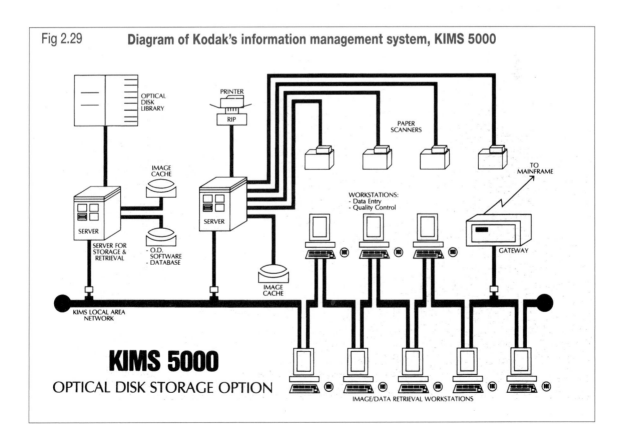

Fig 2.29   **Diagram of Kodak's information management system, KIMS 5000**

single piece of microform divided into as many as 400 frames, depending upon the photographic reduction ratio employed.

Microjackets and microfiches are read by means of a reader which magnifies each frame roughly back to the same size as the original document. (In fact many readers have screens A4 in size.) Some readers possess built-in printers to take a hard copy of the re-enlarged document and are called reader-printers. In this way, a copy invoice, say five years old can be promptly resurrected from an archive. Microjackets and fiches are very commonly found in libraries, bookshops, spare-parts departments of garages and stockrooms of manufacturers – in fact anywhere in which a large number of individual items needs to be catalogued, stored and located quickly. Where large numbers of microfiches are used regularly, it is common practice to index each frame with a number and to catalogue each fiche with a title, etc., and some readers have a facility to take the operator directly to a predetermined frame.

Aperture cards

An aperture card usually holds a single piece of 35 mm film on to which has been recorded a single image – which may be the draughtboard-sized drawing of a single layer of a microprocessor's complex circuitry. The card (about 17.5 cm x 8 cm) also includes a space to hold explanatory notes, etc., and may be filed in a card index or punched hole storage medium for fast location.

Fig 2.30 **Microfiche reader with microfiches and microfilm roll**

Microform and the computer

The widespread expansion of computer-based records management in the 1970s and 80s caused microform equipment manufacturers to work hard to develop an integrated technology which would preserve their investment – and that already made by many large organisations. As a result, three major areas of joint technology were introduced:

Computer output microform (COM)

COM is a system which enables computer-created data to be transferred during its creation *direct* on to microfilm at speeds which emulate those of a laser-printer. The use of such equipment is perhaps best described by means of an example. A large manufacturing company may run its sales invoices for national accounts customers in batches at intervals throughout the month and in so doing potentially create vast piles of copy invoices for its own records. COM enables such company records to be produced directly on to microfilm and thus to save as much as 95 per cent of the storage space needed and, as the process is simultaneous with the production of the paper invoice for onward despatch, at no extra cost in time.

Computer input microform (CIM)

CIM is a process which enables a computer to read the data held on microform and to transfer it into a computerised electronic file for distribution and examination, etc. In this way it provides a facility very much like that of an OCR scanner.

Computer aided retrieval (CAR)

It is not uncommon nowadays for international companies to hold millions (if not billions) of microform records of past activities in research, production, accounts, sales, and purchases, etc. While the vast majority may remain dormant for years, occasionally – say in the unhappy event of an airline disaster – it may prove necessary to locate quickly the records of parts, specifications, sources of supply and personnel involved in manufacturing an aero engine or wing part which go back 5–10 years. In such cases CAR is invaluable, since it links the memory and classification power of the computer with the vast records storage capacity of the microform media.

Frequently computer and microfilm frame are linked by 'blip' squares – tiny boxes to record serial numbers, etc. – which are printed on to each frame. As documents are microfilmed, a unique number is imprinted on to each frame which is also built into an indexing system on computer file. Thus the calling up of a given serial number enables the computer to find the file-roll or fiche in question and to display the desired frame in a matter of seconds!

Records management and optical disks

While great strides have been made in integrating computers and microform systems – even to the extent of including a microform reading and printing facility on LAN/WAN systems – the development of the optical disk offers even more economical records and archive management systems. For example, a single 35 cm (14-inch) optical storage disk (rather like an LP record in appearance) is capable of holding the equivalent of 1,000 computer floppy disks or 250,000 sheets of typescript A4! Some CD-ROM disks are 'WORM'-produced (Write Once, Read Many times), and the convenience of holding vast quantities of data in such a small space, and within a medium which is considered very safe from accidental damage or corruption is already proving very attractive to personnel managers, lawyers, librarians and scientists, despite the comparatively high cost of optical disks and associated equipment. A new interactive video (IV) technology, also called multimedia technology, is rapidly becoming established as a highly effective self-learning medium. It allows the user to access sequences of text, video film, graphics and photographs etc. and to interact with them.

Summary

Microform technology has rightly earned a central place in the records management systems available to managers of all kinds of data. Its plus factors include:

- Enormous savings in the space (and hence cost) needed to store paper documents.
- Data security and completeness: with microform storage, individual files and records do not go astray and are not easily destroyed by accident.
- Costs: once the capital costs of installing equipment are recovered, the actual cost per frame of microforming can be measured in fractions of a penny.
- Information in microform is cheap and easy to send to widely distributed branches, offices or sites.
- Linked to a computerised management information system (MIS) microform can handle millions of records safely and swiftly.

As with any modern technology, a period of rapid technological change inevitably means that minus factors occur:

- To acquire a fully versatile microform facility is expensive in terms of cameras, lenses, reader-printers, and computer-linked equipment.
- A high standard of indexing and cataloguing skills is needed to manage a large system.
- Some processes, such as obtaining printouts and film copies, are time-consuming.

■ Computerised filing systems

PC
2.2.2
2.2.3
2.2.5

Computerised, electronic filing of records is fast becoming the established norm. Indeed, in organisations using a LAN/WAN system, many communications are only ever made in electronic file form. One of the most important features of a computerised information system is its ability to handle enormous amounts of stored and archived information.

Basically, computerised records systems operate in two modes:

1 Centrally held files (in electronic form) are stored on a mainframe or mini-computer and are available for access by organisational users within a carefully controlled security system which restricts access to authorised personnel by means of passwords, etc.

2 Files are held in desktop PCs and distributed throughout the organisation. If such PCs are linked on a LAN/WAN system, then a file created, say, in the export section of a sales department may be made accessible to another PC user in, say, accounts. However, files maintained in decentralised systems tend to be used only by that part of the organisation.

There are distinct advantages in maintaining a centralised records system (sometimes called a unified information database). Note also the growth of computerised management information systems (CMIS).

- All the information is held in a database which is continually being updated. Its value and credibility ratings are therefore high.

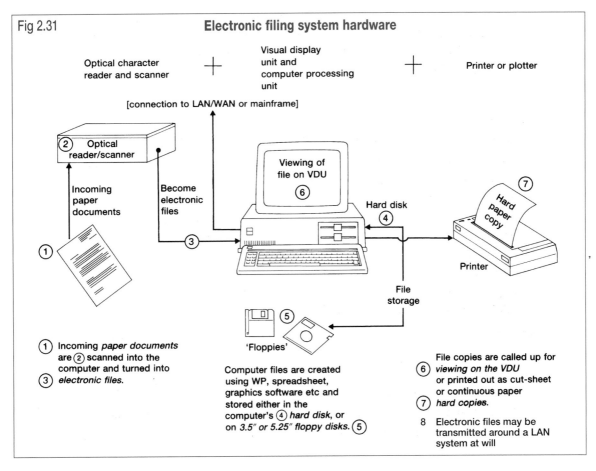

Fig 2.31   **Electronic filing system hardware**

- Careful control may be exercised over the data input process so that 'garbage in' is less likely to occur.
- All information accessed at all levels may be guarded by a coordinated security system.

Disadvantages of the centralised system are

- The costs of producing and maintaining the centralised database are comparatively high.
- Access to information and its updating may be adversely affected by the 'bureaucratic tendency' which tends to slow up entrepreneurs and go-getters in the organisation.
- Managers may not be able to influence the ways in which data is obtained and organised and so not have available the information they most need to do their jobs well.
- Centralised systems are vulnerable to data loss through computer or energy failure and so expensive back-up and fail-safe systems are needed.

■ Filing features of desktop PCs

Nowadays, intelligent PCs (as opposed to dumb network terminals) commonly embody as much as 100mb of memory. This capacity (equivalent to some 40,000 pages of A4 typescript) has revolutionised record-keeping in many offices. The memory storage available to managers and support staff through desktop PCs has led to the following significant changes in office procedures:

- Incoming letters and similar documents may now be transformed into electronic files by means of Optical Character Readers (OCR scanners) linked to the LAN system and distributed as computerised files to interested staff. Only the most important of the incoming paper letters – tenders, written job offer acceptances etc. are kept in paper filing systems, since a printout of the electronically transformed letter is available at any time.

- Retained paper file copies of correspondence sent out are no longer kept, nor are paper informational file copies distributed internally.

- Documents which were originated in paper form may be archived in microform and the need for paper documents minimised by a computer output microform system allied to computer aided retrieval (CAR).

- Managers' job roles have been modified. They now do much more file creation (using WP, spreadsheet or database software etc.), and file distribution (directly via email) and therefore have to maintain personally their own records management system.

Fortunately, today's software applications packages (supported by utility packages like Xtree Gold and PC Tools) enable individual users readily and simply to:

- create and erase directories and subdirectories (the electronic counterpart of filing cabinets and suspended file wallets);

- move a subdirectory to different directory;

- keep a check on how many megabytes of memory space are still available within a given hard-disk drive and the amount currently being used up within each create directory;

- find *an individual file among, say, hundreds* by setting up a search for the file based upon either its known filename or a particular keyword or phrase likely to have been used in it, such as appraisal, depreciation, European Community, etc. In seconds the user is provided with a short list of files to scan which may also be undertaken by means of the utility program, before going into a major applications package.

■ Filing and applications packages

In addition to support from a DOS-supporting utilities package, major software applications packages greatly assist the filing process through their branching-tree system for creating directories and subdirectories:

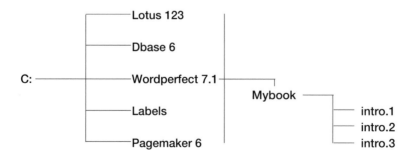

In the above example, five software applications packages have been installed in the computer's C Drive. Within the Wordperfect 7.1 a subdirectory has been created called 'MYBOOK' – perhaps a novel being written. The author has so far created a number of files within MYBOOK which have been labelled INTRO.1, 2, 3 etc. By moving through the branching tree displayed on his VDU, the user may call up the desired file – say, INTR0.3 – within seconds, either to view and modify on screen, or as a preliminary to securing a hard copy printout.

■ Electronic file security

While such electronic files occupy a tiny physical space, they need to be backed up regularly as part of a file maintenance system. This may be effected either by taking a floppy disk copy and keeping the disk safely in a remote location, or by tapestreaming (making a back-up copy) from the hard disk on to a magnetic tape disk. Either way, such precautions are an essential if loss through file corruption or overwriting etc. are to be avoided.

■ Electronic filing and optical disk technology

Further impetus has been given to electronic filing by the introduction of optical disk storage systems. Canon (UK) Limited marketed in the early 1990s a system – their Canofile 250 – which was based upon document scanning input and a 5.25-inch magnetic optical disk capable of storing 13,000 A4 sheets of typescript. The Canofile has a remarkably compact footprint – 57 × 42 centimetres and is capable of scanning documents at 40 A4 pages per minute. Retrieval is effected by four alternative methods – index cell, which identifies an 'attached' visual symbol, a filename using up to 32 characters, a file number using up to nine digits or date. Additionally, documents may be easily cross-referenced. A print facility enables up to 99 copies of a retrieved document to be printed automatically.

At present, optical disk storage systems are expensive – R&D costs have to be recovered – but as with most IT innovations, competition will shortly ensure that prices tumble and purchasers multiply.

ADVANTAGES AND DISADVANTAGES OF ELECTRONIC FILING SYSTEMS

Advantages

- **Speed of set up** – files are made of created documents at the press of a key.
- **Small storage requirements** – electronic files occupy tiny spaces within a hard disk.
- **Speed of access** – practised terminal users can call up one of many thousands of records in seconds.
- **Ease of distribution** – with the aid of LAN/WAN systems, electronic files may be transmitted across office blocks or continents in seconds.
- **High standard of security** – with proper back-up and file maintenance, electronic files are very secure.
- **Long-term cost-effectiveness** – once the comparatively high costs of equipment purchase have been recovered, operational costs are low: document creation, storage and distribution may be carried out by a single employee.

Disadvantages

- **Partial use of system** – problems occur at the interface between paper and electronic systems, where electronic filing is only partially used in an organisation.
- **High costs of installation** – effective electronic filing requires a terminal on each desk linked to a LAN.
- **Acceptance of electronic culture** – older staff feel much more comfortable using paper-based filing systems; it takes time and determination to introduce electronic filing across the board.
- **User disciplines** – computer 'crashes' can be dire if backing-up procedures are overlooked; staff using electronic filing have to be most conscientious in their records housekeeping.

DISCUSSION TOPICS

1 What case could you make as an influential senior manager of an organisation for introducing a policy aimed at removing as a matter of priority as many paper-based information systems as possible in order to replace them with computerised ones?

2 If you had been given the go-ahead to 'go for' the computerised information system option, how would you tackle its introduction so as to avoid alienating your staff in, say, a national head office?

3 The uncontrolled use of IT systems in terms of posture at PC terminals, interacting with VDUs and using keyboards for long periods is proving increasingly hazardous to employees' health. If you were responsible for your organisation's HASAW obligations, what steps would you take to ensure that all employees worked in a healthy and protective environment?

LEGAL REQUIREMENTS AFFECTING BUSINESS SYSTEMS

While business systems are primarily designed and integrated so as to bring logic and order into an organisation's activities, the over-arching system must make provision for the legal requirements with which *all* business enterprises have to comply.

Set out below are details of the principal legal requirements which need to built into an organisation's systems management:

■ The Data Protection Act 1984

This Act was introduced to protect employees and individuals from the unauthorised use or exchange of information held in computerised databanks, following upon the rapid growth of information technology applications in business in the early 1980s.

Essentially, organisations which hold on computer personal data – about employees, customers, patients, pupils or students etc. – who are living and who are identifiable from the data held must:

■ register with The Data Protection Registrar details of the data stored and the uses to which it is put

■ keep to specific principles relating to this type of retained data, which must be fairly and legally obtained and processed, used only for legal purposes, be accurate and correctly maintained, be deleted once its purpose has been fulfilled, be protected by adequate security systems

Individuals and employees have particular rights under The Data Protection Act, which include:

■ right of access to information being held by an organisation about the individual which is personal data within the definitions of the Act

■ the right to be given a copy of such data being held in a computer system

A fee fixed by the Registrar is levied by organisations which supply data in this way, and provisions are established for individuals who have been affected by incorrect or inaccurate information, as a result of negligence or lack of due care by the organisation, to receive compensation through the courts.

There are some exemptions to the Act, which concern payroll and accounting practices. Also, some categories of data being held do not fall within the scope of the Act. These include:

■ crime prevention and prosecution activities

■ privileged data (as between a lawyer and client)

■ data held for statistical or research purposes

■ data covered by the Consumer Credit Act

■ data held by regulatory public bodies for the protection of the public against dishonest, fraudulent and malpractice in financial matters

■ data held in connection with physical/ mental health or social work – on the order of the Secretary of State

The Act also provides for a series of disclosure clauses which the government may deem to be in the public interest.

The effect of the Act has been to reassure the public that a state of Big Brotherdom would not be allowed to develop, where sensitive or private information held on computer could be used in such a way as to damage the affected person's reputation, business, private relationships or credit-worthiness etc. or could be used or moved around inter-connected computer networks without an individual's knowledge or permission. Note that the Act does **not** include information retained in paper-based systems.

■ The Health And Safety At Work Act 1974

The rights and needs of employees to have a safe working environment also make demands upon business systems in that organisations have statutory duties imposed upon them to:

- maintain and distribute to each employee details of the organisation's HASAW policies and operational practices
- maintain displays in the workplace of bulletin sheets relating to HASAW requirements and the HASAW executive
- maintain signs – such as Emergency Evacuation, Hard Hat Area, Emergency Exit etc. – in prominent positions
- keep a register of accidents which must be reported by employees and made available to HASAW inspectors on demand
- maintain a register of COSHH (Care of Substances Harmful to Health) register and maintain/disseminate clear instructions as to the use, storage and disposal of such substances
- (for organisations over a given size) provide sufficient qualified first-aid staff in support of in-situ nursing and/or medical provisions

■ Statutory requirements

By the same token, business organisations are required under various clauses of the Companies Acts to:

- produce on an annual basis business sets of accounts which comply with standing Inland Revenue requirements
- keep accurate and up-to-date records of deductions, payments and receipts in respect of:

  employees' pay (and directors' withdrawals)
  PAYE (Pay As You Earn) tax records
  NIC (National Insurance Contributions)
  SERPS (State Earnings Related Pensions Scheme)
  Details of staff pension/superannuation contributions
  Pensions payments made to retired personnel etc.
  Income from share dividends, rents etc.

- maintain accurate records of all input and output transactions relating to VAT (Value Added Tax), and pay the amounts due on time

Directors' Activities

- produce and maintain all the documentation required under the Companies Acts relating to the activities of company directors or partners – Articles and Memoranda of Association, Partnership Agreements, minutes of directors' and shareholders' meetings etc.

Employment Law

- issuing of contracts of employment

- maintain as required records relating to grievance procedures, disciplinary actions, redundancy procedures, terminations of contracts of employments, maternity leave, sick pay etc.

- records of details sent to employees which change arrangements which are made under statutory obligations (within the legal framework in place at the time)

SETTING UP A BUSINESS INFORMATION SYSTEM

PC
2.1.1
2.1.3
2.3.2
2.3.3
2.3.5

In large organisations it often falls to a computer specialist called a systems analyst to design a computerised information system, which is usually the result of a change in technology employed or procedures in use. Also, in a mature organisation, the system required is most likely to be a relatively small component part of the network of systems in use.

Small businesses, however, rarely possess the luxury of a systems analyst, and so it often falls to an individual manager within a department to design an information system to meet a need by using commercially available software as opposed to a custom-designed, 'bespoke' piece of programming. Nevertheless, the principles of setting up an information system large or small follow the same sequence:

STEPS IN SETTING UP AN INFORMATION SYSTEM

PC
2.1.4
2.2.3
2.3.5

1 **Clarify desired outcomes** What the system is to achieve needs to be painstakingly clarified and agreed by both designer and end-user.

2 **Undertaking of a feasibility study** Before any large-scale work is commenced, careful examination must be made of whether the desired outcomes are possible, and if so, by the use of what resources, at what cost and with what return or advantage, etc.

3 **Submission of formal proposal** All information systems cost money – to design, implement and maintain. Therefore it is prudent to obtain outline approval from senior management at the outset of any systems project.

4 Research and analysis Methodical collection of the small nuts and bolts of relevant data must be collected and analysed. Usually this process takes the form of a project which is managed by systems analysis staff. The project would establish who (exactly) currently does (exactly) what (exactly) when and how frequently, etc.

5 Designing the new system With the assistance of the techniques and program logic (if a customised program is being written) a careful sequence of activities and/or processes is set down. Such a design will systematise aspects such as the type of data to be created or classified, the needs of its main users and how to route the data to them, means of storing and accessing the data, the form the data should take for different types of user – e.g., management summary or full report and the formats in which to present the data, etc.

6 Testing the new system Prior to its announcement and implementation, a freshly designed system must be field trialled and tested – for bugs and other design defects, user acceptance, and delivery of the originally desired outcomes.

7 System documentation The principal steps or phases of the system need to be set down as a user operations manual for ready reference by all who will be involved in the new system.

8 Personnel training and orientation The introduction of new systems inevitably means changing established ones, which can cause some stress and discomfort among staff. Therefore training programmes also need to be designed and introduced if the whole process is to succeed.

9 Ongoing monitoring and refinement Once the system has been introduced, care must be taken to ensure that it is regularly checked for positive/negative feedback. Most systems are capable of improvement once in operation, and almost certainly, the dynamics of business will ensure that the system ages and becomes obsolete sooner or later !

■ Summary

Managing a business information system

Any system involving human beings is likely to be highly unpredictable and prone to Murphy's Law, which states that if anything can go wrong it will, but at the worst possible moment.

The development of western civilisation may be seen as an attempt to impose a rational view and meaning upon an illogical and inscrutable universe. Business information systems attempt a similar interpretation.

It is therefore timely at the end of this Unit to emphasise a number of cautions and caveats:

■ Human beings are not always rational or logical. It therefore pays to have systems in place which can cope with the irrational side of human nature, especially contrariness in the light of clear and fully disseminated instructions.

■ Business activities tend not to occur in obliging tidy designs (like textbook diagrams) but in patterns of surge, turmoil, and inactivity. Effective systems therefore have to cope with problems like overload, interference, lack of use and ignorance of available support.

■ While computing is catching up, the human brain is still infinitely more versatile and imaginative. It is therefore dangerous to prefer computerised information systems to human ingenuity, intuition and lateral thinking, despite the growing popularity of expert systems (software which offers rules and approaches derived from analyses of the outcomes of previous occurrences).

Nevertheless, no business large or small can function for long in the absence of systematised procedures. The following checklist therefore suggests the main criteria to be kept in mind when seeking to manage a business information system:

PC
2.1.1
2.1.4
2.3.5

CRITERIA FOR MANAGING A BUSINESS INFORMATION SYSTEM

1 **Credibility** Most important of all. If employees cannot see the advantages of using a given system, they won't. They'll continue to use the old one, which, for all its faults, actually works.

2 **Accuracy and currency** Managers have to ensure that the information available in the system is accurate and up-to-date. Once in place and accepted, users tend to trust the data in the system. If it is corrupted by error or lack of updating, then the costs this can cause to an organisation will be enormous, since they may be compounded many times.

3 **Flexibility** The principal danger of established information systems is that they keep churning out data which has become old-hat and superseded. It is therefore vital that the system in use is capable of being quickly and simply modified to take changes into account, and that a manager is assigned the duty of monitoring which systems reports are used and which are not, the latter being promptly removed in regular systems housekeeping.

4 **User-friendliness** To be universally accepted and used, an information system needs to be even more user-friendly than the informal 'it grew like Topsy' processes it replaced – or staff will simply revert to the old ways. Staff (given the chance) will unerringly opt for the 'shortest way out' in doing a job, whatever tools they may have been supplied with.

REVIEW TEST (ELEMENTS 2.1, 2.2, 2.3)

1 How is ISDN revolutionising telecommunications?

2 How does a facsimile transceiver work?

3 Compare the printing features of 24-pin dot-matrix, ink-jet and laser printers.

4 List five features of a computerised private automatic branch exchange.

5 What does a systems copier do that other copies don't?

6 Explain how one of the following works: COM, CIM, CAR.

7 How can a utilities package assist a PC user?

8 Why are managers becoming excited about the capacities of CD-ROM technology ?

9 What are the major areas to manage in order to maintain a business information system successfully?

CASE STUDY 1

The Henry Perkins Legacy

Henry Perkins (Builders) Limited is a private building company which was established in 1932 in Dilchester, a thriving market town in the middle of a rural area. The district was much favoured by wealthy couples buying retirement properties, London commuters looking for week-end cottages to acquire cheaply and renovate, and, because of its proximity to ports and the motorway network, young industrial companies in the field of electronics and light engineering.

Until recently, the company had been controlled by the iron grip of the 'Old Man', Henry Perkins, a staunch traditionalist who believed that 'the old, tried and tested ways are best,' disliked things he called 'newfangled' and stood no nonsense from his family or employees.

The workforce currently numbers 52 site employees, with some 30–40 self-employed sub-contractors, depending on the number of contracts with work in progress, and an office staff of 13, which is organised as shown in the diagram below.

Three months ago Henry Perkins died peacefully in his sleep at the age of 72, leaving his two sons David and Andrew and his daughter Julie as directors of a prosperous business run on distinctly old-fashioned lines. At a recent meeting of directors, David, eldest son and now managing director gave this report:

'As we agreed, I've spent the past week reviewing our administrative procedures and, broadly speaking, this is the picture. We have at any given time about 100 active account customers, 30 or so large concerns and 70 small works customers. We're kept busy on the accounts side, which is virtually a paper-based system, because we have to maintain careful costing records of jobs over several months or more and because a lot of our purchase ledger work is involved in keeping track of frequent orders, even though some are quite modest.

'Our accountants do our payroll every week, but I can't say they're as cheap as they were. And we're getting more complaints from the site men about mistakes in their payslips and their bonuses and what have you.

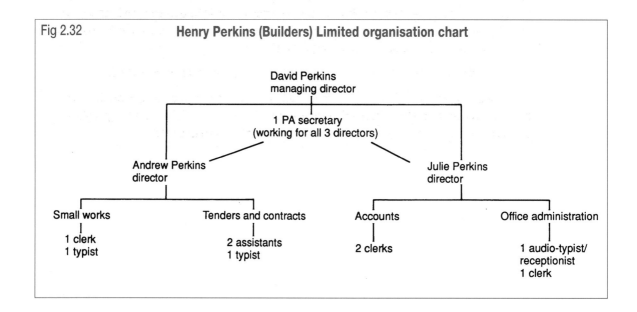

Fig 2.32   **Henry Perkins (Builders) Limited organisation chart**

'On the stock control side, we still seem to be losing money on materials which just seem to disappear. We need a better system for controlling what leaves here and what unused materials ought to be coming back! And our filing system could do with a complete overhaul. I spent half an hour yesterday looking for the Robertson contract, and eventually found it in the Robinson and Parker file. There must be some better way of handling contracts we are regularly referring to while they're active.

'Then there's our company image. If you look at our letterheads and stationery, we look as if we're still in the "jobbing builder pulling handcart age", instead of doing most of our work for the council and the business park. And don't forget that a lot of the people moving into the area have worked for big outfits. I don't think our existing electronic typewriters and vintage copier can deliver the quality of text processing we need now, never mind the time taken to get a mailshot out.

'Lastly, there's what I think the experts call our "informational database". We're always getting in each other's way, or kicking our heels to get at our reference files, suppliers' price lists, contract stipulations, stock sheets and so on. We ought to take a fresh look at how we could organise this aspect better – we're not only wasting time and money, but getting under each others' skin at times.

'Well, that must be enough for starters. Dad did us proud in his way and we've him to thank for seeing us through some sticky times. But time doesn't stand still. If we're to remain competitive, we must undertake a root and branch overhaul of our administration, and be prepared to take a few chances with computers and information technology before our competitors steal a march on us – especially with our tendered contract work increasing.'

ASSIGNMENTS

In groups of three or four, undertake the following assignment:

Consider carefully the information in the case study and organisational chart. Then, as a group, prepare to give an oral presentation (using appropriate visual aids) to the board of directors of Henry Perkins (Builders) Limited on the following:

A specification of the type of computerised business information system (both hardware and software) which you would recommend for installation. Your presentation should be pitched at an informed, non-technical level, and show clearly how your recommendations would be of practical use to the business, both currently and in any middle-term future expansion.

Your presentation should concentrate on a single range of equipment and provide costings.

Each member of the group should play an approximately equal part in the presentation which should last some fifteen minutes. Observer members of the class should assess each presenting group's performance and, in a class wash-up, decide which presentation was best and why.

CASE STUDY 2

A Bit of a Sort Out!

National Car Accessories Limited was founded in 1967 by Phil Sturrock, a live-wire entrepreneur who had begun with a single car accessory centre on the outskirts of Manchester at a time when interest in cars was booming and 'add-ons' were all the rage. In 1978, and some fifty established branches later, National acquired a three-storey building near the centre of Manchester, close to good road and rail communications. The head office building was constructed in the 1950s around a steel girder framework and each floor comprises a series of smallish offices separated by plasterboard partitions.

Having successfully weathered the recessions of the 1970s and 1980s, National now has a network of 120 branches spread across southern Scotland and the north of England. Phil Sturrock remains the company's majority shareholder and managing director, and the company has the following head office departments: Purchasing, Sales, Marketing, Accounts, Personnel, Transport and Branch Administration.

The Marketing Department is headed up by Mrs Jean Watson, Director, and is situated on the western half of the top floor of the building.

The Marketing Department is currently organised as shown in Fig 2.33 below.

Section responsibilities

The three major sections of the Department have the following responsibilities:

Product development
Making sure that National is stocking brand-name and own brand products which are 'up-to-the minute' in design and appeal; close liaison is maintained with a large number of manufacturers, both in the UK and overseas.

Advertising
The Advertising Section is responsible for sustaining effective merchandising within the stores, and for press, promotions and exhibitions, advertising and public relations. Two executives take care of these twin arms.

The Advertising Manager also coordinates the desktop publishing and reprographics work. National recently acquired a DTP system to produce its own masters for stores leaflets and sales brochures, etc. At this time, morale in the unit is low because the two reprographics assistants are being overloaded with photocopying demands from all and sundry.

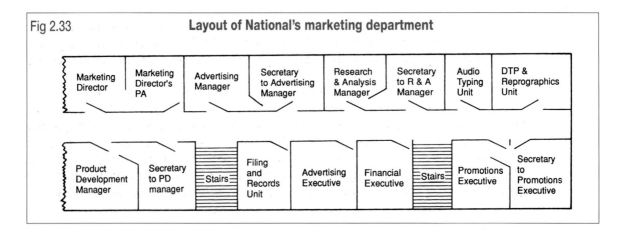

Fig 2.33   **Layout of National's marketing department**

Research and analysis

Phil Sturrock always claims he got where he is by 'keeping a close eye on the competition and keeping one step ahead of the beggars!' So he maintains a keen interest in analyses of buying trends and product popularity and surveying what groups of motorists buy what types of product etc.

The Research and Analysis Manager is also responsible for the department's Filing and Records Unit and Audiotyping Unit. The former is really a store for past survey records and statistics and marketing data is dispersed through all the department's offices. While the Audiotyping Unit is available to everyone in theory, there is much 'behind-the-scenes' grumbling that undue priority is always given to R & A work by the typists.

Financial executive

Andrew Wilson reports directly to Jean Watson and provides advice and information on money aspects of marketing. He has to rely on the Director's PA and the Audio-typing Unit for his text processing etc. and claims that his particular needs are largely underestimated.

Secretarial support staff

The Director and three managers have each a personal secretary; the director's enjoys the title of 'PA' but the other three secretaries resent this because they consider they do just as much demanding work!

Equipment distribution

National Car Accessories Head Office has not exactly moved with the times, largely because every last penny of profit has been put into acquiring and equipping new stores. However, the success of National's rapid growth in the past five years is putting tremendous pressure on Head Office staff – with increasing staff turn-over and morale problems.

In the Marketing Department, the following equipment distribution obtains:

Current equipment distribution

PAs/secretaries to managers: 16K memory electronic typewriters (PA has fax transceiver; Product Development secretary has telex access).

DTP: scanner, PC + laser printer + 'Pagewrite' software recently acquired to do in-house masters for sales leaflets and brochures.

Copying: A3/A4/A5 departmental b/w copier.

Audio-typists: pedal-operated dictation transcribers and electronic typewriters.

Filing and records: largely manual. One PC holds details of press advertising on disk and is 'stand-alone'.

Senior management have woken up to the shortcomings in providing the 'tools to do the job' – witness the acquisition of the DTP equipment and a PC installed in the Filing Unit. The following conversation took place earlier this week after a Board of Directors' meeting:

PHIL STURROCK: 'You can see from my review this morning that something must be done as a matter of urgency! Over the years some of our managerial staff have been "featherbedded" by under-utilised secretaries, while others have had to cope as best they can on a goodwill basis by getting their work done a bit here and a bit there. It's high time we had a bit of a sort out on how we are using our secretarial and clerical support staff and on what equipment and systems they could do with to get the job done. If it's going to cost money, so be it! We'll grow no more until we get this right!'

JEAN WATSON: 'I think you're right. We've managed fairly well so far, but this time it's Head Office that needs investing in and not the branches. I'll set up a Task Force Team in my Department and let you have a written report and recommendations within a fortnight – well before the next Board Meeting.'

PHIL STURROCK: 'Right, And while you're at it, give a thought to your Departmental layout. If we're going into this, we might as well go the whole hog!'

ASSIGNMENTS

1 As the manager of National Car Accessories newly introduced Computer Services Department, Phil Sturrock has asked you to consider the information currently available (the above case study), and to produce for him a feasibility study outline, which would indicate how you would introduce the sort of information system needed to enable the Marketing Department (see Fig 2.34 below for current organisational chart) to work effectively.

2 What do you think may be the human problems likely to arise in the department if the sort of changes which Phil Sturrock envisages are put into effect? How might they be minimised?

3 In pairs, draw up an organisational chart and floor layout which illustrates the changes you would make. You may assume that the building's structure would allow total flexibility within the floor space occupied by the department, other than the location of the stairs and double swing door access to them.

4 What changes would you make to the ways in which the Marketing Department works in the light of the shortcomings which Phil Sturrock reviewed? How would you reorganise:

a the current structure of the Marketing Department's secretarial and office support services?

b the layout of the department so as to optimise access and ease of communications between managerial and support staff?

c the range and type of equipment and systems the Department should have, so as to be able to market the 120 stores and their products more efficiently?

5 Can you identify any new/additional staff needs which the department would have in your development plan? What would be the comparative advantages of advertising for new staff or providing updating training for existing staff? Which option would you take? Why?

6 What particular training needs do you think the managers and executives would need, assuming a large-scale reorganisation of work patterns and organisational structure was put into effect?

7 Where would be the best place to start in introducing a reorganisation of some 21 staff within such a department? What sort of approach is likely to prove most effective?

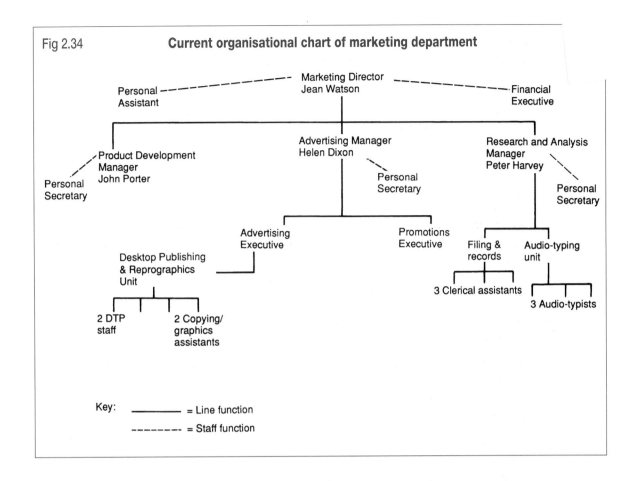

Fig 2.34   **Current organisational chart of marketing department**

Key: ―――――― = Line function

―――――― = Staff function

IDEAS FOR PROJECTS

1 In an effort to improve records management, the head of your department (at work, college or school) is considering going over to an electronic filing system as far as is possible – even to the point of converting incoming correspondence etc. into electronic files.

PC 2.3.1 2.3.2

Team up with a partner, and then:

a find out what record-keeping needs there are at present (and likely to be)
b detail how records are currently kept and what systems are employed
c research into what electronic systems might be worth installing in terms of costs and effectiveness.

Then produce a report with recommendations to your head of department on what is possible, realistic and how the conversion process should be undertaken.

2 In pairs (and by arrangement) undertake a survey of the type of printed communications your organisation sends out to external customers, associates, agencies and contacts, etc. and collect samples if possible.

PC 2.2.1 2.2.2 2.2.5

Then research into the scope of a mid-range DTP system: what it is capable of producing, what it would cost to set up a DTP unit to produce outgoing documents, which documents should be DTP'd and what the likely improvements would be for the organisation.

3 Your department wishes to update its photocopying facilities. As a result, you and a partner have been asked to undertake a survey of what model would best suit your department's needs over the next two to

PC 2.1.2 2.2.3

three years, and which company would provide the most cost-effective deal (whether for leasing or outright purchase).

First carry out your research and then produce a written briefing which survey two or three models and makes recommendations.

PC
2.1.4
2.2.3

4   Increasingly the managers in your organisation (firm, college or school) are seeking to take advantage of video-recording for training purposes.

In pairs, research into the camcorder and monitor/playback systems on the market and provide a written report with recommendations on the 'best buy', giving your reasons.

EVIDENCE-BUILDING ACTIVITY FOR YOUR PORTFOLIO

Element 2.1: Investigate administrative systems

With the active help and support of your teacher, parents, relatives or friends, make contact with a local business or public sector organisation in your area. *Note:* your local Chamber of Commerce, Rotary Club, Training & Enterprise Council (TEC), School Governors or College Corporation may also be able to provide help and introductions. In selecting a suitable organisation, do not overlook the administrative systems which enable your school or college to function, or that today, many local councils undertake work for the educational institution you attend on a competitive tendering basis – which also has to be administered.

Arrange to link in with a manager of the organisation you select and obtain approval to talk to his or her staff on the administrative tasks and duties they carry out, and also, what equipment they employ.

Research objectives

Your research objectives are as follows:

1   To obtain a clear understanding (backed up by suitable evidence) of how the administrative system works
    a   in overview for the whole organisation
    b   in particular for the section or department you are linked with
        You may find the diagram on (page 115 helpful in this regard)

2   To make suitable notes on the key processes you discover and what communications – between what staff – are essential to make them work. Your notes should cover what is routine and what is 'one-off', what procedures exist to check that what should be happening *is* happening and what feedback loops exist to alert staff if an operation is going wrong.

3   Lastly, your investigations should include an examination of how the administrative systems which are in place help the organisation to achieve its objectives, and how they are likely to change as changes in technology, the economy, the market-place or in society impact upon the organisation.

Presentation of evidence

When you have collected your evidence for 1, 2 and 3 above, organise it as a report which meets these terms of reference (in which you simulate the role of Assistant to the Office Administration Manager):

I'd like you to investigate the current administrative systems of the organisation in overview, and to examine them in more depth in relation to one of our departments (or units); take into account where possible what people involved in administration think about the part they play in what we do. Finally, give some thought as to how our administration is likely to have to change – as we respond to external changes. Present your findings in the form of a report which I can use as a reference source when giving the board/governors/corporation an updating briefing on how our administrative systems are working and where we should be going in admin. systems terms.

Method of producing evidence

Produce your report by using a PC and word-processing applications package with which you are familiar.

Performance criteria covered:

2.1.1, 2.1.2, 2.1.3, 2.1.4, 2.1.5

Core skills Level 3

Communication:

3.1.3, 3.1.4, 3.2.1, 3.2.2, 3.2.3, 3.2.4

Information technology:

3.1.1, 3.1.2, 3.1.3, 3.1.4, 3.1.5, 3.3.1, 3.3.2, 3.3.3, 3.3.4

Element 2.2: Investigate communication systems

Again, with help from your teacher, parents, or friends etc, make contact this time with a local business organisation in your area. Note: it could be the same one as you linked with in the activity you undertook relating to Element 2.1

Your principal task in this activity is to concentrate upon the communication systems and equipment which your chosen organisation uses to support its business activities and operations. The communications systems and equipment you investigate may include:

- a PABX (now often computerised) internal telephone network
- stand-alone or LAN/WAN networked personal computers
- ISDN messaging systems for CCTV, telephone,
- transmission of digitised computer data etc.
- facsimile or telex communication systems
- dot-matrix, ink-jet, laser printers
- black and white/colour photocopiers
- electronic and microform filing systems

You may also encounter a wide range of applications software in use, supporting word and number processing, the management of databases, graphics design, project management, desktop management, desktop publishing, order-processing and so on.

On the other hand, you may discover some communication systems which rely exclusively upon oral or paper-based means of transmitting or storing information.

Research objectives

In this activity, your research objectives are as follows:

1 To carry out an audit of the communications equipment used by the organisation and – by designing suitable diagrams – to illustrate what range of equipment is employed to 'drive' what kind of communication systems.

2 You should then arrange to interview a cross-section of the communications systems and equipment users in order to establish their views on what type of communications systems and equipment are best suited to what kind of communications activities and operations having regard to:

- efficiency and effectiveness
- costs: to buy/lease, to operate, to maintain etc.
- user-friendliness and ease of access
- accuracy and reliability
- best use of time
- security and confidentiality where appropriate

3 In the context of **the work of a single department or unit,** you should research into the ways in which the organisation's use of communications systems and equipment are likely to change and evolve in the light of the developments taking place in the field of information technology (the availability, cost, user-friendliness in use, power, sophistication and capabilities of IT systems etc).

You should also consider how such changes will affect the personnel involved in using them in their daily working lives.

Presentation of evidence

You may present your evidence for this activity in one of the two following ways, at the discretion of your teacher:

1   As an individual activity

Present your findings as an **illustrated briefing paper** which the senior management of the organisation you selected could use as a helpful source of up-to-date and accurate information when considering the organisation's future policies and strategies for improving its communication systems and equipment base and the ways in which could be used in the future.

2   As a group activity involving three to five students

Present your findings as a 15–20 minute oral presentation to your class which is supported by suitable hand-out and audio-visual aids material. Your presentation should be so structured as to ensure that each team-member plays an equal part in the researching of data and its presentation. You should also write up a set of group notes which explain to your teacher how you undertook and carried out this activity.

Methods of producing evidence

- Use of diagrammatic illustrations
- Production using WP software of a briefing paper
- AVA-supported oral presentation with WP-produced hand-out and graphics-supported illustrations

Performance criteria covered:

2.2.1, 2.2.2, 2.2.3, 2.2.4, 2.2.5

Core skills Level 3

Communication

3.1.1, 3.1.2, 3.1.3, 3.1.4, 3.2.1, 3.2.2, 3.2.3, 3.3.4, 3.3.1, 3.3.2, 3.3.3

Information technology

3.1.1, 3.1.2, 3.1.3, 3.1.4, 3.1.5, 3.2.1, 3.2.2, 3.2.3, 3.2.4, 3.2.5, 3.2.6, 3.3.1, 3.3.2, 3.3.3, 3.3.4, 3.5.1

Element 2.3: Investigate information processing systems

Using the contacts and network available to your class, make contact with an organisation which uses both manual, paper-based **and** IT, computerised information processing systems.

Your aim in this activity is to investigate its use of information processing systems. In the organisation you have linked with, you are likely to find the following systems in use:

Paper-based

- photocopied forms to capture and record routine information
- 'no carbon required' (NCR) sets of forms used to record and distribute information which is written or typed once only on colour-coded, attached sets of documents
- purchased sets of forms (e.g. Kalamazoo) on which to record linked sequences such as accounts data

Information technology based

- mainframe, mini or PC file-server driven computer terminals (or stand-alone PCs) used to 'drive' various kinds of application software (wp, spreadsheet, database graphics, DTP) etc.
- associated peripheral equipment – communications modems, printers, scanners etc.

The kind of system (paper or IT) and the type of use to which it and its associated equipment are put will depend on the work its users do. In this activity, your tasks focus upon finding out what systems your selected organisation employs, what equipment it uses, what effects of using the systems affect the staff concerned, and how effective the systems are in supporting the operations of the organisation.

Research objectives

Either individually or in pairs, you should undertake these research tasks:

1 Through a series of interviews with selected managers and their staff, draw up **a list of major information processing systems the organisation uses** (e.g. sets of forms to process credit sales, a computerised database to store information on products, customers, detailed records etc.).

2 For each selected system, set down a brief detail of the purposes of the system (e.g. to maintain records on all staff as part of the personnel function).

3 Find out from staff using the systems you identify how helpful and effective they find the systems and equipment in effecting the operation(s) involved and what suggestions they have for improvements.

   In particular, find out what changes have been made as a result of legislation such as HASAW, the Data Protection Act and EC Directives on the use of PCs to the ways in which the systems are operated.

Presentation of evidence

Having assembled your information on systems, equipment and use, write an article which would be suitable for publication in the monthly magazine of your local business community, – say *Midshire Business News* – which explains how a typical local organisation is responding to changes in the ways in which information is captured, processed, stored and disseminated. Your article should bring out the following key features:

- the respective pros and cons of using paper-based or IT-based information processing systems in terms of efficiency and effectiveness, cost-effectiveness and security
- the impact upon users of IT-based technology in terms of: HASAW, Data Protection Act, work practices and routines
- the ways in which current information processing trends are affecting the ways in which employees communicate and interact
- a 'guesstimate' of likely future trends in organisational information processing over the coming ten years

Your article should convey your information clearly and in a structure and tone suited to a range of larger and smaller business owners and managers (as well as their supervisory staff); it should be readable and visually appealing, since no one will be obliged to read your article!

Methods of producing evidence

Produce your article in the form of **either** a word-processed text on A4 sheets **or** a hand-written version on lined paper.

In either version, include three or four illustrations (sketches, diagrams, photographs etc.) to support important points in your text.

Where appropriate, you may import into your article textual excerpts or examples which have been supplied either by your selected organisation or which you have found in your researches.

Performance criteria covered:

2.3.1, 2.3.2, 2.3.3, 2.3.4, 2.3.5

Core skills Level 3

Communication

3.1.1, 3.1.2, 3.2.1, 3.2.2, 3.2.3, 3.2.4, 3.3.1, 3.3.2, 3.3.3

Information technology

3.1.1 to 3.1.6, 3.3.1, 3.3.2, 3.3.3, 3.3.4, 3.3.5, 3.5.1, 3.5.2

FURTHER SOURCES OF INFORMATION

Analysis and Design of Information Systems, J A Senn, 2nd edn, McGraw-Hill, 1989. ISBN: 0 07 056236 9

Analysis and Design of Information Systems, L Seymour Smith, Stanley Thornes, 1990. ISBN: 0 7487 0409 4

Information Technology: An Introduction, 3rd edn, P Zorkoczy, Pitman Publishing, 1990. ISBN: 0 273 03238 0

New Office IT: Human and Managerial Implications, R J Long, Croom Helm, 1990. ISBN: 0 7099 4130 X

The Electronic Office and IT, H Armour, Hutchinson, 1988. ISBN: 0 09 173008 2

The ABCs of Novell Networks, J Woodward, Sybex Publ., 1989. ISBN: 0 895588 694 6

Planning IT: Creating an Information Management Strategy, D Silk, Butterworth, 1991. ISBN: 0 7506 0326 7

Understanding PC Software, R A Penfold, Bernard Babani Publ., 1991. ISBN: 0 85934 248 4

Inside Information, J Megarry, BBC Publications, 1985. ISBN: 0 563 21102 4

Webster's New World Dictionary of Computer Terms, 3rd edn, 1988. ISBN: 0 13 949 23 3

Dictionary of Computing and IT, 3rd edn, Meadows, Gordon, Singleton and Feeney, Kogan Page, 1987. ISBN: 1 85091 262 9

3

MARKETING

Element 3.1
Analyse market research

Element 1.2
Use consumer trends to forecast sales

Element 1.3
Investigate marketing activities

PERFORMANCE CRITERIA AND RANGE

Pages

Element 3.1: Analyse market research
202–36

Performance criteria

1 relevant sources of information are identified which establish potential market need · 210–23

2 appropriate research methods are identified and the criteria for selection explained · 224–36

3 research instruments to collect data are described · 224–36

4 data is analysed and conclusions are drawn · 224–36

5 a report on the findings of market research is prepared · 286–91

Range: **Sources of information:** experts, general public, primary material, secondary material · 224–6

Research methods: postal questionnaires, interviews, telecommunications · 226–36

Criteria for selection of research methods: time, cost, speed, accuracy, ease of use, accessibility of sample · 224–36

Research instruments: closed questionnaires, open questionnaires, interview schedule, electronic monitoring · 224–36

Analysis: statistical techniques (e.g. tend analysis), qualitative techniques · 224–36

Evidence indicators: A report on market research which includes analysis of data, presentation of findings and evaluation of methods used. (If original research is undertaken it must be valid. Analysis of secondary research is more likely to be valid.) Evidence should demonstrate understanding of the implications of the range dimensions in relation to the element. The unit test will confirm the candidate's coverage of range.

Element 3.2: Use consumer trends to forecast sales
256–76

Performance criteria

1 characteristics of consumers are investigated · 256–9

2 economic information is analysed to identify effects on consumption · See Unit 1

3 economic information and consumer trends are used to predict demand for products and services · See Unit 1

4 consumer information is used to forecast sales for a business organisation · 230

Range: **Consumer characteristics:** demographic, age, gender, taste, lifestyle, conscience spending (e.g. 'green' spending) · 256–9

Consumption patterns: increasing, decreasing · 256–76

Economic information: social trends (e.g. income and spending patterns), Gross National Product (GNP), employment statistics, growth indices · See Unit 1

Evidence indicators: A short-term prediction (one to five years) of consumer demand based on identified consumer trends and economic information and a sales forecast (one to five years) presented in graphical text format. Evidence should demonstrate understanding of the implications of the range of dimensions in relation to the element. The unit test will confirm the candidate's coverage of range.

Evidence indicators: A study comparing the effectiveness of marketing activities for two competing products; a representation of the life cycle of a product and a discussion of the ethics of sales and marketing activities referring to current examples. Evidence should demonstrate understanding of the implications of the range dimensions in relation to the element. The unit test will confirm the candidate's coverage of range.

INTRODUCTION

This Unit explains in detail the marketing process. It provides definitions of what marketing is and does, and how it integrates other organisational activities. An overview of twentieth-century marketing developments and achievements is provided to put the Unit into perspective. The three sectors of the economy – primary, secondary and tertiary are described and the main characteristics of both industrial and consumer markets. Major market influencers are examined; economic, political, demographic, etc., and the four components of the marketing mix – product, price, promotion and place – explained. The market research function is examined carefully, as well as product development and pricing policies. The four main stages of the product life cycle are considered along with pricing strategies relating to them.

The buying behaviour of consumers is surveyed and the major phases of the sales process outlined. The role of advertising and sales promotion in the marketing process is examined. The legal aspects of advertising are indicated and, finally, the stages in devising a marketing plan are explained.

Note: In the checklist below, wherever the term 'product' occurs, read also 'service'.

In particular, Unit 3 examines:

- helpful definitions of marketing and its integrative links with all departmental activities
- the components of the marketing function
- the twentieth-century marketing backdrop – the rise of consumerism and 'green' issues
- marketing in the primary, secondary and tertiary sectors of the economy
- principal features of industrial and consumer markets
- macro and micro influencers on markets
- advertising and sales promotion: the work of the advertising agency
- branded goods, house lines and unbranded goods
- the marketing mix: product, price, promotion and place
- the role of market research in the marketing process: primary and secondary research, surveys and questionnaire design, sources of secondary data
- market research and statistical analysis and interpretation – graphs, charts, diagrams, etc.
- creating and bringing a product to the market – concept, design, pre-production, production, costing, and promoting
- marketing and pricing: elasticity of demand, pricing techniques – penetration, cost-plus, top-down, fixed rate of return, premium pricing, milking, etc.
- the product life cycle from launch to obsolescence and product positioning in the market
- marketing and buyer behaviour: psychological triggers and the buying motivators – security, status, self-esteem, the feel-good factor, the nest-making instinct, etc.
- the sales function and its relationship to marketing: sales arm structures, techniques of selling, sales promotion and merchandising
- effective advertising strategies and approaches – hard and soft selling, above and below-the-line advertising
- advertising and the law: the relevant Acts, from the Sale of Goods Act 1893 to the Consumer Protection Act 1987
- devising an effective marketing plan: relationship to the mission statement, SWOT analysis, internal and external audits, evaluating the options, costing the plan, appropriate timescales for delivery

MARKETING: DEFINITIONS AND FUNCTIONS

'Marketing is producing the right goods or services at the right time, in the right place, for the right customer, at the right price and the right return.'

A classical definition

■ 'Marketing is everything!'

Behind this sweeping statement lies the truth that marketing an enterprise successfully involves every aspect of its various activities. In another way it might be said that the marketing function of an organisation is the cement which holds all its parts together. The marketing of an organisation is essentially forward looking, it is concerned with securing the organisation's future in terms of the products or services it sells, the kind of customers it wishes to serve and the profits it wishes to make.

Once viewed in this light, it is easier to see that marketing is vitally interested in each of these departmental functions of the organisation:

Research and development

So as to check that avenues of research are being directed into fruitful areas, centring around products or services which will satisfy a demand and for which a market already exists or can be created.

Production

So as to make sure that whatever is being produced is being made to a design which has been field-tested by a sample of customers for whom it is intended; that it is being made at an agreed price (so that it does not become too expensive), and that it will be available at the right time and in sufficient quantity.

Sales and sales promotion

So as to ensure that the product or service is distributed and packaged with a maximum appeal and availability to the customers at whom it is targeted; that wholesalers and dealers are well briefed on its selling points and provided with appealing point-of-sale merchandising, and that local advertising will aid its launch and raise public awareness of its existence, and where it may be readily purchased.

Accounts

So as to provide company accountants with feedback on, for instance, what retail price the market will bear for the good or service, what the likely annual costs of advertising and sales promotion are likely to be, and what the estimated growth in demand for the product or service will be, and so on.

Personnel – staff training and development

So as to supply information on what new features and specifications are central to a new product, so that company staff may be suitably trained in, say, new production procedures, sales techniques, advertising approaches and customer service aspects.

If the marketing function is broken down by identifying areas of involvement in an organisation's major departments, as illustrated above, it is then easy to see why marketing is seen to be involved in everything an organisation does.

■ Definitions of marketing

PC
3.3.1
3.3.2
3.3.3

Because of its central role in an enterprise's activities, many definitions of marketing have been conceived over the years. Here are some of the more enduring ones:

> **Marketing is getting the right goods (or services) to the right place for the right customers at the right time and at the right price.**

Much depends here on what is meant by 'right'. But this definition does emphasise the amount of effort needed in successful marketing. Design a product the consumer does not like and failure results. Fail to get your new-style Christmas card into the shops by October and, 'forget it'! Fail to make your targeted group of customers aware of your product and sales won't even begin to take off. Over-price your product or service and it will simply age on the shelf !

> **Marketing is selling goods that won't come back to customers who will !**

Such a definition emphasises the importance of a product's quality, utility (being good at what it has been designed for) and the nurturing of the organisation's customers so as to foster their goodwill and brand loyalty – 'Thanks, but I've always worn Nordica ski boots.' This definition centres upon an extremely important aspect of marketing which is called customer orientation, by which is meant focusing all the organisation does upon meeting the customer's needs and expectations.

> **Marketing is the effective exchange of goods or services between suppliers and buyers, so that the needs and wants of consumers and industry are satisfied.**

This definition concentrates upon the economic aspect of marketing. It emphasises the creation of a market-place where seller and buyer meet to exchange commodities – goods (or services) for money, and it also highlights the difference in an economy between satisfying essential needs like food, housing, heat and light and wants – the endless stream of products and services for which mankind seems to have an insatiable appetite – the latest marque of Porsche or Ferrari, the newest release of Prince or Madonna, a videophone or a holiday in Sri Lanka etc.

The idea of the purchaser being satisfied also implies that the supplier has got the design, specification, packaging, price, and warranty of his product right because the buyer has no complaints or dissatisfactions.

Marketing is all about identifying – and then providing – what customers will want in one to four years' time.

The impact of this definition is upon the crucial importance of finding out what the market will want – not today, but some years into the future. It highlights the marketing challenge in, for example, the car-making industry where the lead time from beginning to design a new model to wheeling it into showrooms all over the world is some three to four years. In order to ensure that the enormous financial investment involved is secured, market analysts take extreme care to survey all interested parties in depth so as to take their preferences, desires, dislikes, ideas, proposals, past experiences, etc. into account. In this way, market researchers try to ensure as best they may that their design will meet not current, but future customer requirements and expectations – not to mention incoming government regulations and new laws.

Marketing is the art of getting – and staying – one step ahead of the competition!

In this definition the competitive nature of a free market is emphasised. The refrain which all good marketing executives keep constantly in mind is:

Never forget that the public has a choice!

In order to make that proverbial jump to become a brand or industry leader, many companies spend high proportions of their income on activities listed below:

PC
3.3.1
3.3.2
3.3.3
3.3.4

EFFECTIVE MARKETING REQUIRES INVESTMENT IN:

- Testing (to destruction) the products of a competitor – food-mixers, trainers, cameras, etc., in order to establish precisely how they work, what new technologies they employ and what their likely production costs are.

- Surveying and sampling consumer and industrial markets – and what are called niches or segments of markets – slices of the buyer pie – so as to find out in minute detail what makes them tick and what kind of good or service they are most likely to choose and why.

- Interviewing and consulting wholesalers, distributors, retailers and mail-order houses to ascertain the trends in buyer behaviour and the ever-changing moods and whims of the market.

- Seeking intelligence on how well competitors are doing, how a newly launched product is selling or what the demand is for, say, a novel mortgage offer to first-time buyers, or the discount being offered on a new, fitted kitchen.

- Trying to find out what new models, upgrades, revamped packages of services, etc. competitors are developing in order to leap-frog them and go one better themselves.

- Determining what new needs or wants are emerging in the High Street, such as electric bikes, pocket phones, Nicam TV, or teenage fashions, in order to come to the market ahead of the competition and thus establish a 'pole-position' before too many alternative models arrive to provide the inevitable choice a free market supplies.

DISCUSSION TOPICS

1 How would *you* define what marketing is?

2 Do you agree that consumers' buying trends and habits can be successfully analysed so as to tailor products and services to particular groups? Or do you think that it all boils down to trial and error – or luck?

3 Having produced your definition of marketing in 1 above, how would you distinguish between what is marketing and what is selling? Is there a meaningful difference, or do they both merge into each other?

4 'The best definition of marketing that I know is: developing and introducing strategies which enable the organisation to survive!'

Do you agree? Or is this too simple a view of marketing?

MARKETING IN THE TWENTIETH CENTURY

PC
3.1.1
3.2.1
3.3.1

■ 'Any colour, so long as it's black'

This quotation, attributed to Henry Ford the American motor car tycoon, has long been used to emphasise the concentration upon the manufacturing side of industry which characterised marketing before the two World Wars. It refers to the Model T Ford, which was among the very first motor cars to be produced specifically at low cost through the then innovative method of mass production, so as to sell in high volume and at low cost to the typical 'man in the street'. Ford's point, made with typical succinctness, is that: 'if you want a cheap car, it'll be in black, so as to keep the price down and because coloured paints cost more'. Marketing experts termed this the production-orientated approach to marketing – the customer's range of choice was limited by what the producer chose to supply.

Before the advent of mass production, made possible by the mechanisation of the first industrial revolution, products were generally hand-made in small quantities. Also, since the broad mass of the people were poor or only moderately affluent, products were made to be practical rather than pretty. They were also limited in design by what could be effected by hand and simple tools, and what manufacturing materials were locally available.

As a result of this manufacturing-centred culture, there was a tendency right through the Victorian and Edwardian ages for the makers of goods to design and produce what they thought was serviceable and well-made and then to sell it through wholesale and retailing outlets. Naturally they were responsive to fads and whims, especially in the fashion and building industries, but the science of market analysis and customer survey and feedback was still in its infancy.

PC
3.1.1
3.1.2
3.1.3
3.2.1
3.2.4
3.3.1
3.3.2
3.3.3

The marketing function

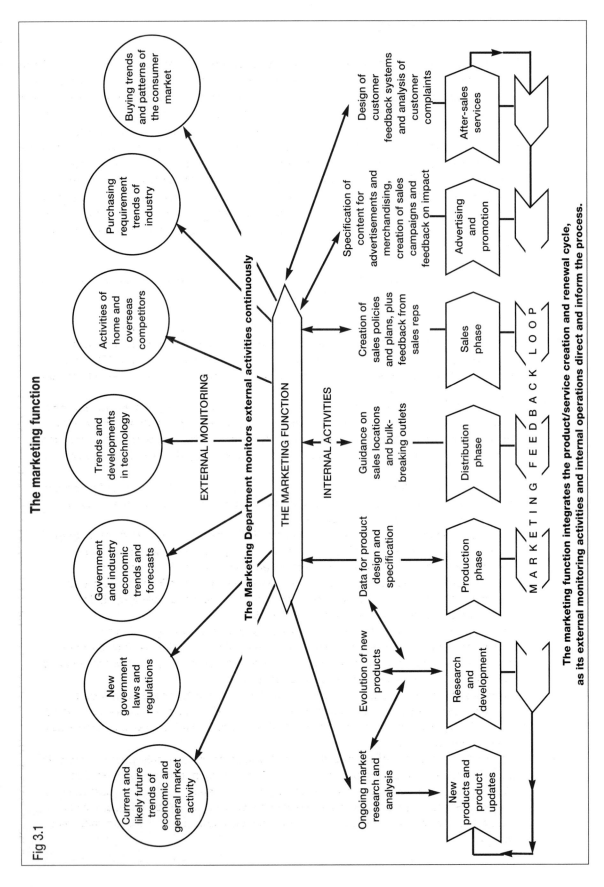

Fig 3.1

The **marketing function** integrates the product/service creation and renewal cycle, as its external monitoring activities and internal operations direct and inform the process.

The rise of consumerism

What changed the manufacturing-led marketing approach radically in the course of the twentieth century was the reliance of mass production upon the rapidly expanding mass-media communications industry. In order to take advantage of economies of scale – long production runs reduce costs, large volume sales recoup research and development charges – the makers of consumer products needed to build and sustain high volume markets. Thus they came to rely upon the blanket coverage and persuasive skills of mass-media advertising delivered through the press, radio, cinema and then television.

In this way a market-place dominated in the nineteenth century by production-led marketing evolved (for consumer goods and services) into a customer-led counterpart.

The following table illustrates how this worked, through a mix of economic, social and cultural change, hastened by the technological breakthroughs engendered by two World Wars.

THE RISE OF THE CONSUMER-LED MARKET, 1900s–1990s

1900–10	An era ends with the death of Queen Victoria in 1901; Britain begins to lose its supremacy as an industrial, exporting nation; the rising power of the working class is acknowledged in the founding of the Labour Representation Committee in 1900; the Board of Education is set up to run all state schools – education is provided between the age of five and fourteen.
1911–20	The First World War (1914–18) causes radical social changes: the gap narrows between rich and poor; women work as factory operatives to aid the war effort; war technology brings advances in the internal combustion engine, paving the way for faster distribution of goods with reliable lorries; the aircraft industry is born; rapid growth in retail sales outlets.
1921–30	International slump forces manufacturers to find ways of making and distributing goods more cheaply; rise of cinema and 'talkies'; stars endorse ranges of products; rise of popular newspapers between 1900 and 1920.
1931–40	Rapid development of mass media communications: 'tabloid' newspapers, photographic magazines, cinema, radio and television broadcasting; education advances improve literacy and discernment; rapid growth of advertising based on branded goods – Ovaltine, Brasso, Hoover etc; road and rail transport communications improve; long-haul airlines develop, e.g. Imperial Airways; Hitler introduces the Volkswagen, 'the people's car'; outbreak of Second World War (1939-45).
1941–50	The Second World War provides a massive boost to manufacturing design and telecommunications; war effort propaganda and public information services develop mass-media visual advertising techniques; arrival of American forces in Europe enlarges perceptions of a consumer culture across the Atlantic.
1951–60	Six years of wartime deprivation fuels an insatiable demand for consumer goods as economies are rebuilt across Europe. The UK absorbs US consumer culture, as national broadcasting develops mass audiences; Radio Luxembourg advertises and commercial radio is born in Europe.
1961–70	The 1960s mark an era of boom and full employment; commercial television develops as a highly effective medium of advertising and of influencing public taste and opinion; Ralph Nader in USA becomes the conscience of the consumer and leads a crusade for better consumer-supporting sales legislation; the concept of consumerism arrives in Europe; the rise in owner-occupied houses promotes marketing of domestic consumer goods.

1971–80	In the 1970s and 80s extensive reforms take place in consumer legislation in UK – in areas of advertising, sales ticketing, credit sales, guarantees etc; the introduction of credit cards (nicknamed 'plastic money') encourages spending sprees and a sharp increase in mailshots to people's homes, urging 'buy now – pay later'; Asian-built electronic consumer durables flood into the UK and undercut European counterparts.
1981–90	As a result of a stop-go economy alternating boom and recession between 1960 and 1993, the UK consumer market becomes highly segmented with a wide variation in spending power; goods are therefore marketed across extensive product ranges, with optional extras and add-ons; foreign competition secures large slices of UK markets, with consumer durables built to higher specifications and quality standards.
Present day	Most consumer purchasing takes place through national chain stores and out-of-town malls and hypermarkets; TV, radio and newspaper advertising increase their influence; user groups are set up to protect the interests of buyers and consumers as business enterprises merge into ever more conglomerates; a backlash starts against plastic, mass-produced goods in favour of hand-crafted alternatives; ecological 'green' lobby forces manufacturers to rethink their use of raw materials and production techniques; public opinion moves from the throw-away to the recycling society.

MILESTONES IN TWENTIETH-CENTURY MARKETING

1900	First mass-produced Kodak camera.
1901	First British gramophone record.
1903	Birth of the *Daily Mirror*.
1905	Pathé France develops colour moving pictures.
1907	First newspaper picture transmitted by wire.
1908	Henry Ford markets first Model T Ford.
1919	RCA-Radio Corporation of America launched.
	Alcock and Brown fly the Atlantic.
1920	Magnetic tape recording developed.
	First commercial radio station KDKA broadcasts from Pittsburgh.
1924	First photographs transmitted from UK to USA.
1927	Movietone News founded – first newsreel made by Fox Films.
	USA manufactures 3.5 million motor cars.
1928	Television transmissions start development in UK and USA.
1929	First colour TV experimental transmissions.
	Germans develop magnetic tape recording.
	Motorola market first car radios in USA.
	29 million phones installed in USA.
	Pre-prepared baby foods launched.
1930	PVC discovered in USA – age of plastic dawns.
	Sliced bread launched in USA.
	First electric kettle.
1931	First UK teleprinter (telex) exchange opens in London.
	Alka Seltzer comes to the aid of the hung over.

1932	First automatic dishwasher marketed.
1934	First launderette opens in Texas.
1935	IBM successfully market their electric typewriter.
1937	Chester Carlson introduces the first Xerox photocopier.
1938	Non-stick Teflon developed by Dupont.
1938	27 per cent of British homes have a vacuum-cleaner, 3 per cent a washing machine, 18 per cent an electric cooker and 3 per cent a refrigerator.
	Nescafé first marketed by the Swiss.
	First Volkswagen sold – 'the people's car' – in Germany.
1939	ICI develop polythene – for a myriad of applications.
	Birdseye pre-cooked frozen foods launched.
1941	Aerosol sprays developed.
1945/6	BBC introduce Home, Light and Third Programmes.
1946	Bikini swimsuit launched.
	First car phones in USA.
1947	Alec Issigonis designs Morris Minor – forerunner of the Mini.
	First large supermarket opens in North London.
1953	IBM develop commercial computer market.
1955	Independent television first broadcasts in UK.
	Wimpy Bars introduce the hamburger to the English.
	Sony markets its portable transistor 'tranny' radio.
1958	BBC pilots stereo broadcasting.
1961	Pentel introduce the felt-tip pen.
	IBM launch their golfball typewriter.
1963	Polaroid film and cameras marketed.
	Word processing developed by IBM.
	Microfilm archiving technology marketed.
1966	Fibre optic technology developed.
1967	Americans experiment with laser beams.
	BBC launch colour television service.
1970	Early version of video disk developed in West Berlin.
1971	Intel Corporation USA market first microchip.
1975	BIC introduce first disposable razor.
1976	IBM market ink-jet printers.
1981	Post Office records 711 million private and 336 million business items of direct mail posted in UK.
1982	34 national daily and Sunday newspapers published regularly in UK.
	Channel Four independent television broadcasts.
1984	Breakfast TV is launched in UK.
1985	Miniaturised hi-fi 'stacks' become popular.
1988	Mobile, cellular phones become an essential 'yuppie' accessory.
1990	CDs oust plastic LPs in recorded entertainment market.
1991	Interactive TV or a mix of video, film, slide, sound and computing arrives.
1992	Nicam stereo enhances television sound reception.
1994	QVC home shopping TV channel starts broadcasting.

Reproduced from data kindly provided by Marshall Editions Ltd: 'The Time-table of Technology' © 1982

DISCUSSION TOPICS

1 In what ways did the social changes brought about by two World Wars influence the evolution of twentieth-century markets?

2 How did the development of first the popular press, and then radio and television broadcasting affect consumers' buying habits?

3 In terms of the twentieth century, the development of the consumer market could be described as the consumer's search for individuality. Yet at the same time, mass production provided millions of identical products for consumers to buy. Can these two opposites be readily reconciled ?

4 Is the most serious charge to be levelled against marketing experts this century the fact that they have actively encouraged the 'use-it-once-and-throw-it-away' mentality in society?

5 If this is the case, how do you expect marketing to change in the next ten to twenty years ?

■ What *is* the market-place?

The above table illustrates the growth of a consumer-led market in the UK over the past century, but satisfying the needs, wants and whims of people as consumers of goods and services is only half the story.

The ability to display goods in a High Street store or services in a building society shop window is based upon a highly developed economy in which an industrial base is needed before consumer goods (or services) can be created. Economists have therefore devised labels for what they see as the three essential sectors of a developed and mixed economy (mixed because it is based upon a blend of both private sector enterprise and public sector services and utilities):

The primary sector

This sector is logically positioned first and carries this label because it describes the process of securing the raw materials which form the basis of all industrial production:

■ coal, iron, bauxite, natural gas, uranium, oil, clay, copper, diamonds, etc.

This sector also embraces the agricultural, fishing and timber industries, as well as the management of utilities like water.

The primary sector of an economy provides the foundation upon which all other sectors are built, since it furnishes the raw materials from which both factory plant and equipment and their end-products are fashioned.

The secondary sector

The heartland of this sector is manufacturing industry, which refines and transforms basic raw materials either into chemicals or materials from which may be made the myriad of tools, machines, fabrics, dyes, oils, paints and finished goods, etc upon which our culture and civilisation depend.

Important examples of this manufacturing and processing sector include:

- Chemical, gas and oil refineries
- Plants processing agricultural herbicides and insecticides
- Steel, copper and aluminium rolling and smelting mills
- Power stations
- Ship, aircraft and railway locomotive assembly works
- Car, computer, television and textile factories
- Food processing factories
- Commercial construction and house-building companies

The secondary sector of industry performs the function of transforming the hewn and harvested raw materials of the primary sector into finished goods or into semi-finished components needing further processing.

The tertiary sector

Because of the nature of the processes involved, many plants and factories engaged in secondary sector manufacturing may be located at a distance from centres of population – they may even be sited on the other side of the world, if that is where the raw materials are. The tertiary sector therefore includes the national and global process of distributing assembled goods to where they can be sold. This sector also includes the all-important phase in the economy of retailing – of bringing goods for sale to the consumers' locality.

A developed economy depends not only upon goods, but also services; the functions of banks and credit houses in lending money, the role of insurance companies in underwriting risks, the legal advice and representation of solicitors and barristers all come under the umbrella label of service industries. Businesses rely not only upon tangible and concrete items like goods to sell, but also upon intangibles like financial advice, timely information, auditing expertise and intelligence upon competitors' activities etc.

Principal examples of tertiary sector organisations include:

- Transporting and freight-carrying firms, parcel couriers, removal companies, postal services
- Wholesale distributors, cash-and-carry warehouses, mail-order companies, factory and farm shops
- Retail shops, departmental stores, supermarkets, petrol filling stations, mobile shops, travel agencies, restaurants, hotels, public houses, theatres, cinemas, football and cricket stadiums
- Telecommunications companies, advertising and employment agencies, office bureaux, merchant and clearing banks, insurance companies, building societies, dry-cleaners, citizens' advice bureaux, charities, tourist information offices and so on.

As the above outline checklist shows, the tertiary sector embodies a host of business and public service organisations which market services ranging from financial to leisure, travel, clothing, information, dining and recruitment needs and so on.

■ Marketing in the three sectors of the economy

The above analysis illustrates the interdependence of the three sectors: raw materials are obtained, processed, distributed and sold. Supporting this process are the underpinning functions of finance, insurance, distribution and advertising, etc.

Nevertheless, the marketing function tends to specialise in each of the three sectors separately, since their characteristics and key activity features are very different and therefore need to be marketed in differing ways.

For example, the techniques of extracting oil from beneath the sea are highly specialised. The companies engaged in this primary sector activity worldwide are relatively few. At the same time, the development and construction costs of designing, building and installing drilling platforms are immense. As a result, the marketing of such complex equipment and systems depends upon **developed technical expertise**. It relies upon long-term forecasting of worldwide oil needs, the rate of expiry of land-based wells, the marketing plans of the oil-mining multinationals themselves, accurate estimates of platform construction and delivery times and highly developed engineering skills.

Prospective buyers, since they are dealing in millions, will require minutely detailed design-and-build specifications and costings. They will also expect and get non-completion penalty clauses, 'bullet-proof' construction warranties, and escape clauses in case of sudden changes in demand.

As you can see, such a marketing environment is worlds away from the sweets rack by the supermarket checkout which invites the departing shopper to make one last impulse purchase!

This being so, it is more accurate to think of marketing as an activity which goes on in at least three different and contrasting market-places. The market-place for an oil-rig is the multinational boardroom and factory; for six-pack lager beers it is the supermarket or off-licence, for the mortgage loan it is the High Street building society or bank. However, while the nature of each of the above products is very different, they do all share the following market-place characteristics:

MAJOR CHARACTERISTICS OF THE THREE-SECTOR MARKET-PLACES

- They all rely on the relationship of supply and demand.
- They must all embody key attractions for prospective purchasers and meet wants or needs they have identified.
- The costs of acquiring the goods or services on offer must prove acceptable to the buyers.
- The resultant sales profits must be acceptable to the sellers.
- The sellers must have identified their target buyers and effected successful sales campaigns to make their products attractive and desirable.
- The sellers must also have found suitable locations in which to display their products for appraisal and trial.
- They must also have found ways of reassuring likely customers that their products will do what they are supposed to and that the customer's expenditure is protected by some form of after-sales warranty.

Successful marketing in any sector is the matching of customer-expectations with the selling organisation's mission statement and goals

DISCUSSION TOPICS

1 What are the likely outcomes for a UK company manufacturing domestic heating systems (which employ extensive copper piping) if the world supply of mined copper falls significantly? What options would be open to the company's board of directors?

2 A recession in one sector of the economy has a domino effect upon the next. What can a shopping mall carpet retailer do when faced by a sharp downturn in demand for the carpeting of newly-built but unsold houses in his locality?

3 Supposing a major car-making firm has a breakthrough in engine design and is ready to market a battery-powered saloon car which will do 0–60 mph in 10 seconds, has a range of 300 miles and thus needs recharging on average once weekly.

As the firm's marketing executives, how would you maximise the profit potential of such a motoring innovation?

4 How would you go about marketing a newly developed nitrates-based fertiliser for cereal crops which was environmentally 'green', with no adverse side-effects in the water-table?

Bear in mind that most agricultural fertilisers are sold through distributor dealers in farming areas.

5 Assume that you and three partners had just set up a local employment agency or printing services bureau. How would you set about marketing your business to potential customers?

MAJOR FEATURES OF INDUSTRIAL AND CONSUMER MARKETS

Industrial markets

- Are highly specialised and segmented into areas of specific expertise – e.g. deep mining, satellite telecommunications, four colour printing, etc.

- Deal in products and services which are highly technical – e.g. computerised drilling machines or acquisitions and mergers consultancy.

- Buy and sell goods and services which are very costly; re-equipping a production line can cost millions.

- Therefore the decision-making process of what to buy takes a long time and involves committees and teams of expert people.

- Selling organisations have to produce extensive tenders which include specifications and prices which are binding if accepted.

- Sales promotion tends to take the form of equipment demonstration and extended loan 'on approval' to allow prospective buyers to check if a system does what its sales force say it will do.

Consumer markets

- Meet not only staple needs, such as food and warmth, they also cater for 'wants' in the forms of fads, whims and fashions.

- Extensive research is conducted into identifying different kinds of consumer – from rich landowner to impoverished pensioner – and into what impels them to buy what they do, and the prices they are prepared to pay.

- Thus consumer products are designed, produced, promoted, distributed and priced with very specific buyers in mind.

- As a result advertising and sales promotional material is placed with media which are known to have high readership, listening and viewing rates among targeted customers.

- Consumer markets are highly competitive and thus product life cycles tend to be short, with continual improvements, upgradings and replacements.

Industrial markets

- Industrial products and services tend to include extensive agreements on warranties, servicing and customer support activities.

- With highly expensive plant and systems on offer, sellers often design 'one-offs' or modify designs in order to tailor a product or service to a specific need.

- Highly skilled support teams are needed to help advertise industrial products, such as technical writers and illustrators.

- Because of high acquisition costs, many industrial products and services are expected to have a longer life cycle than their consumer market counterparts.

Consumer markets

- The prices of many consumer products are relatively low and therefore encourage impulse purchasing; thus product merchandising and packaging is very important.

- Also, many consumer products are made in high volume quantities and need expensive advertising/sales campaigns to sustain a required high level of demand.

- Many consumer goods and services producers design and package several similar products – like tea or pension plans – to suit various sectors of the market – they 'position' their products according to the incomes and life-styles of their customers.

REVIEW TEST

1 How would you define the marketing function?

2 Explain why marketing is regarded as a function which integrates all other organisational functions.

3 What do you understand by the term 'customer orientation'?

4 What caused consumerism to develop in the twentieth century?

5 Why were markets producer-led between 1870 and 1930?

6 Distinguish between the primary, secondary and tertiary sectors in an economy.

PC
3.2.1
3.2.2
3.3.1
3.3.2

■ Industrial and consumer markets

Branded goods and brand loyalties

An interesting contrast between industrial and consumer markets lies in the emphasis placed upon branded goods and brand loyalties. While sellers in both markets seek to 'brand' their products – Perkins diesel engines, Otis lifts, Kelloggs cornflakes, Heinz baked beans, etc., their respective buyers possess different purchasing habits. Industrial buyers using the tender process may opt for a relatively unknown product, if it will meet tender specifications on performance, price, warranty and so on. Brand loyalty in industrial markets is less impulsive and more hard-bitten. In consumer markets, however, marketing departments go to great lengths to promote brand loyalty – with special offers, discounts, self-liquidating 'free' offers, etc. This is generally because there is, intrinsically, little to choose in terms of ingredients and performance between, say, any one of a range of petrols, toothpastes, baked beans, cornflakes or toilet papers.

Also, an intriguing feature of the consumer market, especially in retail food, clothing, DIY and motorists' outlets, is product labelling or branding. Here, some products carry manufacturers' labels which are given high promotional prominence! – Pringle sweaters, Gucci shoes, Jaeger fashions, etc. Other products carry the outlet's brand name: St Michael's underwear (Marks & Spencer), Sainsbury's cornflakes or Halfords' engine oils etc. Sometimes manufacturers seek to enlarge their sales by selling one part of their output as **premium branded goods** carrying their own house labels, another part (often from the same production run or batch) carrying the label of the outlet, and a further proportion as unbranded goods for distribution to small retailers, open markets, mail order houses and so on.

In this way, a manufacturer can achieve economies of scale by marketing **a single production design** and run at the top, middle and bottom of the consumer market spectrum. By contrast, industrial goods manufacturers tend to design and market equipment and systems, say, photocopiers, in a stepped sequence which satisfies varying levels of performance. These are then targeted at specific customers.

Finance and markets

A further area of contrast lies in the differing ways in which industrial and consumer goods are financed. In industrial markets, investment in capital goods – car-making sheet metal presses, newspaper computerised printing systems, chemical refinery plant and so on may run into millions of pounds.

As a result, the sellers of such plant and equipment very often have to work with merchant banks and finance houses in order to market financial loan packages alongside the industrial products – not merely as a service to the customer, but as an essential part of the sales-securing process. And manufacturers generally lobby government continually in order to secure some kind of subsidy on capital expenditure, say in the form of tax allowances or credits. It is for this reason in particular that manufacturing industry puts a premium on interest rate cuts, so that the costs of investment (in the form of bank loans) are less expensive.

In the consumer market, while manufacturers do not need to package loan schemes to aid the sales of washing machines or hi-fi stacks, they do have an interest in encouraging consumer demand as much as possible. For this reason, the clearing banks and High Street retailers have developed a very sophisticated credit purchasing system, based upon the plastic credit card.

Consumers applying for a Barclaycard, Access Card or TSB Trust Card, etc. are given a credit limit (£200, £500, £1,000) depending upon their income levels. Once issued with their cards, consumers are then enabled to make credit purchases up to the given limit each month. Provided they pay for the goods when billed monthly, their cost is interest-free (to the consumer). However, failure to pay within the time limit initiates an interest charge currently running at some 30-plus per cent per annum. As many consumers prove slow payers, the clearing banks make very high profits from this source of deferred payment. In addition, retailers pay a percentage of the price of each sale (2–3 per cent) to the bank running the card system as the price not only of the bank's administrative costs, but also for supplying the means of increasing sales (which would fall significantly if goods purchased had to be paid for on the spot).

Because of the increasing bank charges for servicing credit-card sales, an increasing number of retailing multiples are promoting their own in-house credit sales facilities or attempting to charge more for goods purchased on credit.

Advertising and sales promotion

Another area of contrast between the two markets lies in the way in which advertising and sales promotion are employed to support marketing strategies.

Consumer advertising

Since we are all consumers, it is natural that the promoters of sales and advertising campaigns use communications media which have a high degree of visual or aural impact in those locations which capture and hold our attention:

- Roadside hoardings, football stadium billboards, signs and placards fixed to buildings, names on sports people's kit, etc.
- Television, radio, video film and cinema commercials
- Newspaper, magazine, free local paper display advertisements, home and office-delivered advertising mail, telephone sales, etc.

  Such widescale advertising is also reinforced by point-of-sale merchandising:

- Hanging signs and placards, stickers, counter-standing advertisements, self-service stands and shelves with advertising slogans, uniformed sales staff, advertisements on sales receipts, etc.

Such is the extent of the available media for promoting consumer goods, that companies exist solely to sell space in newspapers or on hoardings, and advertising agencies employ staff to plan a suitable mix of such media for a given sales campaign.

Industrial advertising

Most consumers are blissfully unaware of the tremendous efforts which industrial marketeers put into the promotion of their goods and services. This is because the effort is carefully targeted to known potential customers within industrial sectors by means of:

- trade fairs and exhibitions relating to a given industrial sector such as electronic data interchange (EDI)
- in-company presentations and demonstrations of products and systems
- seminars and briefings given by manufacturing companies to potential industrial customers, e.g. on the advantages of computer-aided design and manufacture, demonstrating the equipment being offered for sale
- extended visits and discussions between technical sales representatives and company buyers
- display advertising and feature articles in specialised trade journals like *Network* (for data communication) or *Business Equipment Digest* for office equipment and systems
- high-quality technical literature and briefing/updating journals
- summarising papers, updates and bulletins sent to industrial companies' technical libraries

While many large organisations in the consumer market employ advertising agencies to design and coordinate their advertising and promotional activities, because of the highly technical (and often confidential) nature of industrial goods and services, their manufacturers and suppliers tend to have developed in-house departments to undertake similar work, liaising closely with their colleagues in R & D and production.

MAJOR INFLUENCERS UPON MARKETS

1 Macro influencers – affecting an entire economy

The current level of spending in the economy: represented in both consumer and industrial markets as a demand for products and services. In the recession phase of the economic cycle the downturn in demand has a knock-on effect – a drop in demand for manufactured consumer durables, say, impacts upon the need for the companies making them to invest in new plant.

Government intervention: in order to prevent too much money circulating in the economy (which may cause inflation) a government may increase interest rates; this makes it more expensive for both industrialists and consumers to borrow money from banks and thus damps down demand.

Government legislation: a government may introduce laws which are intended to have a direct impact on certain markets. For example, the Californian legislation outlawing motor-vehicle exhaust pollution has caused basic redesign and retooling work among car-makers wishing to continue to sell their cars in the States.

Demographic trends: changes in the age distribution of the population and extensive migrations of people (say to find work) have far-reaching consequences for markets; the significant increase in both the USA and UK of citizens in the 55–85 age range, together with their spending power has caused marketing experts to resegmentise their markets so as to benefit from this phenomenon, where more 50-plus year-olds buy sports cars than their 30-year-old offspring !

Rapid technological change: the pace of innovation in both industrial and consumer-based technology causes radical changes in society and its markets; for example, the development of home videos and satellite TV affects eating-out activities and paves the way for home-delivered meals ordered by phone or viewdata services.

Changes in culture and life-styles: the way people live is constantly changing and is a major influence upon markets. Consumer markets like fashion, popular music, entertainment, leisure, travel and sport constantly modify their offerings in the light of consumer trends and buying habits. For example, the animal-rights led campaign has caused many furriers to close down and major departmental stores to cease to stock fur coats; correspondingly the makers of synthetic furs and leather look-alikes are flourishing. Again, the insistence of every family on owning at least one motor car has had the effect in the USA and Europe of so clogging up inner cities that retailing multiples, supermarkets and supportive small stores have established themselves in out-of-town shopping malls with ample parking.

2 Micro influencers – affecting individual markets and localities

Localised and sector-specific effects of the macro influencers: while the above list illustrates general, economy-wide influences upon markets, some specific sectors may be affected more than others. For example, in a region suffering from structural economic decline (where, say, shipyards or steelworks are forced to close), the local market in house sales may collapse, since no one is moving in, and no one can sell a house in order to leave the area.

The activities of close competitors: more than any other factor, businesses are influenced by the success or failure in the market of their close competitors. At the small retail business level, the opening of a superior, better stocked outlet with easier parking down the road has often put a small trader out of business. In product terms, the successful launching of a new product or trading concept embodying superior design and utility frequently causes competing firms to rush out their 'cloned' version as soon as possible – The imitators of Filofax and The Body Shop spring quickly to mind.

Technological developments: just as macro technological developments influence entire societies, so those impacting upon individual market sectors cause radical changes. For instance, the introduction of Jacuzzi and whirlpool tubs and baths into Europe has brought about the inclusion of water jets in traditional baths for bathroom installation, since a market niche has been identified and a demand is there to be met.

Localised spin-offs from major developments: very often small and localised markets are affected by events in much larger ones and benefit (or lose out) from spin-off effects. For example, the eventual take-up of the myriad of offices in the Hays Wharf development within London's dockland will result in a host of local service trades like dry-cleaners, florists, cafés, heelbars, sock shops, newsagents and the like slip-streaming in to meet the needs of a new and expanding market.

Fads, whims and trends: these occur just as much within the micro, individual market as they do in the macro economy. The fashions in ladies' shoes provides a ready illustration, where winkle-picker toes, stiletto heels and platform shoes are but three of dozens of variations in design over the past thirty years, introduced to stimulate demand and to follow 'on the heels' of fashions originating in other countries. Many observers of the consumer market believe that manufacturers manipulate their markets in order to increase demand by introducing sharp swings in fashion in consecutive years and seasons – say from mini to maxi skirts, from short to long hairstyles, from single- to double-breasted suits and so on.

PC
3.2.1
3.2.2
3.1.4
3.3.4

THE MARKETING MIX IN INDUSTRIAL AND CONSUMER MARKETS

Essentially, the term marketing mix stands for the interplay and interrelationship of all the activities which are needed to transform a product or service idea into a reality and to sell it successfully to its intended customers.

This complex chain of operations was simplified by an American marketing expert, Professor E J McCarthy in 1975 into a set of four P's: **Product, Promotion, Place, Price**.

Over the two decades, these four P's have become internationally famous as a shorthand way of remembering what the central components of the mix are.

The chart in Fig 3.2, page 219 illustrates the major activities which make up each of the four P's.

■ Managing the marketing mix

At the beginning of this Unit, emphasis was placed on the integrative nature of marketing. The comprehensiveness of the marketing function is further illustrated by illustrating the components of the marketing mix.

Fig 3.2   **Products do not market themselves and success relies on careful planning and monitoring**

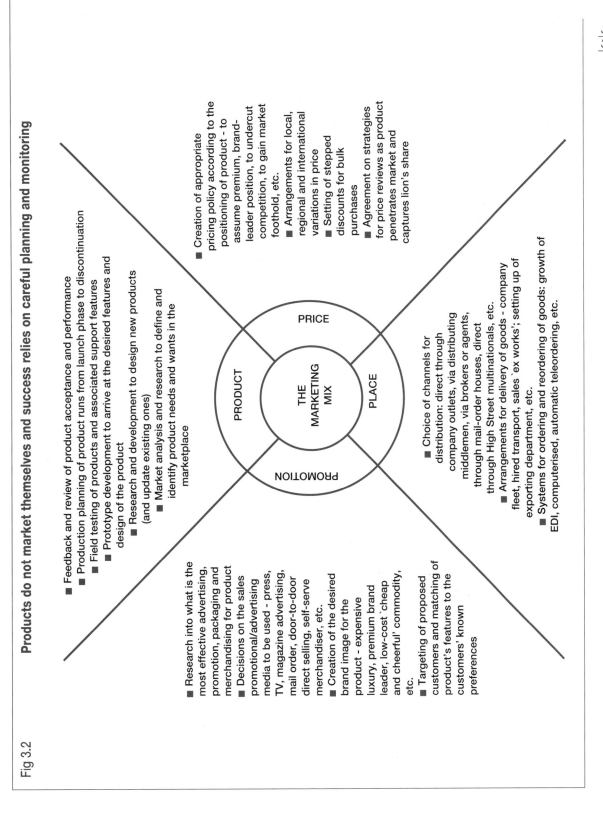

- Creation of appropriate pricing policy according to the positioning of product - to assume premium, brand-leader position, to undercut competition, to gain market foothold, etc.
  - Arrangements for local, regional and international variations in price
  - Setting of stepped discounts for bulk purchases
  - Agreement on strategies for price reviews as product penetrates market and captures lion's share

- Feedback and review of product acceptance and performance
  - Production planning of product runs from launch phase to discontinuation
  - Field testing of products and associated support features
  - Prototype development to arrive at the desired features and design of the product
    - Research and development to design new products (and update existing ones)
      - Market analysis and research to define and identify product needs and wants in the marketplace

PRICE

PRODUCT

THE MARKETING MIX

PLACE

PROMOTION

- Choice of channels for distribution: direct through company outlets, via distributing middlemen, via brokers or agents, through mail-order houses, direct through High Street multinationals, etc.
  - Arrangements for delivery of goods - company fleet, hired transport, sales `ex works'; setting up of exporting department, etc.
    - Systems for ordering and reordering of goods: growth of EDI, computerised, automatic teleordering, etc.

- Research into what is the most effective advertising, promotion, packaging and merchandising for product
  - Decisions on the sales promotional/advertising media to be used - press, TV, magazine advertising, mail order, door-to-door direct selling, self-serve merchandiser, etc.
    - Creation of the desired brand image for the product - expensive luxury, premium brand leader, low-cost `cheap and cheerful' commodity, etc.
      - Targeting of proposed customers and matching of product's features to the customers' known preferences

The product

A number of key questions are central to the product dimension to which correct answers must be found if the launch of a new product is to be successful:

- Who, exactly, is the product aimed at?
- What specific needs/wants must it satisfy?
- What are the criteria and specifications for its development, design and production?
- What is the boundary of acceptable costs within which it must be placed?
- What package of ancillary features must it embody: warranty, operations manual, servicing requirements, consumables – like copier toner cartridges, printer ribbons, etc?
- How long is it expected to last?

The price

Arriving at a suitable price for a product or product range depends upon a number of interlocking factors. Very often the fixing of a sales price is the result of a compromise between what the firm would like and what the market will bear, given the state of competition and demand. (*Note*: a detailed examination of pricing strategies is provided on pages 245–53.)

- What are the factors which will influence the price of the product?
  - development costs, costs of raw materials and components, production costs, contribution to overheads, contribution to targeted company profits, competitors' prices, quantity likely to be sold, etc.
- What price will the market bear given the positioning of the product and the income of its identified purchasers?
- What pricing policy does the company wish to adopt:
  a during the launch phase of the product?
  b during its various product life-cycle phases?
- How will the prices of competing products affect the company's pricing strategy?

The promotion

An appropriate promotional strategy is crucial for the effective marketing of any product or service. Essentially product promotion brings together the choice of channels and media through which to announce and present the product, the creation of a clear identity and image for the product (which will include the all-important aspect of its packaging), and the training and briefing of all those having a part in its sale and post-sales service.

- What is likely to be the most successful choice of promotional activities and media in launching the product – and then sustaining it?
- Where and how will the product be sold?
- How should it be packaged and presented?
- What sort of brand image should be created for it?
- How can its unique selling benefits best be brought to customers' notice?
- How can it best be distinguished from competing products?

- What levels of sales training and support will be needed by:

  a company sales personnel *b* dealers and/or agents?

- What level of after-sales service is appropriate?

The place

The creation of a successful 'place' strategy involves careful logistical planning – in order to get sufficient numbers of the product to a selected mix of outlets. It also involves the planning of availability, or in other words, the establishment of a networked delivery system which will ensure that no wholesale warehouse or retail store is without goods to satisfy an ongoing demand.

A place strategy also involves costings. It may be more profitable to deliver the product to relatively few regional wholesalers and let them absorb the cost of breaking down the bulk by deliveries to large numbers of retailers in repetitive penny numbers.

- What will be the most effective kind of outlet for the product?
  - wholesaler, retail shop, mail order company, departmental store, out-of-town shopping mall, door-to-door direct sales, craft fair, overseas agents, etc.
- What is the most cost-effective means of distributing the product?
  - own fleet of articulated lorries, contracting of transport, use of British Rail, use of Post Office or private sector courier services, etc.
- What production and distribution planning should be undertaken to ensure a continuous availability of the product in its outlets?

Note: there are two options open to a manufacturer of either selling to a wholesale firm and allowing it to benefit from the adding of value in the distribution chain, or of setting up its own distribution and retail networks so as to retain at each stage the profit attributable to the adding of value to the product (by being in the right place at the right time).

The second option is called **vertically integrating the organisation**.

PC
3.2.1
3.2.2
3.2.3
3.2.4
3.3.2

DISCUSSION TOPICS

1 To what extent and in what ways do government policies and activities affect industrial marketing strategies?

2 What promotional ploys are open to an industrial organisation whose sales in its home market are being attacked by undercutting foreign competition?

3 Since the Second World War, the UK economy has been subject to recurring cycles of growth and recession, variously called 'boom-bust' and 'stop-go' cycles. To what extent can a manufacturing company minimise the adverse effects of the 'stop' phase of the cycle, as the economy slides into a recession? Or is its marketing strategy of no use in such circumstances?

4 Very much effort in consumer marketing is put into understanding the buying habits and patterns of the UK shopper. Do you consider such aspects as 'understanding the psychology of the customer' and 'creating a positive buying mood in the new shopping malls' as worth investing time and effort in, or do you consider that a product that is well designed and made will sell itself? To what extent are consumers manipulated into buying products or services by 'artful' businesses?

5 How important in a consumer marketing strategy is public opinion? Consider the impact of public opinion upon stemming the manufacture of CFCs in aerosol sprays, the recycling of packaging materials by supermarkets and bodycare multiples, and the sale of unleaded petrol by filling-station chains.

Since each of the above developments increased operating costs, why did the firms concerned feel constrained to introduce them?

Should the impact of public opinion be included as a component in the production of an organisation's marketing plan?

6 We live in a world of rapidly increasing population and decreasing natural resources. How do you think these two trends will affect the marketing of consumer products over the next decade?

PC
3.1.1
3.1.2
3.1.3
3.1.4
3.1.5

GROUP ACTIVITY

Promoting another Supersnax product!

In groups of two or three, carry out the following activity and give your oral presentation to your class in turn:

The scenario

You are a unit within the Marketing Department of Supasnax plc, a national company manufacturing a range of sweets and confections which sell in supermarkets, newsagents, general stores and cinemas, etc. Your Research & Development Department has recently developed a new snack bar with the following features:

Dimensions:	12 cm × 4 cm × 1.5 cm
Weight:	80 grams net
Calorific value:	75 kcal per 100 grams
Ingredients:	chocolate, cane sugar, artificial sweetener, caramel flavouring, raisins, oatmeal biscuit

The snack's particular characteristics which were first market-researched and then built in to the manufacture of the bar are that it is low in calories and high in food value. Your market analysts identified a market niche for a new product which weight-conscious and dieting consumers could include in their daily intake without feeling guilty or worrying about calorie counting.
This is essentially the product's 'unique selling benefit'.
It is also intended to appeal to consumers who buy snacks in health food shops, because of its high 'natural food content'.

The test market locality

As part of your promotional research, first:
Investigate your local market for sweet snack bars – like Yorkie, Snicker, Topic, etc. Then, make notes on the following aspects:

- Type of sales outlet.

- Location of sales outlets.

- Profile of the type of customers purchasing sweet snacks.

- Methods for point-of-sale promotion and merchandising.

- Price comparisons – between competing snack bars and competing outlets.

Try to find out which bars sell best and why.

Presenting a promotional plan

Then, design a presentation to your senior management for launching the newly created snack bar in your locality, which has been selected as a test market. Your presentation should include:

- an outline of your promotional strategy;

- a point-of-sale promotional placard;

- a design for a 'self-serve' box which also serves as the packaging of the snacks (in packs of 50);

- the design for the wrapper of the bar;

- a name for the snack bar;

- a suggested sales price with reasons for it based on the local situation (assume that your manufacturing, distribution and promotional cost amount to approximately 15p per bar);

- a draft sales letter to existing dealers to promote the launch of your new product;

- a draft sales letter to retailers with whom you do not as yet trade, to introduce yourselves and your new product.

As a class group, observe critically each presentation and decide which was the most effective and why.

DISCUSSION TOPICS

1 How price-sensitive is the snack bar market?

2 How important in the snack bar market is a product's name?

3 To what extent do product packaging and point-of-sale merchandising appear to influence sales?

4 How do the retailers present snack bars for sale?

   Do approaches vary, or are they closely similar?

5 As a sales representative for Supasnax who regularly calls on a range of local retailers (i.e. the ones you researched), what advice could you give the marketing unit on the best way to design point-of-sale merchandising material?

6 What advertising media in your locality would you recommend be used to support the launch of your new product, and why?

MARKET RESEARCH – IT PAYS TO KNOW!

The use of the terms market research and marketing research sometimes cause confusion. Marketing research is the label for the activity of enquiring into and analysing the wide range of activities which make up the marketing function – product development, customer profiling, research into advertising media, the effectiveness of customer service systems and so on. Market research occupies a much narrower sphere of activity, it is the investigation into and analysis and evaluation of the key features, trends, tendencies and activities of a specific market – say for the purchase of satellite TV receivers or for polyunsaturated margarines.

The diagram in Fig 3.3 below illustrates the relationship of market research to the overall process of conceiving, producing and then selling a product or service.

At base, the market research function is to remain 'in the know' about two types of market:

a the market or markets in which the organisation is active

b the market or markets which the organisation is thinking of entering in the future

In the first type, market research staff maintain a monitoring function for existing products. They set up regular surveys in order to check that acceptance of a product or product line is holding up, or whether industrial buyers, wholesalers, retailers or consumers are migrating or 'defecting' to competing products or services. If a company wishes to enter into a new market, perhaps as part of a corporate strategy of diversifying as a means of long-term security, then its market researchers will survey that new market in order to ascertain:

- its current size

- its future potential for growth

- its ability to generate profit both currently and in the future

- the nature and size of existing competitors and their share of the market

- a detailed analysis of the type of customers who make up the market and how they segment into 'slices of the pie' according to factors like age, income and life-style

In order to secure the raw data from which to extract meaningful analysis, researchers of markets devise various methods for obtaining research data. These methods are divided into primary and secondary research.

Primary research

This type of research tends to comprise:

- 'tailor-made' interview questions for in-depth, probing of attitudes and preferences

- 'one-off' questionnaires designed to survey specifically targeted groups of buyers and/or consumers

- carefully designed discussion topics and questions for use in group discussions with, say, a set of consumers in a common category who are test-marketing a new product

Fig 3.3

The role of market research in the marketing process

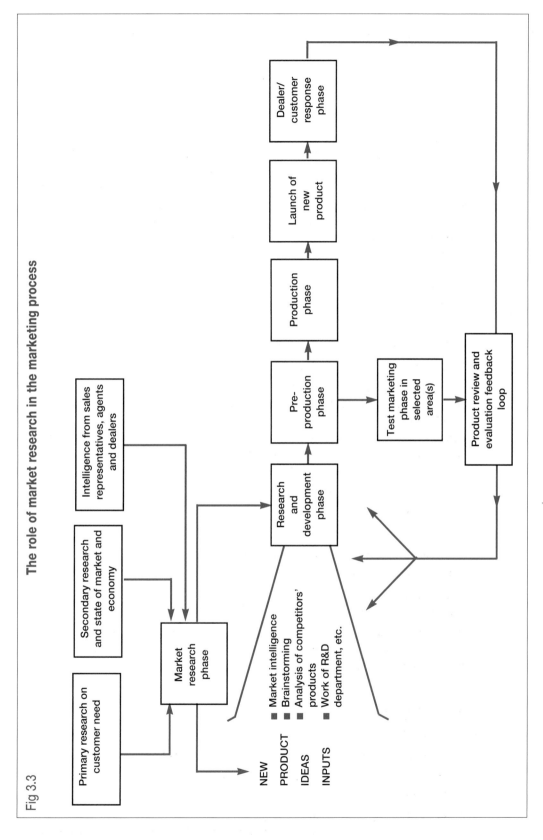

- briefing of sales personnel on what information to seek, say, about competing products, during their visits to existing and new dealers

Such data is expensive to acquire but is essential in preparing a new product or service for a national or international market.

Secondary research

This type of research concerns the acquisition of potentially useful information from published, readily accessible sources such as:

- Government publications: HMSO Reports, Treasury Statements, briefings from the Department of Trade and Industry and British Overseas Trade Board, etc.
- Monthly, quarterly, annual reports and reviews published by organisations like: The Economist Intelligence Unit, The Market Research Society, The Financial Times Business Information Service, etc.
- On-line databases like: Datacards, Dataline, Data-ease, Exstat and Dialog
- Articles in relevant trade journals and magazines
- Cuttings from national and local newspapers
- Regular reports sold on subscription by specialist companies like: Mintel Information Services, Jordan's Business Reviews and Surveys and Phillips & Drew Monthly Forecasts

A number of government departments – such as the Department of Trade and Industry – publish regular newspapers and bulletins (such as *British Business* and *Export Times*) sent free of charge to interested organisations to assist the process of market research. For example, during the run-up to the European Community's Single Market in 1992, the DTI was very active in regularly updating bulletins on EC directives and regulations for exporters.

PC
3.1.2
3.1.3

■ Methods of securing primary data

The following represent major ways of acquiring primary research data used in market researching.

Face-to-face surveys

A common sight nowadays is the researcher with clip-board and pen patrolling the High Street to secure direct responses (the survey questionnaire is clipped to the board) from shoppers and the proverbial man or woman in the street. Such local residents may be chosen at random, but it is more likely that the researcher has been given a particular brief to interview a specific type of consumer who is being targeted and who meets a profile involving his or her age, sex, apparent socio-economic group, occupation (e.g. housewife).

The questionnaire is likely to seek information about:

- what type of product (in a given range) is preferred and why
- what expectations the interviewees have of particular products
- the degree of satisfaction with a given product
- how the type of product might be improved, etc.

Usually the questionnaire has been designed to secure structured and valuable responses about a particular product whose identity is concealed within generalised questions. This is done in an effort to obtain impartial and unprejudiced responses.

Telephone surveys

Less expensive and time-consuming to conduct – if the respondent is a willing telephone conversationalist – is the telephone survey. Again, respondents are asked to provide answer questions which may be of the yes/no kind or the scalar variety; 'To what extent are you satisfied with . . . ?'

Such interviewees are likely to have been selected from listings which are sold to market research firms and which are compiled through individuals:

- living in particular residential areas
- having purchased a motor car of a set value
- having purchased a foreign holiday, etc.

A number of market research support organisations exist to provide national, regional and local information of this kind. One such, CACI Consultancy, with the assistance of the Official Census Database produces 'A Classification of Residential Neighbourhoods'. This database breaks down all UK residential areas into some 38 types, according to the socio-economic status, income, possessions etc. of the inhabitants. Such databases are used by researchers and sales organisations to target various kinds of consumer.

Exit profiles

Another source of primary data is for survey teams to stop customers upon exiting from a store and ask them to complete a short set of questions from a prompt card which lists the questions and range of available responses:

How often do you shop at the store?

Daily	Weekly	Fortnightly	Monthly	Occasionally
❏	❏	❏	❏	❏

How easy do you find it to park?

Very easy	Fairly easy	Easy	Fairly difficult	Very difficult
❏	❏	❏	❏	❏

Such on-the-spot responses are used to monitor (in the above example) shopping habits and acceptance levels of store facilities.

Postal surveys

Another way of securing information is by the use of mailed returns. Public inertia provides a very low response to unsolicited mail surveys (commonly 2–3 per cent). However, manufacturers and suppliers achieve higher responses in these ways:

- attaching a questionnaire to a warranty card which has to be returned to the manufacturer
- making the completion of a questionnaire a condition of continuing to receive a free copy of an informational magazine

■ offering a reward in return for the completion of the questionnaire – perhaps an additional monthly copy of a magazine being bought on subscription

KEY TERMS IN MARKET RESEARCH SAMPLING

The undertaking of surveys through the completion of questionnaires and other forms of information gathering is governed by a series of statistical rules and procedures which have to be scrupulously followed if a survey may be relied upon to give accurate information. The following is an introductory checklist to some of the major terms and concepts which are used in statistical analysis:

Sample: a representative proportion of a whole.

Population: the name given to the whole, from which the sample is taken.

Random sample: one taken by selecting units/people from within the total population in an unstructured and fortuitous manner; a refinement of this process is multi-stage sampling, where a second random sample is taken of an initial larger series of random samples.

Bias: the introduction into the sampling process of data which affects the overall outcome so that it is no longer truly representative.

Sampling error: even when large samples (l,000-plus) are taken from large populations, it is possible that a degree of statistical error creeps into the resultant analyses; for this reason many samples are described as correct to + or – 3 per cent (or whatever the calculated margin of error is).

Survey: a structured enquiry into a chosen area of interest which displays common features and characteristics.

Percentile: a one hundredth part – e.g. the forty-first percentile would be 41/100.

Quartile: the divisor which divides 100 by 4: e.g. the top quartile would be 75–100 per cent.

Index: An index is an average taken of a series of individual numbers over a period of time; indices are used to show the general movement – up or down in, for example, a basket of typical food items or pay rates over set periods of time.

Averages: a number of different types of average statistical analysis:

a   ARITHMETIC or MEAN: this average is calculated by dividing a whole by its component parts – if five batsmen score 85 runs, then their arithmetic/means average is 85 ÷ 5 = 17.

b   MEDIAN: the median average is the middle point in a series; for example, if there are eleven items in a series or scale, then the sixth number or item would be in the median position, with the same number of items above it as beneath it – X X X X X X̲ X X X X X

c   MODE: this type of average identifies a number or item which occurs most frequently in collected data; for example, if in a population of randomly selected people most were aged 38, then this would be the mode average of the population.

CHECKLIST OF TYPES OF QUESTION USED IN SURVEYS

Market researchers employ different types of question in order to secure data. While the questions vary in the responses they seek to elicit, almost all share a common feature – they are all capable of being collated into percentage groups of the total sample being surveyed:

1 The closed question

This question is designed to obtain a single response from two alternatives

Example: Are you a smoker?   YES ❏   NO ❏
              Can you drive a motor car?   YES ❏   NO ❏

2 The open question

This type of question is reserved for acquiring personalised responses to questions for which no simple response is appropriate. Since the responses of each member of the sample will vary, open questions are not designed for percentage analysis:

Example: How are you affected by the design and colour combination of this particular fabric?

3 The prioritising question

This question is used to ascertain relative preferences in ranking order and can be numerically analysed:

Example: Place the following features of the proposed optional extras in order of importance to you: where 1 is most important and 7 least important:

    central locking system   ❏
    quadraphonic loudspeakers   ❏
    adjustable steering wheel   ❏
    detachable car-radio   ❏
    self-locking wheel nuts   ❏
    alloy wheel-trims   ❏
    metallic finish   ❏

4 The scaled question

This is a semi-closed question as respondents are required to select an answer from a given scale which is expressed as a set of intervals along a continuum.

Example: Indicate how easy you found it to use the operating manual which you received with your personal computer:

Extremely easy	Fairly easy	Neither easy nor difficult	Fairly difficult	Very difficult
❏	❏	❏	❏	❏

EXAMPLES OF IMPORTANT SOURCES OF SECONDARY MARKET RESEARCH DATA

From HMSO:

Annual Abstract of Statistics
Economic Trends
Family Expenditure Survey
Financial Statistics
National Income & Expenditure (Blue Book)
Central Statistical Office Reports, e.g. Social Trends 1992
Overseas Trade Statistics of the UK
Guide to Official Statistics

From Government Departments:

British Business DTI
Commission of the European Communities: *Europe on the Move.*
Department of Employment: *Euro Action*

From Market Research Specialists:

The Market Research Society
Directory of Information Sources in the UK
Dun & Bradstreet: *Key British Enterprises*
Kompass: *UK and EC Company Information, Products and Services*
Extel: *Handbook of Market Leaders*
Eurostat: *Statistical Yearbook*
British Statistical Office Newport Gwent
Euromonitor Ltd: *The A–Z of UK Brand Leaders*
　　　　　　　　The A–Z of UK Marketing Data

From Organisations Publishing Frequent Reports and Updatings:

Jordan's Business Reviews and Surveys
Phillips & Drew Monthly Economic Forecasts
Economic Intelligence Unit – Quarterly Reviews
OECD: Regular Reports
Financial Times Business Information Service
Mintel Information Services

From Online Databases:

ICC Database – Dialog
ICC Eurocompany Information Service
Extat
Datastream
Dataline
Datacards

Focus groups and consumer panels

Customer attitudes and responses to products and services on offer have become increasingly important to their sellers as a result of increasing discrimination among consumers and the sophisticated mix of advertising to which they are nowadays exposed.

Market researchers have therefore devised carefully managed group discussions which examine in depth a range of attitudes to, say, a product's design, packaging, major features and cost, etc. Usually the consumers brought together share a common background and profile – they are representative of the targeted market segment at which the product is aimed.

The conduct of such a focus group meeting may, for example, involve the sample of consumers examining three or four different types of package design for, say, a blend of Kenyan coffee and putting them into a preferred ranking, while supplying reasons for their decision.

Such responses – considered in depth and arising from the group's consensus is likely to influence the eventually selected packaging design, especially if the group's choice is replicated by other groups in other regions.

■ Graphs and charts chiefly used to present statistical analysis

PC
3.1.3

Pie chart

A known quantity is broken down into a set of component parts and displayed as segments of a circle – hence the image of 'slices of a pie'.

Fig 3.4

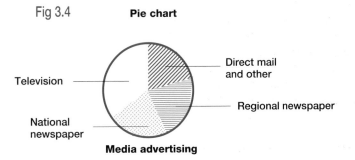

Pie chart

Television

National newspaper

Direct mail and other

Regional newspaper

Media advertising

Line graph

Collected data is plotted against a vertical and lateral axis; variables such as quantity are plotted vertically and invariables such as time laterally.

Fig 3.5

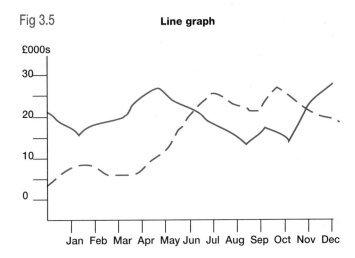

Line graph

£000s

Jan Feb Mar Apr May Jun Jul Aug Sep Oct Nov Dec

Bar chart

Bar charts are plotted in the same way as line graphs, except that amounts are shown as columns of varying height (but of an equal width) (Fig 3.6).

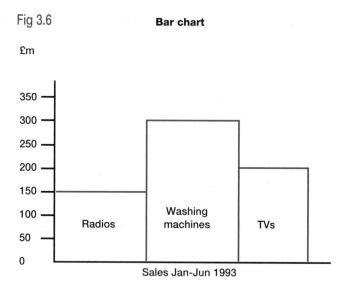

Fig 3.6   **Bar chart**

Stacked bar chart

Designed the same way as bar charts, the stacked version embodies two or more different items in its column height – quantities are 'stacked up' and displayed in contrasting colours or patterns (Fig 3.7).

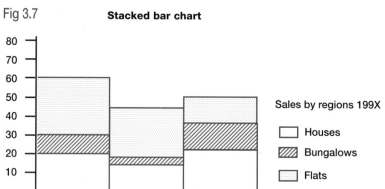

Fig 3.7   **Stacked bar chart**

Three-dimensional bar chart

This chart is also a bar chart, may also be stacked, and is drawn to show three dimensions as a means of providing visual appeal (Fig 3.8).

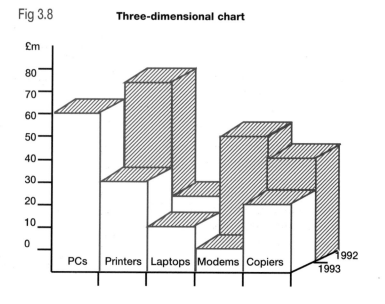

Fig 3.8   **Three-dimensional chart**

Frequency curves, frequency polygons and histograms

These three diagrams represent different ways of showing how data is distributed across a known range of intervals – say ages from 1–100.

The histogram is a set of bars of varying height, where the level of each bar shows the proportion of the total for the part of the range in which the bar is placed (Fig 3.9).

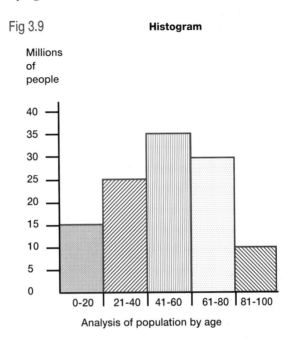

Fig 3.9

Histogram
Millions of people
40
35
30
25
20
15
10
5
0
0-20
21-40
41-60
61-80
81-100
Analysis of population by age

The frequency polygon is arrived at by connecting the points (as for a graph) which lie in the middle of the top of each bar (Fig 3.10).

Fig 3.10

Frequency polygon

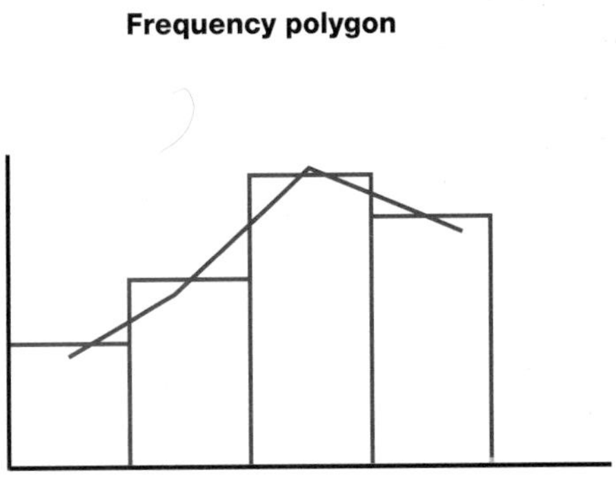

The distribution curve is very much like that of the polygon, except that it has a smoother appearance because of an increased amount of data plotted as a means of defining its shape (Fig 3.11).

Fig 3.11

Distribution curve
0-20
21-40
41-60
61-80

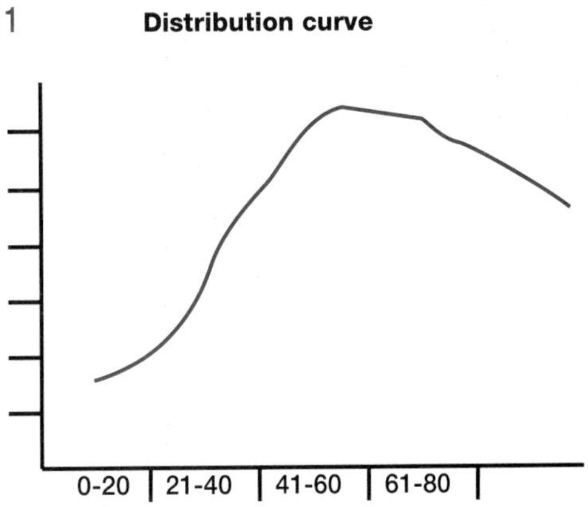

Scatter diagram

A scatter diagram is drawn along two axes, where a set of data is plotted in order to ascertain the nature of the relationship between two known variables; for example, a scatter diagram could be used to demonstrate the effect of unemployment upon the purchase of foreign holidays or the sale of ice-cream during the interval in a cinema as the heating is turned up! (Fig 3.12).

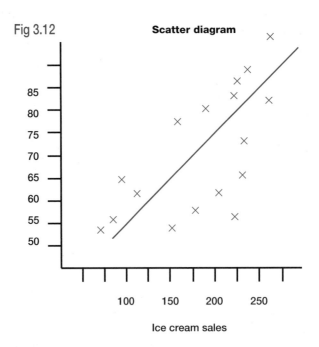

Fig 3.12 · **Scatter diagram**

Ice cream sales

Z chart

The Z chart is used to plot data over a moving period, say, the calendar year, as one year moves on from its predecessor; the chart shows three sets of data:

- current data – plotted week by week or month by month
- a moving total – say, January 1993– January 1994 which becomes February 1993–February 1994 as time moves on in the 1994 calendar year
- a cumulative total – as the year progresses, each month's total is added to those preceding it

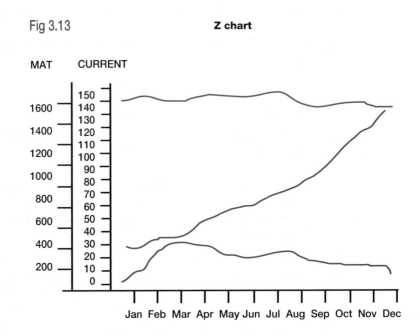

Fig 3.13 · **Z chart**

Pictograph

This chart depicts amounts in the form of appropriate icons or images of relative size in order to make the chart more visually appealing (Fig 3.14).

Fig 3.14

Pictograph

TV satellite dish sales UK

2 million   5 million

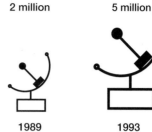

1989   1993

KEY FEATURES OF GOOD QUESTIONNAIRE DESIGN

PC
3.1.2
3.1.3

The characteristics of a good questionnaire.

The list of desirable qualities that a questionnaire should possess given below would seem to be a matter of common sense. Nevertheless, the drafting of questionnaires is one of the most difficult tasks of an inquiry. A pilot survey – that is, a trial survey, carried out prior to the actual survey – invariably leads to alterations and improvements in the questionnaires.

1. *Questions should not be ambiguous.* This means that the question must be capable of only one interpretation.

2. *Questions must be easily understood.* Technical terms should be avoided, except where the questionnaire is addressed to specialists.

3. *Questions should be capable of having a precise answer.* The answer should take the form of 'yes' or 'no,' a number, a measurement, a quantity, a date, a place; facts are required, not opinions (except where opinions are wanted, as in opinion polls).

4. *Questions must not contain words of vague meaning.* To ask if something is large or if a man is unskilled are examples of such questions. When does something become large? What jobs are unskilled?

5. *Questions should not require calculations to be made.* Such questions give rise to unnecessary sources of error. If for the purpose of the inquiry it is necessary to know annual earnings, but the respondent is paid weekly, the weekly earnings are asked for. The calculations necessary are done by the statistician's staff.

6. *Questions should not require the respondent to decide upon classification.*

7. *Questions must not be in such a form that the answers will be biased.* The questions will not therefore contain emotionally coloured words, they will not be leading questions – that is, they will not put answers into the respondents' mouths – and, of course, they must not give offence.

8. *The questionnaire should not be too long.* If a questionnaire is too long, the respondent will not be co-operative, and this may mean inaccurate answers; often a way out is for some of the respondents to answer part of the questions and other respondents to answer other questions.

9. *The questionnaire should cover the exact object of the inquiry.* However, provided the questionnaire is not made too long, advantage can be taken of the arrangements made to obtain information on another subject of interest.

From: *Wheldon's Business Statistics* 8th edition by G.L. Thirlkettle.
Reproduced by kind permission of Macdonald and Evans.

GROUP ACTIVITIES

Market research

1 Design a questionnaire which identifies among a representative group of students in your college or school the reasons which made them choose it for their course of study.

Also use the questionnaire to discover how they rated the advertising material used to promote the course, the application and interview process and their induction on to the course.

First trial your questionnaire and, having surveyed an appropriate student sample, present your findings suitably to your class.

2 Choose **one** item from each of the five categories on page 230 – Examples of Important Sources of Secondary Market Research Data – and produce half an A4 page summarising the way in which it assists the market research function.

Arrange this activity so that each class member receives a copy of the full set of summaries each group produces.

3 Make arrangements to visit one of the largest commercial companies in your locality and interview its marketing staff in order to find out what kind of information it seeks in its market research activities and how it uses it.

4 Choose **one of the items** listed below, carry out your research on it and report back to your group orally on what you discovered:

1 JICNARS, 2 ITCA, 3 BARB, 4 BOTB, 5 OECD.

5 Find out what sources of information are available locally to assist a small retail business owner in researching his or her market in your locality – in one of the following businesses:

1 newsagent, 2 antique shop, 3 carpet shop,

4 bed and breakfast guest-house, 5 sports shop

Having carried out your research, produce a briefing sheet which could be supplied to your local Chamber of Commerce for issuing to its members.

REVIEW TEST

1 What differentiates an industrial from a consumer market?

2 Explain why some products display an elasticity of demand and others do not.

3 Describe the four main components of the marketing mix and how they interrelate.

4 Explain the difference between primary and secondary marketing research.

5 In what different ways can market researchers secure survey information?

6 List the various types of question which may be used in a questionnaire.

7 Provide examples of four different sources of market research secondary data which are available.

8 Describe the different types of graphic presentation used to communicate statistical data.

9 List the key features of good questionnaire design.

THE PRODUCT IN THE MARKET PLACE

PC
3.2.1
3.2.2
3.2.3
3.2.4
3.3.3
3.3.4

■ 'You get what you pay for!'

We have already examined the important activities of the market research function in evaluating existing and possible future markets for a business organisation. The ongoing work of a company's research and development department has also been touched upon as a means of creating entirely new products or of improving and refining existing ones. Both functions need to be integrated in order for a successful product development strategy to be identified and pursued.

The existence in both industrial and consumer markets of tiered segments or subdivisions of a market has been examined and reasons for their existence given, such as supplying 'the luxury end of the market' or meeting what computer salesmen call 'entry level' or basic model demands.

To achieve successful product development, careful thought needs to be given to what exactly a targeted group of prospective customers requires of a given product, and how these requirements can be met, while at the same time generating profits to a preset level.

Thus the process of product development usually follows these steps.

■ 1 The conceptualising stage

- Expert staff – R&D, Marketing and Sales – meet to brainstorm around a central idea for a new product, say, a longer-lasting dry battery or a faster alpine ski.
- The motivation for developing a new product may alternatively stem from the launch of a competing product which embodies a technology rendering all alternatives obsolete.
- Or, a company's market researchers may have identified an entirely new market niche emerging for which no product or service currently exists, say, in the field of foreign holidays in Russia or TV satellite-driven European modern language courses.

During the conceptualising stage, a large company may examine 200–300 proposals for making a film, publishing a thriller or recording a pop tune before narrowing the field to five possibles and, ultimately, one certainty.

■ 2 The design phase

- Once a decision has been reached to invest in a chosen new product, then groups of expert personnel – draughtsmen, designers, toolmakers and marketeers – join together to plan the eventual appearance of the product (or service). At the design phase, answers have to be found to such pertinent questions as:

Q What is the overall budget for product development? And that for production itself?

Q What return upon investment (profit) is sought from the sale of the product: during its first year; over the span of its lifetime?

Q What does its end-user require in terms of its design, range of applications and overall appearance?

Q What are the implications for its overall costs of: development, production, distribution and promotion? Has a Rolls-Royce been conceived when a Ford Escort would do?

Q How does the development of this product fit into the company's corporate marketing plan? Is it seen as a major contributor to future profits or a low-priced, short-term stop-gap while a superior product is being developed?

Q How do the costs of development and production affect the price at which the new product can be successfully launched and then profitably sold through its lifetime?

Q To what extent will the prices at which competing products are being sold affect the price which can be obtained for the new product?

Q Will the new product embody sufficient superior features so as to enable it to be marketed at a higher price than competing products?

Such questions – and their answers – result in compromises and accommodations by the design team in order to produce a product prototype which they consider will prove attractive to its target market while returning a satisfactory profit on the investment given to it.

In an ideal business world, new product launches are always successful because easy answers are found to questions like those above. In reality, product development is likely to be adversely affected by:

1 a shortage of finance to fund ideal R&D, market research and pre-production activities

2 the existence of competing products/services marketed by larger, more affluent organisations being produced via economies of scale at sales prices which are very hard to compete with

3 the limitations of the firm's existing research scientists, designers and production managers

4 the restrictions imposed by:

available production capacity

existing warehousing facilities

available outlets and dealers willing to stock the new product

5 the likely extent of demand for the product generated by advertising and sales promotion campaigns – limited by the budget allocated to them

Unless strategies are devised to overcome such obstacles, then the launch of the new product or service is likely to fail because:

■ the product's design specification was compromised by a lack of investment

■ once produced, the product proved too expensive for its overall perceived worth in the eyes of its buyers

■ production, warehousing and distribution capacity could not keep pace with the demand generated by advertising, sales promotion and the intrinsic demand for the product itself, thus alienating prospective customers

As the above scenarios indicate, coordinating the development of a product is by no means simple. And the executives responsible know their jobs may be on the line if hundreds of thousands or millions of pounds of investment 'go down the tubes' as a result of their mistakes and miscalculations.

In order to minimise the impact of any possible mistakes, extensive care is taken in the pre-production phase of product development as explained below:

■ 3 The pre-production stage

At this stage there are likely to be several alternative versions of the embryonic product in development, each one embodying some variation within a unified design concept. The following factors are particularly important at this stage:

1 that the operation of the product and its appearance are well-accepted by end-users and dealers.

For this reason, product development staff are likely to field-test the product's central features and packaging across a number of representative regions and customer groups, so as to obtain feedback to confirm that selected features and appearance meet with approval.

2 that the costs of the product's design and ultimate production-line build quality remain in line with projected cost estimates.

During the prototype testing phase, a manufacturer's cost accountants and design engineers are likely to monitor closely the relationship between the development design and the production prototype and their respective costs. For example, what a designer commits to a blueprint or CADCAM computer model may prove too costly for the firm's toolmakers to tool up for. Producing the housing for an innovative combustion engine may be beyond a factory's metal-casting resources, so designers and production staff have to work out a compromise, and so on. Alternatively it may prove that the selected sources of raw materials and/or bought-in parts prove too costly and other sources need to be secured.

3 that the prototype evolving into the production model is suited to existing forms of transport and showroom/shop display.

For example, publishers and booksellers dislike textbooks which are printed in an A4 format because they do not fit into existing bookshelves. By the same token a product in development could prove awkward to package in a shrink wrapping or polystyrene knock-proof shell.

4 that the product in its eventual form and design conforms to legal requirements governing HASAW, consumer protection and a host of either factory-based or general consumer legislation.

For this reason all versions and marks of drawings and plans are carefully stored and, in certain industries such as aviation, all design specifications are coded and signed off by the responsible staff as a means of implementing design safety checks.

■ 4 The production stage

Despite all the efforts and attention given to a product during development there are almost always snags which only seem to manifest themselves once a product is in production. For example, the marketing of a computer software application is almost never 'bug-free'; somewhere within some thousands of lines of programming lurks an error which sooner or later surfaces. For this reason Version 1 issues of software are soon followed up by their 1.1 and 2.0 successors.

Therefore, R&D and development staff are likely to be needed to trouble-shoot problems during early production runs. By the same token, the production experts – foremen and operatives – may be able to suggest ways and means of cutting production costs or increasing output without further costs.

Three important factors in the production process should be noted:

1 That the overall design creates a minimum of waste – of raw materials, manpower or time.

   All three cost money and force unwanted contributions on to the costs of producing the product, thus eating into forecast profits.

2 That the product can be built to stringent quality standards.

   Since the Second World War, total quality management (TQM) and 'just-in-time' policies for the delivery of required production materials, as well as the operation of processes meeting British Standard 5750 and ISO 9000 have been introduced into UK factories, warehouses, shops and offices as a means of ensuring that products and services are able to meet and beat overseas and national competition. Thus every new product has to incorporate design and build features which are capable of satisfying a company's quality assurance personnel.

3 That the production runs or batches of the product are planned and executed so as to ensure the optimum cost-effectiveness of production resources.

   Works and factory managers devote much time and effort to the future planning of production runs which are smooth, uninterrupted and which operate at the lowest cost of heat, light and manpower. Rush orders which have to be turned out during a weekend when double-time may be charged are frowned upon when a factory has spare plant capacity during a normal working week. For such reasons, communication and liaison between sales and production are vital in keeping costs down while ensuring that sales are made and deliveries are on time.

■ Product planning: costing and breaking even

At the earliest stage in marketing a new product, a product planning schedule is drawn up which provides – as accurately as possible – estimates of the costs which will be incurred in its:

■ development

■ production

■ distribution and promotion

As the chart in Fig 3.15 indicates, costs are inevitably incurred at each of the six stages of marketing a product or service. And in order to ensure that a profit still ensues, cost accountants must monitor closely the staged costs which are attributable to a given product. Such costs are deemed direct and indirect. Direct costs will include items like the cost of raw materials, specific production processes like firing a batch of chinaware and the work of production operatives on the production line. Indirect costs will embrace factory heating, running a head office and maintaining a salesforce, etc. The cost accountants apportion a percentage of such overheads as fairly as possible to each product in a manufacturer's range.

PC
3.2.2
3.2.3

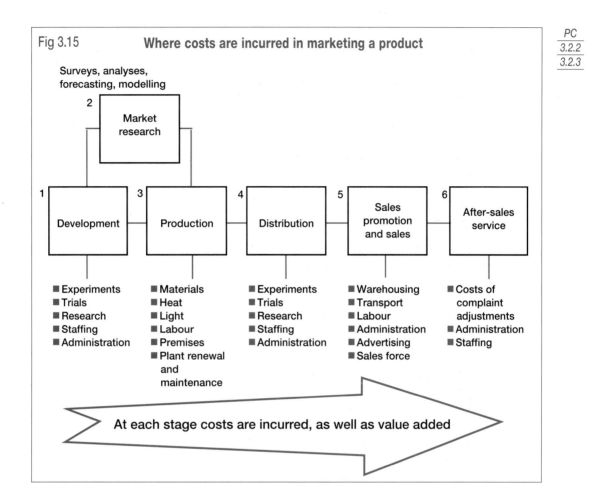

Fig 3.15   **Where costs are incurred in marketing a product**

Fixed and variable costs

Also, the nature of costs incurred in marketing a product or service differ in two essential ways. Some costs – such as the agreed rental of factory or office premises over a financial year remain fixed, as do those for business rates, and charges like road tax, and insurances. The costs of other inputs, such as bought-in raw materials, the fuelling of plant or vehicles and company payroll will vary according to the amount of work done. At peak times more staff may be recruited, more raw materials employed and more plant run over longer periods, while at times of low demand personnel may be laid off, plant left idle and stocks of raw material run down.

Thus the manufacture of each product incurs both fixed and variable costs. A firm's cost accountants as outlined above will apportion fixed costs to each product and will then estimate the amount of variable costs which will be incurred according to the number of products made. The diagram in Fig 3.16 illustrates how a break-even chart is drawn up to provide indications of costs, revenue and a break-even point at which income from sales matches costs incurred.

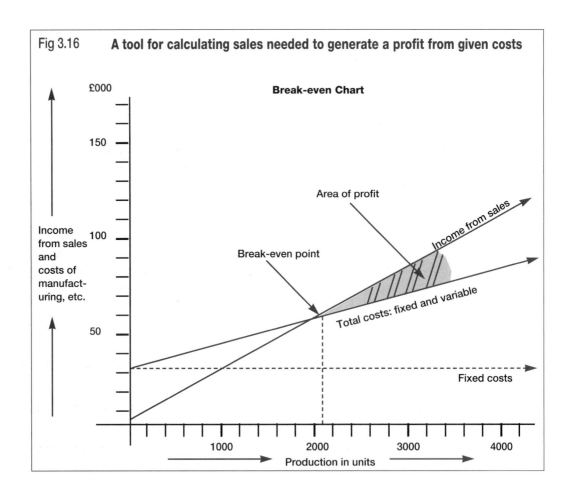

Fig 3.16 **A tool for calculating sales needed to generate a profit from given costs**

As the break-even chart (Fig 3.16) illustrates, it is possible for market researchers to plot anticipated fixed and variable costs for a given product against expected income from sales. By adjusting the levels of total costs and sales prices, different amounts of profit will emerge for the number of units sold. In this way, a long production run may generate acceptable profits from a low-priced unit and a short run from a higher priced alternative – if it can be sold!

Break-even charts are thus very helpful in deciding how to pitch sales prices, control manufacturing costs and yield required profits.

GROUP ACTIVITIES

PC
3.1.1
3.1.2
3.1.3
3.1.4

Product development

In groups of two or three, undertake **one** of the following activities.

1 You work in the Research and Design Department of the British Bicycle Company plc. Your company's market research unit has recently identified what they consider to be an exciting new market niche – a bicycle in both male and female versions for 18-plus-year-olds who are about to enter higher education at a university or college of HE.

Kim Turner, your Marketing Director has, as a result, given you the following brief:

'I'd like you to brainstorm around the design concept for the two bikes in terms of features which a student would really appreciate and find irresistible! We intend to target the bike at mums and dads as a kind of present to a son or daughter for having passed A-levels or BTEC GNVQ Level 3, etc. A rough shot at the recommended retail sales price is some £250–290, so it can't have **all** the bells and whistles!

I'd like you to produce a rough design with explanatory notes justifying the features you think should be emphasised. Oh, and I'll need it by today week for a meeting with yourselves, Market Research and Production.'

First, survey your local bicycle retailing scene for an update on what is available, and then carry out Kim Turner's instructions.

2 First research into **one** of the following and then deliver an oral presentation to your group on why you think the product involved lost its place in the market-place.

   a The Ford Edsel motorcar

   b Sir Clive Sinclair's CS motorised vehicle

   c Sir Freddie Laker's 'Laker Airlines'

   d The BSA motorcycle

3 Make arrangements to interview one or two senior cost accountants in a manufacturing company in your locality. Ask them to explain to you the procedures they follow to cost the development of a product up until the time it goes into regular production.

4 Arrange to interview the manager responsible for quality in **either** a manufacturing or a service industry company. Find out how quality aspects impinge on product development and production-line working.

For both activities 3 and 4, report back orally to your class.

A CASE STUDY IN PRODUCT DEVELOPMENT

1992 – and all that!

Your Head of Department has recently found that an increasing number of enquiries are coming into the Departmental Office about full-time courses which blend business studies with European languages. The impact of the EC 1992 Single Market seems at last to be impacting upon school pupils who are pursuing one or more European languages to GCE Advanced level, and to university undergraduates who are pursuing degree courses in arts subjects, including a European language.

The following represents the most commonly requested features of the sort of business/EC language course requested:

1 It must not exceed 15/16 months of study

2 Intending students must have at least a GCE A-level C grade or equivalent in any EC language they wish to study, and have attained BTEC National/GCE A-level/GNVQ Level 3 standards.

3 The course should result in qualifications in both the business studies and language course areas which, ideally, should be recognised in EC countries as well as the UK.

4 A period of work experience attachment in an EC country should be part of the course, and achievement in it should count to the overall course assessment.

5 The prospective students for this course are in a hurry to find worthwhile first posts and therefore don't want to study within the traditional three terms per academic year framework.

Your HOD has asked you to research into what programmes and syllabuses are being currently promoted by the major national examination boards and to what NVQ/GNVQ levels. S/he also wants you to discuss your outline proposals with representatives of local commerce and industry to see find out what they think would be most appropriate. Having ascertained what is available, your brief is then to:

1 Design a suitable course using, as appropriate, available national assessment programmes or units which meet the above criteria. Your design should form part of a briefing paper which also justifies the recommendations you make.

2 Work out an appropriate cost for the course fees:

 a for UK nationals;

 b for overseas students paying full-cost fees.

 Your familiarity with break-even costing techniques will help here, and your teacher will help with existing cost components and formulae used in your school or college.

3 Draw up a plan for the effective promotion of the course to the target students you identify.

4 Design a course brochure/leaflet which you believe will prompt recruitment.

 As a group, consider how you could obtain feedback on your course design without having to wait some 16 months for the results of a first intake.

5 Give an oral presentation to your class of about ten to fifteen minutes, suitably supported by AVA materials as a briefing on what course you designed, and your rationale for it.

6 In a general class discussion, consider the differences between marketing a manufactured product like an electric kettle, and an abstract service such as this vocational education course.

FIXING A PRICE

■ Elasticity of demand

One of the most difficult aspects of effective marketing of goods and services is arriving at a sales price for a given commodity.

Moreover, a product (or service) may be sold at a range of differing prices during its lifetime as part of an organisation's marketing plan for it, and its overall place in a corporate marketing strategy.

With certain products, there is very little room for manoeuvre. For example, in a mature market for, say, toothpastes or shampoos, a wide range of products jostle for position and consumers purchase to a large extent within a narrow band of prices. If the price of a particular brand moves up significantly, its users are very likely to move across to an alternative. In such markets products are said to be prone to a high elasticity of demand.

With other products, however, where preferences are deeply rooted – say in a favourite pipe tobacco or pop group – a significantly increased price may not result in a fall in demand for the tobacco or compact disk. In such circumstances, the products concerned display an inelasticity of demand. This may also be true of essential items like petrol or sugar provided that all suppliers increase their prices in unison. However, to prevent such price-fixing or setting up of what are called business cartels, legislation has been introduced making it illegal for suppliers to create and manipulate a monopolistic market for goods or services.

At this stage it is important to note that for many markets and their products, goods or services are introduced which are claimed to embody distinct differences from their competitors and so to warrant a higher or lower price – they are deliberately **positioned** to appeal to a targeted market segment.

■ Determinants of a product's price

Wherever a product is positioned in a market, the following factors will affect the price at which it is offered for sale:

■ Unique properties

A product may possess a unique property and be marketed as a market leader, say, because of a technological breakthrough. In this case, the product can command a very high price; for instance just after the Second World War the first biros brought on to the UK market sold for a week's wages because of their novelty value.

■ Development costs

Products with high development costs tend to be sold initially at high prices (compared to other competing goods) since they embody updated features and incorporate the latest technological advances; thus they have more appeal than 'elderly' products which have been around for a long time. Also, most companies are keen to recoup their development costs sooner rather than later so as to be able to invest them in other developments if this is at all possible.

■ **Sales prices of competitors**

Unless a new product possesses some really superior features, it is likely to be 'boxed in' by the pricing patterns of established alternatives; indeed it may have to significantly undercut the prices of well-accepted brands in order to gain a toe-hold in the market-place.

■ **The general state of the market**

Demand for products and services ebbs and flows according to the state of the economic tide. At times of buoyant activity and demand, high prices may be secured for – trainers, garden furniture or Nicam television-sets; in periods or recession, during a wet summer or after the World Soccer Cup or Olympics, prices will fall as retailers chase after sales during a sharp drop in demand.

■ **How the product is perceived by the supplier**

If a product is perceived by its supplier as a premium product – the best they can produce and more than a match for its competition – then it will be deliberately priced at the top end of the continuum. 'Get-in-and-get-out' products consciously made down to a price will correspondingly inhabit the other end of the market.

■ Major approaches to pricing

The cost-plus price

Users of this approach calculate as closely as possible the costs of producing the product and getting it to its point of sale and then include an additional amount to represent the profit to be generated (Fig. 3.17).

The advantage of such a model is that it is likely to arrive at a sales price which truly reflects the accumulated costs of its development, production and sales support. However, when a desirable profit percentage is added on, the resultant price may well prove more than the market will readily bear. It is also rather unsophisticated in that it makes no allowance for, say, spreading particular costs over the lifetime of the product. For example, a more astute pricing policy may add a relatively small charge for development costs on to the price components at the launch of a product in order to help it gain acceptance, and then progressively increase such a charge in stages (and through modest price increases) as demand grows.

Top-down pricing

The alternative to 'cost-plus' pricing may be termed 'top-down'. Users of this pricing strategy tend to start at the retail user price end of the process by posing the question: 'At what price would a product or service sell well in this market?'

The pricing strategies of competitors are carefully evaluated and a new product/service commissioned either to undercut them or match them while supplying superior features. Thus products emerge which have been made to a specific selling price. The quality of the materials used, design and workmanship will have been costed so as to remain within tightly fixed limits.

Many holiday package tour operators price in this way, by estimating what a significant segment of the market, say, blue-collar workers, will pay for a Mediterranean, beach-based holiday and then negotiating with hoteliers, coach firms and airlines to meet specific end-user prices.

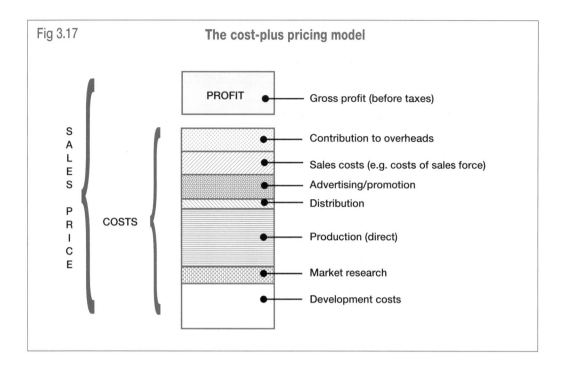

Fig 3.17   **The cost-plus pricing model**

- PROFIT — Gross profit (before taxes)
- Contribution to overheads
- Sales costs (e.g. costs of sales force)
- Advertising/promotion
- Distribution
- Production (direct)
- Market research
- Development costs

(SALES PRICE / COSTS)

Fixed rate of profit return

Some firms seek to obtain a minimum fixed rate of profit on each product as a return on their investment. This may be because they need to generate a known total profit each year in order to:

- pay a sufficient dividend to shareholders
- service loans from banks or credit houses
- cover all operating costs
- allow for depreciation and replacement of premises, plant and equipment
- provide for future developments

While this approach is sound in terms of its good housekeeping it may well come to grief and need intermittent reappraisal if:

- the equilibrium of the market is jolted say by a sudden rise in interest rates
- a strong competitor introduces a hostile, price-slashing campaign to increase market share, or block out a newly-launched product
- an innovative product causes a major change in buying habits among end-users

    and so on

In many ways, a market is like the open sea – at times placid and at times stormy; thus prices, like the trim of a yacht's sails seldom remains constant; they are continually being raised and lowered in response to market conditions.

    For this reason, an overall pricing strategy must be flexible and designed to operate within upper and lower limits.

Pricing for segmented markets

Some firms vary the price of identical products according to the type of customer they target and the nature of the sales environment. Much higher prices are commanded for, say, tins of coke or cans of lager in mountain-top, ski-resort cafes than in city-centre supermarkets. Thus a wholesale supplier may choose to price a product accordingly.

Also, economies of scale play an important part in this strategy, together with the concept of marginal costing. Once fixed costs have been absorbed and total costs are running into profit, the actual cost of producing additional units of production is very small. Therefore, if additionally produced goods can be sold – even at prices lower than their premium-market counterparts – they may still make a significant contribution to overall profits. As already outlined in this unit, such a segmented pricing policy is adopted by many manufacturers spanning the maker's brand, the retailers 'own' brand and unbranded versions of the same good.

■ Mark-ups and discounts

A further factor complicating a pricing policy for a manufacturer is the percentage of mark-up (representing a profit taken) which first a wholesaler and then a retailer add on to a manufacturer's selling price. While such mark-ups or margins are outside the control of the manufacturer, he has to allow in his pricing policy for sufficient space to exist between ex-works prices and ultimate retail prices so as to allow both wholesaler and retailer to live. Failure to do so may of itself result in a new product flopping disastrously, since these margins prove unattractive, given the price the good can be effectively sold for.

Manufacturers and wholesalers may also mask price movements with special price reduction offers, additional contents (say, an extra 10 per cent in a hair conditioner) and self-liquidating offers like 'three for the price of two' built into an overall retail price. Such offers may be introduced to liven up a sluggish demand for a product or to counter competitors' activities.

On the other hand, they may precede a reduction in the price of a product geared to the premium end of the market which is not sustaining its share of this market.

Another ploy in changing price structures surreptitiously is to alter the size of a product's container and therefore of its contents, thus enabling a price to change while retaining a profit margin.

■ Pricing strategies and the product life cycle

In order to examine the various price strategies applied to a product during its lifetime, it is necessary to explain what marketeers see as the key stages in the life cycle of a product or service (Fig 3.18).

The major proposition of the product life cycle model is that no product or service goes on for ever finding a demand in the market-place. Technology moves on, fashions change, fresh fads and crazes arise in all industrial and consumer markets.

And to reinforce such general observations, market research has demonstrated that a product's life typically moves through four stages:

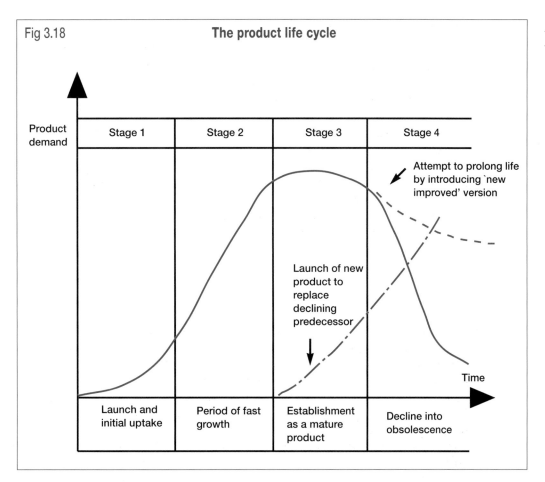

Fig 3.18 The product life cycle

Stage 1: Launch and initial uptake

A successful product tends to start life slowly until sales promotion, determined selling and customer acceptance have done their work. Penetrating a well-established market may be slow going at first, since all sales organisations object to losing market share to a cocky newcomer!

Stage 2: Fast growing demand

Provided that the product has intrinsic worth and appeal, and is effectively supported in advertising and sales promotion terms, then sales are likely to come thick and fast in Stage 2 – especially since the new product benefits from 'bang-up-to-date' design features and packaging.

Stage 3: Consolidated maturity

Once the initial excitement for the product wears out, and it becomes 'newish' rather than 'brand, spanking new', then the rate of climb in demand tends to level off. In fact the product will by then have peaked. Marketing staff during this stage may seek to extend the duration of a high plateau of sales by introducing forceful advertising campaigns which stress the product's status and reliability. And in order to stave off as long as possible the inevitable arrival of Stage 4, they may relaunch the product by giving it a low-cost, cosmetic face-lift. Car makers do this by adding fresh trim and colour schemes to existing bodies, engines and subframes. Washing powder manufacturers tend suddenly to discover a magic new ingredient making the powder wash 'even whiter' than before, and buy extensive peak TV commercial advertising time to prove it!

Stage 4

Despite every promotional blandishment and face-lift, the product begins to look weary and time-worn. Prospective buyers look and inspect but move on to younger models which are more attractive.

Eventually a decision is taken to stop production and the life cycle ends. However, if the marketing department has stayed sharp, the demise of one product is not allowed to take place until its lively and energetic successor is well on its way up the ladder of its own Stage 2! In this way, organisations maintain their profits and market share over decades and dozens of successive product life cycles.

ANOTHER WAY OF REVIVING A TIRED PRODUCT... !

Rover Cars some time ago found another way of prolonging the life of an elderly product. Top executives negotiated with Bulgarian industrialists with a view to selling them the Maestro production line – lock, stock and barrel – in order to help develop Bulgaria's fledgling motorcar industry. Having disposed of the family Moskvitch, Bulgarian motorists might then be flashing around in shiny new Maestrovitches!

And to bear out the validity of the product life cycle concept, Rover had already arranged to replace the Maestro with a Honda-partnered Synchro.

PC
3.3.2
3.3.3

PRICING STRATEGIES

Over a number of years and marketing experiences, companies have evolved a series of pricing strategies which they employ to support a product or service and to optimise the profits secured from sales. The following outlines of such strategies should be examined in conjunction with the four-stage life cycle above.

■ Penetration pricing

This strategy is usually reserved for launching a product, since it relies on undercutting the prices of competing items in order to gain a foothold in the market-place for a new product or service. Wholesalers and retailers may be invited to purchase a new product on a 'trial offer' basis and be wooed by a significant discount on the normal price for such a good.

To counter such attempts at hiving off a share of an existing market, the new product's competitors are likely to respond by announcing to the trade hefty discounts and special offers on their products – even to the point of temporarily cutting their profit margins to zero in order to kill off a potential competitor at birth.

■ Skimming pricing

The name for this pricing strategy is most probably derived from the practice of skimming the cream from the top of a churn of milk, since it describes the process of going into a market with a very high price for a product that embodies pronounced superior qualities from all others. For example, the first company to retail flat, wall-hanging television screens in the UK could expect to obtain a high price for them, representing as they would a distinct technological advance. However, competing TV manufacturers would catch up as fast as possible with their alternatives and force the skimming price to be converted into a competitive one.

■ Market pricing

Here a product or service is offered for sale at a price very close to that of other similar items. The strategy may well be that the product has been produced and distributed at a low cost compared to that of its competitors and that a handsome profit may be obtained by going into the market at the level at which competing products are selling. The conundrum facing marketing decision-makers is whether a significantly larger profit could be obtained by cutting the sales price in such a scenario. As the break-even chart displays, this would, however, require a larger sales volume.

■ Premium product pricing

The term 'product positioning' has been used in this Unit, and the strategy of premium product pricing provides an interesting example of this practice. Experienced marketing staff will decide long before a product is launched which tier or layer of the market it will inhabit, whether it will be sold at the 'silver service' or plastic cutlery end of the market, or somewhere in between. Manufacturers marketing a range of products – like china dinner services or motorcars – will tend to accord to one of their products pride of place as their 'premium' product.

As such – whether or not its manufacturing costs are higher (and they usually are) – it will be priced significantly above its middle and bottom of the range counterparts, both within the in-house product range and among competing products.

In order to give such a product the right image in the market-place, careful attention will paid by copywriting personnel to appropriate colour schemes employing gold, purple or red colours and descriptors like 'exclusive', 'superior', 'extravagant', 'excellent' and so on. As will be examined later in the Unit, there are very good reasons for marketing products in a premium or 'pole' position, since they may be bought in order to supply status and exclusivity to their purchasers.

■ Seasonal pricing

Many products and services enjoy seasonal peaks – turkeys and toys at Christmas, chocolate eggs at Easter, sunshine holidays during July and August, and so on. Their sellers are therefore given the recurrent headache of how to attract interest during off-peak periods. British Rail, for example discounts heavily the cost of rail tickets on commuter lines after 9.00 am when the peak commuting morning rush is over.

Hotel chains commonly market autumn and winter bargain week-end offers to couples aimed at topping up hotels which may be half empty; package holiday operators regularly offer weeks in Mediterranean, North African or southern USA resorts at 'give-away prices' to help in stimulating demand at off-peak times and offsetting hoteliers' and airline companies' fixed costs.

■ Milking pricing

This strategy is normally employed during the final stage of a product's life. By then, it should have earned and repaid the money invested in its development and that spent on advertising and sales promotion in order to build demand for it. Thus the milking strategy is to turn off the tap of all further investment – no more product face-lifts, no more costly sales campaigns, no more supportive discounts or free offers. The product is allowed to move along to its eventual demise at a price which, while a little lower than that enjoyed during its mature stage, nevertheless returns a good profit, given the reduced commitment to the product in terms of updating or promotional support.

■ Loss leaders and self-liquidating offers

Where an organisation markets a wide range of products – supermarket foods, DIY materials, motorists' accessories etc. – then a common pricing strategy is to advertise at regular intervals in highly visible localised promotional campaigns popular items as loss leaders. In other words, a premium brand of cornflakes, paint or engine oil may be advertised at a break-even or even loss-making price. This strategy is used to pull shoppers into the store and the cost of making such an offer is 'liquidated' or covered by the level of profits secured from other items which the store's management expects to sell to the purchaser of the loss leader.

Also, a company may advertise a 'free' give-away as a reward for spending up to a given level, or for purchasing an expensive article. (One entrepreneurial car dealer during hard times offered a free Citroen 2CV with every Citroen XM purchased!) Clearly no firm can afford to do business at a loss for long, and the costs of making such 'free' offers are built into the overall sales price of the expensive item. The offer is thus deemed to be self-liquidating.

■ Sales pricing

Traditionally, special-offer sales in consumer products occur in January and July. After the pre-Christmas boom, January is always a slow month in the High Street and so is July/August when many people are away on holiday. However, during a recession, many retailers are obliged to stage virtually continuous sales in an effort to prompt elusive customers to spend money.

Various Acts of Parliament have been enacted to protect shoppers from being duped by spurious offers during a sale. Goods for example offered at a discounted price – £X OFF! – must have been offered for sale at the higher price for a set number of days prior to the sales offer. While some sales items offer genuine reductions on initially displayed prices, many goods are especially bought in for seasonal sales – often from Third World countries – and offered for sale under a single 'special sales price'. Sales are most commonly held to enable retailers to clear out ageing stock and make room for a new season's sales lines.

DISCUSSION TOPICS

PC
3.2.1
3.3.2

Fixing a price

1 Why do consumers drive miles to buy petrol at lp a litre cheaper, but pay 'over-the-odds' without a qualm for a bottle of wine in a restaurant? Where does customer behaviour fit into the pricing of commodities?

2 Is there ever such a thing as 'a fair price' for something, or is the only 'fair' price what a market will bear?

3 A retailer once said: 'I've been trading for 30 years successfully, and I've never heard heard of your product life cycle!'

To what extent are retailers cushioned from the impact of the rise and fall of products and services? How could being more aware of the product life cycle improve retail business?

REVIEW TEST

PC
3.3.1
3.3.2
3.3.3

1 Describe the process of developing a product for the market-place.

2 Explain (with an example) how a break-even chart works.

3 What is meant by a product's life cycle?

4 Describe briefly the pricing strategies available during the life cycle of a product or service.

PACKAGING: A VITAL LINK IN THE MARKETING CHAIN

A central part of the excitement of Christmas lies in seeing the assembled Christmas presents lying around the foot of a glittering tree, wrapped in a variety of papers – loud and jazzy, quiet and elegant or foil and fun! And a key factor in the excitement they generate lies both in the appeal and promise of their exterior packaging and the concealment they give to what they enclose.

The packaging of more mundane and every-day products also plays a vital role in transforming them from routine items for sale into goods which a consumer cannot resist purchasing.

■ Packaging and brand image

A hundred or so years ago, many fast-moving consumer foodstuffs, such as flour, sugar, butter and eggs, were offered for sale in grocer's shops in plain blue, brown or grey bags or cartons, without any logo, trader's business or product name imprinted upon them.

But as the twentieth century revolution in mass production and mass consumer markets took off, manufacturers and retailers soon came to realise that a given product could be made to sell better if it bore the logo, name and an advertising slogan of its originators or sellers – especially if they already enjoyed consumers' respect and approval. Thus toilet soaps became Pears and Camay and Knight's Castille, while washing powders became Persil and Lux and Omo.

As a result of such powerful advertising campaigns and the reinforcement provided by associated packaging and point-of-sale merchandising, consumers soon came to ask for a Hoover when they were referring to a vacuum-cleaner, or a Kleenex instead of a tissue, or a packet of Kelloggs, instead of breakfast cereal.

Understandably, once manufacturers realised the power of brand image in creating initial and also repeat sales, they lost no opportunity to create an indelible image upon the consumer's mind of the brand name and the key sales features of each of their products through the design of their packaging.

Moreover, as marketing became more sophisticated after the Second World War, advertising departments and agencies exploited product packaging techniques as a means of positioning products in increasingly segmented markets. For example, in the tea market, single manufacturers devised suitable names, such as Earl Grey and Silver Label, accompanied by suitable graphic designs and colour schemes, which ensured that either brand found favour with consumers in the A, B or C1 market segments or in their C2, D counterparts.

GROUP ACTIVITY

Can you think of any other product ranges which manufacturers position similarly with the help of stepped packaging techniques?

Current trends in packaging

The growing influence of environmentalism is having a profound impact upon packaging design and construction. For example, the German Bundeshaus (Parliament) recently passed a law which obliges retail stores and outlets to accept and dispose of in a 'green' way the wrappings and packagings (often in many layers) left by customers on the shop's floor, having unwrapped a product immediately after paying for it. A deliberate intention of this law was to force manufacturers into being more environmentally conscious and less wasteful in the design of their packagings.

Correspondingly in the UK, retailers like The Body Shop actively encourage their customers to use previously purchased cartons, bottles and containers as refill receptacles for their repeat purchases. Multinational companies like Canon are also now providing a free postal and packaging service to enable photocopier toner cartridges to be recycled, and motor-car manufacturers like BMW are even designing the entire motor-car as a recyclable 'package'!

By the same token, manufacturers (and their advertising agencies) are creating good public relations and corporate images by using recycled materials – such as plastic, cardboard and paper – as part of their protective packaging processes.

In addition to responding to 'green' trends, packaging designers are becoming far more conscious of the fast-track life styles of consumers, who as partnered couples may both work and cherish their limited free time. As a result, packaging has become much more time-saving and user-friendly. For instance, oven or micro-oven-ready meals are packaged in trays for instant heating and from which they may subsequently be eaten. Again, boxed wine cartons are designed with inbuilt taps and combine easy dispensing with long-life insulation.

INDIVIDUAL ACTIVITY

Make a checklist of items whose packaging design also influences their sales appeal by incorporating similar user-friendly and ingenious features.

PC
3.3.2

CHECKLIST OF KEY FEATURES OF CONTEMPORARY PACKAGING DESIGN

The following checklist includes some of the most typical and commonly employed features of packaging design:

- **functional design** which assists the user – such as engine oil cartons with funnels to assist easy pouring

- **easy access** – wrappings should be easy to remove and not – like some vacuum-packed plastics – require the teeth of a large carnivore to remove them!

- **environmental friendliness**, so that precious raw materials are not wasted in today's 'throw-away' societies

- **recyclable materials** are employed wherever possible, so as to reduce waste and environmental pollution

- **reinforcement of the product's brand image** and unique sales appeal – luxury, comfort, strength and ease of use etc.

- **ease of use** in terms of the distributor and retailer – good packaging does not overlook the needs of the wholesaler who may store goods in multiple packs on pallets and move them around on fork-lift trucks; similarly, good packaging design takes into account the standardised heights of supermarket gondola shelving, delivery crates etc.

- **safety-consciousness:** highly inflammable or toxic materials should not be used in packaging, and guidance as to disposal of packaging materials should be included with those materials which embody any risk

- **compliance with legal requirements:** text, prices, specifications and contents etc. all come within the scope of the Sales Description Act and may result in legal action if the law is broken

- **and most important: visual and tactile appeal** – unless the packaging, as virtually the last link in the marketing chain, captures the consumer's eye and notice and then confirms the all-important decision to buy, all the work and effort from R&D idea to arrival at the point-of-sale will have been to no avail!

PC
3.2.1
3.2.2

MARKETING AND BUYER BEHAVIOUR

■ What makes people tick?

Buyers, whether industrial purchasing officers, housewives, teenagers or tiny tots, are complex mechanisms when it comes to identifying what motivates them to buy one product or service as opposed to another.

Industrial and social psychologists have undertaken extensive, in-depth studies and identified some of the major reasons for buyer behaviour. They differentiated between perceived needs or wants at a personal, family or social level. Also, they confirmed that buyer behaviour tends to alter as people move from one life cycle phase into another, say from youthful experimentation in buying to deeply entrenched, middle-aged brand loyalties.

■ Needs versus wants

Some goods sell because they form part of the essential prerequisites of staying alive – food, clothing, shelter, medicines and so on. Therefore, little prompting is needed to sell such goods. Indeed, products like fresh bread, flour, sugar, milk and eggs need very little in the way of merchandising, packaging or expensive advertising campaigns. Because they supply a basic need, they tend to sell themselves.

People's wants, however, are a very different matter. Human beings seem never to be satisfied in life. Indeed, they possess insatiable appetites which span a host of goods and services:

> **'Mummy! I want a mountain-bike for my birthday!'**

> **'Darling, I've seen the most gorgeous little eternity ring at Mappins ... '**

> **'You'll love it when you see it – silver metallic finish, Paris grey leather upholstery, 16-valve, petrol injection motor and does 0–60 in under seven seconds!'**

The underlying psychological motivators which fuel such wants are examined below in detail and include: status within a peer group – 'Everyone else's got a mountain-bike', the need to feel good by showing off expensive jewellery, or to feed one's ego in a surge of overtaking power.

Moreover, in a developed consumer market where a number of suppliers exist to supply basic staple needs, then they will seek to differentiate their products from others. They will invest them with a number of benefits and qualities which project an image way beyond any basic function:

> **Wessex Sovereign potatoes are grown in soils rich in nutrients and come to you fresh and wholesome, graded for the size you like and scrubbed clean and sweet!**

> **Baked in their jackets, they're just the job for the hearty appetites you have to cater for on a raw winter evening!**

Such advertising copy seeks to sell the humble potato, not merely as a filling vegetable, but as a convenience food, and one which a loving mum can rely on to satisfy her family when they come in from the cold. In this way advertising develops branded goods from staple products in a needs market by working upon consumers' susceptibilities. And so the line between needs and wants becomes blurred and indistinct as producers' brands and product images take over.

PC
3.2.1

THE BUYING MOTIVATORS

The following checklist illustrates the broad range of buying motivators around which advertising and sales promotion campaigns are created:

Safety and security

People need to feel secure in their daily lives and so the safety/security factor is applied to sales features like central-locking in cars, make-up which is irritant free, tissues which have a 'wet-strength', shoes with waterproof welts, high-performing pensions schemes and so on.

The 'feel-good factor'

Many people spend their lives feeling relatively inadequate and insecure, thus a product or service which reassures them and boosts their morale and ego always finds a ready demand: contact lenses instead of glasses, well-made toupées, a well-cut dress, exclusive pens, lighters and handbags, etc.

Exclusivity

The feeling of being well ahead of the pack, or in American terms, 'ahead of the Jones' is important for many people.

For this reason they may be willing to pay large sums for this year's Jaguar or Mercedes coupé, a month's holiday in Thailand, a Chanel perfume and so on.

Peer group status

People are motivated to buy not necessarily to keep ahead of, but simply to keep up with their peers – co-workers, neighbours or friends. Thus pressures are felt and given in to for buying, say, a gas-fuelled barbecue, a water-softener, an automatic garage door, or a 90-channel satellite dish and decoder.

To win approval

Very many products and services do well because of the natural urge among consumers to look attractive either to existing or to prospective partners – witness the number of hair-stylists, fashion boutiques, fitness centres and jewellery businesses in any population centre. The approval sought may not only be obtained through physical appearance, but through learning to ride, drive, speak French or a host of other accomplishments.

The nest-making instinct

Extensive industries from house-building to Bonzai-tree cultivation rely on the deep-seated urge in people to rear offspring in comfortable or even luxurious surroundings; home-building, DIY and garden-centre firms supply a market which is highly segmented as consumers migrate upwards over time and as income increases.

Value-for-money

While people on occasion 'splash out' way beyond their normal spending power limits, most of the time they are on the look-out for high value-for-money deals which make their income go further. As a result, many firms market goods like food mixers, lawn-mowers, vacuum-cleaners and washing machines as being high on reliability, performance and effectiveness but low on purchase and maintenance costs.

The above list is by no means exhaustive but is indicative of the many psychological prompts which underpin these aspects of modern life:

- Personal esteem and self image
- Sense of personal safety and security
- Status/position in social and work groups
- Mating and child-rearing instincts
- Recreational and leisure life style
- Personal values, beliefs and outlooks
- Personal ambitions, goals, life-plans etc.

■ Unconscious buying triggers

A further complicating factor in seeking to establish what makes a person buy something is that everyone is prompted in purchasing situations as much by unconscious motivations as by conscious ones. For instance, a man or woman who is actively seeking a life partner and is becoming anxious at a lack of success may tend to buy clothes, perfumes or colognes which are more overstated and extreme in fashion terms than he or she would normally buy, as an unconscious means of gaining attention. By contrast, the ageing husband or wife of 30–40 years standing is, more likely to opt for durability and comfort than for stunning visual appeal in a suit or dress.

■ Position in the buying life cycle

Another important aspect of buying behaviour is the phase in the human life cycle in which people find themselves. Young adults, for instance are generally far more willing to experiment – with music disks, hair-styles, food, sports and so on – while their middle-aged parents may be 'set in their ways' with extensive brand loyalties and preferences:

'Your father prefers Coleman's English Mustard!'

'Always bought Pringle sweaters. Needn't bother to get me anything else!'

For such reasons, advertisers often target brand-loyal customers so as to maximise repeat purchasing.

■ Spending power

Though left until last, probably the most important factor in influencing people's buying patterns and traits is their disposable income. It is important to keep in mind that this, too, follows a curve of distribution (Fig 3.19).

In order to keep their fingers on the pulse of buying behaviour, a company's market researchers as well as government statistical offices are continually analysing who bought what from whom and for how much; how sample companies, individuals and families spend their income; what shifts and trends in purchasing habits are detectable and in what directions as a result specific markets are moving. In analysing consumer purchasing trends, there is only one constant: human beings are fickle and, at times irrational, so their buying behaviour can never be taken for granted!

PC
3.2.1
3.2.3
3.2.4

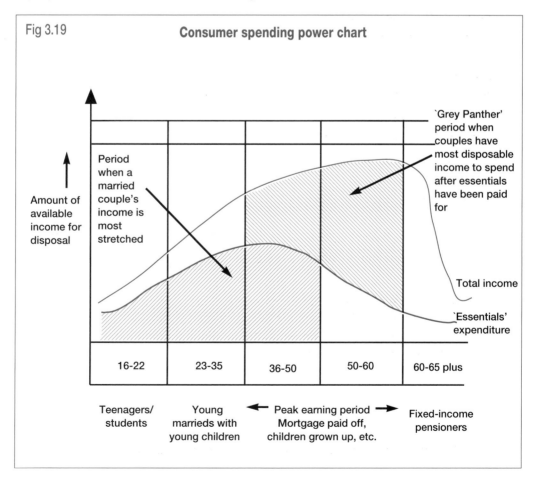

Fig 3.19   **Consumer spending power chart**

'Grey Panther' period when couples have most disposable income to spend after essentials have been paid for

Amount of available income for disposal

Period when a married couple's income is most stretched

Total income

'Essentials' expenditure

| 16-22 | 23-35 | 36-50 | 50-60 | 60-65 plus |

Teenagers/ students   Young marrieds with young children   ← Peak earning period → Mortgage paid off, children grown up, etc.   Fixed-income pensioners

THE SALES PROCESS

A key part of the marketing process is the selling operation. All the work, energy and combined effort of creating, developing, producing and distributing a product counts for nought unless the sales operation is successful.

As in all organisational undertakings, effective selling requires careful planning, administration and the training of personnel.

A typical Sales Department of a national company is structured as shown in Fig 3.20.

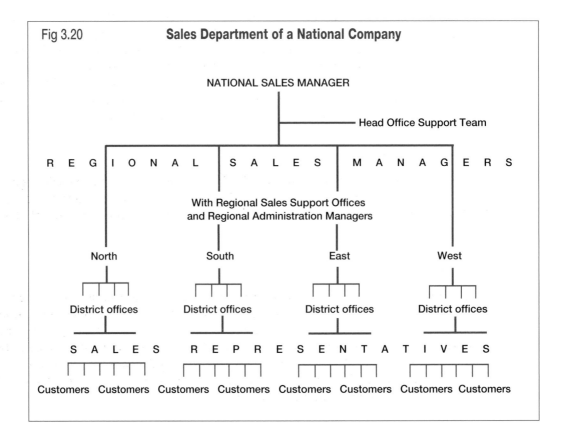

Fig 3.20   **Sales Department of a National Company**

■ Structuring the sales operation

In a national company, say, a company selling motor car tyres and accessories, the breakdown of responsibilities and functions will follow these lines:

National Sales Manager

Negotiates annual sales target with senior management and the budget to support the national sales effort. (Note, this budget will include as cost centres the sales department in a head office complex, each regional sales/administration office and their respective district offices. The budget may also include regional allocations of an advertising/sales promotion budget to support sales which may be run from either regional offices or head office.) Breaks down national sales targets and budgets to regional level. Agrees with regional managers district sub-allocations. Monitors daily/weekly/monthly sales to target statistics. Keeps running costs under review and control, e.g. sales force expenses. Services large national account customers, say, Sainsbury's, Halfords or Boots.

Checks that sales forces are selling to new as well as existing customers. Liaises with marketing department regarding emergence of new markets, product development and market intelligence coming up his management line from sales representatives' customer calls.

Regional Manager

Coordinates regional sales effort, visits major customers regularly with district managers/sales representatives. Monitors sales/expenses for region in same way as national sales manager. Develops sales personnel. Supervises administrative work of regional office – but usually relies on Regional Administrative Manager.

Ensures regional advertising and sales promotional campaigns effective. Works at improving sales in low-achieving districts. Sets targets for new customers and sales of new products etc. Provides regular reports for national sales manager.

District Manager

Primarily organises the selling routines of the district salesforce. May be heavily engaged in selling also. Trouble-shoots customer complaints and problems. In many ways mirrors Regional Manager's role on a smaller scale. Provides regular reports for Regional Manager about sales performance.

Sales Representative

Works at interface with customers to achieve preset sales target. Assists in securing market intelligence from visits. Seeks to enlarge customer base by making new calls. Supports customer services by handling directly any product complaints or warranty problems, etc. Delivers point-of-sale merchandising material. Leaves samples for consideration/evaluation. Provides dealers and retailers with product update briefings and new product sales information, etc. Chases up slow-paying customers whose accounts are overdue. Provides regular reports for district manager.

■ The sales representative's role

The Hollywood stereotype of the successful salesman is usually of a genial, paunchy, flamboyant Old Stager, who's 'been around', who definitely has 'the gift of the gab' but who is not too bothered by unethical or seamy business practices.

This stereotyped caricature is unlikely to sell very well in today's business climate where the sales representative is expected to be:

■ **smartly dressed and in good shape**

buyers or 'prospects' invariably relate the desirability of the product (or service) with the visual appearance of its seller; an old but true proverb says that the salesman must first sell himself, and that includes personal appearance – well-groomed hair, freshly laundered shirt, polished shoes, etc.

■ **expertly informed and up-to-date on their wares**

buyers are always evaluating competing products in retailing or company procurement and no sales representative can sell effectively if his or her information is sketchy, out-dated or invalidated by embarrassing gaps.

■ **expertly informed about sales trends and the market**

the successful sales representative has to be expertly informed about local/regional/national/international sales trends and market characteristics; almost certainly buyers will advance counter-arguments, objections or ripostes during a sales pitch about costs, consumer trends, competitors' activities, etc. which the successful sales representative must be aware of and ready to overcome diplomatically on the basis of high-quality information rather than blind assertion.

■ **skilled and sympathetic in understanding the buyer's needs and problems**

just as 'no one ever won an argument with a customer', so no sales representative ever built sales without first establishing and then developing rapport with the buyer.

■ **able to handle objections, complaints or 'hassles' without giving offence or upsetting the buyer**

most sales representatives are both 'front-line troops' and ambassadors for their companies and so to the buyer, they *are* the company; one reckless remark or rude response can 'blow away' years of goodwill and high-volume purchasing.

■ **a good listener, amateur psychologist and sincere exponent of their chosen field**

invaluable market intelligence stems from casual conversation and gossip if the sales representative has a sympathetic ear; further, abundant sales tend to follow around those sales people who have the skill of putting retailers, buyers and assistants at their ease and who are able to demonstrate a sincere enthusiasm and involvement in their sales sector and product service range.

And as if that weren't sufficient, the successful sales person will be expected by his or her employers to possess developed expertise in self-organisation, sales administration, and follow-up customer maintenance techniques.

■ Selling face-to-face

While there are many other successful means of selling: direct mail, telephone-selling, unsolicited mailing and faxing, etc. undoubtedly the most powerful is the 'flesh and blood' negotiating process where customer and sales person interact face-to-face. In some ways it may be regarded as a ritual process in which both parties are aware of the roles they are expected to play. Certainly this selling process conforms to social and cultural practices – which may vary considerably from country to country. The haggling norms of the Arab souk or bazaar would be treated very dustily in a Rolls-Royce salesroom or Paris fashion-house salon! Nevertheless, there are patterns and sequences which typify the European face-to-face selling which are listed below for you to examine:

Guidelines on face-to-face selling

A well-tried and tested formula is summarised in the acronym AIDA: **Awareness – Information – Desire – Action!**

Awareness: as the first step, this phase seeks to make the customer aware of a product or service; no 'hard sell' is undertaken, rather a consciousness-raising move: 'We're bringing out an improved version of the economy model next month. I'll leave you these brochures to browse through ...'

Information: the next step (on the next visit) may be for the salesman to brief the customer on the product's specifications and attractions, to answer any arising queries and to counter any objections or uncertainties, etc.

Desire: if phases one and two have gone according to plan, the buyer will be signalling evidence of a desire to acquire the product, evidenced by remarks like: 'Well, we might try a case or two – if the price is right! or: 'I might be able to shift a case if you could guarantee delivery before this weekend.'

Action: having created the desire to buy, the final phase is for the salesman to 'close the deal' by initiating actions which cause the customer to make a definite commitment to buy: 'I'll just put you down for the three cases, then, Mrs Harbold, if you could just sign here ... Lovely!' 'I'll just pop over to the car to telephone the warehouse. I'm sure we've got a dozen gross left at the old price. I'll make sure they despatch them this minute, and you'll have 'em first thing tomorrow!'

Other sales specialists sequence the selling steps as:

1 **Re-establishing rapport:** an initial period of small talk about 'the car, the golf, the test match score' – whatever the conscientious rep. has noted as items which interest the buyer.

2 **Lead-in to the desired sales pitch:** general and low-key exchanges about business trends provide a cue for the salesman to introduce his sales item: 'Funny you should say that, we've just modified ours. Look, here's a sample of the new version (hands it to the buyer to examine) see how the cunning devils in R & D have re-routed that circuit ... and that alone has increased its life by 30 per cent!'

3 **Delivery of major selling points, features and benefits for the buyer and his customers:** ever-watchful of the buyers' reactions, the salesman unfolds his practised sales routine, varying it according to the personality of the buyer and the overall context of the sale; depending on the product and circumstances, stress will be given to aspects such as price, performance, design features, durability.

4 **Countering/overcoming objections or buyer resistance:** short of giving away money-trees, the sales person is bound to encounter some resistance to his selling efforts such as cash-flow problems, over-stocking, lulls in trade, and existing loyalty to a competing brand. These must be countered by sales tools like special offers, a one-off extended credit deal, a sale-or return deal, or an introductory extra discount.

5 **Closing the sale:** in all sales transactions, a psychological moment arrives when the buyer is ready to say 'yes'. The practised salesman knows how to spot the verbal/NVC signals, knows when he's said enough and which technique will work to seal the bargain. *Note:* effective sales people never oversell, create overstocking, over-commit their customers financially or sulk if they walk away unsuccessful that day, for 'today's browse is tomorrow's sale!'

CHECKLIST OF A PRODUCT'S SELLING POINTS

- What it costs
- What it costs to run/service/insure
- After-sales support: guarantees, servicing, spares availability and costs
- Design features: reliability, latest model, market-leader, wealth of extras
- Durability: length of warranty, specification of components, tried-and-tested construction, trouble-free track-record
- Availability: order cycle, delivery time, distribution back-up
- Sales support: merchandising, sales literature back-up, dealer training schemes, etc.

What motivates a buyer?

The motivations underlying the desire to buy are many and varied. The psychologist in the sales person will, however, invariably spot these motivators:

- Pack-leader needs
- Vanity
- Status perceptions
- Snob-appeal
- Desire to be one-of-the-boys (or girls)
- Exclusivity of product
- Conspicuous consumption appeal
- Sex-appeal
- Keeping up with Jones
- Last-in scramble

PC
3.2.4
3.3.2
3.3.4

ADVERTISING AND SALES PROMOTION

'Half the money I spend on advertising is wasted; the trouble is,
I don't know which half.'

Lord Leverhulme, Unilever plc.

Businesses spend enormous amounts of money annually on advertising their wares; the amounts tend to vary between two and fifteen per cent of a good's sales price, and run into over £1 billion annually in the UK.

In smaller firms it generally falls to the sales manager to manage the advertising and sales promotion function, but in larger ones, these activities are the responsibility of marketing personnel who very often work in conjunction with appointed advertising agencies.

The role of the advertising agency

The general role of the advertising agency is to assist in-house managers with:

- devising the brand image of a product or service;
- monitoring the advertising activities of competitors;
- positioning new products within an existing product range;
- designing the packaging of a product;
- planning and arranging advertising campaigns on a national or local basis; this service includes liaising with mass-media offices and space sellers;
- designing point-of-sale placards, brochures and leaflets.

At the top end of the advertising agency market, a client account may be worth several million pounds a year in terms of its budget and such accounts are usually serviced by a manager and staff working exclusively to them.

The advertising media mix

As a result of the development of the advertising and telecommunications industries this century, a wide range of media are available for inclusion in an advertising campaign:

CHECKLIST OF AVAILABLE ADVERTISING MEDIA TODAY

- Television commercial, radio commercial, cinema commercial, video-tape film cassette commercial, viewdata entries on Prestel
- Hot-air balloon/trailed airplane poster
- National/local newspaper display or classified advertisement
- Free local newspaper insertion/plug
- Free specialist magazines distributed to key buying decision-makers
- Roadside/sports stadium/forecourt hoarding. Public transport signs and placards – in buses, tubes and taxis
- Leaflets, brochures, pamphlets mailed or delivered by hand to homes and business premises
- Unsolicited sales letters and enclosures
- Trade and public fairs and exhibitions
- Event sponsorship: names of sponsors prominently displayed on racing-cars, sports shirts or power boats
- Give-away items: pens, matches, key-rings, etc. carrying brand names, trade-marks and slogans
- Home selling television channels

- Recorded messages left on telephone answering machines and unsolicited fax messages

The range and scope of available advertising media grows each year as technological innovations multiply and bright media people brainstorm new ways of reaching prospective purchasers.

CURRENT NEWSPAPER AND MAGAZINES IN PRINT IN BRITAIN

- 21 National Newspapers (owned by 11 proprietors)
- 1,500 Weekly Newspapers
- 7,500 Magazines

393 newspapers are circulated in Britain per 1000 of the population

Source: Ms Jane Reed, *British Journalism Review*

PC
3.3.2

■ Planning an advertising campaign

Targeting the right customer

Whether the job is undertaken by in-house marketing managers or contracted out to an advertising agency, the planning and execution of an advertising campaign to promote the launch of a new product is crucial to its acceptance in its chosen market.

Given the wide variety of media options available, the agency staff need first to decide precisely at what type of purchaser the campaign is aimed.

For many years the advertising industry has classified consumers according to the socio-economic groups they belong to. The Institute of Practitioners in Advertising in 1970 produced the following classification:

PC
3.1.3

SOCIO-ECONOMIC GROUPS: IPA CLASSIFICATION

A   Senior/top managers, administrators and professionals: surgeons, barristers, business directors, brigadiers, public utility directors and so on. (3 per cent of population)*

B   Middle/senior managers and public sector personnel – county/district council senior officers, business departmental managers, partners in solicitors/accountants firms, headteachers, smaller business directors and proprietors. (13 per cent of population)*

C1   Supervisory staff/'white-collar' workers in clerical and administrative posts: supervisors, section-heads, factory foremen, assistant managers in branch offices of banks, building societies, etc. (22 per cent of population)*

C2   Skilled manual workers in industrial posts: technicians, maintenance engineers, shipwrights, oil-rig drillers, masons, electricians, etc. (32 per cent of population)*

D   Semi-skilled/unskilled workers: bricklayers' hod-carriers, road-menders, farm-workers, office-cleaners, etc. (19 per cent of population)*

E   Low/fixed income category: old-age pensioners, single parents, widows, long-term unemployed, etc. (11 per cent of population)*

*Source: JICNARS National Readership Surveys

Note: It is important to keep in mind that the examples given above in no way imply a superiority of one type of occupation over another; they are simply intended to provide a rough and ready insight into the spectrum of occupations which have been classified into groups as a result of the life-style, culture and spending power each represents.

Today the income of each group is likely to be distributed as follows:

Group	Income per annum in £s
A	50,000 plus
B	30,000–50,000
C1	20,000–30,000
C2	10,000–20,000
D	4,000–10,000
E	under 4,000

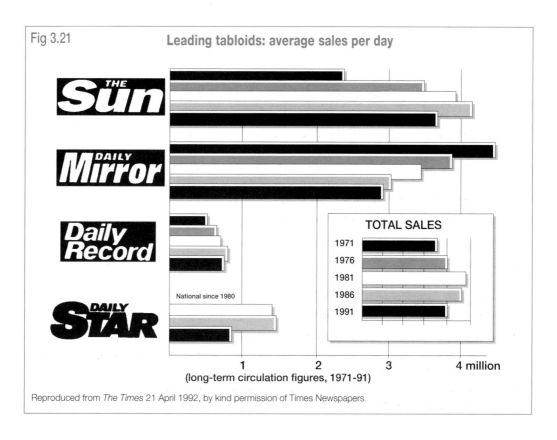

Fig 3.21 — Leading tabloids: average sales per day

(long-term circulation figures, 1971-91)

Reproduced from *The Times* 21 April 1992, by kind permission of Times Newspapers

Once such approximate classifications have been made, further analysis of life-styles reveals, for example, which UK national newspapers and magazines each group subscribes to or purchases on a regular basis:

Sunday Times	*The Times*	*Country Life*
Observer	*Financial Times*	*The Lady*
Sunday Telegraph	*Daily Telegraph*	*Good Housekeeping*
Sunday Express	*Daily Mail*	*Woman's Own*
Sunday Mail	*Daily Express*	*Woman's Realm*
News of the World etc.	*Sun* *Daily Mirror*	*She* *Jackie* etc.

The same kind of market segmentation can be made of each group's television viewing habits, which may range from 'The Money Programme' and 'Panorama' to 'Blind Date' and 'Bruce Forsyth's Generation Game'.

The reason for pin-pointing such reading and viewing habits is to ensure that any commercial or display advertisement placed in a given newspaper or with a specific independent television company will reach its intended audience. There would be little point, say, in promoting installed garden swimming pools among E group families; correspondingly, A and B groups may not have an interest in motor coach day-trips to the seaside. The point being that while no value judgement is being made as to whether one group may be socially superior or inferior to another, their respective life-styles and interests do vary according to what is financially affordable and what interests are demonstrated by the peer groups in each category.

Allocated budgets – cutting the cloth

Each advertising campaign will have a limitation imposed upon it by the amount of finance allocated to it. Therefore agency staff will seek to obtain best value for money. For instance an agency may, over a year, place hundreds of thousands of pounds with a TV company or national newspaper for peak viewing time or 'premium position' advertisements. As a result they will obtain a bulk buying discount, the benefits of which may be passed on to regular customers.

However well spent, the budget is subject to a number of decisions:

Q   How long should the campaign run?

Q   Is it to be national or limited to some regions/districts?

Q   Given the targeted customers and the type of product/service which would be more effective:

  ● Simple posters with a strong visual message on arterial road hoardings and in forecourts?

  ● Run-of-paper display advertisements?

  ● Blanket mail shots to targeted private residences?

Q   How is the product/service to be presented?

   Here the decision will involve design features, colours used, type-faces employed, etc.

Q   What mix of media would prove most cost-effective? e.g. a full-page colour advertisement in a single edition of a 'quality Sunday paper' followed up by three, weekly quarter-page display advertisements in selected regional evening dailies? Or a series of short commercials at peak times on regional commercial radio broadcasts and so on.

Supplying the correct answers to such questions will decide whether the campaign hits home or misfires completely, and when commissioning an advertising agency to run a campaign, a company is often buying into many years of expertise in a range of markets. Expert knowledge of viewing, reading or travelling habits among consumers may enable an agency to achieve its target exposure at a fraction of the costs incurred by inexperienced in-house managers – a point which helps them justify their fees and commissions!

Hard sell or soft sell?

The overall approach of an advertising campaign tends to fall into the category of either a hard or soft sell:

The hard sell

- Emphasises the key selling benefits of a product or service and compares and contrasts its sales price with those of competing items.
- It may indulge in 'knocking copy' a jargon term for making disparaging comments about competing products and their 'inferior' features.
- It may 'push' a significantly discounted special offer price etc.

The soft sell

- Seeks to create a mood in tune with the product's image and to emphasise the 'feel good' effect that buying/owning the product (or service) brings.
- No mention is made of price, x per cent off, competing brands or key selling benefits.
- Colours, music, soft-focusing and textures will combine in the soft selling advertisement to promote a sense of exclusivity, comfort, pride of ownership or whatever response is being sought.
- Soft-selling advertisements are often used to maintain demand for well-established, premium-positioned products.

Advertising reinforcers

In order to gain as much impact as possible throughout a campaign, advertisers seek to reinforce the effect of a mix of media advertised messages by:

- reproducing the logo or trade-mark prominently in every advertisement within each medium
- using the same combination of colours and graphic design so it becomes embedded in customers' minds
- devising a catchy slogan or tune which the public easily memorises:
  'It's the real thing, Coke!'
- replicating in point-of-sale materials key elements of the above reinforcers to stimulate impulse purchasing
- using well-liked and respected sports people and entertainment celebrities to endorse the product
- ensuring that the campaign advertisements and promotional material embody common elements with the product's packaging so as to aid product recognition

Above and below-the-line activities

Not to be confused with 'below-the belt' blows, below-the-line is the term used in advertising to describe the myriad of promotional activities which are devised to support generally a product range or company's activities.

Above-the-line advertising relates to that which identifies a given product or service and then sings its praises. Its below-the-line counterpart includes:

- give-away badges, pens, picture cards for collection, etc.
- free entry into competitions whose prizes are provided by the advertising firm
- give-away, trial samples – at fairs, exhibitions, shows, etc.
- articles written in popular magazines about a company's history and good works
- subsidised items like sweat-shirts carrying the company logo, diaries, tax-disk holders, desktop calendars, etc.
- sponsored stunts which make the headlines – e.g. a round-Britain ride on a tandem for charity, etc.

Building brand loyalty

A number of products – notably in the food industry – are supported by ongoing special offers and discounts. Tins of baked beans, for example, may display detachable coupons worth '5p off your next purchase of Brown's Baked Beans'. Other offers involve collecting stamps or coupons printed on the packaging of a product – cornflakes, beer six-packs – or supplied with every £10 worth of petrol purchased, until the total assembled is enough to send off for a 'free' set of tumblers, table-mats or kitchen knives. Such offers are said to be 'self-liquidating' since the cost of the 'free gifts' is built into the promotional budget and increased sales of the targeted product.

In such sales promotional ways, the marketing team builds brand loyalty and heightens interest in the weekly chore of shopping.

PC
3.2.1
3.2.4

INDIVIDUAL ACTIVITIES

Marketing: buyer behaviour and the advertising function

1 Find out about what Abraham Maslow described as a hierarchy of human needs in his *A Theory of Human Motivation* in 1943. Give an illustrated talk to your class about Maslow's Hierarchy and then, in a class discussion, consider whether they are valid in terms of buyer behaviour.

2 Research into these advertising agency job roles:

   Creative Department Manager, Account Executive, Brand Manager,

   and then brief your class on what each contributes to the work of an advertising agency.

3 Find out the current scale of charges for a national and b regional TV commercials – at peak and off-peak times, and the length of TV transmission times offered for sale. Draw up a table of charges to share with your group.

4 Do the same as for 3 above, but this time for your local commercial radio station.

5 In terms of both 3 and 4 above, find out how TV and radio advertising salespeople convince prospective customers of the cost-effectiveness of using their advertising media.

6 Arrange to interview a senior member of staff in a local company which provides public relations and 'below-the-line' services to private and public-sector organisations. Find out how the costs involved in securing such services are justified and what motivates businesses to invest in indirect advertising activities.

Trading standards and consumer protection

The Office of Fair Trading as an arm of government acts as the nation's watchdog on the many-faceted activities of buying and selling in the consumer market-place.

At local levels, each county council operates its own trading standards department. Its role is to monitor through its inspectors the businesses within its catchment area in terms of the following major activities:

The Weights and Measures Act 1985

The role here is to ensure that all scales and balances in use are correctly calibrated so as to give accurate and 'fair measure', and also to check that vessels used to contain solids or liquids for use in the selling or distributing processes are also correctly sized and marked – such as pint beer glasses, milk bottles and churns etc.

The Consumer Protection Act 1987

The role here involves checking sales goods for safety – such as imported toys which may have dangerous materials in them, or be dangerously constructed – checking on standards of assembly, construction or processing – such as glass being found in jars and bottles in a supermarket and back-tracking this to a production batch and recall etc.

The Trades Descriptions Acts 1968 and 1972

Here the role is to ensure that local business advertisements, point-of-sale merchandising placards and labelling comply with the Act, and often, responding to consumers' complaints of alleged misleading or false descriptions on advertised or displayed products.

Note: The work of the Trading Standards Departments in local authorities is complemented by that of the Environmental Health Office, the Health and Safety Commission and the local Citizens' Advice Bureaux.

The Advertising Standards Authority and Independent Television Commission

There are two principal bodies which act as watchdogs over UK advertising:

for all television advertising: the Independent Television Commission (ITC)
for all other advertising: the Advertising Standards Authority (ASA)

The roles of these twin authorities are as follows

- to monitor all advertising against established criteria for public morality and good taste, compliance with established laws and fair and accurate statements regarding the product or service advertised
- like ACAS, they provide guidelines and models of codes of practice, and many advertising agencies and television companies have incorporated them into their own manuals of operational practice.
- the two authorities may be required to pronounce on a given advertisement or TV commercial, and if they are against it, it is usually speedily withdrawn

GROUP ACTIVITY

In pairs, research into either the ITC or the ASA and the work they do. Then provide upon a factsheet of not more than two sides of A4 a clear set of informational points based on your findings.

Decide in class which factsheet is most informative and then copy it to each class member as a revision aid.

MAJOR ADVERTISING/SALES STATUTES

1893 Sale of Goods Act

1889 Indecent Advertisements Act

1955 Food and Drugs Act (Labelling)

1967 Advertisements (Hire Purchase) Act

1968 Trade Descriptions Act

1971 Unsolicited Goods and Services Act

1973 Fair Trading Act

1973 Independent Broadcasting Act (covering TV Commercials)

1973 Supply of Goods (Implied Terms Act)

1974 Consumer Credit Act

1974 Prices Act (covering clear pricing of goods)

1978 Consumer Safety Act

1979 Sale of Goods Act (updated 1893 Act)

1982 Supply of Goods and Services Act

1987 Consumer Protection Act

These Acts embrace a wide range of powers which ensure that goods sold deliver what they promise, that labels and advertisements supply information which is accurate and not misleading, that residents are not mailed items they have not ordered and do not want, that goods are not sold on credit under high sales pressure, that national safety standards are complied with and so on.

INDIVIDUAL ACTIVITY

Select two of the above Acts, research into their contents and then summarise their principal points in about 300 words. Photocopy or display your findings to share with your class.

DEVISING A MARKETING PLAN

■ 'Marketing is all about the future!'

The final section of this Unit is devoted to the major issues involved in devising and implementing a marketing plan, since this activity embraces all the sections already covered in this Unit.

A company's marketing plan is likely to form a central plank in its overall corporate strategy, which will itself be concerned with general future trading directions and activities, their finance and the most effective use of available resources.

■ The mission statement

Most larger organisations today have embraced the American concept of having a defined Mission Statement which summarises what they believe in and are organised to achieve. Hence a company's marketing plan will need to harmonise with statements about overall goals and objectives like:

To maintain a leading position in the computer manufacturing industry worldwide.

or **To ensure that the company's products and services continue to receive the highest levels of customer acceptance.**

or **To ensure that the company's turnover continues to grow by 10 per cent per annum.**

■ Key stages in the marketing plan

1 Evaluating the current position

Before undertaking reviews of future needs and directions, an effective marketing plan carries out a comprehensive audit or survey of:

a the current 'state of play' within the organisation

b the current state of the market(s) and competitors' activities externally

Such an analysis will involve reviewing the positions of products in their life cycles, the contributions they are making to company profits, and the amount of money they are soaking up individually in terms of their development, production, distribution and advertising costs.

Also, the review will look critically at the quality of the information and intelligence of the firm's market research in order to decide whether it needs reorganising or more financial support.

The in-house survey stage will also cover areas such as:

■ the effectiveness of the retained advertising agency

■ the current share of the market held by individual products and recent trends in sales up or down

■ the overall effectiveness of the salesforce and its impact upon competition

■ the general picture in terms of marketing costs and whether economies can be made in any area – R&D, Production, Distribution, Sales Promotion, etc.

Estimates will be undertaken in similar areas in terms of the activities of competing products and services. Some managers use the SWOT mnemonic to guide discussions here:

SWOT MARKETING ANALYSIS

Evaluating ourselves and our competitors in terms of:

Strengths	–	ours and theirs
Weaknesses	–	ours and theirs
Opportunities	–	how can we capitalise on our strengths so as to take a lead, acquire a position of dominance, boost profits, etc.
Threats	–	to our position and planned activities from our competitors

As a result of both internal and external current position surveys, information inevitably emerges which will affect the nature and direction of the marketing plan, such as:

■ Market share is declining in certain products.

■ Customer acceptance of certain brand images is falling off.

■ The level of profitability in some key product areas has fallen to a point where the required return on investment is marginal.

■ A perceptible swing has been detected towards a major competitor's new product range.

and so on.

2 Defining future marketing strategies

The next stage in devising the marketing plan will depend very much on what the internal/external audit has discovered as well as a number of significant factors like:

Q What is the extent of the finance available for investing in future marketing projects ?

Q Does the company currently have the personnel capable of developing and making the kind of product(s) which will hit back at the inroads of our competitors into our market share?

Q Does the company have access to sufficient distribution outlets so as to deliver an increase in sales of the required 15 per cent?

and so on.

Thus the second stage in designing an effective plan is to arrive at considered judgements as to where the firm's precious resources of:

■ available finance – either generated from profits or loaned from a bank, etc.

■ existing plant, equipment and managerial information systems

■ human resources

■ collective know-how and expertise

■ distribution and sales outlet networks

may best be employed and directed in the future. *Note:* unless an organisation is in dire straits, its marketing plan is likely to take the form of some 60–70 per cent consolidation of products and markets and 30–40 per cent innovation and restructuring.

Given an accurate analysis of the above key resources, decisions may be taken such as:

■ killing off obsolescent products

■ funding the purchase of an urgently needed piece of production machinery; expanding production capacity in a specific area

- prioritising the development of a set of new products/services to replace existing, mature ones
- redefining the company's recruitment and training programmes in certain key areas so as to obtain staff with skills and expertise currently lacking
- restructuring the mix of products to be sold in terms of the volumes to be produced and at what targeted profits
- setting expansion targets to secure additional dealers and outlets

3 Alternative marketing options

Given the results of the analysis of the current position described in 1 above, and the checklist of possible priority activities outlined in 2 above, the company's marketing planners need thirdly to take into consideration a series of available alternatives including:

- **Whether to go for enlarging market share** – as a means of securing market dominance prior to increasing prices or as a strategy for marginalising competition
- **Whether to consolidate in market 'niches' where a high rate of profit can be sustained** – to concentrate on specific market areas which are familiar and supply a good return in investment
- **Whether to diversify into wholly different markets** – declining profits and market shares may force decision-makers to seek 'new pastures'; this strategy also avoids the dangers of having all the marketing eggs 'in one basket'
- **Whether to move into exporting** – saturation of a home market in which too many competitors struggle to survive may encourage a wider marketing vision and strategy
- **Whether to integrate vertically or laterally** – successful organisations with plenty of available finance or collateral against which to borrow may decide to expand vertically, as manufacturers, say, into distributing their own products, or as wholesalers into retailing, or even into all three

Or they may decide to expand laterally by buying more factories, more warehouses or more retail outlets in order to grow in whichever sector they inhabit. Large organisations with many subsidiary companies and divisions tend to restructure in such ways at regular intervals as a means of securing an improved return on their massive investments.

4 Costing the plan

A favourite motto of engineers is: 'All change costs!' And this is certainly true of marketing plans. However, the costs of **not** changing may be considerably higher – if not terminal!

Accurate costing of the marketing plan, both in terms of expenditure and projected income, including profits, is vital. It is not an overstatement to say that the jobs of an organisation's entire workforce may depend upon the forecasts and costings being right – witness the fate of Air Europe, Danair and the Hays Wharf project.

For this reason, accountants will seek to break the plan down as far as possible into components which are readily monitored:

1 *Projected sales*: existing products; new products
2 *Projected cost of sales*: at each stage of the value-adding process from R&D to Customer Service
3 *Percentage contribution of gross profit (by product) to total profit target*
4 *Budget allocations to all cost centres*: such a set of budgets will define the levels of anticipated fixed and variable costs needed for a successful marketing plan

Thus an effective marketing plan will identify all principal sources of planned income and planned expenditure. Moreover, these may be expressed in monthly totals over a financial year so as to provide company accountants with a ready means of monitoring the execution of the plan – sales/profit to target month on month.

Marketing plan time-scales

As marketing plans evolve in a series of successive updatings and revisions, and as product development may take years and not months in some industries, the following tend to be the time-scales employed:

- *Current year*: Planning undertaken in detail for *next year* in terms of costings, sales/profit targets, etc. largely in terms of existing product range.
- *Planning for year after next*: forecasts of movement in the market and product sales – with the emphasis on development and design of products and an analysis of expected customer needs; the laying of plans for the development of new markets and products with outline costings.
- *Subsequent years (3–5 years ahead)*: the marketing plan is updated annually in terms of more distant trends and long-term policies in terms of: building projects, company acquisitions, development of an export division, etc.

As each planning year rolls round, the marketing plan brings into focus the *'Year after next'* as *'Next year'* and puts more detailed flesh on to it.

Review and evaluation

Needless to say, as in all planning, it is essential within the annual planning cycle to include a 'How did we do?' section, which neatly brings the process back to the starting point of the internal/external audit.

PC
3.2.1
3.2.4
3.3.1
3.3.4

REVIEW TEST

1 List the major motivators of buyer behaviour.

2 What does AIDA stand for?

3 Outline briefly the functions of an advertising agency.

4 List five different advertising media currently available.

5 Explain what A, B, C/l, C/2, D and E stand for.

6 What is the difference between a hard and a soft sell?

7 Explain the difference between above and below the line in advertising terms.

8 List three different major Acts of Parliament relating to marketing.

9 What are the major considerations in designing a marketing plan?

10 What does SWOT stand for?

11 Why are marketing plans often three- to five-year rolling plans?

CASE STUDY 1

The Tops Shop: a case study in devising a marketing plan

Pat Roberts, Sarah Williams and Winston Wright were all final-year students at Weston College in Dorset when they decided to form a business partnership. Pat and Sarah were following a business studies diploma programme and Winston was pursuing a fashion design course.

One day in the spring term of their second year at Weston, the three were drinking Coke in the college refectory and Winston was explaining how he and his classmates were designing sweaters, cardigans and jumpers and producing them on knitting machines.

'It's a really great way of expressing your own ideas!' Winston enthused. 'The machines are incredibly versatile, once you get to know how to drive them. Look, I've made this one,' he went on, pulling a chunky sweater out of a plastic bag which was made up of a swirling abstract pattern in pastel shades.

'It's beautiful!' said Sarah. 'I've never seen anything like it – can I try it on?'

'Help yourself,' replied Winston.

Sarah pulled it on over her shirt and pirouetted around the table. 'What do you think?'

'Really something else,' answered Pat, the quiet one of the 'trio, and it's got me thinking. It really is different from anything else I've seen – in a boutique or M & S. How much would a sweater like that cost to make, Winston?'

* * *

Pat's thinking led to a number of off-campus meetings of the three students. At the first Pat briefly outlined his proposal.

'Look, I think Winston's design genius on the knitwear machine could be a real money-spinner. I've had a good wander round town and there's nothing – absolutely nothing – like the sweaters and pullovers his group are producing on the market. If we could sell them at the right price, I reckon they'd go like a bomb!'

'Hold on a minute,' cut in Winston, 'those knitting machines don't come cheap, and what about premises and a retail outlet ...'

'Just let me finish and then I'll listen,' replied Pat. 'Look, I've just received a legacy of £15,000 from my grandma. At the moment it's sitting in a building society and the interest it's earning is just about keeping pace with inflation – it's not **working for me at all!** Why don't we three set up a business making and selling sweaters and jumpers and pullies?'

'Come to think of it,' mused Sarah, who had been looking into the distance, 'my dad's got a small barn he doesn't use now that the EC are cutting back on food production. I wonder if the upstairs could be turned into a workroom?'

'Yeah, well, I have to say the job market's pretty dead at the moment,' added Winston. 'I'm game, but I haven't got £150 quid, never mind about £15,000.'

'My dad might be interested in backing me – us,' said Sarah. 'He's like a bear with a sore head nowadays. Always moaning about not having a real job any more.'

'Are we all in?' asked Pat. 'If so, first we've got a lot of fact-finding to do – devising a marketing plan and so on.'

* * *

The facts which the trio established were set down as follows:

■ The business would be a partnership – at least initially – and would be called 'The Tops Shop'. The three students would be active partners, and Sarah's father, Jack Williams, a sleeping partner with a contribution to start-up capital of £30,000 – £15,000 of which he gave to Sarah and £15,000 he put up as his own contribution.

- As Winston had the manufacturing know-how but no money, Mr Williams agreed to service a loan from the bank made to Winston for £15,000 and also put up the required security. Thus the four partners had each put into the start-up capital for the partnership an equal sum, the total being £60,000.

- Repaying the loan and interest on behalf of Winston would cost the business £9,350 per annum over three years; Winston would have to repay this amount before taking any share of the profits – unless his partners agreed to an alternative 'pay-back' arrangement.

- Pat found a small shop to let at the end of the High Street in Westbridge for £750 per calendar month on a self-repairing lease for three years with an option to renew. It was set between a popular up-market café and a busy chemist's shop. The business rate for the premises was £2,000 per year. Heat and light and water bills were said to be some £150 per quarter.

- Sarah's father said it would cost about £ 5,000 to turn the upstairs of the small barn into a warm and efficient workshop and that he'd secured permission for a change of use. Mr Williams thought a fair rent for the workshop would be £80 a week, and that rates, heat, light and power would add another £50 weekly.

- Winston found a bankrupt knitwear business in the Midlands whose machines and ancillary equipment were up for auction. In the event, all the partners went to the auction and picked up five machines and allied equipment for £4,000. Winston also found a wholesaler who could supply wool and other yarns competitively. Winston's best estimate was that, on average, the raw materials cost for a garment would be £20, if quality was important, which all said it was. But then there was the cost of labour and overheads, etc.

- Mr Williams said he knew of some farmworkers' wives who'd probably be keen to work for the business as machine operatives – if they could be trained up – at about £3.50 per hour. The average time it took said Winston to make a garment by hand was four hours.

- Pat and Sarah did some market research work in Westbridge and district. The most similar types of product to the ones Winston was keen to design were being sold by Briony's Boutique at the other end of the High Street. Sold as 'one-offs', sweaters were retailing at £85–£95, V-necked pullovers at £60–£70, and cardigans at £75–£99. Two national multiples were selling a range of garments of a similar appearance, but manufactured entirely of man-made fibres at prices some £15 cheaper per type than Briony's; they were also mass-produced, not unique models.

- There were three other retail outlets which appeared to sell garments similar to Winston's design concept – one relied on occasional supplies from home-workers and the other two were addressing the 'down market' end, with prices at some £50 for sweaters, £30 for V-neck pullovers and £45 for cardigans in unisex designs; these two were observed by Pat and Sarah to be doing most business locally.

- Rather ominously, a sign over an empty shop by the town-centre cross announced: Acquired By Highland Fashionwear Limited.

Local advertising rates are:

- Display advertisements Westbridge Gazette: £3.80 per column centimetre; circulation: 45,000; Westbridge Freemail (a free advertising weekly): £2.99 per column centimetre; circulation: 22,000; Radio Western: £350 for 30 15-second 'plugs' per week (outside of peak listening times) plus £100 to make commercial.

  (All other rates are as for your own locality.)

ASSIGNMENTS

In groups of three or four, study the above case study carefully. Where prices are not given for items you wish to know, assume them to be at the costs existing in your locality.

1 On the basis of the information provided by the case study, plus any other current prices/costs relevant to it taken from your own locality, devise a marketing/business plan which you think most likely to prove successful in your first year of trading. The marketing aspects of your plan should take into account:

  • Fixing the retail sales price of the three garments you will make – sweater, V-neck pullover and cardigan – bearing in mind the development, production, promotional and overhead costs to be born.
  • What production capacity your workshop will have a) initially, and b) after a period of one year's trading.
  • What the local competition is likely to do once you enter the market.
  • What sort of image you will give your business and its products, and who will be your targeted customers.
  • How your human resources will be organised.
  • What amount of profit before tax you will need to secure in order to cover all operational costs, loan servicing and a suitable return on the partners' investments.

2 Assuming your business survives Year 1 and is successful, the second part of your marketing/business plan should consider how best you might seek to expand the business in Years 2 and 3.
  For example, would it be worth selling as a wholesaler to the retail fashion trade beyond Westbridge?
  How could expansion best be financed?
  For this planning activity, assume that Westbridge is where you live and its surrounding districts are your surrounding districts.

3 Present your group's plans to your class in turn and decide which is most likely to succeed and why. In a general class discussion, identify and agree upon what the most important factors are in launching a small business successfully.

Off-shoot activities

As part of the wider issues addressed by this case study, make a point of finding out about:

  • The legal procedures for establishing a business partnership.
  • The current costs of securing a business loan for a clearing bank.
  • The various current advertising charges in your local media which a small retailer might use.
  • How a business plan seeks to control its monthly cash flow.
  • What tax bills The Tops Shop would face.

CASE STUDY 2

'A Mars a Day'

Clever tactics and famous slogan boost sales of the black-wrapped product born in small Slough factory

Millions of Mars a day add up to healthy anniversary

The Mars bar is still thriving after 60 years. **Nicholas Watt** *reports on a success story that defies the laws of marketing*

BRITAIN'S most enduring nibble has reached its 60th anniversary. The Mars bar, chewed by children and adults alike, was launched with little fanfare from a one-room factory in Slough, Berkshire, in August 1932.

Since then Mars has defied all the laws of marketing. The caramel and nougat filling has not changed; the bar's weight has remained virtually the same at just over 60 grammes; and its black wrapping has resisted the hands of meddlesome marketing men.

The strategy has remained simple: to sell the chocolate from as many outlets as possible. This has been underlined by one of the most successful, and certainly the simplest, of advertising slogans. 'A Mars a day helps you work, rest and play,' runs the ditty launched in 1959.

It is not always a comfortable ride. Kit Kat outsells the Mars bar by £60 million. In 1991 Kit Kat's sales were worth £190 million compared with £130 million for Mars bars.

Last year food watchdogs, led by Action and Information on Sugars (AIS), tried to ban the Mars slogan on the basis that there was no scientific proof that chewing chocolate was of any benefit

Jack Winkler, of AIS, said: 'There is no scientific evidence whatsoever that Mars makes any positive contribution to working, resting or playing.' After a 14-month deliberation the Independent Television Commission ruled in favour of the slogan.

Alan Mitchell, editor of *Marketing,* said yesterday that the Mars strategy has been brilliant. 'They think very carefully and in the long term. For example, they carried out three years of tests before launching Mars ice cream in 1989. This allowed the company to set up their own manufacturing technique that was uncopyable.

'Mars also maintain constant awareness by sponsoring key events such as the London Marathon, and supporting the British Olympic team in Barcelona.'

Mars is working on an ambitious plan to follow the Japanese example of selling confectionery from public vending machines. Mr Mitchell said: 'This would give Mars control of distribution and would mean that the product would be available 24 hours a day.'

What do the food experts think of the bar? Keith Floyd, the television cook, said: 'I have been eating Mars bars since as long as I can remember. I always keep them in the fridge in quarter inch slices which I eat with crunchy sour apples.

'Mars is one of the few things that is so quintessentially British, like HP Sauce and Bird's Eye. When I was once in real trouble in my restaurant I melted down a Mars bar and poured it on to ice cream. The customers were delighted.'

Mars was launched in Britain by the American entrepreneur, Forrest E. Mars senior, after his father, Frank gave him $50,000 and the foreign rights to the Milky Way. Frank had launched Milky Way in America in the 1920s after his son suggested that he should put a chocolate-malted drink in a candy bar. Forrest Mars senior was attracted by Britain's reputation for devouring chocolate which was fed by a line of manufacturers, including

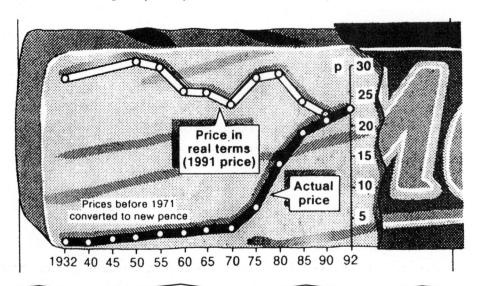

Rowntrees, Terry's and Cadburys.

The British start was relatively modest, with the factory in Slough employing 12 people. Within a year that had shot up to 100, and in the first year two million bars were sold. That was followed by a British version of the Milky Way in 1935 and Maltesers in 1937. Those two were temporarily stopped during the war, but production of the Mars bars continued.

Today the Mars company has 18 per cent of all confectionery sales in Britain. The factory, which is still based in Slough, produces three million Mars bars a day. Mars does not sell just chocolate. Its other brands include Uncle Ben's rice and Whiskas and Pedigree pet food.

The Slough factory is the British side of a worldwide operation which has annual sales of $12 billion. Mars Inc is based in the Washington suburb of McLean, in Virginia, where Forrest Mars senior's two sons share the role of chief executive.

The family is highly secretive and shuns contact with the media. According to *Forbes* magazine the family is worth $12.5 billion, making it the fifth richest family in the world.

Mars received its most impressive accolade when the *Financial Times* suggested that the bar was 'a currency of our time'.

The paper's Lombard column said the Mars bar was a long-established basket of staple commodities, which include cocoa, vegetable fats, milk solids and sugar. It was also a much more reliable unit of account than gold, which is prone to speculation.

Times Newspapers Limited 1992
Reproduced by courtesy of Times Newspapers plc.

DISCUSSION TOPICS

PC
3.2.1
3.3.3
3.3.4

1 To what do you put down the enduring success of the Mars bar as a snack?

2 Do you think that the public would buy Mars bars from vending machines? If so, why? If not, why not?

3 What point is Nicholas Watt making when he refers to Mars bars as 'a much more reliable unit of account than gold'?

4 To what extent does the article satisfactorily explain the success of the Mars bar? Are there any other factors you can think of from your own experience – for example, having to do with consumer buying behaviour?

5 How do you see the future of the Mars bar over the next ten years?

6 What conclusions do you draw from the graph of Mars bar prices?

ACTIVITIES

PC
3.3.3

1 In about 300 words, write a summary of what you understand to be the main strands of the Mars marketing plan since 1932.

2 Having first undertaken your local researches into the sale of Mars bars through various outlets, devise a sales promotion plan as follows:

Aims:

– To increase the local sales of Mars bars by 10 per cent over eight weeks in local outlets.

– To maintain the increase for the subsequent two months.

Budget: £3,500

Pricing strategy:

– Discounts to established customers:

3–7 per cent on purchases depending on volume for the promotional period.

– Discounts to new customers:

5–10 per cent on normal RRP less 30 per cent for promotional period for orders as follows:

50–100 bars:	5 per cent
100–250 bars:	7.5 per cent
250–500 bars:	10 per cent

Your sales promotion plan should include details of:

- sales communications to a) existing customers, b) new customers;
- outline of design concept for point-of-sale material;
- a rationale for the expenditure of the £3,500;
- a statement on pricing policy.

PC
3.1.1
3.1.2
3.1.4
3.1.5
3.2.1
3.2.4

CASE STUDY: 3

Consumer Characteristics and Trends

'Our Five-Year Plan!'

In groups of three or four, first study the following scenario carefully, and then carry out the activities detailed:

Scenario

Your class (and your year in your Department) have been selected for an in-depth study of consumer characteristics and trends being undertaken for a multinational company – Transglobal Incorporated – which is planning to open in the UK a string of High Street departmental stores which cater exclusively for people in the 15–25 age range.

The stores will be structured on identical lines, having these departments:

- **Clothing and Footwear**
- **Sports and Leisure**
- **Music**
- **Holidays**
- **Education and Training**
- **Bodycare**
- **'Wheels' (bikes and motor-bikes)**
- **Pastimes and Gifts (including books and videos)**
- **'Nico's' – a fast food cafeteria and meeting-place**

Your group has been briefed to carry out a survey of the tastes, buying characteristics and trends which people **in your current age range** are likely to possess **in three to five years' time** (which is when the stores will be going 'on stream' and be progressively ready to open).

Global's commission to which you are working therefore requires you to research (in your class and department) into the following aspects of your co-students' current life styles and what they are most likely to develop into during the coming 3–5 years:

- **Clothing**: for work/leisure/party-going/informal socialising etc.

- **Footwear**: for work/leisure/dancing/training/sport etc.
- **Sports and Leisure**: what main activities will be popular and what sort of kit and equipment will be in demand
- **Music**: what types of music will be in fashion, and what sort of equipment will be used to relay it
- **Holidays**: what kind of holidays and breaks the target consumers will want and where, and how they will pay for them
- **Education and Training**: what types of education and training programmes will be on offer and what sort of learning materials, personal equipment etc. will prove to be in demand to support them
- **Bodycare**: what kinds of toiletries, cosmetics, body treatments, equipment and devices will be popular and enjoy a widespread demand
- **'Wheels'**: what sort of transport consumers in the age-range will wish to buy – for work, social and domestic purposes. (*Note*: Global are considering whether or not to include a small car department in their out-of-town stores.)
- **Pastimes and Gifts**: what sort of hobbies, pastimes and spare-time activities the target consumers will follow, and thus what sort of items this department should stock.
- **'Nico's'**: what sort of products the cafeteria should sell and what decor it should have

Research guide-lines

Your group's research should take the following factors into consideration:

- how your age range differs in needs, wants, pursuits and tastes etc. from younger–older age ranges
- what contrasts and what similarities in goods (or services) purchased in Global's stores will arise from the differences in gender of your age range
- how likely changes in life-style will alter the type and range of items stocked in 3–5 years' time
- what impact there will be on the stores' decor, image and stocks for sale resulting from: 'green'/environmental issues, the conscience and sense of social needs the targeted consumers will possess (e.g. cosmetics not tested on animals), goods for sale which exploit poor, Third World economies (e.g. hand-made goods requiring many hours of skilled labour being sold 'dirt-cheap').
- what sort of disposable income the targeted age-range will have to spend, and how this will affect the prices of the goods/services for sale and what policy the stores should adopt in this area
- what areas of consumer spending in the age range are likely to increase and what decrease

ACTIVITIES

1 In a group meeting discuss and decide how you will tackle the overall assignment. Think about allocating activities among group members fairly and effectively.

2 Design a questionnaire or interview set of questions which will help you to obtain the data you need.

> 3 Find out what other sources of data (e.g. secondary) are available which you can tap into for your report.
>
> 4 Present your findings as a group oral presentation of 15–20 minutes and support it with a suitably designed text-processed hand-out.
>
> 5 Decide which group gave the best presentation and why.

IDEAS FOR PROJECTS

PC
3.1.1

1 Select **one** of the following:

The Institute of Practitioners in Advertising

The Advertising Standards Authority

The Independent Television Commission

The Market Research Society

The Institute of Marketing

Carry out on your own initiative research to find out what the organisation was set up to accomplish, and how its work impacts upon marketing. Design a factsheet on its activities for circulation among your class.

PC
3.1.1

2 Find out which on-line market research databases are available in the UK and how they are used by researchers.

PC
3.3.1

3 Choose a charitable organisation which is active in your locality and arrange to interview its officers to obtain a closer understanding of its mission. Then, devise a marketing plan for the office in your area for one to two years. If possible, discuss your plan with the charity's officers for feedback on its validity.

PC
3.1.4

4 In a group of two or three, examine the magazines in each of these magazine groupings:

Group A: *Company Magazine, Options, New Woman, Prima, Me, Chat, Annabel, Cosmopolitan, She.*

Group B: *Woman, Woman's Realm, Woman's Weekly, Woman's Own.*

Group C: *Elle, Vanity Fair, Harpers & Queen, Tatler.*

Decide which age-range and which socio-economic grouping each appeals to (A B C/l C/2 D E) and devise a chart which would be useful to an advertising agency wishing to purchase space.

PC
3.2.1
3.1.4

5 Examine the following daily newspapers in a group of two or three:

Today, Daily Star, Daily Mirror, Sun, Express.

Decide whether they all appeal to the same type of readership, or if not, which different groups might purchase which paper. Justify your conclusions in a class presentation.

PC
3.3.3
3.3.4

6 At present the sales of satellite TV dishes and decoders are at the commencement of the growth phase in their life cycle.

For this project, assume that two or three of you are responsible for the marketing function of Home TV, a retailing chain with five stores in your district. You have been given a budget of £8,000 to promote the sale of the dish and decoder you sell at most profit (choose one of the popular current models). Devise an advertising/promotional campaign which you think would boost sales in your five outlets over the coming 12 months. First research into your local market, then present your campaign strategy (with specimen advertisements etc.) to your class for them to evaluate. Give a rationale for your strategy in your presentation.

7 In a group of two or three arrange to visit in your locality a representative of each of these types of business: PC 3.2.2

a A shop selling teenage clothes/fashions

b A building society branch

c An estate agent

d A carpet retailer

Find out what strategies and actions each took to overcome the decline in demand caused by the last recession. Present your findings in an oral presentation to your class.

8 In groups of three or four, choose one of these products: PC 3.3.2

a a cotton crew-neck sweatshirt with the logo/crest of your school/college/company on it:

bought-in price: £8.95

colours: light blue, pillar-box red, orange, bright green and sunshine yellow.

b a duffle-bag made of vinyl with a fabric outer covering and draw-string closure/shoulder strap – useful for carrying books, sports kit etc; dimensions – about 50 cm high and 35 cm in diameter:

bought-in price: £6.50

colours: black, pine green, tartan, honey.

c a plastic boxed students' study kit containing:

six inch plastic ruler, protractor, compasses, HB pencil, red and blue ballpoint pens, fountain pen, liquid paper (water-based), ink-erasing pencil, rubber eraser, bookmark, staple gun (junior size) and standard file-paper hole punch:

bought-in price: £ 3.25

box colours: royal blue, bottle green, white, pink.

The profit on all sales (after operational costs have been deducted) will go to a Third World children's charity and the task of your group is to devise a marketing plan to sell as many of the products of your choice within the next eight weeks. Produce the plan you think will optimise profits while minimising costs, present your plan to your class for a critical evaluation. Then decide whether you wish to market such a product for real to raise money for charity in your college, school or firm. PC 3.3.2

Element 3.1 Analyse market research

Scenario

You are one of a group of four or five students who, for the purposes of this activity are to role-play a research team working for a local market research company called **Surveypros Limited**. Your company and your team have been commissioned to undertake a market research project on unemployment in your city/town/council district. The organisation which has given you the commission is a newly-formed charity called Workaid. The mission of **Workaid** is to channel its funds into helping unemployed people (who meet their criteria) to find full-time employment.

As the charity has only recently opened a branch in your area, it wishes you to carry out the following research brief:

1 To obtain accurate and up-to-date information on the nature of local unemployment in terms of:

   ● gender, age, and total of unemployed people over a period spanning: the past month, quarter and year.

   ● the extent and duration of unemployment in age groups spanning 16–25, 25–35, 35–45, 45–55, 55–65 ages

2 Information regarding the local trends in unemployment, and in particular, trends likely in the coming 12 months.

3 Information regarding those industrial, commercial, public sector areas which are a) most and b) least likely to see an upturn in employment in the coming:

   a six months

   b year

   c five years.

4 the views of a sample of unemployed people

   a of less than six months unemployment

   b of over a year's unemployment

   on the support locally available to them and what changes, additions or discontinuations they would like to see in the ways in which they are helped to find jobs.

5 the views and forecasts of organisations like:

   the Training & Enterprise Council, County Planning Department, Job Centres on the most likely areas where growth will occur and what training programmes for unemployed people are available locally to assist unemployed people to acquire skills which are most likely to be in demand over the coming two to three years.

Research objectives

Your research objectives are:

1 to secure data from local secondary sources to satisfy the informational requirements of Workaid

2 to devise a survey method which will obtain the responses asked for in 4 and 5 above

Note: your research methods should demonstrate a cost-effective use of time, speed, accuracy, ease of use and accessibility of your samples and sources.

Presentation of evidence
Your research should be presented in a suitable report form which includes the following sections:

a a preliminary section detailing your research methodology which communicates the fact that your research is up-to-date, accurate and reliable

b a description of the research methods used

c a clear analysis of the findings of your research which satisfy the criteria required by Workaid

d a summary of your major findings

e your recommendations as to:

- which groupings within the unemployed population in your locality Workaid should target as being most likely to secure employment with their support

- which employers Workaid should seek to liaise with since they will provide most employment opportunities over the coming 12 months.

- what local training programmes Workaid should support financially as being those most likely to lead to full-time employment in the short term

Methods of producing evidence

Produce your evidence in the form of a word-processed report which includes illustrative data of a graphical nature (charts, graphs etc) and which shows tables of data which communicate via number.

Performance criteria covered

3.1.1, 3.1.2, 3.1.3, 3.1.4, 3.1.5

Core skills Level 3

Communication
3.1.1, 3.1.2, 3.1.3, 3.1.4, 3.2.1, 3.2.2, 3.2.3, 3.2.4, 3.3.1, 3.3.2, 3.3.3, 3.4.1, 3.4.2, 3.4.3

Information technology
3.1.1–3.1.7, 3.2.1–3.2.7, 3.3.1–3.3.5

Application of number
3.1.1–3.1.6, 3.3.1–3.3.6

Element 3.2 Use consumer trends to forecast sales

Either individually or as one of a pair, select **one** of the following products or services:

- a middle-of-the-market UK-built family saloon motor-car (e.g. Ford, Rover, Nissan, etc)

- a personal computer (486 chip) suitable for home use

- a UK-marketed brand of mobile phone

- a micro-wave oven on sale nationally in the UK

- a brand of oven-ready foods (which just need microwave heating)

- an entry-level type of mortgage for first-time home-buyers

- a private, family health insurance plan

- a national package-tour operator marketing summer holidays to Greek islands

- a national chain of fast-food outlets (e.g. Macdonald's, Wendys, Burger King, Happy Eater etc.)

Your main task in this activity is to research into the consumer trends which will influence the growth (or decline) of the product's sales you have chosen to investigate. You will then be in a position to produce an informed forecast and prediction of the likely trends to be expected in the sale of the product in the next three to five years.

Research objectives

1 Having chosen your product or service, undertake an investigation of the characteristics of the consumers who form the core purchasers of the product or service, having regard to their demographic distribution, gender, tastes, life style, attitudes to environmental issues etc.

   You should also concentrate on the likely extent of their patterns of expenditure in the coming three to five years, given the probable economic scenario which will affect them.

   Your investigations should concentrate upon secondary sources of information, but you should also design a survey questionnaire to elicit suitable data from a sample of local consumers who are active purchasers in your selected field.

2 Next you should research into the economic and social trends which will impact upon the consumer group in your locality which forms the major consumer base for your selected product/service.

   Your research should concentrate on: emerging life styles, tastes, purchasing behaviour, employment trends, income and expenditure trends, likelihood of growth or decline in the major business and public sector organisations in your locality.

Set down your research notes in a suitable format and undertake a statistical analysis of your survey questionnaire(s).

Presentation of evidence

For the presentation of your market research data, you should simulate the following situation:

   You work as a senior market researcher for Datanalysis plc, and you have been commissioned by a major 'player' in your selected area (motor-cars, mortgages, holidays etc.) to aid the production of their forthcoming marketing plan (which will inform the organisation's three to five year corporate plan).

Your customer has asked you to present your findings in a well structured and presented briefing document which conveys its information logically, clearly, with immediacy, so that the generalists who form the board of directors may easily assimilate it.

To this end, you have been asked to present data in graphical and diagrammatic form whenever this is likely to be helpful.

Method of producing evidence

Produce your evidence in a suitably structured and formatted briefing paper. You may include as appropriate excerpts and extracts from source documents but must acknowledge them fully.

You should word-process your paper and should process your statistical data by means of a spreadsheet applications package. If possible, merge your wp and spreadsheet inputs into your single paper.

Performance criteria covered

3.2.1, 3.2.2, 3.3.3, 3.3.4

Core skills Level 3

Communication
3.1.1–3.1.4, 3.2.1–3.2.4, 3.3.1–3.3.3, 3.4.1, 3.4.2, 3.4.3

Information technology
3.1.1–3.1.7, 3.2.1–3.2.7, 3.3.1–3.3.5, 3.5.1

Element 3.3 Investigate marketing activities

ACTIVITY 1

As a member of a group of three or four students, select two well-known, competing brands from one of the following categories of product:

washing powder

motor-cycles

petrol

perfume/toilet water

cross-trainers

snack-bars

lager beer

Research objectives

Your research objectives are to:

1 investigate the ways in which each product is marketed having particular regard to: size of sales, market share, product/brand image, customer acceptance/brand loyalty, current probable position in its life cycle.

2 Analyse the approach taken to the marketing mix for both in terms of: price, promotion, place and product positioning

3 Evaluate the respective approaches taken to advertising, promoting and merchandising the products

4 Investigate the after-sales, customer service provisions relating to either product

5 Review the marketing of the products in terms of: how honest information about them is and how fairly and straightforwardly they are promoted.

Presentation of evidence

Present your evidence as a 10–15 minute illustrated oral presentation to your class.

Method of presentation

Ensure that each member of your group undertakes a fair share of the researching and presenting activities. With your presentation, provide your teacher with a short report detailing how you conducted your researches, and produce at least three OHP foils and at least two hand-outs to support your presentation.

ACTIVITY 2

In pairs, select a pop/rock group band which formerly had songs in the Top Twenty, but which has now disappeared from view. Consider the band and its music as a product, and research into it in terms of the product life cycle it enjoyed.

You should refer to the Product Life Cycle Chart on page 249 and seek to explain the way in which the band's popularity and music changed during each phase of its life-cycle. Also, you should provide a rationale to explain why its life in the entertainment world came to an end.

By contrast, you should select a band which has survived over many years (The Rolling Stones, Queen, Status Quo, The Who etc.) and provide your rationale on the tactics it employed to extend its product life cycle as expressed in its music.

Presentation of evidence

Present your evidence as an oral – and audio if you can obtain music tracks – presentation to your class of 10–15 minutes. Your presentation should ensure that both students play an equal part in its research and delivery.

ACTIVITY 3

In groups of three or four students, select **one** of the following products or services:

- timeshare purchase of a holiday apartment
- the purchase of life insurance

- the sale of cosmetics and perfumes

- advertising commercials on independent television

- second-hand cars

- mail-order and telltale products

Research objectives

Investigate the codes of practice, statutes and local government by-laws and agencies which exist to ensure that the consumer is protected from unethical 'sharp' practices from some sellers of such products. Find out also what avenues for redress are open to duped consumers.

Make contact with three to five sales organisations and survey a sample of its sales personnel on what they see as the content of an ethical sales code which should underpin all consumer-based selling.

Presentation of evidence

Part 1
Arrange to tape-record a 10–15 minute discussion in which your group airs the issues concerning honest, ethical selling of the product you chose, and the relevant legal powers which aim to protect the consumer. Include advice which consumers should heed when purchasing a product in your chosen sector.

Part 2
Using the information you gleaned from your contact with selling organisations, draw up a code of practice for sales personnel and their employing companies which would reassure consumers purchasing their products or services.

Performance criteria covered

3.3.1, 3.3.2, 3.3.3, 3.3.4, 3.3.5

Core skills Level 3

Communication
3.1–3.4, 3.3.1–3.3.3

Information technology
3.1.1–3.1.6

Application of number
3.1.1, 3.1.2, 3.1.4, 3.1.5, 3.1.6, 3.3.1, 3.3.2, 3.3.4, 3.3.5, 3.3.6

FURTHER SOURCES OF INFORMATION

Basic Marketing: Principles and Practice, 3rd edn, T Cannon, Cassell Education, 1992. ISBN: 0 304 31673 3

Elements of Marketing, 2nd edn, A R Morden, DP Publications, 1991. ISBN: 1 870 941 70 5

The Fundamentals of Marketing Practice, 2nd edn, J Wilmhurst, Butterworth Heinemann, 1984. ISBN: 0 7506 0433 6

Do-It-Yourself Marketing Research, 3rd edn, G Breen and A Blankenslip, McGraw Hill, 1989. ISBN: 0 07 00751 8

Effective Industrial Selling, M Macdonald and J Leppard, Heinemann, 1988. ISBN: 0 434 91264 6

The Principles And Practice of Selling, A Gillan, Butterworth Heinemann, 1982. ISBN: 0 7500 0109 4

Selling: Management & Practice, 3rd edn, P Allen, M & E Business Handbooks, 1989. ISBN: 0 7121 1027 5

Retail Management, 2nd edn, P Cox and P Brittain, M & E Business Handbooks, 1993. ISBN: 0 7121 1825 X

The Fundamentals of Advertising, J Wilmhurst, Butterworth Heinemann, 1988. ISBN: 0 7506 0250 3

The Marketing of Services, D Cowell, Butterworth Heinemann, 1984. ISBN: 0 434 90263 2

The Customer Service Planner, M Christopher, Butterworth Heinemann, 1992. ISBN: 0 7506 0149 3

The Practice of Advertising, 3rd edn, N Hart, Heinemann, 1990. ISBN: 0 434 90796 0

Public Relations, 3rd edn, F Jefkins, M & E Business Handbooks, 1988. ISBN: 0 7121 1026 7

The Marketing Dictionary, 4th edn, N Hart and J Stapleton, Butterworth Heinemann, 1992. ISBN: 0 7506 0208 2

Macmillan Dictionary of Retailing, S Baron, B Davies, D Swindley, Macmillan, 1991. ISBN: 0 333 56499 9

Macmillan Dictionary of Marketing & Advertising, 2nd edn, M J Baker, Macmillan, 1990. ISBN: 0 333 51605 2

Getting It Right the Second Time (Marketing Case Histories), M Gershman, Mercury Books, 1991. ISBN: 1 85251 160 5

HUMAN RESOURCES

Element 4.1
Investigate human resourcing

Element 4.2
Investigate job roles in organisational structures

Element 4.3
Evaluate job applications and interviews

Pages

Element 4.1: Investigate human resourcing   297–309, 361–93

Performance criteria

1	responsibilities in human resourcing are explained	297–309
2	systems for employee relations are described	297–309, 370–93
3	training and development opportunities are identified	308–10
4	legal requirements regulating employment practices are explained	361–70
5	types of redress available to employees when legislation is not upheld are described	361–70
6	human resource management which improves business performance is identified	370–93

Range: **Human resourcing:** recruitment, retention, performance, termination; health and safety; employee representation and consultation; training and professional development   297–309

         Employee relations: representation, consultation; trade unions; staff organisations; multi-skilling; team work   370–93

         Training and development: vocational qualifications; professional qualifications   308–10

         Legal requirements: conditions of employment, individual rights, equal opportunities, equal pay, health and safety at work   361–70

         Types of redress: industrial tribunal, civil legal action   361–70

         Business performance: productivity; level of absenteeism; quality of service; profit   297–309

Evidence indicators: A report on one business organisation identifying how its human resource management is improving the performance of the business. Evidence should demonstrate understanding of the implications of the range dimensions in relation to the element. The unit test will confirm the candidate's coverage of range.

Element 4.2: Investigate job roles in organisational structures

Performance criteria

1	organisational structures in different types of business organisations are described	See Unit 1
2	job roles within structures are described	See Unit 1
3	purposes of job descriptions are explained and examples are produced	314–18
4	purposes of person specifications are explained and examples are produced	314–18

Range: **Types of business organisation:** sole trader, partnership, co-operative, franchise, private limited company, public limited company, public corporation   See Unit 1

         Structures: hierarchical, flat; centralised, devolved; static, dynamic   See Unit 1

         Job roles: director, manager, team member   See Unit 1

         Job description: job title, position in the organisational structure, responsibilities, competences   314–18

         Person specification: personal attributes and achievements, qualifications, experience   314–18

Purposes: to match applicants with vacancies; to match business objectives to jobs;
to train and develop job holders   314–18

Evidence indicators: Prepare job descriptions and person specifications for two different roles in two different structures showing how different structures may influence the job descriptions. Evidence should demonstrate understanding of the implications of the range dimensions in relation to the element. The unit test will confirm the candidate's coverage of range.

Element 4.3: Evaluate job applications and interviews   318–50

Performance criteria

1 recruitment procedures are identified   312–13, 344
2 letters of application are evaluated for clarity and quality of presentation   348–50
3 curriculum vitae are evaluated for clarity and quality of presentation   325
4 interviewer techniques are practised and appraised   327–47
5 interviewee techniques are practised and appraised   396–9
6 legal and ethical obligations in recruitment are explained   310–12, 351–6

Range: **Recruitment procedures:** application methods, selection methods   318–27

Interview techniques: preparation, assertiveness, body language, framing questions,
listening   327–47

Legal obligations: equal opportunities, contract of employment   351–6, 361–70

Ethical obligations: honesty, objectivity   400–3

Evidence indicators: Two application letters and two curriculum vitae produced by the candidate, at least one handwritten and others using IT with a judgement of the strengths and weaknesses of the content, clarity and quality of presentations. Also appraisals of the interviewee and interviewer in two mock or real interviews. Evidence should demonstrate understanding of the implications of the range dimensions in relation to the element. The unit test will confirm the candidate's coverage of range.

To say that an organisation's most precious resource is its workforce has become a truism today, and in times of widespread redundancy, some might consider the concept cynically. However, the difference between an organisation which manages its human resources well and one that does not invariably becomes evident, in a wide range of performance indicators – such as increasing revenue, innovative product development, stable levels of staff turnover, wider margins of profitability and so on. This is because well-motivated and well-treated staff harness energies and enthusiasms which attain corporate goals while dispirited and demoralised employees don't.

This is why anyone who is a manager in training needs to work hard to develop the expertise and skills needed for effective human resource management. After all, the computer that can emulate the complexities of the human brain and interpersonal behaviour isn't yet on the drawing board!

This Unit examines in detail the following aspects of human resources in organisations:

- the major facets of the personnel function
- organisational functions and structures
- manpower planning and skills auditing
- the recruitment and induction of employees
- personnel specifications and job descriptions
- recruitment advertising
- personnel selection interviews
- contracts of employment
- appraisal systems
- grievance, disciplinary, dismissal and redundancy procedures
- ACAS and industrial relations
- leadership, motivation and management of staff
- negotiating and decision-making techniques
- managing conflict and stress
- self-management and self-organisation techniques
- organisational groups and team-working

PEOPLE: THE ULTIMATE RESOURCE

PC
4.1.1

'An organisation's most precious asset is its people.'

A well-worn observation, which nevertheless bears repeating, is that it is not the bricks and mortar, not the factory machines, not the office systems and equipment and not the availability of money which ensure an organisation's success or failure, it is the ability, determination and morale of its people.

Over the past one hundred and fifty years, a number of terms and descriptors have been used as labels for the people who work in organisations – from labour and hands to staff and personnel. Of all these, the term human resources is probably the happiest and most accurate, since it acknowledges the contributions made by people working at every level in the organisation as a resource which costs money to provide, which is finite, and which should therefore be employed wisely. It is also a term which avoids overtones of us-ness and them-ness, which sometimes characterise poor industrial relations.

This Unit has adopted the title Human Resources since it is now widely used in organisations, not only as a collective term for the workforce, but also to embrace many of the management and administrative activities which support employees as they go about their work, as in 'human resources management'. The other term widely in use is, of course, 'the personnel function'. Of the two perhaps human resource management has a broader meaning, while 'personnel' describes the activities of the department or unit which discharges the responsibilities set out below. For the purpose of this Unit, human resources and personnel take on the same meaning.

THE PERSONNEL FUNCTION

PC
4.1.1
4.1.6

In many ways, the personnel function in organisations operates across a kind of 'cradle-to-grave' spectrum. It certainly spans the progression of employees from recruitment to retirement and beyond, in the management of company pension schemes and involvement in company social activities.

The following checklist identifies the major responsibilities of the personnel function in organisations:

THE PERSONNEL FUNCTION EMBRACES:

Manpower planning and skills auditing

Monitoring the organisation's human resource needs and providing for them; this function involves manpower planning, auditing the skills and expertise of the workforce and designing staff development programmes for existing employees.

Recruitment and personnel selection

Maintaining a recruitment policy which ensures a continuity of supply of personnel in all arms of the business so as to meet human resource needs caused by retirement, resignations, promotions, maternity leave, changing organisational activities and so on.

Staff training and development

Once on the payroll, all staff need to be included in a rolling programme of personal development in order to grow and to maintain their job interest; moreover, the organisation constantly needs to ensure that its workforce is up to the challenges of change – in the market-place, in technology, in terms of foreign competition, in product development and so on – if it is to survive.

Staff appraisal and performance review

Many organisations relate employees' pay to their performance in the job, and so personnel departments are required to devise and maintain systems which appraise every member of staff at least once a year and to relate such appraisals to carefully structured pay scales and bonus tables.

Industrial relations

It generally falls to the personnel department to coordinate on behalf of the board of directors company policy on pay and conditions of service. These are regularly updated in rounds of negotiations with the trade unions and associations recognised by the company and its industry. In addition, personnel will design and implement procedures for handling complaints and grievances from employees and also any disciplinary measures deemed necessary and warranted by management. It will also handle issues like voluntary and involuntary redundancy and early retirement schemes, as well as the termination of contracts of employment. In this context, personnel staff need to be expert in matters of industrial and employment law.

Employment conditions analysis

In order to sustain a competitive position in the market for employees, personnel managers need to obtain regular analyses of local and national labour market trends.
The 'rate for the job' – what employers will pay and employees accept in any recruitment process – is continuously changing due to supply and demand, boom or recession, specific local circumstances, like the winning of a massive government contract by a single engineering firm and so on.
Thus personnel managers need to keep fully abreast of employment trends and developments, like government subsidised youth training schemes, in order to ensure that recruitment advertisements are effective and that pay scales and packages are attractive enough to ensure that key personnel are happy and stay with the company or public service organisation.

Employee welfare

All enlightened organisations extend the personnel function to include support for the social and recreational needs of the workforce. Thus many personnel departments are responsible for organising outings – to the theatre, pop-concert or sports event – at subsidised prices; for the running of a works social club and allied sports facilities for retired employees, which may include Christmas parties and so on. The contribution of such welfare services to staff morale should not be underestimated. Moreover, some organisations will support their employee associations in helping aged former employees fallen on hard times through the setting up of trust funds, etc.

Pensions administration

It usually falls to the personnel department in an organisation to manage the firm's pensions programme. Normally the actual payment of pensions and maintenance of records is undertaken by the pensions company which holds the contract to manage a company's scheme – in much the same way as a bank or chartered accounting partnership will manage a company's payroll for a set fee.

In many organisations a joint body representing both employers and employees acts as a watchdog to ensure that pension payments in and out of the scheme are made within the law. Recent cases of gross misappropriation of pension funds are likely to bring about changes in the law and devolve more responsibility on to the personnel function.

HUMAN RESOURCING: OVERVIEW

Human resourcing may be viewed as a process very much like marketing, and just as important. Like marketing, human resourcing is concerned as much with the future as the present. It works, not only to ensure that the organisation's workforce is able to meet its current goals and objectives, but – by implementing far-sighted planning, staff development and recruitment policies – it is also able to do so in three to five years' time.

This section, therefore, provides an introductory overview to Unit 4 which emphasises the systematic approach taken by effective human resource managers to ensure that their organisations are never let down by any of the situations listed in the following table.

CONSEQUENCES OF POOR HUMAN RELATIONS MANAGEMENT

- manpower shortages in key/ specialist areas
- a workforce whose skills lie at the 'trailing' as opposed to 'leading' edge of the technology they work with
- an ageing and elderly workforce resulting from a failure to introduce 'new blood' posts, and to monitor the distribution curve of employees' ages
- output and continuity of operations hampered and diminished by high levels of absenteeism or labour turnover
- a poor morale resulting from adversarial employee relations, 'MI6' management cultures or a lack of effective employee representation/consultation systems
- adverse publicity arising from media reporting of industrial tribunal awards on upheld unfair/constructive dismissal complaints etc.

Failure in human resources management in areas such as those indicated above leads inevitably to the following:

- the organisation being overtaken by its competition
- the research, design, production and servicing of its products or services becoming obsolescent in terms of the technology employed and of poor quality in terms of design, build and eventual use
- a decline in overall productivity and profit levels

and ultimately to:

- take-over, buy-out, asset-stripping or bankruptcy

This being the case, intelligent company directors and senior executives go to great lengths to anticipate the dangers of poor human resource management and use these policies and practices to make quite sure that their staff – truly their greatest asset – is maintained at a peak of effectiveness and efficiency:

■ Recruitment

Before anyone is recruited to a given post, it will be carefully analysed by expert managers who carry out these tasks:

Job Analysis: Have the job requirements changed since the post was last advertised? If so, how?

How do the changes impact upon the person specification and job description to be drawn up (see pages 314–18)?

Person Specification: How accurately does this identify and detail the abilities, skills and personality traits needed in the ideal applicant? If it is an existing specification, how does it need changing?

Job Description: Is this still current and up to date? If not, what changes need to be made in the light of evolved: technology, work practices, company policy etc?

Interviewing Procedures: Who will select candidates' long-list/short-list (in-house personnel department or recruitment agency?)

Who will interview? Who will chair panel?

Who will 'orchestrate' the selection questions?

■ Induction process

A frequently quoted saying among engineers is 'Start right, stay right!'. and this is certainly true of an organisation's induction procedures (see also pages 354–5), which should include those listed in the table.

INDUCTION PROCEDURES

- A tutor-led study and discussion of the organisation's policies and procedures on:
- Conditions of service
- Training and development
- Health and safety at work
- Grievance and disciplinary procedures
- Trade unions recognised by management
- Equal opportunities/pay policies
- Sickness reporting procedures etc.
- Emergency evacuation procedures

New employees should also be given a tour of that part of the offices, factory, or campus in which they will normally work (and a map if appropriate) and should be introduced to their immediate line manager and co-workers. Note that most large organisations provide summaries, brochures and legally required data sheets in an induction pack or binder which the new employee retains. Also, some of the induction components indicated above have to be communicated by law – such as the HASAW and emergency evacuation procedures – and these have to be displayed in readily available manuals and on bulletin boards throughout the organisation.

LEGAL REQUIREMENTS AND EMPLOYEE RELATIONS

As a result of the Employment and Employment Protection Acts of 1975, 1978, 1980 and 1982 (see pages 361–5) and the Trade Union Reform and Employment Rights Act of 1993, the whole area of employment relations is extensively underpinned by statutory rights and obligations on the parts of both employers and employees. The 1993 Act includes these notable consolidating features:

- written employment particulars – place of work, any collective agreements in place, working outside the UK – must be given to a new employee within 2 months instead of 13 weeks
- maternity leave rights and protection from dismissal arising from maternity leave have been strengthened
- employees are increasingly protected from unfair dismissal as a result of their involvement in HASAW activities
- employees' rights to join the trade union of their choice have been strengthened, and their consent must be obtained before any trade union subscriptions are deducted from their pay
- trade unions must now seek a mandate for a strike by conducting a fully-postal ballot and give employers 7 days' notice of strike action
- unlawful organised industrial action can now be legally restrained by any individual deprived of goods or services as a result of it
- ACAS is no longer required to encourage collective bargaining (by which an employer negotiates with a trade union to agree a 'collective' agreement binding upon all the union's members).

■ Collective bargaining

Historically, many employers have preferred to negotiate on pay and conditions with the trade union(s) it recognised on the basis that such agreements were then universally binding upon all its employees. Collective bargaining covering specific time-spans (of, say, 1–3 years) has the attractions of providing stability and general acceptance, along with minimising the likelihood of strikes or industrial action during the period of the agreement. Thus continuity of production or operations can be virtually guaranteed.

■ Trade union representatives and consultation

Since good employer–trade union relations are generally also good for business, most enlightened employers consult and involve trade union shop stewards, convenors or otherwise titled employee representatives as a matter of routine. For instance, trade union representatives are likely to be members of an organisation's:

Health and Safety Committee

Pensions Committee (as a trustee)

Employee Social and Welfare Committee

Quality Council

Staff Development Advisory Committee

Equal Opportunities Committee

Disciplinary and Grievance Procedure Administrative Groups

It is also worth noting that, in Germany, employees are, by law, entitled to representation on a company's board of directors. In addition to formalised consultation and representation as indicated above, trade union representatives are also often called in to confidential meetings of senior managements whenever initiatives or changes in policy or practices are being considered. The basis for this type of involvement is simple, but all too often ignored by some managements.

If the employees' trade union representatives are happy with a new development (and if they are respected by their co-members) then the workforce is most likely to follow their lead. And, most people, including trade union activists, are more likely to accept change and innovation if they are involved and consulted.

■ Reforms in trade union legislation

Trade union legislation over the past fifteen years has had the effect of outlawing the unofficial and wildcat strikes, and secondary and 'flying' picketing which characterised the confrontational industrial relations in the UK during the 1970s.

Also, the scandals in some unions of ballot-rigging over the past ten years or so have led to a much more rigorous (and fair) process which union executives have to follow in order to obtain a mandate for certain types of industrial action; and it is now illegal for unions to require a new employee to join a 'closed shop' trade union.

DISCUSSION TOPIC

The pendulum of 'industrial clout' of the 1970s, when the UK was paralysed by strikes and unofficial industrial action has swung far away from the days when trade union leaders held immense industrial and economic power – which was sometimes used to secure pay increases in excess of inflation (thus contributing to inflationary spirals)

Today, the number of per capita working days a year lost in the UK owing to strikes and allied industrial action is at an all-time low. Correspondingly, employees in many firms (as part of a labour market in which 3 million are long-term unemployed) are having to accept pay cuts in the annual pay round, work longer hours and accept eroded conditions of service. Would-be employees are also being required by many companies to work to fixed-term contracts of less than two years at a time, with the result that they sign away the employment rights (on redundancy pay and other employment protection rights they would receive after being in a post for more than two years).

Given this current scenario and historical background, what answers would you give to these questions:

Q Are the trade unions nowadays too weak to ensure that employees are fairly treated?

Q What do you see as the role in the future for trade unions?

GROUP ACTIVITIES

In pairs, undertake one of the following activities:

1 Arrange to interview a personnel manager of a large local organisation and, before your visit prepare a checklist of questions to ask him or her about the main tasks – routine and occasional – which the personnel department currently undertakes, and what its current preoccupations are, such as the impact of the 1993 Trade Union Reform and Employment Rights Act.

2 Similarly, arrange to interview a full-time district or regional official of a nation-wide trade union, and armed with a similar set of questions, seek to establish the current preoccupations of the trade union and how it sees its future relationship with local employers and their confederations.

3 Undertake an outline survey of the type and range of vocational qualifications which are currently available to employees in each of these types of employment:

- craft/operative work

- technician work

- clerical administrative work

- supervisory/managerial work

4 Research into the types of legal redress available to an employee who has a case of unfair treatment in the context of employment law.

5 Carry out a survey of the extent of legal protection which is available to people in work concerning their roles as employees.

Having obtained your data for one of the above activities, brief your class by **either** producing a two-sided A4 factsheet, **or** a 10–15 minute oral presentation to your class – with a summary hand-out.

MANPOWER PLANNING AND SKILLS AUDITING

An organisation's personnel operations are as much concerned with the future as are its marketing activities. For instance, if a company wishes to embark successfully upon a new policy, say to export its products to EC countries following upon the creation of the 1992 Single Market, then its personnel department will need to plan for this new development well in advance. It will need to undertake, for example, employee surveys and audits so as to ascertain:

- who can speak what European language(s) and to what degree of fluency
- who has experience of European business cultures and has travelled in targeted export countries
- who would be best suited to be developed into new roles involving documentation in European languages, selling in Europe, coordinating European advertising and so on

Also, the company's directors may decide to set up a new export department to handle the extra business. This decision would in turn require the personnel department to create and implement a plan to:

- identify which staff would be offered posts in the new department
- what implications this would have for promoting or recruiting staff to the department(s) which lose personnel
- to devise in consultation with sales and marketing managers an organisational structure for the department, including the compilation of fresh job specifications and descriptions (see pages 316, and 317–18); also, to produce conditions of service and salary scales which fit in with existing company schemes and policies
- plan for the future growth of the export department in terms of additional staffing, which may in turn require in-house staff training and development programmes or further recruitment
- brief as necessary employment bureaux on the newly created posts and booking space in selected recruitment newspapers and journals, etc.

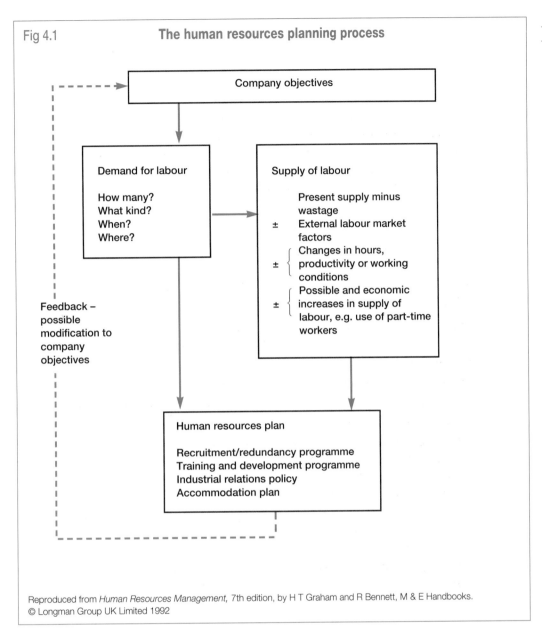

Fig 4.1   **The human resources planning process**

Company objectives

Demand for labour

How many?
What kind?
When?
Where?

Supply of labour

±   Present supply minus
wastage
External labour market
factors

±   Changes in hours,
productivity or working
conditions

±   Possible and economic
increases in supply of
labour, e.g. use of part-time
workers

Feedback –
possible
modification to
company
objectives

Human resources plan

Recruitment/redundancy programme
Training and development programme
Industrial relations policy
Accommodation plan

Reproduced from *Human Resources Management*, 7th edition, by H T Graham and R Bennett, M & E Handbooks.
© Longman Group UK Limited 1992

As the above example illustrates, implementing changes which involve either moving existing staff to other posts, or recruiting new staff cannot be undertaken effectively overnight. Furthermore, the above example is likely to be just one of many personnel projects going on side-by-side in a large organisation.

For this reason, an effective personnel team takes pains to manage the organisation's workforce as a coherent whole. That is to say, it maintains a manpower planning function which continually monitors what qualifications, skills, expertise and experience are required – currently and in the future – to enable all departments to meet their goals and objectives without staffing crises or emergencies.

TYPICAL FEATURES OF MANPOWER PLANNING

Future human resource needs

Liaising with departments so as to anticipate what kind of and how many employees will be needed by when in order to maintain each department's business plan – in terms of expansion, product development, restructuring, relocation, etc.

Staff development and training

Negotiating with managers and their staff over personal career development programmes which mesh with both departmental and corporate strategic plans; commissioning suitable training courses, either in-house or from external agencies.

Age analysis

Maintaining a database of all employees broken down into departments, sections and units which shows employee distribution by age. Graphic representation of this data assists personnel managers in devising and implementing 'new blood' recruitment programmes which fit in with retirement frequencies and also voluntary redundancy or early retirement offers at timely intervals. Failure to undertake this aspect of manpower planning can have dire consequences for companies when, say, a quarter of its R & D staff retire almost simultaneously!

Abilities, experience and skills analysis

Undertaking regular audits of all employees and keeping database records of their:

- existing qualifications
- programmes of further study leading to additional qualifications
- training courses attended
- on-the-job work experience leading to additional skills development
- updating conferences and seminars attended, etc.

Such records may be studied in order to identify specific staff with expertise which has come to be needed, such as engineers with some Russian who are familiar with Russian industry, or to help senior managers in drawing up human resource requirements in strategic plans.

Staffing costs and cost centres

A further important element of manpower planning is to monitor the costs of the workforce as divided into appropriate functions like production, direct labour, salesforce, and office administration staff. Working with departmental managers, Work Study and O & M units, the personnel team may be able to devise strategies for using the workforce more cost-effectively and undertake plant bargaining productivity negotiations based on the information they have extracted from this monitoring process.

Local and national demographic trends

Companies occupying the same industrial or commercial sector inevitably find themselves in competition for specific kinds of personnel, say, CADCAM software engineers, cost accountants or trilingual personal assistants. Therefore, an effective manpower plan undertakes systematic monitoring – not only of the salaries paid and conditions of service offered to key staff like those above but also of the pay-rates for factory operatives and shop assistants who are recruited locally.

Further monitoring activities will include areas such as: the numbers of school or college leavers coming on to the job market, the mature returners being retrained at local colleges of technology, local employment areas where skills shortages have been identified by county council planning departments, national employment trends and statistics (by industrial/commercial sector) published by HMSO, the nature and extent of local and national unemployment, regional and local pay rates, etc.

Personnel managers in large companies will also liaise with local planning authorities so as to ensure if possible that a sufficient supply of low-cost housing is available for its plant or warehouse workforce, and that their needs are being catered for in county strategic plans.

Ratios of workforce occupancies

In liaison with facilities managers, a personnel team may also maintain records of staff occupancy of, say, open office or factory floors, so as to ensure that UK and EC HASAW requirements on personal working space are complied with, and also to anticipate when additional premises may be needed to accommodate an expanding unit, and so on.

■ Why skills audits are needed

PC
4.1.1
4.1.3

Successful organisations are always changing and re-shaping their activities to enable staff to meet fresh challenges or overcome new problems. As a result, line managers may need their staff to embark upon various kinds of self-development like:

- **distance learning degree programmes** such as the Master in Business Administration or a BA in European Business

- **part-time study professional diplomas and certificates** like the Diploma of the Institute of Marketing

- **intensive two to three day short courses** in, say, desktop publishing or developments in EC legislation

- **in-house training courses for two to three hours per week o**n, for example, selling a new product or how to service and maintain a new item of plant

- **home-study programmes** on, say, organisational procedures and operations techniques

- **secondment to another department or unit** for specialist training or updating

and so on

Thus a busy organisation may have several hundred members of its workforce simultaneously undertaking a wide range of personal development activities like those outlined above. Such staff will also be enlarging their banks of skill and expertise simply by becoming experienced in new routines and working procedures. For example, an office assistant working daily on a word processing or desktop publishing package will come to master many of its features through trial and error and by swapping successes and problems with co-workers.

As a result of all this multifarious activity, a personnel department can quickly get out of touch with the developing skills and experiences of its workforce. This can be both dangerous and wasteful. For instance, new personnel may be recruited to posts which could have been filled by existing members of staff, whose relevant skills and experience had become unrecorded and thus overlooked. Moreover, failure to carry out a continual monitoring of organisational human resource needs against existing capabilities may lead a company into dire straits as its personnel become less and less able to cope with new processes, changing market conditions and technological innovations.

Fig 4.2

Personnel Record update

NAME   DEPARTMENT   DATE

In order that we may keep our personnel records up-to-date, please show below any changes since

Date of Last Update   show changes only.

Address   Phone   Weight

Marital Status:

I have joined/left   Trade union

Number of dependants including yourself

Dates of birth of children born since last update

Have you joined/left our pension scheme?

Describe any physical defects you have developed since last update

Describe any major illness you have had since last update, explain

If you received compensation for injuries since last update, explain

Do you now have a car available for your own use?   Registration number

ADDITIONAL SCHOOLING OR SPECIAL TRAINING

Dates	School/college etc.	Name of course and brief description

New memberships in technical or professional societies

New professional offices or honours

Any other changes you would like us to note

Employee's signature   Reviewed by

                                                              Supervisor

NOTE TO SUPERVISOR: Describe on the reverse side any special projects or assignments which you feel have aided this employee's development and increased his value to the Company.

© Copyright 1963, 1968, 1979 — V. W. Eimicke Associates, Inc.
Produced by Waterlow Business Supplies (A Division of Oyez Stationery Ltd)
Oyez House, 16 Third Avenue, Denbigh West Industrial Estate, Bletchley, Milton Keynes MK1 1TE

Form 108

2/87

Reproduced by kind permission of Waterlow Business Supplies

■ Designing and storing a skills audit database

The advent of relational databases – those which can be created so as to permit various kinds of specified data retrieval – proved a boon for personnel managers wishing to create and maintain an accurate record of staff skills and abilities.

CHECKLIST OF TYPICAL FEATURES OF HUMAN RESOURCES SKILLS, ABILITIES AND EXPERIENCE

- Qualifications on joining the organisation.
- Membership of professional bodies (e.g. Institute of Chartered Engineers).
- Details of any particular abilities potentially useful to the organisation – for example:

  degree of fluency in specified foreign languages;

  levels of expertise in various computer programming languages.
- Details (in chronological order) of all in-house and externally commissioned training courses undertaken and results/reports on outcomes.
- Particulars of degree/diploma /certificate work-related programmes of study pursued.
- Records of all experience and training on specific machines and equipment – for example, which passenger aircraft a pilot is qualified to fly and how many hours he/she has logged on which jets, etc.
- Extent of experience in various particular posts both prior to joining and within the organisation with dates of transfers and/or promotions including job titles, etc.
- Notes of hobbies and leisure pursuits which could prove of value to the organisation, e.g. expert photographer or computer buff.

Such particulars are surveyed on a regular basis, say, by distributing questionnaires, which are then used as data entry pro formas for keying into the database. The creation of the database file into specific fields for qualifications, short courses, operation of equipment and work experience, etc. enables personnel managers to produce analyses and individual profiles in skill-specific areas such as:

- bilingual personal assistant (French and German to post-degree level) with Wordstar 7.1 word processing skills

- Doctor of Philosophy in plant sciences with diplomas in crop-spraying and marketing

- factory foreman with National Examining Board in Supervisory Management certificate with three years experience of robotic spot-welding and four years of car body paint-spraying techniques

Access to such a staff skills and abilities database – kept up to date by regular skills audits – provides an invaluable human resource planning and deployment tool.

DISCUSSION TOPICS

1 Given the nature of its work, what kind of problems do you think a personnel manager might have in his or her interactions with a company's senior managers?

2 What range of skills do you think a successful and effective personnel manager needs to possess?

3 What sort of problems would you expect an organisation to encounter which has not undertaken any structured manpower planning over the past 15 years?

4 How would you organise a skills audit in, say, a manufacturing and exporting company of some 800 employees? To whom would you provide what collated data?

THE RECRUITMENT AND INDUCTION PROCESS

A central function of human resource management is the process by which people are recruited into the organisation. Nowadays, there are many legal considerations (stemming from Acts like the Employment Protection Act 1978 and the Employment Act 1982) which render the process of terminating an employee's contract both involved and lengthy (see pages 361–5). For this reason, personnel and line management departments take particular pains in their efforts to recruit people who can do the advertised job well, and who are likely to become cherished, long-serving members of the workforce.

The chart on pages 312–13 illustrates some 17 steps in a typical staff recruitment process. It offers, however, only a mainstream indication of the procedure, since appointments at varying levels within an organisation require different degrees of attention and involvement. For example, a post for a supermarket baker may simply be advertised within the store under VACANCIES: BAKER, and the interview process may be informal and fairly short. Even so, whatever the level of appointment, the law underpinning recruitment remains the same in terms of what constitutes:

■ a fair and non-discriminatory job advertisement

■ binding letters of job offer and acceptance

■ a legally satisfactory contract of employment

■ Contents of a contract of employment

PC
4.1.4

A contract of employment must contain details of:

- job role and job title: details of what the precise nature of the job is, and its title
- pay: hourly, weekly or monthly rate and position on any scale or spine: circumstances in which overtime may be worked and/or details of any bonus or commission entitlement
- working periods: normal starting and finishing times and total hours/week before any overtime may be claimed, etc.
- paid holidays: the number of working days each year (excluding public holidays) of paid leave entitlement
- sick leave and payment: details of the duration and nature of entitlement to sick pay, maternity leave, etc.
- pension/superannuation scheme: details of the contributory or non-contributory schemes the organisation offers; grievance procedure: clear details of the procedures in operation and the identity of the grievance officer; period of notice of termination of contract: the number of weeks/months of notice normally required on either side to effect resignation or termination

In addition, the organisation will probably include in the employment contract package:

- a handbook of practices and procedures or code of behaviour expected
- a schedule/booklet of regulations to be observed
- particulars of any sports, recreational or staff welfare activities
- an organisational chart relevant to the job role of the employee

THE RECRUITMENT PROCESS

Job need identified

Personnel specification produced

Job description updated

Advertisement placed

Applicants respond

Applications sifted

Shortlist drawn up

References taken up

Line managers and personnel department consult

Defines: who the employee reports to and to whom he may report to him: lists in detail the duties and responsibilities of the post-holder.

Sells the job by briefly indicating what benefits – pay, prospects, 'perks' etc are offered in return for an applicant possessing the expertise displayed as needed in the advertisement.

Smaller organisations sometimes ask only for 'letters of application'; large firms want the 'full application package'.

National and international companies receive hundreds of applications for key posts

This schedule gives the interviewer a means of 'marking' the candidate for aspects like:
Appearance
Alertness
Knowledge/expertise
Potential
Rapport

1 Need for new post identified.

2 Line manager details needs: reviews post for changes if it already exists, or lists fresh requirements if a new post is to be established.

3 *Personnel specification* is revised or a fresh one drawn up.

4 *Job description* is revised or a fresh one devised.

5 A *classified* or *display advertisement* is composed for insertion in local/national press.

6 *Duplicated particulars of the post* and application forms are made ready for posting to applicants; the job description may be included in pack to applicants.

7 *Initial letters of interest* are received and application packs despatched

8 Completed applications are received which include *formal covering letter of application, completed application form(s)* and a copy of a *curriculum vitae.*

Note: many organisations hire *employment consultants* to sift through initial applications and to propose candidates for shortlisting.

9 Shortlisted applicants are sent *letter invitation* to attend for interview.

10 *Acceptance letters* received from shortlisted applicants.

11 *Confidential references* are obtained from referees cited in application forms and copied for interview panel, along with shortlisted candidates' application forms and CVs.

Interview panel also provided with *interviewing schedule* on which to record impressions and ratings.

Lists the physical, educational, experience, aptitudes, skills and personality requirements needed in the person who could do the job successfully. Prioritises requirements as 'essential' or useful'.

These may include potted history of the organisation and details of successes as well as outline of job location, duties and prospects.

During this period, line managers and personnel staff meet to organise interview procedures and agree who will assess what.

It is common practice in private sector companies for employees to make very confidential applications for new jobs. Their references will only be taken up with the candidate's permission, and usually after an oral job offer has been made and accepted – 'subject to satisfactory references being received'.

Interviews take place

Job offered and accepted

Resignation submitted

Employment contract issued

Some organisations advise the successful candidate by letter after the interview process as this may take place intermittently.

While a contract of employment may be deemed to exist on the basis of witnessed oral offers and acceptance, the process is confirmed by the exchange of letters.

12 Interviews take place. Candidates provided with expenses claim forms to return after completion. Oral offer of appointment made and orally accepted (subject to acceptable references being obtained).

13 Written letter confirming job offer despatched to successful candidate, and courtesy letters despatched to unsuccessful applicants.

14 Written job acceptance letter returned.

15 Letter of resignation sent to current employer by successful applicant.

16 Written contract of employment sent to new employee and countersigned by both parties.

17 Job description also provided to new employee with company manual and prospectus etc.

Usually a pro forma to detail road/rail fares, hotel and meal costs; employers usually state in application pack whether expenses for interviews attendance will be paid.

It is good manners and good public relations to thank all applicants for their interest in the post.

This must be received by the new employee within 8 weeks of starting in the job: it will include details of pay, holiday entitlement, hours of work, sickness pay and pension agreements, periods of notice required on either side, job description details and appropriate information about company rules and regulations.

Acts and statutes underpinning the recruitment process:

- Employment Protection (Consolidation) Act 1978
- Sex Discrimination Act 1975
- Equal Pay (Amendments) Regulations 1983
- Fair Wages Resolutions (House of Commons)
- Race Relations Act 1976
- Misrepresentation Act 1967
- Trade Union Reform and Employment Rights Act 1993

PERSON SPECIFICATIONS AND JOB DESCRIPTIONS

■ The difference between a person specification and a job description

Some people find it difficult to distinguish between a person specification and a job description. Essentially, a person specification is a checklist drawn up to identify what particular physical characteristics, general and/or vocational qualifications, skills, aptitudes and previous work experience **an ideal candidate for a given post should possess.**

A job description sets out clearly **the most important responsibilities and duties which make up a given job**.

The person specification

Set out below is an example of one type of person specification. The essential features of the specification are graded into Necessary, Helpful and Optional since an organisation would be extremely lucky to obtain the services of an employee who possessed all the characteristics identified.

Depending on the type of post to be advertised, the personnel specification will place more emphasis on either educational qualifications, analytical and communication skills, say, for a personnel manager, or manual dexterity, conscientiousness and the ability to perform routine tasks repetitively if for a production-line operative.

In some jobs, like that of an RAF pilot, 20-20 uncorrected vision (doesn't wear glasses) is deemed essential, while physique is of little or no importance in, say, a computer programmer.

Managers use the process of designing or updating the person specification as an opportunity to reconsider how a job has changed or developed, what aspects have become more or less important and thus what emphasis should be given to the redesigned job occupant's profile. The specification also provides advertising copy writers with a stripped-out summary of the key features of the ideal applicant and thus assists the advertising process.

The job description

The main purpose of the job description is to define as clearly as possible for both its possessor and his or her line manager what the key ingredients of the job are. Compilers of job descriptions seek to identify the priority aspects of a post:

> **To meet agreed company sales turnover targets and to maintain the operations of the sales function within allocated budgets.**

and the list of job responsibilities are usually set out in descending order of priority.

The job description also places its possessor clearly into a line management hierarchy with items entitled: Responsible To: and Responsible For:

In addition to setting out main job functions, the job description may also include details of any equipment, records, security systems or parts of premises for which the possessor is responsible.

Good job descriptions also include the date of first issue and the dates of any subsequent revised issues.

Job descriptions are helpful tools in the personnel appraisal process, but should not be taken too literally as the 'tablets of stone' which define all possible aspects of a post. The statement: 'That's not in my job description!' sometimes betrays a sign of a deteriorating manager–subordinate relationship. And in the case of staff in the higher reaches of the organisational hierarchy, the complexities of jobs and their capacity for open-ended transactions make it virtually impossible for job descriptions to cover all aspects of the work to be undertaken.

CHECKLIST OF MAIN COMPONENTS

PC
4.2.2
4.2.3
4.2.4

Person Specification

Date compiled

Location in management line

Physical characteristics
Vision, hearing, manual
dexterity, etc.

Qualifications
GCSEs NVQs GNVQs GCE A-levels
BTEC/RSA/LCCI/CGLI
Professional Institute, etc.

Experience
Previous posts, full/part-time,work
experience, HND sandwich blocks, etc.

Personality
Self-starter, tact/discretion, sense of
humour, etc.

Interests and hobbies
Foreign travel/languages computer buff,
etc.

Circumstances
When available, willing to work
overtime, willing to work overseas,
clean driver's licence, etc.

Job Description

Date compiled
Date of previous review

Job Title

Department
Location of post
Responsible to
Responsible for

Scope of post
Brief of summary of major features of the post.

Major responsibilities
Checklist of the main priorities of the job set
out in descending order as numbered
sentences.

Other responsibilities
– for, say, security, office equipment or works
plant, supervision of the work of others, etc.

Education and qualifications
Some job descriptions include a summary of
the education and qualifications needed for the
post.

Name of Compiler
Name of Approver
Date of issue

Specimen person specification for a personal secretary

Date: Date of previous review:
Job title: Personal secretary
Reporting to: Middle tier manager

Characteristics	Necessary	Helpful	Optional
Physical:			
20-20/Corrected vision	✓		
Good hearing	✓		
Manual dexterity for keyboarding	✓		
Good carriage and well-groomed appearance	✓		
Qualifications:			
RSA/LCC Secretarial			
Diploma/Certificate		✓	
Shorthand to 100 wpm	✓		
Typewriting to 40 wpm	✓		
Word processing to NVQ Level 3	✓		
Information processing to NVQ Level 3		✓	
English to GCSE A–C	✓		
French to GCSE A–C		✓	
Experience:			
Previous personal secretarial post		✓	
Coordination of overseas travel arrangements		✓	
Working under pressure to tight deadlines	✓		
Personality:			
Tact/discretion	✓		
confidentiality	✓		
Self-starter	✓		
Sense of humour		✓	
Interests/hobbies:			
Foreign languages		✓	
European culture		✓	
Fashionwear/clothes sense			✓
Circumstances:			
Able to start work 1.5.19—		✓	
Clean driving licence			✓
Willing to travel abroad		✓	
Willing to work late at times		✓	

Drawn up by: _____
Approved by: _____
Issue Date: _____

Specimen job description

Date: 12 January 199X Previous Review Date: 15 June 199X

Job title   Personal Secretary to Deputy Sales Manager

Department: Home Sales Department

Location: Company Head Office

Responsible to: Deputy Sales Manager

Responsible for: Work of WP Assistant and Office Information Assistant

Scope of post: To provide secretarial services and informational support to the Deputy Sales Manager and to assist in administering the activities of the home sales force; to coordinate and supervise the work of the DSM's word processing and office information staff; to liaise with field sales personnel, according to DSM's briefings and requests.

Major responsibilities

1 To supervise the opening of correspondence and to ensure its prompt distribution according to house practices.
2 To transcribe and deliver as appropriate incoming fax, telex and Email messages.
3 To accept, transcribe (using appropriate media) and dispatch DSM's correspondence, reports, memoranda and textual messages.
4 To maintain the DSM's electronic appointments and scheduling diaries efficiently.
5 To administer the DSM's paper and electronic filing systems effectively, and to ensure the security of all computer-stored data.
6 To supervise the operation of office equipment so as to maintain efficient, cost-effective and safe practices.
7 To make travel/accommodation arrangements for DSM and designated staff as required.
8 To administer the sales force expenses payment system and to maintain the DSM's office petty cash and purchases systems.
9 To maintain a cost-effective office stationery provision in liaison with the company's office administration manager.
10 To receive visitors and look after their comfort and hospitality needs.
11 To supervise the work of the DSM's office personnel so as to maintain good standards and timely completion of delegated tasks.
12 To monitor office practices and procedures and to advise the DSM on possible improvements and modifications in the light of changing office technology and information systems.
13 To ensure that office security is maintained and that confidences are not breached.
14 To promote an alert approach to HASAW matters at all times.
15 To undertake any reasonable task from time to time at the DSM's request as may be deemed appropriate within the scope of the post.

Equipment/Systems Responsibilities
Office computer terminals for sale operations and malfunction reporting.

Office fax, CABX extensions, photocopying and printing equipment for cost-effective and safe operations and malfunction reporting.

Office-held computer files for safe keeping and prompt accessing and liaison with company DP manager for defect/malfunctioning reporting.

Education and Qualifications

General education to GCSE standard and vocational secretarial education to LCCI Private Secretarial Certificate/NVQ Level 3.

Previous office information processing and secretarial experience essential; the post also requires developed interpersonal/communication skills and developed office applications software and telecommunications expertise as well as word processing proficiency.

PC
4.3.1
4.3.6

RECRUITMENT ADVERTISING AND DOCUMENTATION

■ Advertising the post

Two alternatives are available to a personnel department in recruitment advertising – either to undertake the work in-house, or to subcontract it to a recruitment bureau. Either way, the previously drawn-up or revised personnel specification and job description provide handy summaries of essential requirements and expectations which advertising copywriters can use in designing a display or classified advertisement.

The nature of the post to be advertised – managerial/professional or clerical/factory worker – will affect the decision of national or local advertising and the kind of publishing/ broadcasting media employed.

MEDIA USED IN RECRUITMENT ADVERTISING

- National quality press
- National tabloid press
- Local or (district) weekly newspapers
- Free local papers
- Professional/trade journals and magazines (e.g. *Computing*)
- Regional independent television
- Local commercial radio
- Billboards and notices displayed on company premises

Note: Some jobs are never publicly advertised. Exceptionally able managers and professionals are 'head-hunted' by specialist consultancy firms working on behalf of an organisation needing to recruit. Very discreet approaches are privately made to the 'hunted' expert, negotiations ensue and, if successful, the sought-after person quietly resigns and takes up the new post. This approach is used when it is accepted that public advertising will not attract the type of person required.

■ Advertising rates

All advertising media – national and local newspapers, commercial television and radio – update regularly their advertising prices on what are called rate cards. Not unexpectedly, the costs of advertising vary according to:

■ size and type of advertisement or length of commercial

■ position in newspaper, time and date of commercial broadcast

■ discounts given for repeated insertions or broadcasts

As a result of their market research, commercial television and radio companies are able to advise personnel managers when specific segments of the local or national population will be viewing or listening. Similarly, newspaper advertising managers are able to provide details of the breakdown of their readership (see the Marketing Unit for details of how the public is segmented into socio-economic groupings).

■ Designing the advertisement

There is always a tension in recruitment advertising between supplying too much information in too small a typeface – which people won't read – and providing such sparse information that potential applicants fail to become interested.

Many advertisements provide a brief outline of two sets of details which complement each other:

WE ARE PREPARED TO OFFER THIS: *(Checklist or job offer package)*

FOR THIS: *(Checklist of abilities/experience required in successful applicant)*

Eye-catching headlines play an important part in successful advertisements:

PART-TIME GIRL FRIDAY NEEDED ON SATURDAYS!

JOIN OUR FRIENDLY MADHOUSE IF YOU WANT A JOB THAT'S FUN!

MANAGING DIRECTOR £65,000

Some headlines capture attention by being 'zany' and humorous, others simply by the bald statement of a huge salary. The tone and style of the advertisement will depend entirely upon the nature and level of the post in the hierarchy and how the organisation likes to promote its corporate image.

ADVERTISING ASSIGNMENT

In groups of two or three, study the two advertisements set out below and opposite. Draw up a checklist of the features of their design and layout which you think work to make them effective. Then consider any other approaches which you would adopt in advertising the same posts.
Having completed this evaluation, compare notes with the other groups in your class.

Fig 4.3

Western Riverside Waste Authority

General Manager

£35,000 package including non-contributory leased car (Pay award pending)

We are seeking a committed senior manager to lead this progressive authority now firmly established after its inception 3 years ago which has the major task of disposing of waste from the four inner London boroughs of Hammersmith & Fulham, Kensington & Chelsea, Lambeth and Wandsworth.

The Job

• To be responsible for the operation of two major refuse transfer stations and a civic amenity site located in Wandsworth.
• To provide strategic management, with particular emphasis on planning future waste disposal arrangements for the authority.
• To be responsible for the management of over 80 staff based at two stations and civic amenity site.
• Responsible for the efficient operation of budgetary and administrative systems as well as the negotiation of major contracts.
• To actively promote the running of the operations in a safety conscious and environmentally sensitive way.

The Person

The person we are seeking would ideally possess:
• An engineering background HNC/degree level.
• Significant managerial experience within the waste disposal industry or process engineering.
• Advanced negotiating skills.
• A flair for strategic thinking and priority setting in a dynamic environment.
• The ability to assume 'hands on' control when required.

Although experience in the waste industry would be an advantage, consideration will be given to candidates with other appropriate experience.

Benefits include index linked pension, generous leave entitlement and relocation package if required.

The salary and benefits package attached to this post reflects the fact that we are looking to appoint someone with outstanding qualities which are required to lead the Authority in a period of significant change and the introduction of new developments.

If you would like an informal discussion about this post please contact the Clerk to the Authority, Mr G. K. Jones on 01-871 6001, who should also be contacted for application forms and further details either by telephone or at the following address: Town Hall, Wandsworth High Street, Wandsworth SW18 2PU. Closing date for applications: 6th September 1989.

Fig 4.4

'You're not flogging ad space! I thought you wanted a real job.'

'Yes, I am and it's just the job I wanted. The career prospects are real enough.'

'Don't tell me "young dynamic company . . . due to expansion you'll be a manager next week . . . retire at 30 . . ." – you've been had!'

'Well, the Company has more than doubled in size over the last 2 years, and it's been established over ten years. The average age is early 20's, five of our Publishers are under 30! By the way, they all started in ad sales.'

'Got it! You fell for the line about megabuck OTE. Bet they didn't tell you about the impossible targets?'

'No, I fell for the good basic salary plus the commission opportunity to earn nearly half as much again. My first year's training programme is good news too.'

"Where did you say you worked?"

Centaur Communications Ltd,
50 Poland Street, London W1V 4AX.
Write to the personnel and Training Manager and
tell her why you're right for the U.K.'s fastest growing
business publishing house.'

CENTAUR
L I M I T E D

An equal opportunity employer.

FOLLOW-UP ACTIVITIES

PC
4.2.3
4.2.4

1 First carry out your research, then design a person specification for a trainee manager in a supermarket chain or departmental store.

2 Design a job description for one of the following, having undertaken your research:

   a a college engineer;

   b a school secretary or bursar;

   c a college departmental secretary/personal assistant.

3 Assume that you work in the personnel department of Sentinel Insurance plc, a national company which regularly employs school and college 18-plus leavers as trainee branch managers. Design an application form which you think would capture all the information needed for effective subsequent interviewing.

4 First carry out your research, then design a suitable recruitment advertisement (publication size 12 square centimetres) for the same post for which you designed the job description in Activity 2.

DISCUSSION TOPICS

1 Some organisations have poor track records in providing and updating regularly their employees' job descriptions. Why do you think this is so? What management and employee activities and relationships can you identify which are likely to be assisted by the existence of a reasonably current job description ?

2 Can you anticipate any problems which may emerge from employees working strictly to the wording of their job descriptions ?

3 Can a job description or person specification ever really provide sufficiently detailed information to make it a document worth producing?

4 Why do so many companies nowadays employ recruitment consultants to handle the advertising element of their recruitment needs?

PERSONNEL SELECTION INTERVIEWS

■ The recruitment interview

Different organisations adopt varying approaches to recruitment interviews. The following table illustrates the documentation which is generally employed to assist the interview process:

INTERVIEW SUPPORT DOCUMENTATION PRODUCED BY:

THE APPLICANT

● **Curriculum vitae**
A schematised summary of educational and job experience.

● **Completed application form**
Set of data supplied in response to questions and information requests on the form; some forms include an opportunity for applicants to expand on certain aspects on further A4 sheets.

● **Supportive letter of application**
Posts which are administrative or managerial usually require a supportive letter of application in which the candidate formally confirms his or her application and provides a set of statements, about qualifications and experience, etc. which seek to demonstrate a match with the advertised requirements of the post.

THE ORGANISATION

● **Person specification**
● **Job description**
● **Recruitment advertisement**
● **Factsheet/résumé about organisation and the advertised post**
Many firms produce a briefing sheet which explains the scope of its activities and where the advertised post fits in.

● **Interview assessment form**
Many personnel departments supply interviewing staff with a form for recording on-the-spot responses to the performance of interviewees; such forms are divided into key assessment areas (*see below*)

The recruitment interview is essentially concerned with the following two-way, exploratory process:

The employing interviewers: Seek to obtain confirmation in a face-to-face dialogue that the applicant is able to confirm and elaborate upon the data supplied previously on paper, and that, in the flesh, he or she is able to demonstrate expertise and attitudes which meet up with (or exceed) those specified. The interviewee's potential for growth and development is also evaluated.

The job applicant: Correspondingly, the applicant seeks confirmation that the terms of the advertised job offer match expectations, that the conditions of service are acceptable, and that there are apparently genuine opportunities for career development; and, in times of recession, convincing evidence that the organisation will still be trading in the long-term future!

■ Typical sections of an interview assessment form

PC
4.3.4
4.3.5

While there are no fixed parameters for the design of an interview assessment form, personnel departments over the years have identified the following key areas for evaluation:

- **Physical appearance and deportment**

  Does the applicant communicate the kind of personal image suited to the advertised post? Does he/she have poise and presence?

- **Attainments**

  To what extent do qualifications and previous job roles and work experience meet the needs of the post? Is there any evidence of a capacity for future growth and development from the platform of the attainments to date?

- **General intelligence**

  Can the candidate demonstrate a capacity for 'thinking on his/her feet', analytical thought, lateral and creative thinking, problem-solving and decision-making, etc? Is the candidate a 'quick' thinker, or a more reflective, methodical person?

- **Special aptitudes**

  What particular skills and aptitudes does the candidate possess which are directly relevant and advantageous, such as foreign languages, expertise in the latest software package, a recent qualification in stress counselling etc?

- **Personality/disposition**

  What are the personality traits of the candidate? Serious-minded? Light-hearted? Extrovert? Introvert? Gregarious? Loner? Short-fused? Placid? etc.

- **Interests and hobbies**

  Do the applicant's current recreational pastimes provide any insight into his or her suitability for the post? Do they reveal any capacities which would reinforce the application?

- **Circumstances**

  Are the applicant's current circumstances in harmony with the job needs such as clean driving licence for sales rep's post; length of notice to be worked if urgent need for a quick start in post?

(Adapted from the National Institute of Industrial Psychology, Seven-Point Plan)

Conventionally, interviewers use a schedule which is designed as a matrix so that a rating, say, A to E can be assigned to each of the above areas, with a value like the following:

A Greatly exceeds job requirements.

B More than matches job requirements.

C Matches job requirements.

D Does not match job requirements.

E Significantly fails to meet job requirements.

In addition, panel lists may make further notes in between interviews for later checking on aspects of the interview which were either deemed to go well or badly.

The structure of recruitment interviews inevitably varies, but the following pointers form common denominators of most recruitment interviews:

Whether the interview takes a panel or sequential one-to-one form, good interviewers will have agreed beforehand who will pose what connected range of questions on areas such as:

- education and general/vocational qualifications
- experience in previous posts
- degree of expertise in 'state-of-the-art' processes and systems used in the organisation and related to the post
- outlooks and attitudes upon job-specific and general topics
- capacity for growth and development; determination, tenacity and ambition, etc.

Also, good interviewers make a point of asking the same questions at certain stages to each candidate, so as to obtain an objective assessment of each response.

USEFUL RECRUITMENT PROCESS CHECKLISTS

PC
4.3.1
4.3.2
4.3.3

THE CURRICULUM VITAE

A *curriculum vitae* may be composed by using the following framework:

Personal details
Full name and current address
Telephone number
Age, status - married/single
Nationality
Dependents - wife, husband, children

Education
Secondary school(s)
College(s) ⎫ with
University ⎭ dates
Postgraduate institution
Main subjects taken
Activities, interests
Post(s) of responsibility

Qualifications
Examination passes indicating grades, dates and examining boards.

Work experience
Usually expressed by starting from immediate past and working backwards.
Name of organisation, location, job designation, range of duties, extent of responsibilities, reasons for leaving.

Interests
Leisure activities, hobbies, indicating posts of responsibility – e.g. Honorary Secretary of Drama Club – where appropriate.

Circumstances
Period of notice required to be given.
Mobility – car-ownership, any limiting commitments.

A *curriculum vitae* is usually set out schematically, with appropriate dates and chronological structures.

THE APPLICATION FORM

The following information is generally required on an application form for a job:

Name
Address
Telephone number
Age: date of birth
Status: married/single
Maiden name if married woman
Education
Qualifications
Current/previous experience
Present designation or title
Name and address of employers
Details, with dates, of employment since leaving full-time education
Details of salaries in each appointment
Outline of hobbies, interests
Names, addresses and occupations of referees
Date of availability
Signature and acknowledgement of accuracy of data provided

PERSONNEL REQUISITION

Description of need	date needed: job title and category: recruitment salary range: permanent/temporary: full/part-time:
Reason for need	replacement or addition: if replacement, give reasons:
Requirements	education: qualifications: experience: other please specify:

Approval:
Date vacancy filled: Name:

SHORT APPLICATION FORM FOR EMPLOYMENT

Surname   Forenames

Address   Telephone Nos –
                            private/business

Date of birth   Nationality

Detail of any physical disabilities

Current clean driving licence?

Any criminal convictions other than a spent conviction under the
Rehabilitation of Offenders Act 1974?

Employment:

   Position applied for:

   Pay expected:

   Would you work full-time? part-time? - state hours/week

   If offered this post would you work in any other capacity? please detail

   Have you previously worked for us?

   On what date would you be available?

Note : An extended application form also asks for details of education, employment history, and personal/professional references.

INTERVIEW REPORT (extract)

Candidates are rated in this way:

Poise

☐ Ill at ease, jumpy and nervous

☐ Somewhat tense, easily irritated

☐ Reasonably at ease

☐ Self-assured

☐ Extremely self-assured

(Interviewers tick an appropriate box)

ORAL AND NON-VERBAL COMMUNICATION

■ Introduction

'Considering the amount of oral communication that goes on in all organisations, it never ceases to surprise me how few people can converse well. And, given the importance of oral and non-verbal communication, how little time is devoted to it in in-house training and staff development.'

The above comments made by a senior management consultant highlight both the central importance of good oral communication skills at work and also how they are undervalued in general. Perhaps the underlying reason is that most people consider themselves pretty good at oral communicating, having survived satisfactorily into adult life! There is, however, a world of difference between possessing survival skills and demonstrating a sure-footed mastery of the many work-place activities dominated by oral, and non-verbal communication, such as:

- client/colleague reception
- telephoning
- taking part in meetings
- interviewing and appraising
- giving a presentation
- briefing and demonstrating
- addressing and public speaking
- motivating or disciplining
- selling and persuading
- training and developing staff

Each of the above commonly occurring activities requires differing specialist skills. For example, a hard-pressed company director may have to think very quickly on his feet in order to answer a shareholder's pointed question convincingly at an annual general meeting. Again, a skilled chairman may need to pull out all his oral communication skill stops in order to prevent a crucial meeting breaking down into divisive recriminations and abuse. And the much under-valued sales representative may need to summon up reserves of telephone selling expertise in order to calm a customer upset about the non-delivery of an urgently needed order.

There is, then, little doubt about the need for *all* intending managers and their support staff to become expert in oral communication. Furthermore, this particular set of skills can be improved beyond expectation – even by those people hampered by shyness or self-effacing personalities.

Non-verbal communication (NVC)

Whether we are aware of it or not, we are continuously giving off body language signals whenever we communicate face-to-face or through video/CCTV media, with other people. Body language may be simply divided into expression, gesture and body positioning (posture) signalling. We all know from an early age how to read the signs of anger, anxiety, happiness or irritation in someone's face and gesture. We can also quickly gauge whether someone is sitting or standing in a relaxed, alert, nervous or nonchalant way. Furthermore, as we grow up we learn a host of unwritten rules about the proximity or distance that people like to establish with their contacts, ranging from a close embrace to the cross-desk interview or military inspection.

In the heat of the moment, or because our minds are preoccupied, we often forget at work to remain alert for NVC or body language signals, but they are often vital clues to suppressed or unconscious communication and as such are valuable in providing feedback or responses during the oral communication process.

This section examines the fields of oral and non-verbal communication in detail and supplies you with a series of guidelines and tips to aid your own development. But in order to improve, you must be prepared to take a good look at yourself in an untinted 'communication mirror', and be prepared to remedy careless speech habits, unsuspected NVC signals you give off, or unhelpful attitudes and outlooks. Your ego may take the odd knock in group work role-play and simulation, but if you look upon your study period as a cricketer looks upon a session in the nets, then you will quickly realise the value of realistic trial-goes before the real thing.

DISCUSSION TOPIC

Effective oral communication techniques tend to be overlooked because people are loath to admit – even to themselves – that they are less than expert in any aspect.

The building bricks of oral communication

As with many other subjects, oral communication may be divided into two basic components – the what and the how. The 'what' or content of an oral message requires skill in marshalling thoughts and ideas in a structured and sequenced order that listeners can easily follow and absorb. The 'how' or tone of the message – the way of communicating it by intonation, expression, emphasis and register – serve to help and promote its successful delivery. Thus successful oral communication is a happy blend of message organisation and delivery skills.

Consider, for example, these comments which we typically make in response to observing people communicating orally at work, or contemplating their own gaffes or faux pas:

'I could have bitten my tongue off!'

'Every time Bert opens his mouth, he puts his foot in it!'

'I stood there wishing the earth could swallow me up!'

'The trouble with Helen is that she ought to think before she puts her mouth in gear!'

'You can always rely on Harry to pooh-pooh a new idea...'

'His trouble? I'll tell you what his trouble is – he just never ever listens!'

or,

'Better let Jackie handle the press, she's got the gift of the gab.'

'Mike could do the commentary, he's pretty quick on his feet.'

'Let Charlie go, he could sell ice-cream to Eskimos!'

'I think Anne should chair the meeting, she's got a clear head and is good at handling arguments.'

Whether to praise or blame, we are all quick to assess other people's performances and then to slot them into pigeon-holes as good, bad or indifferent communicators. It therefore matters a great deal in career and advancement terms that your oral skills promote positive responses in others. Rightly or wrongly, for example, it is a known fact that the people who get their way in meetings are those who can speak boldly and who have the self-confidence to dominate the proceedings without becoming boorish.

DISCUSSION TOPIC

The way a person speaks is a highly personal matter. People are best left to 'sort things out' for themselves.

PC
4.3.4
4.3.5

■ Checklist of speaking and listening skills

The following checklist identifies the skills of combining the what and how of oral communication, both as a speaker and a listener:

1 As a speaker

Creating the message

In order to create a well-structured oral message the speaker should:

- decide first and foremost the context of the oral communication and what outcomes are desired
- establish which are the key points to get across and what running order would best link them together in a beginning (to introduce the topic), a middle (to develop main points and arguments), and an end (to emphasise actions needed to be taken by the recipient or general follow-up required)
- select in advance the salient facts and figures which will support the argument/position taken
- decide before embarking on what the delivery style of the message should be: rational/objective, exhorting/enthusing, convincing/persuading, analysing/evaluating, etc since this will fundamentally influence the 'how' of the message's delivery

(*Note:* whenever possible you should make the time – say before a phone-call – to jot down your key points and desired outcomes in advance, to ensure you get across all your message, especially when dealing with a strong personality.)

- once embarked on delivering the message, the speaker should monitor constantly the feedback he receives – whether by watching and hearing or just hearing – and be prepared to modify the message's delivery in the light of misunderstanding, impatience, hostile reaction, etc especially in the cut-and-thrust of two-way dialogue

- lastly, the speaker should know when he has said enough – that the message has been successfully transmitted – and then stop on a positive note.

Styling the message

The extent of the orally delivered message's acceptance in face-to-face communication depends very much on:

- facial signals emitting: friendliness, conviction, warmth, sincerity, even-handedness, rapport

- gesture signals communicating: determination, solidarity with the audience/listener, emphasis, conviction, tolerance

- stance signals conveying: ease and relaxation, respect for a formal situation, authority, physical presence

In enunciating the words of the oral message, a person's speech habits – clipped starts and endings, umming and erring, speaking into his shoes, gabbling, uttering boring monotones etc. – will radically affect the message's acceptance. Important speech features to master are:

accent, pronunciation, enunciation/articulation, intonation, emphasis and projection

- **Accent:** today regional accents are perfectly acceptable, provided that people in other regions can follow them and are not foxed by local dialect words.

- **Pronunciation:** no one likes to hear speech marred by ugly or affected habits: 'Ere! Gissanuvverotdog wujja!' or, 'Hellair! Waive come dine for Arscot, but Jimmie's gorn orf this mornin, for a quick rind of goaf!'

- **Enunciation/articulation:** good oral communication – especially over poor telephone-lines or in large halls – depends on vowels being well-rounded and not swallowed, and consonants not being slurred or clipped: 'Sumfin's appnd to innerupt the eggsekitiv decision-makin' process an conserkwenly a returnawork tommora is definally outadaquestion!'

- **Intonation/emphasis:** nothing causes listeners to switch off faster than the ponderous utterance of drab monotone and the even thud of cadences. Experienced speakers know when to emphasise key words and phrases and when to lift, and drop the voice to provide contrast and colour to their message, or by phrasing, when to make telling pauses or add enlivening pace, etc.

- **Projection:** inexperienced and unsure speakers tend to mumble as if to escape responsibility for their utterances! Effective speakers adopt erect stances and head positions which allow the free and unconstricted escape of air from the lungs and mouth, which are essential to clear delivery – especially in large rooms and halls; their vocal chords are also practised in creating resonant sounds which can carry without harshness or shouting.

2 As a listener

A failure to develop effective listening skills is a vulnerable weak-spot in most people. Most of us constantly feed our ego needs by wanting to dominate conversations as speakers, and by planning what we are going to say next, instead of listening properly to the other person.

Yet at the heart of all effective management and leadership is the ability to keep constantly in touch with staff's views and attitudes and to possess an attuned listening ear for evidence of upsets, disagreements, ideas and suggestions and the like. Acquiring good listening skills like those set out below is vital if you are to become a good oral communicator:

- **Keeping concentration upon what is being said,** and avoiding distractions and mind-wandering which result in blank patches that can last from seconds to minutes.

- **Repeating key words and phrases in the mind** to help retain and recall them – especially important names, dates, facts and figures, etc.

- **Keeping a close eye (and ear) on the speaker's face, gesture and posture** (as well as voice patterns) so as to pick up those aspects which he or she considers important or is in disagreement with; checking whether NVC signals agree or conflict with what is being said.

- **Staying alert for pauses or falls in the speaker's speech rhythms,** which signal opportunities for responding, interposing or putting follow-up questions.

- **Being ready to ask a question or provide a remark** which causes the speaker to explain or amplify a point to aid the listener's understanding of the message.

- **Providing regular feedback responses** which indicate that the message is still being received and understood: 'Quite', 'You're right', 'I quite agree' etc or is being queried or disagreed with: 'No, I think you're wrong there', 'What makes you think that?' 'I don't think I would go that far…', etc.

- **Monitoring and controlling personal NVC signals:** such as those which provide the speaker with positive feedback and help establish rapport and provide encouragement; nipping in the bud signs of boredom or indifference or concealing anger, resentment or irritation, etc unless these are intended for the speaker to pick up.

- **Listening especially attentively for points and sections of personal importance or relevance;** ensuring that actions and personal follow-up requests are fully and clearly understood before the speaker rings off, departs or a meeting is closed.

- **Ensuring that written or tape-recorded notes are made clearly and in sufficient detail** for future reference and follow-up work.

CHECK THESE FEATURES IN YOUR OWN LISTENING SKILLS

- Concentraton control
- NVC signal interpretation
- retention/recall of key data
- Ability to establish rapport
- Ability to elicit information
- Control of personal NVC signals
- Ability to transcribe the spoken word into clear notes

ORAL COMMUNICATION ACTIVITIES

1 Check the clarity of your accent and delivery by tape-recording the following sentences by yourself:

Blue Skies Tours mean fine, warm days!

Mining underground often requires working in confined spaces.

Tempered steel displays both strength and elasticity.

Strict adherence to company regulations is essential.

Advertising is quickly becoming an integral part of people's lives.

Picking grapes is a popular choice for a working holiday.

Baking bricks is a back-breaking business!

Play back your recording and check that:

- the open vowels are really open,
- -ed, -ing endings are not clipped,
- 'h's' have not been omitted,
- 's' and 'z' sounds are clear,
- syllables have not been slurred,
- consonants are clearly sounded.

2 Study the following extracts from three different work situations. Consider how you would use intonation, emphasis, pauses and voice-levels to make them as effective as possible when spoken. Then record them on to tape and submit your version for evaluation by your group:

'I wanted to speak to you about a personal matter as you know I have been with the company now for eighteen months as far as I know my work has always been satisfactory and I feel that I have been a conscientious employee I should therefore like to ask you for an increase in my salary.'

'I have called you in to discuss a most serious matter with you during the past three weeks I have received a number of complaints from customers upset by your apparent rudeness while serving them I propose to outline the circumstances of each complaint from the customer's point of view and then to ask you for your own account of what allegedly took place.'

'Charlie we're in trouble Johnson's have just phoned a large order in but they must have it by tomorrow morning I told them I couldn't promise anything until I'd spoken to you is there any chance of your fitting in another production run I'd certainly appreciate it if you could use your influence.'

3 The following passage is the closing section of a managing director's address to his Annual Sales Conference. Study it carefully and then record it on to tape for play-back analysis. Your aim should be to fire the sales representatives with enthusiasm during a difficult period:

'I know – and you know – that the company, and indeed the country, have been going through a difficult trading period. Equally, I know that the strength of Allied Products lies in its ability to meet a challenge. It hasn't been easy, and I can give you no guarantee that it will get better at all quickly.

What I do know is that if anyone is going to lead the company into a better tomorrow, it is you, its sales representatives. And so my closing message to you all is; the company is proud of what you have done during a difficult year and will back you all to the hilt in the coming months; but it will only be your determination and enthusiasm which will turn the corner during the next year. I know I can rely on you!'

Check the recorded versions for the following:
– audibility–clarity
– delivery–pace, emphasis
– commitment–sincerity
– ability to enthuse
– Where any version may be considered to have fallen short, try to decide the reasons for its lack of success.

4 As a means of gaining practice in using the spoken word effectively, form pairs in your student group and make a recording on audio or video equipment of one of the following situations. When the recordings have been made, play them back to the group for comment and discussion of such factors as: clarity, fluency, persuasiveness, rapport, effectiveness, etc.

Before attempting the recording, the pairs of students should make notes of their aims and objectives and of their roles or attitudes in the situation. Also, a few 'trial goes' may be needed.

a Choose a piece of office or college equipment which you know well and, as a salesperson, seek to sell it to a prospective customer who has to think carefully before spending money on office equipment.

b Sally Jones, audio-typist, is normally conscientious. Recently, however, her work has become untidy and marred by messy erasures. Her supervisor decides the time has come to tackle her on the subject!

c Recently, the wholesaling chain of Office Supplies Limited went over to a computerised system for rendering accounts to its credit customers. Jim/Jane Harris, a customer of long standing, keeps getting demands to pay an account of £243.22 which he/she paid several months ago. Peter/Petra Ford is the sales representative of Office Supplies who has to take the brunt of the complaint when making a call on Jim's/Jane's store.

PC
4.3.4
4.3.5

■ Non-verbal communication

Non-verbal communication (NVC) is a fascinating area of study. It concerns the many ways in which people communicate in face-to-face situations, either as a means of reinforcing or of replacing the spoken word. Sometimes people employ non-verbal communication techniques consciously, at other times the process is carried out unconsciously. In many instances, the response is involuntary. A sudden shock, for instance, may result in someone draining in facial colour, opening his or her eyes wide and becoming slack-jawed.

Non-verbal communication may be divided into three main areas, with rather technical labels for readily observable activities or responses

Kinesics

Facial expressions

Smiles, frowns, narrowed eyes transmitting friendliness, anger or disbelief etc.

Gestures

Pointing fingers, 'thumbs up' sign, shakes of the head, transmitting an emphasising focus, congratulations or disagreements etc.

Movements

Quick pacing up and down, finger-drumming, leisurely strolling, transmitting impatience, boredom or relaxation.

Proxemics

Physical contact

Shaking hands, prodding with the forefinger, clapping on the back, transmitting greetings, insistence or friendship.

Positioning

Keeping a respectful distance, looking over someone's shoulder, sitting close to someone, transmitting awareness of differing status, a close working relationship or relaxed mutual trust.

Posture

Standing straight and erect, lounging, sitting hunched up, leaning forward, spreading oneself in a chair, transmitting alertness and care, self-confidence (or even over-confidence), nervousness or ease.

What NVC signals are being transmitted by the people shown in the following photographs?

(a)

(b)

(c)

(d)

(e)

(f)

Para-linguistics

Feedback sounds of surprise or agreement of annoyance or impatience –
'uh-uh, 'whew!', 'oops!', 'tsk', 'tut-tut' etc.

A heightened awareness of what people are 'saying' non-verbally greatly assists the manager or secretary to read a situation and to act – perhaps to head off a personality clash or to calm an irate customer.

NVC and effective communication

Working successfully in an organisation requires that staff develop human relations skills by becoming more aware of how other people are reacting or feeling. Specifically, it requires the ability to 'read' a situation quickly and correctly. Though information and attitudes may be readily conveyed by means of the spoken word, the constraints of courtesy and staff relationships may result in the spoken message masking how someone is really feeling or relating. At other times, a correct interpretation of NVC signals may allow the interpreter to act positively.

For example, the sales representative who recognises that the nods, smiles and approaching movements of the prospective customer mean that he or she is won over, is able to proceed confidently to close the sale. Equally, the secretary who correctly interprets her principal's frowns and toe-tapping as he or she reads a report, may rightly decide to postpone until a more favourable moment her request for a salary increase! Moreover, the receptionist who recognises annoyance in the hurried approaching steps of a member of staff who bursts into the office, eyes narrowed, chin jutting forward and mouth down-drawn, will have the common sense to ensure that her opening words are calming:

'I'm very sorry, Ms Jones is out at the moment. Is there anything I may do to help meantime?'

rather than exacerbating:

'Ms Jones is out. You'll have to call back.'

Thus the ability to recognise NVC signals and to modify responses in their light is essential to the maintenance and promotion of good human relations within an organisation as well as being a valuable tool in helping the manager, secretary or clerk to achieve objectives involving direct personal contact with others.

DISCUSSION TOPIC
Studying the way people communicate non-verbally is rather like hitting them below the belt.

Expression, gesture and movements

Facial expression

The human face is capable of conveying a wide range of expression and emotion. Various parts of the face are used to convey signals:

A range of responses which are capable of being signalled via NVC:

ACCEPTANCE	SYMPATHY	SURPRISE	PAIN
REJECTION	JEALOUSY	FEAR	PLEASURE
ENJOYMENT	ASSURANCE	IMPATIENCE	ECSTASY
DISLIKE	NERVOUSNESS	FRUSTRATION	TORMENT
FRIENDSHIP	AGREEMENT	ENVY	SATISFACTION
HOSTILITY	DISAGREEMENT	EMPATHY	DISPLEASURE
INTEREST	ATTENTION	EASE	
DISINTEREST	BOREDOM	DISCOMFORT	
ANGER	ACCEPTANCE	ALERTNESS	
LOVE	DISBELIEF	STUPOR	

Facial components which are employed to signal a wide range of NVC responses or feelings:

Forehead – upward and downward frowns

Eyebrows – raising or knitting, furrowing

Eyelids – opening, closing, narrowing

Eye pupils – dilating

Eyes – upwards, downwards gazing, holding or avoiding eye contact

Nose – wrinkling, flaring nostrils

Lips – smiling, pursing, drawn in

Mouth – wide open, drawn in, half-open

Tongue – licking lips, moving around inside cheeks, sucking teeth

Facial muscles – drawn up or down, for grinning, teeth clenching

Jaw/Chin – thrust forward, hanging down

Head – thrown back, inclined to one side, hanging down, chin drawn in, inclined upwards

Though the above check-list of responses may not, perhaps, be manifested in every office or factory, it does indicate the incredible range of emotions and feelings visible in the human facial expression!

ASSIGNMENT

Choose a number of varying responses from the above check-list and, from the list of facial components, make out a description of how the individual parts of the face would act together to form the particular expression for each response.

Gesture

Apart from actors, politicians and public speakers who may rehearse a telling gesture to emphasise a point, many of the gestures which people employ as they speak or listen are used unselfconsciously. When the speaker becomes excited, for example, sweeping movements of the arms or the banging of a fist into an open palm may act to reinforce what is being said. Alternatively, the propping of the head upon a cupped hand may signal that what is being said is boring and failing to interest.

Of course, some gestures are consciously and deliberately made. The car driver who points a finger to their head with a screwing motion is demonstrating what they think about the quality of someone's driving!

The range of gestures that utilise head, shoulders, arms, hands, fingers, legs and feet is indeed wide. Though frequently supporting the spoken word, gestures may either be used, consciously, to replace speech, as, for example, with the finger placed in front of the lips urging silence. Unconscious signals from the listener – the brushing of the hand across mouth and chin may be 'saying', 'I'm not sure that I go along with what is being said'. On the other hand, someone may seek to calm a meeting which is becoming heated by consciously patting down the air with both open palms which transmit the sense of, 'Steady on, let's not lose our tempers over this!'

Commonly used gestures

The following gestures are seen regularly in daily life, either reinforcing or substituting for the spoken word:

Head

- nodding sideways to urge someone along
- nodding up and down
- shaking sideways
- inclined briefly
- cradled in one or both hands

Arms and hands

- widely outstretched
- jammed into trouser pockets
- firmly folded across the chest
- holding the back of the head with fingers laced
- making chopping movements with the side of the hand
- hands pressed together in 'praying' position'
- one or both hands held over mouth
- flat of hand patting desk-top
- hand brushing something away in the air
- both hands placed open upon the chest

Fingers

- running through the hair
- drumming on table-top
- stroking mouth and chin
- stabbing the air with forefinger
- clenched into a fist
- manipulated in an arm-wave
- patting the fingertips together with the fingers of both hands out-stretched
- rubbing the thumb and fingers together

Legs and feet

   leg and foot making kicking motion

   foot or toes tapping the ground

   moving legs up and down while seated

Posture

The way people 'arrange their bodies' as they stand or sit may also be extremely communicative. The candidate at interview, for example, who sits hunched into a chair with arms tight, hands clenched, and legs and feet pressed and folded together is probably 'saying' very 'loudly' to the interviewers, 'I am feeling extremely nervous.' By the same token, the interviewee who lolls and sprawls in the chair may be revealing an unpleasant over-confidence and familiarity. As a general rule, the body frame is more widely spread in a relaxed position, whether seated or standing, when someone feels at ease, and is more tightly held, with arms and legs together when discomfort, nervousness or tension is being experienced.

The ability to interpret such signals and to act as necessary to disarm or reassure is invaluable in promoting good human relations.

GROUP ACTIVITY

PC
4.3.5

Add to the above examples of gesture and posture and then describe the sort of messages sent through each example and identify the contexts in which they may be seen.

■ Communicating face-to-face

Face-to-face communication is the oxygen in the life-blood of business and public service organisations. Despite the efficiency and speed of modern telecommunications – essential in their way – there is no totally acceptable substitute for people talking and reacting in close, direct contact. How often at work are sentiments expressed such as:

'Pop into my office and we'll talk it over.'

'I'm sure we can thrash this out round a table.'

'I'm glad I've bumped into you, Jane, I'd like your opinion on…'

Communicating face-to-face embraces a wide variety of situations:

   private discussions in offices

   encounters in corridors

   conversation over lunch in staff restaurants

   taking part in meetings

   selling across the sales counter

   explaining on the factory floor

   discussing in the large open office

   speaking at conferences

   questioning at interviews

Also, the context of the dialogue may render it formal or informal. A 'natter' over lunch will be expressed in words very different from those used at a formal appointment interview. Also, the way in which a dialogue develops will depend entirely upon its context and the relationship of its participants, who may be conversing with the aim of directing or requesting, informing or persuading, congratulating or disciplining.

Whatever the circumstances, the reason why most people prefer most of the time to communicate face-to-face is that such a medium best provides them with 'a total impression' in a way that written communication or telephone calls do not. This impression derives not only from what is being said, but from the whole manner of a person's delivery, including non-verbal communication factors. Moreover the medium permits instant feedback, the means of asking snap questions and of, sometimes, obtaining prompt answers!

In face-to-face contact many 'tools' of communication are working in concert: intonation of the voice, facial expression, gesture, posture and movement, all of which provide a much fuller and often more accurate indication of the import of any given message.

PC
4.3.4
4.3.5

DISCUSSION TOPIC

The interview process is loaded against the reserved, quiet and introverted. Yet more often than not they may be better in the job than the brash, assertive or plausible candidate.

Factors affecting face-to-face communication

What, then, are the most important factors which affect and influence direct personal contact? Whether the context is formal or informal and whether there has been an opportunity to plan beforehand will clearly make a difference. The following check-list includes some of the main ingredients necessary for effective face-to-face communication:

PC
4.3.4
4.3.5

CHECK BEFORE YOU SPEAK

1 *Plan beforehand* – have supporting notes and documents to hand.

2 *Explore opposing points of view* – look at the situation from the other point of view and have counter-arguments ready if needed.

3 *Check out the location of the contact* – it helps to be familiar with surroundings, whether for a meeting or interview.

4 *Exclude interruptions and distractions* – frequent telephone-calls or staff interruptions prevent concentration

5 *Consider the person or people you will be seeing* – it pays to be as well informed as possible about colleagues, associates or customers, and to know 'what makes them tick'.

6 *Select a mode of speaking appropriate to the situation* – being over-familiar and 'chatty' or reserved and formal may prove blocks to effective communication, depending upon the context of the dialogue.

7 *Check your appearance* – dress is another way of signalling what we represent, or how we wish to be accepted.

DISCUSSION TOPIC

In the interview situation, there is inevitably, a conflict between truth and self-projection.

TIPS ON FACE-TO-FACE ORAL COMMUNICATION

Courtesy

The effective communicator is always courteous.

Avoid:

interrupting,

contradicting,

'showing-off' to impress others,

making someone 'look small',

losing your temper,

being condescending,

showing boredom or impatience.

Listening

Failing to listen to someone is not only a grave discourtesy, but also may result in your looking silly or making a *faux-pas*.

Pay attention, consider the implications of what is being said. Look at the speaker, provide him with feedback to show you are following.

Styling

Strive to ensure that the manner in which you speak is appropriate to the circumstances.

Choose your words and expressions carefully, mindful of the personalities and backgrounds of others present.

It is easy to give offence but difficult to overcome its effects.

Mannerism

Avoid irritating, unpleasant or discourteous mannerisms of speech, gesture or posture.

Do not distract by 'fiddling' with a pencil, doodling or indulging in other distractions.

Thinking

It is vital to think before you speak – once a statement is uttered it may be difficult to retract.

If you agree with a point, try to develop it constructively; if you disagree do not become over-assertive. Show that you can see more than one point of view.

Remember, it is better to say a little which is considered, than a lot which is superficial.

Timing

Choose the right moment to speak; sometimes it is better to let others have their say first.

Listen for the drop in a person's voice, look for a smile or nod which may indicate that someone has finished making a point.

Be alert for the signs a person makes when he wishes to end a conversation or interview.

Know when you have won and leave promptly!

Structuring

If others are to follow your argument and value what you say, it is important that you structure your points logically, and express them in connected phrases and sentences.

It is also essential that you do not speak for too long at a time; people will quickly reject what you have to say if you deprive them of the opportunity to have their say too!

Reacting and contributing

One of the quickest ways of alienating others is to show no reaction to what they have said.

Enthusiastic agreement or determined disagreement both indicate that there is an interest and commitment present.

Ensure you make some positive contribution to the dialogue – if you have nothing to say, people will assume that you have nothing of value to contribute and may assess you accordingly.

INTERVIEWS: GENERAL INTRODUCTION

PC
4.3.1
4.3.4
4.3.5

The interview is used in organisations to meet the needs of many, quite different situations. Some interviews are extremely formal affairs, where a candidate for a post may be examined and evaluated by a board or panel of interviewers. Others are conducted in a much more relaxed atmosphere, in a 'one-to-one' relationship, between, say a manager and a subordinate.

In point of fact, it is very difficult to establish where conversation ends and the interviewing process begins in the work situation.

The interview process is employed to obtain information and responses in a wide variety of areas, from sales performance to accounts collection, from disciplinary proceedings to promotion selection, from counselling on personal problems to personnel appointments. The following table indicates some of the principal areas in which the interview is commonly used.

MAIN APPLICATIONS OF THE INTERVIEW

Job application

Resignation – debriefing

Performance assessment

Counselling

Disciplining

Promoting

Information seeking

Instruction giving

It is therefore important for the members of any organisation to regard the interview not as an intimidating process to be endured, but rather as a tool of communication from the use of which the interviewee has as much to gain as the interviewer. The truth of this observation becomes much more apparent if the interviewee in particular stops to consider that the process *is* two-way.

The following section examines the job application interview process. Careful preparation and probing questions on the part of the interviewee may result in his declining an offered post with a company which is performing poorly and where job prospects exist in theory rather than in practice. It is important therefore, at the outset to interpret the term 'interrogation' as 'a two-way channel for finding out'.

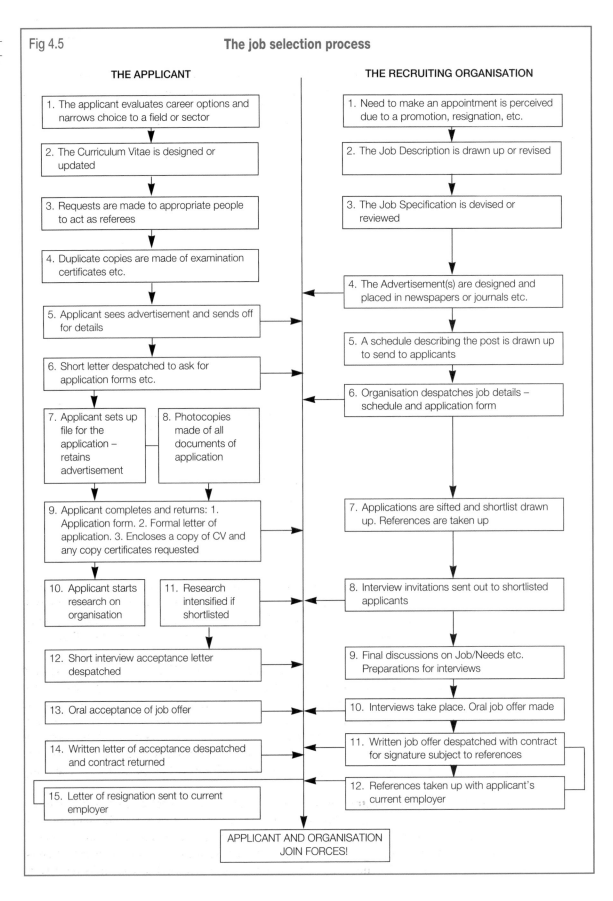

Fig 4.5 The job selection process

THE APPLICANT

THE RECRUITING ORGANISATION

1. The applicant evaluates career options and narrows choice to a field or sector

2. The Curriculum Vitae is designed or updated

3. Requests are made to appropriate people to act as referees

4. Duplicate copies are made of examination certificates etc.

5. Applicant sees advertisement and sends off for details

6. Short letter despatched to ask for application forms etc.

7. Applicant sets up file for the application – retains advertisement

8. Photocopies made of all documents of application

9. Applicant completes and returns: 1. Application form. 2. Formal letter of application. 3. Encloses a copy of CV and any copy certificates requested

10. Applicant starts research on organisation

11. Research intensified if shortlisted

12. Short interview acceptance letter despatched

13. Oral acceptance of job offer

14. Written letter of acceptance despatched and contract returned

15. Letter of resignation sent to current employer

1. Need to make an appointment is perceived due to a promotion, resignation, etc.

2. The Job Description is drawn up or revised

3. The Job Specification is devised or reviewed

4. The Advertisement(s) are designed and placed in newspapers or journals etc.

5. A schedule describing the post is drawn up to send to applicants

6. Organisation despatches job details – schedule and application form

7. Applications are sifted and shortlist drawn up. References are taken up

8. Interview invitations sent out to shortlisted applicants

9. Final discussions on Job/Needs etc. Preparations for interviews

10. Interviews take place. Oral job offer made

11. Written job offer despatched with contract for signature subject to references

12. References taken up with applicant's current employer

APPLICANT AND ORGANISATION JOIN FORCES!

■ The interview

PC
4.3.4
4.3.5

When interview techniques are being discussed, it is usually the formal interview which is considered. It is important to remember, however, that even in informal interview situations the guide-lines which follow will still hold true in principle, if not in detail.

In any interview, the interviewee will be assessed, either directly or indirectly in these areas:

- appearance
- deportment
- manners
- speech
- intelligence
- judgement
- values
- common sense
- initiative
- resourcefulness
- assurance

Basically, the interviewer will be seeking reassurance or information in line with the questions:

- How does the interviewee project himself?
- What has he to offer in terms of specialist skills or knowledge?
- What has he to offer in terms of personality?
- What potential to develop does he display?

Appearance, manners, deportment

As an interviewee, whether making a first job application or an employee before a promotion panel, your personal appearance matters! Rightly or wrongly other people will make judgements about you which will be influenced by your appearance. Looking smart and well-groomed is an asset in any situation and is nowhere more important than at an interview.

The way you hold yourself, move and gesticulate will also affect the way people regard you. In professional and business life attractive people are those who temper assurance with modesty, and who behave calmly, with due consideration for others. On entering the interview room, for example, take care to do so politely but not over-hesitantly and wait to be proffered a hand to shake or to be invited to take a seat. Once seated, avoid the tendency to slouch or lounge and assume a posture which is comfortable, but alert. Also, it is sensible to hold the hands in the lap, and to return them to this position between any gestures.

It is also important to master any feelings of nervousness. Feeling nervous is natural during an interview and you may be sure that the interviewer is aware of this fact and that he or she will go to some trouble to set you at your ease. Nevertheless, allowing nerves to take over, and displaying signs of tension by hunching into the chair, wringing hands, twisting rings or biting lips not only impairs your performance, but transmits a sense of unease to the interviewer as well. The result may be that you do not do justice to yourself and that you leave doubts about your capacities in the mind of the interviewer.

Listening before speaking

Once the interview is under way, perhaps the best advice is to listen! It is all too easy as an interviewee to attend with only half an ear to what is being said or asked. Moreover, you will need to employ all your faculties and to keep extremely alert to ensure that you anticipate, for example, where a sequence of questions is leading you, or to see the probing which may be going on beneath an apparently harmless question!

Listening attentively will also help you to prepare your answer while a question is being framed. It is amazing how fast the brain works in such situations.

Looking at the questioner

Rightly, the ability to 'look someone squarely in the eye' has always been regarded as a sign of honesty and assurance. It helps in any case, during an interview to look at a speaker posing a question since facial expression, gesture or posture often provide valuable insights into what is an interviewer's mind, and shows that you are paying attention.

Similarly, when providing an answer you should make eye-contact with the questioner, but not to the extent of boring into him or her with a transfixing stare!

Think before you speak

This well-worn truism is still excellent advice to the interviewee. Blurting out a nonsense or 'gabbling' on because of nerves are traps into which the unwary often fall. Moreover, it is not possible in an interview to escape from being assessed and both the words you utter and the way in which you express yourself will reveal much about your intelligence, judgement, common sense and *nous*.

In order to answer questions successfully and in so doing to create a favourable impression, you should ask yourself these questions both before and during your answer:

- Have I understood the question?
- Do I appreciate what it is driving at?
- Are there any traps or pitfalls present in the question?
- Can I draw on my own experience to illustrate my answer?
- Am I speaking clearly and convincingly?
- Have I covered the ground and said enough?

Thinking *while* speaking

Just as the practised reader's eye travels ahead before reading a phrase aloud, so the practised interviewee's mind will be thinking ahead and monitoring what is being said. Additionally, the interviewee's eyes will be looking hard at the interviewer for signs of a favourable response to what is being said.

Sometimes the way in which the spoken word is constructed into phrases or sentences allows for 'rest' or 'pause' expressions to be uttered while the brain composes the next important point:

...as a matter of fact I...

…I accept the truth of that but…

…although my initial response might be to…

in this case I would…

Also, there are means of delaying arrival at the explicit answer point of a difficult question by means of a sort of delaying tactic:

I suppose it depends to a large degree upon how the term X is interpreted…

I don't have an easy or quick answer to that question, but on reflection I…

It should be noted that interviewers are only too aware of how much easier it is to pose questions than to answer them, and make natural allowances for initial hesitancy. A word for caution, however: if an interviewee displays a frequent inability to answer questions directly, they are bound to sow in the interviewer's mind seeds of doubt regarding integrity, honesty or, quite simply, lack of knowledge.

Measure what you say

Interviewers are skilled at posing questions which cannot be answered by a simple 'yes' or 'no'. For example, a question would not be phrased:

'Did you enjoy your previous job'

but rather,

'What did you find most satisfying about your previous job?'

In this way the interviewee is invited to expand a reply rather than to offer monosyllabic answers, which inevitably cast doubt upon fluency, knowledge and assurance. It is common, however, for inexperienced interviewees to speak rapidly at great length, as if the assessment were based on words spoken per minute and the range of unrelated topics covered! You must therefore ensure that what you are saying is relevant to the question and forms a summary of the main issues as you see them. It is good practice to pause after having made what you consider an adequate number of points to allow the interviewer either to ask you to continue or to ask another question. Try to strike a happy medium. Saying too little prevents you from demonstrating your knowledge and ability. Saying too much reveals a disorganised and 'butterfly' mind.

Ask *your* questions

Whatever the interviewing situation, the interviewer largely has control of the interview, Nevertheless you should ensure that you make an opportunity to ask the questions *you* have framed. In the context of an application for a job, you wish to establish whether you want the organisation equally as much as it may wish to decide whether it wants you! Such opportunities tend to occur at the end of the interview but clarifying questions may be put throughout. And note: it always sounds lame and lack-lustre to say, in response to an invitation to ask your own questions: 'No, actually, you seem to have answered all of my questions already'.

■ Model letter of application

The post Jane Simmonds applied for:

FINOSA FABRICS LTD require a PERSONAL ASSISTANT to the EXPORT SALES MANAGER (EUROPE)

A knowledge of two EC foreign languages is required and experience of export sales procedures is an advantage. The successful candidate will work on his or her own initiative and be able to handle incoming telephone, fax and telex messages and documentation from French or German agents. He or she must also be prepared to travel abroad.

The company provides excellent conditions of service, including five weeks paid holiday per annum, subsidised insurance and restaurant facilities. Salary negotiable: according to age and experience.

Apply in writing to: The Personnel Manager, Finosa Fabrics Ltd, 4 York Way, London WC2B 6AK

Applications to be received by 30 May 199—

PC
4.3.2

Commentary

Jane Simmonds' letter of application (Fig 4.6) begins by acknowledging the source of the advertisement, makes a formal application statement and refers to relevant enclosures.

In her second paragraph, Jane endeavours to establish a close link between her own career aspirations and vocational education and the essential nature of the advertised post.

Jane goes on to draw particular attention to those aspects of her more recent education which she considers have equipped her with a sound preparation for the post.

In case her prospective employers may be unfamiliar with them, Jane outlines the relevant course components of the Diploma, emphasising those parts which would be most likely to interest her potential principal.

Jane endeavours to display self-confidence without immodesty, and evidence of existing achievement. Since she lacks full-time work-experience, Jane makes the best of her travels and knowledge of the countries relating to the advertisement. She also includes mention of a course of study which has provided relevant insights.

Fig 4.6

Example of a letter of application

Recipient's name and address.
Date

'Appleblossom'
South Downs Way
Burleys
Hampshire PO23 4QR
Tel: 0705–496843

Dear Sir,

I should like to apply for the post of personal assistant to your Export Sales Manager recently advertised in the 'Daily Sentinel', and have pleasure in enclosing my completed application form and a copy of my curriculum vitae.

The advertised post particularly appeals to me, since my own career aspirations and education have been specifically directed for the last two years towards an office administration appointment in the field of export sales.

In the sixth form at Redbrook High School I specialised in Advanced-level German, French and English and proceeded in September 199- to Redbrook College of Technology, where I embarked upon a bilingual secretarial course leading to the Institute of Export's Diploma in Export Studies.

The course includes intensive commercial language studies (I am specialising in German) communication, office administration and export studies with particular emphasis on E.C. procedures and documentation. In addition, the Diploma course provides shorthand, word processing and E.C. telecommunications components, including work in the special foreign language.

I expect to achieve a good pass in the June Diploma examination and to attain shorthand and typewriting speeds of 100/50 wpm, having already secured passes at 80/40 wpm.

During my full-time education, I have travelled extensively in Germany and France, and have become familiar with the customs and outlook of both countries. In August 199- I gained a valuable insight into German business methods during a month's exchange visit to a Handelsschule in Frankfurt-am-Main.

Assisting my father for the past two years in his own company has afforded me an opportunity to use my own initiative and to obtain helpful work experience in areas such as sales documentation, customer relations and the use of data processing in a sales context.

If called, I should be pleased to attend for an interview at any time convenient to you.

My course at Redbrook College of Technology finishes on 30th June 199- and I should be available to commence a full-time appointment from the beginning of July onwards.

yours faithfully

Jane Simmonds (Miss)

Note: It is usual for letters of application such as the one above to be handwritten

Realising that her lack of work-experience could prove a stumbling-block, Jane emphasises the practical work-experience she has had, and highlights aspects of it which she hopes will be relevant to her application.

Availability for interview is made as easy as possible.

Since she needs the job, Jane displays a willingness to start just as soon as possible after the end of her course, thus demonstrating her 'earnestness of intent'.

PC
4.3.2

GROUP ACTIVITIES

1 In groups of two or three study Jane Simmonds' letter from the point of view of Finosa's Personnel Manager and consider the following questions:

Has Jane's letter succeeded in arousing your interest? If so, why? If not, why not? Does Jane's letter succeed in meeting the aims suggested in the commentary? Do you have any criticisms to make of Jane's letter in terms of the information supplied, its structure, its tone and style? Could it be improved upon? Does it adequately match the requirements implied in the advertisement?

2 Draft letters from Finosa to:

   a call Jane Simmonds to attend an interview

   b inform Jane Simmonds of her failure to obtain the post after interview

   c offer Jane Simmonds the post after interview

In 3 groups consider whether the above letters could be created as mail-mergeable standard letters, and if so, how.

PC
4.3.4

INDIVIDUAL ACTIVITIES

1 As Jane Simmonds, assume that, while awaiting news from Finosa after interview, you have been offered, and accepted a post with another company as a result of an earlier application. Write a letter to Finosa appropriate to the situation.

2 As the chairperson of Finosa's interviewing panel, draw up a series of questions that you wish to be passed to each candidate. Compare your list with those produced by your co-students.

PC
4.3.2

DISCUSSION TOPICS

1 Should letters of application still be handwritten?

2 Why do so few recruitment advertisements include details of hourly or annual pay? By omitting such details do they not waste people's time?

■ Legal aspects of recruitment

A number of statutes bear upon the recruitment process:

Disabled Persons (Employment) Act 1958

Employers' Liability (Compulsory Insurance) Act 1969

Equal Pay Act 1970

Sex Discrimination Act 1975

Race Relations Act 1976

Employment Protection Act 1975 and Consolidation Act 1978

Employment Acts of 1980 and 1982

Trade Union Reform and Employment Rights Act 1993

These Acts concentrate on issues such as the following:

- An obligation on firms of more than 20 employees to employ disabled people up to at least 3 per cent of the workforce.
- The requirement of all employers to insure their employees against accidental injury.
- The right of women to enjoy equal pay for equal work (with men).
- The prohibition placed upon job advertisers to discriminate against women in advertising or conditions of service.
- The outlawing of discrimination against employees because of their race, colour or ethnic origin.
- The rights of employees to enjoy basic job security by having a fair contract which stipulates the essentials of the employment agreement: pay rate, notice of termination of contract on either side, sick pay rights, holiday entitlement etc.
- The right for employees to be protected from unfair dismissal and to have access to predetermined procedures for airing a grievance.
- The rights of employees to choose whether or not to join a trade union – whether it is recognised by the organisation or not.
- The rights of employees to reasonable time off work for community duties like being a magistrate or for trade union representative training.

CONTRACTS OF EMPLOYMENT AND INDUCTION

The contract of employment

As the above examples illustrate, taking on employees places significant duties upon an employer. And indeed each employee has a number of obligations to his or her employer, as well as personal rights. Essentially, the act of employing people is regarded as the exchange of a contract binding upon both parties.

The employer is required to exercise a duty of care over all employees and to provide a safe and hygienic working environment (see the Factories Act 1961 and the Office, Shops

To Ms Jane Doe,
350, Elton Road,
Manchester M62 10AS

The following particulars are given to you pursuant to the Employment
Protection (Consolidation) Act 1978

1.   The parties are as follows:

Name and address of Employer: Michael Snooks Ltd,
520 London Square
Manchester M42 145A

Name and address of employee: Jane Doe
350, Elton Road
Manchester M62 10AS

2.   The date when your employment began was: 2 February 1987

Your employment with John Bloggs Ltd from whom Michael
Snooks Ltd purchased the business and which began on
3 February 1986 counts as part of your period of continuous
employment with Michael Snooks Ltd. No employment with a previous
employer counts as part of your period of continuous employment.

3.   The following are the particulars of the terms of your employment

as at ____9 March 1987_____

(a) You are employed at _520 London Square, Manchester M62 145A_

as _a Shorthand - Typist_____

(b) The rate of your remuneration is _£150____ per _week____

(c) Your remuneration is paid at weekly intervals

(d) Your normal working hours are from _9.30a.m_to _5pm_____

Mondays to Fridays inclusive

(e) (i) You are entitled to ___two weeks____ holiday with pay after _one__

completed year of service and to _three weeks__ holiday with pay every

year after _two__ completed years of service.

These holidays are to be taken at a time convenient to the employer between

_1st May_____ and _30 October_ in each year. If an

employee's employment terminates before all holiday accrued due has been

taken, the employee is entitled to payment in lieu thereof on leaving the said

employment. You are also entitled to the customary holidays with pay, i.e.
New Year's Day, Good Friday, Easter Monday, May Day, Spring Bank
Holiday, Late Summer Bank Holiday, Christmas Day and Boxing Day.

(ii) Regulations as to payment while absent during sickness or injury are
available for inspection during normal working hours
in the office of the Secretary/PA to the Personnel Manager

(iii) There is no pension shceme applicable to you.

(f) The length of notice which you are obliged to give to end your contract of
employment is *one week* and the length of notice you are entitled to
receive unless your conduct is such that you may be summarily dismissed is as
follows:—

(i) One week if your period of continuous employment is less than two
years.

(ii) One week's notice for each year of continuous employment if your
period of continuous employment is two years or more but less than twelve
years: and

(iii) Twelve weeks if your period of continuous employment is twelve years
or more.

(g) *NOTE*

If you are not satisfied with any disciplinary decision relating to you or seek
redress of any grievance relating to your employment you can apply in the first
place to *the person in charge of the typing pool*

Details of the procedure available and to be followed in connection with your
employment are *posted in the staff room*

Dated *ninth* day of *March* 19 *87*

Signed

Sarah Snooks

Company Secretary

From *Business Law*, 2nd edition, by Denis Keenan and Sarah Riches.
Reproduced by kind permission of the authors and publisher.

and Railway Premises Act 1963). Further duties include providing work to do and paying for it at due times – weekly, monthly or quarterly, and maintaining records on behalf of the employee in areas like:

- PAYE tax payments deducted
- National Insurance contributions
- Pension/superannuation payments deducted

Correspondingly, the employee has a duty to the employer to work honestly, conscientiously and loyally, exercising due confidentiality. He or she is similarly obliged to accept cheerfully and work to any reasonable (and legal) instructions from superiors acting for the employer. In areas like Health and Safety at Work (HASAW Act 1974), both employers and employees have mutual obligations to maintain a safe working environment. Similarly, both parties may be liable to proceedings (one against the other) if the one has been negligent, in, say, providing security barriers around a piece of potentially dangerous equipment like a steel sheet press.

Such respective duties and obligations are essential parts of the contract of employment which is deemed to exist once employment is offered and taken up. By law, each newly appointed employee must receive from his or her employer within eight weeks of starting work a written contract which includes:

- the title of the job
- agreed pay rates and payment intervals
- arrangements for the payment of any commission, bonuses or overtime
- paid holiday entitlement
- agreed pension scheme payments and conditions
- the level and duration of sick pay entitlement (as an addition to what employees are entitled to from their social security payments)
- details of periods of notice to be worked
- the name, job title and location of the organisation's grievance officer and details of established grievance and disciplinary procedures operated by the organisation

The employer also has a duty to explain how future wage or salary increases are negotiated. Large organisations tend to negotiate directly with the trade union representatives of its employees. However, in some industries, Works Councils (set up by Act of Parliament) negotiate with a representative panel of employers for the industry. Thus both large and small firms accept the overall pay and conditions packages which emerge from such annual pay bargaining.

PC
4.3.1

■ Employee induction

In addition to ensuring that each newly appointed employee is made aware of the legal essentials of his or her employment, many organisations provide a period of initial training and orientation called induction.

The structure of an induction period varies obviously with the type of job. A factory machinist, for example, will be introduced to:

- the person he or she reports to in the management line and the appropriate trade union representative (if applicable)

- the geography of the shop floor and works buildings and location of canteen, toilets, shower rooms, etc.
- the operation of the machinery to be worked
- HASAW safety regulations in force and explanations of company regulations arising, together with disciplinary measures taken if ignored; action to be taken in case of emergency
- works social and sports facilities and social club committee members
- the location and staff associated with issuing pay, providing welfare and counselling (i.e. personnel) and operating grievance procedures

Similar induction processes (with varying emphases on the extent of training on equipment or administration systems) are adopted for office and managerial staff. Many developed organisations also provide induction manuals for newly appointed employees which supply helpful briefing notes on company policy and practices in:

- job rotation and job enrichment schemes
- staff development and further training opportunities
- company policy and approaches to customer care, quality management, equal (male/female) opportunities
- details of pension scheme
- special concessions (e.g. purchasing company products or access to preferential discounts on insurances or holiday packages, etc.)

The essential objectives of employee induction are to provide a specific briefing (with training if needed) on the job's requirements, an introduction to the people with whom the employee will directly work and an orientation towards the culture and practices of the organisation's working environment.

PC
4.3.3
4.3.4

DISCUSSION TOPICS

1 'Despite all the paraphernalia of pseudo-scientific interview techniques and document aids, the process remains one of chemistry and preferences based on personal prejudices.'

2 The job interview is more properly viewed as a sales pitch than as a two-way exchange of information and viewpoints.

3 Women still find it much harder than men to obtain promotion and advancement in organisations. Should all recruitment and promotion interview panels be required by law to include a woman?

4 In many firms, meaningful induction programmes are honoured more in the breach than in the delivery. What other organisational shortcomings can you identify which make the case for creating a separate personnel function in organisations which claim to be able to do without one?

REVIEW TEST (Elements 4.1, 4.2, 4.3)

1 List the principal activities undertaken by an organisation's personnel function and describe briefly the main features of each.

2 Explain what is meant by the two terms: manpower planning, and skills auditing.

3 Why do personnel departments monitor local demographic trends?

4 List the principal steps of recruitment an organisation takes to fill a new or vacant post.

5 What is meant by the term induction? List its component parts.

6 Outline briefly the major features of a contract of employment

7 Explain clearly the difference between a personnel specification and a job description and list the main section headings for each.

8 List the media available to a personnel manager wishing to advertise a professional post.

9 What are the headings under which a curriculum vitae is compiled?

10 What areas would you choose to evaluate in an applicant for a job if you were an interviewer?

11 How does an understanding of NVC signals assist both interviewer and interviewee in recruitment interviews?

PC
4.1.1
4.1.6

APPRAISAL AND PERFORMANCE REVIEW SYSTEMS

■ Performance appraisal

The design and implementation of a system for appraising the work of all employees is a most important part of the personnel function. An effective appraisal scheme will provide a helpful mechanism to aid the delivery of corporate goals and business plans. Employees at all management and operations levels participate in a thorough review of the past year's work and negotiate priorities and objectives for the coming year.

Appraisal schemes may be either open or closed. One type of open scheme provides the appraisee with a copy of the appraiser's review report. Another type proceeds to the joint production (by appraiser and appraisee) of an outcome and future action to be taken document which both agree and initial. In a closed system confidential appraisal reports are produced by line managers to which departmental staff do not have access. Today most organisations operate open appraisal systems since active participation in annual reviews and forward planning by all employees is much more effective in both morale and achievement terms.

Why appraise?

If an organisation is to be successful in its sphere of activity, systems need to be in place which encourage managers and subordinates to:

Look back over the year:

- *Review the scope and nature of the work done* and its relative success and contribution towards meeting departmental goals and objectives.

- *Examine how the appraisee's job may have developed or changed* over the year in ways which may or may not have been recognised by management and to acknowledge such changes by updating the job description.

- *Check to see whether changes in organisational structures and/or policies have impacted upon the job* and if so, whether more human resource assistance or equipment support is needed.

- *Discuss the appraisee's perception of his or her strengths and weaknesses* and where specific personal development or training is required in the light of the past year's performance. Also review longer-term career aspirations.

- *Review any problem areas or difficulties* – say with aspects of internal communication or relations with certain other staff – in order to devise strategies for improvement.

In a similar way, annual (or biannual) appraisal meetings enable the manager and subordinate to negotiate and agree desired outcomes for the year ahead by:

Looking forward to the coming year:

- *Assessing and agreeing what activities should have priority.*

- *Negotiating and agreeing* (wherever possible) what objectively measurable targets should be set for the appraisee to achieve.

  Quantifiable targets may be monitored and checked much more equitably than those described in abstract generalisations like: 'Achieve a more harmonious atmosphere in the office'.

- *Agreeing further training and development activities* to be scheduled during the year.

- *Establishing what support* – extra staff, equipment or materials – is needed to aid the achievement of agreed objectives.

- Where the appraisee is responsible for the work of others, *establishing agreed broad objectives which the appraisee agrees* as achievable outcomes for the department or unit as a whole. These will then be defined in detail when the appraisee resumes his/her manager role as the appraisal process cascades down through the organisation.

Appraisal interviewing models

In many organisations appraisal may be undertaken with an employee's immediate line manager, but there are other, perhaps superior models:

PC
4.1.6

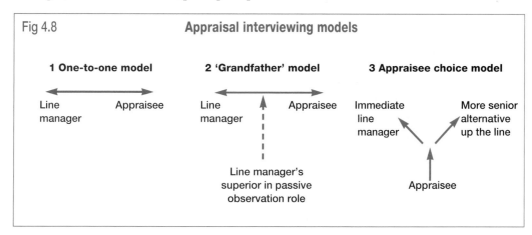

Fig 4.8   **Appraisal interviewing models**

DISCUSSION TOPIC

Which of the above models would you select as likely to be:

   a most effective;

   b fairest;

   c most cost-effective;

   d your overall choice?

The conduct of the appraisal process should be painstakingly planned and supported by appraisal forms and schedules retained as records by both parties.

In many companies the appraisal interview takes the form of three linked stages:

1 Pre-meeting preparation by appraiser and appraisee

2 The appraisal interview

3 The post-interview action plan and follow-up

■ Pre-meeting preparation

Prior to the scheduled meeting – set far enough into the future to allow for meaningful preparation – the appraiser should take pains to familiarise himself fully with the activities and work records of the appraisee relating to the year or review period in question. This may entail assembling:

■ current *Job Description*

■ Any *Confidential Reports* (e.g. evaluations from consultants delivering external short courses)

■ previous *Appraisal Review Documents*

■ intermittent *Activity Reports* from appraisee, etc.

After an updating re-read, the appraiser should formulate a series of key questions in the areas of 'last year–next year' outlined above. Such questions, while not skirting around contentious and sensitive issues (such as an apparent deterioration in the appraisee's motivation) should be couched in a neutral as opposed to inflammatory tone:

   'Do you think you're getting as much out of your job lately as you used to?'

rather than:

   'I think you've been pretty switched off lately! What do you think?'

For appraisal interviews to prove constructive and lead to positive outcomes, it is vital for the appraiser to be **fully briefed** as to the appraisee's overall performance (and difficulties encountered not of his or her making) and **fully prepared** to deal with any contentious issues – whether appraisee shortcomings, or conversely criticism by the appraisee of any organisational mismanagement. Effective appraisal interviews are rarely – if ever – confrontational. Thus the appraiser needs to possess developed interpersonal communication skills and insights.

To this end, many personnel departments design preparation forms for both appraiser and appraisee to help them set down those areas to which they wish to refer during the meeting. An appraisee's form is likely to provide opportunities for listing:

- Outline of year's key activities
- Targets set and met
- Targets missed and causes
- Personal SWOT analysis
- Areas where help/development are needed
- Areas where changes should be introduced
- Perceived priority activities for year ahead

■ The appraisal interview

PC
4.1.6

Care should be taken to ensure that appraisal interviews take place in an informal atmosphere which avoids the creation of stress. The appraiser should ensure that steps are taken to anticipate and avoid potential interruptions like incoming telephone-calls or unscheduled visitors to the office. For this reason, many organisations prefer to hold appraisal interviews in a pleasantly furnished, neutral suite, away from the hurly-burly of line management activities.

Effective appraisal interviews provide for an agenda of areas for discussion which both parties access a few days beforehand. A typical interview agenda looks like this:

TYPICAL STRUCTURE OF AN APPRAISAL INTERVIEW

1 Review of past year's achievements and review of targeted goals/objectives.
2 Identification of areas of problem, difficulty or change during the year.
3 Strategies for resolving any difficulties for direct implementation.
4 Key activities for prioritising in year ahead.
5 Identification of support resources required, including areas for personal development.
6 Creation of an action plan for direct implementation.

Appraiser strategies for effective interviewing include:

- acknowledging and confirming positive achievements
- giving the appraisee enough time to articulate his or her perception of past events
- avoiding the introduction of an 'us and them' or 'the management *vs* the rest' stand-off
- a willingness to concede areas where senior management could improve
- the seeking of joint strategies where both the management of the organisation and the appraisee cooperate mutually to build improved outcomes into the appraisee's job
- the negotiation of an action plan which is reasonable and achievable in the light of resources available to the appraisee

■ Post-interview action

For open appraisal to prove effective, it is important that a jointly agreed record is kept of what was agreed by both parties during the appraisal interview. For this reason, the appraiser and appraisee keep their own notes of negotiated objectives or promised support equipment or ancillary staff, etc.

Either at the end of, or directly after following upon the interview, the appraiser draws up (on a preprinted schedule) a checklist of agreed outcomes for the coming year, together with any supportive commitments made, including staff development to be arranged. If appropriate, areas for the appraisee to improve may be included. This checklist is then passed to the appraisee for scrutiny and acceptance. Ultimately, both parties initial their acceptance of the appraisal interview record, which is retained for future reference as the appraisal process rolls forward.

Monitoring the agreed action plan

Once defined and under way, appraisal action plans need to be regularly monitored by line managers. The entire purpose of job appraisal is rendered futile if a year is allowed to elapse before any further direct involvement in an employee's performance. By this time a team member may have gone so far off course that no amount of last minute corrective action will prevent failure and the interpersonal problems that come in its wake.

For this reason many line managers conduct informal interviews during the calendar year with their staff as a means not only of keeping in touch, but of giving a 'nudge to the tiller' which helps each individual in the departmental or unit team to keep on course and to reach – or exceed – his or her target.

■ Appraisal and reward

Just as managers take pains to provide supportive aid to under-performing employee, so it is natural that rewards should be provided to those who have worked hard and exceeded their annual targets.

For this reason, many organisations link performance with annual salary reviews and employee progression up the promotion ladder. Various mechanisms have been devised to tie in performance to salary. Some firms operate a pay review process which negotiates annual inflation-meeting pay rises with trade unions but then reserve the right to pay out merit-award bonuses on top for those individual staff deemed to have earned them. Other companies link bonuses to percentage increases in turnover or in profit and pay out in proportion to respective employees' job grades. Either way, it is important for continuing employee motivation for all involved in the enterprise to understand how effective work – above the accepted norm – is rewarded, either in promotion or financial terms.

DISCUSSION TOPICS

1 Performance appraisal is sometimes regarded by employees as a kind of back-door route of assessment for promotion and financial reward. In your opinion, should a performance appraisal scheme be conducted quite apart from a salary and progression review, or are the two inevitably linked in a manager's eyes?

2 What procedures should a performance appraisal scheme include to cope with the situation of an employee not getting on very well with his (appraising) line manager?

3 What should happen after an annual performance appraisal interview?

4 Should senior managers be obliged to take part in a performance review of them undertaken by their subordinates in a 'bottom-up' process? Or is this just not realistic?

GRIEVANCE, DISMISSAL AND REDUNDANCY PROCEDURES

Whatever the size of the workforce, large or small, inevitably disputes arise between its members. Wherever human beings interact, sooner or later an individual – or a group – will come to feel aggrieved because of a sense of injustice, unfairness or discrimination.

For this reason organisations adopt carefully worked-out procedures – agreed to by both management and trade union officers – to handle and resolve any grievances which employees may need to air

Many such problem situations are capable of being investigated and resolved at departmental or section level promptly and informally. However, where a deep sense of injustice prevails or significant interpersonal conflict has developed, a procedure needs to be in place to take the grievance to an arbitrator at a higher level.

The flow-chart in Fig. 4.9 illustrates this process.

The point at which a representative of the employee's trade union or association accompanies the aggrieved employee at a meeting depends upon the procedure which has been drawn up. All such grievance procedures are customarily produced by the organisation as a printed document which is supplied to new employees at their induction.

Because some grievances are not easily resolved, a set-down appeals procedure may – in extreme cases – allow for the intervention of a most senior figure, like a governor of a school or a non-executive chairman of the board. However, good procedures are carefully designed to resolve grievances wherever possible at lower, informal levels of the hierarchy and to avoid if possible the involvement of the 'top brass'.

If what starts out as a grievance becomes an industrial dispute, then the organisation's procedures may require the calling in of conciliation officers of the Advisory, Conciliation and Arbitration Service (ACAS) who have developed skills and experience in arbitrating in such matters.

To work at levels within the organisational hierarchy where a grievance may be settled promptly and with least upset, procedures must be designed so as to be seen as fair and

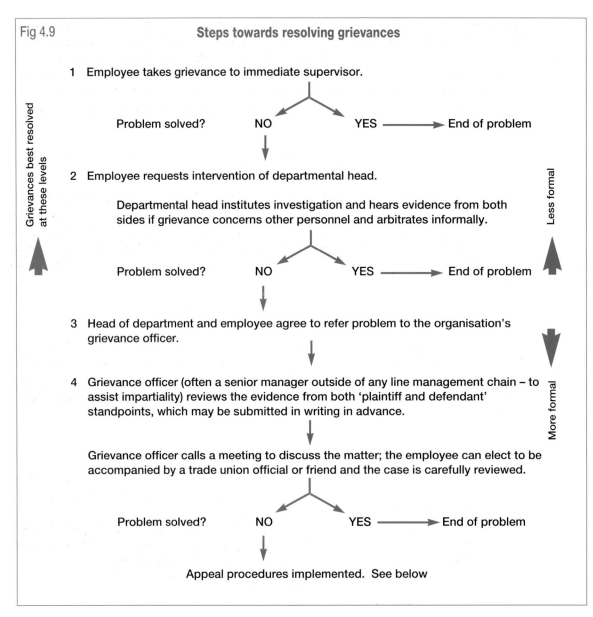

Fig 4.9 **Steps towards resolving grievances**

Grievances best resolved at these levels

1 Employee takes grievance to immediate supervisor.

Problem solved?   NO   YES   →   End of problem

2 Employee requests intervention of departmental head.

Departmental head institutes investigation and hears evidence from both sides if grievance concerns other personnel and arbitrates informally.

Problem solved?   NO   YES   →   End of problem

3 Head of department and employee agree to refer problem to the organisation's grievance officer.

4 Grievance officer (often a senior manager outside of any line management chain – to assist impartiality) reviews the evidence from both 'plaintiff and defendant' standpoints, which may be submitted in writing in advance.

Grievance officer calls a meeting to discuss the matter; the employee can elect to be accompanied by a trade union official or friend and the case is carefully reviewed.

Problem solved?   NO   YES   →   End of problem

Appeal procedures implemented. See below

Less formal

More formal

impartial by all employees. Where good industrial relations exist, management and trade union officials often work jointly to resolve a problem quickly at the informal level. Where relations are confrontational, minor grievances soon escalate because of poor communication and unwillingness to use goodwill – on either side.

■ Termination of employment

The law surrounding the termination of an employee's contract of employment places responsibilities upon both employer and employee. The law provides for notice of termination to be given on either side (see the contract of employment on page 353). In circumstances where an employee has clearly broken the contract of employment with the employer the term dismissal is used to describe the termination. Save for instances such as summary dismissal for gross misconduct, the employee is entitled to be given notice of termination of employment in accordance with statutory provisions. The period of notice will vary from one week to 'not less than twelve weeks', depending on the number of years an employee has worked for the same employer. Employees are entitled to receive in writing a statement of the reasons for termination of contract provided that they have worked for at least twenty-six weeks for the employer prior to the set date of termination.

■ Legitimate, wrongful and unfair dismissal

PC
4.1.2
4.1.4

In general terms, an employee may be legitimately dismissed if the job has properly been made redundant, if the employee is in breach of contract through a form of gross misconduct (such as reckless negligence in lighting a match in a prohibited area of an oil refinery), if legal and reasonable instructions have been disobeyed, if prescribed standards of work performance have not been met or for any other significant and legally acceptable reason.

Wrongful dismissal

In law, an employee is deemed to have been wrongfully dismissed if the employer is in breach of the contract of employment because proper notice has not been given to the employee. By the same token, an employer may seek remedies in law if an employee breaches the employment contract by failing to give and work out notice according to contract.

Unfair dismissal

The Employment Protection (Consolidation) Act 1978 makes provision for employees to obtain compensation and/or reinstatement or re-engagement if they are adjudged to have been unfairly dismissed by an industrial tribunal.

The process of securing a judgement of unfair dismissal is lengthy and complex. The Act particularly identifies the following instances where an employee would be deemed unfairly dismissed if employment were terminated because he or she had:

■ elected not to join a trade union on religious grounds

■ joined or intended to join a trade union

■ been unfairly selected for redundancy

■ become pregnant

■ not been taken on again after confinement

■ been discriminated against by being dismissed for striking (when others had not)

The twenty-six week qualifying period also obtains in cases of unfair dismissal, which can be claimed by employees up to pensionable age.

A formula for compensation is available to the adjudicating industrial tribunal:

For each year of employment

Between 18 and 21 years of age:	½ week's pay
Between 22 and 41 years of age:	1 week's pay
Between 41 and retirement age:	1½ week's pay

The current maximum compensation available for award is approximately £5,200.

While reinstatement may be legally available as a remedy for an unfairly dismissed employee, in practice it may not always be a viable proposition, given the breakdown in relations between employee and employer. An industrial tribunal may therefore take this into account when determining the award, and provisions exist to oblige employers to make further compensatory payments in such instances.

Constructive dismissal

A remedy in law may be sought by employees who believe themselves to have been constructively dismissed. This situation does not occur frequently, but may arise when an employee resigns from his or her job as a result of an action by the employer which effectively causes the job to be materially changed or done away with. For example, a manager might return from annual vacation to find that the significant parts of his job have been allocated in his absence to another executive and that as a result he has nothing meaningful to do. In frustration he may row with his boss and quit but later come to feel that he was effectively forced out. In such a case, an industrial tribunal may adjudge that the action of the company was in effect to have unfairly dismissed the manager.

Given the hardship which many unfairly dismissed employees suffer nowadays in failing to securing other, equivalent employment within a reasonable time, the levels of compensation available may be considered inadequate. Even so, the 1975 and 1978 Employment Protection Acts have proved to be legal milestones in providing protection for employees against unscrupulous 'hire and fire' employers, and the social contract which the European Community is seeking to have adopted by all member states will undoubtedly make further progress in enforcing a civilised compact between the employing and the employed.

■ Redundancy

PC
4.1.2
4.1.4

In legal terms, an employee is considered to have been made redundant if his dismissal has occurred or was mainly due to:

- the employer ending or intending to end the business for which the employee was taken on
- the employer terminating the work of the business in a place where the employee is employed
- the business requirements of the employer ceasing to need (or substantially cutting down) the work which the employee was taken on to perform

Employers have to follow procedures under various Employment Acts which require the redundancy selection process to take place fairly, without discrimination and only after consultation with appropriate trade union representatives, and unfair selection for redundancy provides grounds for action against unfair dismissal.

Many employers consider that the 'last in, first out' approach is a reasonable way to prioritise posts selected for redundancy, but other factors such as level and range of skills, length of employment service and suitability for redeployment, etc. are also used.

Progressive employers take great pains to minimise the traumatic effects which being made redundant can have on employees – especially those in middle age with many years of service behind them. Personnel departments may establish special units to counsel staff selected for redundancy and work together with local and central government agencies to help them obtain alternative employment. In addition, they may be given training while still in employment to assist them in acquiring or improving marketable skills which are in local demand.

Many organisations try to minimise the impact of enforced redundancy by offering packages to employees to encourage them to take early retirement or voluntary redundancy. Such packages may include the payment of lump sums and an addition to the number of years of pension increments to which the employee is entitled – termed pension enhancement.

Redundant employees are entitled to receive payments worked out on a scale similar to that detailed above in the section on unfair dismissal. In certain circumstances organisations may be given rebates by the government to help them meet redundancy payments.

To qualify for redundancy payments an employee needs to have worked for at least sixteen hours a week over an unbroken period of at least two years for the same employer.

ACAS AND INDUSTRIAL RELATIONS

PC
4.1.2

The Advisory Conciliation and Arbitration Service (ACAS) was established under the Employment Protection Act 1975 to promote the improvement of industrial relations in general and, in particular to broaden the base of collective bargaining between employers' confederations and trade unions.

ACAS was also charged with the responsibility of providing a conciliation and settlement service in industrial disputes by supplying individuals or teams of conciliation officers who would act as mediators, listening carefully to both sides of a dispute and helping both parties to progress to a negotiated settlement.

As a rule, ACAS responds to invitations to assist, but it is empowered under the 1975 Act to enquire actively into the activities of an industry or organisation if it is felt that there is evidence of a pressing need to improve relations.

Since 1975, ACAS has been instrumental in encouraging companies and public sector bodies to adopt ACAS-approved codes of practice in, for example, a procedure for handling disciplinary matters. Such a code of practice emphasises what an effective and fair disciplinary procedure should be.

ACAS – APPROVED ASPECTS OF A DISCIPLINARY PROCEDURE

A fair and impartial disciplinary procedure should:

- be written down;
- be made available to all employees;
- explain who operates the procedure and who is party to it;
- detail what disciplinary action is liable to be taken for what kind of indiscipline;
- allow individuals to be accompanied by a trade union official or co-worker/friend if they so wish at disciplinary interviews;
- avoid dismissal for a first disciplinary action, save in cases of gross misconduct;
- include a right of appeal;
- be administered fairly and without discrimination.

Disciplinary Procedure: Example 1 (any organisation)

(1) Purpose and scope

This procedure is designed to help and encourage all employees to achieve and maintain standards of conduct, attendance and job performance. The company rules (a copy of which is displayed in the office) and this procedure apply to all employees. The aim is to ensure consistent and fair treatment for all.

(2) Principles

a No disciplinary action will be taken against an employee until the case has been fully investigated.

b At every stage in the procedure the employee will be advised of the nature of the complaint against him or her and will be given the opportunity to state his or her case before any decision is made.

c At all stages the employee will have the right to be accompanied by a shop steward, employee representative or work colleague during the disciplinary interview.

d No employee will be dismissed for a first breach of discipline except in the case of gross misconduct when the penalty will be dismissal without notice or payment in lieu of notice.

e An employee will have the right to appeal against any disciplinary penalty imposed.

f The procedure may be implemented at any stage if the employee's alleged misconduct warrants such action.

(3) The procedure

Minor faults will be dealt with informally but where the matter is more serious the following procedure will be used:

Stage 1 – Oral warning

If conduct or performance does not meet acceptable standards the employee will normally be given a formal ORAL WARNING. He or she will be advised of the reason for the warning, that it is the first stage of the disciplinary procedure and of his or her right of appeal. A brief note of the oral warning will be kept but it will be spent after .... months, subject to satisfactory conduct and performance.

Stage 1 – Oral warning (continued)

If conduct or performance does not meet acceptable standards the employee will normally be given a formal ORAL WARNING. He or she will be advised of the reason for the warning, that it is the first stage of the disciplinary procedure and of his or her right of appeal. A brief note of the oral warning will be kept but it will be spent after ...... months, subject to satisfactory conduct and performance.

Stage 2 – Written warning

If the offence is a serious one, or if a further offence occurs, a WRITTEN WARNING will be given to the employee by the supervisor. This will give details of the complaint, the improvement required and the timescale. It will warn that action under Stage 3 will be considered if there is no satisfactory improvement and will advise of the right of appeal. A copy of this written warning will be kept by the supervisor but it will be disregarded for disciplinary purposes after ...... months subject to satisfactory conduct and performance.

Stage 3 – Final written warning or disciplinary suspension

If there is still a failure to improve and conduct or performance is still unsatisfactory, or if the misconduct is sufficiently serious to warrant only one written warning but insufficiently serious to justify dismissal (in effect both first and final written warning), a FINAL WRITTEN WARNING will normally be given to the employee. This will give details of the complaint, will warn that dismissal will result if there is no satisfactory improvement and will advise of the right of appeal. A copy of this final written warning will be kept by the supervisor but it will be spent after ...... months (in exceptional cases the period may be longer) subject to satisfactory conduct and performance.

Alternatively, consideration will be given to imposing a penalty of a disciplinary suspension without pay for up to a maximum of five working days.

Stage 4 – Dismissal

If conduct or performance is still unsatisfactory and the employee still fails to reach the prescribed standards, DISMISSAL will normally result. Only the appropriate Senior Manager can take the decision to dismiss. The employee will be provided, as soon as reasonably practicable, with written reasons for dismissal, the date on which employment will terminate and the right of appeal.

(4) Gross misconduct

The following list provides examples of offences which are normally regarded as gross misconduct:

theft, fraud, deliberate falsification of records,

fighting, assault on another person,

deliberate damage to company property,

serious incapability through alcohol or being under the influence of illegal drugs,

serious negligence which causes unacceptable loss, damage or injury,

serious act of insubordination,

unauthorised entry to computer records.

If you are accused of an act of gross misconduct, you may be suspended from work on full pay, normally for no more than five working days, while the company investigates the alleged offence. If, on completion of the investigation and the full disciplinary procedure, the company is satisfied that gross misconduct has occurred, the result will normally be summary dismissal without notice or payment in lieu of notice.

(5) Appeals

An employee who wishes to appeal against a disciplinary decision should inform ...... within two working days. The Senior Manager will hear all appeals and his/her decision is final. At the appeal any disciplinary penalty imposed will be reviewed but it cannot be increased.

Checklist for handling a disciplinary matter

This checklist sets out the key steps which employers should consider when handling a disciplinary matter. All employers regardless of size should observe the principles of natural justice embodied below:

1 Gather all the relevant facts:
- promptly before memories fade
- take statements, collect documents
- in serious cases consider suspension with pay while an investigation is conducted.

2 Be clear about the complaint:
- is action needed at this stage?

3 If so decide whether the action should be:
- advice and counselling
- formal disciplinary action.

4 If formal action is required, arrange a disciplinary interview:
- ensure that the individual is aware of the nature of the complaint and that the interview is a disciplinary one
- tell the individual where and when the interview will take place and of a right to be accompanied.
- try to arrange for a second member of management to be present.

5 Start by introducing:
- those present and the purpose of the interview
- the nature of the complaint
- the supporting evidence.

6 Allow the individual to state his/her case:
- consider and question any explanations put forward.

7 If any new facts emerge:
decide whether further investigation is required; if it is, adjourn the interview and reconvene when the investigation is completed.

8 Except in very straightforward cases, call an adjournment before reaching a decision:
come to a clear view about the facts
if they are disputed, decide on the balance of probability what version of the facts is true

9 Before deciding the penalty consider:
the gravity of the offence and whether the procedure gives guidance as to:
- the penalty applied in similar cases in the past
- the individual's disciplinary record and general service
- any mitigating circumstances
- whether the proposed penalty is reasonable in all the circumstances.

10 Reconvene the disciplinary interview to:
- clearly inform the individual of the decision and the penalty if any
- explain the right of appeal and how it operates
- in the case of a warning explain what improvement is expected, how long the warning will last and what the consequences of failure to improve may be.

11 Record the action taken:
- if other than an oral warning, confirm the disciplinary action to the individual in writing
- keep a simple record of the action taken for future reference.

12 Monitor the individual's performance:
- disciplinary action should be followed up with the object of encouraging improvement
- monitor progress regularly and discuss it with the individual.

ACAS offers further advice for handling the disciplinary process to the effect that all disciplinary matters should be carefully investigated before any hasty formal meeting is arranged, that all employees should have the right to state their side of the matter at issue and if they wish be accompanied by a trade union official. They also suggest that disciplinary codes (except in cases of proven gross misconduct) should provide for warnings and opportunities for employees to remedy any shortcomings before a dismissal letter is issued. Such opportunities are given a time-scale in which an employee may, for example, be given three months in which to demonstrate an improvement. Many disciplinary procedures provide for two orally delivered warnings and a final written one prior to dismissal. At all events, an employer's disciplinary code must be demonstrably fair and reasonable.

Where an employee considers that he or she has not had access to a just disciplinary process leading up to dismissal, the right exists in law to take a complaint of unfair dismissal to an industrial tribunal (*see below*).

While employers are not required to adopt such codes of practice, their acceptance and use on the part of employers may go a long way towards demonstrating in industrial disputes and industrial tribunal actions that an employer has acted with due reasonable care towards a particular, aggrieved employee.

■ Industrial tribunals and appeal tribunals

PC
4.1.2
4.1.4

Industrial tribunals were established by parliament to operate as types of court – with legal powers – to hear cases relating to complaints made under a range of Employment Acts, such as wrongful and unfair dismissal and unfair selection for redundancy, etc.

Such tribunals work through ACAS in the first instance to seek to effect a conciliation, but ultimately have powers to require reinstatements or to award financial compensation where an employee's case is proven to the tribunal's satisfaction.

Employment Appeal Tribunals were established by the 1975 Employment Protection Act to provide both employers and employees access to a higher authority which would adjudicate on appeals lodged after industrial tribunal hearings.

Appeals heard by the Appeals Tribunal include those arising from actions taken under the following Acts:

Equal Pay Act 1970

Sex Discrimination Act 1975

Employment Protection Act 1975

Race Relations Act 1976

Employment Protection (Consolidation) Act 1978

DISCUSSION TOPICS

PC
4.1.2
4.1.4

1 What qualities would you expect to find in an organisation's grievance officer? What could be done if he or she did not possess them in the eyes of employees with grievances?

2 Do you think employees generally are sufficiently aware of their employment rights? If not, what would you propose as practical means of improving the public's levels of awareness?

3 What impact do you think periods of recession and rising job insecurity have on industrial relations?

Do you think that employment legislation goes far enough in securing an employee's employment rights? Or too far? Should all employees accept that they are part of a job market for buying and selling work skills, and if they do not complain when they receive rises and promotion, nor should they if they are laid off or made redundant?

4 Have trade unions had their day? Or are they needed more than ever in organisations which provide employment?

5 Can an employee ever be adequately compensated for unfair dismissal – even if a return to the same job is made available by the judgement of an industrial tribunal?

 REVIEW TEST (Elements 4.1, 4.2, 4.3)

1 Explain briefly the main stages of an open performance appraisal scheme.

2 List in sequence the main steps to be taken in a model grievance procedure.

3 Explain the difference between wrongful and unfair dismissal.

4 What is meant by the term constructive dismissal?

5 Which Acts of Parliament deal primarily with disciplinary procedures, dismissal and redundancy?

6 Outline the steps an organisation should take before making an employee redundant.

7 What are the main functions of an industrial tribunal?

8 What does ACAS stand for and what does it do?

PC
4.1.6

MANAGING THE WORK OF EMPLOYEES

A time-worn, but nevertheless accurate definition of management is:

Helping the organisation to attain its goals by enabling others to achieve their objectives.

Thus managers only achieve themselves if they promote attitudes, climates and motivators which encourage their subordinates – those reporting directly to them – to achieve.

For this enabling function to work effectively, managers first have learned how to lead. Various management theorists have identified different styles of leadership in organisations. Set out below are outlines of what major management theorists considered to be important issues and concepts on the subject of leadership in organisations.

■ Max Weber 1864–1920

Power, authority and their impact on leadership styles

German born, Max Weber made a lifelong study of the structure of organisations and what enabled managers within them to impose their authority on subordinates. He identified three different kinds of organisation: the **charismatic**, like a religious sect or political party, in which authority was based upon a form of devoted loyalty to the leader; the **rational-legal** in which authority was made legitimate because leaders managed from positions of respected expertise and efficiency; and the **traditional** organisation (like the country club) in which authority stemmed from hallowed custom and practice. Weber termed his rational-legal organisation a bureaucracy (not in the modern sense of a bumbling, red-tape festooned set-up) but because its main features were: rational structures, able administrators and impersonal efficiency. Weber's important contribution was to explain how a leader's authority stemmed from the respect given by subordinates to his or her acknowledged expertise.

■ Henri Fayol 1841–1925

Henri Fayol's incisive French logic and intellect marked him as perhaps the most important of the early management thinkers. He produced a series of definitive management activities (see below). Fayol was way ahead of his time, and in particular he helped to bring about clear lines of management, unambiguous job descriptions and coordinated activities in organisations:

The Fayol 14-point management profile

Perhaps the most important of early management thinkers, Fayol formulated a management profile consisting of 14 definitive activities:

1 Division of work,
2 Authority,
3 Discipline,
4 Unity of command,
5 Unity of direction,
6 Subordination of individual interests to the general interest,
7 Remuneration,
8 Centralisation,
9 Scalar chain (the perceived line of authority),
10 Order,
11 Equity,
12 Stability of tenure of personnel,
13 Initiative,
14 Esprit de corps.

His thinking led to developments such as line-management-based organisational hierarchies, specialist departments and the role of senior managers as corporate strategists and anticipated the motivation studies of the 1940s and 50s.

From *General and Industrial Management* by Henri Fayol © 1EE 1984 with permission of Lake Publishing Company

---

Fayol's far-reaching list of management functions led to developments like line management-based organisational hierarchies, the establishing of specialist departments, the role of senior managers as corporate strategists and, in particular, he anticipated the motivation studies of the human relations management school of the 1940s and 50s.

■ Elton Mayo 1880–1949

The Hawthorne Studies – group solidarity and motivation

Elton Mayo, an Australian who worked mostly in the USA, carried out with associates in the early 1930s a series of experiments in the factories and workrooms of Western Electric's Hawthorne Works in Chicago. These researches came to be known as The Hawthorne Studies.

Mayo's team discovered that factory operatives' output and motivation improved significantly when a sympathetic interest (by the Mayo team) was shown in their work. What also came to light unexpectedly was the power of peer group pressure exerted by the group over its members. What the group *chose to do*, and therefore what each member felt able to carry out, was just as important as what management wanted them to do. Mayo's studies brought out into the limelight the importance of a caring and supportive management approach in motivating groups with strong member-centred loyalties.

■ Frederick Herzberg 1923–
Douglas McGregor 1906–1964
Abraham Maslow 1908–1970
Rensis Likert 1903–

Self-actualisation and the human relations school

Mayo's work on motivation and groups was built upon in the period spanning the Second World War (when the need to motivate workers to sustain the war effort was paramount) in a spate of research by social scientists like Herzberg, McGregor, Maslow, Likert and Argyris.

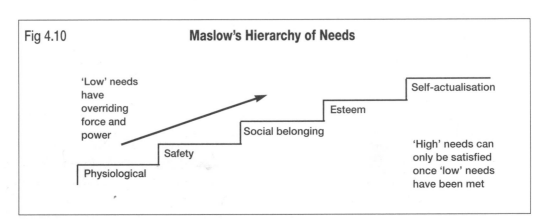

Fig 4.10   **Maslow's Hierarchy of Needs**

In 1943 Abraham Maslow published his *A Theory of Human Motivation*. In it he demonstrated his theory that people in organisations acted upon a tiered hierarchy of needs, where basic life-supporting needs like food, shelter and safety had to be assured before more sophisticated ones (social acceptance, esteem and self-actualisation) could be satisfied (Fig 4.10).

Maslow's insights into the psychological needs of people and the roles they adopt at work was followed in the late 1950s by the famous studies of Frederick Herzberg and his team into motivation among 200 accountants and engineers in Pittsburgh. Herzberg, in a series of in-depth interviews established the following factors as primary motivators of people at work:

Frederick Herzberg's Motivators and Hygiene Factors

Herzberg's Five Major Motivators

- achievement
- recognition
- the work itself
- responsibility
- and advancement.

Frederick Herzberg carried out studies in the late 1950s in Pittsburgh into the motivation of people at work – he listed a number of factors under headings of Motivators (nature of task, achievement, recognition, responsibility, advancement) and 'Hygiene factors' (salary, bonuses, commission, working conditions, acceptability of supervision, pleasantness of working environment, job security). Good hygiene factors help to maintain a person's feeling about work but do not in themselves motivate (a big pay rise soon becomes accepted as the norm).

Above all, Herzberg established, employees needed to be doing a job they believed in and to have their successful efforts recognised and esteemed by their superiors.

Herzberg' s researches also revealed a number of features of which, though they helped to prevent actual demotivation were not in themselves sources of motivational energy. Of these, high pay, acceptable supervision, friendly colleagues, a smart environment and job security featured most. Herzberg called the first set The Motivators and the second Hygiene Factors.

McGregor's Theory X and Theory Y

Douglas McGregor, an American social psychologist and management consultant, identified two contrasting management styles which he observed in the running of different organisations.

He crystallised the key features of both styles or management cultures in his Theory X and Theory Y set of traits. According to McGregor, organisations tended to be run according to either of these fundamentally opposed approaches:

Theory X proposes that, essentially, people are lazy and shiftless and cannot be expected to work hard unless they are closely supervised and 'kept at it' by vigilant, 'hard-nosed' managers.

Theory Y by contrast perceives employees as innately wanting to work hard and perform well, who can be relied upon to 'get on with it' unsupervised in the right supportive working climate.

McGregor's studies examine the inevitable conflicts and tensions which arise when, for example, an organisation's top management strictly adheres to a Theory X style and middle management seeks to work to the Theory Y style. Here frustration and aggression are likely to result in Y-style managers trying to work supportively in a system reliant upon close supervision and stringent line-management control.

McGregor does, of course, concede that organisations are rarely all X or all Y. But he does conclude that, where one style is endorsed, only a full commitment from the top down is likely to have any success in changing it throughout the organisation. Also, it is important to remember that some organisations and units – the armed forces, police, operating theatres, etc – can only work effectively, and when seconds count, within a style of decisive, even autocratic leadership. For who needs a group decision debate on what clamp to use on a severely haemorrhaging patient!

What McGregor's twin scenarios did do, however, was to focus attention on to what style of management was most likely to work in what kind of organisation. It made managers much more aware that directive, Theory X styles are fine in highly structured and disciplined situations, but serve only to put up the backs of professional employees whose education and technical expertise have given them an independence and 'power position' in high-tech or project-centred organisations which only Theory Y styles can successfully harness.

Likert's 'Principle of Supportive Relationships'

Like McGregor, Rensis Likert was an American social scientist. He too was preoccupied with studies of manager/managed relationships. Essentially, his research was based on the premise that effective management and worker output is reliant upon 'mutual respect and trust'. Likert was interested in the potential – often undervalued – of the interlocking work groups which he believed formed the basis of all organisational structures. Management's task was to create a climate in which such groups would interconnect and work harmoniously together for the good of the enterprise. To this end, Likert considered an effective management style to be :

- supportive • helpful and friendly • interested in employee welfare • just but firm
- justifying staff's confidence and respect • committed to staff development
- caring of weaker personnel • able at planning and organising work
- expert in chosen specialism.

In Likert's view, all working groups should be involved in the decision-making process. Even senior ranking managers could be brought into line by a judicious use of consensus decision-making in meetings of a cross-section of staff.

Likert's researches convinced him that a supportive and caring management style was most likely to succeed in motivating groups of workers to give of their best.

The impact of the behavioural or human relations school of management (sometimes referred to as the 'process' school) from 1935–1965 was far-reaching and is still today rippling through current management philosophy. Given that more and more jobs nowadays require advanced technical expertise and professional know-how – NASA space projects, software applications design, defence weapon manufacture and so on – it is little wonder that 'supportive relationships' and 'self-actualisation' management styles are widely and successfully adopted.

■ Current thinking on management and leadership styles

PC
4.1.6

A major swing of the management pendulum away from human relations-based styles occurred in the 1960s and early 1970s, which was founded on a much more task-centred approach. It came to be called **Management by Objectives and Results**.

In MBOR, from the top, through the middle and to the bottom of the organisation, meetings are held at the outset of the work cycle between a manager and his immediate subordinates with the following aims:

- To discuss proposed objectives and targets for the subordinate to achieve within a preset timescale.

- To negotiate these objectives and eventually to agree them and to impose a series of deadlines for their delivery.

- If possible to quantify the targets – e.g. 10 per cent increase in turnover or £2 million increase in net profit.

Once the objectives have been agreed, a process is set up which enables the manager to monitor progress at regular intervals in order to ensure success at the delivery point. In this way, targets may be modified and corrective actions introduced in good time.

MBOR certainly led to a more 'outcome centred' and task-based management style – which in some cases rode roughshod over people in the process and on the downside, senior managers in some firms came to feel that MBOR caused too many high-achieving but individualistic executives to leave and move to other, less regimented organisations.

On the positive side, however, it brought about a sophisticated system of job appraisal and performance rating. In turn, this led to the establishment of fairer salary scales and employment packages being available, because personnel directors had much more informed and realistic ideas of what managers could be expected to achieve throughout the organisation.

DISCUSSION TOPICS

1 Do you agree with Max Weber's identification of three kinds of organisational culture: charismatic, rational-legal and traditional? Can you identify any other types which have emerged since Weber's times?

2 Do you think that Maslow's hierarchy of human needs theory is an accurate predictor of human behaviour, or is he wide of the mark?

3 How far do you go along with Herzberg's motivator/hygiene factor theory of motivation?

4 Does McGregor's X and Y theory over-simplify types of organisational culture and management, or did he 'hit the button'?

5 Is Rensis Likert's view of the role of management: supportive, caring and trusting, etc., idealistic wishful thinking, or the only really effective way of getting the best out of a workforce?

6 Is the quid pro quo or pay-back theory of motivation the only one which, in reality, works today?

CHECKLIST OF MAJOR LEADERSHIP TRAITS AND CHARACTERISTICS

The Trait Approach

Popular in the 1950s and 60s, the Trait Approach identified a series of personal qualities which leaders were supposed to possess. The following list represents those which were claimed to be most widely referred to in surveys as leadership characteristics:

- intelligence;
- articulate and convincing speaking skills;
- decisiveness;
- drive and determination;
- initiative;
- cooperativeness and social skills;
- ability to get things done;
- insight and perception;
- self-assurance and conviction.

The Trait Approach tends to be disregarded by some management specialists and personnel recruiting managers because the list of qualities is endlessly variable and difficult to assess objectively. Nevertheless, few managers would disagree that there are personality traits in leaders which separate them from the pack – not least a stubborn determination to achieve for themselves what they set out to do.

The Style Theory

Supporters of the Style Theory consider that organisations possess different management systems-whether because of the nature of their work or because of an historical kind of management style. Thus various organisations will have a system which leans to being:

● Dictatorial ● Benevolent autocratic ● Consultative ● Democratic

The Style Theory – of which Rensis Likert was a leading investigator – states that leadership in such organisations will tend to reflect that of the system, either by being more task-centred or more people-centred

The Leadership Grid Approach

A number of management experts – Blake, Mouton, Reddin – devised various grids or matrices as handy visual aids to support their theories of leadership, which took the Style view a stage further. Blake and Mouton's grid, for example, plotted a leadership style which could either be high in a task or a people approach: or a mixture of the two:

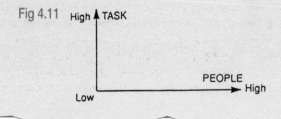

Fig 4.11

The ideal leader would display a style which blended both – neither forgetting the task outcomes in supporting his team, yet neither overlooking staff needs while securing the outcome desired. In a similar way, Reddin's grid identified leadership styles ranging from 'deserter' to 'developer', and detailed instances in which a compromising approach would be legitimate.

Fiedler's Contingency Theory

An American, F. E. Fiedler, published a theory in 1967 which he called a contingency model. This contended that a leadership style – in the same manager and organisation – could vary from being very task-centred to being very people-centred, depending on what the manager's relationship was with his staff at the time.

Funnily enough, a very task-centred approach seemed to be equally successful when the situation was very favourable or very unfavourable to the manager. When it was neither one nor the other, a people-centred approach seemed most successful. While Fiedler claimed to have validated this theory in documented cases, other specialists remained sceptical.

The 'Best Fit' Leadership Approach

More recently, management specialists have supported an approach to leading staff called the 'Best Fit'. Here the leader/manager – whether consciously or unconsciously – emphasises a mix of the basic three ingredients of leadership:

THE TASK   THE SUPPORT STAFF   THE LEADER

Some situations – say where a fast, 'no arguments!' decision is needed may see a fit like this, where the Leader and Task components are high (Fig 4.12):

Fig 4.12

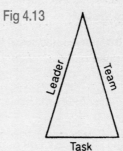

Fig 4.13

Another scenario, say where the situation is dynamic and fast-changing, may require a much more staff–leader consultative style (Fig 4.13):

The 'Pay-Back' Theory

The advent of the materialistic 1980s characterised by the rise and rise of Yuppydom, Dinkies (Double Income No Kids Yet) and 'power-dressing' gave rise to a management approach which acknowledged that 'nothing is for nothing'. Here, support staff were viewed as requiring a quid pro quo – 'If I do what you want, what's in it for me?' In reality this trade-off is as old as man's first social groupings, but the 1980s brought out into sharp focus a hard-nosed, political, organisation man and woman who were much surer of what they were out to achieve in career terms and confident enough to drive hard daily bargains with their bosses on negotiated roles, tasks and activities.

PC
4.1.6

DISCUSSION TOPICS

1 What do you think are the qualities of leadership a good manager should possess?

2 If you were one of an interviewing team of senior managers about to select a junior manager for an important promotion, what sort of evidence of leadership would you look for in those short-listed?

3 Do you agree that an organisation's management style can be either broadly dictatorial or broadly democratic? Or is this a wild over-simplification?

4 Do you think that managers/leaders tend either to be task- or people-centred in their management styles because of deep-rooted personality traits and there's an end of it! Or do you think that a manager could consciously mix the two to achieve a given management task?

5 Can leaders be made? If so, how?

6 'He leads from the front!' is an often quoted response about certain managers. What is meant by it?

CHECKLIST OF EFFECTIVE DELEGATION TECHNIQUES

● Both manager and subordinate(s) know clearly and precisely what the delegated task comprises.

● A reasonable and mutually accepted deadline has been agreed and confirmed (usually best in writing – but it depends on the reliability of the people involved). Once the time-span has been agreed, staff can set about blocking out time in their diaries and planning the sequence of the components of the task.

● Whoever has been delegated to do the job has full access to the resources and tools needed – key data, computer terminal, graphics software, laser printer, etc. If, say, the task is to produce handouts and overhead foils for a presentation.

● The task 'doer' possesses the skills, expertise and experience to enable the job to be achieved proficiently.

● Where doing the job involves other personnel inside or outside of the organisation, the manager has facilitated access (especially if superiors are involved) by a memo or letter at the outset of the project.

● If the task is involved and complex, the manager diaries a series of interim meetings with the subordinate(s) to check on progress towards the deadline and completion, and trouble-shoots any problems or bottle-necks.

● Sufficient time is allowed both to absorb possible delays (within the agreed time-span) and to proof-read or check scrupulously any documents OHPs, models, etc. prior to their final submission – by both manager and subordinate(s) – if the end-product is to be despatched to senior staff or external clients and/or contacts.

Effective delegation requires good organisation and communication – by both the manager and the managed.

■ Effective delegation

Whatever leadership and motivational styles are employed by managers in organisations, for their work to be effective, they have to master the techniques of delegation – of achieving the organisation's preset objectives throughout the work of others.

■ Managing negotiations

PC
4.1.2
4.1.6

A crucial management skill lies in the ability to secure desired outcomes by gaining the acceptance of others for plans, proposals or policies. This objective is often secured through the process of negotiation.

Good negotiations leave both parties feeling that they have achieved most of what they hoped for. Like bazaar bartering, negotiations tend to move from established first positions to a meeting in the middle – where say a pay deal is offered and accepted – compromise having been made by both parties.

Like the direct sales approach, negotiation requires practised skills:

First positions: both parties prepare their ground in first positions – usually what their ideal outcome scenario is.

Preliminary skirmishing: both sides 'test the water' with their proposals. Note: wily negotiators generally decide in advance what their worst situation acceptance point is and also the point at which negotiations would be called off or adjourned.

Agreeing the non-contentious parts: to build an atmosphere of goodwill and a productive working relationship, non-contentious issues and second-tier matters are often negotiated first.

Trading-off the deal: the essence of negotiation lies in trading off some aspects so as to gain others; intelligent negotiators always know what parts of their package are most readily negotiable in this sense. This stage is marked by hard and detailed bargaining; good negotiators make it their business to be expert in the other side's views, specialisms and work. Lack of inside or expert knowledge about the other side is a poor negotiating base.

Spotting the favourable balance and sealing the deal: experienced negotiators become very skilled at knowing when they have wrung as many concessions out as are forthcoming; like all good communicators they know when to stop; at this stage it is vital to have listed mutually agreed conditions, concessions, undertakings and so on for the record and for later issue in a joint statement.

Saving the face and leaving something in the pot

Wise negotiators who emerge victorious from a negotiating sequence always ensure that the other party is not left having totally lost face – especially as in pay-round negotiations there is always a next time to deal with the same team of negotiators. Likewise unless negotiating unconditional surrender, victorious negotiators 'leave something in the pot' for the other side to take back and display as their winnings. In this way a little oil is left on the 'next time' negotiation wheel.

Confirming the deal

The final phase is marked by trade union members or their executive committees or boards of directors or HM Government, for example, accepting negotiated proposals and confirming or ratifying the agreement reached. *Note*: almost all negotiated agreements are given a limited time-span and will almost always list scenarios which could invalidate the agreement or require its modification. For example, a rise in bank rate, the value of the pound, mortgage interest rates, maintenance of productivity increases, etc.

The negotiating manager therefore needs to:

- research and prepare the topic for negotiation thoroughly
- anticipate the other party's proposals and have ready counter-proposals
- study the personalities and susceptibilities of his opponents
- draw up a checklist of pawns which could be sacrificed in the negotiating chess match
- identify clearly the back-stop position which is his sticking-point
- clarify regularly what precisely the other side is proposing or agreeing to and record it as the process unfolds
- spot when he has achieved his aims and seal the deal promptly
- keep superiors in continuous touch while securing ongoing approvals for concessions

Some wheeler-dealer managers love to negotiate; others find it an irksome chore. For all managers, however, developing effective negotiating skills lies at the very heart of successful trading, workforce motivation and the industrial relations which underpin the economy.

PC
4.1.6

DISCUSSION TOPICS

1 What do you think it is today that 'legitimises' a manager's actions and authority in organisations? A mesmerising personality? Hire and fire power? Sweet reasonableness?

2 What features do you think likely to characterise management styles over the next decade? Why?

3 'The systems management approach works brilliantly in textbook models, but is far too impersonal and rigid ever to work in practice!'

4 'The contingency – "Anything goes" model demonstrates the lack today of any kind of business ethic or moral basis for management practice.' Fair comment? Do achieved ends justify any management means today?

5 Is conflict necessarily a 'bad thing' in organisations? Can it ever be productive?

6 How important are recognition and acknowledgement to you?

■ Effective decision-making

One of the simplest ways of distinguishing between a good and a poor manager is to vet the quality of their decision-making. At the top of the managerial tree, company directors and civil servants are charged with making decisions which involve millions of pounds and the jobs of thousands, or outcomes which could affect the material wealth of the country for many years. Middle and junior managers, while limited to making sectional rather than corporate decisions, can also make a significant difference between an organisation's profit or loss. Little wonder, then, that management specialists have given so much attention to the processes of decision-making and decision management.

Most experts see decision-making as moving through five distinct phases:

STAGES IN THE DECISION-MAKING PROCESS

1 Open, free-ranging, brainstorming survey of a proposal

2 Detailed evaluation of aspects and options

3 Selection of most attractive/practical option

4 Implementing the decision; marking its boundaries

5 Analysing outcomes and effecting called-for follow-up.

1 Aims and concepts

The first stage concerns a brainstorming survey of what the issue in question is all about: Why research a new product? Who for? To do what? What market? What's in it for the firm? Long- or short-term prospects? Product life? Do we have the technology? The production capacity?

2 In-depth evaluation of strategies and options

Having undertaken a wide-ranging overview of the background, nature, scope and desired outcomes of the idea, the second phase is to quantify it, cost it, test it in models and prototypes – generally to evaluate it from all angles. From this stage will probably emerge several options. Marketeers refer to optimistic and pessimistic scenarios; R & D scientists may produce high-, middle- and low-cost research programme options and suggest alternative test designs.

3 Selecting the best available option

The third stage is usually marked by a trade-off between identified options – dearest/cheapest, fastest/slowest; needs bought-in experts/we have in-house skills, etc. At this stage some experts refer to the common practice of 'satisficing', where managers opt for the easiest, cheapest, 'least hassle' way out that can convince a majority, even though this may not be the best solution. Important in this stage also is to consider the costs of making *no* decision.

4 Implementing the decision

Once the go-ahead in principle is made, the decision is implemented and boundary positions are identified: limit of injected cash, length of trial period, amount of time available, number of employees committed, etc. Also, the required outcomes of the decision are carefully identified and circulated to all concerned.

5 Post-decision evaluation and feedback

The decision having been implemented, its outcomes (predicted and unpredicted) and its costs and benefits are analysed. In their light, follow-up activities are either reinforced and expanded, stabilised, or reduced or terminated.

Effective managers pursue this kind of decision-making process more or less strenuously depending on the importance of the decision. Ineffective ones allow emotion, prejudice, stubbornness, and a failure to think things through to mar the process. They also generally fail to unearth the relevant facts and factors or to interpret them correctly.

PC
4.1.2

■ Managing conflict

Even the happiest family has its rows and upsets, and organisations are no different. Few managers, therefore, escape an involvement in conflicts from time to time. Conflict scenarios vary enormously, yet most have their roots in human behaviour and psychology:

■ X feels he/she has been slighted, put-down, shown up, made to look a fool, 'wound up', etc. by Y and either reacts angrily or sulks; either way productivity falls as tensions mount until, possibly, one or two people quit.

■ The working group is upset by a new policy/standing order/working condition imposed by management and introduces an official or unspoken work-to-rule to vent anger and frustration.

■ Y gets promoted; X and Z feel by-passed and start a whispering campaign that makes Y's life a misery.

■ Z fails to get appointed to the restructured Project Management Group and therefore feels humiliated, by-passed, put out to grass and overtaken by a younger whizz-kid; resentment smoulders and the working atmosphere suffers.

Such examples serve to illustrate that conflict arises mostly from interpersonal relationships, although we have already seen instances of conflict caused by counter-running interests: management role *v.* union membership, or from a mismatch between a person's ethical code and actions required by management.

Resolving conflict is a highly fatiguing and demanding process. Firstly, the manager has to become skilled in identifying its early warning signs – changes in staff's behaviour patterns in small things, or huddled groups in earnest 'conflab' which dies away on approach, stress-related' absenteeism, etc. Here a discreet secretary can be a great help to the preoccupied manager in alerting him to danger signs.

Having sensed a conflict situation – or having been confronted by it – the manager needs to take immediate steps to defuse it. This usually involves private, individual interviews with affected parties to hear all sides of the dispute. Having decided first upon a fair and attainable solution, the manager then needs to bring the involved parties together to deliver a solution/judgement and – what is quite essential – to secure a clearly expressed acceptance from all sides that there will be no rancour. Of course people say one thing in a manager's office and do another outside on their own patch. Thinking managers therefore make the time to monitor post-reconciliation behaviour and attitudes – and rightly come down hard on those who harbour grudges.

On occasion, a removal from the conflict situation is the only practical solution. Deep-seated personality clashes between two key personnel may require a transfer of one out of the 'aggro arena'. Again, advice may be needed for staff who are unable to square the circle of, say, young children and full-time working so that children are put first and job second, by arranging part-time work until further notice.

Key elements of successful conflict resolution by the manager are:

- strict fairness and impartiality
- trustworthy and sensitive approach to gain confidence
- even-handed examination of each party's position
- identifying root causes and deciding on corrective actions
- outcomes must be enforceable and fair
- resolution of the conflict must be accepted sincerely – by all parties
- loss of face must be avoided/minimised
- reconciliation must be monitored for sincerity/working in practice
- transfers/job-role changes may be necessary

The process of resolving interpersonal conflict in support staff is most stressful in the phases which bring affected parties together. Here the manager will need to have rehearsed a very clear line of argument and be prepared to pull out all his or her persuasive communication stops!

Note: In some conflict situations it may be helpful for a third-party counsellor to be brought in to manage the resolution process as a totally disinterested referee.

■ Managing stress

PC
4.1.2
4.1.6

Stress is a killer. Every day hundreds of people suffer heart attacks aggravated by stress, and many die. Stress also maims minds. Each year thousands of people are hospitalised in psychiatric centres suffering from mental breakdowns, nervous collapses or depression – where stress has proved a contributive factor. Happily many recover from heart attacks and bouts of mental illness to go on to realise their potential and goal aims. Yet their pain and illness could often have been foreseen and prevented.

Thus all managers have a bounden duty to prevent stress becoming a health hazard among their staff. Small amounts of stress are inescapable, and part of living. Indeed, some experts believe that people perform better – in sport, in the theatre or at work – if 'psyched up' with the adrenalin flowing. But this is not the same as this kind of stress:

- *Job overload*

  'My work is piling up with shorter and shorter deadlines and everyone's yelling for overdue WP copy . . . and I just can't cope any more!'

- *Lack of proper management guidance*

  'No one ever tells me what I'm supposed to do and everyone snaps at me for treading on their toes. I can't seem to grasp hold of what's wanted of me and I worry that I'm not doing my job, so I'll get the bullet!

- *Deliberate exclusion*

  'Ever since I had a row with JJ, I've been frozen out; no more informational memos, meetings are called that I don't get invited to any more – although matters are raised affecting my department . . . I think somebody's trying to tell me something!'

Many causes of stress are to do with office politics and the dark side of human nature where ambition, jealousy, envy and petty spite conspire to upset and injure targeted individuals. Some employees are also their own worst enemies in that they have sensitive natures, 'thin skins' and are vulnerable to masked bullying or being 'picked on'. Yet other causes of stress have nothing to do with having become isolated from the pack. They concern:

■ *Not enough responsibility:* a job beneath someone's capabilities can soon lead to frustration and stress.

■ *Too much responsibility:* very conscientious employees may become worriers if promoted too high or too fast, and this may lead to stress and nervous disorders.

■ *Inadequate/non-existent job description:* staff who lack a clearly stated set of responsibilities delegated from their superiors are likely to flounder, yet overwork in an effort to ensure they are doing enough. A failure ever to receive recognition, praise or at least confirmation that the work is going satisfactorily can also lead to stress.

■ *Over-exposure to people and communication overload:* many managers try to maintain an overloaded interface with their staff and contacts, who are thus encouraged to check every decision with the boss and to want his personal ear constantly. This commonly causes stress as the manager tries to keep twenty jobs, forty staff and thirty messages all spinning at once like plates on a juggler's bamboo sticks. Usually the manager's brains end up spinning fastest!

Further causes include conflict situations – between personnel or between employee and the organisation, troubles at home, affairs of the heart especially affairs within organisations, money troubles and so on.

The effective manager needs to tackle stress among his staff in a way similar to that of handling conflict. First, he must be ever-alert to symptoms and signs of stressed behaviour. Secondly, affected staff must be sensitively interviewed and section leaders questioned until the surface and then root causes of the stress are identified. With the staff member and his supervisor, the manager then needs to review work roles, responsibilities, team membership – whatever interfaces or activities are causing the stress and then to devise a programme which will alleviate the stress-causing factors. The affected person's future work and state of mind should be carefully and discreetly monitored for signs of recurrent stress. If the manager has interceded early and well, then the problem may be cured for good.

STRESS SIGNALS

● Increased nervousness

● Shorter fuse – irritability

● Fall in work output

● Increase in making mistakes

● Physical disorders: nervous ticks, shortness of breath

● Absenteeism, idling, vacant moods

● Intolerance increase

● Rise in smoking, drinking, pill-taking

● Apparently unmotivated weeping

● Unwillingness to see staff

Both managers and support staff have a responsibility to counter stress symptoms by:

- engaging in 'switching off' recreations: sport; hobbies, away-days, long weekends, etc
- getting enough of the right food and rest
- pacing work throughout the day – taking time out for a stroll to see a colleague
- balancing work with social life, not taking work home every night
- doing relaxation/meditation exercises
- keeping a sense of humour and perspective
- planning work and rest times in balanced mixes a week at a time and sticking to the plan

The effective manager knows the dangers of stress for himself and his team and keeps its prevention always high on his personal agenda.

MANAGING ONESELF

So far, this Unit has concentrated on the personnel function, aspects of employment law, appraisal procedures, leadership, motivational, delegating, negotiating techniques and the management of conflict and stress – all key aspects of effective human resource management.

And the perspective of this Unit has been general and directed towards the explanation of concepts, principles and current practices. Yet what is undoubtedly the most important aspect of human resource management has been left till last:

Your ability to manage yourself successfully at work

Moreover, a mastery of the skills of self-management is essential at whatever level and location an employee is positioned in the organisational hierarchy. Save for employees whose jobs are governed by repetitive routine under close supervision, all staff are expected to work under their own initiative at times. The ability to work conscientiously while unsupervised increases as the employee moves up the organisation. Middle and senior managers are expected to organise their own time and allocated resources – human, financial and material – in order to meet delegated targets without the constant interference from those above.

Clearly, the faster one learns and employs self-management skills at work, the more likely the work is to be successful – as set tasks are accomplished on or before time – and the more likely the person is to secure advancement through recognition of achievement.

■ Developing self-starting strengths

The strength of the self-starter is that, because of a series of self-imposed disciplines and personal systems, he or she is usually to be found 'ahead of the pack' in terms of efficiency and effectiveness.

However, the self-starters who so often become successful managers do not achieve their career goals by chance. From the outset of their first full-time appointments, they acquire the series of self-starter skills set out below – by dint of their own determination and internal discipline. Indeed it is just such personal traits that prompt others to dub such managers professionals, because they do not expect others to do what they do not practise themselves.

GROUP ACTIVITY

In groups of three or four, consider the following collection of attributes which a successful executive could be expected to possess. Allocate each item with a score of 1–5, where 5 signifies most important and 1 least. Then compare your scores with those of the other groups in your class and discuss the reasons which supported your rating of each attribute.

Able to meet deadlines	Does not hoard information
Respects confidences	Does not pass the buck
Always punctual	Able to identify key priorities
Stands by decisions	Organises time effectively
Always open to suggestions	Knows how to delegate

PC
4.1.3

KEY TRAITS OF A SUCCESSFUL SELF-STARTER

- Makes a point of arriving at work well before the day's start and of being punctual for appointments.

- Maintains an orderly desk top, where telephone message pads, addresses, telephone numbers, working papers, reference data and directories etc are always readily to hand.

- Keeps up-to-date a memory-jogging list of active jobs – tasks which have to be progress-chased or completed within set dates, either on his VDU or as a paper checklist. Checks and amends this list at least daily! Chivvies staff for due feedback and output accordingly.

- Ensures that appointments, meetings, deadlines, memory-joggers are recorded in an electronic or paper diary to which assistants or secretaries have access. Remembers to keep secretarial/support staff advised of freshly made commitments!

- Does not forget to carry out follow-up requests from the manager.

- Makes careful notes of any due deadlines of work assigned and devises a detailed plan of what needs to be done by when if the deadline is to be met. Gives support staff enough time to complete tasks delegated to them well before deadline falls due.

- Checks the progress of a time-constrained task on a regular basis and at predetermined dates which support staff know about in advance. Makes sure that backsliding support staff meet deadlines and provides help if needed.

- Knows how to find out where the organisation's information resources are kept.

- Ensures that his or her work is backed up by a reliable management records/filing system. Takes trouble to remain fully acquainted with the location of files in case of late working etc.

- Keeps a constant eye upon security and confidentiality. Does not leave sensitive material on the desk for visitors and night cleaners to read and disseminate.

- Knows how to keep secrets and shared confidences.

- Is always alert for useful information – from colleagues, clients, competitors, neighbours, etc. and makes sure senior staff are informed of potentially important items.

  Replies to letters, Email notes, phone calls, faxes, etc. promptly. Sends copies to interested colleagues. Lists arising tasks in jobs checklist.

- Makes a point of nurturing relationships with colleagues and contacts who are in a position to provide help in emergencies, such as the reprographics assistant or office caretaker.

- Checks with his or her manager any matter relating to an assigned task which is unclear or becoming problematical. Advises the manager early of any likely problems or tricky matters in the offing – does not 'drop the boss in it'!

- Is willing to share ideas rather than acting as an information hoarder and blocker.

- Does not duck a difficult decision. Involves colleagues and support staff in the decision-making process as part of an open-management approach to the work of the group. Has strength of will to stick to a decision – but also the nobler ability to admit to it when wrong.

Above all, self-starters are self-reliant!

DISCUSSION TOPICS

PC
4.1.3

1 Can self-starting skills be learned, or are people only born self-starters? What makes some people better able to impose discipline upon themselves than others?

2 Are self-starters really only just people with high task orientation who eventually become workaholics?

3 Why is it that successful people at work often become targets for the deadly sins of jealousy and envy within their departments or working groups? Is such an outcome inevitable in the general clamber after promotion? If so, what can a self-starter do to minimise the effects?

■ Managing time successfully

How often is heard in the office or on the factory floor:

> **'Is that the time? I just don't know where today's gone!'**

Frequently this is because the speaker has been so busy that to him or her, the time has flown by. The feeling of time passing rapidly is also experienced by people who become totally absorbed in the task in hand, to the exclusion of all else. Yet time can fly just as fast when it is wasted and frittered away – on juicy but idle gossip, on trivial and low-priority jobs, and in allowing a constant stream of phone-calls and co-workers to take over and redirect a person's day.

The inevitable end-product of personal mismanagement of time is that:

- deadlines get missed
- quality of work deteriorates
- errors and omissions creep into tasks
- uncompleted work piles up along with that which subsequently arrives

Such outcomes make both managers and their assistants irritable and frustrated. No one likes to finish their day's work without some sense of accomplishment. Moreover, the failure of one member of a team to complete an allocated task on time may act as a total block on the work of the rest, which of itself causes tension and stress among working groups.

As a result of such experiences among people at work, many papers and chapters have been written by management gurus on how time at work can be better managed. The following checklist outlines some of the most effective techniques.

TIPS ON EFFECTIVE TIME MANAGEMENT

Effective executives:

- never allow days or weeks at work just to happen – they always devise daily and weekly schedules of work which allocate their time in direct proportion to current priorities;
- ration carefully the time they spend in meetings – too many meetings are really just chatshops and often more is accomplished in an executive's personal office 'workshop';
- keep an eye on the clock, so that ten-minute discussions with staff or visiting sales representatives, etc. do not last half-an-hour;
- encourage their secretaries to filter out low-priority phone-calls or visits by either handling them personally or directly delegating them to other departmental staff;
- manage their time constructively through a mix of blocks of daily time allocated to:
  - a uninterrupted personal work;
  - b discussions with groups or individual staff;
  - c meetings with clients or more senior managers;
  - d taking and making telephone-calls;
  - e reading job-related internal documents and professional journals, circulars and bulletins, etc.;
  - f external appointments with customers or field sales staff, etc.

A number of support devices and techniques exist to aid the management of personal time. For example, office services firms sell eye-catching placards for fixing on office doors which announce:

PERSONAL WORK IN PROGRESS

PLEASE CALL BACK AFTER:

[Space here for erasable marker pen entry]

Similarly, the computerised PABX telephone systems of today enable all users to re-route incoming calls automatically to another extension. Also, such systems can be programmed by staff to provide alarm calls to herald the end of a dedicated period of time for private work or to announce that a meeting or appointment is imminent.

Another technique used to bring home to executives how their time is being used is that of producing a daily time log over a period of a week or so. Preprinted forms are employed, upon which a manager is required – every 30 minutes – to record precisely what he or she has done during the period, whether it was dealing with correspondence, using the phone, trouble-shooting in the department or visiting another part of the office-block or complex.

While such logs take time and a willingness on the part of the executive to complete, they do reveal at times extravagant, time-devouring activities of which the executive is often totally unaware:

TIME-WASTERS REVEALED BY TIME-LOGGING

Over-accessibility

The executive allows too many staff and visitors without appointments to take over his day.

Too much telephoning

Talkative people tend to spend far too long on the telephone, and some managers insist on taking personally all incoming calls.

Out too much

While it is important to keep in personal touch with customers and personnel in the field, too much time out of the office can lead to staff not being properly supervised and the 'tricky' jobs being left . . . and left. . . .

Important documents left unread

Some managers are only happy when interacting with other people; they therefore give too little time to essential reading and become ever more ill-informed about their business sphere of activity – with predictable results

Diary scheduling not adhered to

The easily-swayed manager allows others to change the structure of the day; the boss or a crisis can make this inevitable at times, but for some executives, each day is a mystery tour adventure!

Poor prioritising

When analysed in retrospect, the time-log reveals that the manager's week could have been used much more effectively, given his or her own listed priorities. The fault often lies in a failure to reprioritise activities at the beginning of each day or before leaving work the previous day.

Poor communication

A failure to synchronise diaries with secretary and section leaders can lead to visitors coming to see an executive who has gone out, meetings being missed and key tasks being left undone.

THE IMPORTANCE OF TEAMWORK

To achieve an all-round high performance at work, not only does the aspiring manager need to develop enduring self-starting skills, he or she must also be able to work effectively as a member of a team.

These two facets of working life do not conflict, they complement each other, since working in organisations is a mix of individual and team-based activities. The techniques of team-working and team-building set out in this section are important to acquire, since many of them will involve you in going against your natural instincts. For example, most people would rather lead than follow, talk than listen and enjoy the limelight of success personally, rather than as just one participant in a group enterprise.

Set out below are the generally accepted attributes or characteristics which people in groups tend to adopt and accept.

THE ATTRIBUTES OF A GROUP

Identity	It is identifiable by its members and (usually) by those outside it.
Norms of behaviour	It requires its members to conform to established norms or patterns of outlook, attitude and behaviour.
Purpose	It has aims and objectives either clearly defined or intuitively understood which direct its activities.
Hierarchy	It evolves either formally or informally a leadership and 'pecking-order' or hierarchy which its members accept.
Exclusivity	It has the power to grant or deny admission and also to expel anyone from membership.
Solidarity	It demands loyalty of its members and is capable of experiencing internal conflict while displaying an external front.
Capacity for change	Its life may be either long or short. It may form, disintegrate and re-form depending upon external circumstances and stimuli.

■ Belonging to a group

What makes a group? Certainly it is quite different from a random collection of individuals waiting for a bus or train. Firstly, a group has an identity which its members recognise. This identity may be formally acknowledged, as in a committee or working party, or it may be totally informal, as in a children's gang or a set of commuters using the same train compartment daily. The establishment of a group identity leads anyone to being an 'insider' or an 'outsider' as far as the group is concerned.

The next aspect affecting the creation and composition of groups is that all human beings share the need to belong to one group or another. Very few people survive long periods of isolation. Indeed, long periods of solitary confinement have been proved to be positively injurious. Similarly, few actively seek the life of the hermit or recluse.

Belonging to a group involves an individual in accepting and being accepted. The whole purpose of some groups seems to lie in maintaining a jealously guarded exclusivity and in setting often very extensive formal or informal entry 'exams'. What the individual has to demonstrate is that he or she accepts and is willing to comply with the 'norms' of the group – that is to say the established outlooks, attitudes and behaviour patterns which the group displays. For example, it would be a reckless probationary golfer who never replaced divots, frequently picked up other golfers' balls, cheated on his scorecard and always wore his spiked shoes in the teak-floored club lounge! It is only by clearly demonstrating similar ideas and behaviour that an individual becomes accepted by a group.

In society groups exist in many forms. The basic, indeed fundamental group is, of course, the family. Extensions to this group are formed through relatives and close family friends.

Yet further, separate groups are readily identified in the local sports or social club, residents' association or parent-teacher association etc.

As well as possessing a discernible identity and norms of behaviour, groups also exist to achieve aims and objectives, whether commercial, cultural, sporting or community centred. Such groups will evolve, either formally or informally, procedures for choosing leaders and will also establish 'pecking orders' which derive not only from official status, but also from length of membership, degree of assertiveness or demonstrated expertise. Most cricketers, for example, defer to the club's fast bowler or move aside to allow the 'Father of the House' to reach the bar.

It is interesting to note that within any group of reasonable size subgroups will also exist or come together temporarily. Within a music society, for example, there may lurk a secret, hard-core nucleus wishing to oust Gilbert and Sullivan to put Mozart on the throne! Such a group may only be identified when the future programme comes up for discussion and they form a solid caucus at a meeting. Once the purpose has been achieved, however, such a group may disperse as quickly as it was formed.

DISCUSSION TOPIC

'The best working group is a committee of one!' Is this an autocratic management view, or is there some truth in its implied criticism of the quality of work undertaken by working groups like committees?

■ Groups in organisations

Companies strive to establish a corporate identity among their employees and to build a corporate image through advertising and publicity to make themselves readily and pleasingly identifiable to the general public. Both private and public service organisations encourage staff to feel more involved and committed by circulating house journals, newspapers and magazines and by staging social and sports events. Also, in many organisations there is tremendous loyalty and a will to survive in members facing external competition and adverse circumstances.

If it is true that work-centred organisations embody characteristics shared by most groups, how are they to be identified? Firstly, it should be pointed out that, although an organisation as a whole may have a recognisable identity and character, the whole is, in fact, made up of many smaller groups, and, within them, subgroups. As we have discovered, organisations are divided into specialist divisions, which themselves may take on the characteristics of a distinctly identifiable group 'the marketing wallahs', 'those whizz-kids from R & D', 'the Scrooge brigade in accounts'. Indeed, groups are often formed as a kind of self-defence and means of survival in the face of other groups. In addition, within any specialist or departmental group there will form subgroups of people who associate together for a variety of reasons – shared activities, outlooks, physical proximity, common goals and so on. The following represent some of the reasons why groups are formed within work organisations:

1 It is difficult for an individual to feel a part of a large organisation.

2 People need to have a sense of belonging and to feel that they make a meaningful and accepted contribution somewhere.

3 People are drawn together by striving to achieve common goals and objectives.

4 People often form groups by reason of daily proximity and shared work-places.

5 Common expertise may be the basis of a group as may also be common outlooks and interests.

6 Positions in similar grades may also form a group characteristic.

7 People may wish to join a group because its activities make it look desirable.

Some groups within organisations are created and then develop extremely tight-knit relationships as the result of a formal activity. For example, a committee may be set up to make an investigation or develop a product. Though its members may not, initially, know one another very well, being drawn from different departments and levels, nevertheless, if the work is protracted, and if the members become thoroughly committed to the group's defined goals – especially if the committee faces external criticism – then very often it will become distinctly recognisable as a group. Other groups, however, are formed quite informally, springing from likings which A and B and C may have for one another. Such groups are often found within departments, but may also span them.

■ Working as an effective team member

People who become successful and effective members of working groups, whether in the form of committees, task forces or quality circles, tend to possess the following characteristics:

■ The ability to cooperate and share in decision-making.

■ A willingness to listen to and accept other people's ideas and suggestions.

■ The capacity to modify their own ideas so as to fall in with evolving proposals and decisions.

■ A preparedness to undertake within preset deadlines tasks which form only a part of a greater design or project under the direction of a group leader and to see praise and recognition go to the group rather than to the individual.

■ A willingness to come up with ideas which could be 'shot down' rather than merely coast along as the group's 'sleeper', and so to do a fair share of the group's tasks.

■ An inclination to support other group members and the group's work rather than to undermine it.

■ A willingness to accept responsibility as a group member for the outcomes of the group's activities.

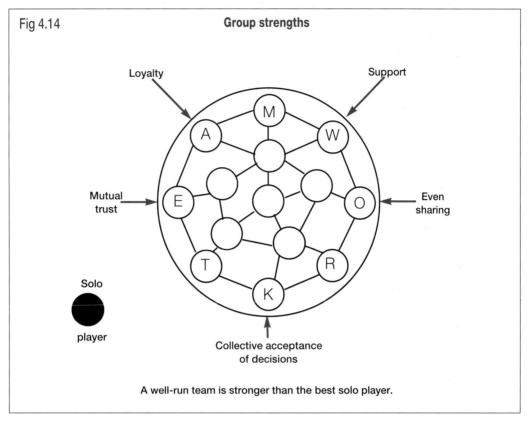

Fig 4.14

Group strengths

Loyalty

Support

Mutual trust

Even sharing

Solo

player

Collective acceptance of decisions

A well-run team is stronger than the best solo player.

DISCUSSION TOPICS

PC
4.1.6

1 How much notice do you think managers should take of the creation and self-maintenance of informal groups within their departments, but outside of recognised line management structures?

2 What techniques are available to members of official working groups within organisations to deal with members who do not pull their weight?

3 What is the difference between an effective and ineffective team leader in your opinion? What signals should a team leader look for to provide feedback on whether or not his leadership is working?

REVIEW TEST (Elements 4.1, 4.2, 4.3)

1 What did Henri Fayol mean by 'a scalar chain'?

2 Explain briefly the structure of Abraham Maslow's Hierarchy of Needs model.

3 Why are The Hawthorne Studies still talked about today?

4 Explain Frederick Herzberg's theory of motivators and hygiene factors.

5 List what you believe to be the main characteristics which a good leader should display.

6 What factors comprise an effective approach to delegation?

7 How can stress at work best be managed?

8 What characteristics does a self-starter at work possess?

9 List five techniques for improving personal time-management.

10 List five time-wasting practices to be avoided.

11 What are the main characteristics of a group in a work environment?

12 What approaches are most likely to help an employee in becoming an effective team worker?

PC
4.1.6

▌ CASE STUDY 1

'You're the manager – you sort it out!'

In groups of three or four in a general class discussion, consider the following brief scenarios and decide what immediate action you, as the manager, would take.

Jo Stacey was appointed by you as your department's Information Processing Supervisor some four weeks ago. She is responsible for coordinating all information and text processing and maintaining your communications facilities. Reporting to her are eight employees who work on desktop terminals and operate your fax, telex and photocopying equipment. The longest serving member of the group is Diane Jackson, who thought that getting the supervisor's job was a foregone conclusion. Since Jo Stacey's arrival, there has been a tension in the group and you are getting vibrations that they are giving Jo a hard time, although she has said nothing. You believe Diane is 'stirring it up'.

PC
4.1.3

What do you do?

You are the Accounts Manager of Midland Counties Transport Limited. Jack Whitley is your Senior Accounts clerk, responsible for some twelve ledger clerks and clerical assistants. Jack's section looks after the company's accounts, payroll, etc.

Jack is now 58 years old and has been with Midland for the past seventeen years. His work record is good; while not a high flier, he has proved loyal, steady and reliable – if more than a little conservative and traditionalist in his outlooks. Once Jack has devised a system to his satisfaction, it takes a lot to get him to change it. His section get on well with him, because they know where they stand with him, and have become thoroughly familiar with his accounting and bookkeeping routines.

However, the advent of the EC single market has caused Midland's directors to invest heavily in an expansion programme which will take their articulated lorries from the Midlands, through the Eurotunnel and across the European Community. At the same time, you and the board have decided that the firm's accounting procedures must be completely transferred from your predominantly paper-based system to a fully networked, integrated accounts software application, in order to cope with your growing business, and to provide the sophisticated management accounting information your board now expects.

When you first briefed Jack on this, as you had anticipated, he took the news hard: 'Waste of money if you ask me. These programs you're talking about – from what I hear, they're littered with bugs or viruses or whatever and staff spend most of their time trying to sort out, what do they call 'em – crashes! My set-up hasn't crashed once in seventeen years!'

You quickly realise you have a problem on your hands. Your board has given you the clearest of instructions. The new integrated system has to be installed, up and running with staff trained to use it competently within twelve weeks, in time for it to be operational for Midland's new financial year.

How are you going to manage this situation?

PC
4.1.2

You are the Sales Manager of West Country Ice Cream Limited, a manufacturing company which makes and distributes a range of ice-cream based products throughout the West Country. Your firm sells mainly to retail stores, sea-front kiosks, sole trader mobile vendors, smaller hotels and guesthouses. Jim Ackroyd is one of three of your District Managers, with a territory extending over Cornwall. He has three sales personnel reporting to him. Traditionally, West Country's management style has been aggressive and rather 'macho' – bustling in with sharper discounts to win business, and so on, pushed on relentlessly by 'Big Barnie Baggott' West Country's ambitious and hard-bitten owner.

This summer sales have been disastrous. A succession of wet depressions have hit the holiday trade hard and sales of ice-cream are down some 50 per cent. Over the past two weeks you have noticed unexpected signs of stress in Jim Ackroyd. Once or twice in afternoon phone conversations he sounded as if he'd been drinking; reports have filtered back to you of confrontations with customers – unheard of before, given Jim's easygoing nature. Yesterday by chance you overheard him relating his worries over his latest sales figures. A family man with young children, Jim's financial position, as you already know, is stretched. This morning, he looks grim and pale as you see him checking orders in an adjacent office.

You decide you must talk to Jim privately. How will you handle the situation? What options are open to you?

CASE STUDY 2

PC
4.1.2
4.1.4

Mending the cracks in Plastimould

Plastimould Ltd is a company manufacturing a range of household utensils from a chemical base – bowls, buckets, pipes, brushes etc. For the past six weeks it has had a serious industrial dispute on its hands. One of the stages in the production process has been declared 'unsafe' by the unionised factory staff.

This stage concerns the cleaning out of vats which have contained the material for moulding into the various products in the company's range. It is accepted by both management and union representatives that it is possible during the cleaning process for fumes to be generated which are dangerous to the skin and which under no circumstances should be inhaled.

Recently three men have collapsed not long after working on the cleansing of the vats and they are still off work sick. After the third man had fallen ill, the union decided after a full meeting of the factory union membership to ban any of the union's members from working on the vat cleansing process. The effect of this ban was to halt production completely.

The union want an independent enquiry into the dangers and effects to health stemming from the cleansing process. For their part, management have declared that the cleansing process is perfectly safe, provided that the protective clothing and equipment provided is worn and used as specified in company regulations.

The union's position is that the clothing is old-fashioned, having been designed more than ten years previously, and that no one to their knowledge had carried out any recent tests to confirm the effectiveness of its protection. The men have complained that it is too hot to wear, and that its bulkiness makes it impossible to work in the more inaccessible parts of the vats. The respirators are also, according to the men, inefficient, especially when any physical exertion is required.

Management has pointed out that the protective clothing and equipment conforms to the safety specifications laid down for such work in the relevant section of the industrial safety legislation. The men, says management, have been cutting safety corners to boost bonus earnings by not wearing all the equipment and clothing when there is a clear need to. If there have been instances of men becoming sick, which management will not accept as being a direct consequence of the cleansing process, then it must be the result of contributory negligence.

The union regards this last attitude of management as totally hypocritical. It claims that in the past management has turned 'a blind eye' to total adherence to factory safety regulations. Only now that the company is faced with a law-suit for damages arising from the medical condition of the three workers currently sick in hospital has the accusation of 'contributory negligence' arisen. In any case, the company has failed in its obligation to inform its factory staff adequately of the potential dangers involved in the cleansing process, and now, 'caught red-handed', was trying to prevent an independent inquiry from being set up.

The latest rejoinder from management is that unless a formula can be decided to restart production with immediate effect, there may well be a possibility that the parent company of Plastimould will divert its production to another factory in another country, thus causing widespread redundancy. The union is inclined to see this as bluff, although some members concede that the six-week lay-off must have had crippling effect on the company's financial position.

ASSIGNMENTS

1 From the management or union team viewpoint, prepare your case for a 'return-to-work' negotiating meeting and then simulate the meeting. Observers or a team member should take notes and produce narrative minutes.

2 Depending upon the outcome of the meeting draft either a 'joint communique' or separate statements for circulation to Plastimould staff.

3 As an individual student write an essay on the problems implicit in the case study and suggest how you think the management and the union should resolve their differences.

PC
4.2.3
4.2.4
4.3.4
4.3.5

CASE STUDY 3

Wanted! Trainee Sales Manager for Excel Computers Ltd

The company

Excel Computers Limited manufactures, markets and retails an extensive range of computers and ancillary equipment, selling to both public and private industry.

Among its other duties, Excel's Sales Department provides an administrative and information service to its 75 sales representatives. The service helps them to perform effectively in what is a highly sophisticated market – both in terms of advanced product technology and the presentation of technical information.

Excel has established a policy of appointing each year, as trainee managers, a number of school and college leavers. They are provided with excellent, in-service training opportunities, including day-release to higher education courses. In addition, their training programmes include experience periods in all departments before taking on specific departmental responsibilities.

The vacancy

Personnel Manager: 'I see young Sara Maxwell has just got the job she's been hoping for in Marketing. I suppose you'll be asking me to find her replacement!'

Sales Manager: 'You're absolutely right! I'll miss Sara, of course, but I suppose Sales' loss is Marketing's gain! At all events, we ought to press on directly with the selection process in order to beat the rush at the end of June. Good college-leavers are at a premium these days! I'd better revise the person specification and job descriptions straight away! The following was Sara's job description.

JOB DESCRIPTION

TITLE: TRAINEE SALES ADMINISTRATION MANAGER

DEPARTMENT: SALES DEPARTMENT

HOURS OF WORK: 37.5 hour week. Flexible Working Hours:
                      Monday–Friday Core Time: 1000–1600

RESPONSIBLE TO: The Assistant Sales Manager

RESPONSIBLE FOR: Designated junior clerical and secretarial staff.

AUTHORITY OVER: Designated junior clerical and secretarial staff.

GENERAL DESCRIPTION

To become proficient in performing duties related to sales administration, with particular regard to providing a supportive service to company sales representatives. To undertake work delegated by senior Sales Department personnel. To attend in-service training courses as required. To direct the work of assigned junior clerical and secretarial staff as requested.

DUTIES AND RESPONSIBILITIES

1 To work within established company regulations and to support determined company policies.

2 To develop sales managerial skills, with particular reference to: sales administration procedures, product knowledge, marketing activities and sales information systems.

3 To assist in the provision of administration and information services provided to the company's sales representative force.

4 To liaise with Marketing Department in communicating sales promotion and advertising programmes to company sales representatives.

5 To deal with arising correspondence, memoranda, reports, meetings, documentation etc.

6 To assist the Assistant Sales Manager generally, or any other senior Sales Department staff as directed by the Assistant Sales Manager.

7 To assist as required with the data processing of sales documentation and sales statistics.

8 To supervise the work of junior staff members as required.

9 To attend courses of training as required.

EXCEL COMPUTERS LIMITED
ORGANISATIONAL INFORMATION

HEAD OFFICE:	Excel House, Guildford Road, Kingston-upon-Thames, Surrey KT12 6GR
	Telegrams: Excel, Kingston-upon-Thames
	Telephone: Kingston 88000
	Fax: 081-639 6848
FACTORIES:	Bristol, Liverpool, Leicester
RESEARCH AND DEVELOPMENT:	Excel Laboratories, Harlow New Town
TRAINING HEADQUARTERS:	Moorbridge Manor, Dorchester, Dorset
PERSONNEL:	16,479 (Head Office: 643)
DEPARTMENTS:	Research and Development, Production, Marketing, Sales, Accounts, Office Administration, Personnel, Distribution and Transport, Training, Communication Services

CONDITIONS OF SERVICE (Head Office Staff)
The company's head office operates a flexible working hours system; staff work in accordance with a job appraisal scheme – all jobs are graded and promotion/remuneration is based upon performance assessed at regular intervals. Company subsidised meals are available in the staff restaurant. Sports and social club facilities are well catered for in the company's leisure complex adjoining head office premises.
Paid Leave: junior – training management grades: 3 weeks per annum plus usual bank holidays.
Company house mortgage loans available at preferential terms.

CAREER OPPORTUNITIES:
The Company's employees are encouraged to develop a knowledge of company activities as a whole and opportunities exist for careers to progress via a number of departments. The company promotes from within whenever possible.

TRAINING:
Excel Computers Limited maintains an ideally situated Training Centre at Moorbridge Manor, Dorchester. Residential course form a central part of management development. Applications to attend day-release higher education courses are reviewed by a standing review committee.

SALARIES:
Management salaries are reviewed annually and paid monthly in arrears. Each management post follows an incremental scale, and annual increases are zoned within defined upper and lower limits according to performance.
Example: Trainee Manager Grade 6

Entering salary:	£14,500
First increment:	£750–1500 p.a.
Second increment:	£900–1700 p.a.

All incremental scales are reviewed annually.

SALES INFORMATION
Total sales turnover last year exceeded £420 million. A new national LAN/WAN system was introduced recently. Business Computer Systems sales rose by 19% last year. Major customers included the Bestbuy Supermarket chain, Sentinel Insurance Limited, Vesco Automotive Products Limited and Harridges Stores.

FUTURE DEVELOPMENTS:
In March of this year, Sir Peter Henryson, Chairman, announced that Excel was strengthening its EC exporting position: 'The time has come for Excel, secure in its very firm UK market, to go on to the export offensive. We have the people, the products, the marketing and the sales expertise. We intend to "excel" in a number of European and transatlantic markets. Our plans are well advanced. You are all familiar with the advertisements placed in the national press reporting the recent Annual General Meeting. Well, I strongly recommend you to "Watch This Space!" '

ACTIVITIES

1 Compose a person specification for the Excel Trainee Sales Administration Manager post, shortly to be advertised.

2 Devise an application form suitable for use in Excel's appointment of the Trainee Sales Administration Manager.

3 Draft an information sheet suitable for sending to candidates who have applied for the Trainee Sales Administration Manager post, outlining the scope of the job and the main features of Excel's business and organisation.

4 Design a display advertisement for the Trainee Manager post and devise an advertising strategy based on your own locality, identifying which newspapers and other media you would use to advertise the post.

5 Make a checklist of questions as follows:

   a   questions which Excel interviewers would wish to ask applicants for the Trainee Manager post;

   b   questions which applicants would wish to ask Excel interviewers.

6 Complete the application form devised in 2 above as an applicant for the post. Compose an appropriate curriculum vitae. Write a suitable letter of application to:

   The Personnel Manager,
   Excel Computers Limited,
   Excel House,
   Guildford Road,
   KINGSTON-UPON-THAMES
   Surrey
   KT12 6GR

7 Set up Excel interviewing panels to evaluate applications received from members of the group. Discuss constructively the strengths and weaknesses of applications.

8 Simulate the interviews for the post of Trainee Sales Administration Manager. Group members should role-play the Excel panel, comprising: the Personnel Manager, the Sales Manager and the Assistant Sales Manager. Other members of the group should role-play successive applicants. Panel interviewers should have time to study applicants. Panel interviewers should have time to study applicants' letters and forms. Applicants should also digest the information in the information sheet devised in 3. Observer-role group members should assess the performances of interviewers and interviewees. Simulations may be tape- or video-recorded for subsequent evaluation.

▌CASE STUDY 4

The Harris Case

On Tuesday 1 February 199–, Jack Harris, a machine operator at Advance Engineering Company Limited, was summarily dismissed . . .

'D' Machines – Extract of company regulations

Extract from the Company Regulations of Advance Engineering Company Limited:

VI SAFETY PROCEDURES

3 Operation of Classified Machinery

Certain production processes (specified below) are effected by machines having a 'D' (Danger) classification. Under no circumstances may such machines be left unattended by operatives while assembly-line work is in progress.

(a) Relief Summoning Procedures
  Operatives working 'D' classified machines are required to summon a relief operator before leaving the machine for any reason while work is in progress.

(b) Summary Dismissal
  In view of the danger to personnel working in the vicinity of 'D' classified machines, operatives who leave them negligently unattended render themselves liable to summary dismissal

  Revised: 1 December 199–

'Try not to worry . . .'

An extract from a conversation which took place in the surgery of Jack Harris's family doctor on Wednesday 19 January 199–:

Doctor Grant: 'Well, Mr Harris, I think I'd better put you on a course of anti-depressants. I don't think you need to stay at home – especially while your wife is in hospital – but you must take things steadily. The pills I am prescribing will help you to do just that. And don't worry about Mrs Harris – she's going to be all right. . . .'

Jack Harris: 'Thank you, Doctor, I'm very grateful. It's been a worrying time ever since the wife was taken ill. Still, they told me this morning she could be out of the intensive care unit in a few days' time, if all goes well. . . .'

'Give us a break!'

An extract from a conversation between Alec Baker, Supervisor, and Jack Harris in the works staff restroom, Tuesday 1 February 199– at 15.35 hours:

Alec Baker: 'Right, Harris, you've had it this time! This time I'm going to have to report you to Mr Watkins! You'd better put that fag out and come with me to his office – straight away!'

Jack Harris: 'Aw, give us a break, Mr Baker, I've only just. . . . You see, I've had a lot. . . . Well, I've not been. . . .'

Alec Baker: 'Save it for Mr Watkins! Come on. It's not as if you haven't been warned about leaving a 'D' classified machine unattended. The line was clearly working when I spotted you missing! Total disregard for your workmates – that's what beats me!'

Summary dismissal

Mr Watkins' reaction on hearing of the incident from Alec Baker in the Works Manager's Office. Tuesday 1 February 199– at 15.55 hours:

'Found smoking you say. In the restroom. Well, it all seems pretty clear-cut to me! Left his 'D' machine unattended and the line in progress when you spotted his absence. You'd think they'd have more sense! Especially after my recent reminder. You'd better wheel him in, Mr Baker! . . . '

The EWA steps in

Extract of a conversation between Jack Harris and Vic Cooper, Convenor of the Engineering Workers' Association at Advance Engineering, Tuesday 1 February 199– at 16.35 hours:

Jack Harris: 'He never gave me a chance, Vic, nor did Watkins! I dunno, I just came over sort of shaky. There was a stoppage further up the line, so I thought I'd just have a quick sit-down in the restroom. I never meant to be away more than a minute or two . . . '

'D' MACHINES – NOTICE TO ALL WORKS PERSONNEL

Notice to all Advance Engineering Works Personnel posted on general works noticeboard 24 January 09.00 hours (*see below at top of next page*).

Vic Cooper: 'Absent only a minute or two you say. Line stopped again! Didn't you tell 'em you weren't feeling well? Anyway, anyone can see you're not right – not by a long chalk.

Didn't give you a chance? Jack, you should have spoken up! Well, I think it's a clear case of victimisation! You'd best go home now. Charlie'll go with you. But don't you worry, you'll keep your job – or my name's not Vic Cooper! Now, I've got some telephoning to do to District Office! . . .'

'. . . on the grounds of unfair dismissal . . .'

Conversation between John Watkins, Works Manager, and Dennis Brooke, Managing Director of Advance Engineering in his office. Friday 4 February 199– at 10.15 hours:

John Watkins: 'Bad business. Not made any easier by Peter Taylor's absence (Advance's Personnel Manager, absent since Christmas because of illness). We could have done with his expertise. Of course, we had to take a firm line. If company regulations are seen to be openly flouted. . . . Open and shut case I'd say.'

Dennis Brooke: 'I'm not so sure. I know things have been too lax in the Works, but by all accounts, Jack Harris was regarded as being conscientious. I hope we haven't acted hastily over this. . . . I've a letter here from the EWA informing me of their intention to advise Mr Harris to take his case to the Industrial Tribunal and to claim unfair dismissal, and that they will be providing him with legal advice.

According to them, Harris was unwell at the time of the incident. Your "open and shut case" had better be as good as you think it is!'

Prior to the Industrial Tribunal's hearing, the EWA secured a written statement from Jack Harris's doctor, to the effect that Jack had been prescribed medication to alleviate anxiety caused by his wife's ill-health.

DISCUSSION TOPICS

1 How well did Alec Baker, John Watkins and Dennis Brooke handle Jack Harris's absence from his D Machine? Can you detect any mismanagement in terms of your knowledge of the Health and Safety at Work Act and current employment protection legislation?

2 To what extent can the summary dismissal of Jack Harris be fairly judged to be the result of his own negligence? Was Dr Grant at fault in allowing Jack to continue to work while feeling under stress?

3 Comment on Vic Cooper's role in the dismissal process. Should he have reacted differently? If so, in what ways?

4 Given the dangerous nature of unattended D Machines, has the company taken sufficient care in briefing their machine operators on procedures to be adopted when wishing to leave them?

5 What do you think – on the basis of the information available in the case study – would be the outcome at an industrial tribunal of Jack's claim for unfair dismissal?

ACTIVITIES

1 First carry out any further necessary researches into summary and unfair dismissal and industrial tribunal procedures, then role-play the industrial tribunal hearing with the following 'cast':

● Industrial tribunal chairman

● Two further tribunal members

● A legal representative for each party

● Jack Harris

● Witnesses to be called

   Each party to the case to produce their own supportive documents, and the panel to produce a written judgement with reasons.

2 Assume you are Peter Taylor, Advance's Personnel Manager, newly returned to work after the tribunal hearing. In the light of the recent Harris case, produce a memorandum to all company supervisors and managers explaining the company's policy on summary dismissal and how to handle potential instances in a legally correct and good code of practice manner.

IDEAS FOR PROJECTS

1 With the help of your teacher (or a supervisor if you are working full- or part-time), find out how your school/college/organisation undertakes manpower planning, so as to ensure a healthy distribution curve in the age of staff in its various departments and centres. Also, with permission, research into the organisation's approach to skills auditing as a means of ensuring that its workforce keeps up-to-date with changes and innovations.

PC
4.1.6

Produce a short report of your findings, graphically illustrated where possible.

PC
4.1.2
4.3.1

2 In pairs, arrange to interview a personnel manager of a local medium to large company. Select one of the following topics for discussion in the context of the company's activities and work culture:

   a   Its recruitment and appointment procedures.

   b   Its approach to staff appraisal and performance review.

   c   Its policies towards staff welfare and sports/recreation facilities.

   d   Its established procedures for handling grievances.

   e   How its pensions programme is administered.

Your teacher may be able to help with effecting an introduction to local contacts, as may also your parents and family friends.

With permission, provide a suitable oral briefing for your class on what you discovered.

PC
4.1.3

3 In pairs, design a set of forms to be used by an appraiser and an appraisee in an open performance appraisal interview process which you think would prove most effective in an organisation in which performance appraisal forms an important part in the achievement of annual targets and objectives.

PC
4.1.2

4 Design a grievance procedure which you think appropriate for your school or college's students, or the department in which you work. Compare your scheme with those produced by fellow students.

PC
4.2.3

5 Design a current job description for one of the following:

   a   Your teacher.

   b   The head of your department.

   c   The departmental secretary/PA.

   d   Your supervisor at work.

   e   Your manager in your part-time job.

PC
4.2.4

6 Assume that the person in 5 above for whom you produced the updated job description is leaving the organisation. Produce a fresh person specification appropriate for his or her successor.

PC
4.3.1

7 Design a display advertisement (to be 12 cm square when published) for your local weekly newspaper which you think likely to prove effective for the person whose job description and personnel specification you designed in Activities 6 and 7.

Display your set of documents for Activities 6, 7 and 8 for your class to contrast and compare.

PC
4.3.2
4.3.3
4.3.4
4.3.5

8 Study carefully the advertisement for advertising space sales personnel on page 321. Make sure you understand the jargon words like 'OTE' etc. In groups of three to five, carry out your researches into telephone space selling (particularly of national and regional newspapers and trade magazines) then arrange your class into groups of **either:**

interviewers (simulating Centaur Limited executives)

or applicants for the space-selling posts

As appropriate – according to the group you are in – design and complete on an individual basis the following forms:

Applicant
- Curriculum vitae
- Letter of application
- Two open testimonials

Interviewer

■ Briefing factsheet about the firm and the job (simulated)

■ Interviewee assessment form

In paired groups of three or four, exchange the above documents and then role-play the interviews for the post of Advertising Space Salesperson. If possible video-tape your interviews for later constructive evaluation.

In a general class wash-up, compare notes on what you discovered about the recruitment process from your researches and role-play.

9 Devise an appropriate induction programme (of about 5 hours overall) for new clerical assistants joining your organisation – either the one in which you work or study. Compare your scheme with those produced by others in your group.

PC
4.3.1

10 First undertake your research, then produce two sections for a company personnel manual which are intended to brief its managers and its staff on how to take part in effective and constructive performance appraisal interviews. When completed, circulate your drafts around your class for interest and comparison and then decide whose versions are the best in terms of their informed approach, readability and clarity.

11 Arrange to interview a personnel officer in a local organisation about its established procedure in the event of having to make anyone on its payroll redundant. When you have carried out your researches, design a flow-chart to illustrate the process, and, having secured the personnel manager's permission, share your chart with those produced by your fellow students.

PC
4.1.2
4.1.4

12 First carry out your researches, then give an illustrated 10–15 minute oral presentation to your class on one of the following:

PC
4.1.2
4.1.4

a The work of ACAS.

b The work of an industrial tribunal.

c The role of a personnel manager in cases of alleged unfair and constructive dismissal.

d The key content of one of the following:

The Sex Discrimination Act 1975

The Employment Protection Act 1975

The Race Relations Act 1976

The Employment Protection (Consolidation) Act 1978

e The role of a full-time trade union official in annual pay and conditions reviews with an organisation's management.

13 First carry out your researches, then give a 10-minute oral presentation on the work and ideas of one of the following:

PC
4.1.6

a Max Weber,

b Henri Fayol,

c Elton Mayo,

d Frederick Herzberg,

e Abraham Maslow,

f Rensis Likert,

g Douglas McGregor,

h F. E. Fiedler

As part of your work for this project, produce a factsheet – of no more than two sides of A4 typescript – which summarises your presentation's points and which members of your class can keep as a useful revision aid.

PC
4.1.6

14 As a member of a large organisation's personnel department, first research, then produce a staff briefing note on how to manage one of the following:

a The delegation of tasks

b Intra-departmental negotiations

c Stress in your job

d Personal and time management

e Working effectively in a group

f Effective team-leading

Your briefing note should impart useful information in a friendly and easy-to-absorb way; it should not be patronising nor appear as a set of regulations to be followed. Illustrations may be included if considered helpful.

Display finished briefing notes on class noticeboards for comparison and evaluation. Decide which ones are most effective and why.

EVIDENCE-BUILDING ACTIVITY FOR YOUR PORTFOLIO

Element 4.1 Investigate human resourcing

Using the support and contacts you have built up during your pursuit of your GNVQ Business (Advanced) course, make an approach to a business organisation in your locality and obtain its permission and help in identifying how its human resource management is improving the performance of the business.

Research objectives

In a series of informal interviews with appropriate managers and their staff, find out and make your notes on:

1 the procedures used to recruit, induct and terminate staff (e.g. natural wastage, redundancy, early retirement etc.)

2 arrangements for staff development and training (including, if in being, schemes for multiskilling, job enrichment, enlargement and rotation), staff social and welfare facilities

3 procedures used to maintain and develop productive employee relations: employee consultation and representation, interface with trade unions, mechanisms in place for handling grievances and disputes; commitments to equal opportunities, equal pay, HASAW

4 systems for monitoring human resource performance and matching of current and future operational needs

Presentation of evidence

When you have assembled your data, produce a report – simulating the role of assistant to the organisation's personnel director or manager (or if a small company, general manager) – which he or she can use as a current briefing source in a series of discussions with the firm's directors on the present state of human resources and how company performance might be further improved.

Note: With your teacher's assistance, you should ensure that the first draft of your report is sent to and cleared by your contact manager before you divulge any of its contents.

Method of producing evidence

If you can, word-process your report, if not, produce a neat hand-written version. Include in your report any tables, charts or diagrams (e.g. organisational chart) which you have been able to acquire; also, include where appropriate any specimen person specifications, job descriptions, company grievance procedure, HASAW operations manual, equal opportunities manual etc. you are able to obtain.

In your report, use a style which is: objective, factual and detached and which is also clear and simple.

Helpful Hint 1: when you make initial contact with a likely company, ensure that you provide a photocopy of the Performance Criteria and Range for Element 4.1 and also a letter from your school/college department which courteously requests assistance and provides assurances that confidentialities will be respected and that the liaising manager will see the draft report first and approve its contents.

Helpful Hint 2: Your county council will almost certainly have a local government officer whose job is to foster commercial and local educational links. He or she would be a good person to contact when seeking to identify a 'friendly' firm. Further help may be obtained through your local Rotary Club, Chamber of Commerce, Training & Enterprise Council and industry federations.

Performance criteria covered

4.1.1, 4.1.2, 4.1.3, 4.1.4, 4.1.5, 4.1.6

Core skills

Communication
3.1.1–3.1.4, 3.2.1–3.2.4, 3.3.1–3.3.3, 3.4.1–3.4.3

Information technology
3.1.1–3.1.6 (also 3.1.7 if a LAN is employed), 3.2.1–3.2.7, 3.3.1–3.3.5, 3.5.1

Note for performance criteria 3.5.1–3.5.5, keep a log of any errors or faults which may have occurred while producing the report and written notes on how you handled them; submit your notes as evidence to your assessor.

Element 4.2 Investigate job roles in organisational structures

Bearing in mind the contacts you have established in local organisations and the help you can expect to obtain from your network of relatives, neighbours and friends in accessing private and public sector managers, select two posts, one private, one public sector, from the lists below:

Private sector	*Public sector*
Milkman	Postman
Shop Assistant	Local Government Clerical Assistant
Assistant Bank Manager, Local Branch	Social Services Care Worker
Personal Secretary	Librarian
Sales Manager	Trading Standards Officer
Chain Store Branch Manager	

Note: With the agreement of your teacher, you may select a post other than any of those listed above, as long as you have one post in each sector.

Research objectives

Your research objectives are to:

1 produce a person specification for each of the posts you have selected based on your research of them using local contacts for data and information

2 produce job descriptions for the same two posts

3 produce a written commentary (with supportive charts or diagrams obtained from your researches which explains how the person specifications and job descriptions reflect the nature of:

- the organisational structure and culture

- the size and type of organisation (e.g. small limited company or district council)

- the kind of work it carries out

- the external influences which are important to it (e.g. central government, High Street customers, industrial purchasing departments)

Your commentary should concentrate on showing how **what the organisation is – as evidenced in terms of its mission statement, goals, and structure,** and **what it does,** as borne out in **its activities and operations and the environment in which it works** all influence the ways in which person specifications and job descriptions are designed.

To enable you to do this, you should convey what aspects of the person specifications and job descriptions are most and what least important, what aspects have not been included since they lie outside the scope of the job role, and what key attributes in the person specification stem directly from the type of organisation the post is for (e.g. 'excellent communication interpersonal skills for a sales representative, or 'methodical attention to detail' for a senior bookkeeper).

Presentation of evidence

Using specimen person specifications and job descriptions you have obtained as format and structure aids, word-process or handwrite your versions. Take particular care in ensuring that your layouts are clear, logically sequenced and make use of techniques of point size of fonts, emboldening, italics, underscoring number referencing and indenting etc. If you are hand-writing your documents, simulate these features as neatly as possible.

Your commentary should be set down in a suitably structured and section/paragraph titling and referencing format.

Method of producing evidence

Use of word-processing document formatting and presentation features or hand-written simulation

Performance criteria covered

4.2.1, 4.2.2, 4.2.3, 4.2.4

Core skills Level 3

Communication
3.2.1–3.2.4, 3.4.1–3.4.3

Information technology
3.1.1–3.1.7 (if LAN used), 3.2.1–3.2.7, 3.3.1–3.3.5, 3.4.4, 3.4.5

3.5.1–3.5.5 [by means of logged notes on how any errors or faults were handled, and how compliance with HASAW requirements was effected].

Element 4.3 Evaluate job applications and interviews

Activity 1

Re-read the advertisement on page 321 for a sales person to conduct telephone selling of advertising space.

Find out what kind of skills and attributes are needed in such a job and then compose a suitable letter of application and a supportive curriculum vitae.

Activity 2

In a similar way, write a letter of application and compose a curriculum vitae (this time simulating a person who is in their mid-twenties and who has been unemployed for six months, having had a variety of posts since leaving school at 18-plus, after achieving a BTEC National Diploma in Business & Finance).

Note: one of the above pairs of application letters and CVs should be word-processed, and the other pair produced in hand-writing.

Activity 3: Group evaluations

Each individual student's letters and CVs should be produced using fictional names so that they may be copied and distributed to evaluation groups of three or four within the class. Each paired letter and CV should then be evaluated by the group in terms of:

- effectiveness in its context
- suitability and quality of content and style
- quality of presentation and visual appeal

In a constructive way, each class group should provide a short presentation to the class which supplies an assessment for each letter against the above criteria. This presentation should be based upon drawn-up notes which are handed to the class teacher as evidence.

Activity 4

In groups, role-play the recruitment interviews relating to either (or both) of the job advertisements for telesales person for Centaur Communications Limited (page 314) and/or the post of Trainee Sales Administration Manager for Excel Computers Limited (page 396–9).

To assist your role-play, first produce:

- an agreed set of interview questions and roles (interviewing panel)
- a completed application form (interviewees)
- a pro forma for recording interviewing impressions and judgements (interviewing panel)

Activity 5

Write a briefing paper of about 450 words on what you consider to be the main aspects of:

1 the legal obligations which both a candidate and an employing organisation must comply with in the recruitment process

2 your views on the honesty, objectivity, fairness and integrity which a recruiting panel should observe during the job selection process

Presentation of evidence

Activities 1 and 2: letters and CVs should be produced as indicated above; one set should relate to your real education and experience (the Centaur post), and the other should supply simulated evidence (for the Excel post).

Activity 3: Your evidence will take the form of a group discussion on the circulated letters and CVs followed by an oral presentation (which will be assessed) and then consolidated by an individually produced set of summarising notes as evidence for your assessor.

Activity 4: If possible you should video your recruitment interview role-play and submit your tape, together with individual sets of letters, CVs, application forms, interview notes etc. as evidence to your assessor. Otherwise, your assessor may elect to sit in and assess your interview simulations as they are delivered.

Activity 5: Your briefing paper should be either word processed or hand-written.

Performance criteria covered

4.3.1, 4.3.2, 4.3.3, 4.3.4, 4.3.5, 4.3.6

Core skills Level 3

Communication
3.1.1, 3.1.2, 3.1.3, 3.1.4, 3.2.1–3.2.4, 3.4.1–3.4.3

Information technology
3.1.1–3.1.7 (if LAN used for 3.1.7), 3.2.1–3.2.7, 3.3.1–3.3.5, 3.4.4

3.5.1–3.5.5 (by means of logged notes on how many errors or faults were handled and how compliance with HASAW requirements was effected.)

FURTHER SOURCES OF INFORMATION

Human Resources Management, 7th edn, H T Graham and R Bennet, M & E Business Handbooks, 1992. ISBN: 0 7121 0844 0

Personnel Management Made Simple, 2nd edn, S Tyson and A York, Made Simple Books, 1989. ISBN: 0 7506 0726 2

Business Law, 2nd edn, D Keenan and S Riches, Pitman, 1990. ISBN: 0 273 03138 4

Negotiating, Bill Scott, Paradigm, 1988. ISBN: 0 9488 25 26 X

Understanding Organisations, 3rd edn, C B Handy, Penguin Books, 1992. ISBN 0 4 009110 6

People in Organisations, 3rd edn, T R Mitchell and J R Larson, McGraw-Hill International, 1987. ISBN: 0 07 100585 4

Hiring and Firing, K Lanz, Pitman, Natwest Business Bookshelf, 1988. ISBN: 0 273 02826 X

Essentials of Employment Law, 3rd edn, D Lewis, Institute of Personnel Management, 1990. ISBN: 0 85292 447 X

Thriving on Chaos, Tom Peters, Pan Books, 1987. ISBN: 0 330 30591 3

EMPLOYMENT IN THE MARKET ECONOMY

Element 5.1
Investigate employment in business sectors

Element 5.2
Analyse external influences relating to employment

Element 5.3
Evaluate the workforce performance of business sectors

Element 5.1: Investigate employment in business sectors

Performance criteria | | *Pages*

1 changing features of employment are identified using a variety of information sources 435, 436, 440

2 employment trends in the UK and EC are identified and explained 427, 429, 438, 468

3 employment trends within different business sectors are investigated and explained 426, 439, 440

4 economic relationships are analysed in relation to different business sectors 416, 417, 426

5 economic relationships used to investigate employment trends are explained 417, 433, 434, 439, 440, 448, 458

Range: **Information sources:** data sets, UK employment law, European Community 491–3, 459, 468

Employment features: full-time, part-time; permanent, temporary; pay and benefits, provision of training and professional development 434

Employment trends: changing contractual arrangements (e.g. full-time, part-time; permanent, temporary); balance of employment between manufacturing and services; balance of employment between skilled and unskilled 426,434

Economic relationships: technological and social change and aggregate labour supply; general and business-specific skills; patterns of wage differentials (e.g. males earning more than females for the same work); skill shortages and unemployment 420, 423, 432, 438, 446

Evidence indicators: A study of two business sectors (e.g. travel sector and textiles sector) using a data set for the UK and the EC. The study will investigate the differences in employment generally and within the specific business sectors. Evidence should demonstrate understanding of the implications of the range dimensions in relation to the element. The unit test will confirm the candidate's coverage of range. 483

Element 5.2: Analyse external influences relating to employment

Performance criteria

1 external influences on business actions relating to employment are analysed and explained 424–5, 447, 457, 464, 466

2 current examples of business actions relating to employment practice are identified 418, 421, 423, 442

3 actions taken by business are explained using economic relationships 418, 420, 434

Range: **External influences:** media, trade unions, legislation, government, technology, competition 447, 457, 459–60

Actions: wages policy; responses to changes in demand; wage differentials 423, 434

Economic relationships: demand for labour and demand for the product; the supply of labour 418–20

Evidence indicators: An explanation of external influences on business employment practices using economic relationships to explain business actions (e.g. energy policy in relation to coal mining, demand for fuel and new technology or food subsidies in relation to farming, single market for food, labour supply and labour-reducing technology). Evidence should demonstrate understanding of the implications of the range dimensions in relation to the element. The unit test will confirm the candidate's coverage of range. 484, 487

Element 5.3: Evaluate the workforce performance of business sectors

Performance criteria	*Pages*
1 features of the workforce performance of different business sectors are identified	440, 470
2 data relating to workforce performance of business is accessed from a variety of sources	443, 475, 479
3 economic relationships are used to analyse the workforce performance of business	470, 473
4 workforce performance of two businesses is evaluated and recorded	475, 479, 483

Range: **Features of workforce performance:** wages; benefits and conditions of work; health and safety record; training policy; equal opportunity policy; productivity; specialisation; motivation; redundancy
440, 444, 470

Data sources: business media; employer and labour organisations; individuals; policies on: training, remuneration, benefits, equal opportunities, health and safety
491–3

Economic relationships: investment in human resources; effects of trade unions and governments on wages, health and safety, training, equal opportunities; effects of foreign investment
440, 442, 444, 470

Evidence indicators: An account of the workforce-related performance of two business sectors (e.g. safety performance in the construction industry or Japanese working practices in car manufacturing) which could be supported by evidence presented in a variety of forms (e.g. statistical, text, video, transcripts of interviews). Evidence should demonstrate understanding of the implications of the range dimensions in relation to the element. The unit test will confirm the candidate's coverage of range.
487, 489

This unit explains employment in the market economy. The employment trends in the UK are identified and explained and the reasons for changes in employment are investigated. The reasons why businesses need labour is examined and why people are paid different wages is explained. The reasons for unemployment are studied. External influences on business performance are examined. The role of trade unions and employer associations are considered in the context of industrial relations. Recent industrial and employment law is examined. Features relating to workforce performance are investigated.

In particular, Unit 5 examines:

- employment and the production process
- the labour market
- why some people earn more than others
- employers' demand for labour
- factors affecting supply of labour
- payments to labour and how they are calculated
- changing trends in employment
- women in employment
- changing contractual arrangements
- projected trends in employment patterns
- health and safety at work
- provision of training
- equal opportunity policy
- employment flows
- unemployment, types
- improving the flow of labour
- unemployment in the UK
- reasons for regional policy
- how regional policy influences employment
- industrial relations and employment legislation
- trade unions and employers' associations
- EC social policy
- External influences relating to employment:
  trade unions
  media
- Features of workforce performance
- Workforce performance of two businesses

EMPLOYMENT

Employment is part of the production process. Labour is the mental and physical effort which adds to the value of the product or service. Labour is distinct from the other inputs which go into the production process because of the human element. Labour needs to be motivated to work and there is often no correlation between effort and pay. Labour can form associations and carry out restrictive practices which influence the production process.

For the labour input to be successful there needs to be an understanding between employer and employee, i.e. a recognition of a relationship between the two.

The level of labour employment in the UK will depend on factors such as the extent of economic activity in the economy, the level of economic activity in countries which trade with the UK and the relationship between labour and technology.

■ The labour market

As with any market there are buyers and sellers. In the labour market the buyers are the employers who are seeking to buy the services, skills and experience of labour, and labour are selling these services.

The labour market in the UK is not an homogeneous or perfect market due to factors such as: differences between individuals, the demands of the job and where the job is located. Factors which affect the labour market include the following:

- workers are individuals with differences in levels of education, skills and experience
- different industries have varying demands for labour, for example in the retail trade there has been a move towards the employment of part-time workers. The demand for skills in the retail trade is different from those in other industries such as manufacturing
- regional differences: some areas of the country are dominated by one industry, for example many people in East Anglia are employed in agriculture
- the industry is either in decline or growing, for example growth in the computer software industry may mean firms have problems in recruiting workers with the required skills
- information that is available may be restricted because of the communication channels used. Job vacancies are normally advertised on a regional basis through local newspapers and job centres. Some jobs are only advertised internally within a business
- trade unions can influence the labour market by negotiating wages and conditions of work on behalf of their members.

The UK's labour force of over 28 million is one of the largest in the European Union. The Union as a whole has a total labour force of 143.5 million. Although Germany has more workers, the UK has the largest number of women in its labour force.

Table 5.1   European Community labour force (millions) 1989

	Total	Male	Female
Belgium	3,910	2,393	1,517
Denmark	2,864	1,550	1,313
Germany	29,063	17,497	11,567
Greece	3,968	2,501	1,467
Spain	14,751	9,652	5,099
France	24,062	13,531	10,531
Ireland	1,306	874	432
Italy	23,394	14,818	8,576
Luxembourg	156	101	54
Netherlands	6,609	4,074	2,535
Portugal	4,818	2,765	2,053
UK	28,682	16,372	12,310
Europe 12	143,583	86,129	57,454

WHY SOME PEOPLE EARN MORE THAN OTHERS

Fig 5.1   Gross weekly earnings by sector

PC
5.1.5

Teachers	£431.20
Police	£429.70
Banking	£344.60
Electricians	£320.60
Civil Engineers	£314.00
Nurses	£304.60
Local Authority	£231.70
Retail Trade	£218.00
Agriculture	£202.00

Average gross weekly pay for male manual workers in the public sector in 1991–92 was £259.70 compared with £270.50 in the private sector. For male white-collar workers the gap is slightly greater, £388.10 in the public sector and £405.40 in the private sector.

Source: *New Earnings Survey 1992*

The information in the table in Fig 5.1 needs to be treated with care: not all people in these professions earn the amounts shown. The figures are the averages, and new starters in these jobs would earn far less than these salaries.

The employer wants labour for the value that it adds to the production process. The demand for labour is a derived demand, wanted for what it can do rather than for itself.

The question facing the business person is:

'How many workers do I need?'

If there are not enough workers, the business does not operate efficiently. If there are too many, the business person is paying higher costs than need be.

One way to look at the question of how many workers to employ is to compare the revenue brought in by the worker compared with the costs of employing him or her.

THE DEMAND FOR LABOUR

■ Marginal revenue product

Each worker produces a physical amount of a good which sells for a particular price. Therefore each extra worker employed makes additional contributions to output. This extra output is called the Marginal Physical Product. Each unit of output sells at a price, so the employer knows the extra value each extra worker contributes to output.

$$\text{Marginal Physical Product} \times \text{Selling Price} = \text{Marginal Revenue Product}$$

$$(\text{MPP} \times P = \text{MRP})$$

PC
5.2.2

The employer is not going to employ anyone whose costs are greater than their MRP.

This means that those businesses that have a high MRP can afford to pay high wages. A business that increases productivity through improved technology or improved organisation will be able to improve the output of its workers. Where the MRP increases, workers can expect higher wages. For example in a car factory where production is done manually, output will be restricted to the slowest worker. However, if automated processes are introduced, the output will speed up and each worker's productivity will increase.

In some situations the MRP can be increased, not through increased output, but by increasing the price of the product for sale. If the demand for a product is price-inelastic (consumers still purchase the product if the price increases), the price part of the MRP equation can be increased without affecting demand. Workers can receive higher wages or perhaps more workers can be employed.

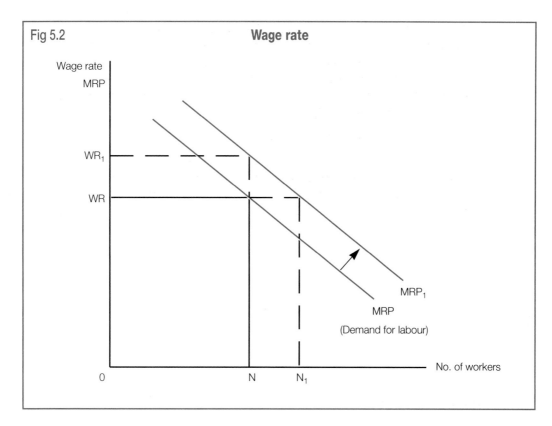

Fig 5.2

Wage rate

Wage rate
MRP

WR₁

WR

MRP₁

MRP
(Demand for labour)

No. of workers

0   N   N₁

In the diagram (Fig 5.2), MRP is the original demand curve for labour where the wage rate is WR and the number of workers employed is 0N. Therefore, if the MRP is raised for each worker, the MRP curve will shift to the right to MRP_1. Therefore, $0N_1$ workers can now receive $0WR_1$ wages or extra $N-N_1$ workers can be employed at the wage rate $0WR_1$.

Note: Not all workers have an easily identified MRP, e.g. nurses and policemen. These workers, for example, do not actually produce a physical product, they provide a service.

■ Elasticity of demand for labour

PC
5.2.2

Elasticity of demand for labour refers to how the employer will respond to a request for an increase in wages.

The elasticity of demand for labour is related to the elasticity of demand for the product. If the price elasticity of demand for the product is inelastic, demand is fairly unresponsive to a change in price, then the employer will be able to pass on extra wage costs to the consumer. When wages are a very small part of total costs, the workers may find wage negotiations easy, whereas those workers whose jobs could be done by machine may find it more difficult to get a wage increase.

Workers who will be able to command high wages are those:

■ in new expanding industries

■ with skills which are in short supply

■ with a high level of education

Workers who may receive low wages are those:

- in declining industries
- with few skills
- of low educational standard

FACTORS AFFECTING THE SUPPLY OF LABOUR

The supply of labour depends upon the number of hours of work offered at different wage rates over a period of time. The labour supply is the number of workers × the average number of hours each worker is prepared to offer.

The supply of labour will therefore depend upon:

- the size of the total population
- the age structure of the population
- the working population
- the working week and holidays
- remuneration

The supply of labour also needs to be seen in the context of labour efficiency. If workers are to work to their full potential and be most proficient, they need education and training, good working conditions and health care facilities.

■ Education and training

Today's industrial society needs highly skilled operatives, engineers and managers. Mundane work is gradually being taken over by automated machinery and the workforce is being trained to work on a higher level and be multi-skilled. Companies need a forward-looking education and training system.

■ Working conditions

'Working conditions' is a term which refers to: the length of the working week, the time allowed for breaks in the working day and the number of days holiday a worker is allowed. Working conditions are regulated by employment law. Employees tend to be more efficient with better working conditions.

The main features of the European Social Charter is to improve and harmonise working conditions for workers as Europe moves towards economic integration. For example, the average hours worked by full-time employees in the UK is 43.6 whereas the UK's main trading competitors, Germany, France and Italy have an average working week of 40.3, 39.9 and 38.9 respectively.

Table 5.2   **Holiday entitlement and public holidays in the EC**

	Annual leave	Public holidays
Germany	15	11
France	25	11
Italy	–	11
Netherlands	20	9
Belgium	20	13.5
Luxembourg	25	12
UK*	–	8
Ireland	15	9
Denmark	25	10
Greece	20–22	13
Portugal	15–21	13
Spain	25	13

* The UK has no minimum statutory annual leave

■ Health

Illness is a major problem facing most firms because it costs money. Keeping workers fit and well and having good health-care facilities will reduce the number of days lost through illness. Some firms offer private health care to their managers, not just as a 'perk' but as a way of making sure that any medical care required is administered swiftly.

■ Individual's supply of labour

PC
5.2.2

The individual's supply of labour will depend upon the number of hours he or she is willing to work. The number of hours worked is normally laid down by collective agreements between employers and trade unions. Sometimes labour is willing to work more than the agreed hours and earn overtime.

As the hours of work offered increase, the worker has to decide between the cost of working in terms of lost leisure time and the payments received for the work. The opportunity cost (the best alternative forgone) of working overtime is lost leisure and the opportunity cost of leisure is lost wages.

The supply curve of labour for an individual will rise from left to right. i.e. as wage rates increase more hours of work are supplied (Fig 5.3)

The worker will supply labour only up to a point, because as income rises so will the demand for leisure. People have their own idea of how much they want to earn. In order to reach their target income, some people may volunteer to work overtime, do shift work, or they may be awarded a pay rise. Once their target income is reached workers will not work more hours if offered to them. If workers get a wage increase, this will enable them to work fewer hours and to afford to substitute leisure for income. This reluctance to supply more labour as wage rates rise causes the supply curve for labour to bend backwards.

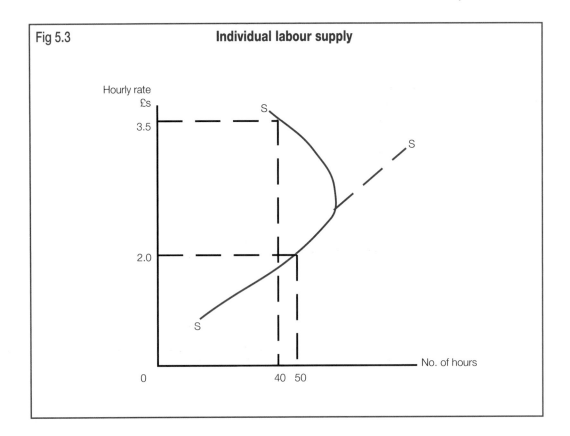

Fig 5.3   **Individual labour supply**

In Fig 5.3 wages are £2 per hour and the number of hours worked is 50. Weekly income is £100. However, if the wage rate is increased to £3.50 per hour the employee need only work 40 hours to earn £140.

Reductions in direct taxation rates such as income tax or national insurance contributions will have the same effect on the supply curve for labour as these are equivalent to a pay rise.

PC
5.2.2

The supply of labour into a particular market will depend upon the factors already described. However, some markets have restrictions placed on supply and it is the effectiveness of these restrictions or barriers of entry which helps to explain why some people can earn more than others.

In the diagram (Fig 5.4), D represents the market demand for labour and S represents those workers who are willing to work in that job market. The higher the wage the greater the supply of labour. With no barriers to entry to the market, the wage rate would be WR and the number of workers employed would be 0Q.

However, if a restriction can be placed on the entry, this will shift the supply to the left and cause supply to be more inelastic. The effect on the market is that now only $0Q_1$ workers will be paid but at the higher rate of $0WR_1$.

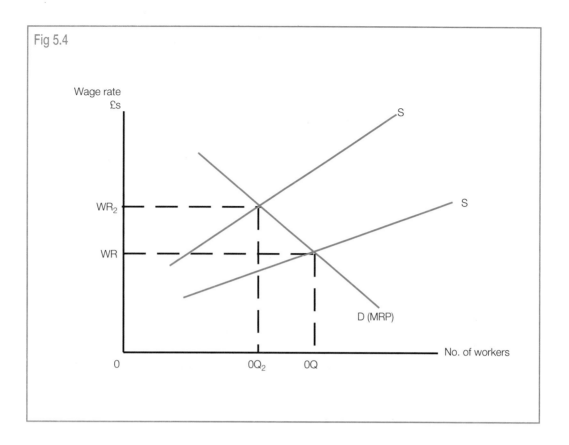

Fig 5.4

FACTORS INFLUENCING THE SUPPLY OF LABOUR AND THEIR EFFECT ON THE WAGE RATE

Age and experience In some occupations workers have incremental pay schemes to reward experience and loyalty.

Skills and abilities If there is a particular skill required for an occupation, then the worker will be rewarded with high wages, as for example professional footballers. In the UK there is a lack of skilled workers in some sectors of industry, for example in engineering, and this shortage of skills enables workers to command relatively high wages.

Qualifications and training Some occupations require people to have specific academic qualifications which can only be achieved after a long period of study as in the case of doctors.

Trade unions The strength of trade unions to negotiate wage levels will depend upon their ability to recruit members. Some occupations are difficult to organise, as for instance the catering industry. In this industry trade unions have little influence compared with those unions operating in the energy supply industry.

PC
5.2.2

Recently there has been a move away from nationally negotiated pay agreements and a move towards local or individual agreements.

Mobility of labour Mobility of labour refers to the ease with which a worker can move between jobs. Difficulties may arise for workers when they try to move between industrial sectors, occupations and different parts of the country.

Immobility of labour may cause a skill shortage. Those people in the industries with the skill shortage therefore are more likely to be paid high wages.

Dirty or dangerous jobs The supply of labour in some jobs is restricted because of the nature of the job. It might be dirty or dangerous such as coal mining. On the other hand some jobs have very good working conditions and attract labour which keeps down wages.

Availability of fringe benefits. Many managerial jobs have payments other than in cash, i.e. 'perks' such as a company car, company house and private health care. Although this cannot be counted as income, it is extra wealth derived from the occupation.

Regional differences Those regions which have high unemployment are going to have a large pool of unemployed workers which will influence the pay rates in that locality. Conversely those regions which are more economically active, especially those having firms in expanding industries, are going to have high wages to pay for the skill shortages in the area.

Government Central and local government are major employers employing people with a wide range of skills and abilities. The government is able to use public sector pay as a means of regulating the economy. For example pay rises in the public sector for 1993 were restricted to 1½ per cent. The government hoped the private sector would adopt this as its norm in its wage negotiations. In previous years, governments have introduced formal and informal pay restraint to try to reduce wage inflation.

■ Payments to labour

In return for selling their skills and experience labour normally receives monetary payment. This is in the form of wages or salaries.

A wage is paid on a weekly basis calculated by the hour or the output of the worker. The wage rate is the sum of money an employer agrees to pay the worker, for example £1 per hour.

Salaries are calculated on an annual basis and paid monthly.

PC
5.2.1

Earnings are what the worker takes home after all the deductions have been taken out, for example income tax and national insurance and include any extra payments such as bonuses.

Nominal wages and real wages The nominal wage is the amount of money paid to the worker, but the real wage is the purchasing power of wages after taking into account inflation.

■ Calculation of pay

Wages can be calculated in a number of ways:

Time rates

Wages are calculated by an hourly rate and are normally applied in situations where:

- work is of high quality
- the rate of output cannot be speeded up
- the work is not a standard operation
- output cannot be measured.

Piece rates

Wages are calculated by output levels and normally takes place where:

- output is measurable
- output is constant
- effort can be encouraged
- workers can work at their own pace
- workers don't need supervision
- costing is easy for the employer.

Measured day work

This method is used to offer pay stability in those industries which used to pay its workers by piece work. Workers are guaranteed a basic weekly sum and then are set measurable and achievable targets of output to earn extra pay.

Merit pay

This is used to encourage workers, as those who work hard get extra pay. Each year an employee will have his or her work performance assessed and may be rewarded accordingly. The assessment tends to be based on the personal qualities of the worker and is concerned with qualities such as, commitment, co-operation, initiative and dependability. Merit pay has come in for criticism because of the way of assessing performance. Some performance is difficult to measure and in some cases the measurement can tend to be subjective. Managers may be influenced by the individual rather than the work completed.

Performance related pay

PC
5.2.1

The trend is now towards performance related pay, recognising the contribution of an individual to the performance of the company. The reward is for output rather than input of the worker. Performance pay will be based on setting the individual objectives and these will be agreed between the worker and his or her line manager. The targets will be clear and measurable and will probably be set after the appraisal interview of the worker. The appraisal interview will highlight the strengths of the person which can be developed and the weaknesses which need help to be remedied. This will then make it easier for the worker to achieve his or her targets.

Performance related pay is a direct move away from nationally negotiated agreements on pay to individual contracts between employer and employee. This method of calculating pay can be used for managers and the shop-floor operative and should do much to change attitudes in the workplace.

1 How do buyers and sellers in the labour market contact each other? Think of as many ways as you can in which this happens and write them down.

2 Find some job advertisements in local or national newspapers. Identify how the organisations wish to be contacted and make a list of skills and experience needed for the jobs.

3 Write a list of skills you possess at the moment and compare this to the skills you think you may need in the future. Prepare an Action Plan for bridging the gap.

4 Compare the quantity of labour supplied by two people you know who work. Enquire what hours they work per week. Multiply this by the number of weeks they work (52 minus holidays). Is there much difference between the two?

5 Is your family occupationally mobile? What different reasons might there be in one family as to why they should not wish to move to the other end of the UK to find work?

PC
5.1.3

CHANGING TRENDS IN EMPLOYMENT

■ The changing industrial base

The main sectors of employment are referred to as:

■ Primary
■ Secondary
■ Tertiary

Industries found in these sectors include:

■ **The primary sector:** agriculture and the extractive industries such as coal mining and quarrying.
■ **The secondary sector:** manufacturing and construction.
■ **The tertiary sector or the service sector:** banking, insurance and education.

Table 5.3   Changes in employment according to sector

	1977 (000)	1991 (000)
Primary	1,086	700
Secondary	839	4,846
Tertiary	12,697	16,245

As a country's economy develops, so the relevant importance of each sector will change.
Before the industrial revolution most people were employed in agriculture. By the 1850s the manufacturing sector of the economy was the most important sector for employment and output. From the latter part of the nineteenth century the tertiary sector grew in importance as it supported or serviced the manufacturing industry. Today the service sector is the largest employer and contributes most to the UK's economy.

The changes in the importance of the manufacturing and tertiary sectors accelerated most during the 1960s and 1980s. For example in 1960 manufacturing accounted for 39 per cent of employment and 26 per cent of output. By 1990 employment in this sector had fallen to 23 per cent and output to 22 per cent. The tertiary sector, however, was employing 70 per cent of the nation's workforce and contributed to over 65 per cent of its output.

The influence of the primary sector continued its decline during the 1980s as both coal and North Seal Oil reduced in output.

De-industrialisation

The decline in the importance of manufacturing is generally referred to as de-industrialisation. De-industrialisation means a decline in manufacturing in terms of:

- the absolute employment level
- the total share of employment in the economy
- a decline in the share of output of the economy

The causes of de-industrialisation include the lack of competitiveness of UK goods with foreign goods both at home and abroad. This lack of competitiveness can be on price, delivery and quality.

During the 1980s UK manufacturers had to contend with a high exchange rate brought about by the exporting of North Sea Oil and high UK interest rates. This made it difficult to export because the high pound made exports expensive and difficult to sell abroad. In the home market the manufacturers had to compete against cheaper imports.

The importance of manufacturing to the UK economy is that other sectors depend on it and cannot operate without manufactured goods. The catering industry needs plates, saucepans, tables and chairs. All items produced by manufacturers can be sold abroad and earn foreign currency, but this is not the case with the tertiary sector. Although the service sector makes a significant contribution to the UK's balance of payments, some services, such as rail travel or the services of firemen and traffic wardens, cannot be sold abroad.

Service industries need manufactured goods in order to provide for their customers. Hotels and restaurants are in the service sector, but they need buildings, furnishings, carpets, crockery and cutlery, cash registers/computers, stationery and a host of other manufactured goods to be able to provide a service.

The decline in the manufacturing sector means that the UK is in a weaker position for competing with countries such as Japan. However, some economists argue that de-industrialisation is just part of the natural development of the economy. The UK was the first to industrialise, so the likelihood is that the UK will be one of the first nations to move on to the next stage in economic development. Other countries such as the United States of America are experiencing similar situations with their secondary sectors.

Changes in labour

As the structure of the economy has changed so there have been changes in the make-up of the labour market. The labour market is vibrant and dynamic and many of the changes in the labour market are related to the labour force. It was stated earlier that the actual size of the labour force will depend on the size of the population, the age structure, the ratio of male to female and the activity rates of those employed.

In 1990 the civilian labour force, i.e. those people in employment plus those who are unemployed and claiming benefit but not including the armed forces, totalled, 28.2 million.

Table 5.4		Civilian labour force: by age		
Great Britain				Millions
	16–24	25–54	55 and over	All aged 16 and over
Estimates				
1971	5.1	15.0	4.9	24.9
1976	5.1	16.1	4.5	25.7
1979	5.6	16.3	4.2	26.0
1983	5.9	16.4	3.7	25.9
1984	6.0	16.7	3.6	26.4
1984	6.1	16.8	3.7	26.6
1986	6.2	17.3	3.4	26.9
1990	5.8	18.8	3.5	28.2
Projections				
1996	4.9	20.2	3.4	28.6
2001	5.0	20.3	3.6	28.9

[1] Estimates for 1971 are based on the Census of Population. Those for 1976, 1984 are based on the GB Labour Force definitions, and from 1984 on the ILO definitions.

Source: Employment Department

Social Trends 22, © Crown copyright 1992

Table 5.4 shows that there has been a steady increase in the total civilian labour force. Part of this change is accounted for by the relatively high birth rates in the 1960s. Within the labour force in 1990, 16–24 year olds made up 21 per cent of the civilian labour force, but by 2001 this is projected to fall to 17 per cent.

There have been an extra 2 million people who have joined the labour force since the 1970s. This has meant that more jobs have had to be created during a period of high unemployment. Between 1983 and 1990 the economy created 940,000 jobs, many of which were part-time and taken up by women.

The difference between those who had jobs and those who had not – the job deficit – gradually closed during the 1980s only to widen again with the onset of the new recession.

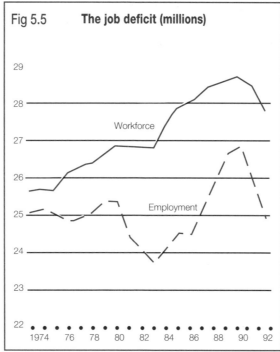

Fig 5.5   **The job deficit (millions)**

Source: Dept of Employment. *Guardian*, Friday, February 19 1993

The self-employed

The 1980s saw a rapid growth in the number of self-employed. Between 1981 and 1990 the number of self-employed increased by 57 per cent. By 1990 almost 3.25 million people were self-employed and half of these people had work either in the construction sector, distribution, catering or the repairs sector of the economy.

Table 5.5   **Number of self-employed persons between 1971 and 1990 in 000's**

	1971	1981	1990
All industries	1,953	2,058	3,222
Males	1,556	1,641	2,449
Females	397	417	773
Manufacturing	129	146	272
Service	1,199	1,274	1,981
Other	625	638	969

In 1989 there was a total of 130.4 million people employed in the EC. Since 1985 over 7 million jobs had been created, while at the same time there was a change taking place to the pattern of employment. Fewer are now employed in agriculture and industry whilst more are employed in services.

Table 5.6   **Number employed by sector in the EC**

	1975	1989
Agriculture (000)	13,942	9,209
Percentage of employed	11.2	7.1
Industry (000)	48,395	43,138
Percentage of employed	38.8	33.2
Service (000)	62,453	77,761
Percentage of employed	50	59.8

Table 5.7   **Numbers of self-employed persons between 1971 and 1990**

	1971 (000)	1981 (000)	1990 (000)
All industries	1,953	2,058	3,222
Males	1,556	1,641	2,449
Females	397	417	773
Manufacturing	129	146	272
Service	1,199	1,274	1,981
Other	625	638	969

The main reasons for the increase in the self-employed include the following:

■ Those people who had been made redundant decided to work for themselves.

■ Government policies encouraged the unemployed to start their own business.

■ Businesses decided to contract out their work rather than employ their own workers.

The 1980s was the era of the entrepreneur.

Activity rates

This refers to the proportion of the population above the minimum school-leaving age who are in the civilian labour force. Recently there have been changes in these rates for both men and women. In 1993 the male activity rate was 74.2 whereas the activity rate for women was 52.8. This represented a fall since 1971 for male activity rates from 80.5 per cent, while women's rates increased from 43.9 per cent. Demographic factors influence women's activity rates, for example firms taking on women because of the shortage of teenage workers, the comparatively low birth rate during the 1970s and a rise in the average age at which women have children. The fall in male activity rates was due mainly to the increase in male unemployment.

The UK activity rate is above the EU average. The activity rate varies between states because of the uneven distribution of:

■ employment in agriculture, industry and services

■ the age structures of the country

■ the percentage of women in the job market.

Table 5.8   **European Community activity rate (%)**

	Total	Male	Female
Belgium	39.6	49.7	30.0
Denmark	56.1	61.8	50.6
Germany	47.9	59.9	36.7
Greece	40.7	53.0	29.2
Spain	38.0	51.0	25.6
France	44.7	52.1	38.8
Ireland	37.9	50.5	25.0
Italy	41.4	54.1	30.0
Luxembourg	42.4	56.1	28.7
Netherlands	45.6	56.8	34.7
Portugal	46.9	56.4	38.3
UK	50.9	59.5	42.6
Eur 12	44.9	55.6	34.9

In the EC there has been a general decline in the male activity rate. This has been offset by the increase in the female activity rate. The main factor influencing female activity rates can be attributed to the number of opportunities available for part-time working.

Changes in the public sector in the UK

The employment patterns in relation to public sector and the private sector changed during the 1980s.

Table 5.9   **Changes in employment in public and private sectors**

	1970 (000)	1980 (000)	1990 (000)
Workforce in employment	24,753	25,327	26,924
Private sector employment	18,238	17,940	20,430
Public sector employment	6,515	7,387	6,071

Most of the decrease in the public sector employment since 1981 is accounted for by a fall in employment in public corporations as a result of privatisation.

WOMEN IN EMPLOYMENT

The fastest growing sector of the labour market is female employment. In 1911, women made up 30 per cent of the workforce, by 1971 this had risen to 42 per cent and by 1993 the figure stood at 48 per cent. It is projected that women will make up 50 per cent of the labour force by the mid 1990s.

Women have always made significant contributions to the labour market, but their contributions depended upon the attitudes of society and the economic climate at the time. The types of employment have also changed over time. At the start of the century women could find employment in factories or in domestic service. Today there is no barrier to the types of job available to women – women on the floor of the Stock Exchange or women Prime Ministers.

In periods of labour shortages women are actively encouraged to work. In times of conflict, such as during both the First and Second World Wars, women took the place of men in the factories or on the farms. However, when the men returned, women were expected to give up their jobs. During the inter-war years it was expected that women would work until they got married and then they would set up home and have a family. Men were the bread-winners.

Since 1970 there has been a shift in attitudes towards women and legislation relating to women in employment. It is now accepted and expected that women make a contribution to the economy. This trend for an increase in women's participation rate in employment is evident in other countries.

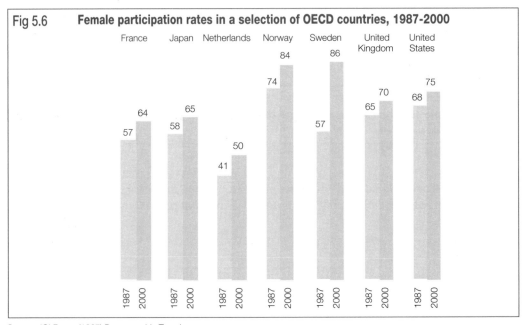

Fig 5.6   **Female participation rates in a selection of OECD countries, 1987-2000**

Source: ICI Paper (1987) Deomgraphic Trends

■ The reasons for the trend in female employment

The rise of the tertiary sector

The growth of the tertiary sector in economic terms has meant a change in employment and employment patterns as more people are now employed in services and are part-time and temporary working has increased. The tertiary sector is now more important than the secondary sector which traditionally employed men in the staple industries of coal mining, ship-building and in the manufacturing sector. These industries have been replaced and their place has been taken by the service industries, for example, banking, insurance and retailing. Service industries are major employers of women.

The rise of part-time occupations

There has been a shift away from full employment to part-time occupations. During the 1990s it is expected that half the UK workforce will be made up of part-time workers. One of the reasons for this is that part-time workers are less costly to employ. Not only are their wages lower than full-time workers but also other employment costs are reduced, for example, sickness benefits and pension contributions.

However, part-time work is useful for married women who have young children and are able to fit working around their family commitments.

The change in the family structure

The trend this century has been for smaller families, i.e. two adults and two children or fewer. Not only has the trend been to have fewer children but to have them later in life and for the women to return to work as soon as possible. The desire is to maintain the standard of living of the family.

Another trend in families has been the rise in one-parent families which has increased the pressure on women to work. However, because mothers have to look after their children they find it difficult to find employment.

Women are cheaper to employ

Women do not earn as much as men despite changes in attitudes and legislation towards women.

Table 5.10   **A comparison of weekly wages in 1990**

	Male	Female
Manual	£237.20	£148.00
Non-manual	£354.90	£215.50

Among the reasons for these differences are that women tend to work in part-time occupations which do not pay the same rates as full-time work and they also tend to work in low-paid industries such as retailing and catering. Women often work in those industries or small firms which are poorly unionised.

Family commitments may mean that women do not wish to work overtime or unsociable hours. This may mean that they miss out on the higher rates of pay.

Women have breaks in their careers when starting a family. The longer a woman is out of a job, the more difficult it becomes for her to get her old job back at the same level and at the same money. For example, a systems analyst who left her job seven years ago would no longer have the knowledge or the skills to do the job now. Women have to restart their careers usually at the bottom of the ladder for pay and prospects, whereas a male colleague who was employed by the firm at the same time at the start of his career would not only be earning more but would have probably gained promotion.

Attitudes of employers

PC
5.1.5

Despite legislation on equal pay there remains a gap between the earnings of men and women.

However, the Equal Pay Act 1970 has required that women performing similar tasks to men must be treated in the same way as men regarding terms and conditions of employment. The Equal Pay Amendment Regulations 1983 allowed women to claim equal pay on the basis of work of equal value if they found it difficult to make a claim based on 'like work' or 'work related or equivalent'.

The Sex Discrimination Act 1975 requires that men and women should be guaranteed equality of opportunity. Since the introduction of the Acts there has been an improvement in women's pay.

PC
5.1.3

■ Measures for bringing more women into the workforce

More women would be able to enter the workforce if constraints on them were removed and employers were more imaginative with the conditions of employment. Employers could be more flexible with their working hours to fit in with the school timetable, offer more child care facilities and give leave of absence to either parent rather than mothers only.

PC
5.1.1

CHANGING CONTRACTUAL ARRANGEMENTS

The tradition of getting a full-time job upon leaving school and staying with the same firm for 40 years seems to be almost gone in the UK economy. The standard full-time permanent contract is still with us, but is becoming rarer. The growth areas in employment contracts are part-time, temporary, outside contractors, agency works and the self-employed. Firms use these contracts increasingly to improve flexibility in the workforce.

Flexibility in the labour market through the use of non-standard contracts has come about as a result of recent recession, the increasingly competitive international market and uncertainty about levels of demand.

TYPES OF FLEXIBILITY IN THE LABOUR MARKET

● **Functional**

Employees are increasingly multi-skilled and can do one another's jobs.

● **Numerical**

Non-standard employment contracts allow employers to increase or decrease employee numbers quickly in response to changes in demand for labour.

● **Financial**

Payment systems are becoming individual, with rewards for performance, or 'market rate' rather than 'across the board' with all employees having the same pay rates.

■ Numerical flexibility and the use of non-standard contracts

PC
5.1.1

Part-time employees

The main reason for the use of part-time permanent employees is to cater for tasks which require a limited number of hours to complete. Examples are cleaners, usually employed for a few hours before or after the company's opening/closing hours, and catering employees, often working from mid/late morning to mid afternoon.

Other reasons for employing part-timers are to match employment levels to peaks in demand, for example, retail trades use part-timers for busy periods during the week. Some employers grant part-time hours because job applicants do not want full-time and others because they can retain valued staff who are unable to continue working full-time.

The growth in the use of part-time staff has come mainly from the retail sector which is experiencing increasing trading hours. Part-time workers rarely get overtime rates for working beyond the standard working day, which increases their attractiveness to employers.

Temporary employees

Employers often need short-time cover for full-time employees who are on holiday or sick. Temporary workers are also used to meet fluctuations in demand, to deal with one-off tasks and to provide specialist skills. The growth area for the employment of temporary workers has been in the health, education and distribution industries. Public sector budget constraints and uncertainty about future funding levels may have influenced the choice to increase the numbers of workers on temporary contracts.

Self-employed workers

'Self-employed' in this sense describes individuals who are given work by companies but are neither employees of that organisation nor of any other organisation. The most important reason for firms to employ these people is for the specialist skills they offer.

There may be an increased demand for specialist skills, or more companies trying to cut costs by buying in skills when needed. Examples of self-employed workers are builders, window cleaners, management consultants and computer specialists.

Costs of employing non-standard labour

Most companies pay the same hourly rate for full-time and part-time employees. Where there are differences, the part-time rate is lower in the majority of cases. The hourly rates paid to agency temps are likely to be higher than for full-time employees.

National Insurance is another major cost item. If employees earn more than a lower earnings limit, both employer and employee are liable for contributions based on total earnings. This provides an incentive to keep total earnings below the limit. Despite this, most part-timers earn more than the threshold.

The majority of part-time and temporary workers are not included in company pension schemes, whereas most permanent full-time workers are. Indirect costs of employing labour are caused by absenteeism (sick leave) and turnover. Part-timers have a slightly higher turnover rate than full-time workers and a lower rate of absenteeism.

The main cost saving associated with non-standard labour is in lower fringe benefit provision.

PC
5.1.1

Flexible hours

Permanent and full-time staff also have experienced greater flexibility in their hours of work over recent years.

Flexible working hours (usually known as 'flexi-time')

This is the longest-running of the flexible hour systems; it became widespread by the 1970s. Two and a half million people are now working flexible hours, most of them office workers.

The firm's working day has to be longer than the working hours for individuals. People then flex their hours according to the needs of the business and their individual preference.

There is a band of time, say, from 8 am–6 pm when employees could work their contracted 7 or 8 hours. The employees can choose what time to go into work, and as long as they work a 'core time' of approximately 10 am–4 pm, their employer is happy for them to work their contracted hours when they wish. Some organisations allow workers to build up time off by working long days. Employers control this by having a 'settlement period' within which time off must be taken so that build-ups of days off do not get over-large.

Compressed working week

Some organisations close early on Fridays, or do not work on Fridays, and therefore longer hours are worked on the other working days.

Compressed annual hours

Some employees are contracted to work a certain number of hours per year. Compressed annual hours involve working many hours in a short period of time. This is suitable for people working away from home such as oil rig workers. They can work intensively for a period of time and then take a long break.

Job sharing

Two people agree to share a single job. The employer has two contracts of employment, one with each person. The distribution of work is for the workers themselves to decide.

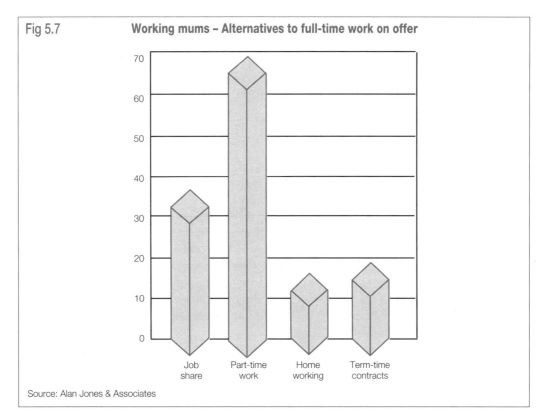

Fig 5.7 **Working mums – Alternatives to full-time work on offer**

Source: Alan Jones & Associates

Employees find the arrangement beneficial as the job is usually of a more interesting nature than many part-time jobs. Most job shares disappear when one person leaves and the other takes it over as a full-time job.

Homeworking (Teleworking)

It is technologically feasible for people to work at home with a computer terminal connecting them to their office. It was once thought that future generations would all be working from home. This has not happened due to problems of isolation and loss of personal contacts. Women who work at home tend to do jobs related to the textile industry, for example making cushions and cuddly toys.

PROJECTED TRENDS IN EMPLOYMENT PATTERNS

■ Technology

Companies which fail to innovate and stay with outdated technologies will eventually go out of business. There is a reluctance by the workers to accept new working practices because of the fear of losing their skills, status or their jobs. However, where new technologies are introduced the conditions for workers improve.

The practical uses and application of micro-electronics, computers and information technology are limitless, whether they are used on the production line, in offices or shops. They change the way people work. In retailing, for example with the introduction of the Electronic Point Of Sales systems selling and stock control has been revolutionised. The laborious manual pricing of individual items can be eliminated and workers can be released to do more interesting jobs.

Communications are continually being improved as technology advances. The way in which people communicate is now more flexible and quicker because of portable telephones, fax machines and telecommunications. Businesses are able to store, process and evaluate information more quickly, and administration is more effective and efficient with the developments being made in computers and information technology.

Advances in technology have enabled the process of production to become more efficient. Manufacturing firms which introduce Just-in-Time stock control are able to reduce their costs of production. The use of robotics on the production line has removed some of the more tedious operations performed by workers and has improved the quality of output.

New materials such as carbon fibre have enabled new products to be produced or have improved old ones. Tennis rackets are now made out of graphite rather than wood.

■ Activity rates

The labour force in the UK is projected to increase by 800,000 people by the year 2001. Almost all of the projected net increase will be among women who are expected to make up 45 per cent of the labour force by this date. This means that there will be higher activity rates for females, particularly those aged between 25 and 44. This change reflects changes in the social and economic factors such as the availability of part-time work and child care facilities. The activity rates for males and females aged between 16 and 24 will increase as more students enter the job market to finance their studies. During the 1980s the male activity rate was influenced by unemployment. The rate is predicted to fall further because of men taking early retirement.

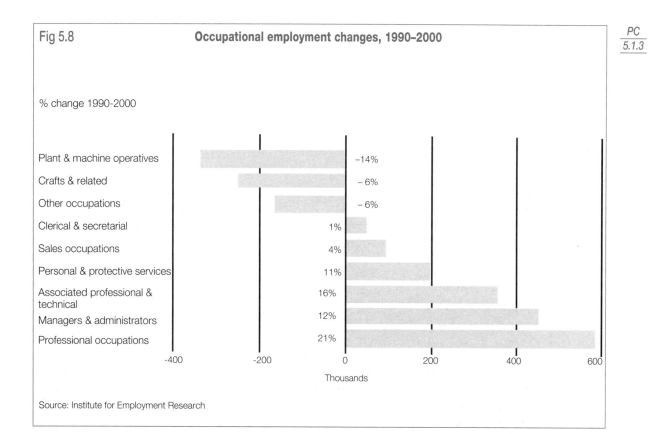

Fig 5.8   **Occupational employment changes, 1990–2000**

% change 1990-2000

Occupation	% change
Plant & machine operatives	–14%
Crafts & related	– 6%
Other occupations	– 6%
Clerical & secretarial	1%
Sales occupations	4%
Personal & protective services	11%
Associated professional & technical	16%
Managers & administrators	12%
Professional occupations	21%

Thousands

Source: Institute for Employment Research

■ New jobs

These are expected to be created in four groups of service industries:

- ■ Hotel and catering   240,000
- ■ Business services   400,000
- ■ Other services   650,000
- ■ Health, education and other public services   670,000

About 200,000 jobs are likely to be lost in primary industries and utilities such as gas and oil. One million jobs are likely to be lost in manufacturing, except motor vehicles. Engineering is expected to lose about 250,000 jobs. There will be a continued shift to white-collar jobs for women, as well as an increase in part-time working.

DISCUSSION TOPICS

1 Put the following into one of the sectors of – Primary, Secondary or Tertiary.

(a) Postman

(b) Oil rig worker

(c) Fashion designer   *(continued overleaf)*

(d) Architect

(e) Fisherman

(f) Farmer

(g) Musician

(h) Builder

(i) Welder

(j) Nurse

(k) Toolmaker

PC
5.1.3

2   Does de-industrialisation matter? Can the UK become a service specialist and do without manufacturing industries?

PC
5.1.1

3   By the year 2001 there will be fewer young people in the labour force. What measures can employers take to find other sources of labour?

PC
5.1.5

4   Using examples of women known to the group who work, discuss why they work, what they do, their qualifications and promotions they have achieved.

PC
5.1.5
5.1.5

5   Draw up an organisation chart for your school or college and identify women in managerial posts.

6   Do attitudes in society towards women working affect women's activity rates?

PC
5.1.5

7   Why are some firms replacing some of their full-time and Saturday staff with part-time workers? How will this change working patterns?

PC
5.1.5

8   Many organisations are increasing the numbers of part-time staff and reducing the numbers of full-time. What effect do you think this might have on the motivation of staff who have been working full-time and have their contracts changed to part-time?

9   Why do people decide to work for themselves and what problems may they face in running their own business?

10 How is technological change affecting how people do their jobs?

FEATURES OF EMPLOYMENT

PC
5.3.1

■ Health and safety at work record

Health and safety at work is important from an employee's point of view because his or her life and health might be at risk from hazards at work. It is also in the employer's interest to support good Health and Safety at Work policies as many working days can be lost through accidents at work, production may fall if workers are unwell and employees who are cared for by their employers may be more productive and loyal.

■ Legislation

The Health and Safety at Work Act 1974 brings up to date the previous legislation:

■ The Factories Act 1961

■ The Offices Shops and Railway Premises Act 1963

■ The Fire Precautions Act 1971

Specific areas of legislation have also been expanded by The Control of Substances Hazardous to Health Regulations 1988 (COSHH).

The Health and Safety at Work Act covers very wide-ranging aspects of health and safety, both for people at work and the public. It also created the Health and Safety Commission. The Commission is responsible for carrying out the policy of the Act and provides advice for businesses and local authorities on how to implement Health and Safety policies.

■ Employer health and safety policy

Every employer is required to prepare a written statement of their general policy on health and safety, and details of the arrangements for carrying out the policy. All employees must be advised of what the policy is.

Employers should take actions to put the policy into practice. They should also give information in their written policy on how particular hazards should be dealt with. Management should take responsibility for Health and Safety matters along with designated safety representatives. In the case of negligence, proceedings, can be taken against the manager responsible, as well as against the organisation.

Duties of employers

Employers should:

■ provide and maintain plant and systems of work that are safe and without risks to health

■ provide a safe place of work, with safe access and exits

■ provide a safe working environment that is without risks to health

■ ensure safety, the absence of risks in the use, handling, storage and transport of articles and substances.

■ provide adequate welfare facilities and arrangements for welfare at work

■ provide any necessary information, including information on legal requirements, to ensure the health and safety of his employees

■ provide adequate supervision as is necessary to ensure the health and safety of his employees

Duties of employees

Three general duties are placed on employees

■ to exercise reasonable care for the health and safety of themselves and others who may be affected by their acts or omissions at work

- to co-operate with the employer, as far as may be necessary, to enable him to carry out his legal duties in health and safety matters

- not to intentionally or recklessly interfere with anything provided in the interests of health, safety or welfare.

UK businesses now have to operate within a European legal framework as health and safety issues are part of the European Union social policy.

Regulations imposed by the European Union cover the following six areas:

1 Management of health and safety
2 Work equipment safety
3 Manual handling of loads
4 Workplace conditions
5 Personal protective equipment
6 Display screen equipment

■ Provision of training

Training is:

'Developing the necessary skills, knowledge and attitudes in the employees of the organisation.'

Training is an investment in the employees which can be carried out in-house or externally. New recruits to a company need training in order to learn their new jobs and existing employees may need training for different or future requirements.

Training is a cost to the organisation and as such it is often cut back during hard times when it is needed most. The return on the investment in training is often difficult to see or long-term in nature, which can make it appear unnecessary. There are still many firms in the UK which do not have a training officer or a training department. This is unfortunate as an investment in training will increase the effectiveness of the organisation.

If the organisation invests money in training, it should expect to receive a return on that investment. It is important that the firm should identify the training needs, select appropriate training methods and monitor and evaluate the effects of training after it has taken place.

■ Identifying training needs

The following need to be decided:

- Organisational goals
- What needs to be done to achieve these goals?
- What should each employee be able to do to carry out their job?
- What gaps are there in the knowledge, skills or attitudes required by employees to carry out jobs?

The area for training is the last question; it identifies the training gap. There are indicators that there is a training gap such as low productivity, accidents, customer complaints. Another way of assessing the training gap is through the idea of competencies. The training or competency gap is identified by assessing whether the employee can perform all the tasks required to do one job. This has taken the training world by storm and is being adopted in education, vocational training and management training.

Competency-based training specifies tasks related to a job which the job holder should be able to perform. Once the employee is deemed to be competent in performing all the tasks associated with a job, he or she can be awarded a qualification. A National Vocational Qualification (NVQ) comes in various levels and is awarded by an 'awarding body' such as City & Guilds, RSA or BTEC. The Management Charter Initiative is a competency-based management qualification and is equivalent to NVQ level 3 (Supervisory Managers), level 4 (First Line Managers) and level 5 (Middle and Senior Managers).

■ Induction

PC
5.3.2

New employees need to be familiarised with the workings of the organisation, safety matters, general conditions of employment and the work of the department in which they are employed. Many large firms have formal induction programmes which aim to integrate new employees into the organisation.

STEPS IN AN INDUCTION PROGRAMME

- History and management of the organisation
- Personnel policies and terms of employment
- Employee benefits and services
- Facilities of the organisation
- General nature of the work to be done
- Introduction to supervisor
- Rules and safety measures
- The relation of various jobs to the new job
- Details of the job
- Introduction to fellow workers
- Follow-up after several weeks.

Induction will have been successful if the new employee is confident in his or her situation.

■ Training for different kinds of employee

PC
5.3.2

Shopfloor

Training can be carried out by a training instructor if there are large numbers of new recruits. If not, then the supervisor can be trained on how to instruct new starters. Shopfloor or manual jobs are often specific to a particular organisation and therefore training is needed even for those who had the same job title in another establishment.

These jobs seldom receive adequate training, resulting in a lower level of performance and less job satisfaction than if training had been in place.

Administrative

Computers and word processors are prevalent in office settings. Employees will usually enter the organisation with the required skills, training only being given when a new computerised system is installed. Often, the only training office workers receive is during the induction period.

Technical

Technicians and apprentices go through long periods of on-the-job training as well as part-time attendance at college to gain the relevant qualification.

Recessions have made the five-year apprenticeship scheme in companies more unusual and workers are becoming multi-skilled and able to do many jobs.

Youth training

The Youth Training Scheme (YTS) began in the 1980s as a one-year programme, and became two-year in 1986. Training and work experience was provided for school leavers on a large scale. In 1989 Youth Training was transferred to Training and Enterprise Councils (TECs) which are local bodies, with the intention of the training being appropriate to local needs.

Equal opportunity policy

In society there are always groups that are discriminated against unfairly due to the prejudices and preconceptions of the people with whom they come into contact. Disadvantaged groups are:

- women
- people from other racial backgrounds
- disabled people
- older people

There is no legislation concerning discrimination against older people. It may be that legislation is not the most effective way of dealing with prejudice. Companies that discriminate against disadvantaged groups in their employment policies are reducing the amount of talent available to them and contributing to social instability outside the organisation.

Equal opportunities policies are not required by law, but for those employers who wish to have an equal opportunities policy, the Equal Opportunities Commission produces a model policy for adaptation to particular organisations.

These policies spell out what constitutes unfair discrimination and what the organisation hopes to achieve through the policy. Some employers have appointed an Equal Opportunities Officer to implement the policy.

Equal opportunities policies involve monitoring how many employees fall into categories of sex, different races and disabled people, where they work, what jobs they do and what training and career development they might have received. This information can be used for deciding where discrimination may be occurring.

A MODEL EQUAL OPPORTUNITIES POLICY

1 **Introduction:** Desirability of the policy and that it is required to be strictly adhered to.

2 **Definitions:** Direct and indirect discrimination defined.

3 **General statement of policy:** A commitment to equal treatment and the belief that this is also in the interests of the organisation. Staff in the organisation should be made aware of the policy and key personnel trained in the policy.

4 **Possible preconceptions:** Examples of preconceptions that may be erroneously held about individuals due to their sex or marital status.

5 **Recruitment and promotion:** Care to be taken that recruitment information has an equal chance of reaching both sexes and does not indicate a preference for one group of applicants. Care that job requirements are justifiable and that interviews are conducted on an objective basis. An intention not to discriminate in promotion.

6 **Training:** An intention not to discriminate with some further details.

7 **Terms and conditions of service and facilities:** An intention not to discriminate.

8 **Monitoring:** Nomination of a person responsible for monitoring the effectiveness of the policy and with overall responsibility for implementation. An intention to review the policy and procedures. Intention to rectify any areas where employees/applicants are found not to be receiving equal treatment.

9 **Grievances and victimisation:** An intention to deal effectively with grievances and victimisation.

Source: Summarised from EOC (1985). *A Model Equal Opportunities Policy.*

EMPLOYMENT FLOWS

PC
5.2.3

In 1944 full employment in the UK was defined in a White Paper on Employment Policy as a situation where the recorded unemployment does not rise above 3 per cent of the working population. During periods of full employment there will always be some people who are unemployed, i.e. those who want a job but for some reason are not able to get one.

The official definition of unemployment states that the unemployed are those people in receipt of benefit who are seeking work but are unable to obtain a job and are registered with the Department of Employment as being willing and available for work.

The government official count of the unemployed is probably too low because not everyone who is seeking employment can claim benefits. Also since 1979 the government has changed the definition of unemployment 29 times, which has usually moved the numbers downwards.

When the numbers of unemployed are announced each month by the Department of Employment it is important to remember that people are not constantly unemployed, but different people join and leave the register each day, i.e. it is a flow of labour into and out of employment (Fig 5.9).

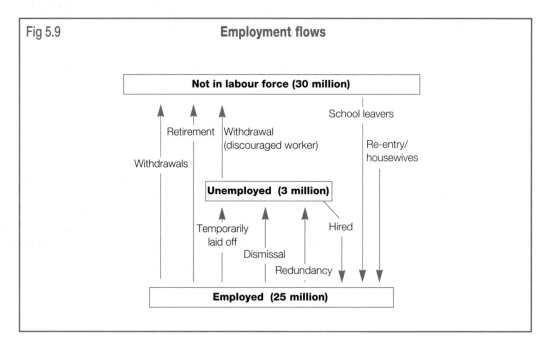

Fig 5.9   **Employment flows**

■ Types of unemployment

The types of unemployment are normally classified as follows:

Frictional This type of unemployment is associated with those people who are seeking their first jobs or are between jobs. It also refers to those who are unemployed in one part of the country but for whom there is a job available in another part of the country.

Seasonal This occurs because some employment is seasonal in character. The tourist industry is a good example as people are laid off during the out-of-season period. Some parts of the country such as Cornwall and Devon have high rates of unemployment during the winter months.

Structural This will happen where there has been a long-term decline in a major industry. The specialist jobs associated with that industry are no longer required. Examples include the coal, steel and shipbuilding industries.

Technological During the last 20 years there has been rapid advancement in the use of labour saving devices which has caused job losses.

Demand deficiency This is sometimes referred to as 'cyclical unemployment' and is usually linked to the business cycle. As the economy moves through various stages of activity from boom to recession the rate of unemployment will fluctuate. The recession between 1980 and 1983 was mainly due to the fall in aggregate demand rather than trade union power or structural decline.

■ Improving the flow of labour

PC
5.2.1

Some economists argue that imperfections in the labour market need to be removed to enable the market to operate more efficiently. Their policies are concerned mainly with improving the supply in the labour market. This includes:

■ reducing trade union power
■ reducing the mismatch of vacancies and skills (immobility of labour)
■ reducing state benefits
■ reducing direct taxation

Trade union power

It can be argued that powerful trade unions are able to distort the market. They can do this by restricting entry into the market by demanding that workers who want to work must join the union. Other union power can be demonstrated by insisting that work done in business is restricted. For example, the only person who is allowed to replace a light bulb is an electrician. Powerful unions are able to negotiate wages above the equilibrium market level.

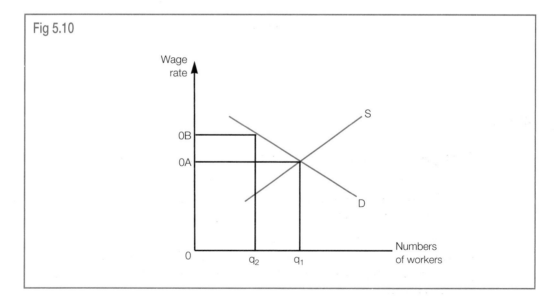

Fig 5.10

In the diagram (Fig 5.10) the market wage rate is 0A and $0q_1$ workers would be employed. However trade union power has pushed up the rate to 0B which means $0q_1–0q_2$ are not employed. These workers would have been employed in a free market.

Reducing union power returns the wage level to its market level. Examples of how union power has been reduced include,

- making unions ballot their members before taking industrial action
- if the union calls a strike, allowing only six union members to form a picket line
- eliminating restrictive practices such as outlawing the closed shop, ending demarcation agreements, and reducing overmanning.

If the latter point is achieved it may allow firms to become more productive. This in turn means that they can employ more workers at a higher wage level as shown in Fig 5.11. The wage rates increase from $0W_1$ to $0W_2$ and employment levels rise from $0q_1$ to $0q_2$ as the demand for labour increases.

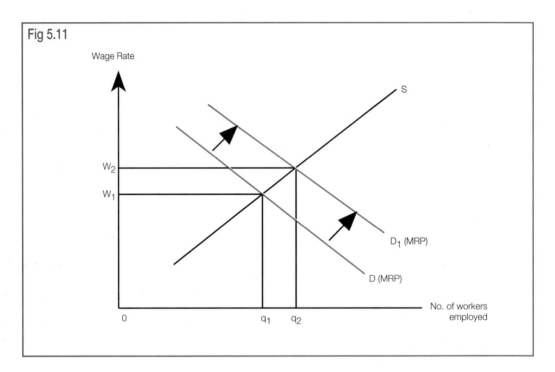

Fig 5.11

■ Mismatch of skills and vacancies

PC
5.1.5

An example of an imperfection in the market-place is the lack of skilled workers. One of the ironies of high unemployment is that there may be millions of people who are unemployed yet at the same time there can be unfilled vacancies for skilled workers.

Governments have tried to reduce the mismatch of vacancies and skills by sponsoring training schemes for the unemployed. The training of teenagers on youth training schemes should improve the skills situation in future years. Improving the *quality* of labour will also improve the *productivity* of labour. Quality can be improved through better education. In the UK today more youngsters are staying on at school and going on to higher education than ever before. There have been changes in the curriculum for example, with the introduction of GCSEs and the competency-based GNVQs which will make the future workforce more flexible.

Other policies to help the unemployed include help with the mobility of labour by improving the information sources about job vacancies. Research has shown that those aged under 24 are more likely to visit the job centre as their main method of job search. Those aged over 35 favoured using the 'situations vacant' columns in newspapers.

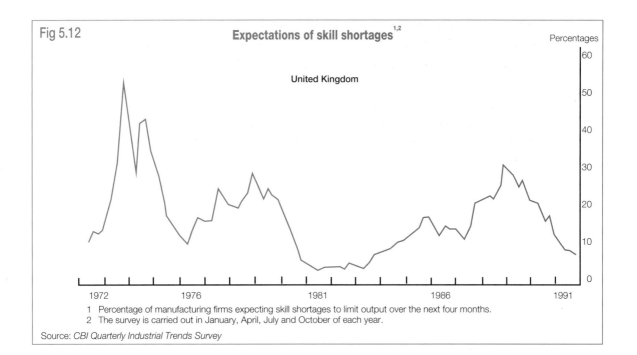

Fig 5.12

Expectations of skill shortages[1,2]

Percentages

United Kingdom

1972   1976   1981   1986   1991

1   Percentage of manufacturing firms expecting skill shortages to limit output over the next four months.
2   The survey is carried out in January, April, July and October of each year.

Source: *CBI Quarterly Industrial Trends Survey*

Table 5.11   **Job search methods of the unemployed: by age, 1990**

Great Britain   *Percentages*

	16-19	*20-24*	*25-34*	*35-49*	*50-59*	*60 and over*	*All unemployed aged 16 and over*
Percentage[1] of each age group using the following as their main method of job search							
Visiting a jobcentre[2]	41	37	28	24	30	23	30
Study 'situations vacant' columns in newspapers	23	28	35	36	35	45	33
Answering advertisements in newspapers or journals[3]	8	9	10	12	9	11	10
Personal contacts	8	10	11	13	11	12	11
Direct approach to firms/ employers	13	10	10	7	9	4	9
Name on private agency books	3	2	2	4	2	1	2
Other[4]	4	3	4	5	4	5	4

1   Percentages are based on data excluding those who did not know or preferred not to state their job search methods and those temporarily not looking for work because they were either waiting to start a new job, temporarily sick or on holiday. The unemployed are based on the ILO definition of unemployment.

2   Includes job clubs, career offices and government employment offices
3   Includes notices outside factories or in shop windows
4   Includes advertising in newspapers/journals and awaiting job application results.

Source: *Labour Force Survey,* Employment Department

In 1986 the government introduced the Restart Programme as help for those who had been unemployed for more than 12 months. In 1987 it was made available to those who had been unemployed for six months. The Restart Programme invited the unemployed to an interview at the Job Centre and offered help towards employment. Other help included employment training, a place on a Restart Course or a place in a Job Club.

Job Clubs help people by providing assistance in finding jobs and free facilities such as telephones and stationery. With the prospects of pit closures the government has made special provisions for the redundant miners by offering advice on setting up a business, retraining, 'upskilling' and help with job search.

Some economists argue that the state benefits are paid at too high a level encouraging unemployment. Because they receive state benefits people do not need to work. Therefore, lowering benefits will motivate people who are unemployed to find work. In Fig 5.13 the benefit is paid at Oc which is above the equilibrium wage level of Ob. Unemployment is q_1-q_2.

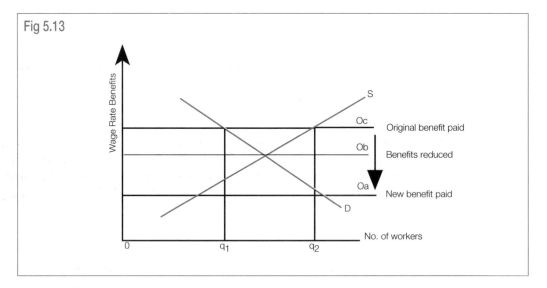

Fig 5.13

However, if benefits were reduced to Oa this would encourage workers to find work because at this point the wage level is higher than the benefits paid.

Governments since 1979 have believed that high income tax discourages people from working. The more their income the higher the tax they pay. If income tax is reduced this means that people have an incentive to work. Also, lower taxation means there is more disposable income available to spend on goods and services. This increase in demand by consumers will encourage employers to take on more workers.

■ Unemployment in the UK

The diagram at Fig. 5.14 shows the path of unemployment over the last 30 years and it is clear that unemployment fluctuated over this time with high peaks in the 1930s and the 1980s.

Unemployment stayed at the low levels after the Second World War, although there was a gradual upward trend when unemployment accelerated during the late 1970s and early 1980s.

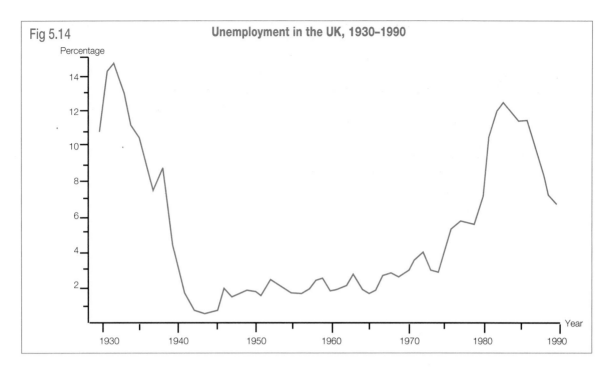

Fig 5.14 **Unemployment in the UK, 1930–1990**

Unemployment was low during this period because government policies were designed to manage the economy to achieve low unemployment. Towards the end of the 1970s, governments changed their economic objectives and instead of maintaining full employment, reducing inflation was seen as more important to the economy. The economy had been hit in the 1970s by the two oil price shocks in 1973 and 1979 which had a profound effect on employment levels.

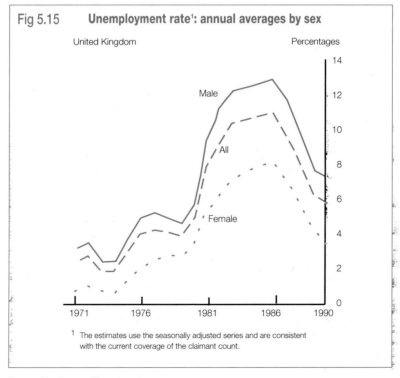

Fig 5.15 **Unemployment rate[1]: annual averages by sex**

[1] The estimates use the seasonally adjusted series and are consistent with the current coverage of the claimant count.

Source: Employment Department

Figure 5.15 shows unemployment rates for both men and women. The pattern of unemployment is similar for both sexes with unemployment rising very sharply during 1980, with male employment worst hit.

Table 5.12   **Unemployed claimants: by duration, sex and age, 1991**[1]

United Kingdom						Percentages and thousands
	Duration of unemployment (percentages)					
	Up to 13 weeks	Over 13 up to 26 weeks	Over 26 up to 52 weeks	Over 52 up to 104 weeks	Over 104 up to 156 weeks	Over 156 weeks	Total (= 100%) (thousands)
Males aged:							
18–19	48.2	24.3	20.7	6.8			119.6
20–24	38.4	22.1	20.9	11.9	3.8	2.8	345.4
25–34	34.4	20.1	19.6	13.5	4.8	7.6	502.8
35–49	32.6	18.7	17.5	12.9	4.7	13.5	417.9
50–59	25.4	14.8	14.5	11.6	5.8	28.0	240.7
60 and over	38.8	23.0	23.5	8.5	1.4	4.9	40.2
All males aged 18 or over	34.6	19.8	18.8	12.2	4.3	10.4	1,666.6
Females aged:							
18–19	51.3	23.1	19.9	5.6			65.8
20–24	45.2	21.6	19.1	9.0	2.6	2.6	128.3
25–34	43.2	20.8	20.5	8.9	2.5	4.2	136.4
35–49	40.7	18.4	17.8	11.6	3.9	7.6	120.0
50–59	25.1	13.3	15.1	12.4	6.5	27.6	77.8
60 and over	5.6	4.7	4.6	6.1	8.1	71 0	0.6
All females aged 18 and over	41.4	19.6	18.6	9.6	3.1	7.6	528.8

[1] At April

Source: Employment Department

Table 5.12 shows the number of people who have been unemployed for various durations. There are important differences between age groups.

If a comparison is made of those males unemployed for up to 13 weeks aged between 20 and 24, the proportion unemployed is 38.4 per cent compared with those aged 50–59 where 25.4 per cent are unemployed. However, the long-term unemployed figures show a changed situation, for example those who have been unemployed up to 3 years, the figures are 6.8 per cent and 11.6 per cent respectively. Clearly it becomes progressively more difficult to find work as one gets older.

The problems of unemployment are not restricted to the UK. In 1990, 12 million people or on average 8.45 per cent of the European labour force were unemployed. The worrying trend is the number of women and youngsters who are unemployed throughout Europe.

Reasons for regional policy

Regional policy seeks to reduce the inequalities between regions which have different unemployment rates

The *laissez-faire* economists might argue that intervening in the market only makes matters worse. Distortions make the markets work less efficiently and, because in the long run, 'you can't buck the market', the pain is just prolonged. The regions should be left to market forces and where there is high unemployment, wage rates in these areas will fall and over time attract firms into these regions. The unemployment problem will disappear.

Unfortunately the market does not always operate too well. The UK has a system for national wage bargaining which means that the wage rate for a postman in Birmingham is the same rate as in Buxton.

There are other factors other than wage costs which may help firms to decide to locate in a particular area. Areas such as Scotland, Wales and Northern England have seen employment fall in industries such as coal and shipbuilding. They were located in these areas because of the availability of raw materials. The newer industries, especially those in information technology, tend to be located near their markets in the South East, especially London. Wage costs would have to fall markedly in some regions if they were to offset the locational advantages of other areas.

Market forces also assume that labour is relatively mobile and can move easily between areas, whereas labour is in fact relatively immobile. Immobility can be one of two types, occupational and geographical.

Table 5.13

Regional variations in unemployment

	Unemployment %						
	1977	*1981*	*1986*	*1987*	*1988*	*1989*	*1990 (June)*
South East	3.5	5.7	8.3	7.2	5.3	3.9	3.7
East Anglia	4.1	6.6	8.5	7.3	5.2	3.6	3.7
South West	5.2	7.1	9.5	8.1	6.2	4.5	4.3
West Midlands	4.5	10.4	12.9	11.4	8.9	6.6	5.8
East Midlands	3.9	7.7	10.1	9.2	7.4	5.6	4.9
Yorkshire and Humberside	4.4	9.4	12.6	11.5	9.6	7.7	6.7
North West	5.7	10.6	13.8	12.5	10.4	8.4	7.4
North	6.4	12.2	15.4	14.3	12.1	10.0	8.5
Wales	5.9	10.8	13.6	12.1	10.0	7.4	6.4
Scotland	6.4	10.4	13.4	13.1	11.3	9.3	8.0
Northern Ireland	8.1	13.1	17.4	17.2	16.0	15.1	13.9

Source: *Employment Gazette*

How regional policy influences employment

Government regional policy can take a number of forms, for example, trying to take work to the workers. It can move its own departments to a particular area such as the Drivers and Vehicle Licensing Department in Swansea, or it can force firms to move to an area of high unemployment. This policy of positive discrimination is one where, if a firm wishes to expand in a growth area, it can only do so if it has permission, i.e. an Industrial Development Certificate. Thus, if a firm wishes to expand, it has to go to a depressed area.

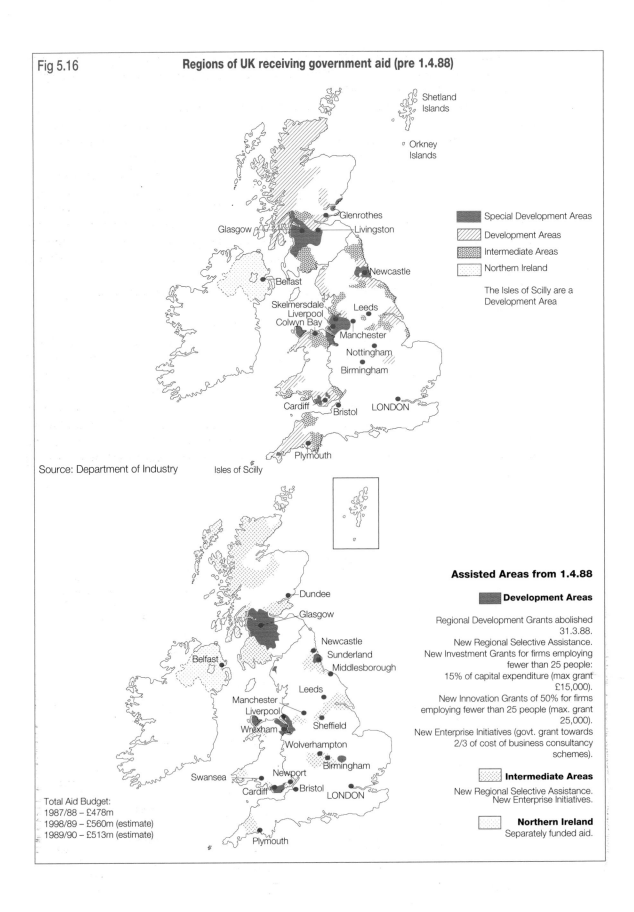

Fig 5.16   Regions of UK receiving government aid (pre 1.4.88)

Shetland Islands

Orkney Islands

Glenrothes
Glasgow — Livingston

■ Special Development Areas
▨ Development Areas
▧ Intermediate Areas
▦ Northern Ireland

The Isles of Scilly are a Development Area

Newcastle
Belfast
Skelmersdale
Liverpool
Colwyn Bay
Leeds
Manchester
Nottingham
Birmingham
Cardiff
Bristol
LONDON
Plymouth

Source: Department of Industry   Isles of Scilly

Assisted Areas from 1.4.88

Dundee
Glasgow
Newcastle
Sunderland
Middlesborough
Belfast
Leeds
Manchester
Liverpool
Sheffield
Wrexham
Wolverhampton
Swansea
Newport
Birmingham
Cardiff
Bristol
LONDON
Plymouth

■ **Development Areas**

Regional Development Grants abolished 31.3.88.
New Regional Selective Assistance.
New Investment Grants for firms employing fewer than 25 people:
15% of capital expenditure (max grant £15,000).
New Innovation Grants of 50% for firms employing fewer than 25 people (max. grant 25,000).
New Enterprise Initiatives (govt. grant towards 2/3 of cost of business consultancy schemes).

▧ **Intermediate Areas**

New Regional Selective Assistance.
New Enterprise Initiatives.

▦ **Northern Ireland**

Separately funded aid.

Total Aid Budget:
1987/88 – £478m
1998/89 – £560m (estimate)
1989/90 – £513m (estimate)

Ford wanted to expand its site at Dagenham but was forced to expand by opening a factory at Halewood on Merseyside. Some firms refused to move so the economy lost those jobs. The IDCs were abandoned in 1982.

Another method governments could use is one of persuasion by offering incentives, for example, by reducing a firm's costs. The building of ready-made factories, lowering the cost of rent and rates in an area or offering tax concessions are methods used by governments to encourage firms to locate in a particular area. Labour costs could be reduced by a subsidy, e.g. the Regional Employment Premium. This blanket subsidy was paid on all employees in selected areas and operated between 1967 and 1976. The major disadvantage of this was that all firms received help in the area selected and not just those the government intended to attract. A further disadvantage was that it did not necessarily influence firms with their location decisions because firms were not sure how long the subsidy would last. This type of help was abolished at the request of the EU because it was deemed to create unfair competition.

Regions can be designated as special areas by the government and, depending upon the criteria, can expect some help and assistance from the government.

Regions of economic growth did not receive any help, whereas those Intermediate Areas with high unemployment levels received some level of support and Development Areas received most help. There are dangers in highlighting these areas because firms might not want to go to a particular area which is said to be depressed. The help in the area has to be discriminating and not blanket coverage because in the depressed areas there will be pockets of growth. Firms may move into the area to get aid, especially if the help is in financing capital expenditure. Once the firms receive financial help they then might move to a more attractive location. Firms will tend not to locate on the boundaries of the neighbouring areas but will locate within the area receiving government help creating deserts around the boundaries of the areas.

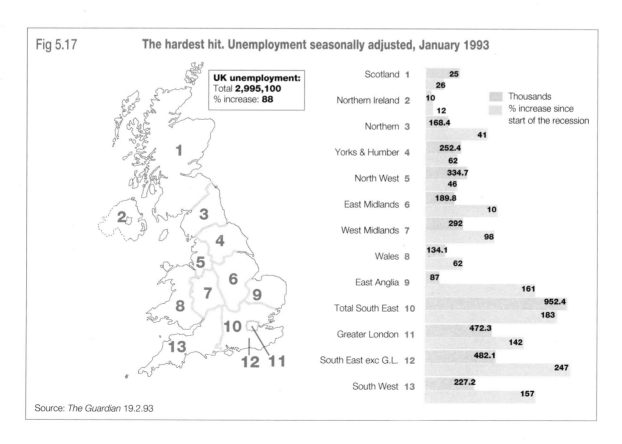

Fig 5.17   **The hardest hit. Unemployment seasonally adjusted, January 1993**

UK unemployment:
Total **2,995,100**
% increase: **88**

Region	Thousands	% increase since start of the recession
Scotland 1	25	26
Northern Ireland 2	10	12
Northern 3	168.4	41
Yorks & Humber 4	252.4	62
North West 5	334.7	46
East Midlands 6	189.8	10
West Midlands 7	292	98
Wales 8	134.1	62
East Anglia 9	87	161
Total South East 10	952.4	183
Greater London 11	472.3	142
South East exc G.L. 12	482.1	247
South West 13	227.2	157

Source: *The Guardian* 19.2.93

The government-designated areas and the help offered in the areas have to be constantly updated because of changes taking place in the economy. The recession of the 1980s hit the Midlands hard, but the region at that time was not covered by government aid. The recession of the 1990s has hit the South-East which again is not covered by aid. The type of aid also has to be reviewed as well as who gets it. Until 1982 it was impossible for firms in the tertiary sector to get aid as it only applied to those firms in manufacturing. Those firms which did locate in the specially designated areas tended to be light industries employing women (Fig 5.17). The Regional Map was changed again in 1993.

The EU does try to help regions with aid through its Regional Development Fund. The aid goes in helping the infrastructure of an area and thus encourages firms to move into that region.

THE COST OF UNEMPLOYMENT

The cost of unemployment to the economy is in four main areas:

1 **Output and incomes are lost** This means that the output of the country is lower than it should be with the resulting loss of goods and services. The standard of living or the level of comfort enjoyed in the country is going to be lower than it could be. Governments lose revenues because of lost Income Tax, National Insurance and reduced VAT. It has to pay out more in benefits to the unemployed and to pay for this extra spending, people in employment have to pay higher taxes. Also the contribution from North Sea oil revenues has gone into paying benefits for the unemployed.

2 **Human capital** This is the value of a person's education and acquired skills. These skills include mechanical and mental skills including work habits and the ability to concentrate on a task. Long-term unemployment makes it more difficult for those unemployed to get a job because they have not been able to update their skills while their present skills lose value over time.

3 **Crime** Crime has risen during periods of unemployment, and when unemployment fell considerably in 1988 crime figures also fell. This is a cost to society as a whole and for individuals.

4 **The unemployed** The loss of a job is a loss of a person's role in society. There is also loss of a sense of belonging to a group. The loss of self-esteem and long periods of boredom can lead to depression. A reduction in income through lost wages can mean poor diets for the family and causes the general health to deteriorate.

THE INFLUENCES OF THE MEDIA ON EMPLOYMENT

The media are a major tool for employers to find out what is happening in their industry. There are general media such as national newspapers and national television and specialist media, such as professional magazines, which give specific information to the industry, for example, *The Caterer* is for the hotel and catering industry.

Newspapers such as the *Financial Times* and *The Guardian* have financial sections which include articles on up-to-date events in industry. For example, the Monday *Guardian* has articles on small businesses. Local newspapers will help the employer to see what is going on in his area. Employment advertisements give information as to who requires staff and often details the rate of pay available.

Television and radio also provide the employer with information as the channels have business programmes such as 'The Money Programme'. Local news is given by regional television and radio programmes. The employer can gain a general overview of events in the economy as a whole.

All of these media provide advertising opportunities, both for firms to advertise their own services and products and to monitor the marketing strategies of their competitors.

There are specialist publications for business which give lists of UK businesses:

> *Kelly's Business Directory*
>
> *Kompass* (products and services directory)
>
> *The Retail Directory of the UK*
>
> *Hambro Company Guide*
>
> *BRAD Advertising Media*

For Europe there is the *Directory of European Industrial and Trade Associations*.

ACTIVITIES

1 Find out from your local Job Centre or Department of Employment:

(a) what services they offer

(b) when you personally would be eligible to sign up for benefit

(c) what procedures you would have to go through

(d) how much the benefit would be

(e) how many new people per week they usually deal with

2 Interview a Personnel Officer of a local firm and ask what qualities he or she looks for when interviewing candidates and how he or she chooses who should be interviewed from application forms.

3 What training do staff in your organisation get? Question a senior person in your organisation to see if they are following the guidelines for 'Identifying Training Needs'.

4 Contact your local TEC (in the telephone directory under the name of the county, e.g. 'Staffordshire Training and Enterprise Council') and ask for information on Youth Training or the National Vocational Qualification. Using the information, compile a fact sheet for your class members.

5 Design an induction programme for new class members.

6 Conduct a survey of people who work and draw up a bar chart showing how many are part-time, permanent, temporary or self-employed.

THE CHANGING ECONOMIC, POLITICAL AND SOCIAL CONTEXT

In 1979 there was a change of government in the UK from Labour to Conservative. The new government made radical changes in the political and economic life of the UK. The following changes in industrial relations took place during the 1980s and 1990s.

■ 1 Political change

- Collective bargaining was rejected and moves by employers toward individual contracts and pay structures were encouraged.
- Full employment was abandoned as a major goal of government objectives.
- Attitudes changed towards the public sector and market conditions were introduced as public sector organisations were expected to make a profit or balance their budget.
- In order to increase labour market flexibility for the unorganised and low paid there has been a reduction in protective legislation so that they can accept work which may have previously been seen as too poorly paid or having unacceptable working conditions.

■ 2 Economic change

(a) Industrial decline during the 1980s has seen approximately two million jobs lost in manufacturing. There has been an increase in employment in the service sector.

(b) Increased uncertainty about economic prospects has led to a reluctance to hire staff on a permanent basis.

(c) There has been an increase in the supply of labour for low paid and insecure jobs, comprising school leavers, the redundant and women returners.

■ 3 Legislative change

Since 1979, the government has taken a step-by-step approach to trade union legislation which has enabled them to bring in many changes. Some of the main Acts and their effects are described below.

1980 Employment Act

Picketing was restricted to an individual's place of employment, making secondary picketing (picketing at a place other than the workers' own place of work) unlawful. Other forms of secondary industrial action such as the 'blacking' of goods were restricted. The action had to be confined to a direct customer or supplier of the employer with whom the union was in dispute.

It became unlawful for an employer to dismiss anyone for non-membership of a union who had conscientious or deeply-held personal reasons for not wishing to join, or who had been engaged before a closed shop agreement was concluded. (A closed shop was a situation in which everyone working in the establishment had to be a union member.) Future closed shops should only come into existence with the overwhelming support of the employees affected. The Act stipulated that if any new closed shop agreement were not approved of by at least 80 per cent of those to be covered by it, it would be unfair for the employer concerned to dismiss anyone for not being a union member.

1982 Employment Act

In this Act the definition of a trade dispute and its immunity from civil damages was narrowed. There were fewer circumstances under which a strike could be considered legal, for example, a union could be sued for damages if workers were in a demarcation dispute with other workers. The Act required that a trade dispute must 'wholly or mainly' relate to employment matters – an attempt to prevent political strikes. Unions could be sued in their own name. Previously only union officials were liable for organising unlawful industrial action on behalf of the union and the union's funds were protected. It was made illegal for an employer to dismiss anyone for non-membership of a union unless a closed shop agreement had been the subject of a ballot within the previous five years and in which 80 per cent of those employees covered by it (or 85 per cent of those actually voting) supported it.

1988 Trade Union Act

This Act stated that industrial action must be formally approved in advance by the union members concerned by secret ballot.

1988 Employment Act

Union members had the right to apply for a court order restraining their union from organising industrial action in the absence of a ballot. Union members could not be disciplined by their union if they did not take part in industrial action. Increased protection was given against the operation of closed shops. The earlier provisions were repealed that had permitted dismissal for non-membership of a union where an 'approved' closed shop was in operation, thereby making dismissal for non-membership of a union automatically unfair.

1990 Employment Act

This Act made it unlawful to deny anyone a job because they were not union members. It outlawed all secondary action by making a union legally liable when it takes action against any customer or supplier of the employer with whom it is in dispute. Unions were made legally responsible for unofficial strikes called by shop stewards or any lay officer – when industrial action is organised by any union official (full-time or part-time), the action will either have to be put to the test of a secret ballot or be repudiated in writing by the union concerned. Workers can be selectively dismissed when taking unofficial industrial action.

The result of the extensive legislation is that trade unions are considerably restricted in their actions now compared with the 1970s and before.

1992 Trade Union Reform and Employment Rights Act

The aims of this Act were to strengthen the rights of individuals and to increase competitiveness of the economy by removing obstacles to the creation of new jobs. Under the Act, individual employees should have:

- the right to a written statement setting out details of their main conditions of employment, including their pay, hours and holidays.
- the right for every woman employee who becomes pregnant to take a minimum of 14 weeks' maternity leave and to be fully protected against losing her job because of her pregnancy.
- for all safety representatives – the right not to be dismissed for carrying out their health and safety duties.
- the right to have disputes with their employer about their contract of employment decided by an industrial tribunal.

Under the Act, trade union members will have:

- the right to decide for themselves which union they join.
- the right to a fully postal ballot, independently scrutinised, before a strike.
- protection against fraud and abuse in trade union elections.
- protection against the mismanagement of their union's finances.
- the right to decide whether or not their union subscriptions are collected by automatic deductions from their pay.

■ Trade union development

The Trade Unions and Labour Relations Act of 1974 stated that a trade union was:

'An organisation of workers whose principal purpose is the regulation of relations between workers and employers or employer associations.'

The original aims of trade unions were:

- to seek and obtain recognition from employers
- to enter into collective agreements on terms and conditions of employment covering union members
- to seek legislation on such matters as compensation for injury at work, state benefits when unemployed and retirement pensions

Trade unions' aims have changed over time and today include improving members benefits in:

■ remuneration, working conditions and status

■ security of employment

■ increasing power of labour in the decision-making process in the workplace

■ welfare, such as help with legal matters related to employment, education and strike funds.

Unions have developed in a piecemeal way, and so has industry, reflecting changes in the economy. Over the last decade unions have gone through rapid change in the structure, composition and their way of working. The rise of the tertiary sector, and especially the public sector has meant a substantial increase in white-collar workers.

■ Types of union

Unions have grown as a result of the need to deal with specific problems, and there is a rich variety of trade union organisations which are difficult to classify. There are four categories which are commonly recognised, although distinctions are becoming increasingly blurred.

Craft unions

These were the early trade unions which catered solely for the skilled craftsmen who had served a recognised apprenticeship. Skilled workers have an affinity with workers with similar skills rather than workers in the same industry. Craft unions are often very powerful in controlling the labour supply. The craft unions were and are powerful because of the specific entry requirements to join and the high member subscriptions payable.

The industrial unions

Initially formed in coalmining, the docks, the railway and gas industries, recruitment was aimed at the entire industry. Industries such as coalmining and the railways were dominated by the NUM (National Union of Mineworkers) and by the NUR (National Union of Railwaymen).

Occupational unions

Members are recruited in a similar occupation although not always in the same industry, for example, a cleaner may work in a hospital, school or council offices and still be a member of NUPE (National Union of Public Employees).

General unions

These unions recruit groups of workers who are not covered by the above categories. Traditionally the members are unskilled and they do not confine themselves to one industry. In contrast to the subscription of craft unions, the general union subscription was low because of the nature of the employment and the pay of the members. The largest union in Britain is the Transport and General Workers' Union (TGWU) which has over time been joined by several previously small independent unions and where membership therefore spans most of the industry.

These categories no longer apply to modern unions as there have been mergers between different unions, certain industries have declined, new industries have emerged and the skills of workers have changed. The Seamen's Union has merged with the National Union of Railwaymen. The Amalgamated Union of Engineering Workers originated as an engineering union, but now includes foundrymen, construction workers, draughtsmen and labourers.

■ Closed and open unions

Another way of categorising unions is by looking at the process of the growth of unions and making a distinction between closed and open unions. Closed unions operate the closed shop rule – organising on a basis of exclusion, controlling entry through training and qualification requirements. Open unions operate on a mass principle and recruit as many workers as possible from the entire spectrum of occupations and skills.

Closed unions have become more open, recruiting skilled workers outside the original skill area, recruiting members with fewer skills or merging with other unions. One of the results of this has been the decline in the number of small unions. Mergers have also taken place between open unions as changes in the economy have taken place, or financial pressures have forced mergers. NALGO (National Association of Local Government Officers) originally only concentrated on the public sector to recruit, but with the introduction of privatisation dropped its exclusive association.

■ Union structure

Unions have rules and regulations which formalise the way they operate and within the organisation there is a formal structure.

General Secretary
|
National Executive
|
Full-time officials
|
Branches
|
Shop stewards
|
Union members

Union members pay a subscription to the union. The income is used to pay for the administration of the union, to pay salaries for full-time officials and provide benefits for the union members. Part of the subscription goes to the running of the TUC. There is also a levy which union members can pay which is used for political purposes.

The shop steward

The shop steward is usually the first union official a new member of the firm will meet.

Shop stewards do their own full-time jobs as well as being the elected workers' representative. They are allowed time off in which to carry out their duties as union officials and the employer will normally give them office facilities. The duty of the shop steward is to recruit new members, collect subscriptions, be the Health and Safety representative for the union and inform the workforce on union matters.

The shop steward is seen by managers as a 'lubricant rather than as an irritant' (Donovan Report 1968). The unions see the shop stewards as the direct representatives for union members, and it can be argued that the shop steward system is an effective way of ensuring that union leaders take care of members and are aware of their views and also of engaging members actively in union affairs.

The branch

The branch co-ordinates the local affairs of the union members. It elects delegates to the union annual conference and ratifies local bargaining agreements. The proceedings can tend to be mundane and most meetings are poorly attended with a few committed members carrying out the work of the branch.

The district

The union branches elect representatives to sit on regional committees. These oversee the running of the branches to present co-ordinated policies. The union will employ full-time staff to administer its affairs.

The Conference

Each year the union holds its conference to discuss issues and decide on policies.

The National Executive

This is the effective leadership of the union which may decide on policy. An important role the executive carries out is wage negotiations with the employers' representatives. The executive is also concerned with the administration and finance of the union.

The General Secretary

This is the person who heads the National Executive. The General Secretary is a full-time employee of the union.

■ The Trades Union Congress (TUC)

The TUC is an umbrella organisation, representing all unions in the UK.

THE AIMS OF THE TUC

- To represent the unions affiliated to it especially on government economic and social policy.
- To help educate and train workers.
- To help settle disputes.
- To aid other organisations with similar aims, e.g. the Labour Party.
- To aid workers in other parts of the world and organisations such as the International Labour Organisation.

The TUC is headed by the General Council which is the TUC's executive body. The Council is the decision-making body for the union movement's policies. The Council is made up of 54 members of the unions affiliated to the TUC. These members are usually Secretaries or Presidents of their own unions.

The TUC has an annual meeting to establish and discuss policy. Each union can send delegates to the meeting, the number of delegates being in accordance with the size of its membership. Each union can vote on policy. The actual voting is done by block votes, i.e. when delegates vote on an issue it is as if all the members of the union are voting, therefore the TGWU delegates will cast over a million votes. The big unions therefore have most say in the running of the movement.

■ The relationship of the TUC to its members

The TUC can only influence through persuasion, although if a trade union has broken the TUC's rules then that union can be suspended or expelled from the TUC. One of the rules is known as the Bridlington Principle which governs the relationships between unions when they are in competition for members or when there is an inter-union dispute. The Electrical, Electronic, Telecommunications and Printers Union (EETPU) withdrew from the TUC after a dispute with the printers about the manning of the printing presses for Times Newspapers.

The TUC cannot call or prevent strikes, but it can offer help and guidance during disputes, usually when there is a national strike or when the strike is called on an important issue.

PC
5.2.1

EMPLOYERS' ASSOCIATION

The Association's function is to represent the employers in the collective bargaining process. The area of discussion is wage rates and conditions of work at industry levels. The agreements set standard terms which are actually applied by the employer, or they are used as standards for local agreements.

In the 1980s collective agreements came under attack and the associations responded by widening their services. They now give help to members on such matters as introducing new pay schemes. The association may provide information or help with training at supervisory and management levels. Legal advice is also offered to members, for example, representing their members at industrial tribunals.

On a national level associations try to influence government policy on industrial relations issues. The internal structure varies from association to association depending on the locality and industry.

■ The Confederation of British Industry (CBI)

The CBI is the employers' equivalent to the TUC.

THE AIMS OF THE CBI

- To provide for British industry the means of formulating, making known and influencing policy in regard to industrial, economic, fiscal, commercial, labour, social, legal and technical questions and to act as a national point of reference for those seeking industry's views.

- To develop the contribution of Britain's Industry to the national economy.

- To encourage the efficiency and competitive power to British industry and to provide advice, information and services to British industry.

The CBI's governing body is its Council, which is chaired by a president elected to office for two years. It is, however, standing committees which work on specific areas such as economic, social and company affairs which are the real policy makers for the CBI.

The CBI claims that its members employ some 10 million people. The organisations not represented include mainly small firms and public sector services. It has formed contacts with central and local government and is represented on various official bodies such as ACAS, The Equal Opportunities Commission and The Health and Safety Executive.

INDUSTRIAL ACTION

If trade union members believe that decisions by management are detrimental to members' pay and conditions, they may take industrial action. Before taking formal action, workers may work less intensively, be less careful in their work, indulge in absenteeism or claim to be sick. Formal collective action may result when there is a formal dispute affecting the workforce which is not properly resolved. Actions may take several forms and can become progressively more severe.

The usual forms of industrial action include strikes, over-time bans and work to rules.

■ Settlement of disputes

Usually the dispute will be settled during the course of negotiations. But sometimes an independent third party is needed. The dispute can be sent to **arbitration** where the two sides put their case and agree to abide by the ruling of the third party. If negotiations are in deadlock, then the two sides might be brought together by a third party, usually the Advisory, Conciliation and Arbitration Service (ACAS). The process of **conciliation** will be to listen to both parties to identify common ground on which negotiations can be built.

■ Collective bargaining

Collective bargaining is a method of attempting to reach an agreement on working conditions and terms of employment between employers and workers. The pay of 60–70 per cent of the British workforce is determined, either directly or indirectly, through collective bargaining.

> ### DIFFERENT VIEWS OF THE COLLECTIVE BARGAINING PROCESS:
>
> 1 That it is a method of exchanging labour for economic reward.
>
> 2 That it is a system of government whereby trade union representative and management together decide on the rules which determine their relationship.
>
> 3 That it is a movement toward industrial democracy. Trade union representatives are involved in decision making in those areas covered by collective agreement and this involvement expands into trade unions participating in the management of the enterprise.

The structure of collective bargaining

Collective bargaining may be organised so that one negotiated settlement determines pay rates and working conditions for the whole industry throughout the country or that each company negotiates with its own workers to decide on a settlement.

Wages councils

The government announced that these were to be abolished in 1992.

Wages Councils could set a minimum hourly rate of pay for those workers who were over 21 years of age. They covered industries such as retailing, catering, clothing and hairdressing where unionisation can be difficult because of the dispersal of workers throughout many small establishments.

Non-union organisations

Certain small and medium-sized companies are not unionised, either because of the difficulties involved or management attitudes may be against unions. This is also the case with large firms. Companies such as IBM and Marks & Spencer have packages of benefits for their employees which may render union membership unnecessary.

Collective bargaining still affects non-union organisations as the settlements agreed through collective bargaining provide a 'market rate' so that employers know the minimum earnings for a particular job. National collective bargaining saves time for both unionised and non-unionised firms in that a 'going rate' is provided and unionised firms do not have to negotiate at a local or establishment level.

Multi-employer, industry-wide agreements have been in decline since the 1950s. By 1986, 87 per cent of employees in plants with collective bargaining had their basic rates of pay negotiated at establishment or company level.

The move from national level bargaining to company plant level bargaining can be explained as follows:

- companies feel free to manage their own employee relations
- companies have specialised personnel departments and managers trained in negotiation
- it is easier to increase job flexibility and relax job demarcation in individualised negotiations
- individual employers have more control over pay determination which they feel is important in competitive product markets
- pay can be related more closely to performance
- owing to increasing competition, labour markets need pay structures which can respond to local demand and supply of labour
- company-level bargaining can involve all trade unions represented in the organisation. Thus 'single table bargaining' is becoming increasingly popular as it is quicker for management to deal with all the trade union representatives together and it avoids inter-union conflict
- company-level bargaining also permits an employer to organise a single-union deal. Trade unions compete with one another to be accepted as the union to represent all the workers in the company

CHANGE IN INDUSTRIAL RELATIONS

- Unions are failing to gain recognition in new firms.
- The scope of collective bargaining has been greatly reduced. Systems of direct consultation and employee involvement are replacing trade union membership as a form of communication between workers and their employers.
- Payment systems are increasingly based on individual and not collective consent.
- Legal regulation now affects all areas of industrial relations: employers can use the legislation as a means of preventing or delaying industrial action.
- Increased productivity and co-operation of trade unions in technical change, suggest that there has been a change in worker attitudes.
- A new form of unionism has emerged, involving no-strike deals and single union agreements.

PC
5.1.2

EUROPEAN COMMUNITY SOCIAL POLICY

The European Social Fund was started to increase the employment of workers and to improve their geographical and occupational mobility within the EU.

■ The social charter

A draft social charter was drawn up in May 1989 by the European Commission. The final draft of the charter was adopted by eleven governments in December 1989 in the form of a declaration. The United Kingdom refused to adopt the declaration, but later a House of Lords Select Committee endorsed the Charter as a 'basis for negotiation'.

The Social Charter is not legally binding. The fundamental principles of the Charter are as follows:

1 Free movement of workers based on the principles of equal treatment in access of employment and social protection.
2 Employment and remuneration based on the principle of fair remuneration.
3 Improvement of living and working conditions.
4 Social protection based on the rules and practices proper to each country.
5 Freedom of association and collective bargaining.
6 Vocational training.
7 Equal treatment of men and women.
8 Information, consultation and participation of workers.
9 Protection of health and safety at the work-place.
10 Protection of children and adolescents.
11 Protection of the elderly.
12 Protection of the disabled.

Images change as joblessness affects all social classes

John Arlidge considers whether there are similarities between the 1930s and present day unemployment

The images have changed. Couples slumped in front of videos on modern estates have replaced cloth-capped men hanging around slum terraces. Queues to the soup kitchens have shortened. With joblessness among men at a post-war high, however, are there similarities between the 1990s and the Depression of the 1930s?

Unemployment was much worse between the wars. In August 1932, joblessness reached 23 per cent among the insured population – those eligible for the benefits of the day. This was about 16 per cent of the total workforce, compared with 10.6 per cent last month.

The jobless were more regionally concentrated. The export-dependent industries hard hit in the slump – shipbuilding, cotton textiles, coal – were located mainly in the north of England, Scotland and Wales, which observers called 'outer Britain'. As sales collapsed, unemployment reached 36 per cent in Wales and 28 per cent in Scotland and the North-east.

Although unemployment rose to 13.5 per cent in London and the South-east in 1932 – today it is about 10.5 per cent – 'inner Britain' saw job growth between the wars. About 3.5 million jobs were created between 1921 and 1938 south of an imaginary line between Coventry and Ipswich.

Dudley Baines, senior lecturer in economic history at the London School of Economics, said: 'There was higher regional industrial specialisation than now. Northern industries lost markets and had nothing to fall back on. But in the South there were vacancies. Developments like the Hoover and Gillette factories in west London, all came in the 1930s.'

'Blue-collar' workers comprised the overwhelming majority of the Thirties' jobless while 'white-collar' workers, who formed a much smaller part of the workforce, were hardly affected. Today the spread is much wider. Half of the 1.5 million jobs lost since the summer of 1990 have been in manufacturing industry. The service sector – financial services, retailing, public service – accounted for about half of the remaining 750,000.

John Philpott, director of the Employment Policy Institute, an independent think-tank, said: 'Today, unemployment cannot be thought of as affecting just one sort of industry or worker. Joblessness extends across the social and occupational spectrum.'

Calculating the number of women who are unemployed is difficult. Mr Baines estimates there are 6 million more married women looking for work today than in the Thirties when about 10 per cent of married women worked. 'Single women worked between the wars but married women were by and large not part of the labour market,' he said.

'It is difficult to know whether married women would have worked had there been jobs. If you accept that most of them would not, then female unemployment in the thirties was far lower than today.'

Women today form half of the 'hidden' unemployed – the estimated 1 million people who are not eligible for benefits, or do not claim them. Although changes in the methods used to measure joblessness make it difficult to make direct comparisons, it is likely that the number of hidden jobless was lower in the Thirties than now.

Using 1931 census data, Charles Feinstein, professor of economic history at All Souls College, Oxford, estimates that unemployment was 'very considerably' less among the uninsured in domestic service, farming, the post office and railways than among the insured.

With high personal indebtedness, life might seem hard now but unemployment was a more devastating experience 60 years ago.

Unemployment benefit for a single man was 17 shillings (85p), when social observers calculated the required minimum income was more than 22 shillings (£1.10), plus rent. Mr Baines estimates that the 1930s benefit for a family of four, in today's money, was £30 per week, compared with £96 now, plus housing benefit of, say, £22.

Only 4 per cent of the population had private cars. The television, now in 90 per cent of homes, was not available, and few people took holidays abroad.

Some who lived through the Depression say today's more divided communities, coupled with the higher standards of living enjoyed by those in work have created a 'crisis of expectations' among the jobless greater than that 60 years ago.

Mr Baines disagrees. 'It is extremely easy to idealise the past. The idea of chumminess of working class society in adversity is a load of rubbish. When times are hard they are hard. If you are hungry, you are hungry.

© *The Independent* 19.2.93

CASE STUDY DISCUSSION QUESTIONS

Images change as joblessness affects all social classes.

1 How has the image of the unemployed changed?

2 Why was unemployment much worse during the inter-war period?

3 Why is it difficult to calculate the numbers of unemployed?

4 In money terms are the unemployed today better off than the unemployed in the 1930s?

FEATURES OF WORKFORCE PERFORMANCE

The owner of a business may set a number of objectives of which survival is a high priority. In order to survive the business must meet the needs of the customer, and to do this the business must be able to:

- produce:
  - the right goods
  - at the right time
  - in the right quantities
  - of the right quality
  - at the right price
- promote the goods in the right way
- sell the goods in the right place

The business must operate in such a way that it can meet the needs of the customer efficiently. Resources within the business need to be allocated in the right proportions, for example numbers of people to machines. The employer needs to make sure that he employs the optimum number of workers who have the right experience, qualifications and training. The employer must ensure that the production process and layout is such that the employees can work to their best performance.

The performance of workers or their productivity can be measured by the actual output, e.g.

$$\frac{\text{Output}}{\text{Number of workers}}$$

The employer will seek to increase output per worker or productivity in order to reduce unit costs. The ways in which the employer will seek to do this are by:

- the encouragement and motivation of the workforce

- analysing the number of workers to machines and their output levels
- the standard in quality of the goods produced
- analysing production methods used

■ The worker

Studies on workers' performance lead to changing ideas on the way to increase workers' performance. For example, FW Taylor believed that the manager should make all the decisions and that the job should be broken down into separate tasks. The Hawthorne experiment showed the importance of the human element in production, the importance of groups and how peer pressure can influence output. Research by social scientists such as Maslow and Herzberg recognised the relevance of motivational factors in increasing the performance of workers.

The workers' performance can be maintained or improved by the following factors:

- Match the worker and the job, making sure that the workers selected for a job have the right experience, qualifications and training.
- Responsibilities of the worker should be made clear. This can be done through a job description. Lack of clarity of duties can lead to frustration, conflict and poor performance.
- Standards of performance should be set. This enables the workers to work to set targets and they can be more responsible for their own output rather than being dependent on a supervisor.
- Have effective channels of communication which enable the workers to know what is happening and enable them to participate in decision making.
- Paying a wage which reflects the skills, qualifications and the nature of the task performed and where feasible, offer incentives such as performance related pay.

- Workers should be trained for the job and training up-dated as the demands of the job change. Training also helps individuals with their careers.

- Workers should be supervised effectively. The supervisor must have the management and technical skills in order to help the workers with their tasks as well as being able to motivate their subordinates.
- Workers should be able to work in a healthy and minimum-risk environment
- Workers should be able to work in a non-threatening environment and be protected by industrial legislation.

■ The use of machines and workforce performance

New machines are bought:

1 to replace worn out machines and maintain output

2 as additional machines to increase output

The workers should benefit because the use of machines usually makes their jobs easier, they tend to make fewer mistakes and machines speed up output. The worker is probably able to produce more with the use of machines and increase his or her performance. Compare the length of time and the work involved in writing a book in the 1790s using a quill pen and ink with the time and work of today's authors who use word processors.

From the employers' point of view the output of workers has increased, but has their overall performance increased? The workers may not need to work as hard as they did before the introduction of machines. Therefore, if pay is related to output, the workers will have an increase in wages because of the performance of the machine rather than increases in their own efforts.

Some businesses are able to utilise machines more than others. In manufacturing the use of machines is commonplace and increases the worker's performance. However, in some occupations, such as teaching, nursing and police work, the introduction of machines will not necessarily increase output. The use of machines, such as computers, will, however, improve the quality of the worker's performance.

THE QUALITY OF THE PRODUCT

Quality is a form of non-price competition. For firms to survive it is necessary to produce goods customers need.

Quality refers to 'the totality of features and characteristics of a product or service that bear on its ability to satisfy stated or implied needs' (British Standard (BS) 4778, 1987).

There are two important aspects of quality:

1 How closely the design and specification of the product meets the customer's requirements.
2 How closely the delivered product conforms to the design or the specification.

These statements show how important it is for firms to design and make goods to the customer's requirements, rather than make a product to a specification determined by a designer who is not interested in the customer's needs.

Workers' performance can be measured by features relating to quality:

■ the amount of waste created
■ the number of rejected parts by internal inspection
■ the number of parts rejected by the customer
■ the number of times the after-sales facilities are used

Workers' performance relating to the control of quality can be monitored by inspection. Parts are produced by operatives and then inspected by supervisors and pay is based on the performance of the worker and his or her ability to produce a specific number of parts to the right quality. Using this method of control creates a division between doing the job and being responsible for it. The result can be conflict as the worker and the quality-control worker dispute whether parts meet the desired specification. Waste created by this method is costly and the product delivered to customers may not be to the standard required.

Workers' performance can be enhanced by attention to quality. Previously it was said that to increase quality of performance, productivity would decline because of the care the worker would have to give the task. However, doing things right first time saves time as the worker does not have to repeat the making of a part. Doing things right first time will also reduce costs.

■ Total Quality Management (TQM)

Improving the performance of workers through improved quality can be achieved by employing Total Quality Management. This approach to quality is based on the idea that quality is everybody's business. This replaces the Quality Control Department whose primary function was control of supply to external customers. Now TQM permeates throughout the whole organisation. People working in the organisation are both customers and suppliers to other departments and therefore each transaction should be based on the policy: 'treat others as you would like them to treat you.'

Employing TQM means preventing errors rather than detecting them. This approach should mean zero defects and the workers performing to the best of their abilities.

■ Quality circles

Japanese industry has been in the lead in striving for perfection in the quality of their goods. One way in which they have been able to reduce the number of defects to a few parts per million is through the adoption of quality circles. A quality circle is a small group of workers who come together voluntarily to solve work problems. They are trained in the basic methods of statistics and communication and the results of their investigations are passed on to other quality circles.

■ Kaizen

The Japanese objective is to have continuous improvement. This idea is known as Kaizen. The workforce is continually moving to a higher level of performance as the quality of the product improves.

THE PRODUCTION PROCESS AND THE WORKFORCE PERFORMANCE

The main type of production process is the automated mass production method. The production process is split into a large number of individual operations and each operation is performed by a worker or a group of workers performing the same task. Each task is timed so that production is continuous and workers operate at the rate of the moving good being produced. In a car factory, workers may fit the seats in a car, while other workers put on the wheels and a different group of workers test the engine.

The advantages of this method of production are as follows:

- people perform the same task, they find ways of doing the job quickly and efficiently, they become experts at their particular job.
- people do not have to move between jobs, the work comes to them.
- Each worker requires little training.
- Machines can be employed to do repetitive tasks.

This method of production was used by Henry Ford to great effect building cars. However, automated mass production brings disadvantages which reduce worker performance.

- **Monotony** Workers are expected to perform their task each day. There is no opportunity for them to use their initiative, be part of the decision-making process or take responsibility for their work.
- **Job alienation** The workers only complete one small task of the whole job and therefore cannot relate to the product being built.
- **Skill reduction** Each task is reduced to the simplest operation and this enables machines to be used. Other operations are broken down so that there is little need for craftsmanship.

This type of work leads to poor workforce performance, indicated by high labour turnover, high absenteeism and poor industrial relations.

The trend is to improve workers' performance by increasing job satisfaction through enlarging the role and responsibilities of workers. Methods employed include the following.

Job rotation
The workers are trained to do a number of different tasks so that they can perform a range of tasks and be able to move from job to job. By doing different jobs, acquiring new skills, team-work is encouraged and allows workers to see problems that other people face.

Job enlargement
In this method of production, workers also do the tasks which were either done before or after the work performed in the original job. The job becomes larger and more varied with the worker being able to use more skills.

Job enrichment
Building more tasks into a job is not necessarily going to increase the performance of a worker, i.e. increasing the number of 'boring' tasks a worker has to perform is not going to increase job satisfaction. Job enrichment tries to expand not just the scope of the job but the depth of the job as well. The individual has some say in the way in which he or she works, and workers are now allowed to use their initiative to solve problems.

Team-work
This is where production has moved away from the specialisation on a production line and groups of workers complete the whole task. The team has the equipment, skills and expertise to produce the whole product. The disadvantages of specialisation are reduced and the workers' morale, motivation and performance are increased.

Just-in-Time (J-I-T)
Just-in-Time refers to the production process receiving the stock as it needs it. This means that the business orders stocks from suppliers at very short notice, i.e. in a few hours or days. Only stock which is required for immediate production is kept on site.

Traditional methods of holding stock are based on buffer stocks and the economic reorder quantity. Stock levels are kept high to ensure a ready supply of materials and there is a 'buffer stock' of materials which is an amount of stock below which the level of stock is never allowed to fall. Each part is ordered in bulk to obtain a discount from the supplier. This method disadvantages the producer because of the cash tied up in stock, and problems in stock control and stock distribution can be hidden within the production process. In some cases stocks of material which are infrequently used may be held at a high level, not only absorbing cash but also taking up factory space. These stock levels may be higher than required because the supplier is unreliable with regard to the quality and delivery of his materials.

Besides reducing waste J-I-T involves the worker in the production process. Workers are responsible for the quality of their work which is produced just in time for the next production process. If they cannot meet this responsibility, workers stop the production process and seek help. Workers are also expected to contribute to improving the production process. This is done through participation in quality circles, suggestion systems and working in teams.

The performance of the worker is greatly enhanced using this production method. However, it is not used as a motivator but as a way to improve profits.

CASE STUDY 2

Siemens Works, Congleton

The business

Siemens Works, Congleton is in Cheshire. Four hundred people are employed at the site. The site is split into two sections. Two-thirds of the workforce are employed in electronics, making a range of drives used in the automation industry, the other one-third make a range of switchgear. Siemens have been in Congleton since 1971. Their parent company is Siemens AG of Germany. A Total Quality programme was introduced two years ago aimed at continuous improvement of all work processes.

In 1992 the Congleton Works increased their turnover by 40 per cent and made a profit for the first time ever. Their German parent company had been supporting them until that time.

Features of workforce performance

Wages

There are three different wage structures:

1 Hourly paid

2 Staff

3 Management

Every July hourly paid people are involved in a collective bargaining process. The union is the Amalgamated Engineering and Electrician's Union (AEEU). All other staff are on individual contracts and they are assessed individually by their managers each October.

Each manager has a budget and makes pay awards within that budget.

Managers receive a bonus related to earnings (Results Related Earnings). Everyone is paid monthly into their bank account.

Benefits and conditions of work

1 **Pension scheme:** This is contributed to by employees. 'It is one of the top ten occupational pension schemes in the country', says Personnel Manager, David Kruze.
2 **Subsidised private health care**
3 **Subsidised restaurant**
4 **Holidays:** 26 days per year, which rises to 30 days with length of service.
5 **Sickness scheme:** Employees can get up to 30 weeks on full pay, depending on length of service.

The working week is 37 hours for shopfloor workers and 36¼ hours for all other employees.

Shopfloor:
8 am–4.30 pm Monday–Thursday
8 am–1 pm Friday
Office:
8.30–4.30 Monday–Friday

Health and safety record

Siemens plc have the following objectives for health and safety:

- 'The elimination of all unsafe practices and conditions of work both at our own premises and while working at client's installations.'
- 'The maintenance of high standards for health, safety and the environment at our own premises and client installations.'
- 'The development of controls to ensure safe working systems are established for all E & A (Energy and Automation) activities, with particular emphasis on off-site working.'
- 'The provision of appropriate training and information on matters of health and safety for each employee/contractor commensurate with their work activities.'
- 'The promotion of co-operation by consultation with employee representatives on health, safety and environment issues.'
- 'The development of promotional campaigns to stimulate and encourage health, safety and environmental awareness throughout E & A.'

There is a Health and Safety Manager and an Occupational Health Nurse.

David Kruze: 'The company has an excellent health and safety record. It's due to the type of work we do, it's fairly light engineering. As a major employer we have to make sure that we adhere to regulations and introduce procedures in line with the latest legislation.'

Siemens plc Energy and Automation produce a booklet on Health & Safety Policy. This states that the Health & Safety Manager:

'…has a responsibility to the Managing Director for policy, co-ordination and audit concerning health, safety and the environment. He also advises General Managers, Departmental Managers and E & A employees/contractors on matters relating to health, safety and the protection of the environment.'

There is a Health and Safety Committee which looks at all the processes in the company and makes sure that potential problem areas are being addressed. Members of the Committee tour round the site every two months and identify problems. They then attempt to resolve those problems during committee meetings.

David Kruze: 'Health and Safety is the individual responsibility of all the managers for their area.'

Training

There is a company Personnel Development Training and Development Policy. It reads as follows:

'Policy Statement

1.1 The aim of Training and Development is to facilitate change within the organisation and individuals, with a view to:

    1.1.1 improving performance/productivity per head

    1.1.2 developing organisational capability

1.2 In our Corporate Mission statement, we state: "The creativity and commitment of our employees are the foundations of our success."

Management fully endorses the role of training and development as a crucial determinant of our organisational growth and profitability. Consequently, this policy document exists to identify the ways in which cost effective training and development activities will be implemented throughout Siemens plc.'

The Training and Development Policy also states that training will be by different methods:

> In-house courses and workshops
> External/Open Training Courses
> Distance/Open Learning including Computer Based Training
> Secondment/Job Rotation
> Assessment/Development Centres
> Performance Coaching
> Mentoring

The present training consists of:

Off-site at local colleges

For example

> HNC in Engineering course
> HNC in Business Studies course

Open University

Siemens pay for the first 50 per cent of course fees on commencement of the course and the remaining 50 per cent on successful completion.

On-site

Corporate training and development department

■ All managers do a mandatory course 'Management by Co-operation'.

■ Managers immediately below the senior management team go through a modular training scheme which includes:

1 Introduction to quality

2 The problem solving discipline

3 Team-work

4 Interpersonal skills

- Hourly paid employees have all received a one-day training session on the aims and philosophy behind Total Quality.

David Kruze: 'We make sure that all the rest of our training fits in with Total Quality.'

The training course for introducing Total Quality was devised by management consultants for Siemens. Siemens Congleton Senior Management deliver the courses themselves.

Training needs are identified during the performance appraisal interview. This information is used by David Kruze to analyse training needs. *David Kruze*: 'From there we decide how we're going to address those needs over the coming year.'

Every employee on the site has been involved with training for Total Quality.

Equal opportunities

The company has an Equal Opportunity Policy. This is given to all staff in the form of a booklet and staff sign a form to say that they have received it. One of the General Statements of Policy in the booklet is:

'The company affirms its commitment to the development of positive policies to promote equal opportunity in employment regardless of a person's colour, race, nationality, ethnic or national origins, sex or marital status. This principle will apply in respect of all conditions of work including: pay, hours of work, holiday entitlement, overtime and shiftwork, work allocation, sick pay, recruitment, selection, training, promotion or re-deployment.'

The company states that it is an Equal Opportunities Employer.

Specialisation

David Kruze: 'We believe in multi-skilling and job rotation. This enables us to have total flexibility on the shop-floor to increase worker motivation. We try to do job rotation even on the more technical jobs.'

Employees are trained in the Company's training school for multi-skilling and flexibility. It is written into employment contracts that new employees agree to undergo training to become multi-skilled.

Motivation

There is a Suggestion Scheme to encourage employees to put forward ideas for improvements in the production process.

David Kruze: 'The Total Quality programme is aimed at motivating every employee through empowerment. People are actively encouraged to come up with ideas.'

Every employee has a Personal Action Plan – they have a chart on the wall near their workplace and they monitor their own progress. This is not checked upon by supervisors or management, it is purely the responsibility of each employee to take charge of their own planning.

Redundancy

No one has been made redundant since early 1992. Until recently Siemens has been unaffected by the recession in Britain. The German recession started in 1993, much later than in the UK, and Siemens' sales are affected by the German experience.

Siemens have a redundancy policy which states:

'Redundancy, as defined by Statute arises if:

(1) The employer has ceased, or intends to cease, to carry on the business for the purpose for which the employee was employed, or

(2) The employer has ceased, or intends to cease, to carry on that business in the place where the employee was so employed, or

(3) The requirements of that business for employees to carry out work of a particular kind, or for employees to carry out work of a particular kind in the place where he/she was so employed, have ceased or diminished or are expected to diminish, or

(4) Employees have been laid off, or kept on short time for either:
  (a) four or more consecutive weeks, or
  (b) six or more consecutive weeks within a period of thirteen weeks.
  Under (4), employees may resign and claim redundancy, provided they follow the appropriate statutory procedure.'

Selection criteria for choosing those to be made redundant is based on a points system. Points are awarded for the following:

1 Skills

2 Performance/flexibility

3 Discipline

4 Attendance

5 Timekeeping

6 Service

Weightings are designed to ensure that the best workers are kept on. 50–40 points can be awarded for 'can competently do all/vast majority of jobs', whereas one point is given for each year of service up to 30 points.

Data sources

Siemens is a member of the confederation of British Industry (CBI). David Kruze uses IDS Studies (Income Data Surveys) and liaises with local employers for information on wage rates. Information is also gained from local and national newspapers on going rates for certain professions.

David Kruze is a member of the Institute of Personnel Management and receives information from them. The company receive information from the Health and Safety Executive, Equal Opportunities Commission and they buy into various companies that offer salary surveys.

CASE STUDY 3

Halifax Building Society

The business

The Halifax is the world's largest building society. It was formed as a result of the merger of Halifax Permanent Building Society and Halifax Equitable Building Society in 1927.

There are over 700 branches in the UK and a network of almost 2000 agencies which provide a counter service. They have recently opened a branch in Spain.

Forty people are employed at their Crewe office, 10 of whom are part-time. There are six managers – the Branch Manager John Richardson and 5 deputies with functional titles such as 'Sales Manager'.

Features of workforce performance

Wages

There are 12 grades within the Halifax Building society:

1–5 Managers – Branch/Service Centre/Area, depending upon the size of the operation

6–7 Assistant Manager Level/Small Sales Outlet Manager Level/Function Manager in Service Centre

8–9 Supervisor of larger teams/Local Branch Manager level

10 First Line Supervisor/Interviewer

11 Complex Clerical/Counsellor

12 Routine Clerical/Cashier

All staff are salaried and are covered by this 12-point grading system. The pay system is performance related. All staff are assessed in an annual appraisal against targets agreed at the beginning of the year with their line manager. Pay rises are agreed 3-6 months after the appraisal interview. If someone is assessed as being effective in their work at grade 3 and their pay is below the mid point for that grade, they receive a higher pay rise than someone who had the same assessment and whose salary was above the mid point of grade 3.

The performance related pay rises are agreed between the Halifax Building Society and the Staff Association of the Society.

There is also a profit sharing scheme which is based on the end of year results of the Society. This scheme is registered with the Government PRP office and can, up to a certain limit, be paid free of tax.

Benefits and conditions of work

1 **Pension scheme:** Occupational pension scheme which includes life assurance arrangements.

2 Concessionary mortgage scheme: Available when employees have been with the Society for one year.

3 Holidays: 22 days per annum, rising to 30 depending on level of service and grade.

4 BUPA membership: For management grades and those with long service.

The working week is 9 am–5.15 pm Monday–Friday and in addition branches are open on Saturdays.

The 10 part-time staff have been mainly recruited for counter service on busy days. Many of the part-time staff were full-time and have returned to work after having families. *John Richardson*: 'We're delighted to accommodate them as they're already trained and know the environment.'

Staff turnover is very low: Absenteeism also is not a cause for concern. *John Richardson*: 'If someone is absent regularly, we counsel them about it and find out what the problems are. If they need further help, we can point them in the right direction.'

Health and safety record

The Society is committed to the health, safety and welfare of staff and other people.

Safety policies, guidance and instructions assist Managers in fulfilling their statutory responsibilities.

Managers carry out a quarterly inspection of their premises, accompanied by Staff Association representatives. They look for possible hazards and evaluate the risks to staff and then ensure any necessary remedial action is taken.

Managers also carry out risk assessments relating to display screen equipment and train staff in correct posture and other risk reduction measures.

Training and development

John Richardson: 'The Halifax Building Society is dedicated to training and development. Working for the Halifax is a career and someone who wants to stay with us can be developed towards a management role. We have recruited graduates and managers from other companies, but most of our managers are developed within the Society.'

The Society has a large in-house training centre in Halifax developing and delivering its own training courses. The Society divides its branch network into eight regions and there is a training office in each region. There is also a Field Trainer who is responsible for workplace training in each area. Each branch office has a Training Co-ordinator who is usually a member of the management team and is responsible for induction training and the co-ordination of the monthly training plan in the branch.

John Richardson: 'Part of our mission statement emphasises development of people, the whole operation is dedicated to it. We are selling something quite intangible. The service staff give to customers is the be all and end all of our existence. You can get a mortgage anywhere on the High Street, although not as quickly and efficiently as we can give you one.'

Promotion depends on ability and potential. People selected for promotion or 'accelerated development' (achieving promotion more quickly than is normal) may attend assessment centres. Here they take part in a range of tests such as group exercises, individual presentations, in-tray exercises, numerical and analytical reasoning tests. These assessment centres provide the staff member and the Society with information on their skills and abilities.

Staff are encouraged to take the Chartered Institute of Bankers' examinations, either at local colleges or through a correspondence course. *John Richardson*: 'People can plan their own development. We are looking for people who are self-motivated to develop.'

Managers can also study for the Diploma in Management Studies or an MBA (a Masters degree in Business Administration).

Equal opportunities

There is a statement about the Halifax being an Equal Opportunities employer in the Staff Manual. *John Richardson*: 'We are very dedicated to equal opportunities and getting more women into senior management.' John's principal assistant is a woman and there are three female supervisors and one male in the branch.

A growing number of branches are managed by women. *John Richardson*: 'Already women are running the largest branches'.

Staff are given career breaks for bringing up families. They are encouraged to return for short periods during the break. This updates them with current practice. *John Richardson*: 'The vast majority of women return after having children. We are a difficult employer to leave. We have good working conditions.'

The Halifax's North West region has won awards for their employment opportunities for disabled people. The Crewe branch employs a deaf person.

Productivity

Managers have daily review meetings for around 10 minutes at the end of each day to discuss progress of work flows in each job.

There are weekly management meetings to look at the weekly figures. These look at throughput, backlogs, work flows and anything outstanding. They focus attention on exceptions. Backlogs of mortgage applications would be a major concern and would be given urgent attention.

John Richardson: 'I know the staff who are doing well because I see them through the week. I spend very little time in my room. We try and balance the jobs out, to give everyone a fair day's work. Staff will say that they're not busy and need moving onto something else. If that is the case, I rotate their roles. Some people have lots of experience such as Sales Interviewers because they have to have done other jobs in the office before they can attain that position. Their roles are flexible.'

Specialisation

John Richardson: 'Most of the people we recruit are selected for their ability to learn and adapt. Not everyone is trained to do every job, but people are trained sufficiently so that we have good cover for absences. People are specialists in the sense that they work on an area for a period of time and gain expertise.

The Society tries to design jobs so that employees can see an end result of their work to attain a feeling of job satisfaction.

The Society also attempts to empower people by giving them decision-making authority. *John Richardson*: 'There are certain key jobs I look at – I talk to the mortgage applications team, the arrears team, the sales team, and give them recognition for their work.' Employees' achievements are recorded on charts which are displayed on the office walls. There are communication meetings every week. *John Richardson*: 'If something has gone well we'll make sure the team know about it and praise those involved.'

Redundancy

There is a Security of Employment Agreement between the Society and the Staff Association which has been in force for many years. *John Richardson*: 'We've never made anyone redundant to date. We've kept tight control of numbers we employ during boom years. We run a tight, efficient ship.'

Social activity

Staff are encouraged to get involved in social events. The branch has a Sports and Social Club and around three-quarters of the staff are members. The Society gives the Club financial support.

John Richardson: 'They tend to do things as a group, they go out together. Today they have organised fund raising for Children in Need. They decided what they wanted to do and did it, it's their idea.'

PC
5.3.4

DISCUSSION QUESTIONS

Case studies, Siemens Works, Congleton and Halifax Building Society

1 Compare the Training and Equal Opportunity Policies of the two businesses.

2 What difficulties are there when evaluating the productivity of firms in manufacturing and service industries?

3 What employee benefits do the two firms provide? What other benefits could they include for their employees?

ASSIGNMENT

You are required to compile a study of two business sectors (e.g. travel sector and textiles sector) using a data set for the UK and the EC. The study will investigate differences in employment generally and within the specific business sectors.

Research

Use a variety of sources (some suggested sources are listed at the end of this chapter). For example, the *Employment Gazette,* November 1993 shows:

8.1 TOURISM

Employment in tourism-related industries in Great Britain

Employees in employment (000s)

	Restaurants, cafes, etc.	Public houses and bars	Night clubs and licensed clubs	Hotels	Libraries museums art galleries and sports	All
1991						
March	291.2	322.6	142.7	286	358.9	1401.3
September	287.7	338.6	141	313.1	402.4	1482.8
1992						
March	283.4	315.3	138.7	270.9	382.5	1390.6
September	298.1	329.1	137.9	304.9	399.8	1469.8

CSO provides an abstract of statistics which shows all aspects of the UK economy, e.g. industries, output, employment.

Eurostat provides information on European countries.

You should show that you know and understand:

a general trends in UK and EU employment

b trends in employment within different business sectors

c economic relationships which influence employment trends

CASE STUDY 4

Energy policy in relation to coalmining and demand for fuel

The UK has always had a strong coal industry as this was once the major source of power. It fuelled the ships that carried British goods to her trading countries and coal was a major export. Factories needed coal for their power plants. Every town in Britain had its own gas supply as gas was extracted from coal. Trains, the major means of transport until the 1960s, were driven by steam locomotives using coal as their fuel. People used coal fires in their homes as a means of heating. Electricity was generated by coal.

However, the demand for coal has gradually fallen away. UK export markets were lost to other countries, especially during the Second World War as the country concentrated on winning the war. In other situations UK coal became too expensive. During the 1950s and '60s there were changes in the types of fuel used for transport, ships and trains. People travelled less by train because as they became better off, they bought cars. Owning a car gave people the freedom and flexibility that a train could not give them. The flexibility of the road systems and the low running costs of lorries moved freight off the railways.

Oil became a major competitor of coal when cheap oil was imported from the Middle East, and in the 1970s oil from the UK's own oilfields in the North Sea came on stream. Electrical power stations started to convert to oil as a fuel to generate electricity. The use of coal for burning in homes from the 1950s was restricted by the Clean Air Acts. This legislation was introduced after people had died during winters from the effects of smog, a potentially lethal concoction of fog and smoke from coal. Gas companies looked for a less dangerous and cleaner gas. Originally, liquified natural gas was imported from North Africa, but again the UK was discovered to have large reserves of its own natural gas. Houses were converted to use natural gas, and because gas was cheaper than coal more people used it for their heating.

Table 5.14   **Coal output in million tonnes**

	1947	1950	1960	1970	1980	1990	1992
Deep mines	187.5	205.6	186.8	135.5	110.3	72.3	61.8
Opencast	10.4	12.4	7.7	8.1	15.3	17.0	15.0
Licensed	2.1	1.5	2.3	2.2	1.1	2.3	4.0
Total	200.0	219.6	196.7	144.7	126.6	91.6	80.8

As the demand for coal fell, the coal industry had to look at ways in which it could compete in the energy market. Uneconomical mines were closed down and the miners were either made redundant or they were encouraged to work in another coalfield. The coal industry also opened 'Super Pits', those which could use more efficient machines. Technology increased the productivity of each miner and the unit cost of coal fell. However, another consequence of introducing machines was the need for fewer miners. The total number of miners has fallen in the last 25 years and especially during the last 10 years.

While coal was important, miners could expect to negotiate high wages. As coal lost importance, so miners' wages fell behind those of other workers. However, in 1973 the price of oil quadrupled and as a consequence energy derived from that source became expensive. Coal again was seen as the important fuel for generating electricity. It was recognised to be unwise to depend on one fuel as the source of power. The miners were able to demand a substantial pay increase in 1974.

Coal as an energy source not only had competition from other fossil fuels but the government, until the mid 1980s, saw nuclear energy as the natural successor to finite fuels and embarked on a policy to produce electricity by nuclear power. The research and development costs were subsidised by governments as were the heavy costs of building the power-stations. The government's aim to generate a substantial amount of electricity by nuclear power was called into question by nuclear incidents in other countries. One occurred in America at a nuclear plant on Five Mile Island and during the 1980s a serious incident occurred at Chernobyl in Russia. The safety of nuclear power plant was called into question. At the same time the nuclear energy industry was struggling with the problem of waste disposal.

This should have been an opportunity for coal. However, during the 1980s the government decided to speed up its closure of uneconomical mines, cutting the cost of subsidies to coal to reduce government spending and taxation. The result was a year-long miners' strike which lasted until 1985. The strike was not about increased wages but saving miners' jobs. Not all miners agreed with the National Union of Mineworkers' approach to the strike and miners in the Nottingham coalfield broke away from the NUM to form another union called the Democratic Union of Mineworkers. The split in the miners' ranks reduced its power.

Privatisation of the electrical companies meant that government control was relinquished and the electricity companies no longer had to buy from British Coal but could seek supplies from the cheapest source e.g. Australia and Poland. The demand for British coal gradually fell as it could not compete with the cheaper, cleaner coal from abroad. Mines were forced to close. At the same time mines were closed the industry was prepared for privatisation.

By December 1993 there were 22 deep-mine collieries employing 15,000 workers earning an average £350 per week.

Energy policy

The President of the Board of Trade is responsible for energy matters in the UK.

The UK's energy policy is to ensure the secure, adequate and economic provision of energy to meet Britain's requirements. The government encourages the exploitation of Britain's energy resources. It wants all economic forms of energy to be produced, supplied and used as efficiently as possible without endangering the environment. The government sees the profitable development of the UK's oil, gas, coal and nuclear energy as important to the country's economic future.

European Energy Charter

In 1991 Britain signed the European Energy Charter
The main objectives are:

- An open competitive market for trade in energy, including a framework for investment promotion and protection.
- Co-operation in the energy field through the co-ordination of energy policies.
- Promotion of energy efficiency and environmental protection

Data

Table 5.15 **Inland energy consumption (in terms of primary sources) million tonnes oil equivalent**

	1981	1986	1989	1990	1993
Oil	65.2	66.2	69.5	71.3	71.1
Coal	69.6	66.8	63.6	63.8	63.3
Natural gas	42.2	49.2	47.4	49.0	52.8
HEP	1.4	1.4	1.4	1.6	1.4
Net imports of electricity	–	3.1	3.0	2.9	3.9
Total	186.6	199.2	200.2	202.7	207.7

Table 5.16 **The coal industry**

	1947	1950	1960	1970	1980	1990	1993
Output (million tonnes)							
Mines	187.5	205.6	186.8	135.5	110.3	72.3	61.8
Opencast	10.4	12.4	7.7	8.1	15.3	17.0	15.00
Licensed	2.1	1.5	2.2	1.1	1.1	2.3	4.0
Total	200.0	219.6	196.7	144.7	126.6	91.6	80.8
Number of pits							
At year end	958	901	698	292	211	65	50
Output							
Per man year (tonnes)	267	298	310	471	479	1,181	1,611
Per manshift (tonnes)							
Production					9.09	22.62	30.39
All underground			1.81	2.92	10.92	29.24	43.39
Employees (000s)							
Colliery manpower	718.4	688.6	588.5	286	230.7	57.3	31.7
Other			42.6	70.3	62.2	17.0	12.5
Accidents							
No. of fatalities	–	476	316	92	39	11	3
Disputes							
Lost tonnage (millions)	1.7	1.0	1.6	3.1	1.5	0.2	0.1

Accidents	1992/3
Fatal	3
Major	326
Others (over 3 days absence)	1,711
Total	2,040

Number of operating pits end of March year 1992/93

Scottish	1
North-East	5
Selby	8
South Yorkshire	12
Nottinghamshire	12
Midland/Wales	12
Total	50

ASSIGNMENT

Using the case study on energy policy, or a case study of your own, explain the external influences on business employment practice using economic relationships.

Other business employment practice cases may include:

■ food subsidies in relation to farming and the single market for food, labour supply and labour reducing technology

■ the introduction of compulsory competitive tendering or deregulation to local authority services and the effect on the demand and supply of labour

■ Sunday trading and late shopping trends in retailing and the effect on the demand for labour

You should demonstrate that you know and understand:

a How business actions concerning employment are influenced by external forces

b Current examples of employment practice

c Actions taken by business, using economic relationships in terms of demand for the product and the demand for and supply of labour

CASE STUDY 5

The UK car industry

The British car industry at one time was a major force in the world market. However, during the 1960s and '70s, the car industry was troubled by producing cars of poor quality, the firms tended to be product-led rather than customer-orientated, there was lack of investment, overmanning and poor industrial relations. Car firms merged to form larger businesses to take on foreign competitors. However, the mergers tended to be unsuccessful. Some Biritsh firms were taken over by foreign companies and eventually the sole remaining British car manufacturer, British Leyland, was taken into public ownership. Later this company was sold to British Aerospace and sold cars under the Rover badge. In January 1994 British Aerospace sold the Rover company to the German car manufacturer BMW.

During the 1980s and early '90s, the car industry went through radical changes. Japan invested heavily in Britain, opening car factories in Washington, Derby and Swindon. They introduced Japanese methods of production, and their British competitors soon followed these working practices. Production is leaner than previous operations – fewer people are employed, and productivity is higher. New methods included just-in-time, zero buffer stocks and quality built into the production process. There is a delegation of responsibility. For example, workers are responsible for the quality of parts produced. In other aspects of quality control, workers join quality circles to help each other to solve problems relating to quality. The attitude now is 'getting it right first time' rather than 'that will do'. Quality is not sufficient, the processes must be 'continuously improved'.

In Japanese-owned companies, people are encouraged to identify with the company. Although there is no guaranteed job for life, as in Japan, there is greater job security. Recently Nissan in Britain were suffering from a drop in world demand for cars. No worker has been threatened with compulsory redundancy and the firm is not asking for voluntary redundancy. However, the workforce has recognised that there needs to be a reduction in their numbers. The companies believe job security helps to motivate the workers.

Team spirit and single status are an important part of Japanese working practices. Managers and workers share a common goal rather than work against each other in an 'us and them' situation. Everyone is referred to as an associate. Everyone wears the same uniform, eats in the same canteen and there are no reserved parking spaces for managers. There is no grading between workers, but each worker is a member of an identifiable team and all workers expected to be multi-skilled and able to move between jobs. Managers and everyone else, including office workers, are expected to work on the production line if the need arises. Managers do not have offices and often have experience on the shop-floor so that they are technically competent and are available if the workers need to contact them.

To help reduce internal demarcation disputes and to help negotiations on wages and working conditions, car firms are moving to a reduction in the number of unions they will deal with. The Japanese companies tend to have single union agreements.

The production targets the British car industry are aiming for are those set by the Japanese in Japan. The time needed to produce a car in Japan is 13.2 hours while in North America it is 18.6 and Europe 22.8. Rover Cars produced 500,000 per annum in 1992, which is equal to 35 cars per man employed per year, compared with the European average of 31 cars per man employed per year.

There are potential problems with the Japanese methods of production. The type of work could be stressful because of the demand by management for constant innovation, quality improvements and the need to intensify workers' efforts. Just-in-time puts greater dependency of workers on each other. The pressure is on the workers to keep the production line moving. In Japan, workers are expected to make up lost production in their own time. Managers, for example, who are called to work on the line, are expected to do their managerial tasks later in the day. Labour is just part of the production process and their major function is to increase productivity, quality and profit.

The introduction of Japanese working practices in the British car industry is enabling it to compete with the rest of the world, especially Japan. The problem facing the car industry is that it is introducing the practices now, but by the time they have fully implemented Japanisation, the Japanese will be further down the road of increasing productivity!

ASSIGNMENT

Arrange to visit two different businesses, such as local factories, retailers, banks, travel agents, building societies and compare the businesses' policies in one of the following areas for a new employee aged 16–18.

Wages

■ What is the basic wage? Are there any regular bonuses?

■ How do they compare with the national/regional average?

■ How does the employer calculate the wages?

■ How are the employees paid (cash, cheque, bank account)?

■ Does the payment system improve business performance?

Benefits and conditions of work

■ What benefits (pensions, holidays) does the organisation provide for the new employee?

■ Do the benefits increase with length of service?

■ Where will the new employee be working? Is it comfortable and well heated and ventilated?

■ What hours is the new employee expected to work? Are weekends and evenings involved?

Health and safety record

■ Ask to see the written health and safety policy.

■ What actions has the organisation taken to implement this policy?

■ Does the policy mention particular hazards and how they should be dealt with?

■ How is the workforce informed about health and safety policies?

■ What training do employees receive in safety procedures?

Training

■ Is there an induction programme? How long does it take and what does it consist of?

■ How many different jobs in the organisation have training programmes? (Does the organisation have a policy of employing people who are already qualified?)

■ How long would the training last for the new employee?

■ What is involved in the training? Does the new employee have the opportunity to have off-the-job training, such as college courses? If so, does the organisation pay for these or give the employee any time during working hours to attend the courses?

Equal opportunities

■ What is the proportion of the workforce who are:

   female, from ethnic minorities, handicapped?

  Are these groups represented in the organisation?

- Compile a breakdown of the numbers of each group within:

    managerial, administrative, operational jobs.

  What proportion of the people doing these jobs is female, from ethnic minorities or handicapped?
- What proportion of the total workforce is over 50?

Productivity

- How is this measured?
- Does the business measure the productivity of its competitors' workforces?

Using evidence presented in a variety of forms (statistics, video, transcripts of interviews, written report, documentation from the organisations), critically review the organisations as employers. Contrast the two organisations studied and present an argument, supported by the evidence you have gathered, as to whether you believe the organisations to be good employers to work for or not. Make recommendations as to how they could improve their performance.

 REVIEW TEST

1 Describe how labour differs from other factor inputs in the production process.

2 What factors does labour employment in the UK depend on?

3 Why is the market for labour 'imperfect'?

4 Define the term 'marginal revenue product'.

5 Name two ways in which marginal revenue product can be increased.

6 How can businesses reduce their costs following wage rises to their workers?

7 Define the 'labour supply'.

8 What factors affect the labour supply in the UK?

9 With the use of a diagram, explain why less labour may be supplied at higher hourly rates of pay.

10 List the ways in which supply of labour may be restricted to particular occupations.

11 How is the relative importance of the primary, secondary and tertiary sectors of the economy changing?

12 Define 'de-industrialisation'.

13 How many people are in the UK labour force – how is this calculated?

14 How have employment levels between private and public sectors changed over the past 20 years?

15 What is meant by 'functional flexibility'?

16 Which industries have seen the largest growth in the use of temporary contracts for workers?

17 Explain 'flexi-time'.

18 What is the Management Charter Initiative?

19 Explain what is meant by an 'induction programme'.

20 Explain the difference between wages and earnings.

21 Give the official definition of 'unemployment'.

22 What forms can regional policy take?

23 What are the costs of unemployment?

24 What have been the main changes in industrial relations over the past 15 years?

25 What is 'single table bargaining'?

26 Name four ways of maintaining or improving the workers' performance.

27 What is meant by quality and how might an organisation improve the quality of its products or service?

28 Explain job enlargement and job enrichment.

29 What is meant by 'Just-in-Time'?

30 How can productivity be measured?

SOURCES OF INFORMATION

Central Statistical Office, Great George Street, London SW1P 3AQ

Central Statistical Office, Cardiff Road, Newport, Gwent, NP9 1XG

HMI Customs and Excise (monthly trade statistics), Tariff and Statistical Office, Unit 51, Room 711, Portcullis House, 27 Victoria Avenue, Southend on Sea, Essex SS2 6AL

Employment Department (employment census), Headquarters Building, PO Box 12, East Lane, Halton, Runcorn WA7 2DN

Employment Department (labour force survey), Caxton House, Tothill Street, London SW1H 9NF

Department of Employment (training), Moorfoot, Sheffield S1 4PQ

Department of Environment, 2 Marsham Street, London SW1P 3EB

Health and Safety Executive, Daniel House, Stanley Road, Bootle, Merseyside L20 3LZ

Department of Health, Hannibal House, Elephant and Castle, London SE1 6TE

Office of Population Censuses and Surveys, St Catherine's House, 10 Kingsway, London WC2B 6JP

Department of Trade and Industry (overseas trade analysed in terms of industries), 151 Buckingham Palace Road, London SW1W 9SS

Department of Trade and Industry (fuel and energy statistics), 1 Palace Street, London SW1E 5HE

The Scottish Office Library, Publication Sales, Room 1/44, New St Andrew's House, Edinburgh EH1 3TG

The Scottish Office (Scottish economic statistics), Alhambra House, 45 Waterloo Street, Glasgow G2 6AT

Welsh Office, Economic and Statistical Services Division, Crown Building, Cathays Park, Cardiff CF1 3NQ

Northern Ireland Departments (economic statistics), Stormont, Belfast BT4 3SW

Northern Ireland Departments (employment and manpower statistics), Netherleigh House, Massey Avenue, Belfast BT4 2JS

Eurostat (information office), Jean Monnet Building, L 2920 Luxembourg (tel. 352 4301 4567)

Eurostat (data shop), Rue de la Loi 120, B 1049 Brussels (tel. 32-2 235 1504)

British Broadcasting Corporation, Broadcasting House, London W1A 1AA

Central Office of Information, Hercules Road, London SE1 7DU

Office of Fair Trading, Room 306, Field House, 15 Bream's Buildings, London EC4A 1PR

Society of Motor Manufacturers and Traders, Forbes House, Halkin Street, London SW1X 7DS

Sports Council, 16 Upper Woburn Place, London WC1H 0HX

Sports Council for Wales, Sophia Gardens, Cardiff CF1 9SW

Trades Union Congress, Congress House, 23-28 Great Russell Street, London WC1V 3LS

House of Commons, London SW1A 0AA

Independent Television Commission, 70 Brompton Road, London SW3 1EY

Low Pay Unit, 27 Amwell Street, London EC1R 1UN

Channel 4, 60 Charlotte Street, London W1P 2AX

Confederation of British Industry, Centre Point, 103 New Oxford Street, London WC1A 1DU

Equal Opportunities Commission, Overseas House, Quay Street, Manchester M3 3HN

For local information, try local offices of organisations. The local Chamber of Commerce and local authority may help with information in your area. For European information, there are a number of publications and you can also try the relevant embassy.

FURTHER SOURCES OF INFORMATION

Priest and Coppock's The UK Economy, A Manual of Applied Economics, M J Artis, Weidenfeld and Nicolson. ISBN 0 297 79691 7

Industrial Relations in Britain, G S Bain, Basil Blackwell. ISBN 0 631 15859 6

Economics, A Student's Guide (3rd Edn), J Beardshaw, Pitman Publishing (1992) ISBN 0 273 03772 3

Economics Theory & Practice, D J Browne, Edward Arnold Publishers. ISBN 0340 49664 9

Understanding Industrial Relations, D Farham and J Pimlott, Cassell Publishers (1990) ISBN 0 304 31794 2

European Community Law, M & E Handbooks, Penelope Kent, Pitman Publishing (1992) ISBN 0 7121 0798 3

Economics, M Parkin and D King, Addison-Wesley Publishing Co (1992) ISBN 0 201 41611 5

Introductory Economics, G F Stanlake, Longman ISBN 582 036 95 X

Personnel Management A New Approach, D Torrington and Laura Hall, Prentice Hall (1991) ISBN 0 13 658667 8

The National Economies of Europe, D Dyker, Longman. ISBN 0582 058813

Europe in Figures (3rd Edn), Eurostat, HMSO

European Economic Integration, F McDonald and S Dearden. Longman. ISBN 0582 082250

The Economics of the Common Market (7th Edn), D Swann, Penguin Books.
ISBN 0 14 014497 8

Economic Trends, CSO

Social Trends, CSO

Employment Gazette, the official journal of the Employment Department, published monthly by HMSO, Subscription enquiries HMSO, Tel. 071-873 8499

Newspapers, *Financial Times, The Independent, The Guardian* and *The Sunday Times.*

FINANCIAL TRANSACTIONS AND MONITORING

Element 6.1
Explain financial transactions and supporting documents

Element 6.2
Complete documents for financial transactions

Element 6.3
Identify and explain data to monitor business performance

PERFORMANCE CRITERIA AND RANGE

Evidence indicators: A clear explanation of the purposes and use of financial transaction documents regularly used in business with an explanation of security checks for payment documents. Evidence should demonstrate understanding of the implications of the range dimensions in relation to the element. The unit test will confirm the candidate's coverage of range.

Evidence indicators: A full set of clearly and accurately completed financial documents with an explanation of the need for clarity and accuracy in documentation. Evidence should demonstrate understanding of the implications of the range dimensions in relation to the element. The unit test will confirm the candidate's coverage of range.

Evidence indicators: An explanation of a given set of accounting data (e.g. case study material) for a business identifying the key components for monitoring it and explaining the implications of the data in judging the performance of the business. Evidence should demonstrate understanding of the implications of the range dimensions in relation to the element. The unit test will confirm the candidate's coverage of range.

Unit 6 explains the key purposes of a business's accounting system and provides a clear and straightforward examination of the transactions which are recorded and processed in a business's double entry book-keeping and accounts operations.

It also provides ample models and illustrations of the documents which are created in order to maintain the sales and purchasing functions and which are used to record and track receipts and payments as they flow into and out of the business.

Lastly, Unit 6 examines the methods which are employed to ensure the security and integrity of a business accounting system, both in a paper-based and computerised environment.

In particular, Unit 6 explains:

- the main functions and purposes of a business accounting system.
- the relationship between assets and capital + liabilities, which forms the basis of the double entry book-keeping system
- the rules for debiting and crediting in the double entry system, and its overall structure
- the books of original entry: sales, purchases, returns inwards, returns outwards, cash book and general journal
- types of account: personal, impersonal
- the credit sales cycle and its documentation, from purchase order to stock requisition order, delivery note, invoice, debit note, credit note and statement.
- posting to sales and general ledgers
- the main features of an integrated accounts software system
- the credit purchase cycle and its documentation, from the raising of a purchase requisition order to the purchases day book, postings to the purchase and general ledgers, the purchase control account and the payment remittance advice
- the systems relating to receipts and payments: daily takings recording, bank paying in books, bank giro credits, business cheques, bank statements
- the format and structure of the cash book
- the imprest petty cash system and its related documentation
- techniques and practices which assure the security and integrity of a business accounting system

Every business – from the humblest sole trader's to the mighty multinational's – needs to keep careful 'books' or accounts, for a number of compelling reasons:

PC
6.1.1
6.3.2
6.3.3

THE KEY PURPOSES OF THE BUSINESS ACCOUNTING SYSTEM

Businesses are obliged to keep careful bookkeeping and accounting records so as:

● to meet legal requirements to present audited accounts (by an independent chartered accountant) at the end of each trading year or period to the Inland Revenue for the purposes of calculating the taxes due from the business

● to ensure that the selling, purchasing and payments transactions which the business undertakes are free from error (billing mistakes can quickly lose customers' goodwill and paying too much for goods bought in can erode or eradicate profits just as quickly)

● to provide continuous feedback both in terms of the minutiae of individual transactions and of summarised financial analyses (called management accounting reports) which inform management in a variety of ways on how the business is doing, and which are used extensively in the production of corporate and business plans

● to ensure that financial processes, especially those involving cash and items which might be converted into cash (such as an open cheque), are securely handled and not liable to misappropriation or theft

● to form the source data for the production of year end or final accounts, which provide feedback on how the business has performed overall; this information is also legally required to be made available to the shareholders of both private and public limited companies, and is naturally desired by the business's owners and/or directors; again, the potential purchasers of a business will undoubtedly request details of, say, the last five years of trading to inform their decision

Unit 6 provides a simple and clear overview of the essential features of a double-entry bookkeeping accounts system, with particular emphasis being placed upon the documentation which accompanies each principal transaction in the sets of books and ledgers which make up the system.

In his excellent text *Bookkeeping & Accounts, 3rd edition*, Frank Wood explains the fundamental accounting equation upon which the double-entry bookkeeping system is based as the need to demonstrate the relationship or balance between the assets or capital (which its start-up directors have put into it) with the liabilities (or monies owing to others) who have lent out finance etc. to it.

In other words,

ASSETS ALWAYS EQUAL CAPITAL + LIABILITIES

Frank Wood explains this simply this way:

Resources: what they are (Assets)	=	Resources, who supplied them (Capital + Liabilities)

Essentially, the assets of a business represent all its sources of wealth, either in the form of premises, land or machinery, or money due to the business from customers who owe it for goods or services purchased on credit or account, or money balances (in credit as opposed to being overdrawn) being held on behalf of the business in its bank.

A business's liabilities, on the other hand, comprise all the debts it owes to others – its suppliers of stock, its stationery suppliers, its accountants, its insurance company etc. the various expenses incurred in its business operations – payroll, heat, light, cleaning etc. and the debts incurred by borrowing money from a bank, building society or finance house in the form of business premises mortgages, money to finance expansion or to purchase new and expensive equipment.

THE DOUBLE-ENTRY SYSTEM: DEBITING AND CREDITING – DR AND CR

To avoid any confusion – which commonly occurs – between the everyday meaning of **debit** and **credit** and the quite separate and specific, double-entry bookkeeping meaning, commit the following table to memory:

THE KEY RULES OF DEBITING AND CREDITING

Accounts	To record	Entry in the account
Assets	an increase	Debit
	a decrease	Credit
Liabilities	an increase	Credit
	a decrease	Debit
Capital	an increase	Credit
	a decrease	Debit

Source: *Frank Wood's Bookkeeping & Accounts*, 3rd Edn, Pitman Publishing, 1992

The following table provides some helpful examples of how the debiting and crediting system works with regard to assets, capital and liabilities:

EXAMPLES OF DEBITING AND CREDITING

Transactions		Effect	Action
199– May 1	Started an engineering business putting £1,000 into a business bank account.	Increases *asset* of bank. Increases *capital* of owner.	Debit bank account. Credit capital account
May 3	Bought works machinery on credit from Unique Machines £275.	Increases *asset* of machinery. Increases *liability* to Unique Machines.	Debit machinery account. Credit Unique Machines account. *Continued overleaf*

Transactions	Effect	Action
199– May 4 — Withdrew £200 cash from the bank and placed it in the cash box.	▼ Decreases *asset* of bank. ▲ Increases *asset* of cash.	Credit bank account. Debit cash account.
May 7 — Bought a motor van paying in cash £180.	▼ Decreases *asset* of cash. ▲ Increases *asset* of motor van.	Credit cash account. Debit motor van account.
May 10 — Sold some of the machinery for £15 on credit to B Barnes	▼ Decreases *asset* of machinery. ▲ Increases *asset* of money owing from B Barnes.	Credit machinery account. Debit B Barnes account.
May 21 — Returned some of the machinery, value £27 to Unique Machines.	▼ Decreases *asset* of machinery. ▼ Decreases *liability* to Unique Machines.	Credit machinery account. Debit Unique Machines.
May 28 — B Barnes pays the firm the amount owing, £15, by cheque.	▲ Increases *asset* of bank. ▼ Decreases *asset* of money owing by B Barnes.	Debit bank account. Credit B Barnes account.
May 30 — Bought another motor van paying by cheque £420.	▼ Decreases *asset* of bank. ▲ Increases *asset* of motor vans.	Credit bank account. Debit motor van account.
May 31 — Paid the amount of £248 to Unique Machines by cheque.	▼ Decreases *asset* of bank. ▼ Decreases *liability* to Unique Machines.	Credit bank account. Debit Unique Machines.

Source: *Frank Wood's Bookkeeping & Accounts*, 3rd edn, Pitman Publishing 1992

In the middle ages in Europe, when the double-entry bookkeeping system was invented by merchants, a single book or ledger was sufficient to record the transactions which took place. Today, however, in an age of national chainstores, supermarkets, conglomerates and multinationals, businesses would need an articulated lorry to carry such a book to its various accounts department staff!

Therefore, it has become common practice to separate the books and ledgers which make up the modern double-entry accounting system in this way:

1 **Books of Original Entry,** into which every transaction is recorded on a daily basis, or as and when it occurs. These books are also referred to as journals, e.g. the Sales Journal, the Purchases Journal. Books of Original Entry record these data:

- the date of the transaction
- its details
- the money totals involved

The journals which make up the books of original entry in a business are:

- Sales
- Purchases
- Returns Inwards
- Returns Outwards
- Cash Book
- General Journal
- Petty Cash Book

Note that both the sales and purchase journals record credit transactions only, while the cash book records receipts and payments for cash, and that the general journal picks up other types of transaction.

2 **Ledgers** which summarise transactions in specific sectors:

- **Sales Ledger**
- **Purchase Ledger**
- **General Ledger**

Thus every transaction which increases or decreases a business's assets, capital or liabilities is entered as a debit or credit, first into a book of original entry (journal) and thence into the appropriate ledger as the following diagram (Fig 6.1) illustrates:

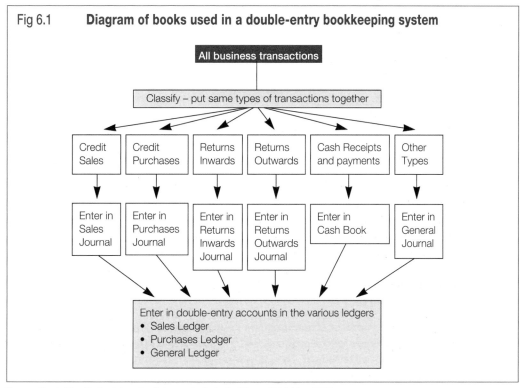

Fig 6.1 **Diagram of books used in a double-entry bookkeeping system**

Source: *Frank Wood's Book-keeping & Accounts*, 3rd edn, Pitman Publishing 1992

■ The basic structure of double-entry bookkeeping

The diagram shown in Fig 6.2 shows clearly the overall structure of the double-entry bookkeeping system and the relationships in debiting and crediting terms which interconnect the various books and ledgers.

PC
6.1.1

■ Types of accounts

The accounts which hold the detailed transactions of the double-entry bookkeeping system are also given specific names, and these are explained in the checklist.

PC
6.1.1
6.3.2
6.3.3

TYPES OF ACCOUNTS

Some accountants describe all accounts as **personal** accounts or as **impersonal** accounts:

● **Personal accounts** – These are for debtors and creditors.

● **Impersonal accounts** – Divided between real accounts and nominal accounts.

● **Real accounts** – Accounts in which property is recorded. Examples are buildings, machinery, fixtures and stock.

● **Nominal accounts** – Accounts in which expenses, income and capital are recorded.

A diagram may enable you to understand it better:

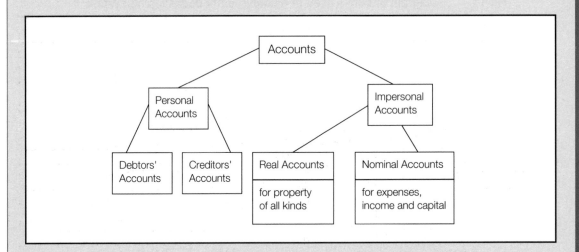

Nominal and private ledgers

The ledger in which the impersonal accounts are kept is known as the **nominal** (or general) **ledger.** Very often, to ensure privacy for the proprietor(s), the capital and drawing accounts and similar accounts are kept in a **private ledger**. By doing this office staff cannot see details of items which the proprietors want to keep a secret.

Source: *Frank Wood's Bookkeeping & Accounts*, 3rd edn Pitman Publishing 1992

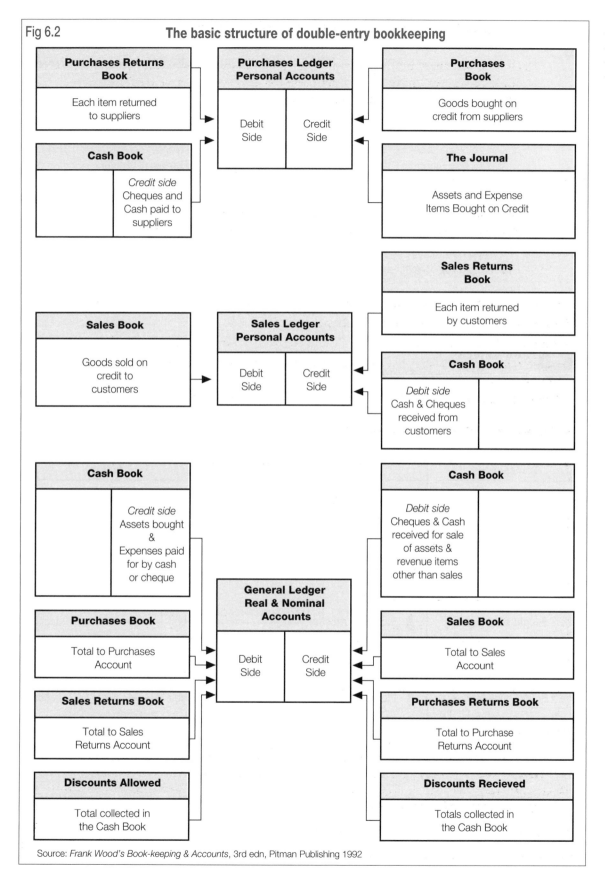

Fig 6.2 **The basic structure of double-entry bookkeeping**

Purchases Returns Book
Each item returned to suppliers

Cash Book
Credit side
Cheques and Cash paid to suppliers

Purchases Ledger Personal Accounts
Debit Side | Credit Side

Purchases Book
Goods bought on credit from suppliers

The Journal
Assets and Expense Items Bought on Credit

Sales Book
Goods sold on credit to customers

Sales Ledger Personal Accounts
Debit Side | Credit Side

Sales Returns Book
Each item returned by customers

Cash Book
Debit side
Cash & Cheques received from customers

Cash Book
Credit side
Assets bought & Expenses paid for by cash or cheque

Purchases Book
Total to Purchases Account

Sales Returns Book
Total to Sales Returns Account

Discounts Allowed
Total collected in the Cash Book

General Ledger Real & Nominal Accounts
Debit Side | Credit Side

Cash Book
Debit side
Cheques & Cash received for sale of assets & revenue items other than sales

Sales Book
Total to Sales Account

Purchases Returns Book
Total to Purchase Returns Account

Discounts Recieved
Totals collected in the Cash Book

Source: *Frank Wood's Book-keeping & Accounts*, 3rd edn, Pitman Publishing 1992

PC
6.1.1
6.3.2
6.3.3

DISCUSSION TOPICS

1 The two sides of Frank Wood's 'accounting equation': assets = capital + liabilities need to balance in the double-entry bookkeeping system.

What help does this necessity provide to the business owner in the effective running of his or her business?

2 Can you think of any advantages which might stem from managing a double-entry bookkeeping system by means of a computer software application? Would there be any disadvantages?

3 Is there a danger in a large business of its accountants becoming too preoccupied with the processing of number-based information, and too divorced from direct interactions with suppliers and customers?

4 Why do so many managing directors of limited companies have accounting backgrounds do you think? Do you consider that an accounting route is the most appropriate to achieve this type of post?

ASSIGNMENT 1

a) Using the examples of 'debiting and crediting' given on pages 499 and 500 complete the following transactions. Remember that each transaction has its own debit entry in one account and a credit entry in another, and most firms have many such accounts. Fill in the blanks. If you do not want to write in the book, make a photocopy and use that.

Transactions	Effect	Action
June 1 Started business by putting £35,000 in a business bank account	▲ Increases asset of ———— ▲ Increases capital of ————	Debit ———— account Credit ———— account
June 2 Bought shop paying £25,000 by cheque	▲ Increases asset of ———— ▼ Decreases asset of ————	Debit ———— account Credit ———— account
June 3 Bought shop fittings on credit from Jones Ltd costing £4,000	▲ Increases asset of ———— ▲ Increases liability of ————	Debit ———— account Credit ———— account
June 4 Withdrew £1,000 cash from bank	▲ Increases asset of ———— ▼ Decreases asset of ————	Debit ———— account Credit ———— account

Transactions	Effect	Action
June 5 Paid for shop equipment £800 in cash	▲ Increases asset of ——————— ▼ Decreases asset of ———————	Debit ——————— account Credit ——————— account
June 10 Bought a motor-van paying £6,000 by cheque	▲ Increases asset of ——————— ▼ Decreases asset of ———————	Debit ——————— account Credit ——————— account
June 12 Received £15,000 loan from X Bank plc	▲ Increases asset of ——————— ▲ Increases liability of ———————	Debit ——————— account Credit ——————— account
June 13 Paid Jones Ltd £4,000 owed for shop fittings	▼ Decreases liability of ——————— ▼ Decreases asset of ———————	Debit ——————— account Credit ——————— account

b) The following accounts relate to the above business. Using your responses in the 'Action' column make the required entries in the following accounts. (Note that in the 'Details' column you write the name of the other account involved in the transaction.)

Debit   BANK ACCOUNT   Credit

Date	Details	£	Date	Details	£
June 1			June 2		
June 12			June 4		
			June 10		
			June 13		

Debit   SHOP PREMISES ACCOUNT   Credit

Date	Details	£	Date	Details	£
June 2					

Debit   JONES LTD ACCOUNT   Credit

Date	Details	£	Date	Details	£
June 13			June 3		

Debit   SHOP EQUIPMENT ACCOUNT   Credit

Date	Details	£	Date	Details	£
June 5					

Debit   X BANK PLC ACCOUNT   Credit

Date	Details	£	Date	Details	£
			June 12		

Debit   CAPITAL ACCOUNT   Credit

Date	Details	£	Date	Details	£
			June 1		

Debit   SHOP FITTINGS ACCOUNT   Credit

Date	Details	£	Date	Details	£
June 3					

Debit   CASH ACCOUNT   **Credit**

Date	Details	£	Date	Details	£
June 4			June 5		

Debit   MOTOR-VAN ACCOUNT   **Credit**

Date	Details	£	Date	Details	£
June 6					

c) Having made all of your entries in the above accounts, you must now balance them off in order to find the value in each account. To do this leave a space after your last entry and using a ruler draw the 'total' lines. Add up both sides and write in the difference – the balance – that will make both sides add up to the same total. This balance could be either on the Credit side for assets or the Debit side for liabilities and capital.

Debit   BANK ACCOUNT   **Credit**

Date	Details	£	Date	Details	£
June 1	Capital	35,000	June 2	Shop premises	25,000
June 12	X Bank plc loan	15,000	June 4	Cash	1,000
			June 10	Motor-van	6,000
			June 13	Jones Ltd	4,000
			June 14	Balance c/fwd	14,000
		50,000			50,000
June 14	Balance b/fwd	14,000			

Notes

1 We have used June 14 as the date of the balance.
2 C/fwd means 'carried forward' and is often referred to as C/D meaning 'carried down'.
3 B/fwd means 'brought forward' and is often referred to as B/D meaning 'brought down'.
4 The brought forward balance of £14,000 for June 14 above is a debit balance. This means that the entries in the account prior to this date had £14,000 more on the debit side than on the credit side.

d) Having balanced all of your accounts, you should have produced the following balances:

Account	Debit balance	Credit balance
	£	£
Bank	14,000	
Capital		35,000
Shop premises	25,000	
Shop fittings	4,000	
Cash	200	
Shop equipment	800	
Motor-van	6,000	
X Bank plc loan		15,000
Totals	50,000	50,000

Note that the above list of balances is called a 'Trial Balance'. Each value column for Debit and Credit must add up to the same total. If an account has no balance at the balance date, it can be left out of the trial balance as was 'Jones Ltd' above.

ASSIGNMENT 2

Write out your own set of accounts to record the following transactions. When you have finished, balance off the accounts and draw up a trial balance in the same way as in Assignment 1.

July 1   Started business with £20,000 in a business bank account

July 2   Bought a lock-up garage for £10,000, paying by cheque

July 3   Bought tools costing £5,000 on credit from Tools Ltd

July 4   Bought a breakdown truck on credit costing £12,000 from Commercial Motors Ltd

July 5   Borrowed £8,000 from X Bank plc

July 8   Paid £5,000 by cheque to Tools Ltd

July 9   Withdrew £1,000 cash from Bank

July 10 Paid Commercial Motors Ltd £12,000 by cheque

DOCUMENTING CREDIT SALES

Most private sector organisations need to generate sales constantly in order to survive – hence the need for mail-order catalogues, calls by sales representatives, direct selling door-to-door or by phone and so on.

However, the most persistent and energetic sales efforts invariably prove futile if they are not accompanied by a well-designed and painstakingly monitored sales documentation system, which records each step of the sales process clearly and free from errors (as far as is humanly possible). Without such a system being in place and vigilantly monitored, a company can soon run into cash-flow problems and ultimately into bankruptcy, since its account customers may be encouraged to defer payment endlessly and to sell on goods wrongly priced in their favour and so on.

The chart in Fig 6.3 illustrates the main stages in the sales process which need to be documented in a sequence if the initial purchase order from an account customer is to be delivered and paid for within a previously agreed time-frame.

■ Eight key stages in documenting credit sales

1 Receiving the purchase order

Today customers order goods or services in a wide variety of ways: by phone (*not recommended – no written record*), by letter, or by mailing a purchase order with a unique reference (*much better*), by faxing a purchase order (*quicker than the post but more expensive*) and by electronic data interchange (EDI) – the buyer's computer 'talks' to the supplier's computer and orders goods directly; this expensive but fast ordering system is used by large manufacturers such as Ford UK Limited and Lucas plc.

Naturally enough, the key data on a purchase order will include the details shown in the following checklist.

KEY DATA ON A PURCHASE ORDER

- the purchaser's name and address for both delivery of the order and for the receipt of the associated accounts documentation (which may not be the same)
- name and address details of supplier, including any named person under 'for the attention of' who normally deals with such orders (to speed up the ordering process)
- date and accounting system references e.g. the purchase order number, say: JUN/1234/ABC
- quantity of items ordered: 100 cubic metres...
- key specification details: make, type, brand name, specifications, model number, unit price, extension price (i.e. total being ordered, reference to VAT rate payable etc.
- clear instructions on whether order is to be delivered or collected, or, if urgent, deadline date for delivery etc.

Fig 6.3   Sales documentation: manual system – monthly cycle

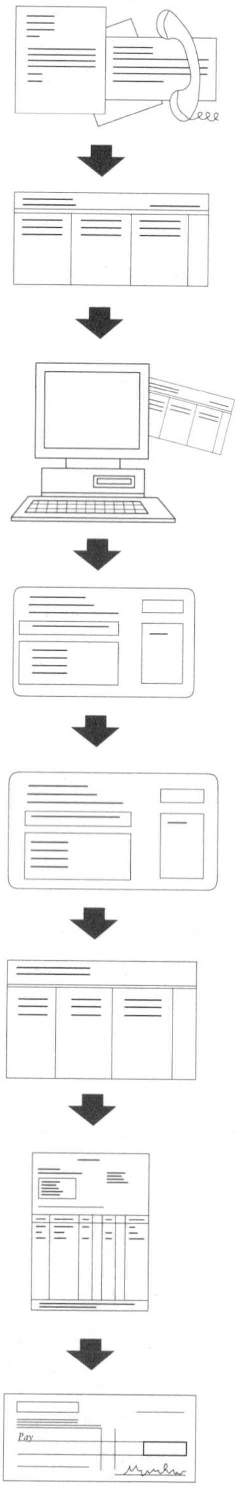

1   **Order received**
This may be by letter, telephone, fax or sales representative's order book

2   **Stores requisition raised**
This authorises the movement of the goods ordered from the warehouse to the dispatch department

3   **Stock record is amended**
The record may be kept on computer database or in a manual system using cards. The stock record is amended to show the reduced balance

4   **A sales invoice is issued**
The sales invoice shows the quantity and description of the goods supplied, price, customer's account number and the amount of VAT due

5   **A delivery/advice note is made out**
This is usually a copy of the invoice but without the pricing information. The delivery-man obtains a signature on one copy as evidence of receipt by the customer

6   **The transaction is recorded in the sales ledger or in the computer record**
The customer's account is brought up to date by adding the total of the invoice to the existing balance

a) **A credit note** is raised if the customer reports that the goods received are faulty or damaged in transit, and are returned to the supplier.

b) **A debit note** is raised if a pricing error is made on a sales invoice in favour of the customer in order to correct the pricing

7   **A statement of account is issued**
This is sent to the customer at the end of the trading period (usually monthly). The statement lists all invoices and credit notes raised during the month and shows the balance payable by the customer and the payment terms, discounts etc.

8   **The customer settles the account**
The customer sends a cheque with a remittance advice note. The payment will be entered in the sales ledger or computer record and the balance owing amended accordingly. Note: subsequent invoices will have been raised before the statement in 7 is due for payment

THE PROCESS BEGINS AGAIN

Most purchase orders indicate the agreed purchase price per item. This is normally the retail price before any deduction for discounts allowable, since such discounts are usually only shown at the later invoicing stage.

The examples shown in Fig 6.4 below illustrate two typical ways of organising the key data of a purchase order:

Fig 6.4 **Two styles of purchase order**

PC 6.1.2

PURCHASE ORDER Order No. 1079

BURGESS & SON
27 Frith Street
Birkenhead B21 3RZ

Tel: (0601) 41732 VAT Reg. No. 632 117381

Roberts Suppliers Co.
Liverpool Road
Liverpool

Date: 3rd Sept 199X

Quantity	Cat. No.	Description	Price
2	LM713	Easi-ride mowers complete with collection boxes Delivery included	£1,527.30 each plus VAT

PURCHASE ORDER Order No. KT27

RUDKINS SUPERSTORES
Market Place, Runcorn

Tel: 0631 233152

Roberts Suppliers Co.
Liverpool Road
Liverpool

27th August 199X

Please supply:	Price £
6 Garden Forks (Aluminium)	22.30 each
10 Wheelbarrows	67.95 each
2 x 24" Quickmow Machines (Electric) with cable	324.00 each
Will collect, please advise	Plus VAT

Source: *Frank Wood's Business Accounting AAT Student's Workbook*, Sheila Robinson, Pitman Publishing 1993

2 and 3 The stock requisition order and stock control system

Once a purchase order has been received by the supplier, the next stage is for a stock requisition order to be made out. This order gives authorisation for goods to be moved from the place where they are being stored (warehouse or stockroom) to dispatch (a point from which they may be loaded on to vans or lorries for delivery).

The stock control system (whether on paper cards or computer) maintains records of stock movements (of a given item) in and out and the current resulting balance of stock-in-hand.

The stock requisition order and stock control systems carry out these important functions:

- they enable a close record to be kept of levels of stock being held, thus ensuring that re-ordering takes place before a 'stock-out' situation arises where orders cannot be promptly met
- they help to prevent stock losses from pilferage, theft or unauthorised movement of goods
- they aid the tracking of goods ordered (if a customer calls to complain of non-delivery of ordered goods, their progress along the sales order/delivery chain can be monitored)

Fig 6.5

STOCK CONTROL CARD

DESCRIPTION	Grade A Tent Cloth (Gold)	BAY NO	13
		MAXIMUM	500 metres
CODE NO	60 TC A/G	MINIMUM	100 metres
		REORDER LEVEL	150 metres

| Date | Receipts | | Issues | | Balance in stock | Remarks Goods on Order and Audit check |
	Goods Rec'd Note No.	Quantity	Reqn. No.	Quantity		
199-		metres		metres	metres	
July 1					300	
" 4			734	100	200	
" 14			823	100	100	15/7 Order No. 97324
" 28	7629	200			300	

Minimum stock level reached

Re-ordering process activated

Source: Adapted from *Finance, First Levels of Competance*, John Harrison, Pitman Publishing 1990. By kind permission of the author

Fig 6.6

STORES REQUISITION FOR STOCK				NO. 734

MATERIALS REQUIRED FOR:

DATE ..4/7/9-....

JOB NO .... RUN NO ......4321..............

Quantity	Description	Price per unit		Cost		Notes
		£	p	£	p	
100 metres	Code No. 60 TC A/G Grade A Tent Cloth (Gold)					

Works Foreman ....P. hong..............	Storekeepers Initials	Cost Office Ref:
Operative ....J. Hills........................	....	....

Source: *Clerical Accounting*, J Harrison & R Dawber, Pitman Publishing 1976

Note that, today, most medium to large firms have their sales systems fully computerised. A computerised system will ensure that, once a purchase order has been entered (into an integrated accounting software system), the stock control details and requisition authorisation will be automatically passed on to the stock-room personnel and the appropriate deductions made to stock levels and printout documents raised etc. The advantages of an integrated computerised accounting system include:

■ fewer data entries, therefore less risk of error

■ faster administration resulting in customers' orders being delivered and recorded much more quickly

■ fewer sheets of paper clogging the administrative system.

4 The delivery/ advice note

PC 6.1.3

Once authorisation has been given for the goods ordered to be moved, they are taken to the organisation's dispatch point. In the case of a regional warehouse servicing a national supermarket chain, this is likely to be a covered (secure) area with loading bays raised some 1 – 1.5 metres above ground level to allow pallets to be loaded directly on to backed-up articulated lorries by means of fork-lift trucks. In a book distribution company, goods which comprise various books ordered by booksellers are first 'picked' by staff moving along shelving set out in a computerised sequence of book sets, and then packed into cardboard boxes for moving to despatch, where a national carrier collects them and delivers them according to a route masterminded (again!) by a computer.

In order to ensure that security requirements are satisfied and to obtain a record of

Fig 6.7 **Examples of sales invoices**

Account customer's address →

OFFICE SUPPLIES CO.
Market Place,
Knutsford

Invoice No. 012040 ← Unique invoice number

Date 13th June 199X

Quantity	Details	Cat No.	Unit Price	£
4	Euroline Waste Bins	0243 X	4.75	19.00
6	Magazine Files	0868 F	2.25	13.50
100	PVC Clear Binding Covers (packed 100)	40321	30.00	30.00
2pkts	Fibre Tip 330 pens Wallet of 10	21470	4.24	8.48
1 pkt	Traditional Pencils	1185 X	2.69	2.69
				73.67
			Add VAT	12.89

Combined total before addition of VAT

← VAT levied

Supplier's VAT registration number →

VAT No. 527 8843 67 £ 86.56 ← Total payable

HOMERS DIY Invoice No: P. 1083
Sandbach Date: 9th June 199X

VAT 279 6689 43

Quantity	Description	Cat No.	Unit Cost	Total Cost
2	Tine Gyrostar VAT	57061	4.20	8.40
				1.47
			£	9.87

THANK YOU FOR YOUR CUSTOM

CHESHIRE GARAGES Invoice No: P. 279
Knutsford
Chesire Date: 3rd June 199X

VAT 420 8163 66

Customer:	£
SUBARU Remove timing covers & faulty timing belts & fit two new ones.	60.34
Labour Charges	35.00
	95.34
Add VAT	16.68
	112.02

Four Wheel Drive Specialists

HEATH MFR CO LTD Invoice No: B. 39766
Knutsford Road
Chesire Date: 16th June 199X

To supplying Parts to your Drawing No. ZS 37/5441	357.70
VAT	60.20
£	417.90

VAT 863 2730 33

SEDDON & SONS (Painters & Decorators) 79
Northern Road, Middlewich 24/6/9X

To Decorating office and reception area including supply of materials	£
As per quotation	525.00
VAT	91.87
	616.87

Source: Adapted from *Frank Wood's Business Accounting AAT Student's Workbook,* Sheila Robinson, Pitman Publishing 1993

prompt delivery, most suppliers provide the delivery driver with an advice or delivery note for the receiving customer to sign. This note provides the same information as the purchase order (unless some goods on the order are omitted because they are out of stock, in which case this fact will be advised under a reference like: 'to follow'), and is, to all intents and purposes, a version of the invoice to come but with all pricing details omitted. The omission of such details is to prevent confidential buying terms from becoming common knowledge and perhaps being leaked to the customer's competitors.

While the delivery driver may only want to obtain his signatures and date (in order to speed off to his next drop, the prudent receiver of the goods is well advised to check all deliveries for breakage or damage in transit before accepting delivery (which may limit his ability to obtain recompense for goods later found to be faulty). Often, the receiver – especially in a small business – is occupied with customers when a delivery occurs, and so signs for the delivery with the added reservation: 'goods received uninspected' in order to reserve the right to return faulty goods and thus to obtain a credit note for them.

5 The invoice

Before examining the invoicing stage of account sales documentation, it is important to recall that, before any account sales transactions are begun, a business supplier will have obtained satisfactory financial references (from, say, a would-be account customer's bankers or other existing suppliers). The supplier of goods or services on account will then have agreed a ceiling amount for orders placed within any trading period (four weeks, a calendar month etc.), as well as the period of credit extension (for example 30 days) immediately following the receipt by the account customer of the statement relating to goods purchased in a given trading period. In this way an account customer is expected (under the terms of the agreed credit given) to pay for goods delivered say, during March by the end of April. Note that during periods of rapidly rising inflation or when high interest rates make money 'dear', traders may shorten significantly the length of credit time given to account customers.

The examples shown in Fig 6.7 provide some typical examples of current invoicing layouts.

Just as for a purchase order, there are a number of key data entries required on a sales invoice in order for it to prove an effective accounts document.

KEY DATA ON A SALES INVOICE

- the customary postal address details for both supplier and customer
- the account customer's unique account number
- a unique reference number for each individual invoice (for ease of later reference or query); note that some invoices also include a reference to the trading period in which they were issued
- entries for: quantity and description (model, make, specification etc.) of the goods
- a catalogue or goods stock number if appropriate
- the gross (i.e. retail or pre-discount price) price of a single good – its unit price
- the extended price of the total number of goods of an identical type ordered (for example 3 × Gardenade Rustless Wheelbarrows)
- an entry for the combined total value of the goods appearing on the invoice (Total: £149.99) before the addition of VAT

PC
6.1.3

- an entry showing the deduction of agreed discounts – for example 'Less 30% trade discount... £130.50'
- an entry for the VAT (at its current rate, say, 17.5%) in £s to be added to the invoice total
- the unique VAT registration number of the supplier: e.g. VAT 863 2730 33

Note: In some account sales transactions the deduction of any allowed discounts is taken from the payment due for an issued monthly statement; this practice keeps the details of net buying terms confidential – between the accountants of the supplier and accounts customer.

PC
6.1.1
6.3.2

■ Posting credit sales to the sales ledger

1 The credit sales are posted, one by one, to the debit side of each customer's account in the sales ledger.

2 At the end of each period the total of the credit sales is posted to the credit of the sales account in the general ledger.

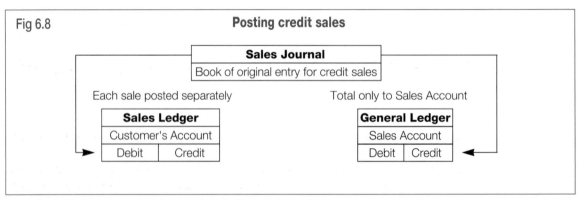

Fig 6.8 — **Posting credit sales**

Source: *Frank Wood's Book-keeping & Accounts,* 3rd edn, Pitman Publishing 1992

PC
6.3.3

Fig 6.9 — **Example of posting credit sales**

Sales Journal

			Invoice No	Folio	(page 26) £
199X					
Sept	1	D Poole	16554	SL 12	560
"	8	T Cockburn	16555	SL 39	1,640
"	28	C Carter	16556	SL 125	200
"	30	D Stevens & Co	16557	SL 249	1,100
		Transferred to Sales Account		GL 44	3,520

Source: *Frank Wood's Book-keeping & Accounts,* 3rd edn, Pitman Publishing 1992

6 The sales ledger entry

Just as documents need to be raised to provide records of delivery and pricing details for credit customers, so they need to be entered into the supplier's accounting system – in this case into the sales ledger – before being passed on in summary form (via sales journal or sales returns books) to the nominal or general ledger.

In the accounting system, it is the sales ledger which records against individual account sales customers' entries the financial details of goods sold to them on credit (in the left-hand Dr column) and payments received for goods purchased by them (in the right-hand Cr column:

Fig 6.10

				SALES LEDGER				
Dr				Halshaw Printing Co. A/c		SL1	Cr	
Date		Fol	£	Date		Fol	£	
31 July	Balance	b/d	117.90	13 July	Bank	CB7	57.90	

Source: *Frank Wood's Business Accounting AAT Student's Workbook*, Sheila Robinson, Pitman Publishing 1993

In this way, the supplier maintains careful records of what is owed and what is paid for at any time for any account customer.

The details of each invoice issued will be retained on a sales ledger card (or its computerised equivalent) in order to enable the monthly statement to be compiled, printed and delivered.

6A and B Credit and Debit Notes

Sometimes, despite every effort to avoid them, mistakes occur, or goods prove faulty at the delivery stage. For example, a clerical error may result in 21 and not 12 identical stock items being charged for on an invoice. This mistake, having been picked up by a vigilant accounts clerk or sales assistant, is pointed out to the supplier, who therefore needs to rectify it by reducing the items charged for by 9. Such a transaction is accomplished by the issue of a credit note for the amount. In order for the sum involved to be credited (so as to prevent any ensuing overpayment by the account customer) the sum will also be shown as a credit in the Cr column of the monthly statement and be deducted from the gross total amount shown as due for payment. Note also that when credit notes are issued, there will be a corresponding reduction due in the amount of VAT payable.

When, on the other hand, a mistake occurs in the account customer's favour – perhaps this time spotted by an equally alert accounts clerk working for the supplier, then a debit note is issued in the same way as for its credit note counterpart. The debit note amount will also be clearly shown on the relevant statement as an extra item of expenditure incurred.

Both credit and debit notes will supply cross-references to the issued invoices to which they refer.

E & OE: Errors and Omissions Excepted

In order to enable mistakes in arithmetic or textual reference to be rectified at a later date, many firms include the abbreviation E&OE at the foot of their account sales documents (invoices, credit/debit notes and statements) so as to avoid a customer claiming that the issued document represented a firm, contractual price for goods received and accepted.

7 Statements of account

A statement of account is 'rendered' or sent to each account customer on a regular basis. Usually, the basis employed requires that statements are sent to account customers a week to a fortnight after the end of the trading period, say, four weeks or a calendar month, to which they refer. The reason for this particular timing is two-fold:

Batch runs of computerised statements

First, suppliers need some time after the closing of the trading period to produce (usually on computer by means of an integrated accounts software package) the summary details (the invoice references and billed totals) of all the invoices relating to a single customer's account on to the statement, including any issued credit or debit notes. In large companies, the calculations for each statement and the statements themselves – which may run into thousands – are processed in a series of batches through the computer, starting with customers' trading names A–E and so on. Naturally this takes some time to achieve, added to which is the time taken for statements to arrive through the post.

Customer checks on statements received

By the same token, customers' accounts departments need some time to check that the statements' details and totals coincide with their own records (in their purchase ledgers) before authorisation is given for the account to be paid. This can mean cross-checking each received invoice against the statement manually in many small businesses – hence the need for strict care and attention to be paid to delivery acceptance procedures. In larger firms, the computer handles much of this work and concentration is paid to reconciling totals – the statement's total, minus and credit notes raised for goods returned, plus any debit note amounts which rectify suppliers' errors.

Settlement discounts

In order to assist the prompt payment of an account within the agreed settlement period (for example: *twenty-eight days after the end of the related trading period*) suppliers often include at the foot of a statement a calculation of a settlement discount which the customer may deduct from the bill if payment is made within, say, the stipulated twenty-eight days:

Total:	£1545:55
Less Settlement Discount 3.75%	£ 57:95
Nett:	£1487:60

Note that in times of high inflation suppliers tend to shorten the settlement time for accounts to be paid and increase the 'carrot' of settlement discount deductible (which is probably built into the agreed account sales price terms in the first place!)

The following example illustrates what a typical statement looks like:

Fig 6.11

STATEMENT OF ACCOUNT

STARCELL OFFICE SUPPLIES

UNIT 8 HANDYWELL INDUSTRIAL ESTATE, NORTHTOWN NO6 IEU

Tel: 039 843 3291   Telex: 986243   Fax: 039 2196743

VAT Registration No. 2538758 32

Date: 31 March 199X

To: Pitman Publishing
     128 Long Acre
     London WC2E 9AN

Terms; 5% 7 days
2½ 28 days
Otherwise net

Date 199-	Details	Ref No.	Dr £	Cr £	Balance £
1 Feb	To account rendered Jan				460.27
9 Feb	To invoice	10862	103.80		564.07
12 Feb	By credit note	566		24.20	539.87
15 Feb	To invoice	10876	91.40		631.27
23 Feb	To debit note	195	11.60		642.87
28 Feb	To invoice	10933	84.32		727.19
28 Feb	By cheque			500.00	227.19
	Amount outstanding				227.19

E & O E

Statements and overdue accounts

Some companies take the opportunity on monthly statements to draw attention to any invoices which remain unpaid from earlier trading periods. Also, if payment proves tardy, copy statements may be sent to slow-paying customers as the first of a series of strategies aimed at securing overdue payment for goods or services sold on account. If this proves ineffective, then the accounts department will activate its debtors' collection system (usually 2–3 letters in total), which tend to culminate in terse warnings such as:

> ...*Unless payment is received within seven days of the receipt of this letter,* [which is sent by recorded delivery] *the company will have no hesitation in taking legal actions to recover the debt.*

Such sentiments represent the final effort to recover an overdue debt, when retaining the customer's goodwill is no longer deemed necessary, since once payment has been received, the account will be closed.

Age analysis of debtors

An important part of the management of credit sales is to keep a watchful eye on the time taken by account customers to pay for goods or services received. Failure to collect monies due can quickly lead to cash-flow problems and, if the business is heavily reliant upon account sales, to crises. It is common practice, therefore, for an age analysis of credit sales debts to be undertaken – preferably automatically by an accounts package computer program, or manually from the sales ledger.

PC
6.3.3

8 Remittance advice and cheque in payment

Having received the supplier's statement and checked it out against its own internal purchase account documentation, payment is authorised by accounts and a remittance advice note raised detailing precisely what payment is being made for, along with a cheque (crossed a/c payee for security) for the agreed amount.

The account sales cycle begins again ...

By the time the payment has been received, recorded and processed, it will not be long before it is once more time to batch and run the statements for the succeeding month's sales...!

PC
6.1.3
6.3.3

DISCUSSION TOPICS

1 What dangers exist for a business which has, say, 75 per cent of its turnover in credit sales?

2 What parts of the credit sales process can you think of (or add to) which help to make the 'sale on account' a financially safe and secure transaction for the seller involved?

3 Do you think that legislation is needed to ensure that firms pay for the goods or services they have bought on credit within a set time? Note that at present many firms deliberately hold back on payments due in order to assist their own cash flow etc.

ACTIVITIES

In groups of two or three, carry out one of the following activities and report back suitably to your class:

1 Draw up a flow chart (relating to a medium-sized company) which shows the sequence of actions taken in order to process a credit sale from start to finish, including the activities of the salesperson, the accounts staff, and the stockroom and delivery personnel. Indicate which documents are issued at each stage, and which department or section receives which top or copy item.

When you have completed your flow chart, copy it to other groups in your class and hold a discussion to see how it might be improved so as to cut down on activities and time taken without sacrificing reliability and security.

2 Find out what legal support a company can rely upon when seeking to recover debts owing from a 'bad account customer' who refuses to pay for goods or services received.

Design a factsheet to record your findings and circulate it around your class.

ASSIGNMENT 3

Alan Thornton & Co. made the following credit sales and returns during the month of February.

Feb 1	Credit sales	F Pickle	£100
Feb 5	Credit sales	S Plank	£125
Feb 9	Returns	F Pickle	£10
Feb 15	Credit sales	P Oak	£75
Feb 20	Returns	P Oak	£15
Feb 23	Credit sales	A Mahmood	£95
Feb 25	Credit sales	C Greaves	£85
Feb 27	Credit sales	A Mahmood	£45
Feb 28	Credit sales	P Oak	£65

All of the above figures need to have VAT charged to them at the rate of 17½% before invoicing. No payments were received during February.

Task 1
Enter the above transactions in a Sales Day Book and a Sales Return Book.

Task 2
Enter the above in the accounts provided below, properly balancing each account at the end of the month and bringing forward the balance at 1 March.

SALES LEDGER

F Pickle A/c	S Plank A/c	P Oak A/c
Feb 1 Bal B/fwd 100		

A Mahmood A/c	C Greaves A/c
	Feb 1 Bal b/fwd 10

Task 3

Open any accounts you see fit in the General Ledger and make the appropriate entries.

Task 4

Advise Alan Thornton as to a suitable credit collection system so that you may receive payment for your goods as efficiently and quickly as possible.

Task 5

Would you treat cash sales any differently in the books? If so, how?

REVIEW TEST

1 List five key purposes of a business accounting system.

2 Write down the accounting equation upon which the double-entry bookkeeping system is based.

3 Set down the table which illustrates the key rules of debiting and crediting account entries which increase or decrease: assets, liabilities and capital.

4 State what debit and credit actions you would take if your business purchased a motor-van for cash which cost £180.

5 What information is stored in books of original entry?

6 List the books which make up the full set of books of original entry.

7 List the ledgers commonly used in the double-entry accounting system.

8 Explain briefly the difference between a personal and an impersonal account.

9 What is a private ledger?

10 Set down the main steps in the processing of a credit sale and list the accounting documents involved at each step.

DOCUMENTING PURCHASES

At the outset of this section it is worth remembering that, in an accounting context, both the sales and purchasing processes are closely connected in that the supplier's sale is the customer's purchase. And so the information you have now acquired about the sequence of account sales documents will stand you in good stead during the following examination of purchase-related documents.

Figure 6.12 illustrates the monthly cycle through which purchases are documented and paid for.

Fig 6.12 **The monthly cycle of purchases documentation**

1 Completion and dispatch of a Purchase Order

When goods or services are required, a numbered Purchase Order is completed and sent to the specified supplier

2 Delivery Note and Invoice for goods recieved

The goods delivered are checked against the delivery note's contents and the delivery is recorded on a goods received note; when the invoice arrives, prices (and discounts) are checked against established trading terms

3 The Purchases Day Book

Arriving invoices are entered into a summary Purchases Day Book which records: date, details, purchase account folio (of the purchases ledger) for the supplier concerned; invoice number and total value; also a VAT column records VAT sums which may be reclaimed if the goods represent business input costs

4 The Purchases Ledger

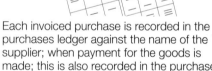

Each invoiced purchase is recorded in the purchases ledger against the name of the supplier; when payment for the goods is made; this is also recorded in the purchases ledger and balances carried forward. Note: details of any credit or debit notes issued are also posted to the appropriate purchase account folio

5 The General Ledger – Purchases and VAT Accounts

Totals of purchases from suppliers and VAT totals are posted to the General Account on a monthly basis

6 The Purchases Ledger Control Account

The totals of purchases made within a given trading period are entered (for each supplier) in the Purchases Ledger Control Account as a means of checking and reconciling them to the statements from suppliers as they arrive. Note that balances on the Purchase Ledgers and Control Account should always agree.

■ 1 Drawing up and despatching the purchase order

Most organisations have established procedures which preface the drawing up of a purchase order. These usually involve obtaining estimates or quotations (if goods are priced below an agreed ceiling, or going out to tender if goods (or services) exceed, say, a four-figure sum.

Once it has been satisfactorily established that a potential purchase is available from a given supplier at an acceptable price, then the purchase order may be drawn up for the signature of a manager or director with the assigned authority.

The key data comprising a purchase order is shown on page 509.

■ 2 The delivery and goods received notes

The ordered goods will arrive in due course and the supplier's driver will require a signature on his delivery note as proof of safe delivery. In turn, the recipient of the goods will make out a goods received note for the assistance of the appropriate accounts, purchasing and stockroom staff, each of whom will require such information as part of their record-keeping systems.

■ 3 The purchases day book

Every day, in medium to large organisations, hundreds of invoices arrive in twice-daily postal deliveries to accounts departments. These invoices may relate to stock purchases, stationery supplies, laundry costs for overalls, the redecoration of branch premises and so on.

In order to create some order out of the multi-coloured, multi-sized bunch of newly arrived invoices, they are carefully entered into a purchases day book (Fig 6.13).

Fig 6.13

PURCHASES DAY BOOK						
Date	Details	Folio	Invoice	Total	Goods	VAT
Nov 1	Bould & Co. Motor oil	C1	SR2103	104.26	88.75	15.51
" 3	Hambleton's: Sparking plugs	C12	SR2114	140.57	119.63	20.94
" 7	Monktons Ltd: Swarfega	C24	SR2123	29.14	24.80	4.34

The purchases day book ensures that a prompt and accurate detail is kept of the essential details of all incoming invoices:

- date of arrival
- invoice details, i.e. name of supplier and details of goods
- purchase ledger folio reference of supplier concerned
- the organisation's unique purchase order number
- the combined total value of the invoice (goods and VAT)
- the total value of the goods excluding VAT
- the VAT total for the goods supplied

The purchases day book entries may then be posted to the purchases ledger. Note that daily totals need only be posted to the purchases and VAT accounts, and that some firms organise their purchases day books to reflect their principal purchase areas (Fig 6.14).

Fig 6.14

PC
6.1.2

	Date	Supplier	Inv. No.	A/c No.	Total	Electrical	Motor	Office	Telephone	Sundries	VAT
	A	B	C	D	E	F	G	H	I	J	K

PURCHASES DAY BOOK

Example of a purchase requisition

PURCHASE REQUISITION

THE BODY SHOP

Date:................... 17 AUGUST 1993 ....

Raised By:........ G RAINHAM .... Dept:...... MATERIALS ......

DELIVERY DETAILS:

Suggested Supplier's Name: (address if applicable):
.... MIMICK MANUFACTURING ....
.... MANCHESTER ....

Purchase Order No.: (if apllicable):........ 570157 ....

SPECIAL PACKAGING/LABELLING:

Confirmation Order: Yes [X]   No [ ]

FOR ANY SINGLE CAPITAL ITEM OVER £250 A CAPITAL
EXPENDITURE PROPOSAL FORM IS REQUIRED.

Delivery Date:........ ASAP ....

N/L CODE	QUANTITY	FULL PRODUCT DESCRIPTION	STOCK CODE	UNIT PRICE	TOTAL (excl VAT)
022-476-002-30	2	CENTRIS 610E 4/80			
		(INCLUDING 2 X 14" COLOUR SCREENS			
		FROM RESERVED STOCK)		956.00	1,912.00
		Note			
		This requisition is produced in a			
		set of three attached copies,			
		colour-coded white, pink, and			
		blue (for distribution) and			
		employs NCR technology			

SPECIAL INSTRUCTIONS TO PURCHASING DEPT:

Authorised Signatory:... Date:....... 18/8/93 ....

Courtesy of Body Shop Supply Company

Fig 6.16

Example of a purchase order

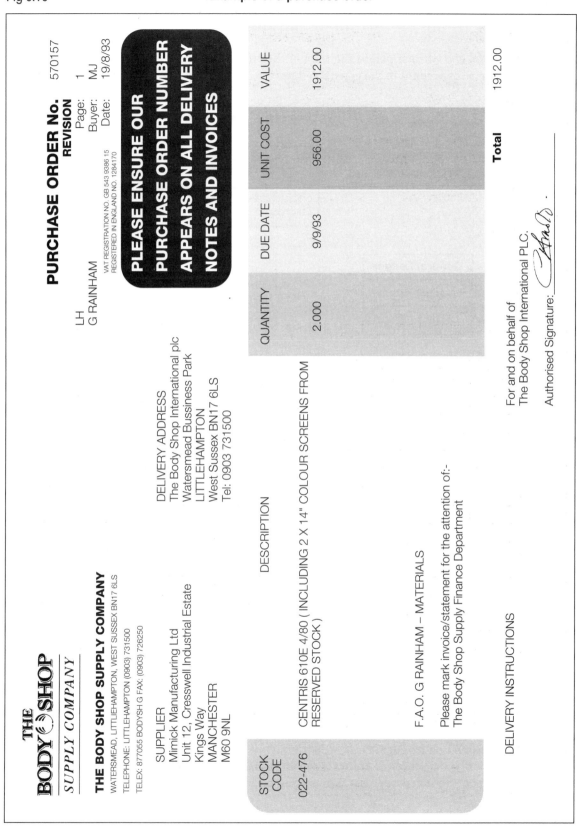

Courtesy of Body Shop Supply Company

Posting credit purchases to the purchases ledger

1 The credit purchases are posted one by one, to the credit of each supplier's account in the purchases ledger.

2 At the end of each period the total of the credit purchases is posted to the debit of the purchases account in the general ledger.

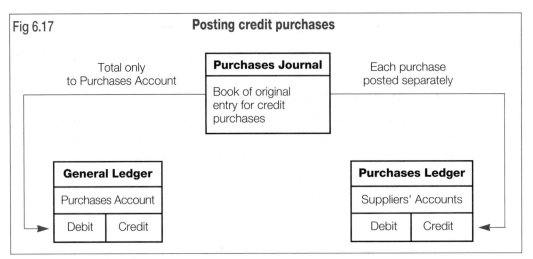

Fig 6.17   **Posting credit purchases**

Source: *Frank Wood's Book-keeping & Accounts,* 3rd edn, Pitman Publishing 1992

Fig 6.18   **Example of posting credit purchases**

Purchases Journal			
	Invoice No	Folio	(page 49)
199X			£
Sept 2 R Simpson	9/101	PL16	670
8 B Hamilton	9/102	PL29	1,380
19 C Brown	9/103	PL55	120
30 K Gabriel	9/104	PL89	510
Transferred to purchases account		GL63	2,680

Source: *Frank Wood's Book-keeping & Accounts,* 3rd edn, Pitman Publishing 1992

■ 4 The purchases ledger

The purchases ledger includes the details of purchase transactions with a company's suppliers in the form of summarised financial data extracted from invoices, credit and debit notes received, together with any amendments needed to remedy any input errors.

A data source for the nominal ledger

Also, the purchase ledger provides a source of data needed for the purchases and purchases returns accounts in the nominal ledger (in which are recorded general summaries of income and expenditure of a business – rents received, sales, purchases returns, incoming fees, dividends etc., and also wages, heat and light, purchases, sales returns and so on.

Documents generated from purchase ledger data

Other accounting operations (and their documentation) which derive from purchase ledger entries include:

- summarising monthly purchases per supplier
- producing data for the purchase control account as a means of preparing to reconcile incoming suppliers' statements against in-house purchasing records
- producing the documentation relating to the payment of goods purchased on account
- remittance advices, cheques and cash book entries for goods paid for by cash
- management accounting information in the form of reports or analyses of purchases

■ 5 and 6 The nominal ledger and purchase control account

PC
6.1.2

The purpose of the general ledger (sometimes also referred to as the nominal ledger) is to record in summary form those transactions which go to make up the income and expenditure activities of a business's operations – sales, purchases, income or profits from various sources, running expenses, and so on. This ledger also holds details of the company's assets and liabilities.

In terms of purchase transactions, the nominal ledger holds summary details of the purchase control (or creditors') account for ease of reference, unencumbered by masses of detailed, daily purchase transactions such as receiving and cross-checking the details of delivery notes, invoices, debit and credit notes and statements etc.

■ Summary

The accounts documents which record the sales and purchasing operations of a business form in essence its lifeblood, circulating as they do around each month's trading period. So important is it to exercise control over both the sales and purchasing operations that larger firms employ accounting personnel called cost and management accountants, whose primary role is to set up systems which provide regular reports on sales and purchasing activities such as:

- sales to target charts (weekly, monthly, quarterly, annually)
- break-downs on costs of sales – direct and indirect costs attributable, including the purchase of stock and contribution to overheads.
- trading and profit and loss accounts – to monitor profitability, which will include the cost of goods and services purchased

A natural follow-on from documenting sales and purchasing operations is, of course, to record just as carefully the resultant flow of cash and other forms of money in and out of the business, and this topic is examined in the next section.

PC
6.1.2
6.1.3

DISCUSSION TOPICS

1 What advantages to a business do you consider stem from setting up a centralised purchasing department and system?

2 The practice of pilferage and petty theft – in the form of taking home items of office stationery, small items of office equipment, products manufactured, pirated copies of computer software applications etc. has been considered by some employees in organisations as part of the 'perks which go with the job'.

What types of security checks and processes can you think of which an accounts (and other involved departments) manager could introduce into a purchasing process to minimise endemic petty theft?

3 'One organisation's sale is another's purchase.' Can you think of any ways in which an ongoing supplier–customer relationship could be streamlined so as to simplify and speed up the credit sale/purchase process for both parties?

ACTIVITIES

In pairs, carry out one of the following activities:

1 Make arrangements to visit the accounts department of a medium to large local firm so as to obtain an expert briefing on how the credit sales and purchasing accounting operations are carried out in practice.

Give your class an (authorised) oral briefing of about 10 minutes.

2 Make arrangements to visit the offices of a company purchasing manager and find out what makes up his or her job role.

Report back to your class with an oral briefing of about 10 minutes.

3 Find out if any local companies in your locality (likely to be manufacturers) are using the electronic data interchange (EDI) system to manage their purchasing from suppliers.

If so, make arrangements to obtain a briefing from the manager responsible on how the system works and what advantages it possesses. If no local operation is on hand, research into the subject with the help of your school/college/public reference library.

Brief your class orally (with illustrations) on what you discover in about 10 minutes.

REVIEW TEST

1 What key data would you expect to find on a typical purchase order?

2 How does a delivery note differ from an invoice?

3 List the key data you would expect to find on a typical credit sale invoice.

4 Set down a typical entry for an individual account customer's purchase of goods in a sales ledger.

5 Explain the difference between a credit note and a debit note and how they affect the statement to which they relate.

6 What does E & OE stand for? What is it used for in credit sales documentation?

7 Why are credit sales statements batch run through the computer in a large business?

8 What is a settlement discount and what is its purpose?

9 What is a letter of collection? How is it used in the documentation of accounts?

10 What is meant by 'age analysis of debtors'. How does this concept impact upon an accounting system?

11 Why do firms send remittance advice notes with cheques paying for goods or services received?

12 List five advantages of employing an integrated accounts software application package to process a company's accounts.

13 What is meant by EDI? How does it assist the accounting process?

14 List the key steps in sequence of a credit purchase and state which document is used at which step.

15 What is the purpose of a purchases day book? What information does it record?

ASSIGNMENT 4

Alan Thornton & Co. made the following credit purchases and returns during the month of February.

Feb 2	Credit purchases	K Hoyle	£60 (inc. £8.94 VAT)
Feb 6	Returns	M Leake	£10 (inc. £1.49 VAT)
Feb 9	Credit purchases	P Horton	£60 (inc. £8.94 VAT)
Feb 16	Credit purchases	N Clayton	£125 (inc. £18.62 VAT)
Feb 18	Credit purchases	P Horton	£50 (inc. £7.45 VAT)
Feb 21	Returns	N Clayton	£25 (inc. £3.72 VAT)
Feb 24	Credit purchases	K Hoyle	£50 (inc. £7.45 VAT)
Feb 26	Credit purchases	N Clayton	£45 (inc. £6.70 VAT)
Feb 27	Credit purchases	G Wood	£35 (inc. £5.21 VAT)

No payments were made during February.

Task 1

Enter the above transactions in a Purchases Day Book and Purchases Returns Book.

Task 2

Enter the above in the accounts provided below, properly balancing each account at the end of the month and bring forward the balance at 1 March.

PURCHASES LEDGER

K Hoyle A/c	M Leake A/c	P Horton A/c
	Feb 1 Bal b/fwd 10	

N Clayton A/c	G Wood A/c
	Feb 1 Bal b/fwd 85

Task 3

Open any accounts you see fit in the General Ledger and make the appropriate entries.

Task 4

Would you treat cash purchases any differently in the books? If so, how?

Task 5

How do the purchase order, the delivery note and the goods received note relate to the purchase invoice?

PC
6.1.4
6.1.5

PAYMENTS AND RECEIPTS DOCUMENTS

In most businesses, payment for goods or services received is made either by cash or cheque. And it is upon these two forms of income that this section concentrates.

However, it should not be overlooked that payment for goods or services can take other forms than cash or cheque (see checklist)

■ Processing cash and cheques

During the course of daily trading a host of organisations large and small – supermarkets, newsagents, football clubs, leisure centres, departmental stores, market stallholders etc. – accept both cash and cheques as payments for goods or services sold.

Accepting cash today may seem the least of a businessman's problems, except that counterfeit money is increasingly in circulation, and many firms pass notes through scanning machines especially designed to identify counterfeit notes.

Similarly, clearing banks circulate among bona fide traders details of chequebooks and cheque guarantee/credit cards recently stolen in order to minimise the effects of cheque fraud. Currently the clearing banks undertake to honour cheques issued by their customers to whom they have supplied a cheque guarantee card up to amounts of either £50 or £100, and the appropriate amount is shown clearly on the customer's card.

Paying into the bank

Prudent business proprietors and branch managers pay their takings of cash and cheques into their banks daily by means of a night safe facility and a paying-in book. This avoids the need to keep money overnight in empty premises.

Nevertheless, businesses such as departmental stores with large daily turnovers still feel it worthwhile to purchase a safe into which to transfer takings hourly from their various sections and floors, and to make regular daily deposits at the nearest branch of the company's bank.

■ Recording and processing money paid in to the business

Each organisation evolves its own system for receiving, recording and banking money flowing into the business. In the following section the major stages in a typical system are illustrated.

KEY STAGES IN RECEIVING, RECORDING AND BANKING INCOMING MONIES

■ 1 In the small business

Cash sales

When a cash sale transaction takes place, customers are provided with a written/till receipt detailing the item(s), cost and VAT (if applicable). The small trader retains a copy of the receipt (note that most cash registers record and analyse all transactions to aid cashing up at the end of daily trading.

The coins, notes and cheques received in payment are kept in a cash register (till) until the end of the day's trading. They are then totalled and after leaving aside for the next day a 'float' or small amount of mixed coins and notes for change etc. the total money taken during the day is entered on a Takings Summary Form (Fig 6.19)

Fig 6.19

TAKINGS SUMMARY FORM			
ASSISTANT'S NAME _Peter Jones_		DATE	4-5-9X
			£
1	Opening Float		15.90
2	Total of Payments Rec'd Analysis Sheet (re: Customers' Accounts)		245.25
3	Total of Cash/Cheque Petrol Receipts		642.80
	TOTAL	£	903.95
4	Deduct Opening Float		15.90
	TOTAL AMOUNT TAKEN	£	888.05
ANALYSIS OF CASH/CHEQUES			
Cheques Total			392.15
Cash Total			495.90
		£	888.05
DISCREPANCIES (if any)			

Source: Adapted from *Frank Wood's Business Accounting AAT Student's Workbook,* Sheila Robinson, Pitman Publishing 1993

Some small businesses, say a garage family business, may use a payments received analysis sheet on a daily basis to record the payment (by individual invoice) of, for example, a service to a delivery van. Since payment has been either by cash or cheque, such transactions need to be set down separately and by account customer (Fig 6.20).

Fig 6.20

PC
6.1.5

PAYMENTS RECEIVED ANALYSIS SHEET				Date 10-5-9X
Customer	Total amount received £	By cash £	By cheque £	Invoice No.
B. Simpson	14.62	14.62		06931
Ace Taxis	32.50		32.50	06932
K. Stone	7.00	7.00		
H White & Son (Builders)	24.95		24.95	0693
TOTALS	£ 245.25	£ 86.20	£ 159.05	

Source: Adapted from *Frank Wood's Business Accounting AAT Student's Workbook*, Sheila Robinson, Pitman Publishing 1993

Accounts documents and audit trails

Such an analysis sheet provides a record of individual payments of account and may also serve as a source document in any audit trail. The audit trail is a documented system or route through which an accounting activity may be checked, so as to ensure that each step in the accounting process is error-free.

For example, should an account payment cheque become mislaid prior to being banked, the fact that it was received is evident on the payments received analysis sheet. Both internal accountants, a company's chartered accountants and the Inland Revenue may need to sample a company's accounting systems and procedures by using the audit trail approach in order to be satisfied that the summarised totals on, say, a trading and profit and loss account are correct. This is especially the case when a firm makes extensive use of a computerised accounts package.

Paying money into the bank

Once the day's takings have been summarised and details noted of any account payments made, the cash and cheque takings (less the float) may be banked. It is good practice to use a night safe, money pouch/sack and plastic coin bags (provided by the bank) in order to deposit a day's takings in the bank' vaults rather than in a shop or filling-station till etc.

The clearing banks provide paying-in forms in book sets to this end. Note that the retained counterfoil provides the trader's record of what has been deposited:

Fig 6.21(i)

Example of a bank paying-in slip

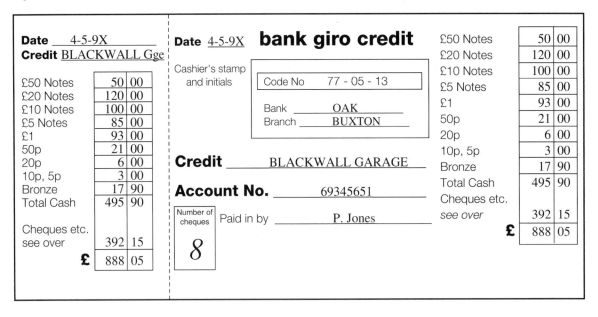

Fig 6.21(ii) Reverse

Source: Adapted from *Frank Wood's Business Accounting AAT Student's Workbook*. Sheila Robinson, Pitman Publishing 1993

The components of a business cheque

Each of the cheques received by a business displays a set of key information – for its issuer, recipient and the two banks involved in debiting and crediting it to the respective interested parties:

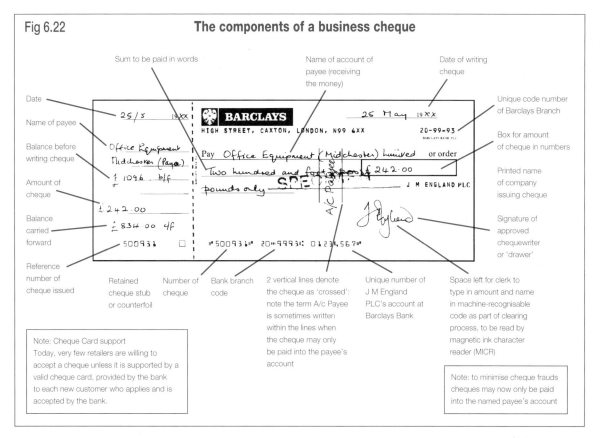

Fig 6.22

The components of a business cheque

Labels (left side, top to bottom):
- Sum to be paid in words
- Name of account of payee (receiving the money)
- Date of writing cheque
- Date
- Name of payee
- Balance before writing cheque
- Amount of cheque
- Balance carried forward
- Reference number of cheque issued

Labels (right side):
- Unique code number of Barclays Branch
- Box for amount of cheque in numbers
- Printed name of company issuing cheque
- Signature of approved chequewriter or 'drawer'

Cheque handwriting:
- 25/5   19XX
- BARCLAYS
- HIGH STREET, CAXTON, LONDON, N99 6XX
- 25 May 19XX
- 20-99-93
- BARCLAYS BANK PLC
- Office Equipment Midchester (Payee)
- £1096 b/f
- Pay Office Equipment (Midchester) Limited   or order
- Two hundred and forty-two pounds only
- £242.00
- SPE
- A/c Payee
- J M ENGLAND PLC
- £242.00
- £834.00 c/f
- 500931
- ⑈500931⑈ 20⑈9993⑈ 0123456 7⑈

Bottom row labels:
- Retained cheque stub or counterfoil
- Number of cheque
- Bank branch code
- 2 vertical lines denote the cheque as 'crossed': note the term A/c Payee is sometimes written within the lines when the cheque may only be paid into the payee's account
- Unique number of J M England PLC's account at Barclays Bank
- Space left for clerk to type in amount and name in machine-recognisable code as part of clearing process, to be read by magnetic ink character reader (MICR)

Note: Cheque Card support
Today, very few retailers are willing to accept a cheque unless it is supported by a valid cheque card, provided by the bank to each new customer who applies and is accepted by the bank.

Note: to minimise cheque frauds cheques may now only be paid into the named payee's account

The alternative to paper cheques: 'smart' plastic shopping cards

In the UK, millions of cheques are processed by the clearing banks each working day. However, bank guarantee cards like those using the Switch system and so-called smart cards, which store electronically in a built-in micro-chip the current balance of a person's account (so as to ensure that enough money is in the account to pay for goods or services about to be purchased) are replacing the issuing of paper cheques. Not everyone likes the instant debit/credit transfer of funds which the Switch systems operates, but then, not everyone liked at first the introduction of self-service in petrol stations in the early 1970s!

The bank statement

Unless requested at more frequent intervals, a small company is likely to receive a monthly statement of account from its bank.

This statement shows clearly each inflow and outflow of money by means of individual entries in either the credit or debit column and the resultant balance. The bank statement also indicates whether an account is in credit (CR) or overdrawn (DR) as a result of more cheques having been issued than money paid in at a given point in time:

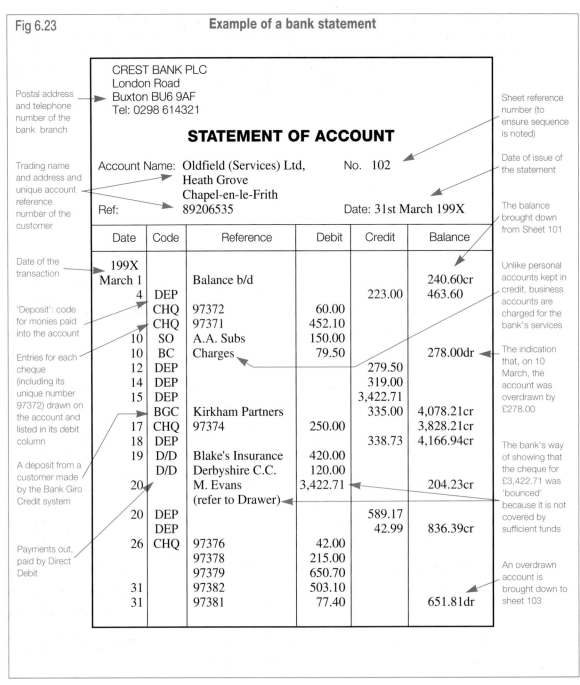

Fig 6.23   **Example of a bank statement**

PC
6.1.4
6.1.5

Postal address and telephone number of the bank branch

CREST BANK PLC
London Road
Buxton BU6 9AF
Tel: 0298 614321

Sheet reference number (to ensure sequence is noted)

STATEMENT OF ACCOUNT

Trading name and address and unique account reference number of the customer

Account Name: Oldfield (Services) Ltd,   No. 102

Heath Grove
Chapel-en-le-Frith
Ref: 89206535   Date: 31st March 199X

Date of issue of the statement

The balance brought down from Sheet 101

Date	Code	Reference	Debit	Credit	Balance
199X March 1		Balance b/d			240.60cr
4	DEP			223.00	463.60
	CHQ	97372	60.00		
	CHQ	97371	452.10		
10	SO	A.A. Subs	150.00		
10	BC	Charges	79.50		278.00dr
12	DEP			279.50	
14	DEP			319.00	
15	DEP			3,422.71	
	BGC	Kirkham Partners		335.00	4,078.21cr
17	CHQ	97374	250.00		3,828.21cr
18	DEP			338.73	4,166.94cr
19	D/D	Blake's Insurance	420.00		
	D/D	Derbyshire C.C.	120.00		
20		M. Evans	3,422.71		204.23cr
		(refer to Drawer)			
20	DEP			589.17	
	DEP			42.99	836.39cr
26	CHQ	97376	42.00		
		97378	215.00		
		97379	650.70		
31		97382	503.10		
31		97381	77.40		651.81dr

Date of the transaction

'Deposit': code for monies paid into the account

Entries for each cheque (including its unique number 97372) drawn on the account and listed in its debit column

A deposit from a customer made by the Bank Giro Credit system

Payments out, paid by Direct Debit

Unlike personal accounts kept in credit, business accounts are charged for the bank's services

The indication that, on 10 March, the account was overdrawn by £278.00

The bank's way of showing that the cheque for £3,422.71 was 'bounced' because it is not covered by sufficient funds

An overdrawn account is brought down to sheet 103

Source: Adapted from Frank Wood's *Business Accounting AAT Student's Workbook*, Sheila Robinson, Pitman Publishing 1993

The clearing banks provide a range of abbreviations to help the customer to interpret the statement:

CR credit	CP card purchase
DR debit	BGC bank giro credit
OD overdrawn	CC cash or cheques
SO standing order	AC automated cash withdrawal (e.g. Cashpoint)
DD direct debit	EC eurocheques etc.
DV dividend	

The takings of a business paid into a bank's night safe deposit will be checked by a bank cashier the following morning and the pouch and paying-in book will be ready for collection at the start of the next daily paying-in cycle. The cash and cheques (once processed and safely cleared against their issuers' bank balances) will be credited to the paying-in firm's account and the banked total will appear as a credit entry on the statement.

■ In the large business

PC
6.1.4
6.1.5

The sequence of steps explained above are followed by larger companies, which also employ some additional procedures and security practices.

The cash book

In order to avoid cash being lost or misappropriated on its way to the bank, large organisations use a cash book to record and track precisely its progress within the accounting system in use. The cash book is also used to record the routine deposits of cash and cheques into a company's bank account.

Fig 6.24   **Example of a two-column cash book**

PC
6.1.5

Cash Book

199X	Cash £	Bank £	199X	Cash £	Bank £
Aug 1 Capital		1,000	Aug 7 Rates		105
" 2 T Moore	33		" 8 Rent	20	
" 3 W P Ltd		244	" 12 C Potts	19	
" 5 K Charles	25		" 12 F Small Ltd		95
" 15 F Hughes	37		" 26 K French		268
" 16 K Noone		408	" 28 Wages	25	
" 30 H Sanders		20	" 31 Balance c/d	49	1,204
" 30 H Howe	18				
	113	1,672		113	1,672
Sept 1 Balances b/d	49	1,204			

Source: *Frank Wood's Book-keeping & Accounts*, 3rd edn, Pitman Publishing 1992

Handling payments received in large companies

PC
6.1.4

An apocryphal story about one particular branch of a famous High Street clothing retailer recounts that, as the nearest branch of the plc's bank was some distance away and the tills were too small for the current boom in sales, the floor supervisors used to hide various parts of the day's takings in brown paper bags stuffed into the pockets of ladies' and gents' overcoats. These would then be retrieved at the end of the day for checking and banking!

Nowadays, large firms pursuing whatever business activity are much more systematic

Fig 6.25

Example of bank column cash-book layout

CASH BOOK (Bank Column Only)

Dr								Cr
Date	Details		Folio	Bank	Date	Details		Folio	Bank
199X					199X				
March 1	Balance		b/f	240.60	March 3	Wage	371		452.10
3	C. Mellor	161.00							
	M. Bennett	25.00			4	Post Office Counters			
	E.Proudlove	37.00		223.00		M/Van Tax	372		60.00
12	Cash Sales Banked			279.50	6	J. Ashton	373		121.42
14	F. Ball	134.00			8	Rent–			
	B. Green	185.00		319.00		Sims & Co.	374		250.00
15	M. Evans			3,422.71	12	Fountains			
						(Stationery)	375		102.63
16	Sales			589.17					
					17	S. Brown	376		42.00

Source: *Frank Wood's Business Accounting AAT Student's Workbook*, Sheila Robinson, Pitman Publishing 1993

and careful about the ways in which they process their payments received. In large stores, accounting staff remove takings from tills for banking at regular intervals during the day. Firms with large numbers of account customers have all associated payments routed either to a regional or head office accounts department which employs specialist staff to handle them and nothing else.

Such payments are processed as explained earlier in this Unit via the sales account day journals and postings to the sales and nominal ledgers. It is worth noting, however, that large firms usually introduce stringent internal security systems to forestall the accidental loss or theft of cash or convertible money orders etc. For example in some organisations *all* incoming mail (save that for the most senior executives) is opened by trusted mailroom/ accounts staff. All cheques and other monies despatched as payment for goods and services are carefully extracted from postal envelopes and recorded on to a type of payments received schedule and signed for by the clerk responsible for accepting the payments. In this way, the likelihood of any incoming payments being 'lost' internally is minimised.

Processing payments for purchases

In large organisations, the staff responsible for paying for all goods and services are likely to be just as busy as their account sales counterparts. Therefore systematising the process is just as important:

1 Departmental personnel requiring a good or service start the process by filling out and submitting to, say, the purchasing department **a purchase requisition order.**

2 This order is routed to the purchase department for scrutiny and authorisation. (Remember that in many large organisations the cheapest and best buying terms result from centralised purchasing, so the requesting department's requisition is checked so as

to ensure that it specifies the approved stockist and the correct buying terms and discounts etc.) From the purchase requisition order **a purchase order** is made out.

3 The next steps may be viewed as a kind of mirror image of the steps explained in the sales accounting process, in that the purchasing company despatches the purchase order to the supplier and awaits the receipt of:

- **a delivery note**
- **a sales invoice**
- **any debit or credit notes issued**
- **a statement**

4 These incoming documents are checked against the company's own purchase accounts system – goods-in docketing, entries in the purchases day book and postings to the purchases and nominal ledgers.

5 Once the purchase accounts section is satisfied that a supplier's statement agrees with its own records of what has been received (allowing for any purchase returns arising from incorrect or faulty goods supplied etc.) payment will be authorised for the account rendered by the incoming statement.

Payment for goods or services received

PC
6.1.5

In a large organisation, a section of its accounts department is likely to handle all payments due, including any expenses claims by its own salesforce, petrol purchased by maintenance staff etc. This role is undertaken by a cashier, who will also issue 'top-ups' for imprest petty cash accounts kept in departments (see below).

Where payments are processed against purchase orders placed with established suppliers, then (just as for the issue of sales account statements) a batch run will be undertaken with the aid of specialised purchase account software which automatically computes, prints and records the cheques issued against each individual account. Similarly, a printed remittance advice note will be produced to accompany the cheque:

Fig 6.26

REMITTANCE ADVICE

TO: Gripsure Trainers Ltd
41 South Street
London SW4 6AJ

**SQUIRES SPORTS
Booth Avenue
Birmingham**

| Account Ref | JC 102 | Date | 12.1.9X | Page | 25 |

DATE	DETAILS	INVOICES	CREDIT NOTES	PAYMENT AMOUNT
4.12.9X	Cross-Country JX	G42193		124.92
7.12.9X	Jogger JT3	G42241		96.82
12.12.9X	Ladies' Badminton	G43211		130.25
16.12.9X	Circuit Trainers		F4 321	−24.95
28.12.9X	STATEMENT		BALANCE DUE	£327.04

Source: Adapted from *Frank Wood's Business Accounting AAT Student's Workbook*, Sheila Robinson, Pitman Publishing 1993

THE PETTY CASH ACCOUNT

While the cash book is used to record the principal inward and outward flow of cash and cheque monies of a business, it has been found much more convenient in larger organisations to 'delegate' the purchase of and payment for a host of small cost consumables to its various departments and cost centres. The procedure employed to facilitate this is called the petty cash imprest system.

The imprest system works upon the principle of the accounts cashier making available to each department a type of float – say of £100:00 – to finance the intermittent purchases of tea, milk and sugar, postage stamps, inking pads, air-freshener and the like.

A petty cash book in each department is used to record each individual purchase transaction (including the totalling of VAT in a separate column where applicable). When the departmental clerk responsible for managing the petty cash sees that the balance being brought down in the book is running low, he or she requests and obtains another £100:00 top-up, and the cycle starts again. Note that the employee who buys any item through the petty cash system must obtain a petty cash voucher from the departmental petty cash clerk describing the purchase and its cost, and pass over the receipt relating to the purchased item. This procedure helps to keep the system secure from abuse.

Each time an imprest (of say £100:00) is made to a department, the accounts cashier will credit the sum to the cash book so as to maintain the balance of the company's cash holdings and appropriate debit entries will be made to nominal and personal accounts. The receipts obtained from petty cash purchases are also retained to satisfy any arising auditing needs.

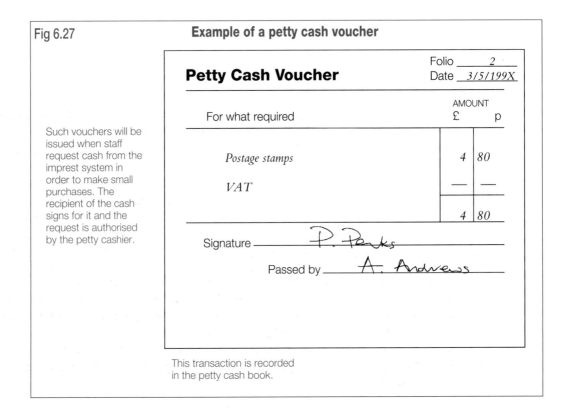

Fig 6.27

Example of a petty cash voucher

Such vouchers will be issued when staff request cash from the imprest system in order to make small purchases. The recipient of the cash signs for it and the request is authorised by the petty cashier.

This transaction is recorded in the petty cash book.

Fig 6.28   Example of a petty cash book

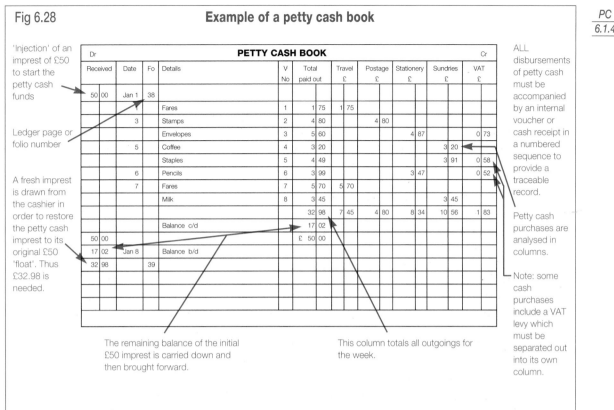

'Injection' of an imprest of £50 to start the petty cash funds

Ledger page or folio number

A fresh imprest is drawn from the cashier in order to restore the petty cash imprest to its original £50 'float'. Thus £32.98 is needed.

The remaining balance of the initial £50 imprest is carried down and then brought forward.

This column totals all outgoings for the week.

ALL disbursements of petty cash must be accompanied by an internal voucher or cash receipt in a numbered sequence to provide a traceable record.

Petty cash purchases are analysed in columns.

Note: some cash purchases include a VAT levy which must be separated out into its own column.

Received		Date	Fo	Details	V No	Total paid out		Travel £		Postage £		Stationery £		Sundries £		VAT £	
50	00	Jan 1	38														
				Fares	1	1	75	1	75								
		3		Stamps	2	4	80			4	80						
				Envelopes	3	5	60					4	87			0	73
		5		Coffee	4	3	20							3	20		
				Staples	5	4	49							3	91	0	58
		6		Pencils	6	3	99					3	47			0	52
		7		Fares	7	5	70	5	70								
				Milk	8	3	45							3	45		
						32	98	7	45	4	80	8	34	10	56	1	83
				Balance c/d		17	02										
50	00					£ 50	00										
17	02	Jan 8		Balance b/d													
32	98		39														

PETTY CASH BOOK   Dr ... Cr

ACCOUNTS DOCUMENTS AND SECURITY

A major advantage that a sole trader of a small business enjoys is that of being personally responsible for the financial security of the business. He or she alone handles all the payments received, effects all banking activities and makes all outgoing payments for purchases.

Contrastingly, in a national chainstore group this activity may involve literally hundreds of employees. Given such numbers of staff involved, it is statistically very probable that at the 'least trustworthy' end of any related distribution curve a number of employees will exist who would be 'on the fiddle' where movements of cash are concerned – if given the chance. Each clearing bank, for example, employs a division of inspectors who visit branches – sometimes without warning – to carry out spot checks on their transaction systems and routines. Large national chains and conglomerates do likewise.

Also, the managers of both private and public sector organisations are constantly aware of their accountability – to shareholders, building society members, elected councillors and governors etc. – for the finance left in their charge.

As a result, a number of key security practices have evolved to protect the integrity of that part of the organisation's operation which is responsible for the stewardship of its financial transactions.

PC 6.1.4

PC 6.1.6

KEY PRACTICES WHICH ASSURE FINANCIAL INTEGRITY

1 The double-entry bookkeeping system and its accompanying regular production of trial balances and reconciliations prevent errors being compounded and misappropriations going undetected.

2 Bookkeeping and accounting systems employ carefully sequenced checks on the movement of money around the organisation through the maintenance of, for example, the purchase control ledger, the cheque requisition form and the petty cash voucher procedures.

3 Both paper-based and computerised accounts systems have to be capable of sustaining audit trails through which sample checks may be undertaken to follow an individual sales or purchase transaction from start to finish.

4 Apart from the requirement for signatures and authorisations to accompany the movement of monies, use is made of safes' alarm-systems and allied security measures to protect cash and valuable documents – both in house and at the bank.

5 Recording mechanisms, inward and outward such as goods inward dockets, stock requisition orders, purchase orders, etc. are cross-checked to appropriate external source documents, such as incoming invoices and despatch notes to ensure that no unauthorised activities have occurred.

6 The centralisation of the accounts function – which controls all financial activities within large organisations – limits the number of employees handling money and facilitates the effective management of accounting systems.

7 Similar centralisation (on a smaller scale) of the opening of incoming mail and the recording of payments in an inward remittance book etc. prevents potential accidental loss or theft of money.

8 The commissioning of external chartered accountants (together with the work and responsibilities of the company accountant) helps to ensure that a company's accounts are audited by a professional, disinterested third party. Any temptations a chartered accountant may have to connive at illegal financial practices in the company which retained him or her are quickly dispersed by the thought of being struck off the practising register by the Inland Revenue.

9 The scrutiny of the accounts and performance of public limited companies by their shareholders.

■ The consequences of incorrect accounting actions

The liability for prosecution under one of the various Companies Acts for having committed an illegal act in an accounting context is not the only danger that may face a company with lax accounting procedures which seduce staff.

Other serious consequences may accompany the distribution of account sales statements which are all GIGO (garbage in, garbage out) as a result of an error in data processing. Once good account customers become aggravated by the involved process of having to put right incorrect accounts documentation, they may well move across to another supplier – especially if there is little to choose in terms of quality and net buying-in prices. Customer goodwill takes a long time to earn and may be lost for good and all in a trice!

Not only can a good account be lost as a result of unspotted, uncorrected accounting errors, the senior management of a company may make calamitous wrong decisions on a strategic scale if the source data employed in a management accountant's financial reports and analyses is wrong. For example, an error in the costing of a prototype product which is subsequently successfully test-marketed may result in production being authorised on a national sales scale which results in millions of pounds of income failing to materialise. Again, a failure to back up the personal sales accounts in a computerised accounts system has resulted in many companies being bankrupted, since, in the absence of a firm's ability to send out statements for accounts rendered, few customers bother to pay up, and an irretrievable cash-flow crisis ensues.

PC
6.1.6

DISCUSSION TOPICS

1 Is an organisation justified in setting up a procedure which requires that *all* incoming mail – even that marked confidential or personal – addressed to staff below the level of, say, director, be opened in the mailroom so as to ensure security in the case of payments being made to it?

2 What steps would you introduce into your own business to ensure that daily cash takings were not subject to pilferage by your employees?

3 Do you think that the clearing banks currently provide sufficient services in terms of the banking and paying-in activities of traders? How would you extend or improve them?

4 Have Switch cards made paper cheques obsolete? If so, why are millions still being processed by banks daily?

5 Why is 'telebanking' from home or office taking so long to arrive? Will it catch on, and should it?

PC
6.1.4
6.1.5
6.1.6

ACTIVITIES

As an individual, carry out one of the tasks below and report back to your class:

1 Find out what the range of services are which a clearing bank typically provides to a local business, which ones are free, and how much is charged for the others. Collect some of the brochures and leaflets which banks employ to promote their services and display them in your base-room.

2 Research into the ways in which a company may make or receive payment for goods or services, *other* than by cash or cheque.

Brief your class on your findings with a suitable factsheet and examples.

3 Design an imprest petty cash system (for your department) which employs a computer spreadsheet application.

Arrange to field test your system for two weeks and report back to your class on the outcomes.

4 Find out how an audit trail system works within an integrated accounting software system and report back to your group on your discoveries.

5 Interview a practising accounts manager and find out what techniques are available to ensure the integrity of a system in operation. Brief your class on your findings.

ASSIGNMENT 5

Using the example of a two-column cash book on page 539 enter the following transactions into the cash book provided.

Sept 1	Received £150 cash from T Moore
Sept 2	Paid rates £210 by cheque
Sept 3	Paid rent £40 by cash
Sept 4	Received £47 cash from F Hughes
Sept 5	Paid wages £75 by cash
Sept 8	Paid T Smith £295 by cheque
Sept 9	Paid K Jones £305 by cheque
Sept 12	Paid £75 wages by cash
Sept 14	Received a cheque for £425 from I Singh
Sept 15	Received £103 cash from B Patel
Sept 19	Paid wages £75 by cash
Sept 20	Paid for office stationery £25 by cash
Sept 24	Received £275 cash from H Howe
Sept 26	Paid wages £75 by cash
Sept 27	Paid rent £40 by cash
Sept 28	Received cash £30 from L Bird

CASH BOOK

Dr	Receipts				Payments		Cr
Date	Details	Cash	Bank	Date	Details	Cash	Bank
		£	£			£	£
Sept 1	Balances b/d	49	1,204	Sept 2			
Sept 1				Sept 3			
Sept 4				Sept 5			
Sept 14				Sept 8			
Sept 15				Sept 9			
Sept 24				Sept 12			
Sept 28				Sept 19			
				Sept 20			
				Sept 26			
				Sept 27			
				Sept 30	Balances c/d		
Oct 1	Balances b/d						

ASSIGNMENT 6

Using the example of a petty cash book on page 543 enter the following transactions into the petty cash book provided.

	Payments	Voucher No.	Amount
Jan 1	Stamps	9	£10.00
Jan 2	Envelopes	10	£8.00 (inc. £1.40 VAT)
Jan 4	Coffee/tea	11	£4.00
Jan 9	Bus fares	12	£4.50
Jan 11	Milk	13	£2.00
Jan 14	Bus fares	14	£3.60
Jan 16	Stationery	15	£4.00 (inc. £0.70 VAT)
Jan 19	Stamps	16	£5.00
Jan 24	Milk	17	£2.00
Jan 27	Staples	18	£4.49 (inc. £2.79 VAT)

Having made the entries, balance the book as at 31 January and then enter the 'Reimbursement' of £47.59 from the Chief Cashier, i.e. the cashier repays the Petty Cashier for the amount spent.

Dr   PETTY CASH BOOK   Cr

Receipts £	Date	Details	Voucher No.	Payments £	Travel £	Postage £	Stationery £	Sundries £	VAT £
50	Jan 1	Balance b/d							

REVIEW TEST

1 List the key information which appears on a crossed cheque.

2 What information is recorded on a payments received analysis sheet?

3 What information would you expect to input on to a bank paying-in slip?

4 What do these abbreviations (taken from a bank statement) stand for:
   OD SO DD BGC EC ?

5 What role does the cash book play in a double-entry accounting system?

6 Explain briefly how an imprest petty cash system works, and the documentation it employs.

7 Explain briefly five procedures you would adopt as an accountant in your accounting system to ensure the integrity and security of its operation.

8 Give three examples of serious problems which can ensue if incorrect accounting actions go unspotted and uncorrected.

PC
6.1.1
6.3.3

'Open all hours!'

Arun and Lata Patel's lives had been 'open all hours', ever since they first bought their business – a minimarket in a suburban shopping precinct – some five years ago. Then, the 150 houses on the Westbury Park development had been only half completed and business had been slow and hard to build. Thanks to the Patels' relentless hard work and willingness to rise at the crack of dawn and retire well after midnight, the minimarket had prospered, as the Westbury suburb of Grafton, a busy industrial town, had rapidly expanded. The store, called the Minimax Grocers & Newsagents, was in the middle of five shops in a parade lying back from a busy through-route to the A6. The Patels, with their 16-year-old daughter, Sonal and 10-year-old son, Naresh occupied a flat over the store.

Minimax had started out as a run-of-the-mill general stores, specialising in those small order items which local shoppers had forgotten to buy at the supermarket or did not want to make a special journey for. With a bus-stop into town just opposite, and room for parking out front, Arun quickly realised, however, that there was ample scope for selling newspapers, magazines and sweets, etc. Before much longer, he was employing six newspaper delivery youngsters. They also picked up orders for home-delivered groceries, which Arun delivered mid-mornings around the adjacent estates in his elderly but trusty van. The delivery side of the business expanded rapidly to a point where Arun had to stop taking on new customers - much against his will.

About a year ago, with the completion of the up-market Westbury Park development, customers who had acquired a taste for exotic micro-oven ready meals, gave Arun and Lata the idea of making room for another open freezer which would stock the spicy and different dishes which innovative food manufacturers were marketing under Chinese, Indian, Mexican and Indonesian brand names.

By this time, the Patels badly needed more helping hands. As luck would have it, two of Arun's nephews moved into the district looking for work in Grafton's textile industry. Both in their early twenties, they were just the trustworthy help that the shop urgently needed. Nor did they need much persuading, when Arun outlined his longer term plans for acquiring additional outlets. Ramesh, the elder brother took over the newsagency and confectionery side, while his brother Raj delivered the grocery orders and with his easy humour and persuasive ways quickly extended business.

Soon after, an incredible stroke of luck occurred – the butcher's shop next door came on to the market. The sitting tenant had been content to provide a mediocre service, and as a consequence could not afford the new lease's increased rents. Arun was quick to see his chance and had clinched the deal before the local estate agent had even displayed the particulars in his front window!

This time it was Mrs Patel who had her say. 'You know,' she had said, 'what Westbury needs is a really good fast-food takeaway!' Always with an eye to market trends, she had overheard snippets of conversation among teenagers and young married couples about the nearest fast-food

outlet some two miles away which had a good reputation for ample portions and really tasty dishes. 'If they'll drive over there, they'll walk in here,' she observed shrewdly. 'We could also fit in a few tables for people who want to eat here, too,' she added. After meeting some demanding requirements, Arun obtained planning permission for the change of use and early in November, the grand opening of Arun's 'Tandoori Takeaway' took place, with Mrs Patel in charge!

*　　　*　　　*

Some eight weeks earlier, Sonal had started working towards a GNVQ Business (Advanced) Award at Grafton College of Technology. From day one, with business in her bones, she had never looked back. She seemed to devour the Units and Elements – especially those parts dealing with business accounting.

She had a natural flair with software and had achieved a Grade A in her Business Information Studies GCSE.

One evening, having just finished an assignment, she poked her head round her father's upstairs office in the flat. He was almost buried under paper! It bulged out of cardboard wallets, ring-binders and box files; it was festooned around the walls, suspended from rows of bull-dog clips, it littered his desk and window sills. Advice notes, invoices, handwritten orders, catalogues, price-lists, special offers and bank statements! It seemed as though Arun had kept every single piece of paper since the first day's trading. Sonal scooped up a handful and let it drop back on to the desk.

'Stop that you silly girl!' shouted Arun. 'Now look what you've done. I'd just sorted those invoices into sequence!'

'Daddy, look at you! You're drowning in a sea of bumf!'

'What do you mean, bumf – I know exactly where everything is kept – or did until you interfered – now go away and let me finish!'

'Not until you make me a promise you'll keep.'

Sonal paused dramatically, for she well knew she was the apple of her father's eye.

'Certainly not! What promise?'

'That first thing tomorrow you go down to Computerama and get fixed up with a decent PC set-up and some suitable accounting software – before you go down for the third time and all your past flashes before your eyes! I don't know how you've managed up till now, but with the new shop and the deliveries expanding, soon you won't need to stop for sleep – you won't have time!'

*　　　*　　　*

For several days Sonal's words echoed around Arun's brain like an advertising jingle that wouldn't go away. Eventually he brought the matter up with Lata. 'I think she's probably right. You should move with the times,' Lata responded. 'How can you even think of new outlets when you're drowning in the paper from just two!'

Outnumbered and out-argued, Arun was waiting the next morning outside the front door as they opened up Computerama for business!

GROUP ACTIVITIES

In pairs, first carry out your fact-finding and then undertake the following tasks.

1 Basing your approach and decision-making on the information in the case study, research into the types of bookkeeping/accounting software currently on the market which you consider would best meet the needs of the Patel's business – both currently and allowing for likely future developments.

Brief your class with an illustrated oral presentation on the package(s) you selected and why.

2 Using the information in the case study and your knowledge of small business trading, draw up a checklist of the input data which would need to be collected systematically and keyed into the Patel's computer in order for them to be able to interpret and analyse what you believe would be useful management accounting information.

3 Using the knowledge you have gained from Tasks 1 and 2 above, draw up a factsheet of what you consider to be the advantages (to the Patels) of using a computerised bookkeeping/accounts system, as opposed to a manual, paper-based one. Compare your list with those of your co-students.

IDEAS FOR PROJECTS

1 Research more fully the principles of double-entry bookkeeping and then write an introductory manual intended to explain simply and clearly to a new entrant to the accounts department of a medium-sized firm on how the system works.   *PC 6.1.1*

2 Research into the ways in which an integrated accounting package like Pegasus or Sage works, and then produce an illustrated factsheet to explain the system clearly to your co-students.   *PC 6.1.1*

3 Find out what accounting services a chartered accountancy partnership can provide to the small business and brief your class on what you discovered in an oral briefing.   *PC 6.3.1*

4 Find out what commercially available paper-based systems (like Kalamazoo) are available to the small business proprietor to help him or her maintain the accounts and issue the related documents to customers and suppliers.   *PC 6.1.1*

Report back to your class with an illustrated presentation.

5 Find out how computerised (daily) stock and sales analysis techniques are used by multiples and franchise businesses – like Marks & Spencer plc, Tesco Stores Limited and the Body Shop – to make their restocking and purchasing faster, simpler and more cost-effective.   *PC 6.1.6*

Compose a factsheet which communicates what you discovered.

6 Find out how audit trails are used with computerised accounting systems to provide security and integrity checks. Brief your group orally on what you know about how they work.   *PC 6.1.6*

7 Find out what techniques large companies employ to control their credit sales and what the legal position is on seeking payment from defaulters.   *PC 6.1.3*

Set down your findings in the form of an article intended for the monthly newsletter of your local chamber of commerce.

8 Find out what support a clearing bank provides for its local business community in the general area of paying takings into the bank and dealing efficiently with receipts and payments.   *PC 6.1.4 6.1.5*

Brief your class with an illustrated presentation.

PC
6.1.2
6.1.3
6.1.4
6.1.5
6.3.3
PC
6.1.1
6.3.1

9 Research into the ways in which information technology developments are changing the ways in which the documentation of accounts is carried out.

Produce your findings as a 10–15 minute talk to your class.

10 Invite one or more of these managers to speak to your class on the current trends and developments of their particular specialism insofar as it relates to the accounts documentation process:

- a clearing bank manager or his deputy

- a central purchasing officer of a large organisation

- a sales representative for an integrated accounts package, or one of his/her experienced users

- a manager in a company that uses the electronic data interchange (EDI) system

- the branch manager of a local High Street retail multiple which employs IT techniques to process stock re-ordering and daily sales analysis data.

EVIDENCE-BUILDING ACTIVITY FOR YOUR PORTFOLIO

Element 6.1 Explain financial transactions and supporting documents

This activity requires you to collect a series of accounting documents (see below) and to provide an explanatory set of notes for each document which explains:

a) what its essential purpose is in the accounting process

b) how it is used (in conjunction with relating accounts documents)

c) how it fits into the procedures its users employ to maintain financial integrity and security

Research objectives

With the help of your school/college administrative staff (e.g. for purchases documents), your parents, relatives, friends or contacts, collect an example of each of the following accounts documents. Note: you may ask to be provided with a photocopy or to have the words 'specimen document' printed on a document if this makes it easier for you to obtain your set of the following:

The purchasing process

1 a purchase requisition document

2 a purchase order

3 a goods received note

4 an invoice for goods purchased

5 a credit note for goods returned

6 a statement of account rendered

The sales process

7 a despatch/delivery note

8 a sales invoice

9 a statement relating to goods sold

Note: If possible, seek to obtain documents 1–6 in a linked sequence relating to a unified purchase process. By the same token, if you can, seek to do the same for the sales sequence which may start with a form of goods release docket from a stores and conclude with the issue of a relating statement.

Payments Documents

10 a clearing bank paying-in slip

11 a completed petty cash voucher

Receipts Documents:

12 a receipt issued at the point of sale

13 a completed business cheque

14 a bank statement

Note: If you experience difficulty in obtaining any of the above documents because of business confidentialities, you may – with the approval of your teacher make use of the examples given in this textbook as substitutes. But, your first aim is to secure real business documents!

Presentation of evidence

You should present your evidence in a binder, with each document positioned as a left-hand page, and your explanatory notes on the facing right–hand page.

Method of producing evidence

Present your documents either as originals or as photocopies, and present your explanatory notes in word processed or hand-written form. Set out your notes as a series of 'bullet points', but make sure you write them in grammatical sentence form.

Performance criteria covered

6.1.1, 6.1.2, 6.1.3, 6.1.4, 6.1.5, 6.1.6

Core skills Level 3

Communication
3.1.1–3.1.4, 3.2.1–3.2.4, 3.4.1–3.4.3

Information Technology
3.1.1–3.1.7, 3.3.1–3.3.5
3.5.1–3.5.5 (by means of logged notes on how any errors or faults were handled, and how compliance with HASAW requirements was effected).

Element 6.2 Complete documents for financial transactions

ACCOUNTS DOCUMENT COMPLETION SIMULATIONS

1 Purchase requisition

You work as Administrative Assistant to the Production Manager of Vulcan Engineering Limited, manufacturer of engine castings for the motor trade. Part of your job role is to order cleaning and hygiene materials used in the production process. Your teacher plays the role of your Production Manager, who authorises your purchase requisition forms.

Use the purchase requisition form on page 555 to order the following goods:

> 10 five-gallon drums of Kleenahand cleaning gel which has a retail price of £35.50 per drum; 20 tins of Skincare protective skin ointment priced at £3.95 per tin; 12 bales of cotton waste priced at £12.50 per bale; 2 dozen bottles of lavatory disinfectant priced at £1.95 per bottle and 10 packs of paper towels priced at £3.45 per pack.

2 Purchase order

Your role has now changed to that of Assistant Purchasing Officer for Vulcan Engineering Limited. You have before you the purchase requisition from your Production Department. Your task is to complete the purchase order on page 556 which is to be sent to:

Industrial Cleaners Limited
Cleaner House   Waythorpe Industrial Park
Waythorpe Lancs. BT15 3RG

The Production Department is in urgent need of the order you are to process and so you have instructions to advise your supplier that it be considered urgent and sent on the first available delivery van.

The next purchase order number in your running sequence is: AX 46572. When you have completed your purchase order, it has to go to your Chief Purchasing Officer for signature – a role played by your teacher.

3 Sales order book

The scenario shifts, and you now find yourself playing the role of a sales ledger clerk working for Industrial Cleaners Limited. You have before you the purchase order numbered AX 46572. Your task is to enter its particulars on to your Sales Order Book schedule (page 557). The first column entitled 'Our Order Number' is used to contain a sequence of the company's own order numbers, the next of which is S 4582. Your sales catalogue reveals the following references for the products ordered:

[Product]	[Sales Catalogue Number]
Kleenahand cleaning gel	C239
Skincare protective ointment	H45
Cotton waste bale	I 375
Lavatory disinfectant	T278
Paper towels	I 29

Any particular delivery requirements are to be entered into the column marked: Delivery Comments, and the delivery date in the final column.

4 Delivery note and invoice

Your next task is to make out both the delivery note and invoice for the order from Vulcan. On pages 558–9 are the simulations of the two forms. In reality, they are likely to be printed in contrasting pastel colours as NCR or 'no carbon required' sheets, where the delivery note lies on top of the invoice and is lightly affixed to it at its head. This enables the details of the order to be filled out once only and for the pricing – including the all-important discount allowed – to be printed on the invoice only (which is sent directly to the accounts department). On many delivery notes – as is simulated below – the pricing components are obliterated on the delivery note.

The next delivery and invoice number on your NCR pad is: KB 12684 and your internal transaction number is 12 4 9X. Vulcan's account number is: IND 23692. Note that Industrial Cleaners uses the alphabetical letters which form part of its Sales Catalogue reference numbers as its product codes – e.g. H and C, standing for hygiene and cleaning products. Also, all the products ordered by Vulcan are standard rated for VAT purposes.

Make out first your delivery note using the above information, and then, using the following terms negotiated with Vulcan produce the associated invoice:

VULCAN ENGINEERING LIMITED
Credit purchase sales discount allowable:
12.5% off retail prices for purchase orders over £300:00
15.0% off retail prices for purchase orders over £600:00
Terms: strictly 30 days   Settlement discount: 3.75%
Credit limit: £3,000 per calendar month

---

5 Goods received note

The scenario moves back to Vulcan Engineering's Goods Inwards Department, where you are now working as a clerk. Your next task is to check the goods which have just been delivered by Industrial Cleaners and to complete the next goods received note on your pad, the reference number of which is F 1383. The goods have been delivered by van and your teacher is role-playing its driver and must therefore sign for their delivery to you as your – and his/her – proof of delivery.

On inspection, you find that one of the drums of Kleenahand gel has been damaged – apparently in transit – and is leaking pink gel.

Use the Industrial Cleaners Limited delivery note and the goods received note on page 560 to complete this task.

6 Statement of account

Your role for this task is Sales Ledger Clerk at Industrial Cleaners Limited. Among your responsibilities is the administration of a number of customer credit sales accounts, including that of Vulcan Engineering Limited. You are therefore currently tasked with producing the statement of account for Vulcan in respect of last month's credit sales transactions. Employing the information you have acquired in undertaking the above five tasks, make out the appropriate statement of account to send to Vulcan Engineering using the statement form on page 561. Remember that Vulcan's account number is: IND 23692. The following data relate to last month's account sales transactions:

Invoices issued

Date	Invoice No	Amount £
03/5/9X	KB11892	321:39
12/5/9X	KB11992	95:45
17/5/9X	KB12236	409:26
21/5/9X	KB12684	664:46
28/5/9X	KB13468	102:89

Credit and debit notes issued

On 24 May 199X, a credit note, number FG 3489, to the value of £35:45 was issued to Vulcan in respect of a damaged drum of Kleenahand gel. On 27 May 199X a debit note number XC 4591 was issued to rectify an undercharge on invoice KB12236. The debit note was issued against a pack of 25 medium-size rubber gloves and amounted to £12:63.

Balance carried forward

Note that a carried forward balance of £12.86 is shown on Vulcan's account as still outstanding and should be shown as the first item on your May statement of account.

7 Payment by cheque

Assume that you work as the Senior Purchase Ledger Clerk at Vulcan Engineering Limited, and that part of your job role is to verify, authorise and effect account purchases, including those made from Industrial Cleaners Limited. Using the cheque on page 562, make out the payment due from the rendering of their account which you produced in Task 6.

8 Paying-in slip

As Chief Cashier of Industrial Cleaners Limited, your next banking transaction involves you in paying the following amounts into your bank, using the paying-in slip on pages 562/3:

Cheques			£
			128:93
			45:80
			2396:35
			346:72
			15:84
			1015:99
Cash:	Notes:	50s	250:00
		20s	320:00
		10s	610:00
	Coins:		
		£1	296:00
		50p	29:50
		20p	14:80
		10p	16:30

Note: Before completing your paying-in slip, find out what multiples of coins a typical clearing bank will accept in its pre-printed plastic coin bags. Then make out your paying-in slip accordingly, leaving your balance of coins in your safe for your next banking.

9 Completing a receipt

For this task, assume that you work part-time as a voluntary assistant in Vulcan Engineering's Social and Welfare Club. Among the many facilities which the club offers are reduced prices for tickets to shows and pantomimes etc at various times of the year, when numerous employees go together on a Club Outing.

At present you are busy issuing tickets and providing receipts for the next Club Outing, which is to a Saturday evening performance of *Phantom of the Opera* at the Adelphi in London's West End. The performance starts at 7.30p.m. on Saturday 21 September 199X, and Bill Tomkins wishes to pay you for four tickets, priced £32.50 each, including return coach fare.

Using the receipt form on page 563, make out a suitable receipt.

Performance criteria covered

6.2.1, 6.2.2, 6.2.3, 6.2.4, 6.2.5

Core skills Level 3

Communication
3.1.1–3.1.4, 3.2.1–3.2.4

Application of number
3.2.1, 3.2.2, 3.2.4, 3.2.5

FORMS TO BE USED IN ELEMENT 6.2 ACTIVITIES

Use this form for Task 1

Fig 6.29

PURCHASE REQUISITION				
Date...../...../.....			Ref No..............	
Department:...				
Quantity	Descripton of goods	Unit price	Supplier's reference	Supplier
Requisition raised by:... Authorised by:..............................				
Purchase Order No...(to be completed by Purchasing Dept.)				

Use this form for Task 2

Fig 6.30

VULCAN ENGINEERING LIMITED
Bramshott Works Foundry Way
BRAMSHOTT Lancs OLD14 6AJ
Tel: 0902 653291 - 4 Fax: 0902 372985

PURCHASE ORDER

To:

_____

----
post code: _____

Date: / /

Purchase Order No:_____
(to be quoted in all correspondence)

Please deliver to the above
address unless otherwise instructed

Quantity	Description	Your Cat No.	Unit price £	Extension £
			Total:	

For and on behalf of:
VULCAN ENGINEERING LIMITED

signed:_____   Chief Purchasing Officer

Use this form for Task 3

Fig 6.31

SALES ORDER BOOK

Date: /   /

Our Order No.	Customer	Qty	Cat No.	Delivery	Comments	Delivered

Source: Adapted from *Finance, First Levels of Competence*, John Harrison, Pitman Publishing 1990. By kind permission of the author.

Use this form for Task 4

Fig 6.32

INDUSTRIAL CLEANERS LIMITED

Cleaner House Waythorpe Industrial Park Waythorpe Lancs BT15 3RG

Tel: 0864 678341   Fax: 0864 658362

VAT REG NO. 204 9975 42

DELIVERY NOTE

To: _____

_____

_____

_____

Date: / /

Delivery Note No.

_____

Transaction No.	Your Order No.	Delivery No.	Invoice Date	Account No.	

Product Code	Description	Unit Price	Quantity	VAT Code	

Use this form for Task 4

Fig 6.33

INDUSTRIAL CLEANERS LIMITED
Cleaner House Waythorpe Industrial Park Waythorpe Lancs BT15 3RG
Tel: 0864 678341   Fax: 0864 658362
VAT REG NO. 204 9975 42

INVOICE

To: _____   Date: / /

    _____   Invoice No.

    _____   _____

Transaction No.	Your Order No.	Delivery No.	Invoice Date	Account No.	

Product Code	Description	Unit Price	Quantity	VAT Code	Price £

	Gross:	
	Less Discount:	
	Nett:	
	Plus VAT at %:	
	Total Payable:	

Terms: Net 30 Days E & OE
VAT Code: V = added at standard rate   Z = zero rated
E = exempt

Use this form for Task 5

Fig 6.34

VULCAN ENGINEERING LIMITED

GOODS RECEIVED NOTE

Date: /   /   Ref No._____

Goods Supplied By: _____

_____

Our Purchase Order No. _____

Supplier's Delivery Note No. _____

Name, signature and company of delivery person:

Name_____ Signed:_____

Company: _____

Quantity	Description of Goods

Inspected By:

Name_____ Signature:_____

Enter below details if found damaged on inspection:

_____

_____

_____

Use this form for Task 6

Fig 6.35

INDUSTRIAL CLEANERS LIMITED
Cleaner House Waythorpe Industrial Park Waythorpe Lancs BT15 3RG
Tel: 0864 678341 Fax: 0864 658362
VAT REG NO. 204 9975 42

STATEMENT OF ACCOUNT

To: _____

_____

_____

Post code: _____

Date: / /

Customer Account No.

_____

Date	Invoice / Credit / Debit Ref.	Cr £	Dr £	Balance £

Total: £

Less settlement discount: £

Balance due: £

Cr: Amount credited
Dr: Amount debited

E + OE

Use this form for Task 7

Fig 6.36　　　　　　　　　　　　　　　　**Business cheque**

Date _____	⬡ **NATIONAL WESTCHESTER BANK**　　65–34–56
	Bramshott Branch 31 High St. Bramshott, Lancs BT4 9KL　　　_____19___
	Pay _____
Pay _____	_____ Account Payee _____
Bal. Bt Fwd ___ _____	
£ [ ]	£ [ ] VULCAN ENGINEERING LIMITED
Other items _____ Bal. Cd Fwd _____	
02451	Cheque No.　Branch Sort Code　Account No.　Transaction Code 02451　　　65–34–56　　　64431192　　　　03

Use this form for Task 8

Fig 6.37　　　　　　　　　　　　　　　**Paying-in slip (front)**

Date _____	_____19___ Paid in by:_____ bank giro credit ⬡
A/C _____	
Cashier's Stamp	Cashier's　**NATIONAL WESTCHESTER**　Notes £50 Stamp　　 **BANK**　　　　　　　　　£ 20
	£ 10
	2　　　　65 34 56　　　　£ 5
	Bramshott Branch　　　　Coins £ 1
Cash _____	Cheques ☐　　　　　　　　　Other coins
Cheques _____	Fee box ☐　**VULCAN ENGINEERING LIMITED**　Total Cash
£ [ ]	Cheques etc.
01692	01692　　65 34 56 95567342 98　　£ [ ]

Paying-in slip (back)

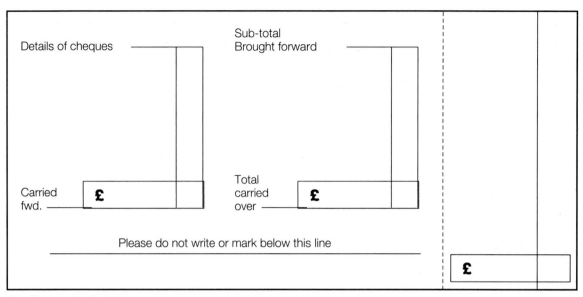

Details of cheques

Sub-total
Brought forward

Carried
fwd. _____ £

Total
carried
over _____ £

Please do not write or mark below this line

£

RECEIPT	*VULCAN ENGINEERING LIMITED* *SPORTS & SOCIAL CLUB* *Bramshott Works Foundry Way* *Bramshott* *Tel: 0902 687453*	No.

Manager: Jack Bastow

Date: / / 199X   VAT REG NO. 347 9857 23

To _____

Description	£	p
Total		
Plus VAT		
Price		

Received with thanks _____ Chief Cashier

Element 6.3 Identify and explain data to monitor business performance

Study carefully the information concerning the Trial Balance and accompanying notes set out below relating to TUV plc, a manufacturing company. Your tasks in this activity are then to:

a) prepare a profit and loss account

b) a balance sheet

for TUV plc and then to provide an analysis of the company's performance and financial status based upon the data you have processed.

TUV plc Trial Balance as at 31 December 19X7

	Debit £000	Credit £000
Sales		1,000
Machinery – Cost	588	
Machinery – Depreciation		180
Computer – Cost	250	
Computer – Depreciation		50
Warehouse – Cost	700	
Warehouse – Depreciation		96
Delivery Vehicles – Cost	230	
Delivery Vehicles – Depreciation		80
Disposal		10
Stock at 1 January 19X7	20	
Purchases of Materials	250	
Repairs to Machinery	27	
Rent – Factory	28	
– Offices	32	
Manufacturing Wages	49	
Directors' Salaries	35	
Clerical Staff Salaries	18	
Office Heating and Lighting	9	
Sales Commission	68	
Road Tax and Insurance on Vehicles	30	
Bad Debts	50	
Provision for Bad Debts		1
Loan Interest	20	
Debtors	84	
Bank	105	
Creditors		26
10% Debenture Loans		400
Interim Ordinary Dividend	30	
8% Preference Shares		250
Ordinary Shares		310
Profit and Loss Account		220
	2,623	2,623

Notes

1 Stock was counted on 31 December 19X7 and valued at £25,000.

2 The company's auditors have discovered that the acquisition of a piece of machinery costing £12,000 has been posted incorrectly to the repairs account. No adjustment has been made in respect of this error.

3 The balance on the disposals account represents the proceeds of the disposal of a delivery vehicle which had originally cost £30,000 and which had been depreciated by £13,000. No other entries have been made in respect of this transaction.

4 Depreciation has still to be charged as follows:

Machinery	10% straight line
Computer	20% straight line
Warehouse	2% straight line
Delivery Vehicles	25% reducing balance

5 The computer is used mainly for accounting and payroll purposes.

6 The following expenses have been incurred but not recorded:

	£000
Manufacturing Wages	1
Factory Rent	2
Clerical Salaries	2
Office Heating	4

The company paid £10,000 during the year in order to insure the delivery vehicles for the 12-month period from 1 July 19X7 to 30 June 19X8.

7 The provision for bad debts has to be increased to £4,000.

8 The directors propose to pay the preference dividend in full and to make a final ordinary dividend payment of £50,000.

Reproduced by kind permission of the Longman UK Group from: *Accounting – An Introduction for Professional Students* by John Dunn, published by Pitman Publishing.

Activity Tasks

1 Produce the Profit and Loss Account

2 Produce the Balance Sheet

3 Produce a commentary on 1 and 2 above which addresses the following questions:

Activity Questions

a) How satisfactory is TUV's (i) gross profit and (ii) net profit?

b) How healthy is TUV's financial position at the end of December 19X7?

c) What recommendations would you make to TUV in terms of employing its available financial resources in its next trading year?

d) How healthy is TUV's situation regarding its debtors?

e) What advice would you give to TUV's board of directors regarding TUV's distribution costs?

f) Should TUV pay off its loan interest?

g) In your view, were the directors right to propose to pay the preference dividend in full and to make a final ordinary dividend payment of £50,000?

h) If you were the entrepreneurial chairman and tycoon of Global Consolidated plc, would you consider making a hostile takeover bid for TUV? If so, why? If not, why not?

Presentation of evidence

Present your evidence in the form of a report to TUV's board of directors.

Method of producing evidence

Your accounting documents should be set out using an accepted set of layout conventions. Your report should be word-processed if possible, and should incorporate a layout which makes your points easy to assimilate. Your report's presentation should also reflect that it is to be presented to TUV's top management tier.

Performance criteria covered

6.3.1, 6.3.2, 6.3.3, 6.3.4, 6.3.5, 6.3.6, 6.3.7

Core skills Level 3

Communication
3.2.1–3.2.4, 3.3.1–3.3.3, 3.4.1–3.4.3

Information Technology
3.1.1–3.1.7, 3.2.1–3.2.7, 3.3.1–3.3.5
3.5.1–3.5.5 (by means of logged notes on how errors or faults were handled and how compliance with HASAW was effected).

FURTHER SOURCES OF INFORMATION

Frank Wood's Book-keeping & Accounts, 3rd edn, Pitman Publishing, 1992. ISBN: 0 273 03770 6

Book-keeping Made Simple, G Whitehead, Heinemann, 1987. ISBN: 0 434 98484 1

Frank Wood's Business Accounting AAT Student's Workbook, Sheila I Robinson, Pitman Publishing, 1993. ISBN: 0 273 60188 1

Book-keeping & Accounting, G Whitehead, Pitman Publishing, 1991. ISBN: 0 273 03516 9

Commerce, D T Williams (revised by M Pincott), Pitman Publishing, 1985. ISBN: 0 273 03279 8

Business of Banking, D Wright and W Valentine, 2nd edn, Northcote House Publishers Ltd, 1988. ISBN: 0 7463 0535 4

Finance for BTEC National, J Hopkins, Pitman Publishing, 1988. ISBN 0 273 02877 4

FINANCIAL RESOURCES

Element 7.1
Identify sources of finance for a business plan

Element 7.2
Produce and explain a projected cash flow for a single
product business

Element 7.3
Calculate the cost of goods or service

Element 7.4
Produce and explain profit and loss statements and
balance sheets

Evidence indicators: A financial plan outlining the financing requirements, sources and methods of acquiring financial support in relation to a given business plan. The plan may be the candidate's own plan produced for Unit 8 or a plan from a case study. Evidence should demonstrate understanding of the implications of the range dimensions in relation to the element. The unit test will confirm the candidate's coverage of range.

Evidence indicators: A cash flow forecast for a twelve month period for a single-product business together with an explanation of the significance of in-flow and out-flow timing and the use of a cash flow to support the seeking of finance. (This element does not require evidence of book-keeping.) Evidence should be computer-generated using spreadsheets. Evidence should demonstrate understanding of the implications of the range dimensions in relation to the element. The unit test will confirm the candidate's coverage of range.

Element 7.3: Calculate the cost of goods or service   595–619

Performance criteria

1 direct and indirect costs of businesses are explained   597–609

2 a unit of the goods or service is correctly identified   607, 675–6

3 number of units of the goods produced or service provided in a time period is calculated   675–6

4 direct costs of the goods or service for a time period are calculated   675–6

5 indirect costs of the organisation for a time period are calculated   675–6

6 allocation of indirect cost to unit production cost over the time period is calculated   675–6

7 total cost of a unit of the goods or service is calculated   675–6

Range: **Direct costs:** labour wages, materials, depreciation, power   595–619, 675–6

        Indirect costs: management, administration, marketing, running expenses   595–619, 675–6

Evidence indicators: A breakdown of the cost of goods or service with calculations together with an explanation of a business's direct and indirect costs. Evidence may be computer-generated using spreadsheets or manually-generated. Evidence should demonstrate understanding of the implications of the range dimensions in relation to the element. The unit test will confirm the candidate's coverage of range.

Element 7.4: Produce and explain profit and loss statements and balance sheets   620–67

Performance criteria

1 purposes of profit and loss statements and balance sheets are explained   631–41

2 trading periods are correctly identified and explained   631–41

3 single column trial balance is extracted from given accounting records and correctly totalled to zero   621–30

4 each account on the trial balance is correctly identified as relating to trading profit and loss or balance sheet items   636–9, 669–70

5 profit and loss account and balance sheet are correctly extended and the profit or loss for the period is entered in each column as the number required to produce a zero total   669–70

6 profit and loss and balance sheets are restated in conventional form and explained   631–41, 669–70

Range: **Purposes:** secure finance, maintain finance, monitor performance   619–67

        Trading period: quarterly, annually   631–41

        Overheads: administration, wages, rent, telephone, interest, travel expenses   635–6

        Profit and loss conventional form: sales, cost of sales, gross profit, overheads; net profit   635–6

Balance sheet conventional form: assets, current assets, current liabilities; share capital, profit and loss brought forward, profit and loss for period   632–6

Evidence indicators: A profit and loss statement and balance sheet for a single product outlet (e.g. an ice- cream kiosk, a mini-cab or a self-employed decorator) together with an explanation of the use of profit and loss statements and balance sheets to secure and maintain finance from lenders. Evidence can be computer-generated using accounting software or spreadsheets or manually-generated. Evidence should demonstrate understanding of the implications of the range dimensions in relation to the element. The unit test will confirm the candidate's coverage of range.

INTRODUCTION

Financial resources

In Unit 7, the various financial resources available to an organisation are identified and explained – such as the assets of land, buildings, production machinery and office equipment. Similarly the nature and deployment of working capital – raw materials, bought-in stock, money due from debtors etc. – are examined in the context of sustaining a healthy cash-flow during business operations. The Unit also explores the means of securing loans for start-up and business development, from banks, building societies, stock-market flotations, lease-back etc., and their associated costs.

The cash-flow forecast

The methodology and rationale for drawing up projected cash-flow (twelve-monthly) schedules is also explained in detail, including the key roles of timing the payment of creditors and securing monies owed to the business, as well as the need to interpret the significance of *actual* performance against targeted outcomes.

Costing and budgeting

The key functions of costing, cost-control and budgeting are examined in depth, including direct and indirect costs, absorption and marginal costing and break-even analysis.

The documentation of accounts: from double-entry bookkeeping to published final accounts

Unit 7 finally provides clearly illustrated explanations of the principles of: double-entry bookkeeping and drawing up a trial balance; the production of a balance sheet and a trading and profit and loss account; key management accounting ratios; the compilation of sole trader, partnership, company and non profit-making organisational final accounts.

With the help of the many models, specimens and worked examples, Unit 7 supplies an ideal study aid and reference to support financial resources activities and assignments – including those dispersed through its detailed sections.

In particular, Unit 7 examines:

- sources of finance for a business plan
- venture and investment capital
- sources of external and internal funding – long, medium and short term
- financial resourcing and share issues – preference, debenture, ordinary shares, flotations and rights issues
- types and sources of finance available to the small business
- the use of working capital and cash-flow forecasting in the business operating cycle
- the production and interpretation of the cash-flow forecast
- the role of the operating budget in start-up business planning
- the costing of goods and services: raw materials, direct labour, overheads etc.
- absorption, cost-centre, marginal costing and break-even analysis principles and applications
- budgeting and budgetary control
- double-entry bookkeeping: principles and key processes, including extracting a trial balance
- drawing up a balance sheet
- producing a trading and profit and loss account
- methods of calculating depreciation: straight line, reducing balance
- interpretation of final accounts
- management of accounting ratios: profitability, return on capital employed (ROCE), current and liquid ratios (acid test), debtors collection period, creditors payment period etc.
- sole trader, partnership, company and charitable organisation and club accounts
- published final accounts: balance sheet, profit and loss account, cash flow statement, notes to these statements, directors' report, auditors' report

SOURCES OF FINANCE FOR A BUSINESS PLAN

PC
7.1.1
7.1.2
7.1.3
7.1.4

No business will succeed for long without a carefully drawn up plan of action – what it intends to do. Such plans are generally referred to as business plans, and are employed both in the preparatory stage of starting up a business and in undertaking a fresh business project or initiative in established organisations. (A detailed examination of business planning is provided in Unit 8.)

A major component of any successful business plan is its financial forecasting and allocation of financial resources – to underpin research, production, marketing, sales and personnel activities etc. A prerequisite of constructing the financial parts of a business plan is to establish clearly what financial resources may be available for deploying in it.

■ Long-term assets

As you are aware, long-term assets in a business include land, premises, plant and machinery, equipment and fixtures. While such assets are essential in order to run a business, they are not always readily turned into capital which might fund a start-up business or fresh business initiative.

However, assets of the above type may well be employed to provide sources of finance in one or more of these ways:

- surplus land may be sold or leased to provide cash

- premises owned by the organisation may be 'leased back' to, say, an insurance company or bank, thus releasing cash for investing in the business plan.

- surplus expensive equipment could be sold or leased

- a loan could be secured from a bank or finance house using the organisation's assets as security for it. (For example, a mortgage could be taken out on premises owned by a company.)

■ Venture and investment capital

Very often the entrepreneur wishing to start up a business has insufficient capital with which to do so. Some (reckless) would-be entrepreneurs offer their own private houses up as security for, say, a bank loan, and run the risk of finding themselves and their families 'out on the street' if the business fails.

However, as there has been an expanding market for several hundred years in the business of lending money to entrepreneurs (medieval merchants financed speculative voyages of sea-captains seeking gold, silver, silks, spices etc.), it is no wonder that, today, there exist numerous private and merchant banks clustering around the financial centres of the world – London, Zurich, Frankfurt, Hong Kong, New York and Tokyo – whose main purpose is to lend out risk or venture capital to those entrepreneurs who can convince them that a particular business venture's 'likely return on capital invested' balances with an acceptable degree of risk. Such sources of finance do not, however, come cheap and may levy up to 70–80 per cent interest charges per annum or loan period.

■ Other sources of finance

Other sources of business lending include:

- clearing banks
- building societies
- finance houses
- private, individual investors (e.g. sleeping partners)
- hire-purchase companies (if the finance is needed for plant, vehicles or equipment etc.)
- government agencies (which may on occasion provide grants or loans to assist business start-ups as a means of regenerating a depressed regional or local economy)

■ Interest charges – the costs of servicing a loan

PC
7.1.3
7.1.4

A main factor in deciding which source of loan finance to accept is, of course, the charges (interest) which are required to service the loan. These will vary from time to time, depending upon the level of the base interest rate imposed on clearing banks by the Bank of England, and thus the extent of the supply of money in the economy. It is not uncommon for start-up and business project interest rates to exceed 30 per cent annual interest charges. For this reason, business directors continually clamour for decreases in prevailing interest rates, so as to make borrowing for capital investment less expensive.

■ Internal equity

PC
7.1.4

Because borrowing money from external sources is so expensive, many companies prefer – if they can manage it – to provide investment capital from within. There are a number of ways in which this may be achieved:

- as outlined above, from the sale or lease of long-term assets – land, premises etc.
- by drawing upon reserves: many larger organisations (especially public limited companies) retain significant proportions of their post-tax profits in the form of reserves and thus do not usually distribute all their generated profits as dividends to shareholders
- by making use of accumulated finance which has been set aside to replace depreciated equipment (thus giving themselves, in effect, an interest-free loan)
- by the company directors providing interest-free loans to the business from personal sources in the form of a cash injection (though this source is bound to have strings attached in some form or other)

■ The offer of shares for sale

PC
7.1.3

A popular way of obtaining capital for business expansion is to offer for sale shares in the company concerned. Smaller, private limited companies may achieve this by inviting one or more people to purchase shares in the firm and to join the board of directors. While this may promptly provide welcome cash to finance a business plan, it may well also alter the balance of control by redistributing the available shares among an enlarged board of directors, giving overall control to whichever grouping holds more than 50 per cent.

The issue of shares is more commonly undertaken for public limited companies by national and international issuing houses via stock exchanges and market makers, which will quote a new share issue at a specific, opening price. Depending upon the degree of interest shown in the shares, they will, thereafter, float up or down. New shares offers are often advertised through prospectuses (which provide relevant details of the company's track-record, financial strength and other reassuring data) published in financial newspapers and journals.

Sometimes – as with some goverment privatisation share flotations – financial houses, pensions organisations and banks etc. are invited to tender for sets of shares which are then sold to the highest bidders. At other times, existing company shareholders are given a 'first-refusal' of buying freshly marketed shares in what is termed a rights issue, where they may be enabled to purchase newly offered shares as a percentage of their existing holding, and sometimes more cheaply than the general public in a subsequent open offer.

■ Types of share issued

Ordinary shares

These are most generally issued and will be given a (nominal) face value price at the time of issue. What they subsequently cost to buy and sell (including the stock-broker's commission) will depend on what value is placed upon them by the money market at a given time. For example, the original shares of the privatised British Telecom were issued at £1.00 and are currently trading at £4.30. Ordinary shares tend to appreciate most dramatically in value in a buoyant economy, but are last in the queue for paying out if a company goes into receivership, and neither automatically qualify for the payment of an annual dividend.

Preference shares

As their name suggests, preference shares enjoy superior benefits, which (in the form of debentures) include the payment of a fixed rate of dividend each year (e.g. Harridges 8%). Preference shares are entitled to be paid out during a receivership before any ordinary shares.

PC
7.1.4

■ Short-term finance (up to 3 years)

Bank overdraft

This is usually the simplest type of finance to arrange and often the cheapest. Interest is only charged on the overdrawn balance, but the rate will vary according to current interest rates. It must be remembered that technically an overdraft is repayable on demand and this can occasionally prove a problem.

Traditionally overdrafts have been used to finance stock and work in progress as the sale of the finished goods will generate funds which will repay the loan. Many seasonal businesses rely on overdrafts to finance periods when sales are low.

Today, however, some firms have almost a permanent overdraft which is used to finance the purchase of fixed assets.

Creditors

It is often forgotten that this is a way of obtaining finance. Most companies obtain their stock on credit and pay within agreed credit periods.

Factoring or invoice discounting

Factor agencies will give a firm around 80 per cent of the value of invoices as soon as they are sent. The balance will be paid as the money is received, less the charges of the factor company.

■ Medium-term finance (3–10 years)

PC
7.1.4

Bank loans

This is a more formal arrangement with a bank than the overdraft facilities. The bank agrees to a loan at a fixed rate of interest. Repayment of the loan and interest payments are scheduled at the beginning and are usually directly debited from the current account to the loan account.

Hire purchase

This has been described earlier in the section, but it is worth noting here that the interest is an allowable expense for tax purposes and that other tax allowances can be claimed in the year in which the goods were bought, even though the full cost has not been made to the finance company.

Leasing

A company may choose to lease fixed assets rather than buy them. The ownership of the assets remain with the finance company and the rent charged is sufficient to cover the cost of the asset and to provide the finance company with a reasonable return on their investment.

■ Long-term finance

PC
7.1.4

Bank and other loans

In these cases the institution will usually require security for the loan. This is often by a charge over the company's property even though the loan is not being used to buy the property.

Debentures

Debentures are loans and their characteristics are similar to preference shares described earlier in this section.

Share capital

Share capital is sometimes put in a separate category known as permanent capital as a company must have some issued share capital to exist.

Other sources

There are many other sources of finance available in particular circumstances including:

- Venture capital and export finance available through banks.
- Grant Aid Schemes initiated by the Government. These include Assisted Area Grants, Regional Development Grants and others.
- European Economic Community Funds provided by the Community's budget to promote the Community's objectives by providing finance for suitable projects. These

funds include the social and regional development funds. Additionally the European Investment Bank will provide finance for projects in industrial, energy and infrastructure fields.

- Local forms of assistance

  Many local authorities will give assistance for particular projects. The assistance given will vary from authority to authority and full information can be obtained on local schemes from the relevant body.

- Department of Trade and Industry

  One of the functions of this government department is to encourage research and development into new uses of, for example, computers, microprocessors and fibre optics. It will provide expertise and financial assistance towards equipment and development costs.

The advantages and disadvantages of the common types of finance available to small businesses can be summarised as shown on p. 577.

PC
7.1.3

CAPITAL GEARING

As we have seen, long-term finance can be satisfied by issuing shares or raising loan capital. The relationship between equity and loan capital is termed the *gearing ratio*. There are various ways gearing can be measured, but generally a company will be described as *highly geared* when it has a high proportion of fixed interest capital compared with ordinary share capital. Low gearing occurs when a company makes little use of fixed interest capital. The effect of gearing on a company is shown by the example in Table 7.1. Companies A and B have raised the same amount of capital but in different ways. Company A makes little use of fixed interest capital – we can say it is low geared with a ratio of 1:9. Conversely Company B, with its greater use of loan capital, is highly geared having a ratio of 9:1.

In situation 1, both companies – after paying the debenture interest – have a residue available for ordinary shareholders which is equivalent to a 10 per cent return on capital.

In situation 2, profits have increased by £10,000. The impact on Company A with its greater use of equity capital is to raise the return to shareholders by 1 per cent to 11 per cent. However, in Company B the profits have to be spread between far fewer shareholders. Thus the impact of this profit rise is far greater. The return on capital has doubled from 10 per cent to 20 per cent.

In situation 3 though, where profits fall by £10,000 the return to ordinary shareholders in Company A falls from 10 per cent to 9 per cent. However, for Company B, the reduction in profit means that the shareholders will receive no return on their capital this year. Summarising, we can say that profit fluctuations will have a smaller impact on a low-geared firm than a high-geared firm. High gearing benefits firms in prosperous times, but in a recession, when sales and profits fall, the very existence of the firm may be at risk through an inability to service (pay interest on) its loans.

Types of finance available to small business

	Advantages	*Disadvantages*
Short term		
Bank overdraft (from clearing	Usually cheapest finance available; flexible; quickly obtainable; no minimum sum; interest paid on usage only; normally renewable.	Technically repayable on demand; vulnerable to change in government and banking policy; temptation to use for wrong applications (because of cheapness and convenience); may require personal guarantees.
Short-term loan (from clearing banks and finance houses, often owned by clearing banks)	Term commitment by lender; often quickly obtainable; can often roll over; improves overdraft flexibility.	Dearer than overdraft (except in special circumstances); uneconomical if funds not really required; may involve some restrictions.
Credit factoring (from specialist finance houses, often owned by clearing banks)	Can save costs if properly used – but often doesn't; credit linked to sales; used properly can be very convenient over a bridging stage; flexible; factors may carry bad debt risk (for extra payment); high percentage advance.	Can be some loss of contact with customers; difficult to terminate; regarded by some financiers as sign of weakness; might reduce overdraft facilities; dearer than it looks at first glance; minimum invoice/account value £100/£1,000 puts it beyond reach of some who need it most.
Invoice discounting (from specialist finance house)	No loss of contact with customers; can be ended easily; credit linked to sales; flexible; inexpensive and fairly quick to arrange can be great help in tight liquidity situation.	Might reduce overdraft facilities; dearer than overdraft facilities; regarded by some financiers as a sign of weakness.
Medium term		
Hire-purchase (from specialist finance houses, mostly owned by clearing banks)	Quick and inexpensive to arrange; ideal for short life, heavy use assets with guaranteed return, costs and repayment terms fixed for period; does not normally affect bank overdraft; capital allowances available straight away	Fairly expensive; default may be prosecuted over-vigorously; interest expressed as flat rate can be misleading (a rough rule of thumb is to double the flat rate to get the true rate).
Leasing (usually from same finance houses as hire-purchase)	Same advantages as hire purchase except since ownership does not pass, tax allowances are not available to leases but they are reflected in a lower cost.	Ownership does not pass, therefore no tax allowances.
Medium-term loans (from specialist financial institutions, clearing banks, merchant banks, government and EC sources)	Term commitment by lender – costs and repayment known; ideal for financing fixed assets; low minimum sum from some sources; inflation lessens real cost.	Might involve borrowing and other restrictions; dearer than shorter period finance; early repayment may involve additional interest charges.
Long term		
Long-term loans (from specialist institutions, insurance companies, government and EC sources)	Improves financial flexibility; other advantages same as for medium-term loans; improves balance sheet; cumulative effect of inflation makes it highly economic in real terms.	Same disadvantages as medium-term loans; insurance company loans dearer than they look when linked to life policies; lengthy to arrange (allow four months); may be partly convertible into equity.
Share capital (from specialist institutions, venture capital funds, merchant banks, pension funds)	Improves the platform on which borrowings can be raised. No repayments.	Can be expensive and, if in equity form, will reduce the owner's stake.

Reproduced from *Starting a Business* by Hargreaves, published by Heinemann.

Table 7.1	The impact of gearing upon profitability		
		Company A (£'000)	Company B (£'000)
Ordinary shares		900	100
Debentures (10%)		100	900
Total long-term finance		1,000	1,000

Situation 1

	Company A	Company B
Profit	100	100
Debenture interest	10	90
Residue available to equity shareholders	90	10
As a % return on ordinary share capital	10% $\frac{(90)}{900}$	10% $\frac{(10)}{100}$

Situation 2

Profit increases by 10%

	Company A	Company B
Profit	110	110
Debenture interest	10	90
Residue available to equity shareholders	100	20
As a % return on capital	11%	20%

Situation 3

Profits decline by 10%

	Company A	Company B
Profit	90	90
Debenture interest	10	90
Residue available to equity shareholders	80	Nil
As a % return on capital	9%	Nil

Source: *A-Level Business Studies*, M. Buckley *et al.*, Longman 1992

PC
7.1.3
7.1.4

DISCUSSION TOPICS

1 What do you see as the dangers in running a business which is heavily indebted to a bank or finance house?

2 Is there any such thing as a 'reasonable' interest rate to charge in return for lending out sums of money? Or should the extent of the interest rate be limited only by 'what the market will bear'?

3 What do you see as the consequences in an economy of 'expensive money'?

4 It has been said by financial commentators that obtaining cash injections from the issue of shares by large companies enables their managers to gain extensive (even unbridled) control, since shareholders rarely attend annual shareholders' meetings in any significant numbers. Should shareholders be given more power and rights? If so, of what kind?

5 How does high and low gearing affect a company's security?

ACTIVITIES

In pairs, undertake *one* of the following activities:

1 Find out the current interest charges levied by a local clearing bank on a loan to start up a small business, and what kind of planning documentation is required from the would-be entrepreneurs.

2 Find out the going rate for a medium-to-large company to secure a loan of, say, £250,000 to finance a business project, and what sort of securities a bank or finance house might require.

3 Find out what type of financial support is currently being made available by your local Training & Enterprise Council (TEC) and/or Department of Trade and Industry to assist business start-ups, expansion or development.

4 Research into three to five sets of published company accounts and find out what proportion of profits is retained in the form of reserves, and what proportion of turnover is paid out in the form of shareholders' dividends – seek to provide a rationale for your findings.

5 Research into the issue of shares as a means of obtaining additional injections of capital.

 Report back to your group on your findings in the form of a 5-10 minute oral presentation and summarise your key data as a factsheet for distribution to your class as a revision support tool.

WORKING CAPITAL

Working capital is traditionally referred to as the difference between current assets and current liabilities. it is also a crucial factor in the financial component of any business plan, since it is the source of finance which pays for the day-to-day bills and running expenses, such as the payment for goods purchased for stock, petty cash items, payroll, services (cleaning, laundry, vending machines) and so on.

In both start-up and mature business planning, a key component is the cash-flow forecast, which itemises all the components which go to make up:

■ sources of income

■ sources of expenditure

during a given trading period (which may be the duration of the business plan). A detailed examination of cash flow forecasting is given below.

The term 'working capital' is used to describe the money which circulates around the business during its normal trading activities:

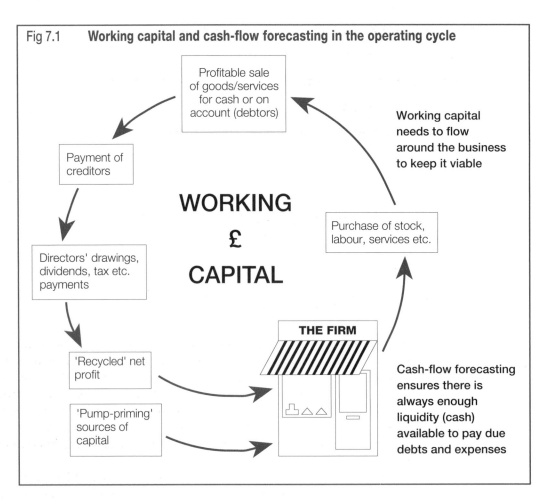

Fig 7.1 Working capital and cash-flow forecasting in the operating cycle

As Fig 7.1 illustrates, all businesses need, basically, two forms of finance:

1 Start-up, pump-priming capital, which may come from directors' investments, loans or the issue of shares etc.

2 Money earned in the form of an operating profit – stemming from the profitable sale of goods or services

Additionally, it may be that a company invests some of its profits and derives income from interest payments or dividends from time to time.

REVIEW TEST

1 List four long-term assets a business is likely to possess.

2 Explain briefly how these assets might be employed to provide the finance needed for a new business project.

3 Explain briefly what is meant by the term 'venture and investment capital'.

4 List the main sources of finance available to a small trader wishing to expand his or her business, and to a public limited company wishing to do the same.

5 What is meant by the term 'internal equity'?

6   Explain the difference between preference and ordinary shares.

7   What is a rights issue, and what is it used for?

8   List three kinds of long, two medium and two short-term types of finance.

9   How does capital gearing affect a company's profitability?

10   Explain briefly how working capital is employed in a business.

CASH-FLOW FORECASTS

PC
7.2.1

■ The role of the cash-flow forecast

Prudent companies employ accountants to monitor continually the relationship between money flowing out of the enterprise (in the form of payments for raw materials, stock purchases, support services, payroll etc.) and revenue coming in from debtors (in the form of payments for goods or services sold to them), as well as any income from any investments. If income received always preceded in time payments out, there would be little or no need for cash-flow forecasting and analysis. Problems arise, however, when there is insufficient hard cash (liquidity) at the bank or in the safe to pay bills which have become due.

For this reason, management accountants tend to look for a ratio of 2:1 for current assets against current liabilities as a measure of a firm's financial viability or robustness in its business operations. (*Note:* current assets are those assets which can be readily converted into cash within, say, one year – payments for goods/services sold, finished goods ready for sale, stock in hand etc.; current liabilities represent the monies owed to creditors.) The 2:1 ratio reassures interested parties that the enterprise is most unlikely to fail as a result of a cash-flow problem.

Since 1992, companies have been required to include a cash-flow statement in their presentation of accounts, an example of which is shown in Table 7.2.

■ Producing and interpreting a cash-flow forecast

PC
7.2.1
7.2.2

The following section (reproduced by kind permission of the National Westminster Bank plc from *Profit by Planning*) provides an excellent illustration of the way in which methodical cash-flow forecasting helps a new business through its all-important first twelve months of trading. *Note:* the following section has been written to address directly a would-be business start-up entrepreneur.

Completing cash-flow forecasts

Once you have completed your operating budget you are ready to move on to your cash-flow forecast. Again, there are two forms enclosed, one for you, and, if appropriate, one for your bank manager.

Table 7.2   **Example of a cash-flow statement**

	£000	£000
Sandal PLC		
Cash flow statement for the year ended 30 April 1992		
Net cash inflow from operating activities		4,765
Returns on investment and servicing of finance		
Interest received	2,435	
Interest paid	(56)	
Dividends paid	(1,890)	
Net cash inflow from returns on investments and servicing of finance		489
Taxation		
Corporation tax paid	(1,546)	
Tax paid		(1,546)
Investing activities		
Payments to acquire fixed assets	(857)	
Receipts from sales of fixed assets	280	
Net cash outflow from investing activities		(577)
Net cash inflow before financing		3,131
Financing		
Issue of ordinary share capital	200	
Repayment of debenture loan	(40)	
Net cash inflow from financing		160
Increase in cash and cash equivalents		3,291

Source: *Business Studies* (Longman Revise Guides), M. Buckley *et al.*, Longman 1992

Completing a cash-flow forecast is not just a question of transferring the figures from your operating budget. We will discuss some of the differences a little later on. First though, let's consider the objectives of a cash-flow forecast:

Cash is the life-blood of the business and neglecting to give attention to this vital element is one of the main reasons for business failures.

Time spent assessing the cash requirements and monitoring cash-flow is time well spent because it can:

- identify potential cash shortfalls before they occur
- enable potential surplus cash to be identified and used efficiently
- ensure that adequate cash is available for any necessary capital expenditure
- encourage more efficient use of resources and reduce costs
- lead to soundly-based decisions

How do you complete a cash-flow forecast?

Like your operating budget, your cash-flow forecast will be based on assumptions. Again ensure these are realistic and make a note of all the assumptions used.

Unlike your operating budget, your cash-flow forecast is not concerned with profit and loss. It merely represents your best estimate of the timing of cash receipts and payments, through your bank account, over a period.

Please bear in mind:

a) The period of credit you give to your customers or take from your suppliers. If, for example, you allow 30 days credit, your operating budget could show invoiced sales in say January, which should not feature in your cash-flow forecast until February, and then only if you have adequate systems in place to ensure that customers pay on time.

   If yours is a new business without a track record, you may well have to settle with your suppliers immediately. This will obviously have a material effect on your cash-flow.

b) You should show all cash to be paid and received, including capital expenditure, and loans received and repaid. These items are not in the operating budget. Conversely, remember that depreciation should not be included in a cash-flow forecast as it is purely a book entry and does not involve cash going in or out of the business.

c) VAT will be included in a **cash-flow forecast**, although it is excluded from an **operating budget** as it is not a charge against profit or loss but is a cash settlement with H M Customs and Excise.

NB. Where the business is not registered for VAT – and therefore not charged on sales – include as part of expenses figures shown in operating budget. The reason for this is that since you will be unable to claim tax back from H M Customs & Excise, it will have an effect upon your projected profit.

To help you to complete the form, let's run through some of the headings in more detail. Again, it will be helpful if you have the form in front of you while reading the next section. See page 587 for the form referred to.

Line 4 Exclude your Bank overdraft, but include all other loans, including those from the Bank.

Line 5 Show all money of a permanent nature that you or your fellow directors/partners are putting into the business.

Line 7 Show such items as grants, selective financial assistance and so on.

Line 10 Show all remuneration and withdrawals from the business.

Line 13 All items should tie in with the information shown in your business plan.

Line 16 Include items such as electricity, gas, oil, water, telephone, insurance and so on.

Line 21 Include such items as Solicitor's fees, Accountant's fees, Consultancy fees and so on.

Lines 23-25 Include any other appropriate items.

Line 29 Show the opening current account balance in the Bank's book, but exclude Bank loans.

Monitoring

Now you've completed your forecasting, you may feel that all the hard work is over. Far from it. Although you've given a lot of thought already to the future of your business, monitoring your performance is probably more important.

You must now use the information you have compiled in an effective way and compare your actual performance against your projections.

If there is a difference, you need to find the reason and decide whether you need to take any corrective action.

Let's look at some figures for a possible cash-flow forecast and compare the actual performance with the projections. While we will concentrate on just the 6 and 12 monthly accumulated figures, you should be looking at your performance on a monthly basis to ensure you have the earliest possible warning of any difficulties. In practice the 6-monthly figures will not appear on your cash-flow forecast form but the 12-monthly will be your total column.

		Trading Periods			
		6 months to June		12 months to December	
Line	Receipts	Projected	Actual	Projected	Actual
		£	£	£	£
2	Sales (inc VAT) debtors	41,400	41,400	103,500	92,000
5	Capital introduced	10,000	10,000	10,000	10,000
A	Total receipts	51,400	51,400	113,500	102,000
	Payments				
8	Cash purchases	32,200	40,250	59,800	58,850
11	Wages /salaries (Net)	13,000	13,000	26,000	26,000
12	PAYE/NI	2,500	2,500	5,500	5,500
13	Capital items	5,000	5,000	5,000	5,000
15	Rent	2,250	1,500	3,750	3,750
15	Rates	240	240	480	480
16	Light and heat	450	475	900	1,000
16	Telephone and post	210	190	440	420
16	Insurance	400	400	400	400
19	Interest	680	750	940	1,465
20	Bank/finance charges	200	300	400	500
21	Bookkeeper	1,000	1,000	2,000	2,000
21	Professional fees	400	400	950	950
23	General expenses	400	500	800	1,000
26	VAT	1,000	800	5,500	4,375
B	Total payments	59,930	67,305	112,860	111,690
C	Net cash-flow (A–B)	(8,530)	(15,905)	640	(9,690)
29	Opening bank balance	Nil	Nil	Nil	Nil
D	Closing bank balance	(8,530)	(15,905)	640	(9,690)
	(C + or – Line 29)	Overdrawn	Overdrawn	In credit	Overdrawn

Reproduced by kind permission of National Westminster Bank from *profit by planning – Services for the Smaller Business*

Comments on actual figures for the first six months

a) Cash from sales at £41,400 is as anticipated, following a firm order.

b) Wages, PAYE, rates, insurance, book-keeping, professional fees and capital expenditure are as predicted.

c) Light, heat, telephone, general expenses, interest and Bank/Finance charges: these differ from the projection which, without previous experience to suggest likely expenditure, is hardly surprising. Still, there's no significant difference so, now the accounts are settled, there's no need to worry.

d) Although rental payments seem reduced, this is only because the June payment of £750 was put off until early July.

e) However, the purchases differ significantly from the forecast: not £32,200 but £40,250!

Here are some (but not all) of the possible reasons for the difference with comments on potential remedies:

Possible reasons	Possible remedies
(i) More material has been used than originally estimated. Result: a reduction in gross profit margin.	(i) If the contract is to continue, you might try and renegotiate the price to allow for use of more materials or look for means of reducing wastage. Otherwise you have to shop around to buy them more cheaply.
(ii) Suppliers have raised the price of materials. Result: once again, a reduction in gross profit margin.	(ii) As above you have learnt the hard way that you must allow for price rises when quoting for a contract of several months. Another time you won't underestimate on materials. You might buy more materials in advance but see (iii) below.
(iii) Stock is building up because buying and production are out of line.	(iii) While this does not affect the gross margin, is it wise to carry stock surplus to immediate needs? True it avoids price rises, but with stock possibly financed by bank borrowing, the interest costs may cancel out any savings.
(iv) In a business where credit is taken from suppliers, the increase in purchase payments could mean a shorter credit period allowed by the supplier.	(iv) You need to balance prompt payment to the supplier with the impact on bank borrowing.

Of course, there are many more possibilities. The same lesson will emerge from all of them: comparison of actual performance against original projection is the best way to identify potential problems and possible solutions to them.

Comments on actual figures for 12 months to December

a) At the end of 12 months we now see that cash from sales is £11,500 down; this difference has only arisen in the second half year.

Possible reasons	Possible remedies
(i) You did less business after finishing an initial contract in June.	(i) You should try to get more work. During this time your workforce would not have been at full stretch and with no promise of more work, you might have to consider some cuts in staff. Likewise cuts in overheads, although it is unlikely to yield significant savings at this stage.
(ii) Your customers took more than the originally projected credit period.	(ii) You should be tougher. You should strengthen credit control, and press customers to honour your terms of business.
(iii) While production continued as forecast, invoicing and deliveries fall behind.	(iii) You deliver on completion and invoice promptly.

b) Even when the payment-for-purchases figure is virtually as projected, it is a good idea to ensure that this is for the right reasons as there may be compensating differences. In this instance, purchase payments were:

	12 months	1st 6 months	2nd 6 months
Forecast	£59,800	£32,200	£27,600
Actual	£58,850	£40,250	£18,600

You can see from the record, that the second half of the year is also very different from the forecast. This example shows what might have happened:

Because sales in this period were lower than forecast, payments for purchases were reduced by, say, £4,400.

Having got on good terms with your suppliers over the first six months, you persuaded them to give you credit terms during the second six months. Result: goods delivered from August on were not paid for until September or later. Hence a once and for all cashflow benefit

£4,600
_____
£9,000

This £9,000 is the difference between the forecast and the actual figure for the second six months. It shows why you should always analyse the reasons behind such differences.

Other differences

VAT is down because sales are down offset in part by the reduction in buying.

Interest is up because, during the second half year, the overdraft has been running at a higher level than was originally forecast.

These examples illustrate what might happen to your cash-flow forecast. Similarly you should monitor your performance through your operating budget to ensure that your profit projections are on course.

Example of a cash-flow forecasting schedule

Enter Month													
Figures rounded to £ 's	Budget	Actual	Budget	Actual	Budget	Actual	Budget	Actual	Budget	Actual	Budget	Actual
Receipts 1 Sales (inc VAT) – Cash													
2 Debtors													
3 Other Trading Income													
4 Loans Received													
5 Capital Introduced													
6 Disposal of Assets													
7 Other Receipts													
A **Total Receipts**													
Payments 8 Cash Purchases													
9 Payments to Creditors													
10 Principals Remuneration													
11 Wages/Salaries (net)													
12 PAYE/NI													
13 Capital Items													
14 Transport/Packaging													
15 Rent/Rates													
16 Services													
17 Loan Repayments													
18 HP Leasing Repayments													
19 Interest													
20 Bank/Finance Charges													
21 Professional Fees													
22 Advertising													
23													
24													
25													
26 VAT													
27 Corporation Tax etc													
28 Dividends													
B **Total Payments**													
C **Net Cashflow (A–B)**													
29 Opening Bank Balance													
D **Closing Bank Balance (C ± Line 29)**													

Basic Assumptions – Please specify the following assumptions used in completing this form and list any other relevant ones overleaf

– Credit Taken – the average period taken from creditors. Days

– Credit Given – the average period given to debtors. Days

Note. The cash-flow forecast normally spans 12 months

Reproduced by kind permission of National Westminster Bank from *profit by planning – Services for the Smaller Business*

Example of an operating budget schedule

Enter Month		Budget	Actual	Budget	Actual	Budget	Actual	Budget	Actual	Budget	Actual	Budget	Actual
Figures rounded to £ 's													
	Sales												
1	Home												
2	Export												
A	**Total Sales**												
	Direct Costs												
3	Materials – purchases												
4	Wages and Salaries												
5	Stock Change (Increase)/Decrease												
B	**Cost of Goods Sold**												
C	**Gross Profit [A – B = C]**												
D	**Gross Profit as % of Sales [C ÷ A x 100 = D]**												
	Overheads												
6	Production												
7													
8													
9													
10													
11													
12	Selling & Distribution												
13													
14													
15													
16													
17													
18	Administration												
19													
20													
21													
22													
23													
24	Other Expenses												
25													
26													
27													
28													
29													
30	Finance Charges												
31	Depreciation												
E	**Total Overheads**												
F	**Net Profit before Tax [C – E = F]**												
G	**Sales required to break-even [E ÷ D x 100 = G]**												

Note. The operating budget schedule normally spans 12 months

Reproduced by kind permission of National Westminster Bank from *profit by planning – Services for the Smaller Business*

■ Why cash-flow forecasts are needed in business

As the above example from Natwest's *Profit by Planning* amply illustrates, a clearing bank will usually want to see a carefully compiled cash-flow forecast (and overall business plan) before advancing any start-up business loan to a would-be entrepreneur. Correspondingly, in order to assist the process of preparation and decision-making which precedes the commencement of trading, banks like Natwest go to much effort in order to design and distribute sets of schedules and supporting notes. In this way, the prospective borrower gives confidence to the potential lender by demonstrating that his or her original business idea has been strengthened by a professional, business-like approach to planning and financing.

The following checklist illustrates the ways in which a cash-flow forecast support the business operation:

HOW A CASH-FLOW FORECAST SUPPORTS BUSINESS OPERATIONS

A cash-flow forecast supports business operations by:

- reassuring prospective lenders of finance of the viability and likelihood of success of the business planning process (especially in start-up situations)
- providing a means of measuring on a continuous month-by-month basis the degree to which actual performance is mirroring forecast or targeted performance (so that prompt corrective action may be taken if needed)
- enabling the forecaster to better schedule the payment of creditors and to plan for large items of expenditure such as quarterly VAT payments
- allowing the forecaster to focus attention on possible danger areas, such as an increasing time-lapse between the issue of account statements and their payment
- by monitoring the amounts and frequency of directors' drawings
- by monitoring the sales turnover month on month and comparing this with totals of monthly payments

---

■ Cash-flow forecasts, operating budgets and opportunity costs

In large, established companies, the cash-flow forecast, together with a proposed operating budget may be demanded by management accountants working for enthusiastic managers who put up project proposals, say, to introduce a new product or service. Careful analysis by the management accountants of the submitted forecast and budget will enable them to decide whether the new project is likely to generate a demanded level of profit, or whether the concept of opportunity cost will come into play – whether the finance to be used up in the proposed project might yield a better return on investment from a deployment elsewhere in the company's operations.

CHECKLIST OF KEY FACTORS NEEDED TO PRODUCE AN EFFECTIVE CASH-FLOW FORECAST

When undertaking the production of a cash-flow forecast, the following are the key factors which need to be checked out carefully:

Receipts

Realistic projections of the amount of sales turnover and how it is likely to build, given factors like seasonal demand, customers' likely cash availability (e.g. immediately after Christmas) etc.

Accurate data on the levels of available start-up capital

Prudent projections of any income (and its timing) from investments made with any available capital

Payments

Prudent projections on the number of staff needed and how much they will be paid (including any bonuses or commission). Remember how cost-effectively Marks & Spencer plc deploy their full and part-time staff)

Up-to-date calculations on the levels of PAYE and NIC which will be levied weekly/monthly

The timing and amounts of the purchases of capital items – fixtures, equipment, vehicles etc.

Sufficient allowance for heat, light, telephones and postage and office consumables such as photocopying

Correct calculations for monthly rentals such as PCs, printers and copiers, and the costs of associated materials

Correct calculations of the amounts of interest and service charges payable to: banks, building societies, hire-purchase companies etc.

Close forecasts on fees charged by accountants (note that some companies now ask chartered accountants to tender for auditing the year's accounts

Provisions for emergencies or reserves which may be deemed necessary to cover a potentially slow trading period (say January or February) so as to avoid cash-flow problems

And, most important, *realistic provisions for bad debts*; in today's tough business world, many otherwise sound firms fail early because of bad debts incurred or giving credit to exceedingly slow paying account customers

Realistic projections of how much directors will need to take (and the frequency) in the form of drawings from the business

DISCUSSION TOPICS

1 What do you consider to be the most useful features of a well drawn up cash-flow forecast in terms of aiding a newly established business?

2 What sort of business eventualities does the cash-flow forecast **not** cater for?

   Can you provide examples and suggest other ways of managing their impact?

3 What items in a cash-flow forecast would **you** monitor most carefully in your own, new business over 6-12 months? Provide a rationale for the items you select.

4 Many small businesses fail in their early stages of development because they fail to get in fast enough the money which is owed to them for goods or services sold on account. What strategies can you think of which could be used to secure prompt payment from a firm's account customers?

ACTIVITIES

In groups of two or three, research into one of the following activities and then produce a set of briefing notes for circulation around your class:

1 Find out how a debt factoring service can assist a business with cash-flow problems.

2 Find out how and why management accountants use opportunity cost calculations as a means of evaluating the viability of proposed new business projects.

3 Find out what techniques a company's accountants employ to ensure that its cash-flow remains in a healthy state.

4 Find out some of the ways in which a company's working capital may be used most cost-effectively in, either, say, a manufacturing or retailing business environment.

ASSIGNMENT 1

You are required to complete a cash-flow statement for a new firm 'Smith & Co.' which starts business on 1 April. Use the Cash Budget Form on page 592 to fill in your responses.

1 Smith will put £35,000 into a business bank account on 2 January.

2 Later that week Smith draws cheques to pay for the following:

a) Premises £20,000 for the purchase of a lease

b) Fixtures and fittings £5,000

c) Motor vehicles £9,000

3 All stock purchases will be on credit. Smith will purchase stock costing £5,000 at the beginning of January that must be paid in February. Other purchases will be at the rate of £4,000 per month including purchases for the rest of January. Other than the initial £5,000 purchase all goods will be paid for two months after their purchase.

4 Sales are estimated to be at a rate of £6,000 for January and £8,000 thereafter. All sales are on a credit basis and debtors will pay their accounts in the month after the sale.

5 Salaries will cost £1,000 per month payable in the same month.

6 Other expenses will average £400 per month, payable one month in arrears.

7 Insurance will cost £800 payable in February and rates will cost £500 per quarter payable in March and June.

8 Smith will take £1,000 per month as personal drawings.

9 A bank loan of £10,000 will be received in February.

CASH BUDGET FORM

Months	Jan	Feb	Mar	Apr	May	Jun
Receipts						
(1) Capital						
(4) Sales Receipts from debtors						
(9) Loan						
Total receipts	£	£	£	£	£	£
Payments						
(2) Fixed assets (a) Premises (b) Fixtures (c) Motor Vehicles						
(3) Stock purchases						
(5) Salaries						
(6) Other exps						
(7) Insurance Rates						
(8) Drawings						
Total payments	£	£	£	£	£	£
Receipts less payments	£	£	£	£	£	£
Balance at bank	£	£	£	£	£	£

ASSIGNMENT 2

From the following information you must use the Cash Budget Form on page 594 to record the following receipts and payments:

a) Opening bank balance £5,000

b) Production in units:

Nov	Dec	Jan	Feb	Mar	Apr	May	Jun	Jul
460	540	700	640	560	500	420	380	400

c) Raw materials used in production cost £6 per unit. Of this one-third is paid one month before production and two-thirds in the same month as production.

d) Direct labour costs of £8 per unit are payable in the same month as production.

e) Variable overheads are £16 per unit payable three-quarters in the same month as production and one-quarter in the month following production.

f) Sales at £32 per unit:

Oct	Nov	Dec	Jan	Feb	Mar	Apr	May	Jun
240	360	480	580	620	620	680	520	360

Debtors to pay their accounts: one-fifth as a deposit in the month of the sale and the remainder two months later.

g) Fixed overheads are £900 per month payable each month.

h) Extensions to the premises costing £15,000 are to be paid for in February.

i) A loan of £18,000 will be received in February.

CASH BUDGET FORM

Months						
Total receipts	£	£	£	£	£	£
Payments						
Total payments	£	£	£	£	£	£
Receipts less payments	£	£	£	£	£	£
Balance at bank	£	£	£	£	£	£

THE COSTING OF GOODS AND SERVICES

It has become a truism to say that businesses exist to make profits. However, what is not so widely acknowledged is that, without controlling their costs, businesses are not only unlikely to generate profits, they may soon find themselves making an early acquaintance with the Official Receiver!

This section, therefore, concentrates upon the key role in financial management of efficient and effective costing in all its aspects:

- direct and indirect costs
- fixed and variable costs
- absorption costing
- marginal costing
- break-even analysis
- budgetary control

Whether your career takes you into manufacturing, a service industry or the public sector, a sound grasp of the principles of costing and cost control allied to an ability to produce associated charts and schedules will always stand you in good stead.

■ Costing in a manufacturing environment

As a manufacturing business makes rather than buys finished goods we need an account which will enable us to calculate the cost of the finished goods produced. This is known as a manufacturing account and for Dudley Manufacturing Ltd would look like the following example:

DUDLEY MANUFACTURING LIMITED
Manufacturing Account for the Year ended 31 December 1992

	£	£
Cost of Raw Materials Used		
Opening Stock	3,250	
Purchases of Raw Materials	52,185	
	55,435	
Closing Stock	1,565	
		53,870
Manufacturing Wages		35,625
Prime Costs		89,495
Factory Overheads		
Factory Rent and Rates	6,480	
Factory Light, Heat and Power	7,935	
Machinery Repairs	1,575	
Other Factory Expenses	3,250	

Depreciation of Plant and Machinery	3,765	
		23,005
		112,500
Work in Progress		
Opening Value	1,575	
Less Closing Value	3,890	
		(2,315)
Factory Cost of Goods Produced		110,185

You will see that the above is simply a list of all the expenses incurred in the factory.

- The cost of the raw materials used and the manufacturing wages have been added together to give prime cost.
- Factory overheads have been listed including the depreciation of machinery subtotalled and added to prime cost.
- As a factory has a continuous production line in operation at any one time there are partly finished goods in it. At the end of the year an adjustment has to be made for the change in work-in-progress for the beginning to the end of the year.
- The final figure is the factory cost of the finished goods produced and is transferred to the Trading Account. It is used instead of the purchases figure for a retail firm.
- The Trading Account calculates the gross profit as usual, you can see how the factory cost of goods produced has been substituted for purchases.

For example, the Trading Account for Dudley Manufacturing Ltd might look like the following:

DUDLEY MANUFACTURING LIMITED
Trading Account for the Year ended 31 December 1992

	£	£
Sales		180,835
Cost of Sales		
Opening Stock of Finished Goods	7,590	
Factory Cost of Goods Produced	110,185	
	117,775	
Closing Stock of Finished Goods	8,910	
		108,865
Gross Profit		71,970

- The Profit and Loss Account and the Balance Sheet will follow in the usual way. The only item to remember is that in the Balance Sheet the stock figure will show the stock of raw material, work-in-progress and finished goods.

■ Elements of cost

For a long time, manufacturing firms have found it necessary to analyse their costs in order to control them and thus make their businesses more competitive and profitable. In more recent times all types of businesses have understood the necessity of analysing and controlling costs. There are three main elements of cost:

■ Raw materials: The cost of the materials used in the production of goods.

■ Direct labour. The cost of the work force directly engaged in the production of goods.

■ Overheads. All other costs involved in operating the business.

■ Classification of costs

Costs can be categorised in two basic ways either because of their type or because of their behaviour.

   If we define costs by type we get direct and indirect costs.

Direct costs. These are the raw materials and direct labour

Indirect costs. These are overheads such as rent, rates, light heat and power, etc.

If we define costs by behaviour we get fixed and variable costs.

Fixed costs. These are costs which do not vary with the level of activity of a firm. A good example is the rent paid for the use of premises. The landlord will expect the rent to be paid whether a firm has manufactured and sold 500 or 5,000 widgets. A fixed cost will alter in time, the landlord will review the rent at the end of a set period.

Variable costs. These are costs which vary in direct proportion with the level of activity of a firm, for example, raw materials. If you produce 500 widgets you will need twice as much material than if you produce 250 widgets.

Semi-variable costs are costs which contain a fixed and a variable element. Many costs are like this but we assume that they can be split into their fixed and variable elements.

If we look at simple graphical representations of fixed and variable expenses they would appear as shown in Figs A and B. This is a simplistic way of looking at the costs since if a firm wishes to expand beyond a certain point, it will need to rent bigger premises. At the same time a supplier of raw materials is likely to give a discounted price if more than a certain quantity of goods is purchased.

   In such cases the graphs shown in Figs A and B would need to be amended as shown in Figs C and D.

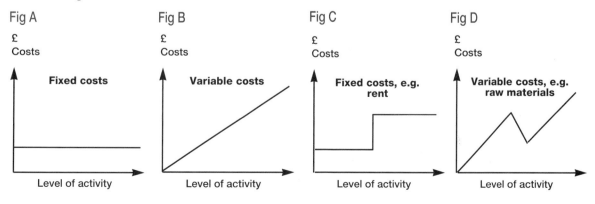

Fig A — £ Costs — Fixed costs — Level of activity

Fig B — £ Costs — Variable costs — Level of activity

Fig C — £ Costs — Fixed costs, e.g. rent — Level of activity

Fig D — £ Costs — Variable costs, e.g. raw materials — Level of activity

Absorption costing

If a firm which produces several different types of product wants to know what a particular item 'costs' to produce, it needs to identify the direct costs and then to add on an appropriate proportion of the overheads of the firm. When the firm has calculated the cost of an item, it will then be able to decide how many it needs to sell in order to make a reasonable profit.

Unfortunately, if a firm has several departments such as machining and finishing departments, it is not always easy to see how to split manufacturing costs between them and thus at times arbitrary divisions are made. Absorption costing does not claim to apportion overheads accurately to each department, it attempts to split overheads between revenue-producing departments and thus finds a 'cost' of a product.

Cost centre

A factory is split into specified sections/departments to which costs are allocated. These could be a service or a manufacturing section of a firm. Expenses are allocated or apportioned to each cost centre in a predetermined way.

The varying stages in absorption costing are as follows:

- The overheads for the next period are estimated as accurately as possible.
- The overheads which are specific to a department are allocated to that section.
- Overheads which cannot be specifically allocated are apportioned to departments in a particular way. There are several methods of apportionment including:

  1 On the basis of floor area.
  2 On the basis of the direct wages allocated to the departments.

- If there are any service areas in the factory, their costs must be apportioned between the production departments. This is usually on the basis of the average time spent by the service department in each of the production departments.

The total overheads of each production department are now known and these are used to calculate an overhead absorption rate for that department. Again there are many methods of calculating overhead absorption rates, some of the most common are:

$$a \quad \text{machine hour rate} \quad = \quad \frac{\text{Department overheads}}{\text{Estimated no. of machine hours}}$$

$$b \quad \text{labour hour rate} \quad = \quad \frac{\text{Department overheads}}{\text{Estimated no. of labour hours}}$$

$$c \quad \text{labour rate} \quad = \quad \frac{\text{Department overheads}}{\text{Estimated cost of labour}}$$

The cost of a job can then be calculated:

$$\text{Cost of job} = \text{raw materials} + \text{direct labour} + \text{overheads using the appropriate rate}$$

The required selling price of the job can be calculated by adding a suitable mark-up to the cost price.

These stages can be shown diagrammatically as follows:

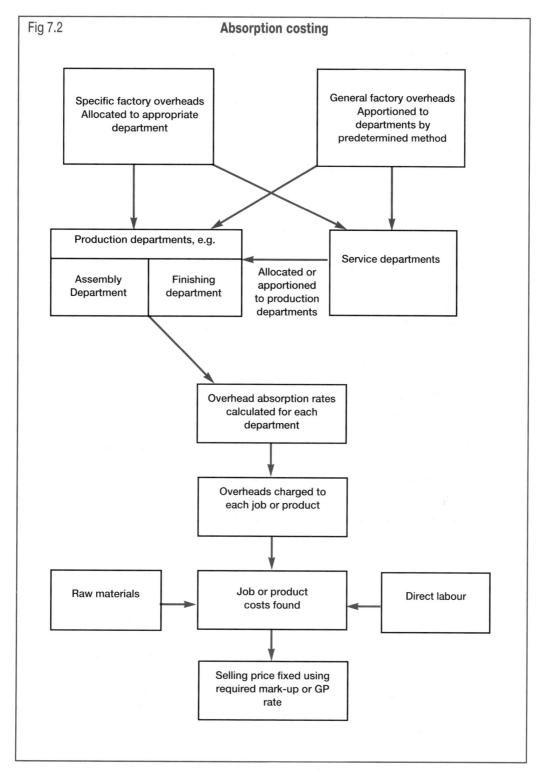

Fig 7.2   **Absorption costing**

Limitations of absorption costing

The first limitation is that the figures that are used to determine the cost of an item are estimates and will not be the actual costs incurred by the firm. This is true of any costing system used and is a general problem.

The other main drawback is that the method of apportioning overheads is purely a matter of choice of the managers of the firm and may become outdated with time. Unfortunately firms are very lax over the updating of their costing system. With the change in production from labour orientated methods to machine methods there is a need to update traditional labour rate methods.

PC
7.3.3
7.3.4

EXAMPLE OF FIXING A SELLING PRICE USING ABSORPTION COSTING

Helmsley Ltd is a small manufacturing company producing a variety of equipment for the hotel and catering trade. It operates from a factory which is divided into three sections, assembly, finishing and service.

The costs for the coming period are estimated to be:

Specific overheads	Assembly	£50,000
	Finishing	£20,000
	Servicing	£7,500
	General administration	£150,000

It is the company's policy to allocate the administration expenses to departments on the basis of floor area. These are:

assembly: finishing: service   8 : 3 : I

During the period it is estimated that the machines in the assembly department will operate for 50,000 hours and the labour force in the finishing department will work 12,500 hours.
The service department, on average, charges the assembly department for 1,500 hours and the finishing department for 500 hours of work.
A regular customer has asked for a quote for a customised product. It is estimated that it will take 12 machine hours and 4 labour hours in the finishing department to complete the product. The direct materials and labour will cost £130.
The firm usually requires a gross profit of 40 per cent on sales.
Calculate the selling price that should be quoted to the customer.

Stage 1

Produce a chart of overhead distribution to find the overheads of each production department.

Cost centre	Assembly £	Finishing £	Service £	Total £
Specific costs	50,000	20,000	7,500	77,500
General admin. apportion (8 : 3 : 1)	100,000	37,500	12,500	150,000
Subtotal	150,000	57,500	20,000	227,000
Apportion service area (ratio 1500 : 500)	15,000	5,000	(20,000)	–
Total Production Dept. overheads	165,000	62,500	–	227,500

Stage 2

Calculate overhead absorption rates for each department.

a Assembly Department. This would be based on the machine hours of the department as the assembly is, basically, a machine intensive process.

$$\text{i.e. overhead absorption rate} = \frac{\text{department overheads}}{\text{estimated no. of machine hours}}$$

$$= \frac{165,000}{50,000}$$

$$= \text{£3.3 per machine hour}$$

b Finishing Department. This would be based on the labour hours of the department as the finishing is usually a labour intensive process.

$$\text{i.e. overhead absorption rate} = \frac{\text{department overheads}}{\text{estimated no. of labour hours}}$$

$$= \frac{62,500}{12,500}$$

$$= \text{£5.0 per labour hour}$$

Stage 3

Calculate the total cost of the product.

Total cost = raw materials + direct labour + overheads

Raw materials and direct labour	£130.00
Overheads for assembly dept.	39.60
(£3.3 ph × 12 hrs)	
Overheads for finishing dept.	20.00
(£5.0 ph × 4hrs)	
Total factory cost	£189.60

Stage 4

Calculate the required selling price.

If a gross profit on sales of 40 per cent is required then the factory cost is 60 per cent of required selling price.

$$\text{Thus the required selling price} = \frac{\text{Total factory cost}}{60\%}$$

$$= \frac{189.60}{60\%}$$

$$= \text{£316.00}$$

■ Marginal costing and break-even analysis

Marginal costing considers costs under the headings of fixed costs and variable costs. It does not try to find the cost of production in terms of raw materials, direct labour and overheads. Rather it considers the variable costs of production and what profit or loss would be made if varying levels of production and sales were achieved.

Marginal costing uses a few simple mathematical ideas.

Contribution

This is defined as: selling price less variable costs. It can be expressed as a contribution per unit or as a contribution from producing and selling a number of units.

It is the contribution that is made towards meeting fixed costs and making a profit.

Break-even point

The break-even point is where a firm makes neither a profit nor a loss, the point where income and expenses are equal.

This is defined as: $\dfrac{\text{Fixed Costs}}{\text{Contribution per unit}}$

It tells us how many units must be sold before the business breaks even.

If you want to know how much the sales income must be before the firm breaks even, then you must multiply the break-even point by the selling price per unit, i.e.

Break-even point in £ = Break-even point in units × selling price per unit

Margin of safety

This tells us how 'safe' a scheme is by looking at how far our estimated sales can fall below the estimated maximum before the scheme is no longer viable, that is before we would be in a loss-making situation.

Margin of safety = $\dfrac{\text{Maximum Estimated sales} - \text{break-even point}}{\text{Maximum Estimated sales}}$

This gives the answer as a percentage. For example the sales can be 10 per cent lower than expected before the firm is no longer profitable.

Example

Assume that a firm makes widgets which it expects to sell for £15 each. The material costs will be £4.50 and the labour £5.50 per widget. The maximum sales are estimated to be 6,000 units and the fixed costs £22,500. Then:

Total variable costs	=	raw material + labour cost
	=	£4.50 + 5.50 per unit
	=	£10.00 per unit
Contribution	=	Selling price – variable costs
	=	£15.00 – £10.00 per unit
	=	£5.00 per unit

$$\text{Break-even point} \quad = \quad \frac{\text{Fixed costs}}{\text{Contribution per unit}}$$

$$= \quad \frac{£22,500 \text{ units}}{£5}$$

$$= \quad 4,500 \text{ units}$$

Break-even point in £ = Break-even point in units × Selling price per unit

$$= \quad 4,500 \times £15$$

$$= \quad £67,500$$

$$\text{Margin of safety} \quad = \quad \frac{(\text{Estimated sales} - \text{Break-even point})}{\text{Estimated sales}} \times 100\%$$

$$= \quad \frac{(6,000 - 4,500)}{6,000} \times 100\%$$

$$= \quad 25\%$$

■ Break-even charts

It is often useful to present break-even information in the form of a graph. If we wish to draw a break-even chart for the above example the first step would be to produce a small table of calculations as follows:

Units	Variable costs (£10 per unit)	Fixed costs	Total costs	Sales income (15 per unit)
	£	£	£	£
0	0	22,500	22,500	0
3,000	30,000	22,500	52,500	45,000
6,000	60,000	22,500	82,500	90,000

We assume that there is a linear relationship between units and costs and units and sales income. Thus the total cost line and the sales income line will appear as straight lines on a graph and it is only necessary to plot two points on each line. However, as a safety precaution it is suggested that three points are plotted. If the points are not in a straight line you have made a mistake!

The break-even chart from the above information would look like this:

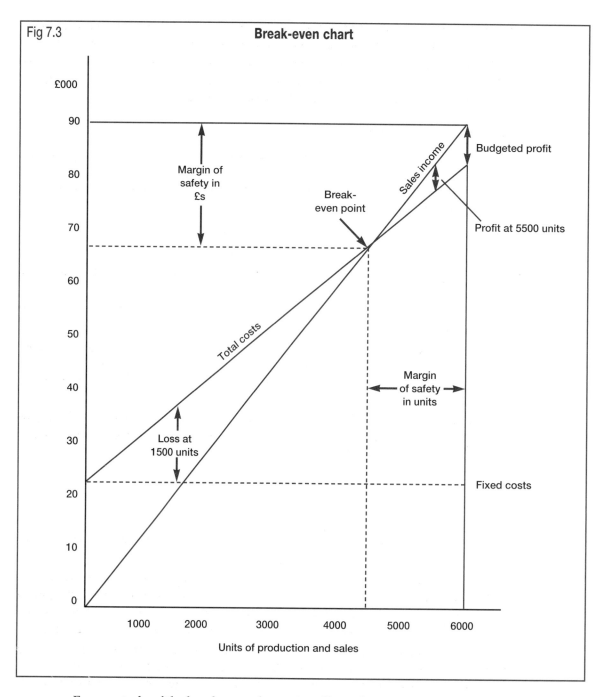

Fig 7.3

Break-even chart

£000

Margin of safety in £s

Break-even point

Sales income

Budgeted profit

Profit at 5500 units

Total costs

Margin of safety in units

Loss at 1500 units

Fixed costs

Units of production and sales

From a study of the break-even chart you will see that:

■ the horizontal axis represents units of activity. This axis needs a scale that starts at zero and extends as far as the maximum level of activity.

■ the vertical axis represents money. This axis needs a scale that starts at zero and extends as far as the maximum amount of sales (or total costs if the break-even point has not been reached).

■ the sales line starts at the origin as no income is received if nothing is sold.

■ the fixed costs line shows that these costs are constant at all levels of activity.

■ the variable costs are superimposed on the fixed costs line to give total costs.

- the point where the total costs line and the sales line cross is the break-even point. This is because at this point total costs equal sales income and thus no profit or loss is made.
- the margin of safety is represented by the distance between the break-even point and the maximum expected sales. It is not expressed as a percentage here as it is possible to see how large it is compared with the maximum estimated sales.

Other uses of a break-even chart

Although it is often argued that the principal use of a break-even chart is to find the break-even point in a given situation, there are other uses of these charts.

It is possible to find the expected profit or loss at any particular level of activity, e.g. using the above chart it can be seen that:

a If 1,500 units are sold then a loss of £15,000 will be made.

b If 5,500 units are sold then a profit of £5,000 will be made.

It should be obvious that below the break-even point a loss will be made, but this is confirmed as the total cost line is above the sales line.

Break-even charts are also used in 'what if' situations. It is possible to use a break-even chart to find relevant information to answer such problems as:

a Would it be better if we sold goods at £15 each when then the estimated sales would be 6,000 units or to reduce the price to £13.50 when the estimated sales would be 8,000 units? By drawing a third line on the break-even chart it will be possible to compare the two schemes.

b Would it be better to make the product in-house or to subcontract the work to another firm? Again by adding another line to the break-even chart to represent the costs of subcontracting the work it will be possible to make a comparison.

■ Absorption costing *v* marginal costing

It will probably be useful at this stage if these two traditional methods of costing are compared.

- Businesses which use absorption costing do so because they wish to attempt to find the total 'cost' of manufacturing a product. Thus they hope to be able to set their selling price at such a level that it will not only be attractive to potential purchasers but generate sufficient volume of trade to cover all their expenses and produce an acceptable profit.

- Businesses which use marginal costing do so because they believe that it is more realistic and assists the decision-making process. Marginal costing is useful in quickly assessing the position for situations such as, what happens if we change our selling price? Would it be better to make or buy one of our products?

  As marginal costing does not attempt to allocate fixed costs to a product, some argue that it is a more accurate method of costing, it does not rely on some arbitrary method of apportioning overheads.

- Additionally, as fixed costs relate to a period not to the level of activity, some people argue that it is fairer to set all fixed costs against revenue of the period and not to carry any fixed costs forward in stock valuation.

It is up to a company to choose which method of costing to use. It should not change the method to suit a particular set of circumstances. One of the basic principles of accounting is consistency.

DISCUSSION TOPICS

1 What sort of *external* factors are currently most likely to impact upon a manufacturing company's operational costs?

2 Of all the kinds of costs which a manufacturing company incurs during its operations, which do you consider to be the least difficult and which the most difficult to control? Give reasons for the choices you make.

3 What advantages do you consider derive from dividing an organisation's departments and units into individual cost centres? Can you think of any disadvantages?

4 As the manager of, say, the production department of a large engineering firm, what action could you take if you felt that your department was having to bear too large a proportion of allocated service department overheads? How would you ensure that absorption costing is objectively carried out?

5 What advantages do you consider marginal costing possesses compared with absorption costing? Is the former better suited to manufacturing and the latter to retail and service industries? If so, why?

ACTIVITIES

Undertake in a group of two or three **one** of the following activities and share your findings with your class:

1 Arrange to visit a local factory and to interview its available cost accountant and production managers in order to ascertain the principles (but not the necessarily confidential costings) which it uses to monitor the value and costs being added to its products in the course of their manufacture.

Your teacher may need to help you obtain an 'entree' for this activity.

2 Find a visiting speaker (say from one of your local management accountants' professional institute branches) who would come and speak to your class on the links between costing, budgeting, pricing, marketing and profit. Brief him or her on what approach you would like the talk to take.

Arrange for notes to be taken of the talk and circulated.

3 In liaison with your school/college refectory manager, produce a break-even analysis chart to calculate sales and profit for a new snack or beverage to be introduced.

ASSIGNMENT 3

Your firm sells a product for an average cost of £50 each. You have identified the following variable costs:
Labour £10
Materials £15
Variable overhead £5

Your monthly production is 95 units and the attributable fixed costs are £1,500.

Calculate:

1 the normal monthly profit for the product

2 the break-even point in units

3 the margin of safety in units

4 the profit that would result if a further 15 units could be made and sold for the same price/cost structure

ASSIGNMENT 4

Your firm makes just one product and its costs, profit and selling price have been estimated as follows for a production/sales run of 10,000 per annum.

	£	£
	(000)	(000)
Sales		1,000
Less costs		
Labour	500	
Materials	100	
Overheads	300	900
Net profit		100

You estimate that 80 per cent of the labour is a variable cost, all of the materials are variable and 40 per cent of the overheads are variable.

Calculate:

1 a profit statement using a marginal costing layout,

   i.e. Sales less Variable Cost = Contribution

   Total Contribution less Fixed Cost = Net Profit

2 the contribution per unit

3 the profit or loss of a) an increase of 20 per cent in sales and b) a decrease of 20 in sales.

BUDGETING AND BUDGETARY CONTROL

The word 'budget' is usually understood by most people. We have already looked at personal budgets but we now have to apply the same principles to a business situation.

A budget can be defined as a financial plan prepared for a future period of time. This period can be short, medium or long. A short period would be one year or less and most firms would budget for this sort of period. Bigger firms would budget in the medium term, perhaps for a five-year period and for the long term of up to, say, ten years. The features of a budget can be summarised as follows:

- It is for a predetermined, future, period of time.
- It contains financial and quantitative data.
- It aims to achieve specific overall objectives for the firm.
- It lays down the policy to be followed so that the objectives can be achieved.

Budgetary control is a technique in which actual results are continuously compared with expected figures and any significant differences investigated.

The purpose of budgeting and budgetary control is to:

- coordinate the activities of the different sections of a company and thus to produce a master budget for the company and individual budgets for the varying sections of the firm.
- communicate the policies of the company to all managers responsible for the operation of the budgets.
- control the budgets by comparing actual results with budgeted figures and to investigate differences.
- compel the formation of a budget, which is better than management just hoping that things will work.

Budgeting and budgetary control are very much management techniques. Many large firms establish a budget committee under the chairmanship of the managing or financial director. This committee must see that the targets that are set are reasonable and attainable.

Any firm's approach to budgetary planning will be unique to that company but a general approach would be as follows:

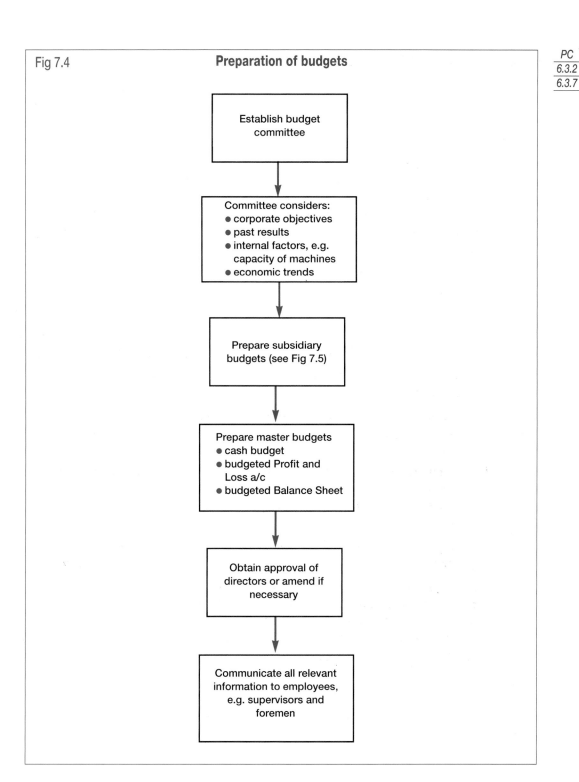

Fig 7.4 — **Preparation of budgets**

■ The limiting factor (or principal budget factor)

In all situations there will be one factor which will stop a firm from further expansion. The most common limiting factor is the sales demand, i.e. there is a finite demand for a company's goods.

Other limiting factors could be the supply of a raw material, machine capacity, skilled labour, etc.

Once the principal budget factor has been identified, it is possible to produce budgets for the organisation. To do this the subsidiary budgets for each aspect of a firm's activities must be prepared and then these must be incorporated into the master budgets which consist of a cash budget, a budgeted Profit and Loss Account and a Balance Sheet.

The processes to be undertaken can be shown diagrammatically below.

PC
6.3.2
6.3.7

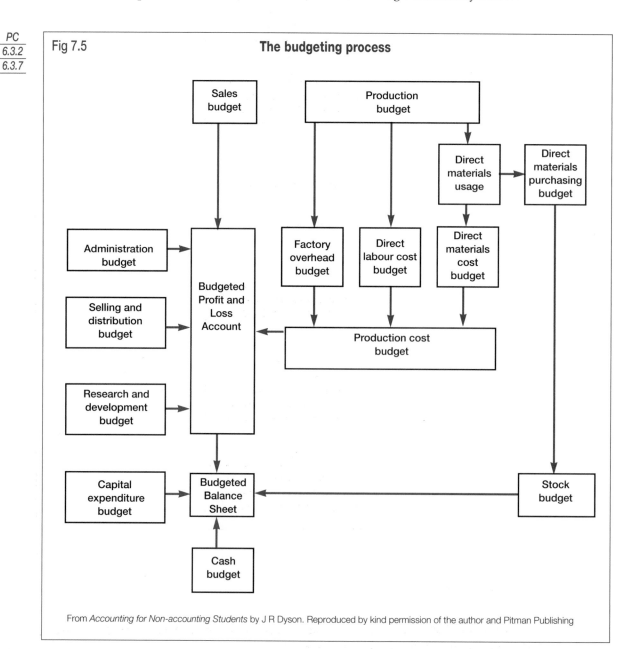

Fig 7.5 **The budgeting process**

From *Accounting for Non-accounting Students* by J R Dyson. Reproduced by kind permission of the author and Pitman Publishing

PC
6.3.3
6.3.7

■ Budgetary control

A budget that has been approved becomes the official policy of a firm and must be put into practice, compared with actual results and any appropriate action taken to remedy problems. Knowledge gained from the operation of the current budget must be used when the next period's budget is prepared.

Again this can be shown diagrammatically as follows:

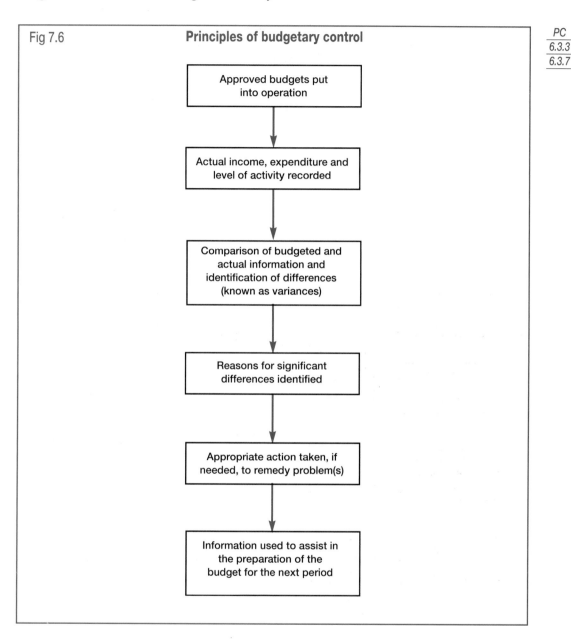

PC
6.3.3
6.3.7

Fig 7.6 **Principles of budgetary control**

■ Methods of budgeting

There are many terms that you will come across if you undertake a detailed study of budgeting. These would include the following.

Fixed budgets

This is a budget that is set at the beginning of a budget period and which remains unchanged even if actual production and sales levels differ from budgeted figures.

Flexible budgets

This is a budget which distinguishes between fixed and variable costs and is designed to change so as to relate to the actual volume of goods produced and sold.

Zero-based budgeting

It is often the practice to base a budget for the next period on the budgeted and actual results in previous periods. Unfortunately this may have the effect of perpetrating wastefulness and inefficiencies.

In zero-based budgeting the budget starts from zero, and all figures entered into the budget have to be justified by the relevant manager. Unfortunately this method of budgeting is complex to operate and can be very time-consuming to construct.

Budget preparation

It will be obvious by now that the preparation of budgets is a complicated matter. The example below is meant to give an outline of how budgets are prepared. In practice the research to establish the information would take many weeks or months to prepare.

EXAMPLE OF THE PREPARATION OF BUDGETS

Lyndhurst Ltd is a long-established firm which manufactures and sells one product.

Its Balance Sheet as at 31 December 1992 is expected to be:

Lyndhurst Ltd

Balance Sheet as at 31 December 1992

Fixed Assets	Cost	Dep. to date	Net
	£	£	£
Machinery	40,000	16,000	24,000
Motor Vehicles	20,000	7,500	12,500
	60,000	23,500	36,500
Current Assets			
Stocks: Raw Materials		10,000	
Finished Goods		13,500	
Debtors (from Dec Sales)		18,900	
		42,400	
Creditors: amounts falling due within one year			
Creditors for Raw Materials		20,000	
(Nov £10,000, Dec £10,000)			
Creditors for Overheads		2,000	
Bank Overdraft		3,000	
		25,000	
Net Current Assets			17,400
Total Assets *less* Current Liabilities			53,900

Capital and Reserves

Share Capital		40,000
Reserves		13,900
		53,900

It is expected that during the coming 6 months:

1 Sales in units, will be:

Jan	Feb	Mar	Apr	May	June
800	800	800	1,000	1,200	1,500

2 Production will be at the rate of 1,150 units per month

3 Goods currently sell at £30 each. It is proposed to increase this by 5 per cent on 1 April.

4 On average 10 per cent of sales will be for cash and 90 per cent will be sold on one month's credit.

5 Purchases of raw materials will be:

Jan	Feb	Mar	Apr	May	June
£12,000	£12,000	£12,000	£15,000	£15,000	£15,000

6 The variable costs of production are:
Materials £12, Labour £4, Overheads £2 per unit

7 Suppliers allow two months' credit.

8 Wages are paid in the month of production.

9 Variable overheads are paid in the month following production.

10 Fixed overheads are £10,000 per month.

11 A new vehicle will be bought in March for £15,000 and paid for in April.

12 The company expects to be overdrawn by £3,000 on 1 January and has a maximum overdraft facility of £15,000.

13 Depreciation for the six months :
Machinery £1,200
Motor vehicles £2,750

From the above information it is possible to draw up the following budgets.

PC
6.3.3
6.3.7

Sales Budget

	Jan	Feb	Mar	April	May	June
Sales in units	800	800	800	1,000	1,200	1,500
Sales in	£ 24,000	24,000	24,000	31,500	37,800	47,250
Cash sales 10%	£ 2,400	2,400	2,400	3,150	3,780	4,725
Credit sales 90%	£ 21,600	21,600	21,600	28,350	34,020	42,525

Production Budget   1,150 units per month

Raw Materials Budget

	Jan	Feb	Mar	April	May	June
Opening stock	£ 10,000	8,200	6,400	4,600	5,800	7,000
Purchases	£ 12,000	12,000	12,000	15,000	15,000	15,000
	22,000	20,200	18,400	19,600	20,800	22,000
Used in production	£ 13,800	13,800	13,800	13,800	13,800	13,800
Closing stock	£ 8,200	6,400	4,600	5,800	7,000	8,200

Wages Budget   Wages incurred per month £4,600

Overheads Budget   Overheads incurred per month £2,300

Finished Goods Budget in units

	Jan	Feb	Mar	April	May	June
Opening stock	750	1,100	1,450	1,800	1,950	1,900
Goods produced	1,150	1,150	1,150	1,150	1,150	1,150
	1,900	2,250	2,600	2,950	3,100	3,050
Sales	800	800	800	1,000	1,200	1,500
Closing stock	1,100	1,450	1,800	1,950	1,900	1,550
Closing stock	£ 19,800	26,100	32,400	35,100	34,200	27,900

Debtors Budget

	Jan	Feb	Mar	April	May	June
Opening balance	£ 18,900	21,600	21,600	21,600	28,350	34,020
Credit sales	£ 21,600	21,600	21,600	28,350	34,020	42,525
	40,500	43,200	43,200	49,950	62,370	76,545
Cast received	£ 18,900	21,600	21,600	21,600	28,350	34,020
Closing balance	£ 21,600	21,600	21,600	28,350	34,020	42,525

Creditors Budget

	Jan	Feb	Mar	April	May	June
Opening balance	£ 20,000	22,000	24,000	24,000	27,000	30,000
Credit purchases	£ 12,000	12,000	12,000	15,000	15,000	15,000
	32,000	34,000	36,000	39,000	42,000	45,000
Cost paid	£ 10,000	10,000	12,000	12,000	12,000	15,000
Closing balance	£ 22,000	24,000	24,000	27,000	30,000	30,000

PC
6.3.3
6.3.7

Cash Budget

	Jan	Feb	Mar	April	May	June
	£	£	£	£	£	£
Opening balance	(3,000)	(8,300)	(11,200)	(16,100)	(35,250)	(32,020)
Receipt of cash sales	2,400	2,400	2,400	3,150	3,780	4,725
Debtors receipts	18,900	21,600	21,600	21,600	28,350	34,020
Total	18,300	15,700	12,800	8,650	(3,120)	6,725

Payments:

	Jan	Feb	Mar	April	May	June
To credits	10,000	10,000	12,000	12,000	12,000	15,000
Wages	4,600	4,600	4,600	4,600	4,600	4,600
Variable overheads	2,000	2,300	2,300	2,300	2,300	2,300
Fixed overheads	10,000	10,000	10,000	10,000	10,000	10,000
New vehicle				15,000		
	26,600	26,900	28,900	43,900	28,900	31,900
Closing balance	(8,300)	(11,200)	(16,100)	(35,250)	(32,020)	(25,175)

Budgeted Operating Statement for the six months ended 30 June 1993

	£	£
Sales (6,100 units)		188,550
Less: Cost of goods sold (6,100 units @ £18)		109,800
Gross profit		78,750
Less: Fixed overheads	60,000	
Depreciation: of machinery	1,200	
of motor vehicles	2,750	
		63,950
Net profit		14,800

Budgeted Balance Sheet as at 30 June 1993

Fixed Assets	Cost	Dep. to date	Net
	£	£	£
Machinery	40,000	17,200	22,800
Motor vehicles	35,000	10,250	24,750
	75,000	27,450	47,550

Current Assets		
Stocks: Raw materials		8,200
Finished goods		27,900
Debtors		42,525
		78,625

Credited: amounts falling due within one year		
Credit for raw materials		30,000
Credited for overheads		2,300
Bank overdraft		25,175
		57,475

Net Current Assets		21,150
Total assets less current liabilities		68,700
Capital and reserves		
Share capital		40,000
Reserves (13,900 and 14,800)		28,700
		68,700

The above budgets show some worrying features:

- The principal problem is that the bank overdraft limit has been exceeded by the end of March. Fortunately the Company will have time to consider what action it needs to take to avoid financial embarrassment.

- Although the firm has made a profit, it is not in a position to pay a dividend. This may not please the shareholders.

- Unless the firm has seasonable sales, it should consider whether it is trying to expand too fast. The sales per month have nearly doubled in six months.

■ Corporate taxation

Taxation is a very complex field of accounting. Some people argue that it is a separate subject. Most companies will employ tax experts to deal with their affairs. The aim of all businesses is to minimise their tax liability; this is tax avoidance and is perfectly legal. Tax evasion is the non-payment of tax that is lawfully due and is illegal.

A company is a separate legal entity and its profits are subject to corporation tax. This is payable nine months after the end of the company's financial year. The current rate of tax is 33 per cent but for companies with small profits, i.e. less than £250,000, the rate is reduced to 25 per cent.

The calculation of the profits liable to corporation tax is complicated as not all expenses that are included in a Profit and Loss Account would be allowed in calculating taxable profits. The rule is that the expense must have been incurred 'wholly and exclusively' in the running of the business. For example, the majority of entertainment expenses are not allowable, depreciation has to be replaced by capital allowances which could be described as Government-controlled depreciation.

Dividend payments also require some tax consideration. When a company pays a dividend to its shareholders it must also pay 'Advance Corporation Tax' to the Inland Revenue. This payment is considered as an advance on the corporation tax and is deducted from the total tax due to give the 'mainstream' corporation tax.

GLOSSARY

Accrued Expense An expense which has not been paid before the end of the accounting period to which it relates.

Authorised Share Capital This refers to the value of shares that a company is authorised to issue as stated in their Memorandum of Association.

Balance Sheet A financial statement showing the assets and liabilities of a firm at a particular point in time.

Break-even Point The level of activity at which a firm makes neither a profit nor a loss.

Budget A financial and/or a quantitative plan of operation for the coming accounting period.

Budgetary Control The continuous comparison of actual with budgeted results and institution of the necessary corrective action.

Business Plan A complete plan for a business including financial forecasts.

Capital Expenditure Money spent on the purchase or improvement of fixed assets.

Cash Budget An estimate of the money that will be received and paid during the following accounting period, and the effect that this will have on the cash held by the company.

Contribution The difference between the selling price and the variable costs of sale.

Creditors The people and organisations who are owed money by a business.

Current Assets Amounts owed to a business and other assets which will be converted into cash within 12 months.

Current Liabilities Amounts owed by a firm which require payment within the next 12 months.

Debenture An acknowledgement of a debt, binding a limited company to pay interest at a specified rate.

Debtors Those who owe money to a business, usually as a result of the firm selling goods on credit.

Depreciation The amount that is written off the book value of a fixed asset and charged as an expense in the profit and loss account.

Dividends The payment to shareholders from the profits of the company.

Fixed Assets Permanent assets held in an organisation which are needed for the firm to be able to function. Firms do not normally trade in their fixed assets.

Fixed Costs The costs of running a firm which do not vary with the level of activity of the firm.

Gross Profit The difference between the sales revenue and the costs of those sales.

Insolvency The condition when external debts exceed the value of assets of a business. This means that the company will be unable to pay its debts as they fall due. It is an offence to trade when knowingly insolvent.

Issued Share Capital This is the nominal value of the shares that have been issued by a company.

Mortgage This is a loan given to an individual or an organisation which is secured against a specific property.

Net Profit The profit made by an organisation after all expenses have been taken into account. It can be expressed as Net profit = Gross Profit – Expenses.

Ordinary Share Capital This is often called 'risk' capital, as the shareholders only receive a dividend if profits are made and after preference shareholders have received their dividend. Ordinary shareholders normally have voting rights in the company.

Partnership Two or more people carrying on a business with a view to making a profit from the business.

Preference Shares Shares which are paid a fixed dividend in priority to any dividend payable to ordinary shareholders. In the liquidation of a company they will receive the nominal value of their shares before the ordinary shareholders receive any money back.

Prepayments Expenses paid for in advance of the accounting period to which they relate. All expenses must be 'matched' to the income of the same period.

Ratio Analysis A technique used for the interpretation of accounts. A comparison is made between the results of a firm in a given accounting period with those of the previous period, the budgeted figures or those of a similar firm.

Sole Trader A person who is self-employed, who is operating a business alone and has sole responsibility for its management.

Stock The goods which a firm purchases with the specific intention of selling or raw materials which it converts into goods to sell.

Variable Costs Costs which vary in direct proportion to the level of activities of a firm.

Variance The difference between a budgeted and actual figure.

PC
6.3.3
6.3.7

DISCUSSION TOPICS

1 What do you see as the 'limiting factor' which would stop your school, college or work place from further expansion?

2 If you were the head teacher (or general manager of your firm if already at work) of your school/college, what key data would you require to be included in an annual budget produced for approval from your Board of Directors, Board of Governors or Corporation?

3 What type of budgeting method do you consider to be most suited to your school, college or place of work?

PC
6.3.3
6.3.7

ACTIVITIES

Working individually, research into one of the following activities, and then produce your findings in an appropriate format for circulating around your class:

1 Supposing that the Chief Finance Officer for your school, college (or Accounts Director if you are already at work) indicated that a saving of some 10 per cent of current running costs had to be made to avoid an overspend situation arising at the end of the financial year (in four months' time), what areas could you suggest for cutting back in order to achieve the saving with a minimum loss of efficiency and effectiveness?

Produce a checklist of your areas for cut-back in order of priority and a rationale for having chosen your selected areas. Compare your selection with those of your class-mates.

2 Find out how the budget for one of the following is produced and monitored:

your county council; your district council; your local NHS/ trust hospital

3 Research into **one** of the following aspects of corporate taxation and then summarise your findings on how the system works:

a) corporate taxation of a private limited company

b) the auditing of a public limited company's annual accounts

c) the roles and responsibilities of the Inland Revenue

d) the VAT collecting function of HM Customs & Excise

e) the work of the Official Receiver's office

4 Find out the procedures to be adopted by a company which elects to go into voluntary liquidation.

5 Distinguish between direct and indirect costs.

Classify the following as either a direct or an indirect cost:

Raw Materials used in manufacture.

Factory rent.

Royalty paid for each item produced.

Bonus pay for production workers.

Electricity costs of factory.

Depreciation of machinery.

Wages of factory foreman.

Cost of leasing machinery.

Cost of leasing specialist factory machinery used in the production of one item.

Employer NI contributions for factory machine operators.

6 A firm manufactures widgets which sell for £8 each. Its fixed costs are £75,000 per annum and the variable costs are £3 per unit. It estimates that the maximum sales are 20,000 widgets per annum.

Draw a break-even chart and show:

The break-even point.

The margin of safety.

The maximum profit.

7 Verify your results by calculating the above.

8 The firm believes that there is likely to be an increase of 50p per unit in the variable costs in the immediate future. If this happens the firm would consider raising the selling price to £9 per widget, which would cause sales to fall by 12.5 per cent.

If the fixed costs remain at £75,000 calculate:

The new break-even point.

The new margin of safety.

The new maximum profit.

9 In small groups discuss whether it would be sensible to increase the selling price to £9. What alternative course of action could the firm take?

PC
7.4.1
7.4.2
7.4.5
7.4.6

BUSINESS FINANCE: BOOKKEEPING, TRADING AND FINAL ACCOUNTS

■ Introduction

It is now necessary to examine the ways in which a business accounts for its business operations and how they can be controlled.

You will probably appreciate that there are many different types of business including that of sole trader, a partnership and a limited company.

Main features of typical businesses

	Limited companies	Partnerships	Sole traders
Type of owner-ship possible	Dividend into 'shares'. There may be any number of shares from two (public companies seven) upwards. Each share carries certain defined legal rights and duties. Shares may be divided into classes with different legal attributes. Any share of a given class is identical with any other as respects legal attributes. A shareholder may hold from one share upwards. Hence very great subdivision of ownership is possible	There normally may be no more than 20 partners. Rights and duties are fixed by agreement. Each partner may have different rights and duties. Subdivision of ownership interest requires agreement of all partners	One owner
Risk to personal estate of owners if business becomes insolvent	Limited to a fixed amount per share, usually paid when the share is first issued	Unlimited. Any partner is responsible for all the debts of the business	Unlimited
Management	In hands of directors elected by shareholders at annual meetings	By agreement between partners	As owner wishes
Information about business available to public	A good deal of information, including annual accounting information, must be registered with the Registrar of Companies and/or sent to shareholders, etc. The public can inspect registered information. The Registrar exercises some supervision over information registered. There must be an annual audit of the accounts, in most cases by qualified accountants	None, except that partners' names must be registered publicly if they are different from the business name	As for partnerships
Withdrawal of funds from the business	Dividends may be paid to shareholders only out of profits. A special legal procedure, involving the consent of the courts, is necessary to repay shareholders' capital	By agreement between partners	At discretion of owner
Financing possibilities	Limited risk, the subdivision of interest, and the law relating to borrowing on the security of 'debentures' makes financing simpler and cheaper than is the case with partnerships and sole traders	Relatively restricted (*see* Companies)	Relatively restricted (*see* Companies)
Constitution	Embodied in formal legal documents copies of which are registered. Alteration requires a special legal procedure, involving the consent of a specified proportion of the shareholders	As agreed between partners. May be informal and need not be in writing	None
Tax on income	Corporation Tax on profits	Income Tax (Sch. D Case I or II)	As for partnerships
Termination	Perpetual succession unless liquidation	By agreement	At will

Reproduced from *Accounting*, R J Bull, published by Butterworth

Sole trader

A sole trader is someone who set up a business for himself. He may employ people to work for him, but he is responsible for the decision-making in the firm.

Partnership

A partnership is a group of people working together in a business. Usually all partners put money into the business and take on responsibilities for various aspects of the running of the firm.

Company

A limited company is a separate legal entity. It is owned by its shareholders who appoint directors to run the company. A company can be a Public Limited Company (a PLC) or a Private Limited Company (Ltd).

The basic differences between the three types of firm are shown in the chart on page 620.

USING A FULL DOUBLE-ENTRY SYSTEM: AND PRODUCING A TRIAL BALANCE

While Unit 7 concentrates on examining the structure of company accounts, it is important that you also gain an insight into the 'nuts and bolts' of the double-entry bookkeeping system.

■ Nature of the full double-entry system

The double-entry system is the basis of all bookkeeping systems, whether they are manual (handwritten) systems or computerised systems. To be able to 'think in double entries' is a great advantage, because it can answer every problem that ever presents itself in accountancy. The whole layout is illustrated in Fig 7.7. The numbers 1–5 guide us through the system and you should look at the part numbered 1 and study the illustration and then read the notes which begin with section 1 below. Having followed that section, proceed to part 2 of the illustration and so on.

1 Every transaction has a business document related to it

A 'transaction' is a business arrangement of any sort whatsoever. The most common transactions are listed below. At the end of each is the document related to it.

- *Purchases* of goods for resale or to be worked into a finished product for resale. (The document is an invoice; the top copy of the invoice from the supplier who sold us the goods.)
- *Sales* (the document is the second copy of our invoice – the top copy having gone to the customer).
- *Purchase returns* (the document is the *credit note*, the top copy of the supplier's credit note which is sent to us when the supplier receives back the returned goods).
- *Sales returns* (this time it is the *second copy of our credit note*, the top copy having gone to the customer who returned the goods to us).
- *Purchases of consumables* (there will usually be an *invoice* or *bill* for the supply of these

items. It will be the top copy of the supplier's invoice. If there is no invoice for a small item the till receipt or some other *petty cash voucher* – perhaps an internal petty cash voucher made out and signed by the proprietor – will be used.)

■ *Purchase of capital items* (there will always be an invoice from the supplier of the capital item, and it will be the top copy). With some items there may be a *deed* (premises) or a formal *hire-purchase document*, etc.

■ *Payments in cash and by cheque.* Here the receipt we obtain (the top copy) or give (the duplicate copy) or the *cheque* (inwards or outwards) will be the valid document. If we use a petty cash book, these receipts will become *petty cash vouchers.*

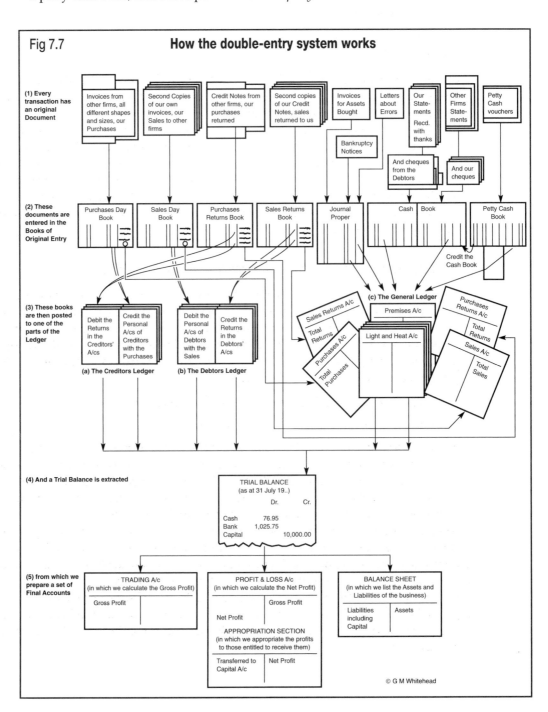

Fig 7.7 How the double-entry system works

© G M Whitehead

2 These documents are entered in books of original entry

Originally, in the Middle Ages, there were only two books: a book of original entry called the Journal, or day book, and the main book of account which was called the Ledger. Later it was found that having only two books was inconvenient, as only two bookkeepers could work on the books at any one time. It was therefore found to be helpful if the journal was divided into five parts. These were:

- The Purchases Day Book
- The Sales Day Book
- The Purchases Returns Book
- The Sales Returns Book
- The Journal Proper

Note that the first four are all to do with the things we buy and sell; activities which repeat themselves many times every day. The Journal Proper was kept for rarer items, such as the purchase of capital items, bad debts and depreciation, etc.

The other two books of original entry are the Cash Book and the Petty Cash Book, which as their names suggest, refer to incoming cash and cheques and outgoing cash and cheques. The chief idea of books of original entry is to make a permanent record of documents which can easily be lost. Keeping books of original entry in this way does give a great deal of work for very little benefit, and it is chiefly in this field that short-cut systems are widely used today. Computers do all such things with effortless ease, and this explains why computerised systems are so popular.

3 The books of original entry are then posted to the Ledger

The Ledger is the main book of account in the double-entry system. An account is a page in the ledger, or rather a leaf in the ledger, because both sides of a page are devoted to each account. If we open up an account with someone it simply means we give them a page in our ledger, with their name and address, telephone number etc., at the top. Every transaction with them goes on the page, either on the left-hand side (the debit side) or the right-hand side (the credit side). The rules are:

- *Debit the account that receives the goods, or services, or money*
- *Credit the account that gives goods, or services, or money*

This rule is usually shortened to: *Debit the receiver, credit the giver*. So if we supply Catherine Timms with envelopes worth £28.50 we debit her account with £28.50, because she is receiving value. She is now our debtor (she has an unpaid balance of £28.50 on her account). Later, if she sends us a cheque for £28.50 we credit her account – credit the giver. This leaves her account clear; there is no balance on her account.

Note that because there are so many accounts (one firm in the United Kingdom has over 8 million debtors alone) the ledger is split into sections. We have a *Creditors' Ledger* (with all our suppliers' accounts in it) a *Debtors' Ledger* (with all our debtors' accounts in it) and a *General Ledger*, with the rest of our accounts. More of this later.

It will not detract from our understanding of Fig 7.7 if we consider for a moment the layout of a traditional ledger account, such as would be found in all the sections of the ledger illustrated in Fig 7.7. You can see this layout in Fig 7.8 and it is described in the notes below it.

Fig 7.8

The layout of a traditional ledger account

Dr							Cr
Debit Side Date	Details	Folio	Amount	**Credit Side** Date	Details	Folio	Amount

Notes to Fig 7.8

- The page is divided down the middle.
- The left-hand side is called the debit side, or debtor side, and often has the abbreviation Dr printed at the top.
- The right-hand side is called the credit side, or creditor side, and often has the abbreviation Cr printed at the top.
- Columns are drawn on each side for the date, details, folio numbers (to be explained later) and the amount received or given.

It is when we make entries in the ledger accounts that the term 'double-entry' comes into use, for every accounting transaction requires two entries not one. Imagine a transaction in which we purchase a piece of furniture worth £100 from A. Trader, on credit, payable in one month's time. A. Trader gives us a piece of furniture worth £100. Can you think in double entries? Which account will receive a piece of furniture worth £100? Obviously it must be the Furniture Account. Debit Furniture Account with £100!

Which account is giving us £100 worth of value? Clearly it is A. Trader. Credit A. Trader's account with £100! A. Trader is now one of our creditors, and we owe him £100 for furniture received.

Later, of course, we shall pay A. Trader £100, probably by cheque. Who will receive the £100 cheque? Clearly it is A. Trader, so we debit A. Trader's account, and that wipes out the debt and leaves his account clear The bank account has given the cheque. Credit the giver, so we credit Bank account, which loses £100 of the money in the bank. The first of these double entries is shown in Fig 7.9.

Fig 7.9 — **A double entry**

Dr				Furniture Account			L.1 Cr
199 Aug. 17	A.Trader	L2	£ 0.00				

Dr				A. Trader			L.2 Cr
				19 Aug. 17	Furniture	L1	£ 0.00

Notes to Fig 7.9

- The two accounts affected are Furniture account and A. Trader's account.

- Each account (page in the ledger) has a reference number written in the top right-hand corner. It is called a 'folio number' (Latin: *folium* = leaf).

- When the entries are made it is usual to record the folio number of the other account in the folio column. This tells anyone looking at an account where to find the other half of the double-entry.

- Note that the Furniture account received value and so it is debited, but A. Trader gave value so his account is credited. Remember the rule: debit the account that receives value, credit the account that gives value.

- Later, when A. Trader is paid by cheque, A. Trader's account will be debited and Bank account (which is giving the money) will be credited.

4 A trial balance is extracted

Under the double-entry system entries are being made in accounts all the time, some on the debit side and some on the credit side. The busiest accounts are probably the Cash account and the Bank account, which are separated out in a special book, the *Cash Book,* kept by a bookkeeper who is fairly high in the accounting team, and called the *Cashier.* Other busy accounts are the Purchases account and the Sales account; like dealings in cash and by cheque, purchases and sales take place all day, every day in many businesses.

As a result of all these efforts we find it helpful to check up on all our entries at least once a month, and this is done by taking out a *Trial Balance.* As the name implies we try the books to see if they balance, because if they do we must have made all our double entries correctly. To draw up a trial balance we balance off each account in the ledger, including the Cash account and Bank account in the cash book. The final balance on any particular account will be on either the debit side or the credit side. If we make a list of these balances and total them, we should find that the two sides reach to the same figure.

In Unit 6 we have only a very brief indication of what the trial balance looks like, so it is helpful now if we look at one more closely. Before we do so, look at the three accounts shown in Fig 7.10 to see how the balancing-off procedure is done. For simplicity the accounts have been shown without the full rulings.

Fig 7.10   **Balancing-off accounts before taking out a trial balance**

Mrs M Jones A/c, 2173 Camside, Cambridge CB4 1PQ   L 32

199–	£		
27 January	137.56		

Commission Received A/c   L 199

		199–	£
		4 January Motor-car sale	25.00
		11 January Motor-car sale	38.94
		23 January Finance contract	72.65

Land & Buildings A/c   L 252

199–	£	199–	£
1 January Balance b/d	147,256.55	19 January Sale of Pett St.	38,250.00
14 January Garages	8,285.60	31 January Balance c/d	122,157.15
29 January Shop front	4,865.00		
	£160,407.15		£160,407.15
199–	£		
1 February Balance b/d	122,157.15		

Notes to Fig 7.10

■ The first account has only one entry on the debit side. Clearly this is a debit balance and we can see at once what the figure is. There is no need to tidy up this account at all – we just record it on our list of balances as a debit balance of £137.56.

■ With Commission Received Account there are several entries all on the same side, the credit side. You might think, with a name Commission Received Account these would be debit entries, because of the rule that we debit the account that receives goods, or services, or money. In fact, this money has been received but it will be debited in the Cash account (or in the Bank account if we received the money as a cheque). This account is the other half of the double entry – the one that says: 'Who gave this money to the business?' The answer is that it has been given by 'Commission Received Account' – though that may be a number of individuals who pay us for the service we rendered them. For example, garages often allow people wishing to sell a car to exhibit it on the forecourt and take 10 per cent of the sale price as commission. This is a profit of the business and goes on the credit side of the account.

   Do we need to tidy up this account? Yes – but we need not balance it off. All we do is add it up in pencil and enter the figure on our trial balance – a credit balance of £136.59.

■ The third account is the Land and Buildings Account and it has items on both sides of the account. What do we do here? The answer is that we balance off the account. One side is clearly larger than the other. There is £160,407.15 on the debit side, and only £38,250.00 on the credit side. Taking the smaller side from the larger we have a difference of £122,157.15. This is the balance on the account; the value of the buildings owned when we balance the books on the last day of the month. Note that we add this balance to the credit side, making both sides equal at £160,407.15, but immediately bring the balance down on to the left-hand side, where it shows clearly in a single figure the balance on the account.

Personal accounts, nominal accounts and real accounts

There is one further point to make about these accounts. They show us the three types of account we have in every business.

Mrs M Jones's account is obviously a personal account, an account with one of the persons we deal with in business. Personal accounts are always either debtors (people who owe us money) or creditors (people to whom we owe money). There is one rather special personal account, and that is the *Capital Account,* the account of the proprietor. Since we owe back to the proprietor everything he or she has put into the business, it is almost always a creditor account, with a credit balance.

Land and Buildings Account is a *real account*; that is an account which tells us about some real asset the business owns. Thus land and buildings, motor vehicles, plant and machinery, furniture and fittings and cash are all real things you can actually touch and handle. This business has land and buildings worth £122,157.15. Assets are always debit balances, and appear on the debit side of the trial balance.

Commission Received Account is not a real account. It is a record of money received, but the real money is in the cash box, or in the bank. It is said to be a *nominal account*, because the money is there 'in name only'. All nominal accounts are either profits or losses, and we keep a record of them only until the end of the year so we can work out the profits of the business.

Figure 7.11 shows a trial balance. This one has been taken out at the end of the year, although trial balances are always done monthly. Written alongside each item are notes showing whether the item is an asset, a liability, a profit or a loss. Some items are called 'trading account items' because they appear in the trading account; don't forget that to prepare a trading account we also need the closing stock figure, which is given separately at the end. One special item is the 'drawings' of the proprietor. This trial balance is worked into a set of final accounts in the next section.

Fig 7.11

A typical trial balance

T SANDERSON

Trial Balance as at 31 December 199–

Ledger Accounts	Notes	Dr £	Cr £	Notes
Premises account	Asset	86,000.00		
Capital account			130,675.70	Liability
Debtors:				
R Green account	Asset	394.00		
P Colne account	Asset	426.00		
Creditors:				
M Shah account			872.50	Liability
P Driver account			729.30	Liability
Plant and machinery account	Asset	38,240.50		
Office furniture account	Asset	7,246.38		
Cash account	Asset	249.72		
Bank account	Asset	13,825.60		
Bad debts account	Loss	238.60		
Advertising account	Loss	3,294.60		
Commission paid account	Loss	25.60		
Discount allowed account	Loss	128.54		
Discount received account			236.35	Profit
Business rates account	Loss	894.56		
Carriage out account	Loss	328.70		
Salaries account	Loss	27,925.50		
Motor expenses account	Loss	1,727.36		
Rent received account			1,850.00	Profit
Stock at 1 January 199–	Trading account item	9,275.50		
Purchases account	Trading account item	29,312.65		
Sales account			98,325.50	Trading account item
Purchases returns account			2,275.56	Trading account item
Sales return account	Trading account item	2,425.50		
Drawings	Special item	12,960.00		
		£234,964.91	£234,964.91	

At 31 December stocktaking revealed that the closing stock figure was £13,925.60.

Fig 7.12   A set of sole trader's accounts

T SANDERSON

Trading Account for year ending 31 December 199–

	£		£
Opening stock	9,275.50	Sales	98,325.50
Purchases	29,312.65	*Less* returns	2,425.50
Less returns	2,275.56	Net turnover	95,900.00
	27,037.90		
Total stock available	36,312.59		
Less closing stock	13,925.60		
Cost of sales	22,386.99		
Gross profit	73,513.01		
	£95,900.00		£95,900.00

Profit and Loss Account for year ending 31 December 199–

	£		£
Bad debts	238.60	Gross profit	73,513.01
Advertising	3,924.60	Discount received	236.35
Commission paid	25.60	Rent received	1,850.00
Discount allowed	128.54		75,599.36
Community charges	894.56		
Carriage outwards	328.70		
Salaries	27,925.50		
Motor expenses	1,727.36		
Total Losses	34,563.46		
Net profit	41,035.90		
	£75,599.36		£75,599.36

Balance Sheet as at 31 December 199–

	£		£
Capital (at start)	130,675.70	*Fixed assets*	
Add net profit	41,035.90	Premises	86,000.00
Less drawings	12,960.00	Plant and machinery	38,240.50
	28,075.90	Office furniture	7,246.38
	158,751.60		131,486.88
Long-term liabilities	–	*Current assets*	
		Closing stock 13,925.60	
Current liabilities		Debtors 820.60	
Creditors	1,601.80	Bank 13,825.60	
		Cash 294.72	
			28,866.52
	£160,353.40		£160,353.40

5 A set of 'Final Accounts' is prepared

The final stage in double-entry bookkeeping is to prepare a set of final accounts to discover *a*) the net profit of the business and *b*) the financial situation of the business at the start of the new financial year. This is done by producing a Balance Sheet. Since we have already learned how to produce a Trading Account and a Profit and Loss Account it is relatively simple to use the Trial Balance given in Fig 7.11 to produce a set of Final Accounts which can be submitted to the Inland Revenue.

Practical requirements to keep a full set of double-entry books

We now come down to the crucial point about keeping a full set of double-entry books: what books do you need, and where do you get them? The answer is that you need:

- A Journal Proper
- Four day books: a Purchases Day Book, a Sales Day Book
- A Purchases Returns Day Book and a Sales Returns Day Book
- A Four-column Cash Book (which used to be a Three-column Cash Book but now that VAT is a constant feature of our lives you need an extra column for the VAT)
- A Petty Cash Book (for small cash outgoings)
- A loose-leaf Ledger, divided into sections for debtors and creditors, and a 'General Ledger' section

■ Conclusions about the double-entry system

What can we say in conclusion about the double-entry system? The chief points seem to be:

- It is the only perfect bookkeeping system, which will answer every difficulty that arises.
- There is everything to be said for getting to know the full double-entry system and being able to think in double entries.
- At the same time it is too cumbersome to be used by a person who is a 'one-man (or one-woman) band'. It really needs a specialist bookkeeper and is thus most suitable for the slightly larger business that has reached the stage where it can afford one. Smaller firms should use one of the simple systems, either Simplex or one of the more advanced systems.
- Even the firm that does have a specialist bookkeeper should consider the use of simultaneous record systems for purchases, sales, wages, etc.

■ In the last analysis the true answer to accounting problems is a computerised system. The computer *does* work on a perfect double-entry system built into the programs provided by the systems analyst. The computer operator is not aware of what the computer is doing, and must ensure only that the data keyed in is correct.

This excerpt has been adapted from *Book-keeping and Accounts*, 2nd edition by Geoffrey Whitehead and published by Pitman Publishing 1989.

REVIEW TEST

1 What information does a cash-flow forecast provide?

2 In what ways does the production and maintenance of a cash-flow forecast help a business proprietor to run the business effectively?

3 Explain the difference between direct and indirect costs and give two examples of each.

4 Distinguish between fixed and variable costs, and provide two examples of each.

5 Explain briefly how the techniques of absorption and marginal costings are used in business.

6 How is the technique of break-even analysis used to predict cost and profit? Draw a break-even analysis chart to illustrate your answer.

7 List the main stages in preparing a budget.

8 What is meant by 'the limiting factor' in a budgetary context?

9 What advantages for an organisation stem from the establishment of cost centres within it?

10 Explain briefly the differences between: a fixed budget, a flexible budget and a zero-based budget.

11 What is the technique of ratio analysis used for?

12 Explain briefly why a company needs to undertake trial balances and bank reconciliations on a regular basis.

PRODUCING THE ANNUAL BALANCE SHEET AND TRADING PROFIT AND LOSS ACCOUNT

The two documents that all firms need to produce at the end of a year are a Trading Profit and Loss Account and a Balance Sheet. A trading profit and loss account looks at establishing whether a profit or loss has been made in the accounting period and the balance sheet is a financial statement which lists the assets and liabilities of a firm at the balance sheet date.

An asset is an item owned by a firm, such as motor-car or stock for sale. A liability is an amount owed by a firm for, say, stock which has been bought on credit.

If you look at pages 632 and 633 you will see a set of accounts for G Campbell who is trading at The White Hart public house. We will examine these in detail.

G CAMPBELL – THE WHITE HART
Balance Sheet as at 30 September 1992

Fixed Assets	£	£
Fixtures and Fittings		12,925
Motor Vehicle		5,100
		18,025
Current Assets		
Stock	9,125	
Debtors	180	
Prepayments	365	
Bank Balance	1,175	
Cash in Hand	790	
	11,635	
Current Liabilities		
Creditors	5,480	
Accrued Expenses	1,725	
Bank Overdraft	285	
	7,490	
Net Current Assets		4,145
Total Assets Less Current Liabilities		22,170
Long-Term Loan		
Bank Loan		3,000
		£19,170
Capital		
Balance at the beginning of the year		18,190
Net Profit for year	15,055	
Drawings	14,075	
		980
		£19,170

G CAMPBELL – THE WHITE HART
Trading and Profit and Loss Account for the Year ended 30 September 1994

	£	£
Sales		142,240
Cost of Sales		
Opening Stock	10,630	
Purchases	72,460	
	83,090	
Closing Stock	9,125	
		73,965
Gross Profit		68,275
Expenses		
Wages	18,245	
Rent and Rates	14,460	
Light and Heat	4,945	
Motor Expenses	905	
Repairs and Renewals	1,665	
Telephone	385	
Printing and Stationery	675	
Bank Charges and Interest	1,755	
Loan Interest	450	
Accountancy and Stocktaking	1,900	
Insurance	1,535	
Laundry and Cleaning	680	
Entertainments	900	
Bad Debts	100	
Sundries	1,485	
Depreciation of Motor Vehicles	1,700	
Depreciation of Fixtures and Fittings	1,435	
		53,220
Net Profit		£15,055

■ The White Hart Balance Sheet

This Balance Sheet shows the financial state of the pub at the Balance Sheet date, 30 September 1994. Hence it is important that the title of the document is correct. The White Hart Balance Sheet shows the assets and liabilities of the pub as at 30 September 1994.

Assets are items which are owned by the firm and which have at some time been bought by that firm. They are split into two categories, *fixed assets* and *current assets*.

Fixed assets

These are items which are owned by a firm which it expects to keep for some years. They are necessary for the firm to trade, but do not form part of the normal trading stock. In our case the pub owns fixtures and fittings such as bar stools and kitchen equipment and a motor car. The last mentioned is probably used for visits to the cash-and-carry and the bank etc.

Other firms would have different types of fixed assets, in general these would be categorised under four headings: land and buildings, plant and machinery, fixtures and fittings and motor vehicles. These titles can be adjusted to suit a particular situation. The purchase of these assets is known as Capital Expenditure.

Current assets

These are items owned by the firm whose value changes on a regular basis. They can be divided into five main categories:

Stock. In the case of our pub this would be the food stock for bar snacks, etc. and the wet stock (the stock of drinks).

Debtors. This is the amount of money owed to a firm from credit sales. In a pub there are very few credit sales and thus the figure for debtors is low.

Prepayments. Although a firm might have to pay some of its expenses in advance, for example, insurance is usually paid before the period covered, these are not included in a Profit and Loss Account until the relevant time. Thus they are a current asset at the balance sheet date.

Bank balances. Current or deposit account balances that can be withdrawn at short notice.

Cash in hand. The notes and coins that form the cash float and any takings not yet banked.

Current liabilities

These are amounts that are owed by a firm that must be paid within the next twelve months and usually much sooner.

Creditors. This is the amount owed by a firm to the suppliers of its stock. In our case this would be the amount due to the brewery and its food suppliers.

Accrued expenses. The amount due to the supplier of services – for example, the amount due to British Telecom for telephone calls since the last bill was paid. This is irrespective of whether an invoice has been received and paid as the service has been given.

Bank overdraft. This is shown as a liability and not as a negative asset. Technically it is repayable on demand from the bank.

Net current assets

This is the difference between the current assets and the current liabilities. It is sometimes called the working capital of a firm.

Total assets less current liabilities

This is the sum of the fixed assets and the net current assets.

Long-term loans

These are loans which are repayable at least one year after the Balance Sheet date.

The final total of the 'top section' of the Balance Sheet is calculated by subtracting the long-term loans from the total assets less current liabilities.

Capital

This represents the amount of money that the owner has put into the firm either directly or indirectly by trading, making a profit and leaving some of that profit in the firm. Drawings are the money or goods taken from the firm by the owner.

Important note: A Balance Sheet must Balance!

Note that the final figure in the Balance Sheet is the same as the total of the 'top section'. This is no coincidence. If the bookkeeping has been completed correctly and the accounts have been properly prepared, then the balance sheet will balance.

■ The Trading and Profit and Loss Account for The White Hart

PC
7.4.1
7.4.6

We will now look at the Trading and Profit and Loss Account. This is a summary of the income and expenditure of a firm over a period of time. Again take careful note of the title of the document. It tells you that it summarises the transactions for the year from 1 October 1991 to 30 September 1994.

Sales

This is the total value of all the sales, cash and credit, made during the year. It is irrelevant at this stage whether the cash has been received for the credit sales. A sale is considered to have taken place when the customer is invoiced.

Cost of sales

This is the amount of money that the sales have cost a firm. It is calculated by taking the stock at the beginning of the year, adding the purchases of goods for the year and subtracting the closing stock. Purchases include cash and credit purchases. It is not relevant whether the goods have been paid for.

Gross profit

This is the difference between the sales and the cost of sales.

Expenses

These are the day-to-day running expenses of the firm. They must relate to the period under review and thus consideration must be given to prepayments and accrued expenses mentioned before. Most of the expenses are self-explanatory, but one or two need further explanation and this is given below.

Net profit

This is the difference between the gross profit and expenses of the firm. It is the profit that the firm has made after all expenses have been taken into account.

Bad debts and depreciation

Bad debts. Unfortunately not all customers are honest. It is likely that in the course of a year a few cheques will 'bounce' or one or more debtors will 'vanish' without settling their accounts. These amounts will be written off as an expense of the business.

Provision for doubtful debts. The majority of business people expect that some debts, not yet identified, will eventually become bad debts. These will probably be associated with sales made in the last few weeks of a financial year. A prudent trader will make an allowance for these in his accounts and update the provision each year.

There is no provision in the accounts of The White Hart as debtors are a relatively minor sum.

Depreciation. This is defined by accountants as 'the measure of the wearing out, consumption or other reduction in the useful economic life of a fixed asset, whether arising from use, effluxion of time or obsolescence through technological or market changes. Depreciation should be allocated so as to charge a fair proportion of cost or valuation of the asset to each accounting period expected to benefit from its use.'

In calculating depreciation the following factors should be taken into account:

- the cost of the asset
- the expected useful economic life of the asset to the business
- the estimated residual value of the asset

METHODS OF CALCULATING DEPRECIATION

(*See Trading and Profit and Loss Account, Page 633*)

The straight line method

This method simply spreads the net cost of an asset to a firm equally over the life of that asset.

Example

A firm buys a car for £12,000. It expects to keep the car for 3 years and then to trade it in for £3,000.

The net cost to the firm is £12,000 – 3,000   = £9,000

The annual depreciation is £9,000 ÷ 3   = £3,000

Some people do not like the straight line method, although it is easy to understand and calculate, because they feel that an asset loses more of its value in the early years of its life than in the later years. These people prefer to use the reducing balance method which addresses this problem.

The reducing balance method

Under this method the value of the asset is reduced by a fixed percentage each year. The loss in value gives the depreciation charge for the year.

Example

A firm buys a car for £12,000. It is the firm's policy to depreciate its cars at the rate of 25 per cent per annum using the reducing balance method. The charges for depreciation are as follows:

Year 1	
Cost of car	£12,000
Depreciation 25% of £12,000	3,000
Written-down value at end of year	9,000
Year 2	
Depreciation 25% of £9,000	2,250
Written-down value at end of year	6,750
Year 3	
Depreciation 25% of £6,750	1,688
Written-down value at end of year	£5,062

Note: As depreciation is only an estimate, calculations are made to the nearest pound.

You will have noticed that two of the three factors are estimates and thus the depreciation charge itself is only an estimate of the amount of the cost used in a particular accounting period.

An additional complication is that there are several methods of calculating depreciation. The two methods most widely used are the straight line method and the reducing balance method.

As depreciation is counted as an expense in the Profit and Loss Account, the Balance Sheet shows the written-down value of the asset at the end of the year.

PC
7.4.1
7.4.6

DISCUSSION TOPICS

1 What financial advantages do you see in a firm electing to become a private limited company as opposed to remaining a partnership? Can you identify any disadvantages?

2 Since a balance sheet represents only a 'frozen frame' picture of a company's finances on a given day, at a given time (for The White Hart, midnight on 30 September 1994), why is it that so much importance is attached to it by: directors, managers, shareholders, would-be purchasers of the business, and the Inland Revenue?

3 Assuming you were the owner of The White Hart, with a newly appointed resident managing couple, how often would you want to receive a trading and profit and loss account for the business done? What measures might you introduce to ensure that the account was an accurate reflection of what business took place (given that the business is largely cash-based and you are an absentee proprietor)?

ASSIGNMENT 5

From the following Trial Balance produce the firm's Trading and Profit and Loss Account for the year to 31 December and a Balance Sheet as at that date.

Notes

1 Use the answer sheet provided

2 Appreciate that the closing stock figure given after the trial balance is used both in the Trading Account and the Current Assets section of the Balance Sheet.

Trial Balance as at 31 December

Account	Debit £	Credit £
Capital		115,400
Sales		150,400
Stock b/fwd	10,800	
Purchases	80,200	
Rent and rates	21,000	
Vehicle running costs	4,000	
Insurances	1,000	
Wages and salaries	15,000	
Telephone and postage	1,800	
Premises	120,000	
Fixtures	10,000	
Vehicles	20,000	
Debtors	16,000	
Creditors		20,000
Bank	11,000	
Drawings	20,000	
Loan		50,000
Loan interest	5,000	
	335,800	335,800

Note that the value of the Closing Stock at the end of the year was £14,100. Ignore depreciation of fixed assets

Assignment 5 Answer Sheet 1

Trading and Profit and Loss Account for the Year ended 31 December

	£	£
Sales		☐
Less the cost of sales		
Stock brought forward	☐	
Add Purchases	☐	
	☐	
Less Stock carried forward	☐	☐
Gross profit		☐
Less Expenses		
Rent and rates	☐	
Insurances	☐	
Wages and salaries	☐	
Telephone and postages	☐	
Vehicle running costs	☐	
Loan interest	☐	☐
Net profit		☐

Assignment 5 Answer Sheet 2

Balance Sheet as at 31 December

	£	£
Fixed assets		
Premises		___
Fixtures		___
Vehicles		___
Current assets		
Stock	___	
Debtors	___	
Bank	___	
	___	
Less current liabilities		
Creditors	___	
Working capital		___
		___
Long-term liabilities		
Loan		___
		___
Financed by		
Capital		___
Add net profit		___
		___
Less drawings		___
		___

INDIVIDUAL ACTIVITY

Working individually, undertake the following activity and then share your findings with your class:

Read through again carefully the balance sheet and trading and profit and loss account of The White Hart (on pages 632 and 633 and then check through the ratios on pages 641–5).

Assume you are a financial consultant working for Hooper & Downland (a national business consultancy firm). The directors of Wheatsheaf Brewery plc have asked you to produce for them a financial analysis and report on the performance and worth as a going concern of *The White Hart* which is on the market.

Produce a suitable report which justifies the recommendations you give, bearing in mind that the asking price for the pub is £200,000 freehold.

INTERPRETATION OF FINAL ACCOUNTS

It is insufficient in today's competitive business world just to be able to understand a set of accounts. It is also necessary to be able to interpret them and to answer such questions as:

- Has my business performed better than last year?
- Is my business as profitable as my rivals?
- If I present these accounts to my bank manager will he continue my overdraft facilities?
- Will the Inspector of Taxes be happy with these results?

In order to interpret a set of accounts it is necessary to calculate a number of accounting 'ratios' and to draw suitable conclusions from these calculations. Although the calculations are given the name of 'ratios', many of them are expressed as a percentage or as a period of time.

It is possible to calculate many ratios. Here we will look at the most important ones under three main headings:

Profitability. Whether a firm is making a reasonable profit for its size.

Liquidity. Whether a firm has sufficient resources available to pay its debts as they fall due.

Activity. Whether a firm has good control over its assets.

Profitability

There are three main ratios in this category.

1 Gross profit rate

This is calculated as follows:

$$\text{Gross profit rate} = \frac{\text{Gross profit}}{\text{Sales}} \times 100$$

This expresses the gross profit as a percentage of the sales.

If we take the accounts for The White Hart, the calculation would be:

$$\frac{68,275}{142,240} \times 100 = 48.00\%$$

This tells us that for every £100 of sales we make a profit before running expenses of £48.00

In practice you would compare this percentage with the corresponding figure for previous years. If there had been a considerable change then it would require further investigation. The reason for the change could be:

a *There has been a change in the 'sales mix'* In our case perhaps more food and less alcoholic drink was sold. As these goods have different individual gross profit rates the overall rate would have changed.

b *There was an increase in the cost of goods sold* which was not passed on to the customers. If this was a deliberate policy to retain customers, a further question must be asked. Has the volume of sales been maintained?

c *There has been a cut in price of some goods*, for example, bar snacks. This would be done to maintain or improve the volume of trade.

d *Theft by members of staff or customers.* This is a problem in all businesses and a lasting solution to it has never been found.

2 Net profit rate

This is calculated as follows:

$$\text{Net profit rate} = \frac{\text{Net Profit}}{\text{Sales}} \times 100$$

This expresses the net profit as a percentage of sales.

If we look at our pub again the calculation would be:

$$\frac{15,055}{142,240} \times 100 = 10.58\%$$

This tells us that for every £100 of sales we make a profit of £10.58 after all expenses have been taken into account.

Again a firm would compare this with its results for previous years and investigate any major difference. The reasons for a change could include:

a *A change in the gross profit rate.*

b *A comparatively large change in one or more of the expenses.* In the case of our pub it could be that there has been an exceptionally large increase in the rent payable due to a renegotiation of the rental agreement.

3 Return on capital employed

This can be subdivided into two ratios:

3.1 Return on owner's equity = $\dfrac{\text{Net profit}}{\text{Capital employed}} \times 100$

This expresses the net profit made by the owner as a percentage of the money that he has invested in it.

The Capital Employed is taken as the opening balance on the capital account or, if preferred, the average capital account balance for the year.

For The White Hart the calculation would be:

$$\frac{15,055}{18,190} \times 100 = 82.76\%$$

This tells us that for every £100 that the owner has invested in the pub a profit of £82.76 has been made. This is an extremely high percentage return but it must be remembered that the profit has got to support Mr Campbell's personal financial requirements.

In addition to comparing this year's figure with previous years etc., a sole trader could look at the return that he could get if he invested the money in, say, a building society. In comparing the two percentages the additional risk involved in running a business and the extra work involved must be taken into account.

$$3.2 \quad \text{Return on long-term capital employed} = \frac{\text{Net profit before interest}}{\text{Long-term capital employed}} \times 100$$

This expresses the profit made on the money invested in a firm as a percentage of the money invested in it on a long-term basis. Interest must be added back to the profit in order to arrive at a figure for the money earned for people who have invested in the business on a long-term basis.

For our business the calculation would be:

$$\frac{15,055 + 450}{18,190 + 3,000} \times 100 = 73.17\%$$

This tells us that for every £100 invested in the pub a profit of £73.17 is made.

Liquidity

There are two main ratios in this category.

1 Current or working capital ratio

This is calculated as follows:

$$\text{Current ratio} = \frac{\text{Current assets}}{\text{Current liabilities}}$$

This ratio measures that relationship between the current assets and current liabilities.

For our pub the calculation is:

$$\frac{11,635}{7,490} : 1 = 1.55 : 1$$

There is no ideal current ratio. However, for a retail business a figure of 2:1 is sometimes quoted. Many firms will have a ratio much lower than this and manage to survive quite happily. If a firm has had a current ratio of 1.5:1 for the past 5 years then it is reasonable to assume that it will continue to survive with a ratio of 1.5:1. A sudden change in a ratio is cause for concern as it suggests that it might not be financially viable.

2 Liquid ratio or acid test

This is calculated as follows:

$$\text{Liquid ratio} = \frac{\text{Current assets excluding stock}}{\text{Current liabilities}}$$

This ratio compares the liquid or near liquid funds of a firm with the liabilities which will be due for payment shortly after the balance sheet date.

For our pub the calculation is:

$$\frac{(11,635 - 9,125)}{7,490} : 1 = 0.34 : 1$$

As a general rule this ratio should be about 1:1. If it is very much lower than this, there is a danger of the business being unable to pay its debts on time. If it is very much larger than this, the danger is that the business is not making the best use of its funds.

The White Hart's liquidity ratios are low, but they might be acceptable. The business is a cash business and it is likely that Mr Campbell will be able to sell his stock in time to pay his creditors. If there is doubt, Mr Campbell could see if the bank will allow him sufficient overdraft facilities.

Activity

In this section we will consider three ratios.

1 Rate of stock turnover

This is calculated as follows:

$$\text{Rate of stock turnover} = \frac{\text{Cost of goods sold}}{\text{Average stock}}$$

If we only have a set of final accounts the average stock is:

$$\frac{\text{Opening stock} + \text{Closing stock}}{2}$$

The answer tells us how many times per year the stock is 'cleared'. For The White Hart the calculation is:

$$\text{Average Stock} = \frac{(10,630 + 9,125)}{2} = 9,877.50$$

$$\text{Rate of stock turnover} = \frac{73,965}{9,877.50} = 7.49$$

This means the same as saying that 7.5 times per year the stock is sold and then replaced. Obviously in practice the pub is never empty, there is always drink in the cellar and food in the kitchen.

Alternatively the rate of stock turnover can be expressed as:

$$\frac{\text{Average stock}}{\text{Cost of goods sold}} \times \text{12 or 52 or 365}$$

This tells us how long, on average, an item is in stock. The answer is given in months, weeks or days. For The White Hart the calculation is:

$$\frac{9,877.50}{73,965} \times 52 = 6.94 \text{ weeks}$$

This means that an item is in stock approximately 7 weeks.

Any business will wish to have as high a rate of stock turnover as possible, within reasonable limits.

This ratio taken with the gross profit rate will give some indication to the pattern of trading of the firm. If the firm has a comparatively low gross profit rate and you believe this is because it hopes to have a high volume of trade then the rate of stock turnover should be comparatively high.

2 Debtors collection period

This is calculated as:

$$\text{Debtors collection period} = \frac{\text{Debtors}}{\text{Credit sales for year}} \times 52 \text{ weeks}$$

This will tell how long, on average, the firm's debtors take to settle their accounts. You should compare this with the firm's credit control policy.

As the vast majority of a pub's sales are for cash, it is not appropriate to calculate the debtors collection period in this case.

3 Creditors payment period

This is calculated as:

$$\text{Creditors payment period} = \frac{\text{Creditors}}{\text{Credit purchases for year}} \times 52 \text{ weeks}$$

This will show how long, on average, the firm takes to pay its creditors. Obviously it does not want to pay its bills any earlier than necessary but equally it does not want to antagonise its suppliers. They may withdraw their credit facilities which will not be to the firm's advantage!

For The White Hart the calculation is:

$$\frac{5,480}{72,460} \times 52 = 3.9 \text{ weeks}$$

General points to note

The interpretation of accounts is a complex issue. The ratios that are calculated can be compared with results for previous years, with budgeted figures or with results of similar firms. If the latter is undertaken, remember that there may be different accounting policies in different firms, for example, a different method of calculating depreciation.

If you are required to write a report comparing the results of two different firms, remember to use the correct format for a report. An informal style will probably suffice. Your detailed calculations are best attached as an appendix to the report and a summary of your calculations should be included in the body of the report. Students usually find it easier to write about each category of ratios and then to draw an overall conclusion.

PARTNERSHIP ACCOUNTS

PC
7.4.5
7.4.6

What you have learned about the accounts of a sole trader are true for the accounts of a partnership. It is, however, necessary to amend the accounts to allow for the fact that more than one person owns the business

ACCOUNTING REQUIREMENTS OF THE PARTNERSHIP ACT OF 1890

Partnerships are governed by the Partnership Act of 1890. This states that in the absence of any agreement to the contrary profits and losses are to be shared equally.

Most partners will ask a solicitor to draw up a partnership agreement for them in which the following would be included:

● The amount of capital to be contributed by each partner.

● The annual rate of interest to be allowed on this capital, if any.

● The amount of salary to be paid to each partner, if any.

● The division of the profit and losses between the partners.

To account for the above a Profit and Loss Appropriation Account is drawn up after the preparation of the Profit and Loss Account and before the Balance Sheet is completed.

This account shows how the net profit is to be split between the partners.

For example, Alan and Jane are in partnership. Their Partnership agreement includes the following:

a Alan will contribute £50,000 as capital and Jane £25,000.

b Interest will be allowed on capital at the rate of 8 per cent per annum.

c In recognition of her particular skills Jane will receive a salary of £16,000 per annum.

d Residual profits and losses are to be split equally.

If in the year ended 30 June 1992 the partnership made a net profit of £42,000, then the Profit and Loss Appropriation Account would be as follows:

	£	£
Alan and Jane		
Profit and Loss Appropriation Account for the Year ended 30 June 1992		
Net Profit for year		42,000
Interest on Capital:		
Alan 8% × £50,000	4,000	
Jane 8% × £25,000	2,000	
Salary Jane	16,000	
		22,000
		20,000
Residual Profit		
Alan 50% × £20,000	10,000	
Jane 50% × £20,000	10,000	20,000

The Balance Sheet also needs to be adjusted as each partner has a fixed amount of capital and in addition they will want to know how much profit each has retained in the firm since this is theoretically the amount that he or she can withdraw from the firm.

The facts that you have learned about fixed and current assets and current and long-term liabilities are as true for a partnership as for a sole trader. It is the bottom section of the Balance Sheet that needs alteration. The Sole Trader's Capital Account is replaced by the Partners' Capital and Current Accounts.

The Capital Accounts show the fixed capital of each partner.

The Current Accounts show the retained profit of each partner:

■ the balance brought forward from the previous year;

■ the interest on capital, if any;

■ the salaries, if any;

■ the residual profit;

■ the drawings for the year;

■ the balance carried forward.

For Alan and Jane their Balance Sheet might be summarised as follows:

Alan and Jane
Balance Sheet as at 30 June 1992

	Alan	Jane	£
Fixed Assets			80,000
Net Current Assets			10,000
Total Assets less Current Liabilities			90,000
	Alan	Jane	
	£	£	
Capital Accounts	50,000	25,000	75,000
Current Accounts			
Opening Balance	1,000	2,000	
Interest on Capital	4,000	2,000	
Salary	–	16,000	
Residual Profit	10,000	10,000	
	15,000	30,000	
Drawings	12,500	17,500	
	2,500	12,500	15,000
			90,000

Note that in practice the details of the fixed assets and net current assets would be shown as for a sole trader.

COMPANY ACCOUNTS

As with the accounts of partnerships, the rules for preparing the accounts of a sole trader apply to those of a limited company but need to be adjusted to account for the different type of business.

There is the additional complication that a company's accounts are controlled by the provisions of the Companies Act 1985 as amended by the 1989 Act.

A company is owned by its shareholders and you need to know a little more about shares before we look at the actual accounts.

When a company is formed it needs to prepare a *Memorandum and Articles of Association*. *The Memorandum of Association* is the document forming the constitution of the company and defines its objectives and powers. The *Articles of Association* contains the rules and regulations for conducting the business of the company, and define the rights of the members and the powers and duties of the directors.

The memorandum will contain a statement of the shares that the firm can issue, i.e. the authorised share capital. A company can issue as many shares as it wishes up to this limit.

The authorised and issued share capital will be divided into one or more different classes of shares. The principal types are ordinary and preference shares. A company must issue ordinary shares, it need not issue preference shares. Each share has a nominal or face value which may be 25p, 50p, £1 or any other amount that the company decides.

■ Types of company shares

Preference shares

These shares will carry a fixed rate of dividend. For example a company may authorise and issue 200,000 8 per cent Preference Shares of £1 each.

For every such share that a person holds he will receive a dividend of 8p (8% of £1) per year. In practice this may be paid in two instalments of 4p each. Preference dividends are paid before any proposed ordinary dividend but only if the company has retained profits.

In the event of the company failing and being wound up the preference shareholders will be repaid the nominal value of their shares before the ordinary shareholders receive any money. This is after external creditors have been paid.

Thus preference shares are considered 'safer' than ordinary shares.

Ordinary shares

As the name suggests these are the most common type of shares. Ordinary shareholders take the greatest risk in a company but when a company is making high profits there is the potential for large dividends to be paid.

Ordinary shareholders normally have voting rights in a company unlike preference shareholders.

Debentures

A debenture is a loan made to a company in exchange for a debenture certificate issued by the company acknowledging the debt. The debenture will carry a fixed rate of interest and this is an expense of the Profit and Loss Account.

Debentures are often 'secured' on one of the assets of the company, e.g. the freehold property. This means that if the company is wound up then the property will be sold and the proceeds used to repay the debenture holders.

Remember debentures are not shares, they are a loan to a company.

■ Limited company accounts

A limited company will prepare a trading and profit and loss account in the same way as a sole trader. There are two expenses that may be found in its accounts which will not appear in sole trader accounts.

Directors' remuneration. This is the amount paid to the directors. Directors are employed by a company in the same way as any other employee and thus their pay is a legitimate expense of the Profit and Loss Account.

Debenture interest is shown in the Profit and Loss Account in the same way as any other interest paid.

Profit and Loss Appropriation Account

PC
7.4.5

In a similar way to that of a partnership there is the need to prepare a Profit and Loss Appropriation Account for a company, this time to show how the net profit has been shared amongst the owners, i.e. the shareholders.

If we assume that a company makes a net profit of £250,000 after all expenses have been taken into account then its appropriation account might be as follows.

Profit and Loss Appropriation Account for the year ended 31 December 1992	£	£
Net Profit for year before tax		250,000
Corporation Tax		60,000
Net Profit after tax		190,000
Dividends paid and proposed:		
Ordinary interim paid	40,000	
Ordinary final proposed	70,000	
		110,000
Retained Profit for year		80,000
Retained Profit brought forward		45,000
Retained Profit carried forward		125,000

If you examine the above account you will see that:

■ the Company estimates that it will have to pay corporation tax on this year's profit of £60,000.

■ this leaves a profit for the shareholders of £190,000.

Financial resources 649

- the company has not issued any preference shares. If any had been issued, the shareholders would be entitled to a dividend which would have been shown in the Appropriation Account.

- during the year the Company paid a dividend of £40,000 to its ordinary shareholders. This was probably based on the half-year accounts which would have shown that the company could expect a profit for the year.

- the Company propose to pay a final dividend for the year of £70,000. This would be paid shortly after an annual general meeting of the shareholders.

- this leaves an undistributed profit for the year of £80,000. A company will very rarely pay a dividend equal to the profit for the year. It needs to retain money in the firm to meet the problems of inflation and to allow the firm to expand.

- there is undistributed profit from previous years of £45,000 which gives a retained profit to be carried forward of £125,000.

- retained profits are called Revenue Reserves which can be distributed in future years as dividend or used to give the shareholders more shares. Such an issue of shares is known as a scrip issue.

PC
7.4.1

■ Limited Company Balance Sheet

The Balance Sheet of a company has the same basic structure as that of a sole trader. Obviously it is adjusted to meet the needs of the shareholders.

A Balance Sheet of a company might look as follows:

Moorgate Ltd

Balance Sheet as at 31 December 1992

Fixed Assets	Cost £000	Acc. Depreciation £000	£000
Tangible Assets			
Land and Buildings	500	50	450
Plant and Machinery	1,993	620	1,373
Office Equipment	330	162	168
	2,823	832	1,991
Current Assets			
Stock		1,589	
Debtors		1,152	
Prepayments		74	
Cash at Bank and In Hand		24	
		2,839	
Creditors: amounts falling due within one year			
Bank Overdraft		518	
Creditors		709	
Accrued Expenses		12	
Proposed Dividend		110	
Corporation Tax		255	
		1,604	

Net Current Assets	1,235
Total Assets less Current liabilities	3,226
Creditors: amounts falling due after more than one year	
8% Debentures	500
	2,726
Capital and Reserves	
Called-up Share Capital	1,575
Share Premium Account	350
Profit and Loss Account	801
	2,726

If you look at the above Balance Sheet you will see the following:

■ The cost and total depreciation to date of the fixed assets are shown. This is a legal requirement.

■ Current assets are the same as for a sole trader.

■ The heading 'Creditors amounts falling due within one year' is used instead of current liabilities. This leaves the reader of the accounts in no doubt what a current liability is.

■ Note the introduction of two new short-term liabilities; corporation tax and proposed dividends.

■ Net current assets and total assets less current liabilities are calculated as before.

■ The heading 'Creditors amounts falling due after more than one year' is used instead of long-term loans.

■ Debentures are included in long-term liabilities.

■ Share capital shows the nominal value of the issued share capital.

■ If shares are issued at more than their nominal value, then the excess must be shown in a Share Premium Account. This is a Capital Reserve and cannot be used to pay a dividend.

■ The Profit and Loss Account shows the retained profit carried forward as calculated in the Profit and Loss Appropriation Account.

■ The total of the share capital, the capital reserves and the revenue reserves represents the shareholders' interest in the company and is known as the shareholders' equity.

■ Note that the Balance Sheet balances!

■ The authorised share capital is shown as a note to the Balance Sheet and gives the shareholders an indication of how much money the company could raise by the further issue of shares.

PUBLISHED FINAL ACCOUNTS

PC
7.4.5
7.4.6

The accounts shown above would be those available to the management of a company. The financial information that would be available to the shareholders and other interested parties would come in the form of a set of published final accounts. These would contain:

- The Balance Sheet
- The Profit and Loss Account
- The Cash Flow Statement
- The Notes to the above Statements
- The Directors' Report
- The Auditors' Report

The Balance Sheet would summarise some of the information that has been detailed on the face of our Balance Sheet. The details required to be shown according to the Companies Acts would be shown in the Notes to the Balance Sheet.

The Profit and Loss Account would not show details of the cost of sales and expenses. The cost of sales would be shown as one figure, the expenses would be grouped under the headings of selling and distribution costs and administration expenses. Again certain details would be shown in the notes as required by the Companies Acts.

The Cash Flow Statement is explained below.

Notes to the Financial Statements would contain the details required above and other information such as details of the accounting policies used by the company such as the method of depreciation used. If any important events have happened since the Balance Sheet date and before the accounts have been completed, these would be detailed in the notes.

The Directors are required by law to issue a report containing:

- a statement of the principal activities of the company
- a summary of the company's performance during the financial year
- a summary of the expected performance for the coming year
- a list of the directors and their shareholdings
- details of the proposed dividend

The Auditors are appointed by the shareholders to report on whether the accounts give a true and fair view of the company's state of affairs at the year end and of its profit and cash flow for the year and whether the accounts have been prepared according to the requirements of the Companies Acts.

■ Summary Financial Statements

It was recognised that the majority of shareholders of public companies did not examine the accounts that were sent to them. This is partly because accounts can appear to be very complicated to the untrained mind. To produce a full set of accounts for every shareholder is an expensive exercise, especially if they end up in the waste-paper basket unread. The government recognised this problem and public companies are now allowed to send their shareholders Summary Financial Statements rather than a full set of accounts.

Summary Financial Statements contain:

- a statement by the company's auditors of their opinion as to whether the statement is consistent with the accounts
- a summary of the Directors' Report
- a summary of the Profit and Loss Account and the Balance Sheet

■ Cash Flow Statements

Cash Flow Statements were introduced in September 1991 by the Accounting Standards Board. Their objective is to report on their 'cash generation and absorption for a period'.

The problem with the traditional financial reporting basis is that the Balance Sheet shows the position of the company at one point in time and the Profit and Loss Account shows the income arising in a year and the expenses relating to that year. Neither statement shows the movement of cash in or out of the business during the year.

An accountant is frequently asked 'if the company has a retained profit for the year of £25,000 why have the bank balances decreased by £2,000? There could be numerous answers to this question and a Cash Flow Statement should supply the correct one.

The main headings in a Cash Flow Statement are:

- Operating activities
- Returns on investments and servicing of finance
- Taxation
- Investing activities
- Financing

The final figure in the statement gives the increase (or decrease) in cash and cash equivalents. It is the net cash inflow or outflow of the business for the year.

'Cash' means cash in hand or bank balances.

'Cash equivalents' means short-term investments that are very easy to turn into cash.

The following illustration (pages 655/6) has been issued by the Accounting Standards Board and shows all the main headings.

The notes must accompany the statement as they give details of the figures used in the example.

You should note the following:

■ There must be a reconciliation between the operating profit reported in the Profit and Loss Account and the net cash flow from operating activities. This should be shown as a note to the statement and can be calculated in one of two ways.

■ *The 'direct' method* shows cash receipts and payments for the year aggregating to the net cash flow from operating activities. It includes cash receipts from customers, cash payments to suppliers and cash payments to and on behalf of employees.

■ *The 'indirect' method* starts with the operating profit and adjusts it for non-cash charges and credits to reconcile it to the net cash flow from operating activities.

The indirect method is shown in the statement and could be compared with the direct method.

The principal advantage of the direct method is that it shows operating cash receipts and payments. Knowledge of the specific sources of cash receipts and the purposes for which cash payments were made in past periods may be useful in assessing future cash flows.

The principal advantage of the indirect method is that it highlights the differences between the operating profit and the net cash flow from operating activities. Many users of financial statements believe that such a reconciliation is essential to give an indication of the quality of the reporting entity's earnings.

Direct method	£000
Cash received from customers	24,765
Cash payments to suppliers	(11,480)
Cash paid to and on behalf of employees	(5,386)
Other cash payments	(1,010)
Net cash inflow from operating activities	6,889

Indirect method	£000
Operating profit	6,022
Depreciation charge	893
Loss on sale of tangible fixed assets	6
Increase in stocks	(194)
Increase in debtors	(72)
Increase in creditors	234
Net cash inflow from operating activities	6,889

■ Examination of the calculations of net cash inflow from operations

Direct method

The items used in the direct method are available from the financial records kept by a company. However, when companies were asked about the proposed standard, some stated that they did not currently collect information in the required form directly from their accounting systems. Thus it has been agreed that at the moment companies do not have to give the information required by the direct method.

It is possible to calculate the required figure using the Profit and Loss Account and the Balance Sheet.

The cash received from customers is: debtors at the beginning of the year + sales for the year – debtors at the end of the year.

The cash payments to suppliers is: creditors at the beginning of the year + purchases for the year – creditors at the end of the year.

Cash paid to and on behalf of employees and other cash payments can be calculated in a similar way.

Indirect method

A company is required to give this information in a note to the statement. The following should be noted:

■ Depreciation must be added back to the net profit as it does not represent cash paid during the year. It is a 'book transaction'.

■ The loss on sale of a tangible asset is the difference between the written-down value of the asset and the sale proceeds. Like depreciation it is not a cash transaction.

FINANCIAL REPORTING STANDARD CASH FLOW STATEMENTS

XYZ LIMITED
Cash flow statement for the year ended 31 March 1992

	£'000	£'000
Net cash inflow from operating activities		6,889
Returns on investments and servicing of finance		
Interest received	3,011	
Interest paid	(12)	
Dividend paid	(2,417)	
Net cash inflow from returns on investments and servicing of finance		582
Taxation		
Corporation tax paid (including advance corporation tax)	(2,922)	
Tax paid		(2,922)
Investing activities		
Payments to acquire intangible fixed assets	(71)	
Payments to acquire tangible fixed assets	(1,496)	
Receipts from sales of tangible fixed assets	42	
Net cash outflow from investing activities		(1,525)
Net cash inflow before financing		3,024
Financing		
Issue of ordinary share capital	211	
Repurchase of debenture loan	(149)	
Expenses paid in connection with share issues	(5)	
Net cash inflow from financing		57
Increase in cash and cash equivalents		3,081

Notes to the cash flow statement

1 RECONCILIATION OF OPERATING PROFIT TO NET CASH INFLOW FROM OPERATING ACTIVITIES

	£'000
Operating profit	6,022
Depreciation charges	893
Loss on sale of tangible fixed assets	6
Increase in stocks	(194)
Increase in debtors	(72)
Increase in creditors	234
Net cash inflow from operating activities	6,889

2 ANALYSIS OF CHANGES IN CASH AND CASH EQUIVALENTS DURING THE YEAR

	£'000
Balance at 1 April 1991	21,373
Net cash inflow	3,081
Balance at 31 March 1992	24,454

3 ANALYSIS OF THE BALANCES OF CASH AND CASH EQUIVALENTS AS SHOWN IN THE BALANCE SHEET

	1992 £'000	1991 £'000	Change in year £'000
Cash at bank and in hand	529	681	(152)
Short-term investments	23,936	20,700	3,236
Bank overdrafts	(11)	(8)	(3)
	24,454	21,373	3,081

4 ANALYSIS OF CHANGES IN FINANCING DURING THE YEAR

	Share capital £'000	Debenture loan £'000
Balance at 1 April 1991	27,411	156
Cash inflow/(outflow) from financing	211	(149)
Profit on repurchase of debenture loan for less than its book value		(7)
Balance at 31 March 1992	27,622	–

- The increase or decrease in stock is calculated by comparing the balances in two adjacent Balance Sheets.

- An increase in stock is deducted from operating profit. It represents a purchase that has not been set against the current operating profit. It must either have been paid for in cash or bought on credit and thus represents an actual or potential cash outflow.

- An increase in debtors is deducted from the operating profit. During a year an entity collects outstanding debts from the previous year and some of the money relating to this year's sales. If debtors have increased, then the company has not collected cash equal to its sales for the year.

- An increase in creditors is added to the operating profit. During a year an entity pays its outstanding debts from the previous year and for some of this year's purchases. If creditors have increased, then the company has not paid cash equal to its purchases for the year.

Returns on investments and servicing of finance

Interest received and paid are self explanatory.

Dividends are those paid during the year and would be last year's final proposed dividend and this year's interim dividend.

Taxation

The corporation tax paid this year would be based on last year's profit.

Investing activities

This shows the amount paid to acquire new fixed assets and the amount received from the sale of surplus assets.

Financing

A company can finance its activities by the issue of shares and debentures. Similarly it can be required to repay its long-term loans or, occasionally, to redeem some of its shares.

Increase in cash and cash equivalents

This should show the change in the cash position during the year.

ACCOUNTS OF NON PROFIT-MAKING ORGANISATIONS

PC
7.4.5
7.4.6

A club will usually want to keep a record of its financial transactions and to present accounts to its members once a year. As a club is not in business, it exists 'for the mutual benefit of its members', and so it is not suitable to prepare trading accounts in the normal way.

■ Receipts and payments accounts

A very small club would be content to summarise its cash and bank transactions at the end of the year. Such a summary would be called a receipts and payments account and would look like the following:

REGIS CHESS CLUB
Receipts and Payments Account for the Year ended 31 March 1993

	£	£
Receipts		
Bank and Cash Balances at 1 April 1992		483
Subscriptions		750
Competition Fees		125
Donations		50
		1,408
Payments		
Rent	200	
Light and Heat	375	
Secretarial Expenses	107	
Printing	46	
Competition Prizes	100	
New Chess Sets	294	
Sundries	33	
		1,155
Bank and cash balances at 31 March 1993		£253

PC
7.4.5

■ Income and Expenditure Accounts

A larger club would want a more formal set of accounts and an Income and Expenditure Account would meet this need.

This is similar to a Trading and Profit and Loss Account prepared by a business. It looks at the income due for the year and the expenses relating to that year. Thus it takes into account accruals and prepayments and accounts for depreciation of fixed assets.

If the club holds a specific event the income and expenses will often be grouped together so the members can see whether a profit or loss was made.

Similarly if the club has a bar or sells refreshments on a regular basis with a view to making a profit then a trading account would be prepared for that activity so that the profit or loss can be determined.

THE ACCOUNTS OF CHAMBERS SOCIAL CLUB

Bar Trading Account for the Year ended 31 March 1993

	£	£
Bar Takings		71,165
Cost of Takings		
Opening Stock	3,765	
Purchases	54,785	
	58,550	
Closing Stock	3,595	
		54,955
Profit transferred to the Income and		
Expenditure Account		16,210

Income and Expenditure Account for the Year ended 31 March 1993

	£	£
Income		
Subscriptions		2,500
Profit from Bar		16,210
Fruit Machine Income		12,345
Hall Hire		1,500
Juke Box Income		1,030
New Year Dance: Income	2,530	
Expenses	1,985	
Profit		545
		34,130
Expenditure		
Wages	19,925	
Rent and Rates	3,775	
Light and Heat	2,460	
Printing and Stationery	450	
Cleaning	750	
Secretarial Expenses	615	
Accountancy and Stocktaking	1,575	
Repairs and Renewals	630	
Sundries	795	
Depreciation of fixtures	2,900	
		33,875
Surplus for Year		255

If you examine the above accounts you will see:

- From the Bar Trading Account that the bar made a profit of £16,210. This is transferred to the Income and Expenditure Account.

- From the Income and Expenditure Account that the club had a New Year dance which made a profit of £545. Overall the club had a surplus for the year of £255.

- A club does not talk about a net profit; as has been said it is not in business.

PC
7.4.6

The Club Balance Sheet

If the club is sufficiently large then it will want to prepare a Balance Sheet to show its financial position at its year end. This takes on the same structure as that of a business, the Capital Account of the sole trader is replaced by an Accumulated Fund showing the accumulated surpluses for the club.

The Balance Sheet of Chambers Social Club might look as follows:

PC
7.4.6

	£	£
Balance Sheet as at 31 March 1993		
Fixed Assets		
Fixtures and Fittings at Cost		
less Depreciation		11,600
Current Assets		
Stock	3,595	
Prepayments	505	
Subs in Arrears	120	
Bank Deposit Account	10,050	
Cash In Hand	1,485	
	15,755	
Current Liabilities		
Creditors	4,560	
Subs in Advance	375	
Bank Overdraft – Current Account	5,320	
	10,255	
Net Current Assets		5,500
Net Assets		17,100
Accumulated Fund		
Balance at the beginning of year		16,845
Surplus for year		255
		17,100

Note: the only items that need some explanation are the subscriptions.

Subscriptions in arrears are a current asset as one or more members owe the Club money for their subscriptions for the past year.

Subscriptions in advance are a current liability as members have paid in advance of receiving a service, i.e. the right to use the club's facilities during the year to 31 March 1994.

ASSIGNMENT 6

The Chambers Social Club keeps its records in an analytical cash book during the year. The Honorary Treasurer provides you with a list of all the analysis columns for the club's receipts and payments. You have to use last year's balance sheet (see page 660) and the list of receipts and payments in order to produce:

a) this year's Bar Trading Account

b) an Income and Expenditure Account

c) a Balance Sheet for the end of the year

Receipts	£	Payments	£
Bar takings	79,140	Bank overdraft b/fwd	5,320
Subscriptions	2,600	Bar purchases	59,100
Fruit machine income	13,190	New Year Dance exps	2,070
Hall hire	1,500	Wages	21,010
Juke box income	1,110	Rent and rates	3,975
New Year Dance income	2,700	Light and heat	2,915
		Printing and stationery	590
		Cleaning	790
		Secretarial exps	585
		Accountancy and stocktaking	1,490
		Repairs and renewals	1,900
		Sundries	1,010
		New fixtures and fittings	1,000
Bank overdraft c/fwd	1,515		
	101,755		101,755

Notes

a) The purchase of new fixtures and fittings is not an expense and it needs to be added to the balance sheet balance of £11,600. You must treat the depreciation of fixtures and fittings as an expense. Use a figure of £3,150 for this year's depreciation (your balance sheet value for fixtures and fittings will then be £11,600 + £1,000 − £3,150 = £9,450.)

b) The closing stock at the bar was valued at £4,095 (this value is used in the Bar Trading Account and the Current Assets in the balance sheet).

c) The prepayment in last year's balance sheet of £505 refers to rent and rates. At the end of this year the equivalent figure is £530. The calculation of this year's expense is therefore:

	£
Amount paid	3,975
Add Prepayment b/fwd	505
	4,480
Less Prepayment c/fwd	530
This year's expenses	3,950

d) The subscriptions income has to be calculated taking into account last year's Subscriptions in Arrears and Subscriptions in Advance as well as their values at the end of this year. At the end of March 1994 the club has £100 of Subscriptions in Arrears and £450 of Subscriptions in Advance. The following calculations of the income from subscriptions has to be made.

	£
Subscriptions received in year	2,600
Less subscriptions in arrears b/fwd	120
	2,480
Add subscriptions in advance b/fwd	375
	2,855
Add subscriptions in arrears c/fwd	100
	2,955
Less subscriptions in advance c/fwd	450
	2,505

e) The Bank Deposits Account now stands at £10,955. No payments out of or into this account have been made during the year and the difference of £905 between this year's balance and last year's figure is due to the interest added by the bank. This figure of £905 must be treated as income in the Income and Expenditure Account

f) The creditor's value of £4,560 in last year's balance sheet relates to Bar Purchases. At the end of this year the equivalent value is £3,950. The calculation of the actual bar purchases for the year is thus:

	£
Amount paid in year	59,100
Less Creditors b/fwd	4,560
	54,540
Add Creditors c/fwd	3,950
	58,490

■ Preparation of a set of sole trader's accounts

A detailed examination of the preparation of final accounts is not undertaken in this unit, but one example follows which will give you an idea of the processes which must be undergone in order to prepare a set of final accounts for a sole trader.

During a year Colorado completed his double entry bookkeeping effectively and at the end of the year, 31 March 1993, the following balances were extracted from his books:

	£
Sales	200,000
Purchases	131,400
Stock 1 April 1992	18,000
Bad Debts	2,028
Wages and Salaries	24,216
Admin. Expenses	30,172
Selling Expenses	5,688
Bank Charges	1,306
Plant and Equipment	76,000
Office Furniture	18,000
Debtors	38,075
Creditors	18,963
Cash at Bank	2,584
Cash In Hand	372
Capital	141,514
Drawings	12,636

It was also known that at 31 March 1993:

1 The stock was £45,308.

2 £2,200 was owed for wages and salaries.

3 £240 was owed for bank charges.

4 Included in admin. expenses was £2,000 for insurance for the year to 31 March 1994.

5 Colorado provides for depreciation at 10 per cent per annum on plant and equipment and 20 per cent per annum on office furniture.

The accounts that would be prepared from these figures would be as follows:

Workings:
1 As wages are outstanding at the end of the year the total incurred during the year is:

From the trial balance	£24,216
Owing at end of year	2,200
Due for the year (P+L)	£26,416

2 Similarly for bank charges:

From the trial balance	£1,306
Owing at end of year	240
Due for year (P+L)	£1,546

3 Total owing at end of year, to be shown in the Balance Sheet
£2,200 + 240 = £2,440.

4 As insurance has been paid this year for next year the total of administration expenses for the year are:

From the trial balance	£30,172
Prepaid at end of year	2,000
Due for the year (P+L)	£28,172

5 The depreciation for the year is:

On plant and equipment 10% × £76,000 = £7,600
On office machinery 20% × £18,000 = £3,600

The Final Accounts can now be prepared and will look as follows on page 665.

DISCUSSION TOPICS

1 If you were in a position to start a business would you prefer to be a sole trader or a member of a partnership?

2 Do you think that published accounts give the right amount of information to shareholders? If not, what changes (more or less) would you make?

3 Accounts are prepared on an historical cost basis. Do you think that a supplementary set of accounts should be prepared to account for inflation? If so, what problems do you envisage in the preparation of such a set of accounts?

4 To compare a set of company accounts with those of another company is not a very meaningful exercise as companies can use different accounting policies for items such as depreciation. Do you agree?

Trading and Profit and Loss Account for the Year ended 31 March 1993

	£	£
Sales		200,000
Cost of Sales:		
Opening Stock	18,000	
Purchases	131,400	
Available Stock	149,400	
Closing Stock	45,308	
		104,092
Gross Profit		95,908
Expenses		
Bad Debts	2,028	
Wages and Salaries	26,416	
Admin. Expenses	28,172	
Selling Expenses	5,688	
Bank Charges	1,546	
Depreciation of:		
Plant and Equipment	7,600	
Office Furniture	3,600	75,050
Net Profit		20,858

Balance Sheet as at 31 March 1993

	£	£
Fixed Assets		
Plant and Equipment		68,400
Office Furniture		14,400
		82,800
Current Assets		
Stock	45,308	
Debtors	38,075	
Prepayment	2,000	
Cash at Bank	2,584	
Cash In Hand	372	
	88,339	
Current Liabilities		
Creditors	18,963	
Accrued Expenses	2,440	
	21,403	
Net Current Assets		66,936
Total Assets *less* Current Liabilities		149,736
Capital		
Balance at beginning of year		141,514
Add Profit for year		20,858
		162,372
Less Drawings for year		12,636
		149,736

INDIVIDUAL ACTIVITIES

1 Draw up a checklist of the main users of financial accounts, and for each state what you think is the reason for their interest in the accounts.

2 You work for a major clearing bank in an office which assists start-up businesses. A new client says in a preliminary interview with you that he has heard of the phrase 'limited liability' and believes that this is the main advantage of trading as a company rather than as a sole trader.

Prepare notes for your client explaining clearly what is meant by the term 'limited liability', whether his personal assets would be safe in practice and what you see as the advantages of trading as a company.

3 You have recently inherited a sizable nest-egg, and so you now have the chance to set up the small business you have always wanted to run.

Compose a mission statement which will communicate the kind of business you want to establish, and what its main goals will be. Then produce a checklist of assets which you think you will need to obtain before you can start trading. Also, estimate the expenses you are likely to incur during the first year of trading.

Circulate your start-up schedule among your class and compare the approaches of your co-students. Decide together which plans have the most likely chances of success and why.

4 A friend of yours has come to you for advice regarding depreciation. During her accounting year she has bought a second-hand car for £5,000 which she hopes will last for about three years and which she then intends to trade in for about £1,250. Her accountant has tried to explain depreciation to her, but she is still a little confused.

Write a letter to her explaining what is meant by depreciation, and why it is necessary to account for it. Suggest to your friend two alternative methods that she could use. Lastly, advise her which method would give her lower profit in the first year of ownership of her car.

5 An acquaintance of yours has recently been appointed Honorary Treasurer of a local club, despite the fact that he knows little about accounting. The club's Annual General Meeting is to be held soon, and as someone who is an expert in such matters, he has come to you asking for some help. After a general explanation of what is involved in keeping club accounts, you agree to provide a set of briefing notes on the following aspects:

a The financial duties of a club's honorary treasurer

b The purpose of the Income and Expenditure Account and Balance Sheet

c How depreciation affects club accounts

d Why the figure for depreciation shown in the Income and Expenditure Account differs from the figure in the Balance Sheet.

As a class, select the three best sets of notes and display them on your baseroom noticeboard.

REVIEW TEST

1 What is the difference between fixed assets and current assets?

2 What are current liabilities?

3 Describe the main features of straight line and reducing balance depreciation.

4 Summarise the main functions of: *a*) a balance sheet and *b*) a trading and profit and loss account.

5 What are the main profitability ratios?

6 What are the main liquidity ratios?

7 List three main purposes to which accounting ratios may be put in a large company.

8 What is a profit and loss appropriation account?

9 What information would you expect to find in a company's cash-flow statement?

10 List the main items which comprise a club balance sheet.

PC
6.3.6
7.4.5

CASE STUDY 1

Caledonian Ltd

Caledonian Ltd is a medium-sized company which wishes to expand its activities. The board of directors has heard that the directors and shareholders of Goodwin Ltd are considering retirement and may be open to an offer to purchase the company.

You work for the accountants to Caledonian Ltd and are assigned the task of analysing the accounts of Goodwin Ltd. You are given the accounts of the last three years and these are summarised below:

Profit and Loss Account
for the year ended 31 December

	1990 £000	1991 £000	1992 £000
Sales	1,700	1,950	1,900
Cost of Sales	900	1,030	1,050
Gross Profit	800	920	850
Selling and Distribution Costs	80	90	95
Administration Expenses	500	575	600
Financial Charges	10	10	10
	590	675	705
Net profit for year	210	245	145

(Note: the Appropriation Account is not available)

Balance Sheet as at 31 December

	1990 £000	1991 £000	1992 £000
Fixed Assets	550	575	500
Current Assets			
Stock	100	110	170
Debtors	210	245	395
Balance at Bank	50	60	5
	360	415	570
Creditors: amounts falling due within one year	160	225	395
Net Current Assets	200	190	175
Total Assets *less* Current liabilities	750	765	675
Capital and Reserves			
Share Capital	500	500	500
Reserves	250	265	175
	750	765	675

ASSIGNMENT

You are to draft a report to the directors of Caledonian Ltd in which you are to:

a use suitable accounting ratios to analyse the accounts in terms of profitability, liquidity and activity;

b make a recommendation to the directors on whether the firm is suitable for purchase.

The draft report will be considered by the partner dealing with Caledonian Ltd and will form the basis of the report which will be sent to the directors of the company.

PC
7.1.2
7.3.4
7.4.5
7.4.6

CASE STUDY 2

Starting your own business

After leaving college you have been unable to obtain employment. By chance your aged aunt has recently died and you discover that she has left you £5,000 in her will. You decide to use the money to start a small business. You investigate the opportunities in your area and discover that the refreshment kiosk at your local station is empty.

PC
6.3.6
7.4.5

ASSIGNMENTS

You realise that you need to make a business plan and that you will probably need financial assistance from a bank.

1 Arrange to visit a similar establishment in your area, e.g. the snack-bar at your local bus or train station, the refreshment area at your local leisure centre. If possible, obtain some information about the sales and expenses of the business. Make a note of the equipment in use at the premises.
2 Obtain a 'business start-up pack' from a High Street bank.
3 Draw up a business plan for your proposed establishment to include:
    a a plan of the layout of your proposed establishment;
    b details of your proposed opening hours;
    c details of what you expect to sell;
    d an estimate of the costs of the furniture and fittings that you will need;
    e an estimate of the sales and expenses for the first six months of operation;
    f a cash flow statement for the first six months;
    g a budgeted profit and loss account for the period;
    h a budgeted balance sheet at the end of the period.

You can use the documents obtained from the bank or design your own forms.

IDEAS FOR PROJECTS

1 With the help of your teacher and/or contacts, acquire three to five sets of annual accounts and reports from public limited companies, such as Shell, ICI/Zeneca, British Telecom, an electricity board etc. Using the techniques you have learned in this Unit, and the accounting ratios it includes, draw up a set of notes which compares the performances of the companies you have selected, and explain what you consider to be the major features of the performance of each one.

PC
6.3.5
6.3.6
6.3.7

2 In pairs, arrange to visit a local clearing bank in order to interview an assistant manager on the subject of business lending. Find out what the bank's approach is to: the amount and type of information required of the would-be borrower, what 'strings' or conditions are generally attached to the lending of money to business proprietors/directors, what type of references may be required and so on.

Brief your class on your findings in an illustrated oral presentation.

PC
7.1.2
7.1.3
7.1.4

3 Research into the role played in business finance by the issue and sale of shares. Produce a factsheet which will suitably brief other students in your class.

PC
7.1.3
7.1.4

4 Find out how a local clearing bank handles business overdrafts and, when you have obtained sufficient data, design a briefing sheet which would prove a helpful reference source for someone about to start up a small business.

5 Assume that your headteacher/principal has agreed to the setting up of a shop on campus which will sell study notes, revision aids, textbooks, stationery materials, floppy disks, etc. direct to students.

PC
7.2.2
7.2.3
7.2.5

Using the information available to you on: student population, current costs of stock, actual hourly rates of pay for the shop's staff, contributions to overheads etc. draw up a cash-flow forecast for the first 12 months' business operations of the shop.

<table>
<tr><td>PC
7.3.1</td><td>6</td><td>Arrange to visit a cost accountant in a local factory and ask him or her to explain how the company approaches the tasks of controlling manufacturing costs and monitoring the process of added value.

Share your findings through an oral briefing to your class.</td></tr>
</table>

<table>
<tr><td>PC
7.3.1</td><td>7</td><td>Liaise with the students and staff in your school/college who are involved in the production of a play, musical or concert etc. which is shortly to take place (with tickets being sold to parents, friends, students etc.). Find out the principal 'ingredients' of the fixed and variable costs relating to the event and produce a break-even analysis chart for the organisers to help them in their marketing of the event.</td></tr>
</table>

<table>
<tr><td>PC
7.4.1</td><td>8</td><td>Liaise with the head of the department in which you are studying and, using spreadsheet software, design and produce a system for controlling the budget allocated to the purchase of learning materials, stationery and 'consumables' which is simple and easy to use, and from which helpful reports may be generated on a weekly/monthly basis.</td></tr>
</table>

<table>
<tr><td>PC
7.2.7</td><td>9</td><td>Find out what happens during the period in which a business becomes bankrupt. Research into the activities of filing for bankruptcy and how they affect a) a sole trader, b) private limited company and c) a plc.

Present your findings in the form of an article included in the Business section of a Sunday broadsheet newspaper – in other words, seek to make your article readable and free from technical jargon and succinct.</td></tr>
</table>

<table>
<tr><td>PC
6.3.3
7.4.1</td><td>10</td><td>Find out more about the principles of double-entry bookkeeping and brief your class accordingly.</td></tr>
</table>

11 Find out how the use of integrated accounting software programs has revolutionised accounting practices in larger firms and give an illustrated presentation on this important subject to your class.

12 Research into current taxation requirements for: small, private and public limited companies – for example, what may be set against tax liabilities, what constitutes legal 'avoidance' and illegal 'evasion' of tax payments, current rates of taxation, how a varied range of business people regard current taxation requirements and what improvements might be made in the UK tax system.

<table>
<tr><td>PC
7.4.1
7.3.1</td><td>13</td><td>Arrange for a local chartered accountant to come and talk to your class on:

'Current trends and directions in business accounting'

Ensure that your class has prepared some suitable questions to ask beforehand.</td></tr>
</table>

<table>
<tr><td>PC
7.1.1
7.3.1</td><td>14</td><td>Find out how the finances of your local county or district council are managed, and how the approaches employed differ from those of the private sector.

Present your findings in either an oral presentation or an illustrated written article.</td></tr>
</table>

EVIDENCE-BUILDING ACTIVITY FOR YOUR PORTFOLIO

Element 7.1 Identify sources of finance for a business plan

First, turn to the Activities at the end of Unit 8 (for elements 8.1, 8.2 and 8.3) which relate to researching data for a business plan and then producing it. Read each Activity scenario carefully, and then make your selection of the type of business (café and cake shop, sports shop, boutique, music centre etc.) for which you will do your research and then produce your business plan. Having made your selection, return to this Activity.

Your task in this Activity is to produce a financial plan which outlines the financing requirements, sources and methods of acquiring financial support in relation to the business plan you produce as part of your Unit 8 Activities.

Research objectives

Your financial plan will naturally depend upon the type of business you decide to start up, but it will also depend upon a number of other factors, such as:

- whether the premises from which you will operate are to be purchased outright (in which case funds for a commercial mortgage will be needed), leased or rented (in which case a start-up loan may be needed to tide you over until business picks up)

- the amount and nature of any alterations needed to make the premises suitable for your type of trading

- the extent of the fixtures and fittings you will need to install

- the amount of opening stock you will need to purchase

- the size of your payroll obligations from day one onwards

- the amount and nature of the advertising and sales promotional activities you will need to undertake to promote your new business

- the cost of any business vehicles you may need to acquire

- the costs of the start-up legal and financial services you may need to obtain (solicitors, bank charges, insurances etc.)

Second, you will need to explore the locally available sources which might finance the above areas, such as clearing banks, building societies, possible investors or sleeping partners, finance houses, government agencies such as the local TEC and so on. You will need to compare their costs and fees and work out which source is likely to offer you the 'best deal' – whether for a mortgage, loan or hire-purchase arrangement etc. Also, you may need consider why a bank loan may depend upon the borrower being able to 'put up collateral' as the security for the loan he or she asks for.

Production of evidence

You should produce your financial plan in two parts:

Part 1: This part should detail your calculations on the amount of finance you will need to acquire your business premises and the fixtures, fittings, opening stock etc. to be in a position to commence trading. You should also state clearly the sources of the finance you estimate you will need and the costs of obtaining it (e.g. the annual percentage rate of a loan etc.).

Part 2: This part should show in broad overview terms the structure of your working capital planning – how you will finance the day-to-day running of your business – replenishing stocks, financing payroll, heat, light and water and other debtors.

Part 2 anticipates the more detailed production of your projected cash-flow plan (see the Activity for Element 7.2).

Method of producing evidence

If at all possible, produce your financial plan with the help of both WP and spreadsheet applications packages in the form of a detailed, schematic report.

Performance criteria covered

7.1.1, 7.1.2, 7.1.3, 7.1.4

Core skills Level 3

Communication

3.1.1–3.1.4, 3.2.1–3.2.4, 3.4.1–3.4.3

Information Technology

3.1.1–3.1.7, 3.2.1–3.2.7, 3.3.1–3.3.5

3.5.1–3.5.5 (by means of logged notes on how any errors or faults were handled, and how compliance with HASAW requirements were effected).

Element 7.2: Produce and explain a projected cash-flow for a single product business

Your task in this activity is to produce a cash-flow forecast for a twelve month period. Your forecast should also be accompanied by a written explanation of the importance of taking into account the timing of the flow of finance into and out of the business (e.g. the quarterly payment of VAT collected), together with the value of a well-produced cash-flow forecast as a means of supporting a request for finance.

Your cash-flow forecast should be based upon the work you did for Activity Element 7.1 and the production of your business plan in Unit 8.

Research objectives

First, turn to page 701 and check carefully through the component parts of the Natwest cash-flow forecasting schedule, so as to re-acquaint yourself with their purpose and format.

Next, collect your 'raw data' of your forecasts in the sequence given in the schedule – from Sales to Insurance.

Use a spreadsheet applications package to communicate your data and to provide the calculations formulae for successive monthly and year-end totals etc.

Finally, compute the amounts and timing of the VAT and total payments etc. to be made and thus your net cash-flow positions and forecast bank balances.

When you have produced your spreadsheet forecast, write a detailed commentary upon it (see above) which also identifies what you see as potential problem items and aspects and how these can be anticipated and overcome.

Production of evidence

Your cash-flow forecast should take the form of a suitable referenced spreadsheet printout accompanied with an explanatory commentary and analysis of the key points of your forecast, together with the explanations referred to in the above scenario and the section detailing how possible problem aspects can be anticipated and forestalled.

Method of producing evidence

Produce your evidence in the form of a report which merges the spreadsheet and word-processed files you create on your PC or network terminal.

Performance criteria covered

7.2.1, 7.2.2, 7.2.3, 7.2.4, 7.2.5, 7.2.7

Core skills Level 3

Communication

3.1.1–3.1.4, 3.2.1–3.2.4, 3.3.1–3.3.3, 3.4.1–3.4.3

Information technology

3.1.1–3.1.7, 3.2.1–3.2.7, 3.3.1–3.3.5

3.5.1–3.5.5 (by means of logged notes on how errors or faults were handled and how compliance with HASAW requirements were effected).

Application of Number

3.2.1–3.2.8

Element 7.3: Calculate the cost of goods or service

CASE STUDY

The head of your department (at school, college or at work) is currently giving active consideration to setting up a departmental reprographics unit to cope with rapidly expanding photocopying work.

The following are the data which he/she has so far collected in order to gain a detailed insight into the start-up and running costs of this important development:

Direct costs

	£
Reprographics Assistant (37.5 hour week): incl. superannuation and NIC	4.70 per hour
It is intended that the Assistant be appointed on a term-time only basis	
A4 copy paper white (ream)	2.35
A3 copy paper white (ream) (Anticipated use: 90:10 ratio in favour of A4 paper)	3.85
Cost of toner cartridges, each (with a forecast life 3,000 copies per cartridge	85.00
Cost of purchasing photocopier: (to be depreciated in straight line mode over four years). Note: Include only the depreciation costs in your direct costings	4,500.00
Cost of heat and light	11.50 per week

Indirect costs

Notional rental of reprographics room (10 square metres)	7.50 per metre per annum
Contribution to management overheads	350.00 per annum
Running costs (including servicing of equipment but excluding replacement toner cartridges and paper)	15.00 per week
Marketing costs (to staff and students)	5.50 per week

The school/college policy is to levy all assigned indirect charges over 52 weeks per year, irrespective of term times.

Note: If more than 12 reams of A4 copy paper are purchased each month, a further discount of 7.5 per cent is allowable.

Research objectives

1 Using the above data, calculate the cost per unit of photocopied paper sheet (assuming single-sided copying only) on the basis of:

   3,000, 6,000 and 10,000 copies made per calendar month

2 For each calculation, break down your costings as: direct, indirect and total

3 Work out the ratio of indirect cost to production cost for each level of production.

Presentation of evidence

1 *Schedule of calculations*

   Bearing in mind that an acceptable cost per single-sided A4 sheet would be about 5p per copy, what advice would you give your head of department on the basis of your calculations using the above data? Produce your findings as a spreadsheet printout accompanied with your explanation of where the major costs were found.

2 *Proposals for achieving viable costings*

   Attach a memorandum to the above evidence which suggests how many copies would need to be made per month (and how many hours per week the Assistant could be employed) for sufficient reductions to be made so as to bring overall costings into line with the 5p yardstick.

3 *Accompanying notes*

   Lastly, produce a set of accompanying notes which provide an account of what you found to be the important factors you identified in undertaking this Activity which affected the costing of the proposed photocopying centre and how what you learned might be applied generally to a factory or office.

Method of producing evidence

Use a spreadsheet application to work out your calculations and produce your commentary, memorandum and notes in suitable formats.

Performance criteria covered

7.3.1, 7.3.2, 7.3.3, 7.3.4, 7.3.5, 7.3.6, 7.3.7

Core skills Level 3

Communication

3.2.1–3.2.4, 3.3.1–3.3.3, 3.4.1–3.4.3

Information technology

3.1.1–3.1.7, 3.2.1–3.2.7, 3.3.1–3.3.5

3.5.1–3.5.5 (by means of logged notes on how errors or faults were handled and how compliance with HASAW requirements were effected).

Application of number

3.2.1–3.2.8

Element 7.4: Produce and explain profit and loss statements and balance sheets

CASE STUDY

In this Activity you have two tasks: firstly to produce a profit and loss account and then a balance sheet.

The following trial balance was extracted from the books of B Jackson on 30 April 19X7. From it, prepare his trading and profit and loss account for the year ended 30 April 19X7, and a balance sheet as at that date.

	Dr	Cr
	£	£
Sales		18,600
Purchases	11,556	
Stock 1 May 19X6	3,776	
Carriage outwards	326	
Carriage inwards	234	
Returns inwards	440	
Returns outwards		355
Salaries and wages	2,447	
Motor expenses	664	
Rent	456	
Rates	120	
Sundry expenses	1,202	
Motor vehicles	2,400	
Fixtures and fittings	600	
Debtors	4,577	
Creditors		3,045
Cash at bank	3,876	
Cash in hand	120	
Drawings	2,050	
Capital		12,844
	34,844	34,844

Stock at 30 April 19X7 was £4,998.

Presentation of evidence

Present your profit and loss statement and balance sheet using one of the accepted current formats.

Include in your presentation your analysis of the financial position of B Jackson and an explanation of how such financial information may be used to obtain finance from lenders.

Method of producing evidence

You may either produce your evidence in hand-written form or employ word processing and spreadsheet applications

Performance criteria covered

7.4.1, 7.4.2, 7.4.3, 7.4.4, 7.4.5, 7.4.6

Communication

3.2.1–3.2.4, 3.3.1–3.3.3, 3.4.1–3.4.3

Information technology

3.1.1–3.1.7, 3.2.1–3.2.7, 3.3.1–3.3.5

3.5.1–3.5.5 (by means of logged notes on how errors or faults were handled, and how compliance with HASAW requirements were effected).

FURTHER SOURCES OF INFORMATION

Frank Wood's Book-keeping & Accounts, Pitman Publishing 1992

Frank Wood's Business Accounting 1, Pitman Publishing 1993

Finance for BTEC National Students, J Hopkins, Pitman Publishing 1988. ISBN 0273 02877 4

Finance, Eve and Langlois, Oxford University Press

A Business Plan, A West, Pitman-Natwest 1988. ISBN 0 273 02824 3

Starting Up, G Jones, Pitman-Natwest 1991. ISBN 0 273 03514 2

Profit by Planning – Services for the Smaller Business, National Westminster Bank

Book-keeping & Accounts 1, G Whitehead, Pitman Publishing 1985. ISBN 0 273 02141 9

Book-keeping & Accounts 2, G Whitehead, Pitman Publishing 1986 ISBN 0 273 02471 X

Book-keeping and Accounting, 2nd edn, Pitman-Natwest 1991. ISBN 0273 03516 9

Financial Accounting: An Introduction, J Blake, Hutchinson Management Studies 1985. ISBN 0 09 161641 7

The UK Equity Market and *What's the Form,* The International Stock Exchange, London

Business of Banking, 2nd edn, D Wright & W Valentine, Northcote House Publications 1988. ISBN 0 7463 0535 4

BUSINESS PLANNING

Element 8.1
Prepare work and collect data for a business plan

Element 8.2
Produce and present a business plan

Element 8.3
Produce a sales and marketing plan

Element 8.1: Prepare work and collect data for a business plan

Performance criteria

	Pages
1 objectives of business are identified and agreed	680–7
2 legal and insurance implications of the objectives are identified	688–91
3 feasibility of proposals is checked through discussion with others	722–32
4 resource requirements to design and produce the goods or service are identified and estimated	722–32
5 resource requirements to sell and market the goods or service are identified and estimated	722–32
6 time constraints on production, sales, marketing and administration are identified on a flow chart	722–32
7 potential support for the plan from external sources is identified	722–32

Range: Objectives: to make a profit; to break-even; to be subsidised   680–733

Legal and insurance implications: employment law; health and safety; environmental protection; trades descriptions; age limits; asset insurance; public liability; product liability   688–91

Resources: human, physical, financial, time   680–733

External support: own organisation, other organisations, individuals   722–32

Evidence indicators: Draft business proposals including a flow chart and showing legal, insurance, estimated resource implications and indications of possible support from external sources. (The candidate does not have to have evidence of design, production, sales and marketing but there has to be evidence that the candidate understands the significance of these items in preparing a business plan.) Evidence should demonstrate understanding of the implications of the range dimensions in relation to the element. The unit test will confirm the candidate's coverage of range.

Element 8.2: Produce and present a business plan

Performance criteria

1 purposes of a business plan are explained	688–733
2 business objectives for a single product or service are identified and explained	688–91
3 marketing plan is identified	705–11
4 production plan is described	716–19
5 resource requirements and ability to meet the requirements are identified and explained	688–91
6 financial data and forecasts to support the plan are produced	697–705
7 monitoring and review procedures for plan are identified	697–705
8 business plan is presented to an audience	722–32

Range: Purposes of a business plan: to seek finance; to gain finance; to monitor performance   688–91

Objectives: supply of goods or service; achieve sales volume; achieve sales value; achieve market share; make profit; break-even   680–7, 688–91

Marketing plan: pricing, promoting, distribution, selling, timing   705–11

Production plan: premises, machinery, raw materials, labour   716–19

Resource requirements: human, physical, financial

Financial data and forecasts: time period, cash flow forecast, start-up balance sheet, projected profit and loss and balance sheet

Monitoring and review: monthly profit and loss and balance sheet

Evidence indicators: A five-part business plan relating to a single product or service in written form with oral presentation to a simulated potential provider of finance. The five parts are objectives, marketing plan (outline only), production plan (outline only), resource requirements, financial support data. (The marketing plan referred to could also be that plan which is produced for Element 8.3.) Evidence should demonstrate understanding of the implications of the range dimensions in relation to the element. The unit test will confirm the candidate's coverage of range.

Element 8.3: Produce a sales and marketing plan

Performance criteria

1 purposes of a sales and marketing plan are explained

2 planning activities to market a product are described

3 marketing budget is estimated

4 timing of sales and marketing activities is scheduled

5 sales and marketing plan for a single product is produced

Range: Purposes: support application for finance; set targets; monitor performance

Planning activities: naming; pricing; promoting; sales targets; timing; distribution; after-market

Evidence indicators: Prepare a sales and marketing plan for a single product, which includes an estimated budget and timing schedule. Evidence should demonstrate understanding of the implications of the range dimensions in relation to the element. The unit test will confirm the candidate's coverage of range.

INTRODUCTION

This Unit explains the relationship between an organisation's mission, its goals and objectives and its various types of business plan. It proceeds from the macro, comprehensive analysis of a corporate plan to the key elements of a start-up business plan. It provides detailed treatments of the design and applications of the following business plans:

- a corporate plan
- a start-up business plan
- a marketing plan
- a sales plan *and*
- a production plan

Throughout the Unit, emphasis is placed upon the need for planning data to be as objective and factual as possible, for detailed, rational analysis and, above all, for types of business plan to cross-refer to and integrate with:

- the central business idea
- financial aspects

- the market-place
- the human resources employed
- the physical resources of stock, plant, equipment and premises
- the part played by IT, telecommunications and communications media

In particular Unit 8 examines:
- the rationale behind an effective mission statement
- the extension of the mission statement into corporate goals and objectives
- the structure and scope of a corporate plan
- the rationale and structure for start-up, marketing, sales and production plans
- how SWOT analysis assists the planning process
- how to use break-even charts in business plans
- how to structure and interpret a cash-flow forecast
- the role of the operating budget in business plans
- how the trading and profit and loss account supports the monitoring of the business plan
- the parts played by information technology and telecommunications in providing helpful tools for business planners

PC
8.1.1

MISSION STATEMENTS AND COMPANY GOALS

Over-arching all business planning functions in an organisation is its mission statement. Effective mission statements express simply and briefly what the organisation has been set up to achieve. Many organisations include a set of company goals with their mission statement as a means of supplying more detail to explain their mission. Such goals aim to be ongoing and act as markers for all staff as they work – in daily or yearly cycles – towards achieving the organisation's mission.

In his well-known set of guidelines, '*Up The Organisation*', Robert Townsend refers to one of the goals which Avis, the USA car-rental company, set itself when he was running it:

'We want to become the fastest-growing company with the highest profit margins in the business of renting and leasing vehicles without drivers.'

Townsend goes on to stress the importance of defining goals which force all employees to concentrate on the crucial and central activities of the organisation. In the case of Avis, the definition emphasises growth and profits. It also cuts out involvement in any activities not associated with the car rental/leasing business. Avis at the time owned sightseeing and chauffeur-driven limousine hire companies; and it vetoes the future purchase of companies operating outside the given remit.

Today many North American (and European) companies devise mission statements which set out their essential reasons for being what they are and doing what they do. References to such statements are frequently published in their annual reports, public relations literature and in-house bulletins in order to engrave them upon the minds of customers, staff and the public at large.

A typical mission statement for a public limited company might look like this:

> **NATIONAL COURIERS (UK) PLC**
>
> MISSION STATEMENT
> JANUARY 1994
>
> - The company aims to provide a fast, reliable national courier service which keeps its delivery promises, no matter what.
> - National Couriers is fully committed to the concept and processes of Total Quality Management and is continually seeking to improve the quality of its operations by putting its customers first.
> - A commitment has been made to doubling sales turnover in the next five years – thus rendering the company 'Number One' in the UK courier business while maintaining existing net profit ratios.
> - The company genuinely believes that its employees are its most precious resource and is committed as an equal opportunities employer to their personal and career development.
> - National Courier appreciates the importance of the environment to the communities around its depots and centres and strongly supports the work of its Community Liaison Groups with local residents.

As the above example illustrates, mission statements seek to provide all-embracing statements of purpose and intent which are meant to stand the test of time. However, good mission statements avoid lapsing into worthy, over-general, abstract ideas. One of the best – of an organisation making and distributing parts to manufacturers is:

'Just In Time – With Us, Not Just A Concept!'

This statement became a painted slogan on the company's fleet of lorries and obliged all involved to ensure that delivery schedules were kept to – so as to avoid becoming a laughing-stock, hoist with their own petard.

National Courier makes the same commitment to customer service and then details its expansion plans – not to increase profit ratios, but to dominate the UK market by doubling sales turnover within five years. Notice also that National Courier takes pains to ensure that its role as a caring employer is given a high profile – both inside and outside the organisation. Lastly, in an era of environmental concern, NC emphasises its commitment to maintaining good relations with the communities around its distribution depots and garages.

In a nutshell – taking only some 135 words – National Courier's mission statement manages to encompass:

- **Its commitment to delivering on time, as promised.**
- **The importance attached to the reliability and quality of its operations.**
- **That it is a customer-oriented company.**
- **That it intends to be UK number one within 5 years.**
- **That profits (and shareholders' dividends) will be maintained.**
- **That it cares about the development of its staff and espouses equal opportunities.**
- **That it is environmentally and local-community conscious.**

As a result, National Courier staff – from directors to drivers – will be able to interpret correctly and carry out the detailed objectives and plans which senior management will tease out of the mission statement and cascade as weekly, monthly and annual targets for achieving.

STRATEGIC PLANNING AT THE CORPORATE LEVEL

The directors and senior managers who inhabit the top-most tier of the organisational pyramid spend a great deal of their time in planning the future directions and activities of the company.

The plan they devise and update on an annual, rolling basis is called a strategic plan, since it is concerned with events and operations some three to five years into the future, which will affect and involve all the company's resources. For this reason such plans are sometimes called corporate plans, as they embrace the whole body of the organisation.

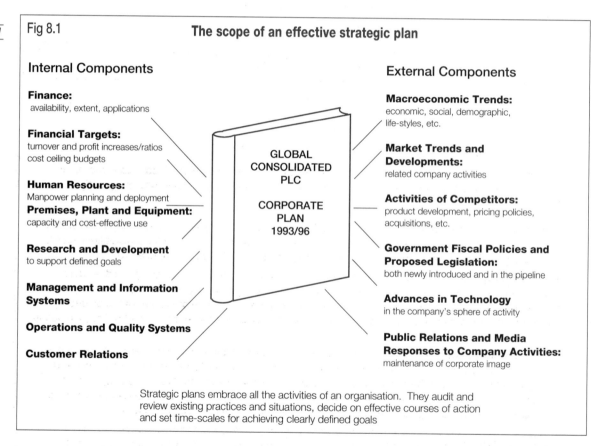

Fig 8.1   **The scope of an effective strategic plan**

Internal Components

Finance:
availability, extent, applications

Financial Targets:
turnover and profit increases/ratios
cost ceiling budgets

Human Resources:
Manpower planning and deployment
Premises, Plant and Equipment:
capacity and cost-effective use

Research and Development
to support defined goals

Management and Information Systems

Operations and Quality Systems

Customer Relations

GLOBAL
CONSOLIDATED
PLC

CORPORATE
PLAN
1993/96

External Components

Macroeconomic Trends:
economic, social, demographic,
life-styles, etc.

Market Trends and Developments:
related company activities

Activities of Competitors:
product development, pricing policies,
acquisitions, etc.

Government Fiscal Policies and Proposed Legislation:
both newly introduced and in the pipeline

Advances in Technology
in the company's sphere of activity

Public Relations and Media Responses to Company Activities:
maintenance of corporate image

Strategic plans embrace all the activities of an organisation. They audit and review existing practices and situations, decide on effective courses of action and set time-scales for achieving clearly defined goals

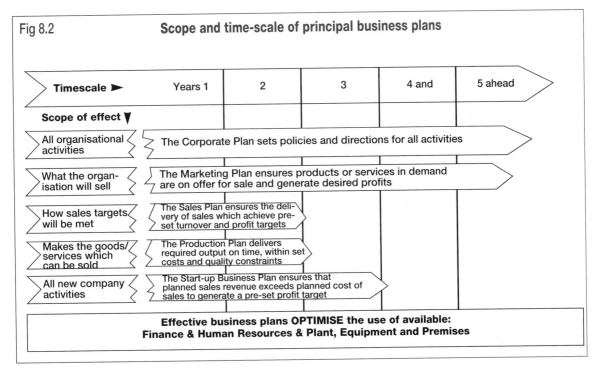

Fig 8.2 — Scope and time-scale of principal business plans

THE PLANNING PROCESS - FROM MACRO TO MICRO

The applications of the disciplines and skills needed to produce effective business plans are many and varied in the world of business. The following table illustrates some of the most frequently employed:

- **The corporate or strategic plan:** Larger organisations produce 3–5 year forward-rolling plans which frame policy and embrace all aspects of business activity; from the corporate plan's guidelines, shorter-term tactical and operational plans – in divisions, departments and sections are devised.

- **The marketing plan:** The marketing plan forms part of the total strategic plan and plots the future directions of the enterprise in terms of what products or services it will develop and sell – and by what means; the plan extends some 2-5 years into the future, depending upon the nature of the business; accurate interpretation of market trends and purchasing habits forms an essential part of the plan, along with timely and well-judged product development.

- **The sales plan:** Once the marketing plan is in place, the sales department produces a sales plan the aim of which is to secure the overall sales needed to generate the levels and volume of turnover and arising profit stipulated in the corporate plan and given direction by the marketing plan. In national companies, such a sales plan will be methodically broken down by region, district and branch or outlet, thus sub-dividing sales targets to be achieved and sales expenses not to be exceeded.

- **The production plan:** Manufacturing companies need to plan and synchronise their production of goods to match closely what has been ordered by regular customers, or what will directly be sold on. Just-in-time production management techniques ensure that precious capital is not tied up in materials waiting to be processed or in finished goods languishing in adjacent warehouses. Production planning also aims to minimise waste and defective products, secure the most cost-effective operating periods and systems and integrate essential plant maintenance with production as smoothly as possible.

- **Project planning** In all kinds of organisation and at all levels of activity, teams of staff are continually working on projects which are undertaken in the process of meeting the organisation's goals and objectives. Effective project planning requires a logical and methodical approach in which key activities are identified and set into the most practical and least time-consuming chronological sequence.

CHECKLIST OF A STRATEGIC PLAN'S COMPONENTS

The following checklist illustrates the principal components which will be included in a business company's strategic planning:

Elements within the organisation

Finance – its likely availability and extent; its planned uses expressed as estimates and forecasts and its distribution within the organisation.

This section will also make a commitment to profit targets – either in pounds sterling or as a percentage of turnover and will set sales targets together with ceiling expenses budgets for company cost-centres.

Human resources – a review of the age, skills, experience and deployment of the company's employees; a forecast of what particular skills and experience will be needed where, in order to achieve the plan's goals and targets; the creation of staff development plans to meet future operational needs.

Premises, plant and equipment – the ability of existing buildings and equipment to meet the future needs of the organisation, and thus the need to plan for constructing, say, a new factory, re-tooling a production-line, or replacing obsolescent computer networks etc.

Research and development – the ability of the organisation's R&D arm to provide the kind of products or services which the company wishes to market in the future, and the possible need to diversify, invest more extensively in R&D or to slim out a product range etc.

Purchasing policies – the need to review the cost-effectiveness of buying-in arrangements and the review of existing suppliers and their terms.

Management and information systems – the ability of existing management structures, methods and communication systems to meet future demands, in say, a period of rapid expansion, relocation or company restructuring; the impact of new office information technology on existing practices and procedures.

Operations – a review of existing business operations – product range, manufacturing techniques, or services; factory/office/distribution/sales administration, customer and technical services etc. in order to reshape them so as to meet future needs.

Quality systems – a review of the standards being achieved and the next steps to be taken towards, say, achieving a total quality management system or 'just in time' production with 'zero defects' etc.

Customer relations – an audit of the extent and nature of customer complaints and the means of their elimination.

The development of policies to improve and develop good customer services in pre- and post-sales phases.

External factors affecting the organisation

Macro-economic trends in the Company's field of activity – surveys and analyses of social, demographic, business-cycle and consumer/industrial activities and future trends which will impinge on the future operations of the company both in national and international contexts.

Markets and market research – analyses and evaluations of current and future behaviour in the company's markets, and from this decisions as to the necessary future markets the company should plan either to develop further or to enter, and from this a detailed analysis of the segments and niches to be targeted

Activities of competitors - a detailed survey of the current and likely future activities and developments to be expected from the competition, and from this the development of strategies for forestalling them with counteractions and developments

Developments in Government Legislation – an examination of current and planned UK laws, regulations and EC directives and their likely impact on the company's activities.

Technological advances – an examination of those technologies related to the activities of the company and how likely future innovations will impact upon the company.

Public relations and environmental factors – a consideration of how future company activities are likely to be regarded by the public and the media and what steps need to be taken to ensure the continuance of 'a good press' and a respected corporate image.

A GOOD STRATEGIC PLAN

- **audits the current situation inside and outside the Company**
- **identifies key trends and opportunities**
- **and makes clear-cut decisions for action**

■ Typical business goals

PC
8.1.1

- To expand the business by x per cent in y years
- To increase net profit by x per cent in the next trading year
- To increase market share by x per cent per year over a fixed period until the company becomes the market leader with a dominant hold on the market (short of arousing the interest of the Monopoly and Mergers Commission)
- To cut operating costs by x per cent in the next trading year
- To acquire x number of additional factories, branches, shops etc. over the coming y years by purchase of existing firms in order to grow and establish a regional or national coverage
- To move into the export market and develop turnover of £x in y years
- To become 'green' and secure an improved corporate image among customers and general public
- To 'give something back' by developing community service roles and commitments
- To move consciously into another economic sector so as to develop the company and improve its long-term profitability
- To make a significant increase in research and development investment in order to 'stay in the game' *and so on*

FROM GOALS TO PLANNING IN BUSINESS ORGANISATIONS

PC
8.1.1
8.2.1

In today's business world the practice of planning – whether for starting up a new business, expanding into a new market or directing the overall development of a large company – has become far more sophisticated than it was some 5–10 years ago.

For example, in the boom period of the mid-1980s, when finance was readily available to any would-be entrepreneur, many sole trader businesses were set up on 'a wing and a prayer' by small traders, whose success or failure were governed more by 'gut-feeling' intuition than by the assembly of key factual and numerical data. Moreover the majority of clearing banks were far more 'laid back' when vetting new business proposals and plans than they are in the much harder business world of today.

■ 'Start right, stay right!' – why planning is an essential business tool

Many would-be successful small traders fail early on because of basic shortcomings in their start-up strategies. They make fatal basic errors like these:

- under-valuing the expertise and know-how needed in the selected business field
- over-estimating the size of the market to be traded in
- exaggerating the size of the market share they will win

- selecting a poor location from which to trade
- mistaking the extent of the profit margins to be secured in highly competitive markets
- under-estimating the challenge represented by established and experienced competitors
- failing to respond in time to significant shifts in market trends and patterns of demand
- failing to start with and to maintain sufficient financial reserves to enable a 'bad trading patch' to be survived
- failing to monitor closely monthly income and expenditure in a detailed cash-flow forecast

Faced with such a developed and sophisticated market-place, expert and detailed business planning forms a vital activity for every starting-out small trader and established business wishing to expand and consolidate its position. In today's competitive business world, no trader is too small to ignore these central planks of his or her business

- **an in-depth knowledge of the chosen market and its customers**
- **a continuous monitoring of the business's financial status**
- **a rolling forward business plan which 'sets the course' for the business and steers it through storm and fair weather alike.**

Acquiring and updating such vital information may be laborious, but 'you can't beat knowing', and having ready access to extensive statistical and factual data from which to devise sound future action plans.

PC
8.2.1

KEY FACTORS IN EFFECTIVE BUSINESS PLANNING

Whatever the sector of the economy a business occupies, and notwithstanding whether it supplies goods or services to meet defined needs or wants, it must address a common set of questions when starting to frame a business plan:

- What business do we *want* to be in?
- What business *were* we in, and *are* we in at present?
- Who are our customers? Who will they be?
- What is it – precisely – that they want now? And what are they likely to want in the future?
- How much of what is wanted can we sell in any given trading period ?
- What will be our cost of sales – both in the short and longer terms ?
- Will the sales we achieve generate profit levels sufficient to enable us to pay out adequate dividends (or directors' remunerations) and to re-invest in plant, stock and other renewals?
- Can we beat our competitors in our chosen market(s) and either increase or maintain our market share?
- Do we possess the financial, physical and human resources needed to deliver the business plan we are devising?

Fig 8.3 **The eight-stage start-up business plan**

PC
8.2.2

Keeps plan 'on track' → **8** Monitor Planning Operation

Refine basic business idea **1** ← Assesses viability and 'unique selling benefit'

Ensures essential 'know-how' available → **7** Match staff skills to business

Research chosen market **2** ← Evaluates competition and customers' profile

EFFECTIVE
START-UP
BUSINESS PLANS
FORESTALL
'DEATH BY OVERSIGHT'
AND
SECURE PLANNED
PROFITS

Prevents errors through ignorance → **6** Acquire legal aspects know-how

Obtain suitable location **3** ← Measures 'traffic' and 'visibility'

5 Produce detailed cash-flow forecast

Secure sufficient start-up capital **4**

Monitors ability to meet obligations →

← Ensures liquidity and sufficient emergency reserves

REVIEW TEST

1 Explain briefly what a mission statement is, and why an organisation needs one.

2 What is a corporate plan? Explain what it covers and why it is drawn up by a business organisation.

3 List five areas which you would expect to find included in a corporate plan.

4 In terms of business planning, explain the difference between a strategic and a tactical plan.

5 List four different kinds of plan which would be devised in the course of a year in a large private sector organisation.

6 List five commonly occurring reasons for the early failure of a small trader, start-up business.

THE START-UP BUSINESS PLAN

No business plan is more important than the start-up business plan. A good plan will result, ultimately in the evolution of a Marks & Spencer or Boots plc, but a poor one will quickly dispatch its creator into the massed ranks of the would-be but failed entrepreneurs.

There are eight main components of an effective start-up business plan:

KEY COMPONENTS OF AN EFFECTIVE START-UP BUSINESS PLAN

- **A basic business idea** – which is imaginative, realistic, viable and achievable.

- **Thorough market research** – which supplies accurate and up-to-date information about the market to be targeted.

- **An affordable but attractive location** – whether the business is to be in manufacturing, distribution or the service industry sector; where it makes, sells or works from is a vital ingredient in its eventual success.

- **Sufficient, available start-up capital** – most new companies which fail do so because they ran out of money prematurely – often as a result of underestimating the extent of the finance required.

- **Careful and detailed financial forward planning** – both the cash-flow forecast and operating budget are highly dependent upon prudent financial estimates and detailed monitoring of income and expenditure on a regular basis.

- **A clear understanding of the legal obligations involved in setting up a business** – both sole traders and small business employers accept extensive legal obligations when setting up a business involving company, employment, health and safety and trading law; and ignorance of the law is never an excuse when things go wrong!

- **A realistic evaluation of the skills and abilities of the people to work in the business** – if there is a mismatch between the expertise needed to run the business and the level of that which is available, the enterprise may well fail while its owners are 'learning by experience', and there are usually few second chances.

- **Ongoing monitoring of the plan in action** – it is essential that sufficient time is given to monitoring 'actual' performance against 'planned' targets and estimates; in a young business there is little margin for error and limited financial reserves to call upon.

DISCUSSION TOPICS

1 Are mission statements merely 'window-dressing waffle', or do they make a genuine and important contribution to corporate communication?

2 Why bother to paint 'Just-in-time – with us, not just a concept!' on the side of an articulated lorry?

3 Having produced the plans listed on page 683, what techniques would you use to ensure that all the relevant staff were made aware of their content, and that they were actually followed?

4 Why do *you* think so many small businesses fail during their first trading year? Should they be given more government support, or not?

■ The basic business idea

Whether as a part of a plan to be vetted by a bank manager in a loan application process, or whether as a self-disciplining exercise, the basic business idea should be painstakingly analysed and exposed to critical scrutiny. Among the key questions to be posed at the very outset are:

PC
8.2.5

QUESTIONS WHICH TEST THE BASIC BUSINESS IDEA

- Is my idea unusual, imaginative, out-of-the ordinary? Or is it 'old-hat', stale and run-of-the-mill, and already over-supplied by existing businesses? What is its 'unique selling benefit'?
- What physical resources does my idea require: Work from home? A shop? Franchised floor-space in a store? Transport?
- How acceptable is my idea to my prospective customers? Who *are* my prospective customers?
- Would my idea generate enough sales and profits to enable me and mine to live and ultimately to prosper? Both in the short and in the long term?

■ Legal and insurance aspects

Legal implications

A key part of the early business planning process to obtain an informed appreciation of the current national – and local – legal implications which will impact upon the business idea.

For example, it is extremely unlikely that a county council planning department will give authorisation to an application for change of use of business premises if someone wanted to convert a village shop and post office in an area of 'outstanding natural beauty' into a fast-food take-away!

The following checklist provides illustrations of the typical legal considerations which a business start-up entrepreneur would need to take into account:

Business premises

What are the current planning consents and authorised uses to which the premises may be put? Are there any restrictions in local county council planning by-laws or covenants in a leasehold agreement which the entrepreneur would have to abide by? Are there any parking restrictions, one-way traffic systems – or *proposed* changes in traffic routing which might affect the value to the entrepreneur of the proposed site for trading?

Health and safety at work

Do the premises under consideration meet HASAW requirements in terms of lavatories, rest-room and personal space requirements, along with safe walkways, general structures and electrical wiring etc? Would it be prudent to have a surveyor's structural report commissioned?

Fire and emergency evacuation requirements

Do the premises meet current fire and emergency evacuation requirements – in many instances a current fire safety certificate will be needed, issued by the county council Fire Brigade Office after a site inspection.

Proposed product or service range

Do the products which will be taken into stock conform to UK Weights & Measures, Trading Standards Office and Environmental Health Office requirements? Especial care is needed, for example, in vetting imported toys from Third World manufacturers, or garments from any foreign (or UK) supplier source so as to ensure they meet legal safety standards. Where services are concerned, can the legal requirements required of, for example, financial services, estate agency, chiropractice, or rest/nursing homes etc. be met?

Environmental protection

Is there any likelihood that the proposed business will fall foul of any environment protection laws ? For example, will outflow from a proposed manufacturing process into a river or stream cause pollution, or will work processes, such as the fitting and testing of car alarms, cause noise pollution?

Advertising and Sales Promotion

While detailed planning in this area will be done when drawing up a later marketing plan, it is important to consider – at the outset – whether any problems are likely to arise from Trade Descriptions, Sale of Goods or Consumer Credit Acts etc. relating to how products or services will be advertised and offered for sale.

Employment law

If employees are to be taken on, it is essential for prospective employers to be fully aware of their legal obligations well in advance for providing:

Employee accidental injury/ death insurance
National Insurance contributions
HASAW safety, clothing, hygiene and rest-room requirements
Contracts and conditions of service details etc.

Public, third party liability (see below)

Legal requirements must also be complied with in order to ensure that any person visiting or shopping in business premises (or liable to be injured by any falling masonry or fixture on the outside pavement etc.) is insured against any arising claim for injury or death.

Insurance implications

As the above listing illustrates, legal and insurance requirements often merge. The following listing indicates some major additional considerations:

Insurance of business premises

If premises are to be purchased freehold, the bank or building society providing any mortgage will insist that the premises be insured at least to the level of the loan in case of fire, flood or accidental damage etc. If they are to be purchased leasehold, the lessor will invariably include in the lease tightly written stipulations about structural and other building related insurances which the lessee will have to pay for.

Product liability

Similarly, it is prudent for business people to take out third party liability insurance in case a sold good causes injury or death through a defect in its manufacture and the aggrieved parties sue both manufacturer and retailer.

Vehicle insurances

It almost goes without saying that all motor-vehicles must be insured in line with the business in which they are used – whether heavy goods vehicle, light van, courier motor-cycle etc.

Private health insurance

An area of business insurance often overlooked, but essential for the small business entrepreneur is personal health insurance which also provides an income (or a lump sum in case the business fails) if he or she becomes ill and therefore unable to direct daily business operations over an extended period.

You would be forgiven for concluding that the above listings of both legal and insurance obligations might daunt the most enthusiastic would-be business person.

And indeed, one of the down-sides of current business management lies in the heavy burden imposed on business entrepreneurs by the requirements of our contemporary society. Given such a burden, not to mention the risk of losing all the invested venture capital, you might also come to appreciate the justification which such business people offer for obtaining a fair – or even handsome – profit from their business labours!

■ Market research

PC
8.2.3
8.3.2

Similar questions need to be framed in the areas of market research and location. Most small businesses tend to operate within a locality or district, and so the market research information is likely to concentrate upon:

- **The size and extent of the local potential market.**

  In terms of: numbers of potential customers, estimated sales turnover, density of likely customers, such as the number of people who walk past a main-street shop in a range of given hours, or who inhabit a large housing estate.

- **The spending power of targeted customers.**

  Successful businesses are those which reach a sufficient number of customers possessing enough disposable income to afford the goods/services on offer. (See Unit 3 Marketing, on the services of companies providing data on local socio-economic groups.)

- **The strength and size of the competition.**

  When too many sellers enter into a given market it is said to have become saturated or over-supplied; in such circumstances, available custom becomes highly segmented – broken up into small sections – and all the traders suffer from insufficient sales income and arising profits. Furthermore, the presence of nearby competitors who are well established, with a loyal customer base, are likely to 'strangle the newcomer at birth' by temporarily sacrificing gross profit margins to a devastating series of undercutting special offers and 'unbeatable' discounts.

■ **Pricing structures that the market will bear.**

The prices for given products and services which can be obtained relate very directly to the extent of demand and numbers of direct competitors. In a market in which demand is low and in which competition is fierce, prices obtained are unlikely to generate sufficient margins to cover the cost of sales and still provide an adequate net profit. In this context, obtainable profit margins are also very closely related to how well a trader can buy his stock – 'you have to buy right to sell right'.

■ **Local prospects for economic prosperity and growth.**

Start-up market research also needs to address the likely future economic trends within the selected locality; this will involve researching into the performance of large employers, the extent of inward investment and the improvement of infrastructure elements such as inner city redevelopment or green field site factory building; negative data, such as the imminent closure of a large works, or relocation of a government agency etc. is also important – there is little point in setting up a business in a locality which is 'dying on its feet'.

PC
8.1.3
8.2.3
8.2.6

MARKET RESEARCH AND SWOT

A very helpful approach to undertaking the market research part of the start-up business plan is to analyse the **Strengths, Weaknesses, Opportunities and Threats (SWOT)** of both the start-up business itself and the businesses which make up the perceived competition. Such a SWOT analysis will include:

● the 'marketability' of the basic business idea;

● the 'sellability' of own and competing product ranges (or range of services on offer);

● the sales prices for the product or service range likely to be obtained;

● the projected arising gross and net profit margins;

● the effectiveness of advertising and sales promotion activities – own and competition's;

● 'draw' and density of customer traffic which the business location enjoys – own and competitors';

● likely impact of competitors' responses to the newly opened business;

● likelihood of 'doom scenarios' such as the construction of a bypass or a new one-way traffic system or widespread car-parking ban which could wreck the business in one fell swoop!

PC
8.2.3
8.2.6
8.3.3

■ Finance and the business plan

One of the most important financial planning tasks to be undertaken early is a calculation of the business's projected break-even point. This is the point at which sufficient goods or services have been sold to cover the cost of sales by the profit they generate. The example on page 694 shows simply and clearly how the break-even point is calculated.

The break-even point for any business's sales can also be calculated with the aid of a graph. The diagram below (Fig. 8.4) illustrates how sales income is plotted against fixed and variable costs. Where the rising volume of sales intersects the plotted rising track of variable plus fixed costs, enough revenue has been obtained to cover all associated outgoings – a break-even point has been reached. The shaded segment indicates the subsequent move into profit from the sustained increase in sales:

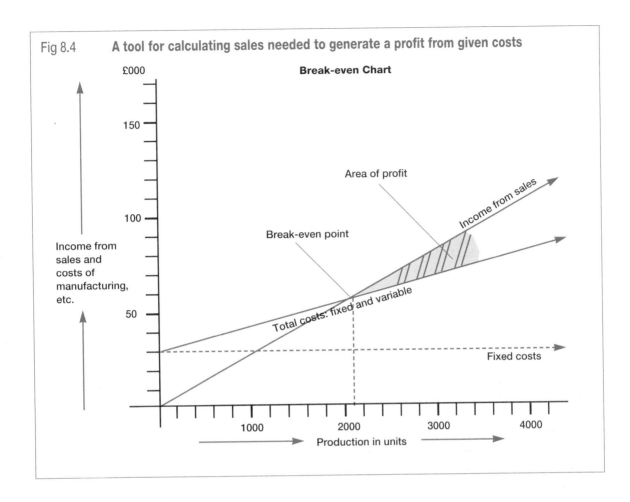

Fig 8.4 **A tool for calculating sales needed to generate a profit from given costs**

Break-even Chart

£000

150

100

Area of profit

Income from sales

Break-even point

Income from
sales and
costs of
manufacturing,
etc.

50

Total costs: fixed and variable

Fixed costs

1000   2000   3000   4000

Production in units

Whether calculated as a table or a graph, it is essential to produce a projection of sales income, cost of sales, gross and net profit early in the planning process in order to establish whether, for example, a high level of costs and overheads would result in the need for an impossibly high revenue from sales in order to generate sufficient profit. If this were to prove the case, then the would-be entrepreneur would need to 'go back to the drawing-board' to see how the components of his break-even chart might be massaged in order to produce a more realistic relationship between projected sales income and profit.

How to calculate the break-even point

Working out your break-even point

Break-even is the level of sales you need to cover all of your costs. Let's see how to work it out, using an imaginary manufacturer. The same calculation applies to any business. Let's say you have stock valued at £38,000 and you are projecting the following over the next 12 months.

	£
Sales	108,000
Purchases	60,000
Closing stock	50,000
Wages or salaries	32,000
Overheads	10,360

From these figures, you can work out your projected gross and net profit. That is to say, your profits before (gross) and after (net) you allow for your overheads.

Sales		108,000
Purchases	60,000	
Wages or salaries	32,000	
Stock (increase) or decrease	(12,000)*	
Less cost of goods sold		(80,000)
Gross profit (profit before overhead costs)		28,000
Less overheads		(10,360)
Net profit		17,640

* Your opening stock is £38,000, and your closing stock is £50,000. The Stock Change figure is always the opening amount with the closing stock taken off.

Now you need to work out your gross profit margin. This is your gross profit, which is your profit before allowing for overheads. It is written as a percentage of sales.

$$\frac{\text{Gross profit} \times 100}{\text{Sales}} = \frac{£28,000 \times 100}{£108,000} = 25.9\%$$

If you can reach the gross profit margin and your overheads do not change, the break-even turnover is worked as follows:

$$\frac{\text{Overheads} \times 100}{\text{Gross profit margin}} = \frac{£10,360 \times 100}{25.9} = £40,000$$

Therefore, this business will need a turnover of £40,000 to cover all overheads, as long as it keeps the gross profit margin.

Looked at another way...

£40,000 turnover at 25.9% gross profit margin = £10,360
This is just enough to cover the overheads.

There are 2 other useful calculations you can do:

First if the business keeps its present level of turnover, but its margins are reduced for some reason, perhaps because of rising costs, you can work out how much the margin can fall by, and still cover your overheads.

$$\frac{\text{Overheads} \times 100}{\text{Sales}} = \frac{£10,360 \times 100}{£108,000} = 9.59\%$$

This is the break-even gross profit margin.

Second work out the amount you need to sell every month just to break even. This figure is important because you can use it to check whether or not you are on target, or need to make some adjustments. But remember that this calculation does not take into account any seasonal changes which might affect your business.

To work out monthly targets, simply take your break-even sales figure for the year and divide by 12.

$$\frac{£40,000}{12} = £3,333 \text{ per month}$$

This model is reproduced with the kind permission of National Westminster Bank from their *The business start-up guide* 1993

DISCUSSION TOPIC

Given the above scenario – of a situation in which the volume of sales needed to generate enough income to cover cost of sales looks impossibly high – how could the would-be small businessman adjust his or her plan to make it more likely to succeed? What components of the plan could be trimmed most readily do you think?

EXAMPLES OF FIXED AND VARIABLE COST ITEMS

Fixed Costs

Fixed costs are those which can be expected to remain unchanged for the duration of the trading period. Typical fixed costs in a small business include:

- Rent of premises
- Business rates
- Insurances
- Heating
- Lighting

(Remember that energy costs may be variable if, say, a firm introduces overtime and thus works equipment for longer periods to make more goods.)

Variable Costs

Variable costs are those which rise pro rata – at a rate which stems from an increase in business activity or increases in operational costs. For example, a successful business may need to employ additional sales personnel to cope with demand. Thus the firm's salary bill will increase. Or, a manufacturer may have to cope with an increase in the cost of raw materials during the trading period.

Typical examples of variable costs in a small business include:

- Salaries
- Raw materials/Bought in stock
- Fuel/energy
- Packaging

In the first months of a business the continuous monitoring of the levels of fixed and variable costs is crucial for, if their total creeps up unnoticed, a business may fail despite a high level of sales, since the profits needed to sustain it will have been eroded and insufficient profit made. Similarly, if sales fall back from projected levels, swift action will be needed to reduce cost of sales correspondingly in order to maintain a sufficient cash-flow (see below).

The following chart illustrates what trading information a prudent proprietor monitors in the course of a trading year:

Example of a business plan monitoring schedule

Trading Periods

Line*	Receipts	6 months to June Projected £	Actual £	12 months to December Projected £	Actual £
2	Sales Debtors (including VAT)	41,400	41,400	103,500	92,000
5	Capital introduced	10,000	10,000	10,000	10,000
A	Total receipts	51,400	51,400	113,500	102,000
	Payments				
8	Cash purchases	32,200	40,250	59,800	58,850
11	Wages or Salaries (Net)	13,000	13,000	26,000	26,000
12	PAYE and NI	2,500	2,500	5,500	5,500
13	Capital items (for example equipment or vehicles)	5,000	5,000	5,000	5,000
15	Rent	2,250	1,500	3,750	3,750
15	Rates	240	240	480	480
16	Light and heat	450	475	900	1,000
16	Telephone and post	210	190	440	420
19	Interest	680	750	940	1,465
20	Bank and finance charges	200	300	400	500
21	Book-keeper	1,000	1,000	2,000	2,000
21	Professional fees	400	400	950	950
23	Insurance	400	400	400	400
24	General expenses	400	500	800	1,000
26	VAT	1,000	800	5,500	4,375
B	Total payments	59,930	67,305	112,860	111,690
C	Net cashflow (A-B)	(8,530)	(15,905)	640	(9,690)
29	Opening Bank Balance	Nil	Nil	Nil	Nil
D	Closing Bank Balance (Net cashflow + or − your opening balance)	(8,530) Overdrawn	(15,905) Overdrawn	640 In Credit	(9,690) Overdrawn

This schedule is reproduced with the kind permission of National Westminster Bank.
(*See also the Cashflow Forecast example on page 699)

Note that in the above planning/monitoring schedule the monitoring periods are shown as six months for illustration purposes. In reality, a business proprietor would monitor the items listed above at weekly and monthly intervals.

DISCUSSION TOPICS

1 What led in your view to the actual overdrawn as opposed to the in credit position at the end of 12 months' trading period?

2 Can you suggest what timely steps might have been taken to retrieve the situation?

CASH-FLOW FORECASTS AND OPERATING BUDGETS

■ Estimating and monitoring the cash flow forecast

Another essential financial aspect of start-up business planning – and indeed, just as important in a mature business – is the rolling cash flow forecast. This forecast is usually set down in a planning schedule which totals each month's flow of money into and out of the business. The trading period may be from January to December or from April to March, depending upon the one chosen for the business. Bear in mind that the Inland Revenue's financial year follows the latter monthly sequence.

In essence, a cash flow forecast is a table of those items which go to make up the component parts of all receipts (money flowing in to the business), and all payments which go out.

Typical composition of receipts

The items termed receipts include:

■ payment for goods received as cash

■ money owed for goods purchased on account

■ injections of capital or personal investment into the business at the outset

■ money received from selling any assets (equipment, unwanted stock etc.) belonging to the business

Typical composition of payments

The items termed payments include:

■ money paid out as cash or cheques for goods purchased – notably stock to sell

■ money paid out for items purchased as an essential part of the business's running costs – advertising, cleaning, insurances, fuel, heat and light etc.

■ payroll for all employees and directors' withdrawals and all associated NIC payments etc.

■ rent, rates and associated physical resources costs such as service charges relating to a lease

- all the repayment charges associated with hiring, leasing or renting plant, equipment, machinery, overalls, indoor plants etc.

- all financial charges such as bank charges, annual accountant's fees, interest and service charges on loans etc.

- all payments made in the form of taxes such as corporation tax, VAT, any shareholders' dividends etc.

PC
8.1.2
8.2.5
8.2.7

DISCUSSION TOPICS

One of the 'dark sides' of the business world is that today many large enterprises dispatch many small ones into receivership because they deliberately defer and delay for as long as possible paying the small trader for goods or services purchased on account. Contrastingly, the large firms seek to obtain payment for the goods or services they sell on account as promptly as possible. Such a practice, of course, helps to assure the future of the larger company through a manipulation of its cash flow which ensures that there is always a positive balance in favour of moneys flowing in.

1 Should a business law be enacted to provide small traders with stronger protection in this area?

2 What actions could the small trader take to obtain prompter payment for goods or services sold on account?

3 What rule of thumb would you suggest to a small trader as the safest ratio or mix of selling of goods a) for cash and b) on account?

What a good cash flow forecast makes possible is the anticipation of potential times when the business's financial viability – indeed its very existence – may be put at risk by the proprietor having to pay out money to meet due bills when there is an insufficient inflow of cash to do so, and for taking preventative action in the case of account customers who are very slow payers.

Mr Micawber in Charles Dickens' *David Copperfield* well knew that 'Annual income twenty pounds, annual expenditure twenty pounds ought and six' resulted in misery. For the new small business it often results in bankruptcy, even though assets may exist of a greater value than the debts incurred, but which are unrealisable in time to save the business.

Set out below is an example of the listing of items which comprise a cash flow forecast schedule. Note the straightforward arithmetic (a – b = c) for calculating the net cash flow and the final position for each month after opening and closing bank balances have been taken into consideration.

Example of a cash-flow forecasting schedule

Business name:

Cash-flow forecast [Note: schedule extends for 12 months] ⟶

	Enter month				
	Figures rounded to £'s	Budget	Actual	Budget	Actual
	Receipts				
1	Sales (including VAT) – Cash				
2	– Debtors				
3	Other trading income				
4	Loans you have received				
5	New capital				
6	Selling of assets				
7	Other receipts				
a	Total receipts				
	Payments cash for goods you				
8	have bought				
9	Payments to creditors				
10	Owner or directors' withdrawals				
11	Wages and Salaries (net)				
12	PAYE/NI				
13	Capital items (for example equipment and vehicles)				
14	Transport and packaging				
15	Rent or rates				
16	Services				
17	Loan repayments				
18	Hire or leasing repayments				
19	Interest				
20	Bank or finance charges				
21	Professional fees				
22	Advertising				
23	Insurance				
24					
25					
26	VAT				
27	Corporation tax and so on				
28	Dividends				
b	Total payments				
c	Net cashflow (a – b)				
29	Opening bank balance				
d	Closing bank balance (c ± Line 29)				

Basic assumptions – please give details of the assumptions you use
Credit taken – the average time your creditors give you to pay.
Credit given – the average time you give your debtors to pay.

Table of useful monitoring calculations

PC
8.2.6
8.2.7

You need to monitor how well your business is doing and keep track of performance. You can spot changes by using the following quick calculations

- Gross profit margin:

$$\frac{\text{Gross profit X 100}}{\text{Sales}} = \%$$

- Net profit as a percentage of sales:

$$\frac{\text{Net Profit}}{\text{Sales}} = \%$$

- Profit azs a percentage of the capital used:

$$\frac{\text{Net Profit}}{\text{Net Assets}} \text{ X 100 } = \%$$

- Rate of stock turnover:

$$\frac{\text{Cost of stock sold}}{\text{Average stock at cost}}$$

- Net working capital (current assts – current liabilities) as a percentage of sales:

$$\frac{\text{Net working capital}}{\text{Sales}} \text{ X 100 } = \%$$

- Working capital ratio:

$$\frac{\text{Current assets}}{\text{Current liabilities}}$$

Any ratio below 1 means that your business is currently insolvent.

- Quick ratio:

$$\frac{\text{Debtors}}{\text{Current liabilities}}$$

This calculations shows whether it would be easy to sell your business using only assets which could be quickly sold or realised. It also shows whether your business can pay debts as they are due. Your debtors should only be trade debts which you will receive within a few months. In this calculation, do not include any stock unless you can sell it quickly for cash.

Example of a start-up cash-flow forecast for a retail shop selling ladies' fashions

Cash-flow forecast

		CASH IN	MAY	JUN	JUL	AUG	SEP	OCT	NOV	DEC	JAN	FEB	MAR	APR	TOTALS
(1)	1	Sales (inc VAT)	1000	1500	2000	3000	3000	2750	4000	8000	1500	1750	2750	3250	34500
	2	Bank or other loans		2000											2000
	3	Owner's Capital	6500												6500
	4	Other Money in													
	5	Total	7500	3500	2000	3000	3000	2750	4000	8000	1500	1750	2750	3250	43000
		CASH OUT (INC VAT)													
(2)	6	Stock/Raw materials	5000	3000	1500	1250	1500	1375	2000	4000	750	875	1375	1625	24250
	7	Advertising & Promotion	200						200						400
	8	Bank Charges/Interest			44			38			9				91
	9	Business Insurance	350												350
(3)	10	Drawings/Salaries/NI		300	300	300	500	500	500	800	700	700	700	700	6000
(4)	11	Electric/Gas/Heat		75		75		75		125		125		100	575
	12	Fees (eg Accountant, Lawyer)	300											400	700
	13	HP/Lease/Loan Payments		80	80	80	80	80	80	80	80	80	80	80	880
	14	Motor – Fuel													
	15	Motor – Other Expenses													
	16	Postage/Carriage													
	17	Rent & Rates	1000	250	250	1250	250	250	1250	250	250	1250	250		6500
	18	Repairs & Maintenance		50			50			50			50		200
	19	Staff Wages													
	20	Staff PAYE/NI													
	21	Stationery/Printing	20					20							40
	22	Sundries	80	50	30	20	10	10	10	10	10	10	10	10	260
	23	Telephone/Fax	250	50			100			100			100		600
	24	Travelling					100							100	200
	25	VAT													
	26	Other Expenses													
	27	CAPITAL EXPENDITURE	1450												1450
	28	TOTAL	8650	3855	2204	2975	2590	2328	4060	5415	1799	3040	2565	3015	42496
	29	Net Cashflow	(1150)	(355)	(204)	25	410	422	(60)	2585	(299)	(1290)	185	235	504
	30	Opening Balance	0	(1150)	(1505)	(1709)	(1684)	(1274)	(852)	(912)	1673	1374	84	269	0
(5)	31	CLOSING BALANCE	(1150)	(1505)	(1709)	(1684)	(1274)	(852)	(912)	1673	1374	84	269	504	504

Figures in brackets are negative i.e. the business bank account would be in overdraft.

© Reproduced from *The Greatest Little Business Book* 5th edition by kind permission of Peter Hingston and Hingston Associates.

**START-UP LADIES' FASHIONS RETAIL SHOP
CASH-FLOW FORECAST**

Commentary

1 *Sales*

Note that the sales forecast allows for peaks in spring, autumn and Christmas trading

2 *Stock*

Similar buying-in peaks occur as well as an initial opening stock purchase of £5,000

3 *Proprietor's drawings*

The sole trader owner is careful to minimise drawings in the early months of June–August

4 *Electricity/Gas/Heat*

Due weighting is given to additional costs during winter months

5 *Cash-flow balances*

Note that a planned deficit in the closing balances from May to November has been allowed for and that the projected closing balance for the first 12 months of trading is a modest £504.

Erring on the side of caution

It is better in drawing up a cash flow forecast to err on the side of caution. This forecast indicates a break-even first year which is likely to move steadily into growth and increased trading profits in the second and third years of trading.

■ The operating budget

Another helpful financial monitoring tool is the operating budget. This is similar to the cash flow forecast in that it extends monthly listings for both projected and actual financial totals over twelve months. However, the items listed and compared in an operating budget are sales and cost of sales – broken down into their component sub-headings.

Sales

The operating budget first totals the turnover value of all sales as each calendar month ensues:

    (a) Income from all sales

Cost of sales

It then facilitates the calculation of a gross profit total by:

    (b) totalling the cost of all goods purchased (in the month)

    (c) adding the value of the opening stock

    (d) deducting the value of the closing stock

    (e) also deducting direct labour costs

Gross profit

The gross profit (or loss) figure, (f) is:

$$f = a - (b + c - d - e)$$

or, Gross profit = sales minus: opening stock, plus goods purchased less closing stock, less direct labour costs

Net profit

The operating budget then provides a listing of all the expenses for each month which are incurred as costs arising from the sales operation. In a manufacturing organisation these will centre upon production costs; in a service industry, they will derive mainly from mounting the sales operation and include the cost of running a sales force, advertising and sales promotion, office administration, the monthly bills for payroll, heating, light, rent, an allocation for equipment and vehicle depreciation and so on.

Thus the calculation for arriving at a net profit total is:

Gross profit: f
less Total expenses: g
equals Net profit: h

Such a comprehensive and detailed business start-up plan is needed, not only to present to a bank manager as a prerequisite for obtaining a loan and overdraft facilities, but also as an essential analysis of the overall business proposal.

Regrettably, each year thousands of businesses fail – last year some 440 were failing each week – and too many fall into the category of those which should never have been started up. That they were and failed in their first year – as about one-third do – is almost certainly due to the failure of their owners to carry out sufficient preplanning and investigation, before a commitment is made and precious assets put at risk.

For this very reason, risk-taking entrepreneurs who first plan carefully and then work 'all hours' to build up a successful business enterprise feel (rightly) entitled to the affluence and high standards of living which may come from their hard work and the initial risks they were prepared to take.

PC
8.1.3
8.1.5
8.2.2
8.2.7

DISCUSSION TOPICS

1 What do you consider the most risky aspects of starting up a business?

   How might the risks you identify be minimised by the entrepreneur?

2 To what extent is a start-up business plan worth the time and effort put into its production, if the 'proof of the pudding' is always in the eating?

3 According to accepted theory, it is crucial to monitor operations closely and frequently during the first months of opening a business. Yet at such a time, its proprietor(s) are likely to be devoting all their time and energy to selling and promoting sales. What advice on the effective management of time could you offer to such small traders? How would you suggest their working week should be organised to ensure that essential data is captured and scrutinised? What IT systems could you recommend which might help?

THE TRADING AND PROFIT AND LOSS ACCOUNT

The trading and profit and loss account for any given trading period – say monthly, quarterly or annually is simply the presentation of the above summarised totals, as the following example illustrates:

Specimen trading and profit and loss accounts

Trading Account			Profit and Loss Account		
Sales		£37,500	Gross profit		£12,600
Opening stock	£4,500		Business salaries		
+ Purchases	£15,000		(including your		
	£19,500		own drawings)	£3,000	
			+ Rent	£1,000	
– Closing stock	£4,600	£14,900	+ Rent	£250	
		£22,600	+ Light/heating	£250	
– Direct labour costs		£10,000	+ Telephone/post	£250	
			+ Insurance	£250	
GROSS PROFIT		£12,600	+ Repairs	£1,000	
			+ Advertising	£750	
Gross Profit Margin			+ Bank interest/HP	£750	
			+ Other expenses	£900	£8,400
$\dfrac{\text{Gross profit £12,600}}{\text{Sales £37,500}} \times 100 = 34\%$			NET PROFIT		£4,200

Note: for simplicity all figures shown are exclusive of VAT.

Reproduced by kind permission of Midland Bank PLC

■ The start-up business plan: summary

While there is no single, correct way to structure a start-up business plan, the following checklist provides a suggested list of key topics in a logical sequence:

CHECKLIST OF KEY SECTIONS OF A START-UP BUSINESS PLAN

1 Reference details of the business:

Owner's(s') personal details: e.g. directors, partners or sole proprietor

Business trading name

Trading address and registered office address

Date of proposed commencement of trading

2 Details of capitalisation – value and allocation of shares among directors or sums invested by partners

3 Details of basic business idea and the rationale for it

4 Market research SWOT analysis and any test marketing undertaken

5 Details of proposed location and business premises, including particulars of cost (e.g. freehold, leasehold or rental) and rates

6 Particulars of goods/services to be sold, including likely suppliers, trading margins (buying in and selling out prices) and likely extent of stocks needing to be held to provide a viable range

7 Breakdown of the costs of start-up plant, equipment, fixtures and fittings needed in order to open up convincingly

8 A detailed cash flow forecast for the first 12 months of trading supplemented by an outline forecast for years 2 and 3

9 A summary trading and profit and loss account projection for year 1

10 Details of the financial support needed to start the business:

   a from personal resources

   b as loans from a bank or similar source

This section will also indicate the extent of any government start-up grants or loans.

Note: This section should also include proposals on how any requested loan will be secured (say against assets in any property owned which is free of any mortgage or similar financial constraint)

REVIEW TEST

1 Make a checklist of what you consider to be the key components of an effective start-up business plan

2 What is meant by the term: unique selling benefit?

3 What areas would you expect the market research section of a start-up business plan to cover?

4 What does SWOT stand for? How is SWOT used in compiling a business plan?

5 What is a break-even chart? How can the compiling of a break-even chart assist the business planning process?

6 Explain the difference between fixed costs and variable costs.

7 List the items you would expect to make up receipts in a cash-flow forecast. Make a similar list for payments.

8 If a number total on a cash-flow forecast is enclosed in brackets, how should the figure be interpreted?

9 Write down the monitoring formulas for calculating:

   a) gross profit margin,

   b) rate of stock turnover,

   c) net profit as a percentage of sales.

10 How does an operating budget differ from a cash-flow forecast?

11 Why is the frequent production of trading and profit and loss accounts so important in the first year of trading?

THE MARKETING PLAN

PC
8.2.3
8.3.1

The marketing plan, while an essential tool in coordinating the overall marketing function over a three- to five-year rolling period, should also be regarded as a central part of an organisation's corporate plan.

This is because its main value lies in auditing the strengths and weaknesses of the organisation's past and present situation and, from an informed position, devising detailed policies and strategies for ensuring that appropriate products or services will come on stream – sometimes four or five years into the future. Appropriate in marketing terms means:

Products or services that will:

■ take the place of mature and obsolescent lines in the product life cycle

■ sell because they meet the expectations of targeted customers and are deemed to be up-to-date and appealing

■ capture a targeted market share

■ generate levels of gross and net profit specified in the marketing and corporate plans

■ ensure the development of the organisation and its survival in a competitive business world

Given the importance of an effective marketing plan to the future of the organisation, it is not surprising that it should be based upon careful research and analysis of 'hard' factual data, rather than the intuitive finger in the air to catch the wind.

Set out below is a chart which lists in chronological order the key stages which are undertaken in producing an effective marketing plan. These stages are as valid for the small, local business as for the globally based multinational.

KEY STAGES IN PRODUCING AN EFFECTIVE MARKETING PLAN

1 Restatement and clarification of the mission

Before embarking upon any collection and analysis of data, it is important that the organisation's mission statement and goals are reviewed. For example, is the company still seeking to win market share at a modest profit, or has the basic strategy changed so that it now wishes to generate profits – say to finance expansion. Such a shift in corporate strategy would fundamentally change the shape and structure of any marketing plan.

2 The internal audit of the strengths and weaknesses of the products/services on offer

An audit to be undertaken early on in the planning period analyses the condition of each product or service which is being offered for sale. Such an audit will examine and evaluate:

- the position of the product in its life-cycle – is it young and thriving, or elderly and waning?

- what is the degree of acceptance for the product? Is it hard or easy to sell ?

- What contribution does it make to company sales revenue and profits? What is its forecast future life and projected contribution to overall sales and profits during the life of the marketing plan? What has it cost and what will it cost to bring to the market? Are these costs acceptable?

- How effective is the organisation's packaging, merchandising, advertising and sales promotion of the product compared with that of principal competitors?

3 The review of product/ service development

All successful enterprises rely on a vigorous and innovative research and development function – to ensure that new products or services are continually being invented, developed and tested as potential new members of the range to be offered for sale. A crucial element, therefore, of the marketing plan is an objective appraisal of the strengths and weaknesses of the products/services under development:

- How do they compare with products/services already being sold and in competitors' pipelines?
- Has test marketing shown that customers will buy the new product/service in sufficient quantities?
- What features does the prototype embody which the sales force will be able to capitalise upon?
- Are enough products/services in development to ensure that smooth transitions will occur as obsolescent ones time out?
- Is R & D matching (and beating!) the efforts of main competitors?

Many established companies go out of business every year through failing to maintain a strong R & D function. They end up with a tired range of products or services which fail to match, say, the technological features of competing ones or fail to meet changed customer expectations.

4 The external audit: researching the market

A particularly important stage in producing a marketing plan is the undertaking of a conscientious and detailed survey of two major – indeed key – influencers upon the business:

> **the customers**
> **the competition**

The market research stage is mainly concerned with checking out:

the customers in a consumer market

- whether the organisation's customers are still made up of the same socio-economic groupings, having regard to age, gender, location, education, spending power etc. if the market is a consumer market – and if not, how the customer base is changing and evolving, and what impact this will have upon aspects like product design, cost, packaging, merchandising in the future; mapping trends in customers' tastes and preferences is crucial to the market research stage.

the customers in an industrial market

- whether changes in manufacturing processing and technological advances are forcing updates and improvements upon product design and working, and what effect, for example, this is likely to have on the pricing structure the organisation devises.

- whether structural changes in the market oblige the organisation to undertake a radical re-think on its marketing strategy; for instance, whether because of the continual erosion of profit margins from selling through wholesalers – such as agrochemical suppliers to farmers – to embark upon a strategy of direct selling and cutting out the middle man.

the competitors: in a consumer market

- whether the organisation's market position is safe, or being threatened by competing firms on the basis of:

    superior products, more competitive pricing strategies, superior advertising, sales promotion and merchandising, more effective (at the time) strategies such as forgoing profit margins by selling premier products cheaply in order to secure significant increases in market share, or by enticing customers by appealing discounts, free gifts or enhanced warranties etc.

the competitors: in an industrial market

- whether the organisation's market position is under threat from the introduction of an innovative and technically superior product

- whether irresistible, supportive financial plans are being offered to manufacturers or distributors to enable them, say, to purchase a new production line or a new fleet of articulated lorries.

In all market research planning, the eventual key factor is:

What do we need to do in order to either:

a ensure we continue to hold our dominant position?

b overcome the threats we have identified in competitors' activities in the market-place?

Summary

The market research stages comprise an external audit and analysis of aspects such as product innovation and design features, pricing strategies, advertising ploys, promotional offers and 'special deals', supportive financial arrangements, product positioning (say of a family saloon car just launched by a competitor) and so on.

5 Auditing the available resources needed to deliver the plan

Sometimes socially ambitious consumers are referred to as having: 'champagne tastes, but beer money!' Similarly, prudent consumers are advised to 'cut their cloth according to their purse'.

In other words, there is little point in devising any marketing plan strategies which cannot be afforded either in terms of:

- the extent of *finance* available to underwrite the plan

- the skills and abilities of the *workforce*

- the capacities and facilities of existing plant and equipment

Clearly, in many organisations sufficient reserves of capital may exist to buy in expert personnel, sophisticated new equipment or meet the costs of designing major new products.

Indeed, effective organisations plan for just such eventualities in their corporate plans. However, for a marketing plan to be effective, it must also be realistic. Sometimes compromises need to be made in the light of the resources which can be directed to the plan's delivery.

Thus the marketing plan of a well-managed organisation will maintain continual contact with:

- the manpower planning of the personnel department
- the equipment replacement and renewal policies of production or retail branch management
- the manipulation of funds by the senior accountant so as to provide available capital for research and development of new products and overall support for the marketing function

6 Costing the plan

An old but true production engineering motto is:

'All change costs!'

This could be extended to include – in a marketing plan context: 'All activity, and especially changed activity costs!' Thus any marketing plan worth its salt will include a summarising stage in which all the activities and operations which go to make up the marketing plan are costed in a detailed schedule.

This schedule will include cost projections for existing and new products (or services) of:

- research and development
- production
- distribution/warehousing
- market research and marketing administration
- advertising, sales promotion and merchandising
- sales support: the sales force and sales administration
- customer and after sales services

Some organisations have established formulas which enable marketing staff to calculate *for each product or service* what proportion of the total income it is expected to generate should be written down against items such as those listed above, and what contribution it is expected to make to net profits. Such an approach is also helpful when it comes to formulating a pricing strategy for the product or service.

7 The marketing plan summary

In large organisations, as you will have realised, the marketing plan is usually a lengthy and complex document. It is therefore customary for a summary section to be included – often at the front of the plan – which lists the plan's key points and issues.

This summary helps managers to gauge the overall thrust and direction of the plan before having to take in extensive factual and statistical data.

■ The monitoring function

Clearly, there is little point in expending the time and costs of producing a marketing plan if no one then takes the trouble to set up mechanisms and systems for providing feedback on how the plan is being followed and implemented.

Thus the marketing department will hold regular meetings with colleagues in R & D, production, sales, personnel, accounts etc. in order to check, say, whether products under development will come on stream according to due deadlines or whether sales are generating the projected gross and net profits.

DISCUSSION TOPICS

1 'The problem with producing good marketing plans is that so much of their content is based on estimates, forecasts, projections and futuring.' What types of 'hard information' can you list which would help to make a marketing plan more specific and less speculative?

2 Establishing likely customer buying trends is always a problem. What techniques can you suggest, say, for a retail ladies' fashions boutique?

3 What would you suggest as the major differences of emphasis and approach between an industrial and a consumer marketing plan?

KEY COMPONENTS OF A MARKETING BUDGET

Naturally, no two marketing budgets will be the same. Not only will they vary from industry to industry – manufacturing to retailing – but they will also vary according to the size and age of the business. For instance, a start-up venture may need to spend a far higher proportion of its marketing budget on advertising and sales promotion in order to achieve market penetration and to publicise the trading name, type of business and its locations.

Nevertheless, it is possible to identify a listing of key marketing budget areas which will form components of the whole.

■ Marketing budget or corporate budget?

In terms of a company's overall corporate budget, the marketing budget component may also include costings and estimates for the relocation of staff and the acquisition and fitting out of premises – if, for example, a retail chainstore group is operating to a policy of expansion, where twenty-five new stores are due to be opened across the UK within a calendar year.

In such instances, it is most likely that the expansion – though planned for by the marketing department – will be funded from a 'development pot', such as a shares rights issue or from retained profits or from a bank loan, rather than from an annual marketing budget, which is usually restricted to paying for the forward planning and daily routines of the department.

■ Financing the marketing budget

The amount of finance allocated depends entirely upon a number of variable factors like:

- the amount of profit generated by a business, from which funds may be drawn
- the level of competition and the position of the organisation in it; a well-established market leader may not feel it necessary to devote as much money to a marketing budget as, say, a young, thrusting company wishing to acquire a larger share of the market in a hurry; however, in a fiercely competitive market all players may feel it necessary to market aggressively and to divert financial resources to this activity
- the degree of complexity or sophistication of the product/service range which may require continuous explanation and support; alternatively – say in the sweet snack market – a constant development of simple but new products may require a continuous, high level of marketing

GROUP ACTIVITY

In pairs, carry out the following activity and then write it up for circulation and discussion among your class:

With the help of your teacher or a personal contact, make arrangements to visit a local company, voluntary or charitable organisation which possesses a marketing department and interview one of its senior marketing managers. Seek to establish what kind of elements and aspects inform its marketing plan and budget – in general terms. Bear in mind that both items will be confidential in other than broad-brush terms, and concentrate, therefore, on the 'ingredients' rather than the 'costs and prices'.

THE SALES PLAN

PC
8.3.1

An organisation's sales plan may be regarded as the tactical follow-up to its marketing plan strategy. Generally, marketing plans span a future period of some three to five years from any current trading year. By contrast, sales plans tend to concentrate upon the single year (or trading period) following upon the current trading year.

■ The key sales plan objective

Not unexpectedly, a sales plan details *the means by which the sales will be achieved which are required in order for the goals of the marketing plan in Year 1 to be attained.* However, within this simple requirement may lie a set of varying objectives. Depending upon the marketing plan's needs and priorities, the sale of goods or services during the sales plan period may need to:

- concentrate upon those products which yield most profit
- direct all sales effort and energy to expanding market share (within preset minimum/maximum) profit margins
- achieve a preset target of winning new customers
- convert existing customers from outright purchase to leasing of sales products or services
- sell and discount a given good heavily against a newly arrived competing item so as to drive it out of the market.

Thus it is essential for an organisation's sales director to possess a clear and specific briefing as to the key objective(s) of the sales plan to be devised.

■ Negotiating sales targets

At the same time, it is important to remember that neither marketing nor sales plans are ever produced in a vacuum. They are always devised against a backdrop of what is happening in the market-place. There is, therefore, little point in senior managers – sitting atop the organisational pyramid – issuing impossibly high sales targets to be achieved. Imposed targets which take no heed of the state of the economy, competitors' existing slice of the market, the 'sellability' of the current product range or the ground the existing sales force can effectively cover are unlikely to be met, but very liable to demotivate.

Thus an effective sales department keeps its marketing counterpart continuously informed with:

- branch, district, regional and national sales turnover totals
- at daily, weekly, monthly, quarterly and annually intervals

It also provides detailed break-downs of sales by:

- individual product
- profit generated
- specified customer
- new customers
- 'head office' accounts etc.

so that an informed analysis of how sales are performing is always available on a rolling basis. By the same token, a company's sales representatives are likely to be involved in the process of forecasting sales in any given trading period, given their in-depth knowledge of their own sales territories. In this way, a mixture of sales analysis and sales intelligence usually informs the design of both the marketing and sales plans and the setting of sales targets.

■ Disaggregating the sales targets

By product mix to achieve turnover and profit targets

A sales director will, ultimately, accept an overall sales turnover target, which may in addition include an overall profit margin to be generated – the difference between the prices at which the goods or services are sold to customers (wholesalers, retailers, dealers etc) and the prices which have been established as the cost prices by the firm's cost accountants.

As some products produce higher margins than others, the sales director will need to arrive at a *product mix* which is considered most likely to deliver both the required level of sales *and* profit margin. Thus a regional and district manager may in due course receive a sales revenue target which is disaggregated into a series of percentages – one for each product in the sales range. Such a technique ensures that both turnover and profit targets are simultaneously met.

By territory to exploit the most economically active areas and to achieve a fair distribution of sales targets

It is common practice in national (and international companies) to break down overall sales targets as follows:

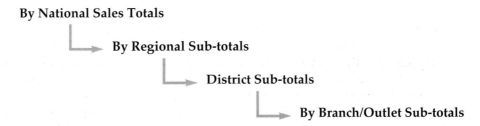

By National Sales Totals

└──▶ **By Regional Sub-totals**

└──▶ **District Sub-totals**

└──▶ **By Branch/Outlet Sub-totals**

Thus national sales targets are broken down into branch sub-totals – and even into branch departmental totals as in a departmental store. Moreover, the sales director is able to provide a weighting – either plus or minus – upon those regions, districts or branches which are deemed either to enjoy a higher sales potential, perhaps because of a concentration of an urban population, a larger industrial base or a more affluent local economy. In some organisations, the regional and district managers respectively are responsible for making their own disaggregations of the delivered sales target.

Fig 8.5 **How a national company disaggregates its sales plan targets within a realistic framework**

A 12-MONTH TRADING PERIOD

Sales targets crystallise from the corporate and marketing plans for turnover and profitability by product

Sales department validates targets against known sales climate/potential and intelligence of market

Total sales targets broken down into regional sub-totals

and regional totals into district sub-totals

and into branch/outlet sub-totals

and into further sub-totals by product/counter sales

Sales turnover and profit needs disseminated down the organisation

Sales forecasts and market intelligence communicated upwards to secure realistic and achievable sales targets.

KEY STAGES IN PRODUCING A SALES PLAN

(This model is set in a national UK sales context)
The following stages represent the major steps to be taken in drawing up an effective sales plan:

1 Negotiating the overall sales plan targets
Meetings of company directors with research and development, production, marketing and sales responsibilities, under the chairmanship of the managing director will hammer out the targets which derive from the organisation's corporate plan. The design of the sales plan depends particularly on decisions taken when agreeing the marketing plan. The outcome will be a negotiated agreement on overall sales targets in the form of turnover, ratios of products to be sold and profits (gross and net) to be achieved.

2 Target allocation strategy
Many sales directors in larger businesses adopt a safety strategy of communicating to sales personnel a series of sales targets some 10 per cent higher than those actually agreed. This approach builds in a safety net in case some sales centres fail to meet their targets and allow for some negative developments – such as an economic downturn or the launch of a powerful competing product.

3 Regional consultation
Once in possession of agreed targets and sales policies, the sales director will meet to consult with his regional managers and agree their respective regional sales targets. The amounts targeted will include not only sales revenue and profit percentages, but also allow for the costs of sales support expenses (such as running the regional sales force), any bonuses or special rewards payable to customers for achieving pre-set purchasing targets and any advertising or sales promotion campaigns for which a budget has been regionally allocated.

4 District consultation

A very similar series of meetings will take place at district level as the national sales targets are progressively allocated down the sales line.

5 Branch/sales force consultations

The final process of target allocations lies at the individual outlet or sales representative level.

6 Design of sales winning strategies

Once the total sales targets have been fully allocated, the next stage is for the sales department to construct its strategies for winning sales. These will involve each sales representative in drawing up a series of call plans which detail the frequencies in which existing and new customers will be visited. The winning strategies will also involve costing in items such as bonuses and commissions to the sales force as well as volume sales rewards to dealers and distributors.

7 Sales reporting and feedback mechanisms

The sales plan will include details of how the process of securing sales is to be monitored. Typically, sales representatives submit weekly reports on the past week's activities in terms of orders taken, overdue accounts moneys collected, new calls made, new business secured, marketing intelligence picked up and operating expenses incurred.

8 Customer support

The sales plan will finally detail the ways in which customers will be provided with sales support – in the form of demonstration models, merchandising packs, product development seminars and after-sales service etc.

■ The need for building in flexibility

The market-place is like a river which is forever changing its course. Unexpected events like a technological breakthrough or government taxing intervention can create radical market changes within hours. Thus all business planning must allow for the unexpected and prove sufficiently flexible so as to enable prompt revisions and reviews, to permit modifications or open up new directions. Hence the need for close monitoring – 'You can't beat knowing what's going on in your own backyard!'

PC 8.2.7

DISCUSSION TOPICS

1 What kind of sales information would you request and at what intervals – if you were a national sales director – in order to ensure that the targets of your annual sales plan were met?

2 What actions would you take as the sales manager of a large organisation, say, selling computing equipment to retailers in the UK, if three successive monthly sales turnover totals indicated a worrying drop in sales?

3 As a marketing manager, in what sales analysis data would you be most interested? Why?

THE PRODUCTION PLAN

The design of the production plan is part of the essential triangular link between the marketing, sales and production processes. It is important to understand that each of these business functions is inextricably entwined with the other two:

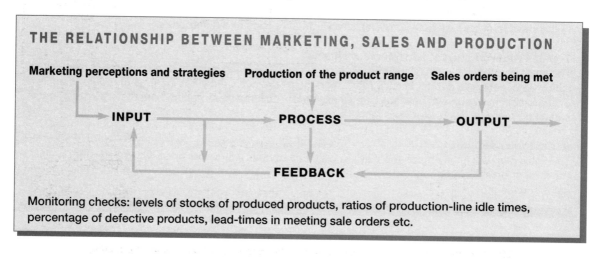

THE RELATIONSHIP BETWEEN MARKETING, SALES AND PRODUCTION

Marketing perceptions and strategies   Production of the product range   Sales orders being met

INPUT ──── PROCESS ──── OUTPUT

FEEDBACK

Monitoring checks: levels of stocks of produced products, ratios of production-line idle times, percentage of defective products, lead-times in meeting sale orders etc.

Manufacturing resource planning (MRP) is a system which integrates the processes of marketing, production and sales. MRP relies upon a fully integrated process and is usually coordinated by a master scheduler, whose role is to ensure that each of the three phases is most efficiently and cost-effectively managed. The diagram in Figure 8.6 illustrates the MRP process:

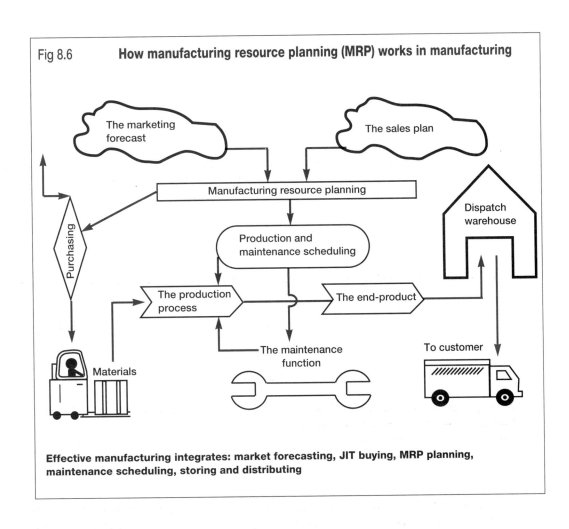

Fig 8.6   How manufacturing resource planning (MRP) works in manufacturing

The marketing forecast

The sales plan

Manufacturing resource planning

Purchasing

Dispatch warehouse

Production and maintenance scheduling

The production process

The end-product

Materials

The maintenance function

To customer

Effective manufacturing integrates: market forecasting, JIT buying, MRP planning, maintenance scheduling, storing and distributing

MANUFACTURING RESOURCE PLANNING TECHNIQUES

Manufacturing resource planning begins with the implementation of the marketing plan, which in effect answers the question:

How much do we want to manufacture?

MRP then manages all the factors present in meeting the 'how much' and 'of what type' manufacturing aspects and then proceeds to meet the sales plan question:

By when?

In other words, all the projections, estimates and forecasts have to be synthesised in a production plan into concrete ranges and mixes of products, the manufacture of which has to be scheduled as cost-effectively as possible, using just-in-time and electronic data interchange (EDI) systems. In MRP, each production stage is given a part coding.

Thus all arriving raw materials or bought-in parts are checked for quality and may not be moved on until set standards have been met. Similarly, finished goods may not be moved to the warehouse until quality checks have been fulfilled. At every stage all materials and items are given unique production batch codings to aid tracking and subsequent identification in case of a defect occurring. In this way a computerised database is built up of each and every production run. In the case of the dreaded product recall newspaper advertisement, any defect problems may be quickly located and the PR damage limited.

For a production plan to be effective, the manufacturing process must be standardised as far as possible in terms of:

- the quality of materials accepted for processing
- the stages of the production process
- the quality standards administered
- the time taken to complete the production process
- the periods of maintenance and safety checks (well within set limits)

PC
8.1.6
8.2.4

KEY STAGES IN PRODUCTION PLANNING

The following are the key stages in production planning:

1   Pre-plan requirements
Prior to the design of a production plan, it is necessary to:

- have agreed the basic product concept and marketing strategy
- have developed the idea via R&D into an accepted and tested prototype, which designers and toolmakers agree is feasible and cost-effective to manufacture

2   Production planning stages
The production planning stage requires close, sequential liaison and coordination with a number of involved process functions as the diagram (Fig. 8.7) illustrates:

3   Post-production planning stages
The production planning cycle – once the finished goods have left the factory – includes evaluation and feedback phases in which levels of production output are compared with targets, actual waste levels with projected levels and so on. Also, the triangular relationship – marketing, production, sales – results in wash-up meetings at which, say, the introduction of a new product or modifications to existing ones are reviewed in order to meet, say, the total quality management requirement of a process of continuous improvement.

Fig 8.7   **The cycle of integrated manufacturing resource planning**

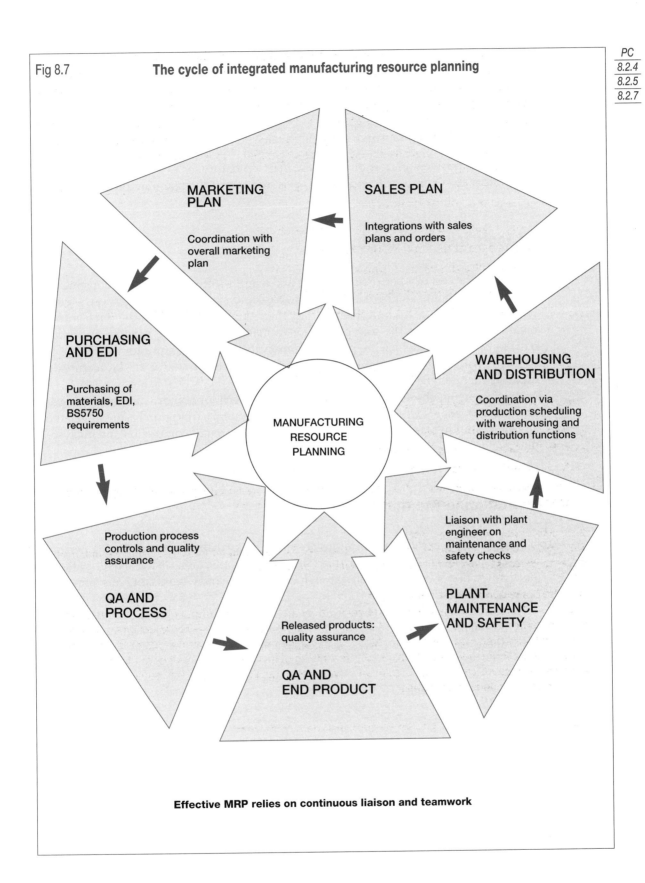

Effective MRP relies on continuous liaison and teamwork

IT AND TELECOMMUNICATIONS PLANNING SUPPORT TOOLS

Whether the business plan is of a modest, start-up nature, or is a mighty, multinational corporate plan, a number of helpful tools exist to support the planning process:

■ Support tools for start-up planning

Nowadays the cost of a personal computer and a multi-software package embracing word processing, accounts and bookkeeping, database and spreadsheet applications – even in windows mode – costs hundreds rather than thousands of pounds. Such a tool is invaluable in enabling the sole proprietor to manipulate textual, number and graphic data, to keep records which are promptly retrievable, and with a printer to produce hard copies at will. Such a personal PC system provides at a low cost all the features of a capable office – in the hands of a trained user.

Now becoming obsolescent – but still helpful for 'technophobics' – are the paper-based booklets and ledgers which have turnkey business systems, from purchasing to inventory, already set out in blank form mode with helpful notes to aid completion and analysis by the small trader.

■ Aids to producing the marketing plan

IT hardware and software applications are similarly available to the marketing personnel of a medium to large organisation. In addition to the applications listed above, marketeers make much use of computer software which models market trends and answers a wide range of 'what if' questions.

The marketing plan is also supported by a wide range of information providers, such as *JICNARS (Joint Industry Committee for National Readership Survey)* and such regular publications as *Phillips and Drew's published monthly forecasts.*

■ And the sales plan

Sales planners make extensive use of customary applications software, but also of particular packages used for 'sales tracking'. Such applications enable sales managers to keep close tabs on how far a sales prospect has proceeded along the sales track – from the first identification of a likely buyer to the physical location of an item (say a photocopier) in the process of being delivered.

■ The production plan

In terms of the all-embracing use made of information technology, of note in the production planning process are:

■ *Electronic Data Interchange (EDI)* computerised systems, through which purchasing and supplying computers 'talk' to each other and synchronise just-in-time manufacturing systems.

■ *Computer-Aided Design and Manufacture IT systems* which enable designers and machine operators to perform complex design and manufacturing operations with the benefits of features like three-dimensional, rotating electronic drawings, computerised design modelling and optimum build routes and processes.

■ Telecommunications

Advances in telecommunications technology have made it possible for architects and builders – on different continents – to amend blueprints and plans electronically through the use of wide area network software. In-house confravision and video-telephones now support planning meetings and the visual examination of diagrams and charts by personnel in remote locations.

■ Support agencies

In addition to technological support, business planners can nowadays call upon a wide range of public and private sector experts, ranging from staff in the Department of Trade and Industry, the local Training and Enterprise Council (TEC), and the Chamber of Commerce, national professional institutes such as the Institute of Marketing and a host of entrepreneurial management consultants.

Local public and college libraries also now stock a broad selection of 'do-it-yourself' planning handbooks, and all the clearing banks offer comprehensive financial support services to starting out business people.

■ The best support

Underpinning the most conscientiously gathered data and statistics, forms, schedules, software and flowcharts is the most important planning tool of all – that inner determination to venture out and to succeed! And the successful business entrepreneurs find that conviction and self-belief from within, rather than from without.

1 List the main sections you would expect to find in the marketing plan of a medium to large plc.

2 What is meant by ' an internal audit' in a marketing plan context?

3 Explain briefly how a sales plan will differ from a marketing plan and why.

4 What is meant by the term 'disaggregation' in the context of sales planning?

5 What do the initials MRP stand for? Explain the process of MRP briefly.

6 What do the following stand for:

   EDI, JIT, CADCAM, JICNARS?

7 Compose a checklist for each of the people you would expect to receive a copy of:

   a) a start-up business plan,

   b) a corporate plan,

   c) a marketing plan,

   d) a sales plan and

   e) a production plan.

8 Explain briefly the techniques you would adopt to ensure that any business plan you are involved in devising is as objective as possible.

PC
8.1.3
8.1.5
8.2.2
8.2.8
8.3.2
8.3.5

CASE STUDY 1

The New College Bookshop

The Board of Governors/Corporation of your school/college has recently given permission for a new bookshop to be established as part of a policy of securing income and surpluses (profits) from enterprises which also help the students.

- The location of the bookshop has been left for a Planning Group to decide, but it must be readily accessible and ideally capable of expansion if the venture proves a success.

- Also, the hours of opening have been left to the Planning Group to decide upon after a suitable survey of customers' needs has been made.

- While it is felt that textbooks are likely to be the largest item of stock, the Governors/ Corporation are keen for the bookshop to be innovative and to meet customers' needs as comprehensively as possible.

- The bookshop must be fully self-funded, so projected turnover and profits must be sufficient to pay for running costs and payroll etc.

- The Governors/Corporation are prepared to lend the bookshop £10,000 as start-up capital and for the closing balances for the first 6 months of operation to be in the red!

- With your teachers' help, decide on an actual (prospective) location and allocated costs of: rent, rates, heat and light.

ACTIVITIES

1 First undertake your researches as the Planning Group of two or three people and then produce a start-up business plan for the bookshop.

2 Using suitable AVA support, deliver your plan to your class in an oral presentation of some 10 minutes and field any arising questions.

3 Invite your Head Teacher or Vice Principal to discuss your plans with your class and to evaluate them from the point of view of their financial soundness and viability.

4 Devise a suitable advertising campaign to excite students' awareness of the new facility and include a sample poster, public-address system commercial and notice-board A4 advertisement in your advertising plan.

CASE STUDY 2

PC
8.1.1
8.2.3
8.2.6
8.3.5

'I want you to market our GNVQs in business!'

With these words Mrs Frances Richardson began a briefing session for the students in the Business and Computing Department of Midchester College who were pursuing a second year of study for the GNVQ Advanced Award in Business.

Sue Crane whispered to a fellow-student, Stuart Wilson, 'I bet she's just winding us up! They'd never let us do it for real!' 'Oh yes they would!' responded the sharp-eared Mrs Richardson, 'But first I want to brief you on the current market situation and background, so you can then decide for yourselves whether you want to accept the challenge.'

Mrs Richardson's subsequent briefing covered the following points:

■ The College's mission is to provide a relevant range of programmes aimed mainly to meet the needs of the students, their parents and local employers throughout the local community.

■ Seventy-three per cent of the local economy is service-industry based; the remainder is concentrated in several high-tech industrial parks and in agriculture. Midchester possesses an affluent number of retired people who use the banking, building society, shopping mall, leisure centre and theatre complex facilities extensively.

■ Midchester is also the seat of the Midshire County Council, which employs over 1,400 staff.

■ GNVQs at Intermediate and Advanced Levels in Business were first introduced into the Department in September 1993, having been especially designed to promote a practical route into either a business career or higher education. However, because they are still comparatively new, many students, parents and employers in the Midchester district know very little about them – they still need widespread publicising in a language free from educational jargon.

■ At present recruitment to the GNVQ programmes in the Department is as follows:

	Intermediate	Advanced
Second Intake:	18	19 (Sept 1994)
First Intake:	17	15 (Sept 1993)

- The reason for the lower than expected recruitment to the 1994–5 programmes has been put down to increasing competition from the three all-through 11–18 schools in the Midchester district, and to a lack of suitable information about the courses communicated in the right media.

- Some students also have expressed the view among themselves that the choice of Option Units is based on subject areas more in tune with the teachers' existing expertise than with the needs of the local economy.

- The current edition of the College's Corporate Plan has targeted an increase in recruitment across the College of 25 per cent over the coming three years. The next academic year has been set to achieve a growth of 8 per cent, and the equivalent target for the large Department of Business and Computing at 12 per cent, since the three-year target for the Department is for a 35 per cent growth rate. Mrs Richardson and her senior colleagues believe this target could be readily exceeded with the right marketing approach.

- Currently, the College publishes a full-time and a part-time prospectus once a year in March. To keep costs down, the print is small and the paper inexpensive. It is left to the Departments to produce additional leaflets and brochures.

- The local advertising media include: a weekly *Midchester Chronicle*, a commercial radio station, 'Wessex Sound', two free, home-delivered advertising papers and the usual spaces for renting on buses, at the railway station and on roadside hoardings.

- The study facilities in the Department comprise: 100 networked PCs, including 25 in an open access suite; major software applications for wp, dtp, spreadsheet, database and graphics work, an electronic training office, 3 CCTV mobile units with video playback, a select business studies library and classrooms equipped with OHP and audio recording equipment. The College Resource Centre and Library provides extensive support and is well stocked.

'Well,' concluded Mrs Richardson, 'that's about it. It's all set down on this handout (*which she circulates*). My staff and I are most eager to receive your help, since we feel that our marketing may have lost touch with the views and needs of Midchester's 16-plus teenagers. So here's what I'd like you to do . . .'

CASE STUDY ACTIVITIES

1 In groups of three or four, reread the case study carefully and then make notes of the points you consider most helpful to your group as data for *a marketing plan* (limited to the academic year of the next intake of students) which Mrs Richardson has asked you to produce. With your teacher's guidance, you may extend the data available to you by using some drawn from your school/college and locality – especially in the areas of financial costs and resources and local advertising media and charges.

2 As part of your data collecting for the marketing plan you have been asked to *design a questionnaire* to survey GNVQ Business students on their views on how they were recruited, how they rate their course of study and what improvements might be made, and so on.

3 Mrs Richardson is particularly anxious to communicate effectively the major features of the GNVQ Intermediate and Advanced Business Programmes and has asked your group to *devise a suitable brochure* in a style and English you think 16-plus prospective students will find appealing.

DISCUSSION TOPICS

PC
8.1.3
8.1.4
8.1.5
8.2.3
8.2.5
8.2.8

1 What marketing strategies do you think most likely to succeed in your locality for spreading information about GNVQ Business programmes?

2 The case study refers to the competition for students between Midchester College and local secondary schools. Do you think competition is 'a good thing' in a public service educational context?

3 What do you see as the major differences in marketing a service as opposed to a product?

4 How would you monitor the effectiveness of the case study's marketing plan?

CASE STUDY 3

PC
8.1.1
8.1.3
8.1.5
8.2.2
8.2.3
8.2.8
8.3.4
8.3.5

Turner Power Tools

Cyril Turner, a former Sales Manager with Brent Power Tools Ltd, decided in 1991 to set up his own business, Turner Power Tools, situated not far from his previous employer. He began his work supported only by administrative help from a business student as part of his industrial training with the aim of promoting certain power tool brand names, becoming a recognised distributor for suppliers, and dealing mainly with account customers. Initial operations were centred on retail premises.

Constraints

Cyril Turner was severely hampered by his previous employment at Brent Power Tools and by the existing power tools distribution system.

a Power tool companies and fixing suppliers generally only trade through distributors. Brent Power Tools Ltd already acted as the local distributor for many firms in the area and the manufacturers were unwilling to cause disruption and uncertainty in the market by encouraging an unknown factor in the shape of Turner Power Tools. The contacts that Turner had made while at Brent Power Tools were therefore effectively closed at the time of setting up his business.

b Turner had signed an agreement with Brent Power Tools undertaking not to approach their customers with the same products for a period of six months.

c The more reputable, well-established companies in the North London area already had distributors in the area; those manufacturers willing to sell through Turner Power Tools were unknown even in the trade with a product quality that was also unknown.

d Turner's intention of dealing with reputable power tool companies required greater cash outlay in holding stocks.

Options

a Many start-up businesses in the power tools market begin by buying and selling to order, depending on picking up any item and make of goods available. This, however, would affect the company's initial intention of dealing with reputable power tool manufacturers.

b The prospects for Turner Power Tools beginning by operating as a retail outlet was extremely limited since the equipment concerned consisted essentially of industrial tools made of hard-wearing parts to withstand heavy duty use on building sites or as part of a hire fleet. They are therefore about four times the price of an equivalent DIY tool.

c The Japanese manufacturer Sanaa was a newcomer to the UK power tools market. The company had made its name in electronic equipment, was well known and had a high reputation for reliability. Their power tools were proven excellent but as yet this section of the company had no distributor in the north and west of London. Turner Power Tools secured this Sanaa distributorship adding substantially to its image. As part of the agreement, Sanaa passed on to the distributor any enquiries about power tools in the area; in return Turner actively promoted the Sanaa equipment. Initially the company stocked about £5,000 of Sanaa tools; this subsequently increased to about 120 tools with a net value of about £15,000. By holding stock of Sanaa equipment Turner Power Tools soon found itself in a position to supply its competitors with Sanaa goods for them to resell.

Finding customers

Cyril Turner's potential customers included local government bodies, building and construction firms, joiners' shops, electricians, and maintenance departments. The trade tends to demand on-site personal service, being on hand to take orders and arrange the delivery of goods when required.

The demand for personal selling was reflected in an initial experiment. Turner's assistant sent a mail shot to all of the 40 names of approved builders on a list supplied by the council. They reasoned that most of those on the list were small firms working from home who would be difficult to contact otherwise and could ideally be canvassed through the post. They were also locally based so the mail shot would at least supply them with information about the new company. However, the mail shot generated no direct response. A similar result came from placing an advert in two local newspapers in consecutive weeks.

The trade was found to be a close-knit one in which personal relationships with clients are very important. The price of goods is often less significant than the quality of the personal service offered: being on hand, supplying a good service including the willingness to supply goods at short notice, sometimes on the day the order is placed. In any case, customers expected deliveries within one to two days, with the sales representative often taking the goods to his own customers. Turner Power Tools were in addition willing to supply customers' requests for goods like specialist engineering tools which are not normally stocked. For those customers, such as the local authority which is only interested in price, the company was willing to match the prices quoted by competitors.

Progress

In the first three months of trading sales were double the figures expected (*see* Table 8.1). By the beginning of the fourth month of trading Turner found more and more of his time spent in the office dealing with customer enquiries and telephoned orders. As the

Table 8.1 Turner Power Tools sales and purchases, 1991–92

Month	Sales	Purchases
November '91	5 458	3 961
December	6 728	10 198
January '92	17 534	8 484
February	30 204	14 752
March	24 424	22 271
April	22 570	16 313
May	34 755	18 821
June	32 311	11 470
July	49 836	17 384
August	33 915	53 423*
September	44 028	7 301
October	45 223	17 633
November	44 653	56 761*
December	25 401	32 328
Total	417 040	291 100

*Distortion caused by payments made for VAT quarter.

enquiries became more complex it was essential that someone with good knowledge of the tool and fixing trades should be on hand to deal with telephone sales enquiries. It had become necessary to recruit a sales representative, someone to deal with telephone enquiries, and a clerk was hired on the Jobskills Scheme to process orders and take in suppliers' deliveries.

Paperwork

As sales increased so did the paperwork:

a Turner's customers placed small orders frequently. There were about 120 account customers and at the end of the month a statement was drawn up for each account. With no ledger system the statements were based on the sales day book and the difficulty in balancing the total outstanding at the end of each month had been increasing. It took between three and four days to prepare the balance statement each month.

b Turner's supplied a very wide range of goods, many of which were not held in house but subsequently ordered from suppliers. The increased use of this mechanism also greatly increased the number of delivery notes, invoices, and statements coming in from a large number of different suppliers – the company dealt with about 70, the majority of which would be involved in each month's trading.

Invoices had to be matched to delivery notes and all prices, discounts, and mathematical extensions checked; these all had to match the statements. As with sales there was no purchase ledger, but neither was there a purchase day book. To ensure that all payments for a certain month were made reliance was placed on memory and checking through all the invoices in the files.

c Each month's sales were based on the sales day book and this supplied the company's VAT analysis for sales. As there was no purchase day book the monthly VAT was calculated on the basis of cheque stubs and invoices marked paid for the month in question.

ASSIGNMENTS

In groups of three or four produce your answers to the following questions as a series of written presentations. In a class discussion, compare your answers to those produced by other groups and decide on the overall most suitable responses.

1 What important factors did Cyril Turner overlook or underestimate in planning his business start-up? Should he have foreseen them? How might they have been taken into account?

2 What do you see as the current Strengths, Weaknesses, Opportunities and Threats (SWOT Analysis) facing Turner Power Tools?

3 Assuming that it is now December 1992 and you have access to the figures shown in Table 8.1, produce the following parts of a business plan for 1993:

   a An organisational structure capable of enabling the business to grow.

   b A company development strategy for the coming two years.

   c A marketing strategy likely to prove effective given the circumstances of the business environment of Turner Power Tools.

   d A sales strategy for the coming year.

   e A policy for handling the increasing paperwork.

This case study was adapted from Turner Power Tools in Alan West's *A Business Plan* and is reproduced by kind permission of Longman Group UK Limited.

IDEAS FOR PROJECTS

PC
8.1.1

1 In pairs, first carry out your research and then devise for your school, college or organisation:

   a a mission statement;

   b 10–12 related goals for the current year.

PC
8.1.4
8.2.6

2 Seek to interview either your Principal/Vice Principal or Head Teacher/Deputy Head or Managing Director/an operational director at work with a view to finding out what kind of information is collected and used in the production of the corporate plan. Make confidential notes of your findings and agree with the staff you interviewed that you may share them with your class group prior to distributing them and giving an appropriate oral presentation to your class.

PC
8.2.3
8.3.1

3 In pairs, arrange to interview a local marketing manager who can brief you on how the marketing plan for his/her organisation is put together. Remember that you are only likely to be given the principles of the approach, as the operational detail is of a highly confidential nature.

Seek the agreement of the marketing manager you interviewed to visit your group and deliver a talk on the planning process in a marketing context.

PC
8.2.2
8.24

4 Arrange in groups of three or four to visit a local factory and to be shown around the production lines. In an ensuing discussion with production managers, seek to find out how production is managed and planned, and make notes which you have vetted before leaving.

In a general class discussion, compare the visits made and information gained. Seek to establish whether there are any features common to production planning of whatever type of product.

5 In groups of three or four first undertake your researches and then produce a start-up business plan for one of the following:

PC
8.2.1
8.2.5
8.2.8
8.3.2

   a A traditional-style 'Tuck Shop' to sell: cakes, sandwiches, snacks, minerals and sweets during break-times in your school/college from hutted accommodation at the centre of the campus.

   b A European foreign language private tuition service at lunchtimes, twilights and evenings delivered by native speakers of French, German and Spanish.

   The 'basic idea' is that your group runs the business and pays for the services of the EC language teachers who do not share in any dividends or profits.

   c A music shop selling second-hand tapes, CDs and LPs purchased from students; the net profits from the business are to go to charity to be decided by the start-up entrepreneurs.

6 Select **one** of the above a), b) or c) topics and produce a marketing plan for the venture you choose. Make your plan as realistic as possible, using your expert knowledge of your school or college.

PC
8.2.3
8.3.2

EVIDENCE-BUILDING ACTIVITY FOR YOUR PORTFOLIO

Element 8.1: Prepare work and collect data for a business plan

Select **one** of the following types of business having regard to its likely success in your locality:

- an 'up-market' café and cake shop

- a sports clothing and equipment shop

- a boutique targeting women in the 16–30 age range

- a music centre selling both hi-fi equipment, tapes, CDs and allied wares

- a fast-food cafeteria which will have a British as opposed to American ambience and image.

Research objectives

Your research and activity objectives for Element 8.1 are to: secure data which will inform the business plan you will produce to meet the evidence requirements of Element 8.2.

Your researches should result in your having secured detailed information which will provide answers to the following questions:

1 **What are your key objectives in starting up the business** – in terms of projected levels of turnover, growth and profitability etc?

2 **Where will you locate your business** – so as to ensure as far as possible that it is situated in an appropriately busy area with good access communications, but not so well sited that its purchase, lease or rent proves unrealistically high in relation to your projected turnover and profit objectives?

Note: look for 'For Sale' or 'To Let' signs above shop premises and obtain details from the advertising estate agent; scan your weekly press for commercial premises advertisements and find out the asking price of rental per square metre etc.

3 Where will you secure a loan in order to finance the acquisition of premises, opening stock and the payment of initial costs like payroll, service installations?

4 What will be the impact upon your running costs and profitability of servicing the loan you secure?

5 What human resources will you be able to afford? You will need to consider the trade-off between securing sufficient sales and administration 'pairs of hands' with their payroll and employer-associated NIC and SERPS costs etc.

6 What will be the effect upon your plan of complying with statutory and employer-protecting requirements – such as: business-related insurances, HASAW, employment protection and fair trading laws etc?

7 What equipment, fixtures, time and know-how resources will be essential to running the business successfully?

8 What steps will need to be taken in order to ensure that the forecasts and projections your plan will make are both feasible and realistic – in terms of likely turnover, fixed and variable costs and gross/net profit percentages?

Your researches should aim to provide concrete, factual data to answer the above questions, and you should also produce a flow-chart which illustrates the timescale of the start-up process and (in Gantt chart format) the stages at which main activities would come on stream.

Helpful hint 1   The more elaborate and extensive your objectives for turnover and profit are, the higher your operational expenses will become.

Helpful hint 2   Your research data should cover in detail the first calendar year of operations; your business plan should make outline forecasts of turnover, costs and profitability – based upon likely growth – for years 2 and 3.

Production of evidence

Decide upon the headings under which you will assemble your research data and then, when you are satisfied that you have collected sufficient for each heading, set it out in a series of brief notes under each section heading

Method of producing evidence

Use word-processing and spreadsheet application packages to assemble your evidence and to produce a series of source draft files which you can expand later in your formal business plan document.

Element 8.2: Produce and present a business plan

Using the data you have collected in your researches for the activity of Element 8.1, your task is now to produce a business plan (covering in detail a period of 12 calendar months and in overview a further two years). Your plan should be for the business you selected in the 8.1 activity.

Before embarking upon this activity, you should first re-read the section in Unit 8 (pages 686, 688–705), and you should ensure that your plan covers these sections:

1 The overall goals and objectives of the business in terms of sales, profitability, market share, and growth etc.

2 What resources will be required in year 1, and how they are expected to increase in years 2 and 3.

3 What you forecast cash-flow will be in the first 12 months (using the schedule on page 699 as your model), a start-up projected balance sheet and a profit and loss sheet for the first 12 months.

4 Your financial planning section should also include your arrangements for monthly and quarterly monitoring of your projected cash-flow and trading profit and loss.

5 Your business plan should lastly include a marketing planning section – which may be the marketing plan you produce for the Element 8.3 activity.

Presentation of evidence

Role-play scenario: Assume that you are presenting your plan at a meeting of officials from a bank which is considering financing your start-up business; in this simulation, your co-students will role-play the officials.

You should produce your business plan in the form of an A4 word-processed brochure which includes suitable graphic/diagrammatic illustrations. A copy of your plan should be distributed to your co-students as a pre-presentation briefing document.

You should explain and justify your business plan in an oral presentation to your class of approximately 15–20 minutes. You should include in your presentation an opportunity for the officials (co-students) to put questions to you on aspects of your plan, which you should seek to answer as reassuringly as possible.

Method of producing evidence

Produce your evidence by merging files you have created using word processing and spreadsheet software application packages (and also a graphics package if possible).

Element 8.3: Produce a sales and marketing plan

Activity 1

Using the data you collected for the Element 8.1 Activity, produce the marketing plan section of the business plan you have undertaken for the Element 8.2 Activity.

Note: before undertaking this Activity, re-read the section on marketing planning pages 705–11.

Activity 2

First select a single product (or service) you are selling in the business you selected at the outset of the Element 8.1 Activity, for example a Reebok or Nike ladies' cross-trainer, a brand of fashion jeans, a compilation CD of a popular rock group etc.

Next, re-read the section on The Sales Plan pages 711–15.

Your sales plan for your selected product/service should include:

1 your target sales turnover figure over a period of four months

2 your forecast cost of sales, broken down into detailed cost headings

3 the gross and net profit which your projected sales will generate

4 your sales promotion, advertising and merchandising strategies, with details as to how they will be structured during the 4 months of your plan.

5 what after sales and customer service support will be required to ensure the success of your sales plan

Note: You should design a matrix using a spreadsheet software package to illustrate your sales plan, broken down into four monthly periods.

Presentation of evidence

You should produce your evidence in the form of a printout of a spreadsheet matrix with suitable headings set against four monthly columns and a totals column. In addition, you should word process a commentary of about three sides of A4 which provides an objective explanation and rationale for your sales plan.

Method of presentation of evidence

Your sales plan should comprise a spreadsheet matrix, word-processed commentary supported by appropriate illustrative material.

Performance Criteria Covered

Element 8.1
8.1.1, 8.1.2, 8.1.3, 8.1.4, 8.1.5, 8.1.6, 8.1.7

Element 8.2
8.2.1, 8.2.2, 8.2.3, 8.2.4, 8.2.5, 8.2.6, 8.2.7, 8.2.8

Element 8.3
8.3.1, 8.3.2, 8.3.3, 8.3.4, 8.3.5

Core skills Level 3

Communication
3.1.1–3.1.4, 3.2.1, 3.2.4, 3.3.1–3.3.3, 3.4.1–3.4.3

Information processing
3.1.1–3.1.7 (3.1.7 if LAN used), 3.2.1–3.2.7, 3.3.1–3.3.5, 3.4.4

3.5.1–3.5.5 (by means of logged notes on how errors or faults were handled and how compliance with HASAW was effected).

Application of number
3.2.1, 3.2.2, 3.2.4, 3.2.5, 3.2.8

FURTHER SOURCES OF INFORMATION

The Greatest Little Business Book, 5th edn, P Hingston, Hingston Associates, 1991. ISBN 0 906555 10 8

The Business Start-Up Guide, National Westminster Bank, 1992.

The Business Planner, I Maitland, Butterworth-Heinemann, 1992. ISBN 07506 0136 1 (deals mainly with financial aspects)

A Business Plan, A West, Pitman/Natwest 1988. ISBN 0 273 02824 3

Modern Business Administration, 5th edn, R C Appleby, Pitman Publishing, 1991. ISBN 0 273 03332 8

Managing Growth, M Bennett, Longman–Natwest, 1989. ISBN 0 273 03103 1

Marketing: An Introduction, 3rd edn, P Kotler & G Armstrong, Prentice Hall, 1993. ISBN 0 13 555244 3

How To Prepare A Marketing Plan, 4th edn, J Stapleton, Gower, 1989. ISBN 0 566 02723 2 (includes sales forecasting/planning)

Production Management Systems, J Browne, J Harhen, J Shivnan, Addison-Wesley, 1988. ISBN 0 201 17820 6.

A checklist of major items and their place in the Conference Project Plan

Major decisions:

When? Where? What?
Who speaks? Who comes?
What will it cost?

Vital deadlines to be met

Speakers secured; programme designed and mailed; bookings secured; budget finalised

Attention to detail counts!

Meeting speakers' needs; ensuring delegates' comfort; anticipating wants and needs; providing good communications

Week: 0 — 1 — 5 — 8 — 25 — 48 — 51 — 52 — 55

'Go' Decision	Strategic Planning	Costing and conference budget	Promotion and sales drive		Detail work run-up	Conference takes place	Post-conference
			Finalising speakers and programme	**Services to organise**			
Form conference planning team and identify roles	Decide:	Identify cost centres and set fees for delegates	Produce and mail first programme	Produce and mail final programme	Prepare venue	'Think!'	Produce:
● Chairman	● Theme	● Fees of speakers	Obtain confirmations from invited speakers and:	Confirm provisional venue and hotel bookings	● Registration/enquiry desk	● Patrol	● Conference accounts
● Marketing	● Dates	● Cost of hotel accommodation	● Photographs	Hire:	● Seating	● Monitor	● Pay bills
● Delegates coordinator	● Duration	● Hire of suite(s)	● Talk synopses	● AVA specialists	● Podium	● Observe	● Write thank you letters
● Hotel and catering, etc.	● Venue	● Catering	● Curriculum vitaes	● Transport – coaches/minibuses	● AVA equipment	● Anticipate	● Hold team debriefing meeting
	● Clientele/target delegates	● Specialist services	Market conference:	● Catering specialists	● Cloaks	● Back-up	● Produce conference report and mail/publish it
	Map out:	● AVA/communications	● Advertisements	● Decor/signs/logos/ backdrops specialists	● Press room	● Maintain PR profile	
	● Target speakers	● Decor	● Mailshots	Design and print day programmes and delegate packs	● Speakers' quiet room	Look after:	
	● Topics	● Transport	● Press releases	Check arrival times of speakers and VIPs	● Car parking	● Speakers	
	● Supportive provisions	● Reprography	● Articles		● Dining facilities	● VIPs	
	● Exhibition	Marketing and publicity:	● Letters to VIPs		Finalise:	● Delegates	
	● Book equipment display	● Advertising	● Phone calls		● Reception		
	● Social programme	● Programme printing	● Free entries in specialist journals		● Procedures		
		● Delegates packs	Set up conference administration unit and coordinator		● Name badges		
		Construct a break-even chart	Devise systems to process bookings		● Parking vouchers		
					● Seating plans		
					● Social programme for spouses		
					● Escorts for VIPs		
					● Mobile phones for organisers		
					● Rehearsals for speakers (identify internal 'stand-by' speakers)		

INDEX